JAMES WRIGHT

JAMES WRIGHT
A Life in Poetry

JONATHAN BLUNK

Farrar, Straus and Giroux

New York

Farrar, Straus and Giroux
18 West 18th Street, New York 10011

Grateful acknowledgment is made for permission to reprint the following material:
"Lorca & Jimenez" by Robert Bly. Copyright © 1973, 1997 by Robert Bly.
Reprinted by permission of Beacon Press, Boston.

Library of Congress Cataloging-in-Publication Data
Names: Blunk, Jonathan, author.
Title: James Wright : a life in poetry / Jonathan Blunk.
Description: First edition. | New York : Farrar, Straus and Giroux, 2017. |
    Includes bibliographical references and index.
Identifiers: LCCN 2017003852 | ISBN 9780374178598 (hardcover) |
    ISBN 9780374717377 (e-book)
Subjects: LCSH: Wright, James Arlington, 1927–1980. | Poets, American—
    20th century—Biography.
Classification: LCC PS3573.R5358 Z55 2017 | DDC 811/.54 [B]—dc23
LC record available at https://lccn.loc.gov/2017003852

Designed by Jonathan D. Lippincott

Our books may be purchased in bulk for promotional, educational,
or business use. Please contact your local bookseller or the Macmillan Corporate
and Premium Sales Department at 1-800-221-7945, extension 5442,
or by e-mail at MacmillanSpecialMarkets@macmillan.com.

www.fsgbooks.com
www.twitter.com/fsgbooks • www.facebook.com/fsgbooks

1   3   5   7   9   10   8   6   4   2

Frontispiece: James Wright in his basement study, Como Avenue, Minneapolis,
circa summer 1960 (Photograph by Liberty Kovacs)

Dedicated to my teachers,
and in memory of the first and best of them,
my father, Theodore Blunk

We are not human beings having a spiritual journey. We are spiritual beings having a human journey.

—Pierre Teilhard de Chardin (1881–1955)

Contents

Preface

James Wright's life was shaped by a rare depth of compassion, a moral shrewdness as keen as George Orwell's, and an almost helpless devotion to poetry. Nearly four decades have passed since the poet's death in 1980, yet new readers are continually drawn to the excellence of Wright's work. The speaker welcomes us into these poems, and readers feel acknowledged and respected. Sharp details from Wright's life are found throughout his work, moments of feeling that are captured with richness and clarity. He wants to tell the human, often painful, truth. Ranging from delicate lyrics to desperate curses, the voice in his poems claims great authority.

From the age of ten, Wright worked hard at his poetry, with the same care and determination he saw in his father, a factory worker. Wright used poetry as a way to survive and finally to escape from the dead-end life that threatened to trap him in the Ohio River Valley. He rarely went back after joining the army at the age of eighteen, but in a way, all of Wright's poems are addressed to the Ohio River and to the people who lived and worked along its banks—the townspeople in Martins Ferry, Ohio. Wright includes them in the audience he creates for his poetry, the hard-pressed, resilient southern Ohioans he knew growing up in a steel town during the Depression. Many of his poems confer dignity on their inner lives.

Wright had an associative, musical intellect, aided by a startling "phonographic" memory that gave him the ability to recite poems and prose for hours on end. After saying poems in Latin, German, Spanish, or French, he would improvise his own translations. His poems first won acclaim for their skillful use of metrical forms and patterns of rhyme—an "academic" verse that valued convention. This "classical streak" in Wright's character proved an asset in his career as a professor of English literature. But in his poetry Wright was fearless, absorbing the free-verse and image-based strategies he found in Whitman and in the wealth of new translations of world poetry in the 1960s. The German and Spanish writers he translated influenced Wright more than the poems of his American contemporaries.

The success of his 1963 volume, *The Branch Will Not Break*—composed almost entirely of free-verse poems—encouraged the idea that Wright had dramatically turned his back on metrical poetry. But like many other stories that have gathered around Wright's name, this is false. He never stopped writing poems in rhyme and meter. Wright wanted only to expand the range of possibilities available to him. In his last decade, he returned to the spoken rhythms and idioms of his native Ohio. His lyrical prose pieces—like his journals and letters—show astonishing fluency of language, thought, and feeling. Over multiple drafts, Wright alternated between prose and line-break versions of his late poems, listening for their proper form. Having achieved a thorough mastery of his craft, Wright found the patience and focus to let the poem at hand emerge in its own good time.

————

As I describe in the acknowledgments, this biography has had a long period of gestation, and it benefits from many years of research. I worked closely with Wright's translations and have also made a study of his personal library, where the margins of his books still shout his praise and invectives. I recorded hundreds of hours of interviews and public tributes to the poet, and found that everyone who ever met Wright could recall him vividly. That strong sense of Wright's physical presence can still be felt in recordings of his readings. I have transcribed more than four dozen of Wright's public talks, readings, and interviews, wanting to keep his voice at the center of this book.

I also quote extensively from unpublished journals, letters, and poems, thanks to the unrestricted access I have been given to Wright's papers. One extraordinary collection of letters, written between 1957 and

1959, chronicles Wright's deliberate creation of a Muse that could sustain his poetry. He sometimes referred to these unpublished letters as a separate journal, and they possess a profound intimacy. Two decades later, in the months of Wright's final trip to Europe in 1979, his journals contain some of his best writing, nearly all of it as yet unpublished. As a result of my focus on this unknown work, Wright's published poems appear here less often. They can be found in his Complete Poems, *Above the River,* or the fine *Selected Poems* edited by Robert Bly and Anne Wright.

My hope has always been to turn attention back to the poems, which include some of the most influential and enduring lyrics of the past century. Wright's life, by turns despairing and inspiring, is always fascinating. But as he would remind us, it is finally the work that matters. I feel grateful to have spent so much time in Wright's company.

JAMES WRIGHT

At a point of beginning

July–August 1958

He knew he had to write one last poem before he could quit. Thirty years old, he had tried many times to give it up, but now he swore to the Muse that he was through. On the morning of July 22, 1958, James Wright began "His Farewell to Poetry."

All that summer, Wright woke before dawn, impatient to get to work. The light grew slowly in his basement study. "Two huge molten glooms of oak trees" shaded the house, and rusted awnings at ground level hooded the small windows near the ceiling. For a desk, Wright had placed a wooden board on sawhorses, with a gooseneck lamp and a typewriter on top. Plank bookshelves stacked on cinder blocks stood against the walls; floor beams and heating ducts were crowded above his head. In the dawn quiet, he heard songbirds and the rough shuttle of freight trains crossing above Como Avenue, where rows of small houses stood on narrow plots a mile from the University of Minnesota campus in Minneapolis.

Wright always felt that daybreak was the best time for writing. "There is something uncluttered and clear and living about the air at that time of day." The basement stayed cool despite the summer's brutal heat, and these early hours were quiet while his five-year-old son, Franz, and his wife, Liberty, slept. As July drew to a close, the Wrights' second child was due any day.

Standing five foot ten, Wright was not tall, but he was solidly built— like a football player, many said. His light brown hair was growing thin;

his wide-set brown eyes bore a sharp intensity until laughter gave him a mischievous squint. On his round face he wore horn-rimmed glasses that slipped from the too-small bridge of his nose. Reflexively, he pushed them snug with a finger stained by nicotine. At his desk, he alternately typed or wrote in a cramped, rounded script. Even with the windows propped open, cigarette smoke hung near the ceiling as Wright worked for hours in what he described as "this crazily organized study of mine (utterly alone in a corner of the basement, partitioned off by stained hardwood walls)."

Though he was freed from teaching for the coming semester, a sense of urgency compelled him and he slept little. Charles Dickens had become his constant companion—a doctoral dissertation—but this one last poem pulled him away. Wright's "Farewell to Poetry," retitled and published five years later after countless revisions, marks a turning point in his art, a moment of crisis that sparked the transformation of his life.

―――――

Wright's anguish over his own poetry had grown crippling. Though he published widely, he now felt "trapped by the very thing—the traditional technique—which I labored so hard to attain," as he confessed to his friend and mentor Theodore Roethke. In a letter to the poet Donald Hall, Wright insisted that he had been "denying the darker and wilder side of myself for the sake of subsisting on mere comfort—both academic and poetic." For Wright, this wasn't an argument over the use of iambic pentameter or emotional restraint. To rely upon "mere competence" amounted to a betrayal of true poetry.

Three weeks earlier, Wright had mailed a caustic, somewhat unhinged letter to the poet and critic James Dickey, a man he had never met. He enclosed an essay he'd written for *The Sewanee Review* condemning Dickey's arrogance and mulishness as a critic; Wright considered it a courtesy to alert him in advance. The essay defended a poet Dickey had just attacked in a review in that same magazine, but its true provocation had been his earlier scorn for Wright's own poems, which Dickey had mocked as "ploddingly 'sincere.'" Wright's letter challenged Dickey to concede that "generosity is not only a moral virtue" for a critic, but "also an act of intelligence." Ignoring Wright's argument, Dickey had seized upon an outburst of profanity to claim criminal offense against himself and his family.

Two days before drafting "His Farewell to Poetry," Wright sent a fawning apology to Dickey for his "paranoid and hysterical" letter, setting the tone for a peculiar yet substantial correspondence. Dickey's rebuke intensified Wright's feelings of anxiety and depression; he confesses to having sustained himself by "the illusion that my gifts might after all be genuine, though minor." As Wright awaited the birth of his second child, he feared the mounting financial burdens and grew convinced of his failure as a poet. Determined to find stability in his academic career and haunted by the image of Dickens "howling at me from the door-knocker," he decided to give up poetry altogether—after writing one final poem.

———

The Wright home in Minneapolis at 2414 Como Avenue near Twenty-fourth Street was remarkably small. The bedroom on the second floor had a steep, peaked roof that left little space to stand. Each room on the first floor opened onto the next: a living room at the front with a narrow, closed-in porch, a dining room, and a kitchen at the back, where a thin plot of grass and dirt lay beyond the looming oak trees and a pair of straggling pines. On July 22, having worked for hours on "His Farewell," Wright climbed the twelve plank steps from the semidarkness of his basement study into the heat of that early afternoon and left to retrieve his mail on campus.

His half-hour walk crossed three separate railroad lines, passing beneath the shade of tall ash trees that bordered Van Cleve Park, and continuing through the student neighborhood called Dinkytown on the eastern edge of campus. Wright mounted the broad marble stairs to his third-floor office in Folwell Hall and threw open the huge window beside his battered oak desk covered with books and papers. Traffic sounds along University Avenue and cigarette smoke filled this small room as he became "absolutely fixed with concentration for more than an hour," reading and rereading a copy of the first issue of a magazine called *The Fifties* that he'd found in his faculty mailbox. He had no idea who the editors were, or that such a poetry journal even existed. The cover showed a drawing of the ancient Norse god Odin, and inside was a startling declaration: "The editors of this magazine think that most of the poetry published in America today is too old-fashioned." In that one sentence, *The Fifties* voiced the same concerns that had consumed him in private. Over the next twenty-four hours, Wright typed a sprawling letter of praise, delight, argument, and disbelief to one of the magazine's editors, Robert Bly.

After a polite expression of gratitude, Wright is swept away with enthusiasm, "wondering at the weirdness of it all"—the coincidence of his quitting poetry and the appearance of *The Fifties* in his mailbox that same day. Wright insists that his widely praised first book, *The Green Wall*, "stank"; it had been "written by a dead man." The mere mention of the Austrian poet Georg Trakl, whose work would appear in a subsequent issue, is a source of bewilderment and joy. Years before, as a Fulbright student in Vienna, Wright had stumbled into the wrong classroom and become transfixed by Trakl's poetry—a fortuitous accident that mirrored the unexpected gift of this new journal. Wright describes how just that morning he had "done the honorable thing, the thing that Robert Herrick tried to do" three centuries earlier: he had written "my own 'Farewell to Poetry' . . . I said—as obscurely and gibberingly as I *felt* like saying—that the hell with it, I was getting *out*. And I got out. And that is really why your magazine meant so much to me. It's really extremely strange that I should receive it today, just after I quit." In paraphrasing his new poem, Wright's determination to *get out* of poetry becomes identical with the cold tenacity it had taken to escape the dead-end factory life and spiritual desolation of the Ohio Valley. Wright was questioning his own poetry at the deepest level, but in the act of writing to Bly, his "*suffering with this sense of failure*" begins to lift. Claiming to have given up poetry, his sheer exuberance contradicts him.

Early the next morning, Wright continued his letter to Bly, adding pages of postscript and marginalia—in all, sixteen pages of single-spaced type, the margins crammed with exclamations, questions, and recommendations. He challenges Bly's categorical rejection of iambic meter, initiating a debate between them that would continue for years. In *The Fifties*' lead essay, "Five Decades of Modern American Poetry," Bly lamented the return of "the old tradition" of iambic verse—a regression from the advances brought about by the great American modernists in the first decades of the century. "An imagination, a style, a content exists that has a magnificence of suggestion and association," Bly argued, championing the work of European and South American poets. Wright is excited by the focus on translation, but instinctively defends the craft he had worked to master and the poet-teachers to whom he was devoted— Theodore Roethke and John Crowe Ransom chief among them. He insists that Bly's critique applies to poets who fail "to build a genuine personal rhythm out of iambic." Wright's close reading of *The Fifties* is an extended form of praise; he quotes passages from Hart Crane and Federico García Lorca, testing the nuances of Bly's argument. "I have this strange compulsion to discover the truth about my failure—ever since I received your magazine."

———

The terms of Bly's rant quickly found their way into Wright's harsh self-criticism. In a letter to Donald Hall on July 25, Wright searches for the sources of his own poetic "failure," naming poets whose work reproaches "mere competence"—especially that of Pablo Neruda and Lorca. In this long and brilliant letter, he equates his personal struggle with that of his peers and introduces the metaphor of a pendulum to describe the pull of his emotions, using a figure of speech that recurs for many months. Wright says he feels "divided—really divided, as on the blade of a sword," between the loyalty he owes to the "intellectual grace" of Edwin Arlington Robinson and the "far more disturbing and ruthless" poetry of his contemporaries who champion Walt Whitman. Robinson and Whitman stand at the opposite poles of his poetic allegiance. Unable to fuse their divergent styles, "I have helplessly and nauseously swung back and forth terrified by great space on the pendulum from the one to the other."

Wright goes on to outline the "two necessary steps" a poet must take to create "a great and original poetry": after mastering the technical demands of tradition, a poet must then "*break through* this formal competence, in order to *create* a poetry which is unique and all one's own: the truly shaped voice of oneself." The command of craft that Horace requires must be joined with an unmistakable, personal voice. Throughout this dynamic letter, Wright sounds vibrant and self-assured. Nevertheless, confronting his own "failure and incapacity," he tells Hall that he has quit writing poetry. Over the coming days, however, he revised multiple drafts of his new poem, now called "His Prayer to the True Muse."

———

"Thank you immensely for the praise," Bly begins his first letter to Wright on August 1. "Your concern is the greatest compliment this magazine will ever receive." From this exchange grew a bond as important as any in the lives of both poets. In his reply five days later, Wright responds to an image that had already appeared in his poems, journals, and letters. "Your own phrase about 'rising from the dead' connotes some of the shock of self-recognition which has got to take place among us." Referring to new poems by Hall, W. D. Snodgrass, and Louis Simpson in *The Fifties*, Wright recognizes how other poets share the challenge he faces, and he articulates a striking vision of poetry as a communal effort.

> It is that we have learned the tricks too well, and that having arrived at a point of beginning, we have assumed that we were completed. All that happened to me is that I was stung awake . . . and if I cannot find [what Bly called the "new imagination"] in myself (though I believe I can), then I will identify and fight for it in others. And this is not mock-humility—I see blood in this matter, I really do. The enclosed poem is the revision of what began as "His Farewell to Poetry."

With its title borrowed from Herrick, the poem's original sixty lines had been "shortened by about ten more lines, and stripped and stripped ruthlessly." This process of revision became characteristic for Wright; over the next decade, successive drafts show him pressing for more concision and immediacy in nearly every poem.

In "His Farewell," Wright's doubts and self-hatred are stubbornly linked to the place of his birth. With each new version, the poem's physical setting—the mounds of factory refuse, scarred sumacs, and hobo jungles of the poet's childhood in Martins Ferry, Ohio, "my grave, the ditch of my defeat"—falls away, while the spiritual landscape intensifies. Disguised as a confession of failure, the poem becomes a prayer for consolation and inspiration. When "Goodbye to the Poetry of Calcium" appeared in 1963 as the second poem in Wright's landmark collection, *The Branch Will Not Break*, just eighteen lines would remain. Throughout years of revision, the poem preserves the tension and density of emotion that first inspired it, capturing a vivid impression of grief and longing.

Liberty gave birth to Marshall John Wright on the morning of July 30, 1958; they returned home from the hospital on August 4. Within a week, Liberty's divorced sister—with her own five-year-old son—moved in indefinitely, and the strain Wright felt is apparent in his letters. Roethke, who suffered from a bipolar disorder, understood the danger that shadowed Wright's self-questioning, depression, and intense activity that summer. "I worry my can off, practically," Roethke wrote from Seattle on August 16. "I've been through all this before, through the wringer, bud, so please respect my advice. Once you become too hyper-active and lose too much sleep, you'll cross a threshold where chaos (and terror) ensues. And believe me, chum, it's always a chancey thing whether you get back or not."

In his reply, Wright tries to reassure Roethke, promising to "take about two weeks off at once." He acknowledges the pressure he's been under, conceding, "This is not the sort of atmosphere in which one challenges Shakespeare." All the stress and excitement, however, inspired a period of astonishing productivity. Wright drafted more prose that summer than at any other time in his life—nearly two hundred pages of his dissertation alone. With uninterrupted hours open to him, he pushed himself relentlessly. Together with an outpouring of letters and three "hack reviews for money," Wright continued revising the manuscript for his second collection of poems, one that Wesleyan University Press accepted in October under the title *The Lamentation of Saint Judas*.

———

In the basement on Como Avenue, Wright turned reams of paper through his typewriter that summer—especially at the end of July, when "everything exploded at once." Following a brief trip in August to visit Donald Hall in Ann Arbor, Michigan, the uneasiness and grim determination evident in Wright's letters began to let up. Looking back over the previous weeks, he realized that he had found "the courage to try self-honesty, and also to admit how deeply and dangerously I *cared* about poetry." For Wright, this argument about poetic craft embodied a choice about how to live. The other significant events in his life that summer—the purchase of a home, the birth of his son, the completion of his doctoral thesis—occurred as if in parentheses, just as they often appeared in his letters. After years of compromise, he believed he must now confront the imperative proposed by Yeats: "perfection of the life, or of the work." Wright's rededication to poetry transformed his writing, but it also damaged his family and his teaching career, altering the course of his life.

In a letter to Bly on August 26, Wright recalls his parting words to Hall earlier that week: "I said that I felt as if I were eighteen years old again—vicious, arrogant, shaking with impatience to work." Over a matter of weeks, the enthralling sense of possibility that poetry meant to Wright had once more canceled out his uncertainty and self-reproach. In the summer of 1958, he treasured his solitude "in the basement, with the furnace, the moths, the skeletons of mice and the necklaces of twilight." His makeshift desk in a narrow, secluded study proved to be the pivot around which his life would turn. Wright had not reached an end of poetry, but a point of beginning. "I feel born again," he told Bly. "All I want is to work. I thought I was finished, I really did, but I'm not finished. But this will take a long, long time."

Goodbye to the Poetry of Calcium

Dark cypresses—
The world is uneasily happy:
It will all be forgotten.
—Theodor Storm

Mother of roots, you have not seeded
The tall ashes of loneliness
For me. Therefore,
Now I go.
If I knew the name,
Your name, all trellises of vineyards and old fire
Would quicken to shake terribly my
Earth, mother of spiraling searches, terrible
Fable of calcium, girl. I crept this afternoon
In weeds once more.
Casual, daydreaming you might not strike
Me down. Mother of window sills and journeys,
Hallower of scratching hands,
The sight of my blind man makes me want to weep.
Tiller of waves or whatever, woman or man,
Mother of roots or father of diamonds,
Look: I am nothing.
I do not even have ashes to rub into my eyes.

—from *The Branch Will Not Break*, 1963

PART I

1

That is my country, that river

December 13, 1927–September 1944

[My parents] are sturdy, steadfast people, poorly educated and—especially
my mother—very well read. My relatives are strangely unpredictable and
rather wildly kind.   —from a letter to Mary Oliver, September 16, 1965

Riverview Cemetery commands the crest of an Appalachian foothill
where the Ohio River flows past Martins Ferry, Ohio. Time and again,
as a teenager in the early 1940s, James Wright climbed to this highest
point above the river, anxious to feel "the sense, the vista" he found in
books. But the smoke and soot from steel mills obscured the steep, matching hills of West Virginia on the opposite shore. Behind him, to the west,
farmland, orchards, and fields had been disfigured by coal and strip
mines; the river, too, was fouled by refuse and waste. Yet the Ohio de-
fines the geography and the essence of the place; it is a boundary and a
dark presence. The once thriving industrial town stretches along a
narrow shelf half a mile wide, a hundred feet above the river's floodplain.
In Wright's youth this bottomland was crowded with factories, tenements,
and docks, whole neighborhoods at risk of flooding each spring. He
counted himself "among the brief green things"—the sumac, trillium,
and weeds—that survived in a ravaged place.

By the time Wright left Martins Ferry in June 1946, he knew every
street and alleyway in his hometown, each muddy footpath that stretched
for miles along the river. He knew the Ohio in all its moods; he knew

what poverty was, and hard work. When Wright enlisted in the army at the age of eighteen, he swore he would never return to the Ohio Valley; he made only brief visits back home.

He climbed to the graveyard's summit again on Christmas Eve 1951, a month before he graduated from Kenyon College. Liberty Kardules, a nursing student and high school classmate, stood beside him. They could see the Blaw-Knox and Laughlin steel mills dominating the northern edge of the flats beside the river and, among the factories, the green rectangle of the high school football field. They saw the train and street-car lines, and the Terminal Bridge crossing at the tip of Wheeling Island. On the upper plateau, the twin blue domes of the Greek Orthodox church stood out from the grid of brick and clapboard houses. Wright gestured to the town below them and cursed the place: "'Give up hope, all ye who enter here.' It's pure hell down there. Just pure hell." Liberty agreed. "We knew that we had to get out of there or it would kill us." Joined in desperation, the couple descended the stairs of that same church six weeks later as husband and wife.

Wright found himself in Martins Ferry once more in August 1953, with Liberty and their infant son, Franz. They had just returned from a year in Vienna and spent one night in her father's house on Pearl Street. During their absence, Liberty's mother had died of cancer, and when they visited her grave near the cemetery's peak, Wright looked out once more on his hometown. Then twenty-five, he was about to take his young family on the long train journey to Seattle to continue his graduate studies. His rage to escape the Ohio Valley remained, but the pull of memory would prove stronger still. Wright's childhood place came to occupy the center of his poetic imagination; over the remaining twenty-seven years of his life, he made it into an unmistakable landscape in American literature.

Wright came to accept the "peculiar kind of devotion" he felt toward Martins Ferry and its townspeople. "I have done a great deal of wandering," he recalled late in his life—to Japan and Hawaii, throughout Europe and the United States. "Yet all of these places taken together do not have the vastness in my mind that I still find when I contemplate, as I've so often done in my books, the small river town of Martins Ferry in southeastern Ohio." Wright remembered with startling immediacy "the dark howlings and twangs of the language I grew up with: the nearly unspeakable violences of the spirit and body, spun suddenly into baroque figures of speech across the sooty alleys near the river and up and down the B&O railroad track that lay peaceful among the hobo jungles like a scar."

Martins Ferry was blighted in ways typical to industrial river towns throughout the early twentieth century: its hillsides gouged by strip mines, the air blackened by coal smoke, and the river polluted by sewage and oil. But as with other towns that flourished in the Ohio Valley, the factories and mines attracted a great diversity of people. The headstones in Riverview Cemetery chronicle the history of Martins Ferry's growth; the older ones on the lower edge bear the names of Welsh coal miners from the mid-1800s. Ascending the slope, the stones describe successive waves of immigrants from Hungary, Poland, Italy, Greece, Romania, England, and Ireland.

In the "Childhood Sketch" he drafted in August 1978, Wright says of Martins Ferry: "I had lived in all of the neighborhoods except the wealthy ones up on the hills away from the factories and the river, and I knew most of the languages, and carry with me today the affections of those words." Wright felt a sharp grief for those he left behind in Ohio; they are both the subject of and the intended audience for his poems. After years of rootlessness, he came to cherish the multicultural, working-class neighborhoods of his youth, and Wright's imagination always returned to the banks of the Ohio River. "In form and body it remains itself one of the magnificent rivers of the world. It could gather into itself the Seine, the Arno, and the Adige, and still have room for a whole mile of drifting lost lives."

―――――

In languages spoken by the native peoples of the Ohio Valley, many names for the river translate as "beautiful." The Ohio flows south and west for a thousand miles, from the confluence of the Allegheny and Monongahela Rivers—the site of Pittsburgh—to Cairo, Illinois, where it joins the Mississippi. Various Algonquian tribes made their home in the valley and defended the land west of the river from both local Iroquois and European pioneers. Beginning in 1744 and continuing for two decades, British and French troops battled for possession of the Ohio River and its surrounding territories. Native warriors prevented settlements west of the river until after the Revolutionary War, when thousands of colonists and more recent immigrants crossed the Allegheny and Appalachian mountain ranges to claim land for homesteading. Indigenous tribes were pushed farther inland, but the battle for control of the river was prolonged and bitter. In some native tongues the Ohio became known as the "River of Blood."

The first permanent settlement on the western shore, across from the fortified military post at Wheeling, Virginia, sprang up around a ferry landing, on a broad stretch of flatland. Absalom Martin had helped his father-in-law, Ebenezer Zane, survey the surrounding land, and Martin's ferry became the starting point of "a good waggon Road," as Zane called it, between Wheeling and Maysville, Kentucky. Zane's Trace, a shorter and more reliable route west, less prone to the seasonal dangers of river travel, opened in 1797. For decades the town of Martins Ferry remained a major crossroads and entry point to the Northwest Territory— what became the states of Ohio, Indiana, Michigan, Illinois, and Wisconsin. The Zane family and other pioneers planted orchards of fruit trees, berry bushes, and grape vines on Wheeling Island and the open fields on the western shore, cultivating tracts they then sold to the steady waves of settlers. In childhood, Wright knew the legacy of those early farmers: along the riverbank, amid tangles of shrub oak and sumac, the fragrances of blossoming pear, peach, and apple trees mingled with the smell of locust trees in springtime.

European immigrants joined colonial homesteaders in the early 1800s, bypassing coastal states to settle directly in the interior. This northern heartland of the Midwest became the first region in the United States to prohibit slavery, and "free-thinkers"—who advocated tolerance and the necessity of education—influenced the region's politics well into the twentieth century. The river formed a boundary between free and slave states prior to the Civil War, and by 1840, Ohio had more safe houses for escaping slaves than any other state. Martins Ferry, across the river from the slave-trading market in Wheeling, became a crucial haven.

Many Scots-Irish immigrants from England's northern borderlands were self-sufficient farmers who raised their own livestock, a kind of plain-folk, hardscrabble farming that took root in the backcountry of Appalachia as a separate way of life. This "Cohee" culture (derived from "yeomen") had enormous influence upon Wright's mother, Jessie, who spent her childhood on a subsistence farm in northern West Virginia. Martins Ferry, too, first developed as a farming community, and in the 1860s was still surrounded by vineyards, orchards, cornfields, and farms.

The discovery of coal seams running beneath neighboring hillsides ignited the town's industrial growth. With limestone, clay, and iron ore also close at hand, the riverfront made an ideal location for an iron-smelting blast furnace. In 1853, the Penn Central Railroad opened the entire area to heavy industry. Steel towns like Martins Ferry, Steubenville, Weirton, Benwood, and many others sprang up all along the Ohio River, which gave access to national and global markets. By the 1870s, Wheeling had become a major rail hub, while in Martins Ferry two separate train lines cut through the river's wide floodplain, known as the Bottom. When the flats grew overcrowded, the town's business district and wealthier citizens moved to the upper plateau above the river. The Ohio is a quarter-mile wide where the prominent brick houses of Martins Ferry ascend the western bank.

Hundreds of English and Welsh coal miners lived in Martins Ferry by the end of the nineteenth century, working in mines sunk straight into the hillsides. Wheeling Steel shuttled carloads of coal from the "tipple" down to the mill on elevated tracks that passed over working-class neighborhoods at the northern edge of town. With the mining boom, Martins Ferry's population tripled by 1900, and this growth continued unabated at the time of Wright's birth in 1927. Immigrants from Italy, Poland, and Hungary joined the local Appalachian workers, together with African-Americans from the South. During Wright's adolescence, Martins Ferry boasted twenty thousand inhabitants, most laboring in the steel mills along the river or the coal mines in interior hill country to the west.

————

When James Wright's parents—Jessie and Dudley—married in March 1916, they united families with roots on both sides of the Ohio River reaching back more than a century. Wright described his mother's parents, born and raised in West Virginia, as "honest-to-God hillbillies to a fare-thee-well." Jacob James Rawley Lyons, Jessie's father, was born April 17, 1859, near the western border of present-day Virginia, and died at the age of fifty-seven in June 1916. Rawley Lyons was twenty years old when he married Elizabeth Bedora Starkey—the matriarch of the Lyons family and a cherished presence in Wright's childhood.

Elizabeth, or "Biddy," was born in Hundred, West Virginia, on September 21, 1862, and married Rawley Lyons at the age of sixteen. Together they worked a subsistence farm in hill country a few miles east of the Ohio River in the West Virginia panhandle. Nearly a decade passed before their first child was born—a girl who died in infancy—but Biddy gave birth to seven more children over the next fifteen years. Jessie, born August 21, 1897, was the middle child, with two older sisters, an older brother, William, and three younger brothers.

Soon after the birth of the youngest, Sherman, in 1905, Rawley Lyons disappeared and was never heard from again. Though Biddy now faced the hardship of raising seven children on her own, a sense of relief followed her husband's desertion. It freed her from Lyons's violent temper, which grew worse the more he drank. The family left the farm Jessie had known as a girl and relocated across the river in Bridgeport, Ohio, the town just south of Martins Ferry. They moved often during her childhood, and though Jessie attended school only through the sixth grade, she became a voracious reader. Wright would later describe how his mother "slaved—it is the true word—in a laundry" from the time she was sixteen. After crossing the river into North Wheeling each day with her sister, Jessie worked the enormous ironing presses known as "mangles." Jim's aunt Grace would work at the White Swan Laundry her entire life.

Dudley Wright's even temper and steady employment made him an ideal suitor for Jessie; he was also handsome, quiet, and kind. Over the course of their marriage, he proved to be a man of great forbearance as well. Like Jessie, he was a middle child from a large family who had grown up in poverty. Dudley's father, Spencer Washington Sterms Wright, was born in 1861, not far from the birthplace of Biddy Lyons, south of Wheeling near the Ohio River. Ellen Louise Beck, Dudley's mother, became Spencer Wright's second wife, and like him had been raised in Belmont County, Ohio, twenty miles west of the river.

Wright spoke often of his Irish ancestry, common to both sides of his family; he regretted his "almost obscene gift of gab, which I learned from my poor frustrated mother." He came to distrust the ease he felt in talking and storytelling. A more debilitating physical legacy, however, also came down to him: both grandfathers were alcoholics. Spencer Wright died in 1932 at the age of sixty-four as a consequence of his drinking. He had fathered eight children and, in many ways, had been as absent from his family as Jessie's father had been.

John Dudley Ira Wright was born June 26, 1893, in Bridgeport, Ohio. By the time his father tried to get sober, he could no longer hold a job, forcing his children to find work. Dudley's four sisters and a brother eventually scattered throughout Ohio and the Midwest, and only his sister Lillian remained close to him and his family. Dudley—who never drank—completed the eighth grade before taking a job at the Hinge Works in Wheeling, a factory that soon became the Hazel-Atlas Glass Company. He was fourteen years old.

Wright's father spent his entire working life on a factory assembly line. He began as a press roller of steel before training as a die setter—a tedious job that nevertheless demanded skill and concentration. The Wheeling plant, an immense brick structure on the southeastern edge of the city, produced the zinc lids and rings used to seal mason jars. Dudley made the precise adjustments necessary to cut the lids from their metal matrix before they were fitted with rubber sealing rings. The home canning industry flourished throughout the Depression, and Dudley was thus rarely out of work—even during the worst years of the early 1930s. On his marriage certificate from March 1916, when he was twenty-two years old, Wright's father listed his occupation as "Press Operator, Glass Works." Jessie was then eighteen and glad to quit her job at the White Swan Laundry. The couple moved a few miles north, crossing the town line from Bridgeport into Martins Ferry.

After four years of marriage, Jessie and Dudley Wright adopted an eighteen-month-old baby girl, Margaret, from an orphanage in Wheeling. Jessie was anxious to start a family, but, as with her own mother, years passed before she first conceived. Marge was seven years old when Jessie's first son, Theodore (called Ted), was born in July 1925. By then, Jessie had begun moving the family practically every year from one rented house to another. She was often nervous and irritable, and only Dudley's return each night brought her some peace.

———

James Arlington Wright was born at home on December 13, 1927. Jessie gave birth in an old-fashioned double bed with a wrought-iron headboard; she often said Jimmy was spoiled from the start. As was common, she spent ten days in bed nursing the newborn, but when she returned to her chores the boy squalled endlessly. In Aetnaville, at the southern edge of Martins Ferry, the Wrights' home stood a few hundred yards from the river. Day and night, they heard the clatter of streetcars and coal cars, punctuated by the whistles of B&O freight trains and of shift changes at the factories. In the silence beneath, the Ohio River remained "part of my spirit," Wright realized. "I always felt, since I was a kid, the need of being near water."

"I was born at 613 Union Street," Wright recalled late in life. "I don't know why I should cling to that particular useless detail." He could remember vast catalogs of detail, but Wright cherished this simple fact—in part because his family moved so often when he was young. Before he was ten he had lived in six different houses in every corner of Martins Ferry. Landlords offered a month's free rent to tenants who stayed a full year, but the family's frequent moves arose as much from Jessie's restlessness as from the struggle to keep ahead. "It was like hopscotch," Marge recalled. "Mother had a little gypsy in her, I think." In many of the Wrights' rented homes—including houses on Broadway, Walnut Street, Pearl Street, and South Third Street—Jessie took in boarders to help pay the rent; men came to town without their families to work in the mines or the steel mills. But Jessie was uncomfortable with the proximity and familiarity of neighbors. She even put bottles of colored water on her windowsills, a superstition she knew would upset the local clergy and churchgoing women.

Dudley's patience and equanimity secured whatever happiness Wright's parents knew in marriage—only he could quiet Jessie's temper. She cursed Dudley each morning as he left for work, even as he bent to kiss her goodbye. The image of Jessie, always a strict disciplinarian, "swearing at the dishes" in Wright's poem "How My Fever Left" is part of a portrait taken from life. Yet her children worshipped her, and she remained ever attentive to their needs and health. As a boy, Jim tested his mother's patience on every walk to the grocery store, "stopping to look at every plant, every twig." A photograph of Wright at ten months, seated between his sister and his brother Ted on a broad porch railing, shows this same curiosity, his left eyebrow slightly raised. This distinctive look appears in another photo taken at Christmas a week after his fifth birthday. Jim's smile beams and his arched left eyebrow makes him seem both cautious and alert—an expression captured in photographs throughout his life.

Though his mother remained a resolute skeptic, two distinct strains of Christianity formed part of Wright's upbringing: the strict mores of Scots-Irish Presbyterians and the animated drama of Pentecostalism. Jessie allowed Dudley to take their sons to church on Sundays, but Marge's religious fervor led to an estrangement from her mother. Marge attended the fundamentalist Assembly of God church on her own, and she rebelled against her parents' authority. At fifteen she left school and crossed the river into Wheeling to marry Paul Pyle, a man six years older who had just returned from California—"hoboing and hopping freight trains." Their marriage lasted more than sixty years, until Marge's death in 1996. The couple married in the depths of the Depression, and while Jim recalled putting cardboard in his shoes to cover the holes, Marge knew that their family had been spared worse hardships.

Skilled laborers like Dudley lived on the "streets with names" on the town's upper plateau—a world apart from the houseboats, shacks, and tenements on the numbered streets near the train tracks and the river. Dudley continued to work, and there was always food on the table; Wright's parents shared what they could and gave odd jobs to drifters in exchange for meals. But in the faces of those around him, Wright saw the daily struggle that life had become.

Martins Ferry had two "hot" mills—the Laughlin steel mill and the Aetna mill—where molten steel was rolled in slabs; day laborers contracted for "piecework" and got paid for the tonnage they produced each day. Towering brick smokestacks sent plumes of coal dust into the air, while every home also burned coal for heat. At night the town and hills above it were lit red from the blast furnaces pouring steel, and workers emerged from factory shifts blackened with soot. Homes quickly became grimy with the powdery ash, as did snow as soon as it fell. Local mining towns met the heavy demand for coal, with trains a hundred cars long— some stretching over two miles—passing every day along the river. These freight trains slowed as they moved through the populous flats, and townspeople jumped onto the open cars to throw coal down to others pushing wheelbarrows through the charred weeds. In winter, many gathered tree branches and logs washed up on the riverbank for fuel.

Vast neighborhoods of homes, businesses, and factories surrounded the thriving industrial commerce on the flatland along the river. The Train (or Terminal) Bridge marked the southern edge of town. On a narrow wooden walkway beside the tracks, Dudley and hundreds of other workers crossed the bridge every day to reach the factories and rail yards in Wheeling. Suspended a hundred feet above the river, the narrow boardwalk became treacherous with ice and snow in winter. Wheeling was then a city of more than a hundred thousand—six times the size of Martins Ferry—with an extensive downtown, five movie theaters, and the Capitol Theatre, which hosted Jamboree, the sole competitor to Nashville's Grand Ole Opry.

Wright could sit for hours in front of the radio, and he listened to everything—not just country music but weekly serials, baseball games, and music of all kinds. He also paid close attention to the cadences and patterns of speech all around him; his "photographic" memory was linked to an uncommon aural acuity. "I have a reasonably good ear for music," he once wrote, "and when I am alone, I can hear voices that spoke to me twenty years ago."

———

Floods threatened towns all along the Ohio River during the snowmelt each spring. In March 1936, during a spell of bitter cold weather, flood-waters rose for three days, ultimately cresting more than eighteen feet above flood stage. The entire river valley, from Pittsburgh south to the Mississippi—including all of eastern Ohio—was ravaged. The swollen river rose nearly to the upper shelf of the town, and Wheeling Island flooded completely. A friend of Wright's watched as the Wheeling Gospel Tabernacle was swept from the northern tip of the island, toppling homes before it into the surging waters. Seventeen deaths were reported in the local vicinity alone.

Wright, eight years old and living at the southern end of town just clear of the cresting river, witnessed the ferocity of the flood and the massive cleanup effort that followed. Families evacuated from the bot-tomland were housed in schools, churches, and fire stations in town—a forced camaraderie among those left homeless. All but the sturdiest brick structures were cleared from the flats; the homes and factory buildings left standing were filled with mud, and most were beyond repair. The tragedy united Ferrians in a profound way, helping define the commu-nity by the determination they shared to restore the town and overcome the devastation. As part of that effort, the Works Progress Administration built a public swimming pool in a downtown city park that summer, and Wright's father and uncles "helped dig that hole in the ground. . . . No grave for once." A luminous epiphany written decades later, "The Old WPA Swimming Pool in Martins Ferry, Ohio" captures the sense of re-newal and possibility he then felt. But Wright and his friends, "children of the blast furnaces and factories and mines, kept faith with the river." They continued to swim in the Ohio.

Swimming in the Ohio River was more common to the generation of Wright's parents; it had always been dangerous. Powerful eddy currents surge at the northern tip of Wheeling Island, where the main course of the river follows the West Virginia shore and a smaller channel separates the island from Ohio. The "bare-ass beach" where Wright and other children swam was beneath the concrete piers of the Train Bridge, beyond the tracks and weeds along the riverbank. After work in the summer, Dudley often took his boys down to the river, and Wright treasured memories of swimming with his brother Ted, who recalled "a kind of a poor-man's beach" where barges off-loaded gravel and sand. But every year brought news of drownings, especially in early summer when the water ran high. The dredging of sand from the river created whirlpools with incredible force, known by the "hideous Ohio phrase—a suckhole." Both Jim and Ted witnessed such deaths. With his friend Thomas Hodge and other Boy Scouts, Jim helped search for boys who were lost to the river. The effort to recover the bodies often demanded the skills of a professional diver named John Shunk, who dragged the river bottom with huge iron hooks. Many times, they searched without success.

————

Just after Wright turned ten at the end of December 1937, his mother moved the family into the first home they ever owned: a large gray house in the southern part of town, beside a streetcar stop and the Nickles Bakery. The two-story structure at 1016 Broadway had a wide front porch and an alley at the back shored up with railroad ties, where a steep slope dropped off to the flats and the river. Ted was twelve years old when they moved in just before Christmas; Marge was already married, with a son the same age as Jessie's youngest, Jack, who was three. The family soon adopted a black-and-white spaniel mutt named Queenie, who chose Jim as her favorite. The front yard had a mulberry tree, two sycamores, and a maple, and Jim could often be found among their branches. He lived in this house for seven and a half years—the longest period he ever spent beneath one roof. More than any other place, 1016 Broadway formed his idea of home.

Tom Hodge knew Jim best between the ages of ten and fourteen, during middle school and their early years of high school. Though two years younger, Hodge was precocious and kept pace with Jim's intense curiosity. In summer they roamed west of town, stealing fruit from arbors and orchards "up on the hill," as shown in "An Offering for Mr. Blue-hart." Hodge lived two blocks away, and between their homes stood the South School, which Wright entered in the middle of fifth grade. As he revealed in an autobiographical essay written at the end of high school, this was when Wright "discovered with a furious awe that he was a poet; a poor one, but a poet all the same."

Encouraged by his parents, Jim had become an avid reader; books filled their home. Jessie had taught Jim to read before he entered school, and she often made her sons sit at the kitchen table and read to her as she did chores. By the age of ten, Wright was constantly seeking out new books and writers, and Tom Hodge witnessed Wright's discovery of poetry through the work of Lord Byron. A boarder in the Hodge home, an itinerant preacher, had left behind a sizable collection of books, and Tom told Wright "he could just go through the books, read any one he wanted and keep any one he wanted. So Jim had his own little library at our place." The two friends would often sit on the porch and talk of poetry. Byron's poems captured Wright's imagination, and even Jack, at the age of seven, remembered his brother declaiming:

The Assyrian came down like the wolf on the fold,
And his cohorts were gleaming in purple and gold.

Of course, Jack could make little sense of "The Destruction of Sennach-erib," but Jim began reciting poems to anyone. He also discovered the heavily rhymed verse of James Whitcomb Riley, which often used mid-western dialects, but the poems of the English Romantics—Byron, Shel-ley, Blake, and Keats—were his earliest infatuation. "One of the strangest experiences of my life," Wright later recalled, "was my first reading, as a child, of the Blake line 'The Ohio shall wash my stains from me.'"

By the age of twelve, he had begun writing sonnets; he drafted hun-dreds of them throughout high school and his service in the army. When he entered Shreve High School in September 1941, he thought of him-self as a writer and treasured the certificate of merit awarded by the American Legion for an essay in his freshman year. But Wright remained an unexceptional student, "solitary and morose," and most of his courses amounted to vocational training. All that fall, from the porch of the Hodge home on Pearl Street or crouched beside the radio's speaker, he and Tom listened to Pirates baseball games from Pittsburgh, Joe Louis prizefights, and serial mysteries, like *The Green Hornet* and *Inner Sanctum*. But reports of the war in Europe began to dominate the broadcasts, and soon many older friends had enlisted and shipped out.

English verse was not the only poetry to claim Wright's attention. For years, he visited Grandma Lyons after school each day, and her warmth and understanding helped him weather his mother's harsh discipline and bitterness. Biddy encouraged her grandson to read the Bible, a practice they came to share. The King James Bible had a profound and lasting impact on Wright's language and thought; he received his own copy in Sunday school at the age of nine. He attended the First Christian Church regularly and was baptized in the fall of his sophomore year, which he considered a decisive event. Fellow churchgoers thought Jim might take up the ministry, and he briefly considered it himself. Wright's deepening interest in theology and metaphysics, however, contributed to the nervous breakdown he suffered as a teenager in the summer of 1943.

His trouble began with the death of Grandma Lyons the previous fall—the first death of someone Jim felt close to. Not only did Wright mourn the loss of a beloved confederate who could ease his mother's temper and agitation, but he also felt that Biddy had understood him better than anyone. Moreover, the war now overshadowed daily life; in the winter of 1943, radio reports chronicled the siege of Stalingrad. Despite the enlistment of so many young men and women, the population of Martins Ferry actually swelled, as the steel mills and factories worked around the clock to fortify the war effort. Ted graduated from high school in June 1943 and enlisted that July, leaving Jim the oldest son at home.

Two other books pilfered from the Hodge family's attic compounded Wright's anxieties that summer. One was *The Bible Unmasked*, which featured explicit pen and ink drawings of erotic scenes from the Old Testament and argued that incidents of incest and prostitution involving biblical patriarchs proved the immoral and contradictory nature of Judeo-Christian religious beliefs. In response, Wright began reading the Bible obsessively. Ted's wife, Helen, believed this helped trigger his breakdown. "When he came home from the hospital, the doctor told him, 'No more Bibles in the house. Get rid of all of them!'"

When Jack questioned their mother, Jessie told him that his brother had heard voices in his head debating the existence of God. She blamed another of the books Jim had found in the preacher's library: *The Mysterious Universe*. Published in 1932 by a noted astrophysicist, the work argues that, given the infinite expanse of the universe, the presence of human beings on a tiny planet at the edge of one of millions of galaxies is utterly insignificant—to say nothing of any one life. As Wright struggled with fundamental questions of theology, the book became a source of anguish. In his application to Kenyon College in the fall of 1947, he confirmed Jessie's suspicion that his reading had worked to undermine his sanity.

> In about my fourteenth year, suddenly I discovered that the uni-
> verse was infinite, that somewhere in the universe spun a tiny clot
> of mud called earth, whereon vegetated an ape-like creature known
> as man; and explosively I observed that I was alive upon the
> earth. The actions which were bound to effect intellectual isola-
> tion were inevitable. . . . Numerous months of my middle adoles-
> cence were spent inside a painful solitary shell.

As Wright later confessed, the mental turmoil he felt when he woke one morning compelled him to put his fist through a mirror. His parents took him to Ohio Valley General Hospital in North Wheeling, where he spent six weeks in the psychiatric ward, from the end of August into October. Doctors there administered insulin shock therapy—a precursor to electroshock treatments—that induced periods of intense hunger. Wright's autobiography, written two and a half years later, gives a glancing description of his breakdown in the summer of 1943: "He became possessed by the flooding conviction that everything he had ever seen, heard, smelled, touched, tasted, and slept with had to be recorded. His fingers sought out volumes of the writings of Milton, Shakespeare, Marlowe, Keats, and any number of earth's most powerful dreamers. Desperately he raged into Darwin's *Origin of Species*, but it was too much."

Recovered too late to begin his junior year, in October Wright crossed the river into Wheeling and found work at Bolton's Cigar Store and Restaurant. Four months later he got a job on the loading dock at Sears, Roebuck & Co., "where he met, and was impressed by, the philosophy of truck drivers, furniture repair men, and trash collectors." In the daily grind of this backbreaking work he also befriended a high school senior immersed in mathematics and physics, and the two talked constantly. Wright would later find joy in recounting this turn of events, calling it "a time when I began to rise from the dead." When he returned to high school, Wright wanted to excel, determined to master Latin and mathematics and to seek a college degree. He knew that to stay in Ohio meant a lifetime of rough physical labor without reprieve. Throughout his adolescence, Wright "abominated the Ohio Valley," and he came to blame this deep-seated hatred for the breakdown he had suffered. In his first letter to Robert Bly on July 22, 1958, Wright cursed Martins Ferry, "that unspeakable rat-hole where I grew up . . . the slag heaps and the black trees and the stool-washed river and the chemicals from the factories of Wheeling Steel, Blaw Knox, the Hanna Coal Co. which . . . are the only images of childhood I can ever have." Later in life, Wright endured a recurring nightmare in which he was stripped of his college degrees and forced to return to work in a factory in Martins Ferry.

2

And I got out

September 1944–July 1946

As a child, Wright loved going back to school; the beginning of autumn brought a sense of hopefulness and promise. In September 1944, these feelings were especially keen. After a year of heavy manual work, traveling every day into Wheeling, he knew that academic success offered his best chance to escape the Ohio Valley. The new school year also meant the start of the high school football season, a communal ritual of great significance throughout Ohio and the Midwest. For a few exceptional athletes, high school sports offer entry to the wider world, ambitions celebrated across generations. "Autumn Begins in Martins Ferry, Ohio" later introduced many readers to Wright's hometown, and it underscores the uneasy distance that grew between the poet and the people he left behind.

In the Shreve High football stadium,
I think of Polacks nursing long beers in Tiltonsville,
And gray faces of Negroes in the blast furnace at Benwood,
And the ruptured night watchman of Wheeling Steel,
Dreaming of heroes.

All the proud fathers are ashamed to go home.
Their women cluck like starved pullets,
Dying for love.

Therefore,
Their sons grow suicidally beautiful
At the beginning of October,
And gallop terribly against each other's bodies.

Though written in 1960—years after Wright's last visit there—the poem occurs in the present, with the speaker simply one among the crowd of spectators. He stands at a curious remove from his fellow townspeople, however, and observes them with the empathy of a privileged insider.

Powerfully built, with a broad chest and shoulders, Wright had the physical skill and tenacity that could have earned him a place on the high school football team like his brother Ted. Though he loved the game, he never tried out for the team. He focused his tremendous energy on his studies and his writing.

Beyond his immediate family, few townsfolk could recall the teenage Wright distinctly before the autumn of 1944, when he seemed to suddenly appear in high school. At this point, the poet becomes recognizable in the memories of his classmates: studious, determined, eloquent, and possessed of an astonishing memory. Wright returned as a more sociable and confident sixteen-year-old, but in many ways the atmosphere was no different from the workplace; the war remained a harsh backdrop. Anticipating enlistment, his friends cared little about school, and many left early each day for afternoon shifts at Wheeling Steel (making bomb fins and "blitz cans") or the Blaw-Knox mill (fabricating anti-aircraft cannons). At sixteen, many of Wright's friends earned seventy-five cents an hour in the mills. There were dozens of bars and beer joints all over town, and when their shifts ended, students stood at the bar beside their fathers and uncles. Wright also joined those who crossed the river into Wheeling on summer evenings, where the streetwalkers appeared on Twenty-third Street near the river.

While some of his classmates didn't bother with high school at all, Jim Wright was different—a quiet, serious guy with a stack of books under his arm. But he was just as conscious of the war. His brother Ted was stationed first in Calcutta and then in Shanghai with a field artillery unit, while their father's glass factory job was designated as critical, "red circle" work, which meant long hours with little time off. In February 1945, Paul Hanson—an older classmate whom Wright revered—died in a railroad accident in France, and the loss left a deep and lasting wound.

Hanson would appear in elegiac poems for years to come, the first of many ghost presences who haunt Wright's poetry. Everything conspired to make him work harder in school. As one classmate put it, "This was wartime—people didn't fool around."

Wright's newfound ambition led him to join the Martins Ferry Hi-Y Club, a volunteer service group sponsored by the Young Men's Christian Association. Already a figure apart, he endured more than the usual abuse from the club's senior members in public hazing rituals famous throughout the city. Each Hi-Y Club fielded a football team against neighboring towns, and having survived initiation, Wright exacted payback that fall when his junior team overpowered the senior squad. He had grown up playing on a rough cinder field called the Dump, with "a hardnosed, tough bunch of sandlot players, real headknockers," one classmate recalled. "Jim was just as violent as the next guy. He was fearless when he was playing football." With Wright as captain the following year, the Martins Ferry Hi-Y team went undefeated; the coach of the high school team refused to let his players scrimmage against them.

————

In September 1944, Wright met two outstanding teachers whose encouragement proved essential during his last two years in high school. His Latin teacher, Helen McNeely Sheriff, and his English teacher, Elizabeth Willerton, recognized Wright's innate gifts, and they both demanded excellence from him. Miss Sheriff modeled her classroom after an English boarding school and she found an ideal pupil in Wright, whose preternatural talent for memorization placed him, literally, at the front of the class. He recognized a strong classical streak in his own nature, and admired Sheriff's rigor and seriousness. Sheriff proved to him "that the use of the mind is not a mere luxury, but rather is itself an exercise of strength even greater than the strength required to drive a coal-truck or flop tin from a steel-stove." Throughout his life, Wright acknowledged the pivotal influence these teachers had on him. "I have never written anything," he admitted, "without wondering, sooner or later, whether or not Miss Sheriff would find it worthy." Many of Wright's poems from high school show the influence of his translations of Latin prose and poetry, a discipline he came to depend on as a strategy for survival.

Miss Willerton helped broaden the range of Wright's reading and introduced him to Tolstoy, Dostoevsky, and other Russian novelists, classical music, and the visual arts. Her friendship would remain crucial to him long after he left her classroom. Susan Lamb first encountered Jim Wright in their junior-year English course. He caught her attention following the IQ test that Willerton gave to all her classes. "I was a good student—that's why he liked me—and I got a real high score, but his was practically off the charts. He was truly in the genius category." Lamb saw the strong attachment that Wright felt toward Willerton; finally receiving the encouragement he craved, he grew prolific. Expanding beyond his first Romantic models, Wright's earliest poems combined traditional themes and rhetoric with vernacular speech. He wrote more than a hundred sonnets in his last two years of high school, many dedicated to writers, artists, and composers in a curious mixture of admiration and possession.

Willerton and Lamb were among the few outside his family with whom Jim shared his poems. More than criticism or advice, he wanted an audience. Jack Wright remembered sitting at the kitchen table, reading to his mother from Jim's notebook as she washed dishes: "I cannot write. The words no longer flow / Across the page, unfettered and profuse." In this untitled sonnet, Wright challenges Romantic notions of inspiration by locating his own Muse in darkness, though he seeks to "write / Eternally, the synonyms of light." From the beginning, this tension between darkness and light appears in his work. Wright's juvenilia often use overwrought imagery and slang to startle the reader and coarsen the language; one sonnet begins, "You made warm mention of some scummy gem / Of 'poetry' I puked, or sang, or wrote." But this same poem goes on to describe a conflict between "one part of me that will not die" and another "drowning in a lake of blood." The poet stands apart, watching, "my feet ensnared in mud." Many of Wright's adolescent poems capture his sense of internal struggle and betray how anxious he was of failing. He thought of poetry as a noble, intellectual calling, and he often signed his work with the pseudonym "J. Wolfingham Wright."

Wright's devotion to Keats encouraged his obsession with the sonnet form. In one, "On Receiving a Copy of the Works of Keats," he worries that his passion for poetry will leave him like "A dying sailor gazing at the sea"—echoing Keats's own early sonnet "On First Looking into Chapman's Homer." Wright's first addresses to the Muse can also be traced to Keats, with poems that name "Fanny" as his inspiration and admirer. The dryads, nymphs, and faeries in so many of these early poems appear as tokens of transformative energy, Romantic assurances of a cultured, exhilarating world beyond the one he knew. Poetry carried this sense of promise, and he filled pages of his notebooks to relieve the fears and anxieties that weighed upon him.

Wright felt "a desire for lonesomeness" and walked for hours through the streets of Martins Ferry and along the banks of the Ohio River, carrying Keats's poems. Though the urban landscape of his hometown was "as ugly as a human place may well be," he could clearly visualize its streets and dirt paths more than a decade later. "If nobody was around me, I used to read, over and over and over again, that marvelous poem 'Sleep and Poetry' by Keats. I haven't looked at it for years, and yet I remember, as though the page were before me, the lines that seemed to me to be carved on the very twilight air itself. . . . 'Oh for ten years, that I might overwhelm / Myself in poesy.' He didn't get his ten years. Nobody ever does."

———

Jessie had always wanted to move out of Martins Ferry into the country, where she could live and work on a farm of her own—a longing that sprang from memories of her childhood in West Virginia. In the summer of 1945 she and Dudley received an offer for their Broadway house from the owner of the Nickles Bakery, which stood adjacent to their property. Weeks later, the Wrights purchased forty-five acres of stony, sloping farmland bordering St. Clairsville Road in Warnock, Ohio, some seventeen miles west of the river. The run-down farmhouse and outbuildings had been vacant for more than a decade and needed extensive renovation; it would be two years before they could move in. For a time, Jim, Jack, and their parents lived with Uncle Sherman and his wife, Agnes, but by Jim's senior year they rented rooms at the northern edge of Martins Ferry, in the blue-collar neighborhood known as Bulltown.

Susan Lamb spent more time with Wright than anyone else during their senior year. Working with Miss Willerton, they coedited their class yearbook, and Jim often walked Susan home after school, carrying her books. He loved classical music and ecstatically recounted a concert he attended in Wheeling with Willerton that featured Tchaikovsky's symphonic poem based on Byron's *Manfred*. Already he talked passionately about E. A. Robinson and Walt Whitman. As Susan recalled: "He was very intense. All brilliant people, I think, who are really good at something are *excessive*. Anything he did—just like when he took up smoking, he smoked too much, when he took up drinking, he drank too much. But that's how he was—single-minded. And when he was on a book, I mean, that was it!"

Wright haunted the public library for hours until chased out of the stacks at closing time. The Martins Ferry historian and librarian Annie Tanks remembered him vividly from this time, dressed in his fatigue coat and rubber miners' boots. "I could always tell he'd been down by the river, because he had mud on his boots. He was always by himself." Wright would walk for hours along the western bank of the Ohio, and it remained his chosen company.

As tall as his father but more robust, Wright was a commanding presence. He wore wire-rimmed glasses and his attire hardly varied: a blue work shirt with blue jeans or overalls, the heavy boots miners wore, an old army overcoat in winter, and always with a cigarette pinched between his fingers. He remained a solitary figure, and his imagination fastened upon the physical and psychic landscape of his childhood even in his earliest poems. By far the shortest to be given a title in his high school notebooks, "Suicide Note" is from the late spring of 1946: "The calm, cool face of the river / Asked me for a kiss."

In his final weeks of high school he wrote the autobiographical essay for Willerton titled "A Sketch of the Life of James Wright, A Young Man Who Is Still Alive." His prose, in a third-person voice, has a lively, inflated rhetoric and deprecating, comic self-regard, taking inspiration from both Laurence Sterne's *Tristram Shandy* and Thomas Wolfe's *Look Homeward, Angel*. Especially in high school, Wolfe's novels had a strong influence on Wright's imagination. When Wright finished his English final exam with more than half the class time remaining, Willerton handed him the autobiography of one of his classmates to read while he waited for others to finish. He became fascinated. Eleutheria Kardules—known as Liberty—was "a beautiful Greek girl with long, dark curly hair, laughing eyes, and a vibrancy about her," recalled a fellow student. Wright introduced himself to her at the end of Willerton's final class. "That's how we met," Liberty remembered. "I think she set us up."

In June, prior to Wright's enlistment, Willerton invited Jim and Liberty to her home, together with a couple of local college students. "We spent an evening at her house, listening to music and reading poetry and talking," Liberty recalled. "I was just thrilled to death, because I wanted to go to college more than anything else." As a firstborn Greek daughter, however, her hopes were rejected outright. Liberty's family lived in a close-knit Greek neighborhood on the flats, in rough tenement housing among factories near the river. Her father, Paul Kardules, delivered coal throughout the area and was known for his drinking and violent temper. An immigrant with little English, he depended on Liberty to translate business documents and keep his books; she also helped care for four younger siblings, though she chafed at her father's cruelty and lived in fear of him.

———

Wright graduated from Charles R. Shreve High School on May 29, 1946, ranked second in his class. His graduation photo shows "a confident sun-burst of a face beneath a shock of dark hair, with a hint of the ruffian about it and only a suggestion, in the vaguely melancholy eyes, that its flesh could sag in sadness from its bones." The only celebration Pete Lan-num recalled was meeting Jim at a local soda shop. Wright had wanted to join the navy—to fly combat aircraft—but was rejected for poor eye-sight. Without further thought, he enlisted in the army.

Wright shared "serious reading bouts" with his brother Jack during his last months in Martins Ferry, and John Steinbeck's just-published *Cannery Row* became a lifelong favorite. Throughout his service in the army, he constantly wrote home, asking for books and demanding letters in return. Wright was thrilled by the sight of Mount Rainier at Fort Lewis near Tacoma, Washington, where he underwent basic training. In his first letter to Susan Lamb as a soldier, he exclaims, "Think of it! 2,500 miles between home and me! I'll feel like Walt Whitman soon."

3

Between the river and
the rice fields

July 1946–February 1948

Wright's journey west by train—through Chicago, across the midwestern plains and Rocky Mountains, to the Pacific Northwest—revealed the true, overwhelming expanse of the country. He had never been farther than Columbus, Ohio. And though he returned to Martins Ferry just a handful of times, he would remember the place and her people in exacting detail. At eighteen, Wright began to learn what homesickness felt like.

Despite the demands of basic training, Wright continued his prodigious reading and writing. His correspondence with Susan Lamb alone was voluminous; he wrote to her every day for weeks at a time. A year younger than Wright and still living at home, Lamb was unsure about where to attend college. "I had quite a time answering those letters. He was very lonely, and you could consider them love letters, but I really wasn't in for that." Wright's letters always included declarations of his love and pleas for her response; from Japan, he sent silk scarves and other small gifts. He wrote candidly and without restraint, knowing he could never speak so openly in person. Wright's letters to her also became at times a kind of journal. Between July 1946 and January 1950, he wrote more than one hundred letters to Lamb, the majority posted during his seventeen months in uniform. As he wrote in September 1946 from Fort Lewis, "It seems that I pour anything at all that is good in me into my letters or my other writing."

In his first letters home, Wright asked his parents to send a collection of Gerard Manley Hopkins and Elizabeth Barrett Browning's *Sonnets from the Portuguese*. After a month away, he assured Jessie that he was fine, both physically and mentally. "But, being my mother, you know that I am a little off balance, and that I require vast chunks of fuel to sate my imagination, which very often rushes hot as a furnace." He pleaded with his family to write, but disowned the Ohio Valley. "I don't give a damn if I ever come home again or not. There is nothing at home for me to possess except imagination, and as soon as I find time I can dream here just as easily." He needed an audience, though, and Susan Lamb became just that.

> I am not a useful citizen. I am not a good soldier. My poetry is poisonous, and my dreams have snaggled teeth and battered mouths. I guess I am not worth a damn. Therefore . . . I ask you, almost implore you, to continue writing, and still to remind me of the thousand holinesses which I knew as a boy, and which are throwing up their pliant arms and vomiting to death.

Though she never felt attracted to Wright, she welcomed his poems and letters in all their "rawness" and "wildness" and let him imagine her as he wished.

———

Summer in the Pacific Northwest made the grueling ordeal of army training more bearable. Wright first glimpsed the Pacific Ocean through a stand of tall pines; he loved the salt air and dramatic landscape at once. Though he lacked the ambition to excel as a soldier, he was a social success in the army. He made friends easily among his fellow recruits, including two Japanese men recently released from internment camps. Nonetheless, Private Wright wanted time alone to compose sonnets and letters, and to continue his translations of Latin and his readings in poetry and philosophy. He kept up a rigorous course of study; following one fifteen-mile march in full field pack, he wrote, "I experienced some of the old sweet exhaustion that used to accompany my Latin homework." After six weeks at Fort Lewis—as one of a company of twenty-two thousand troops—Wright recalled his study of Caesar, and his "lofty visions of the armored Roman legions marching through the wilds of Gaul."

This idealized camaraderie proved short-lived. When he completed training near the middle of September, he crossed the country a second time, assigned to an engineering unit at Fort Belvoir, Virginia, and a twelve-week course in map reproduction. Wright hated to leave "the unspeakable beauty" of the Pacific Northwest and the friends he had made there. On the eve of departing Washington State, two months after his arrival, he wrote that the view of Mount Rainier above Puget Sound had become "symbolic to me of all the inviolable loneliness and grey desolation which I have known all my life."

At Fort Belvoir, Wright soon realized he lacked the background for or, in fact, any real interest in photolithography. He was surrounded by recruits with more "practical knowledge of modern things"—many of whom had been in college—and he became swamped with self-doubt. "I don't care a damn for anything anymore. I was a thousand times more a poet at the age of 13 than I am now," he wrote Lamb soon after arriving in Virginia. By the end of the month he'd sworn to give up poetry "a thousand times," but couldn't control his "fanatical urge to write." In what time he had at night, Wright translated Latin poetry and read insatiably. "All my writings up to this date fill several hundred pages. I want to translate Catullus, more of Horace, and I want to study Virgil."

Wright explored nearby Washington, D.C., that fall and frequented the symphony in the capital. In October he cursed his hometown again—"I don't give a Goddamn whether I ever go back to Martins Ferry or not"—and yet returned there three times in one month, a distance of more than two hundred miles. To Lamb he admitted that his first visit home "to see my folks again was a supreme beauty, because I am absolutely sure that I love my Mother very deeply"—suggesting to the doubts he'd left home with.

Most important, Wright found a copy of *Thus Spake Zarathustra* by Friedrich Nietzsche, "the marvelously wild German philosopher [whose] fiercely charged writings are filling my dreams." Wright carried the book everywhere during his army service; he claimed to have read it five hundred times, and internalized Nietzsche's concept of self-overcoming. "I took the way of complete loneliness from the beginning," he wrote a decade later. "It is a perfect description of my life."

Many of Wright's letters to Lamb in the fall of 1946 included a new sonnet or translation; by December he had begun translations from Ovid. Wright's first experience of "the melancholy ecstasy" of New York

City came early that month when he "raised hell in Times Square" with two friends and attended a concert at Carnegie Hall. Over the Christmas holiday, Wright spent ten days in Martins Ferry with his parents and siblings—his last extended stay in his hometown. On Christmas Day, he talked for hours with Elizabeth Willerton at her home, and then spent the evening with Susan Lamb, scarcely speaking at all. She let Wright kiss her as they parted, but the meeting proved unsettling for them both. Back in uniform in Virginia the first week in January, his next letter to Willerton included his translation of the famous Latin ode to Lesbia's pet sparrow. "Catullus is as dear to me as are sleep and music," he declared. To Lamb, Wright apologized for his silence when they had met, insisting, "I still have a love for you which is as deep as my instinct for death."

On January 13, 1947, a month past his nineteenth birthday, Private Wright found himself on a train traveling across the southern United States, en route to Camp Stoneman, California, awaiting his deployment to "some hole in the Pacific." Writing to Lamb, he tried to appear indifferent. "I am becoming a little accustomed to these blind stupidities in my existence for which Someone or Something is carelessly responsible. The army is idiotic indeed, but not unbearably so. I don't mind saying that I should sooner be dead than live in Martins Ferry again."

A week later he boarded a troop ship for Yokohama, Japan. He had found a copy of Hermann Hesse's *Steppenwolf* in a San Francisco bookstore, and it became indispensable to him. On the long, difficult sea journey, "I pitched over the side my extra pair of combat boots, my heavy overcoat, and some other stuff," Wright recalled decades later. "I never threw my copy of *Steppenwolf* overboard, though. I was willing then to sacrifice many practical necessities for it, and I still am."

Nearly everyone on board "that crummy little merchant ship" suffered from seasickness during a fierce winter storm on the Pacific, and was relieved when the ship broke down for ten days in Honolulu, Hawaii. When they finally arrived in Japan, Wright felt disoriented by the great natural beauty of the islands. The American army base in Zama, twenty-five miles southwest of Tokyo, stood near the Sagami River, and two other rivers flowed through the town. In his first letter to Lamb at the end of February 1947, Wright declared, "I am more utterly and desolately alone than I have ever been in my life." Within days, however, he began to feel at ease among the soldiers who shared "the bleak barn-like casual barracks." In letters to his family, he wrote excitedly about the country and people, recounting visits to the majestic Mount Fuji and to the celebrated temples of Kyoto and Kamakura.

During his seven months in Zama, Wright continued reading intensively, particularly books of philosophy and religion. Along with Nietzsche, which he annotated closely, he studied the Koran and the King James Bible. He underscored passages in James Joyce's *Portrait of the Artist as a Young Man* and transcribed unfamiliar words. Early in the novel, he wrote in the margin: "Wonderful ear for the *real* music of voices in conversation. J's greatest *poetic secret.*" That spring he studied Richard Wright, John O'Hara, and Dostoevsky.

Wright's education in modern poetry also began in earnest. Oscar Williams published *A Little Treasury of Modern Poetry* in 1946, and Wright carried this small, sturdy book throughout his tour of duty and for the rest of his life. He discovered many of the poets he came to love best in this one anthology, including Edward Thomas, D. H. Lawrence, and Robert Frost. With the work of 140 poets and 450 poems across seven hundred pages, the anthology has remarkable breadth. The catholicity of Williams's approach also left a lasting impression. Rather than a chronological ordering, the poems are grouped around subjective themes with italicized headings at the top of each page (for example, "Mortality," "The Human Heart," and "Mourning"). Williams wanted to turn his readers' attention toward the individual poems; works by Emily Dickinson and Thomas Hardy appear side by side with others by Elizabeth Bishop and Delmore Schwartz. In a provisional wooden Quonset hut in Japan, Wright memorized Hopkins, A. E. Housman, Dylan Thomas, W. H. Auden, Hart Crane, and Yeats.

Though he often claimed to have quit—"By God, I am going to keep myself from writing if I have to tape my fingers and thumbs together"— Wright never stopped for long. His letters home often included new poems and translations. When Wright's superiors recognized his skill as a typist, they put him to work as an office clerk. From this point on, almost all his letters and poems appear in typescript, even his journal entries. Though he still complained bitterly about the Ohio Valley, a chance meeting with a soldier from his hometown made him realize how "unbelievably pleasant" it could be to reminisce about "the intricacies of Martins Ferry streets." And as he had always done beside the Ohio River, he made a habit of walking alone along the banks of the Sagami.

Wright knew that thirty months of tuition on the GI Bill would fall short of a college degree, and that he must save more than a full year's expenses. Each month, he sent nearly all his army pay home to Ohio for banking. Though determined to attend college, Wright had not given much thought as to where he might study. In the spring of 1947, he met John "Jack" Furniss, a fellow Ohioan who had already enrolled at Kenyon College in Gambier, Ohio, where the poet John Crowe Ransom taught. Wright applied to several colleges in Ohio, but only Kenyon accepted him. His application praised Nietzsche and Catullus and included an imposing list of the books he'd read over the preceding year: works by Tolstoy, Chekhov, Turgenev, Schopenhauer, Aristophanes, Saroyan, Dos Passos, and many, many others.

With no real explanation, Wright was among the many recruits in the Occupation Forces who received an early discharge from service. In November 1947 he crossed the States once more, returning from the West Coast to his parents' new farm in Ohio. Their property lay a half-mile east of the town of Warnock: a cluster of a dozen houses at a minor crossroads with a post office and a general store. There were coal mines in every direction; the closest town of any size was ten miles north, the county seat of St. Clairsville.

No matter how hard Jessie and her family worked, the farm was doomed to failure—acres of rocky, uneven pasture on a corner lot with a stand of pine trees and a few old-growth oaks. The farmhouse stood across from a stream that ran along the southern boundary road where the field began to rise. The log cabin structure had a stone foundation and basement; partition walls created four rooms with a kitchen at the back that lacked running water. Two huge maples shaded the front porch, with a nearby springhouse and a small, dilapidated barn on a concrete slab. "It had lain fallow for the most part during some fifteen years before my folks obtained it a couple of years ago," Wright told Lamb. "I returned from overseas just about in time to join the general struggle against a wilderness of weeds and other disorganization." The family survived the winter beside the woodstove or huddled over kerosene heaters. "That farm was just Jessie's idea," Marge recalled. "And once she had her mind made up, there wasn't no use in trying to change it."

Wright credited "the fates . . . those three charming sisters" for his surprising early discharge. "They fixed it so that I could spend only a year and a half in the army instead of three years." In early December 1947—a week before turning twenty—he wrote to Susan Lamb:

> I am now situated on a farm, plopped down in the wilderness about 15 miles out of Bellaire. The atmosphere suits me famously. I have music for passivity, books for activity, and a free-thinking mother for conversation. I might add that I have finally given up the shoddy aesthetics of "poetry" in preference for the more applicable world of actual useful ideas. . . . I am entering Kenyon College, Gambier, Ohio, on 12 Feb. 48, for the purpose of pursuing the new attitudes which I have unearthed.

Wright was now determined to focus on coursework in philosophy, believing once more that he had outgrown the excesses of poetry and the "adolescent infatuation" of his letters to Lamb. Gambier was just a hundred miles from the farm, and Wright arrived by bus in his fatigue jacket and work boots, his few books crammed in an army duffel bag.

4

Bitterly hard, sincere work

February 1948–January 1950

The ivy-covered stone buildings on the Kenyon campus had stood for
more than a century by the time Wright arrived in February 1948. Located in the center of Ohio, the college had been the exclusive province
of the sons of midwestern wealth, boasting a flying club and a polo team
even during the Depression. At the end of the war, however, an enlight-
ened student recruitment policy invited dozens of high-achieving public
school students from metropolitan regions on the East Coast to join an
influx of returning veterans. At the northern edge of campus, nineteen
wooden barracks were built to house the swelling numbers of incoming
freshmen; the all-male student body well exceeded the usual roster of
five hundred. For Wright and Jack Furniss, at least the army surplus
housing felt familiar.

The room they shared in "Splinterville" that spring became "a gathering place for all types of usual and not so usual people." Even among
friends, Wright was an imposing figure; in his GI fatigues and a blue
work shirt, he had an air of detachment. To his classmates he seemed
much older, in part due to "his grave, punctilious, modest manner. When
he spoke it was in a surprisingly gentle voice for one of such yeoman
size. He puffed cigarettes with the same intensity that he conceived ideas.
He knew who he was when most of us were still searching."

E. L. Doctorow, who became a close friend of Wright's, arrived at
Kenyon in the fall of 1948. A graduate of the Bronx High School of Sci-

ence, Doctorow was drawn by the reputation of the faculty and *The Kenyon Review*, which had become a preeminent literary quarterly under John Crowe Ransom's editorship. President Gordon Chalmers had lured Ransom away from Vanderbilt University a decade before, and he continued to gather a first-rate faculty, making Kenyon one of the best small colleges in the country. The renowned philosophers Virgil Aldrich and Philip Blair Rice, together with the noted English scholars Charles M. Coffin and Denham Sutcliffe, were among Ransom's colleagues. The increased diversity of the student body became a strong incentive; as Doctorow knew, "The faculty wanted the gratification of teaching students that were worth teaching." The novelist Richard Gibson was one of two black students to arrive in September 1948—the first Kenyon had ever admitted. As another classmate recalled, the veterans "were a little bit more mature and damn serious."

Kenyon's illustrious School of English sessions, held on campus for three summers from 1948 until 1950, helped secure the school's prestige. Ransom wanted "to bring literary criticism into the Academy," and he gathered acclaimed writers such as Allen Tate, F. O. Matthiessen, Yvor Winters, and a young Cleanth Brooks to lecture and teach. These were the New Critics, who, like Ransom, insisted that a literary work must be appreciated on its own terms, apart from the biographical circumstances of its creation. Challenging the Romantic conception of art as self-expression, the New Criticism demanded a rigorous evaluation of a piece of writing as an object unto itself. Literary criticism at Kenyon became an intellectual practice, and every poem had to survive close scrutiny as an exercise of craft and reason.

The lively academic atmosphere of the School of English sessions spilled over into the school year. Undergraduates "vigorously 'explicated' poems in and out of class" with "the kind of exhilaration that [the Beats] had to start with." Wright, however, never became a convert to the New Criticism. He mistrusted reductive readings and the way criticism usurped an immediate experience of the poem. In this and other ways, Wright stood apart, "with nothing in his makeup to be a fraternity man." A growing class consciousness set Wright against the dominant social order. As Doctorow recalled,

> He had a lot of trouble, coming from Martins Ferry on the GI
> Bill in his overalls, accustoming himself to the still quite social

upper-middle-class character of so many of the students—there was a class thing. He was living this conflict, perhaps more painful to him than it was to us urban kids with a degree of sophistication; his provincialism was painful to him and he was climbing up away from it.

In his first weeks on campus, Wright discovered the small, wood-paneled music library in Pierce Hall. The college had a remarkable collection of 78-rpm classical recordings, and friends learned to look for Wright in a listening carrel there, transfixed by the German art songs of the nineteenth century. The direction of Wright's life and his poetry began to turn; he followed his ear. In his second semester, he began studying German, and within months he had drafted translations of Goethe and Rilke.

Returning to Warnock for the summer, Wright pitched in with chores, while writing and reading for hours every night. Dudley endured a hellish commute into Wheeling during the five years they lived on the farm. He woke at 4:00 a.m. every morning to travel over twenty miles by bus and streetcar, a trip of more than three hours each way. Jessie commanded two grown sons and the days' work. At first she tried raising goats, though the pasture was soon given over to a pair of cows; they also kept an unruly brood of chickens and a few pigs. Jim and Jack helped weed and hoe their few acres of corn, repaired fences, and mucked out the cow barn. There was not a full acre of level ground and little shade; the soil was stony and difficult to till, and their primary source of food—a large vegetable garden off the back porch—required constant care.

During Wright's years at Kenyon, the farm became the setting for much of his writing. That first summer, he sporadically typed pages for a journal and even ventured a couple of short stories, "experimental compositions" he described as "raw, semi-Whitmanesque character sketches." Wright made a selection of the poems he'd written since high school and set to work revising dozens of them. He titled the collection *Echoes from the Timeless*. At the end of the summer, in what became a ritual of fatigue and discouragement, he scrawled on the cover page of the manuscript, "To hell with these also. I'm done."

Wright kept up with classmates and friends, writing letters by kerosene lamp in the evenings. A chance meeting with Liberty Kardules on the streets of Martins Ferry the previous December had kindled a regular exchange. Wright's encouragement shored up her decision to begin nursing school that August, though this meant severing ties with her father and eviction from her home. A courtship slowly evolved as their correspondence grew. "I lived for his letters," Liberty recalled. "I think I fell in love with him through his letters. He was so exuberant." Wright's letters—filled with the rhapsodic prose he had once lavished on Susan Lamb—became a "lifeline" for her over the next four years. Only on her wedding day did her father finally permit Liberty to return home.

———

At the age of seventeen, Doctorow first encountered Wright beneath the towering stained glass windows in Kenyon's dining hall, at the table reserved for unaffiliated students.

> He had a round face with particularly small features—small mouth, and small eyes encircled with a pair of colorless plastic GI glasses which he regularly adjusted because his small nose had not a sufficient bridge to keep them up where they belonged. He spoke in a high but richly timbred voice, like a tenor's. His conversation was intense, opinionated, heavy with four-letter words, but what made it astonishing was that it was interwoven with recitations of poetry. I had never heard anything like it. He would glide from ordinary speech to verse without dropping a beat. It was as if recitation was a normal part of ordinary discourse. Sometimes the lines were appropriate to the subject under discussion, other times not, as if he had been running through them silently in his mind and they just happened to break into his speech, or they had been summoned up from some area of his unconscious and he was merely giving voice to them as a madman speaking to himself. But it all made perfect sense, somehow, and left you awed, because it was a whole system of mind. . . . You could not be in Wright's presence for five minutes without understanding what it took to get a true line down on a page. . . . It was an intensity of self-generated perception, a raging, all-consuming subjection to your own consciousness, a kind of helplessness, finally.

Among like-minded students and teachers at Kenyon, Wright had begun to feel at home. Doctorow became one of the few with whom he shared his poems, asking for comments but largely ignoring them. He gathered drafts in spring-bound black binders, and seemed to be continually adding to or revising them; he jotted down lines for new poems in the margins of his class notebooks.

Wright took his first class in German that fall, taught by a strict, "blustering, Baron von Munchausen–like character" nicknamed "Captain" Eberle by students. Wright spent hours listening to recordings of German lieder—lyrics by Heine, Goethe, and others, set to music by Schubert, Schumann, Brahms, and Mahler. In his journal, he named Rilke as a guiding spirit. That same semester, Wright also studied with Ransom. A polymath fluent in Latin, Greek, and German, and well-read in philosophy, Ransom possessed a profound literary intelligence. Three nights a week, twenty students gathered to hear him read from the *Oxford Anthology of English Poetry* in his slow, deliberate manner—from Shakespeare to E. A. Robinson, pausing occasionally to relight his pipe. Throughout these two-hour classes, Ransom demanded "the constant company of the actual poems."

Robert Lowell had followed Ransom to Kenyon from Vanderbilt in 1937 to continue working with him. "It was not the classes but the conversations that mattered," Lowell wrote of his mentor in 1948. "To appreciate the language of Ransom's poems, you must realize that it is the language of one of the best talkers that has ever lived in the United States." Ransom found in Wright a more self-taught poet than Lowell, without the advantages of an elite education but just as driven. Ransom had a deep and lasting influence on Wright; he read Wright's poems closely and made marginal notes on drafts that compliment or correct lines for meter and diction. Though he deferred to Ransom's vast learning, Wright defended the vernacular language and emotional intensity that already distinguished his work. Ransom admired "a certain crude energy" in Wright's verse, and his praise gave Wright the confidence to work harder still.

Wright's Shakespeare course in the spring of 1949 introduced him to a different kind of mentor, the inspiring teacher and formidable scholar Philip Wolcott Timberlake. In contrast to Ransom's reserved and dignified manner, the tall and lanky Timberlake would sprawl across the top of his desk, leaning his head on an elbow, then jump to his feet to recite at length with great passion. He could appear melancholy and withdrawn, until swept up in gusts of enthusiasm—in temperament much like Wright, with whom he grew close. A Kenyon graduate himself,

Timberlake had been born and raised in Steubenville, just upriver from Martins Ferry.

Wright began his sophomore year in February 1949 living in a massive stone dormitory building known as Old Kenyon, together with all the students not pledged to a fraternity. These "campus misfits" formed an ad hoc group known as the Middle Kenyon Association, ironically called the "Mu Kaps." Wright joined in the loud debates that sprang up in the common areas and dorm rooms of Old Kenyon each night, arguing literature and politics. But after three weeks of classes, in the early morning hours of Sunday, February 27, a fire broke out at the center of the Old Kenyon building. While Wright and the majority of students escaped, nine others died in the blaze, several after jumping from second- and third-story windows. The landmark structure was completely destroyed as the fire continued through the night. Many lost everything, while everyone had friends who died. Like others, Wright returned to barracks housing for the remainder of the term; the rebuilding of Old Kenyon continued for the next year and a half. "We were all just shattered," recalled Doctorow. Having begun to rely on this group's society, Wright was struck deeply by the loss.

The entire editorial staff of the campus literary magazine, *Hika*, was made up of Middle Kenyon students displaced by the fire. Wright had also joined the magazine and in the spring of 1949 saw his name in print for the first time beneath two poems: "Sonnet: At a Carnival" and "The Lover." The latter is one of Wright's best early poems, an elegy for an elderly Warnock couple. In the poem's conclusion the husband lies "in delirium" on his deathbed, recalling his wife's youthful beauty: "Look at her hair; / The dark brown coils, that was what I meant— / The brownness in the hair. My God. The hair." Combining the classical theme of time's passage with colloquial speech, the poem exemplifies Wright's first ambitions.

Throughout his life, Wright translated more of Rilke's work than that of any other poet; there are multiple drafts of forty different poems from his years at Kenyon. Wright began drafting English versions of Rilke's early poems that spring, attracted by their simple yet compelling music. Few still read Rilke's work in the years following the war, when anti-German sentiment ran high, but Wright felt an overpowering personal response to his poetry. He began typing out the *Sonnets to Orpheus* in German, to better hear their music.

The summer of 1949 proved to be exceptionally productive for Wright, though nothing from this time ever saw print. There are thousands of typed manuscript pages dated from June through September; besides letters and journal entries, he drafted prose fragments, short stories, German translations, and a seemingly endless profusion of his own poems: sonnets, pastoral eclogues, dramatic narratives, elegies, songs, laments, confessions, verse letters, metrical exercises, and dozens of poems dedicated to writers and composers. All went through multiple typescript versions, copied from handwritten notebook drafts. Wright often folded pages in half and inserted them lengthwise in his typewriter, creating four pages without margins.

Two separate extended sequences were rooted in Ohio. The "Friendly Letters to Hirpinus Snodgrass" are verse epistles in the manner of Horace that he revised obsessively; the eight Wright finally collected fill thirty-three pages. Their conversational tone often creates an unsettling tension with their subject matter. In one he describes seeing a friend drown in the river and the diver named "Flaccus" (Horace's surname) who failed to recover the body.

He will not come back.
The river in Ohio is a black
coffin lid.

Wright called another extended series "Variations," a loose grouping of poems in which he adopts a persona: "Patchen," in tribute to the Ohio poet Kenneth Patchen. A prolific avant-garde artist and poet devoted to Whitman and Blake, Patchen gained renown as a pacifist and was later claimed by the Beat movement as a literary forebear. Wright revered Patchen's poems about the poor and about his Ohio childhood. In Wright's sequence, the name appears in a third-person voice, as in one "Variation" that begins, "Patchen was in a sad distracted mood." Often, though, the speaker takes center stage:

Patchen and Patchen, over and over again
I say my name, the name of a wild Ohioan
Poet who used to live in Warren far
Up north there where the strip mines are not so

Raw as they are here. Patchen, Patchen, over
And over again I say the word, my name.

Wright also began to keep a journal that summer; over the course of his life, his journals came to hold his most personal reflections, becoming a private refuge devoted to his work. "There is no reason at all for me to resort to any kind of verbal device, either in bitterness or sentimentality. Therefore I want it to stay naked and clear." In September, looking back on all the poems he had written that summer, he realized that his strongest work showed only "the power of physical violence," whereas his goal was "simple classical restraint—Mozart, Robinson, Gandhi, Christ." Wright saw how far he stood from achieving such technical command. He began writing letters "with some measure of control. But most of the time a typewriter is for me simply a piano on which to improvise melodies and fragments."

When Wright returned to Kenyon in September, he carried a manuscript of more than two hundred pages. Included among 121 poems in *Folio for Summer, 1949* are a dozen ballads, two dozen sonnets, and four of the "Friendly Letters." Sixteen are "Imitations and Adaptations from the German," most translations of Rilke but including versions of Hofmannsthal, Nietzsche, Lenau, and Eichendorff. Only "Evening Visions"—an imitation of Rilke's "Herbst" ("Autumn")—would eventually appear in *Hika* as a much longer poem titled "Vision and Elegy."

———

Thrilled to be back on campus, Wright entered one of the most fulfilling periods in his life—socially, intellectually, and academically. Together with four other students, he took up residence in Professor Timberlake's home, a "big three-story house in the Gambier woods" at the edge of campus. Not only did Wright have two courses with Timberlake— Chaucer and Old English—but the house also became a gathering place, with impromptu readings of Shakespeare, musical performances, and literary debates that lasted long into the night. For an entire year, Wright and five classmates joined Timberlake to read *Beowulf* in Anglo-Saxon two afternoons each week. Wright continued his study of German with Dr. Andre Hanfman, a multilingual Russian émigré, and took an introductory music course; it seemed natural to study classical music and

German together. Wright also read the Spanish of Pablo Neruda, Jorge Luis Borges, and Rubén Darío aloud to internalize the sound of their poems. As Doctorow observed, for Wright, "a language was not just something to take an exam in, it was a music you heard."

Wright carried his binders of recent poems everywhere, subjecting every page, it seemed, to constant revision. "You'd find him at the Village Inn," Doctorow recalled, "sitting alone with a cigarette and a cup of coffee, or in front of a beer at Jean Valjean's, and he'd be hunched in a booth revising a typed draft in his round, grade-school hand." Wright attracted a wide assortment of independent students—"the social pariahs, the oddballs, the pre-beatniks"—who delighted in his company and acceptance. "They loved to make Jim laugh," and through him felt part of the college community. One night each week, when Kenyon's fraternities marched three abreast down Middle Path, Wright often assembled his friends to follow behind them, singing the Horst-Wessel Nazi anthem.

For his part, Doctorow found this clowning and high jinks tiresome; he wanted to write plays and became active in the campus theater. Wright, too, kept mostly to himself; the two semesters he spent in a room in Timberlake's attic proved to be a year of hard work. On his twenty-second birthday, December 13, he wrote a brief note to Susan Lamb: "I'm so damned buried in German, Middle English, and Anglo-Saxon, that I can't even think in English anymore." On Christmas Day, he was at home with Jack and his parents on the farm in Warnock, but the intoxication of Kenyon's social world lingered.

At the present moment I am listening to a recording of Debussy's second book of preludes. . . . I am attired in a pale, egg-shell blue work shirt with charming frayed sleeves, a new pair of gray work pants, and my army clodhoppers. . . . This is a very rambling letter, as I wanted it to be. I don't care. I have many friends. Edgar Doctorow and I are writing an opera. If no one will perform it for us, we'll do it ourselves. We don't give a damn.

5

Writing like a Dionysian maniac

January 1950–December 1951

On New Year's Day 1950, in a letter to the newly married Elizabeth Willerton Esterly, Wright gave an eloquent introduction to Rilke and detailed for her one of his own translations. "Rilke is as musical in German as Keats is in English, and you know what that means." He tells her of his German professor, Andre Hanfman, whom he frequently visits at his home. In the fall Wright would board with the professor and his wife, who were astonished by his intense, insatiable interest in German poetry. Though Wright was captivated by Goethe in a class with Hanfman that spring, Rilke still claimed his devotion. He called his apprentice versions in English "imitations," "adaptations," or even "thefts." In his own poems, Wright adapted rhyme schemes borrowed from German folk stanzas and songs. After just three semesters of formal study, he had gained remarkable fluency; his classes in Anglo-Saxon, Old English, and Chaucer helped foster his assimilation of German. In one of Wright's notebooks that spring, there is a telling sequence of consecutive pages: a translation of the funeral passage in *Beowulf*; a draft of Rilke's early poem "A Picture of My Father in His Youth"; and a poem of his own titled "My Father."

In the late-night debates that defined Wright's time at Kenyon, politics always vied with literature, and the growing unrest in Korea became an ever-present concern on campus. At Timberlake's home, or at the Village Inn, Dottie's restaurant, or Jean Valjean's in Gambier, the talk was always heated and intense, and Wright often took center stage. "We talked politics and I listened to poetry," Doctorow recalled. "I had known poets in high school, but this guy was clearly a poet all the way through. He was always a poet, even when he wasn't doing poetry."

———

On June 17, 1950, soon after Wright arrived back in Warnock for the summer, the local papers reported the ongoing investigation of the rape and murder of a local teenager. George Doty, a twenty-eight-year-old cabdriver with a pregnant wife and two young children, soon confessed to the crime. He was convicted of first-degree murder for bludgeoning the girl to death "in a fit of anger, fear, and frustration." The crime and its aftermath—especially the righteous outrage that dominated coverage of Doty's trial and conviction—troubled Wright for years. The moral dilemma of capital punishment weighed on him, and as a member of that community he felt implicated. The welter of emotions raised by the deaths of both the victim and the criminal would appear in numerous poems, culminating in Wright's signature declaration, "At the Executed Murderer's Grave."

Wright kept mostly to himself that summer. Marge Pyle had moved with her husband and family to a house near her parents' farm, and she saw Jim often. "He studied hard when he was across the road in the old farmhouse." Wright could now read Heinrich Heine's poems in German "with pretty clear understanding and enormous pleasure." He also re-read Wolfe's *Time and the River*; framed by wild exhortations, he typed out five full pages from the novel in a letter to Jack Furniss. One of the few visitors the family welcomed that summer was Jim's professor Philip Timberlake. He wanted to show Wright "how beautiful Ohio could be," and took him on a daylong driving tour as far south as Marietta, on the Ohio River. Dudley later honored Timberlake with "one of the great accolades," Jack recalled. "'He is as common as old shoes.'"

Whenever he could, Wright returned to his notebooks, his phonograph, and his typewriter. By September, he had gathered hundreds of poems—more than four hundred pages stippled with pencil corrections and marginalia. He wrote more "Patchen Variations"; a new series of "Crazy Mary" poems, inspired by Yeats; and still more ballads, sonnets, songs, elegies, tributes, imitations, metrical experiments, hymns, and odes. "The most characteristic thing about my whole approach to literature is that I always begin by writing like a Dionysian maniac," he told his classmate Al Herzing. "I do not want to relinquish the vitality, but only to control it."

Wright even attempted a few short stories that summer, but the discouragement of a classmate and a rejection slip from *Fantasy and Science Fiction Magazine* convinced him to give up on fiction. One nine-page story returned by these readers, however, includes candid portraits of Wright's parents, as seen from the eyes of an eight-year-old boy named Sonny. As dusk falls in a town much like Martins Ferry, the boy asks his mother if he can go out to play after dinner. "She turned to him with that odd look, in which sternness and tenderness were commingled, and studied him for a moment." Later, his play with friends is "called to a halt by the great voice of his father," a voice "extremely kind and understanding" that nonetheless "possessed that indefinable authority."

In the fall of 1950, Wright studied Spenser and the writers of the English Renaissance with Charles Coffin; as his classmate Roger Hecht observed, teacher and student were well matched. "Coffin's tastes were as huge and all-encompassing as Wright's; he had read everything." Along with Hanfman's German literature courses, Wright took his first of three semesters in French and made quick progress. He also carried an extra course for the rest of his time at Kenyon, a seminar in preparation for his honors thesis on Thomas Hardy's poetry and fiction.

Wright grew ever more ruthless in his study habits and self-discipline. As he recalled years later, "I used to study my guts out for five hours running, each evening" in the library. Near midnight, he joined friends in the dorm room of an amateur musician named John Schmitt, in the basement of the rebuilt Old Kenyon building, where they listened to both classical and modern composers—Copland, Milhaud, Bartók. Passionate about music, Schmitt was one of the few students with a phonograph, and his radio program on the campus station made use of his personal record collection. One classmate remembered Wright "sitting in the fading afternoon light of the Pierce Music Room, listening to classical music while reading *The Faerie Queen* aloud."

Among modern poets, Robert Frost loomed largest for Wright. He met Frost only once, in October 1950, at the peak of the poet's celebrity. Kenyon hosted a three-day conference in his honor—the same week a feature story on Frost appeared in *Time* magazine, with an idealized portrait of the white-haired poet on the cover. At seventy-five, he had just published his *Complete Poems* and was the only contemporary poet most Americans had ever heard of. Wright spoke to Frost briefly and asked about his friendship with Edward Thomas. Frost "responded with a luminous delight, a gratitude to a reader, even a twenty-year-old. At that time I had no idea that his life had been so scarred by loss and pain."

Living poets notwithstanding, the ghost of Rilke continued to haunt Wright. The fall issue of *Hika* included Wright's "Vision and Elegy," one of the *Folio* poems he had begun more than a year before. In this extensively revised and expanded version, Rilke's ghost appears on the Warnock farm and Wright asks a blessing from him, wondering why death seems to touch him so little. As day breaks, however, Wright's vision of the poet fades and the harsh demands of reality return. Over the next few years, many of Wright's poems stubbornly enact this choice again and again: to turn away from private visions and live more fully in community.

———

The previous fall, Liberty Kardules had begun a nursing residency in Cleveland, Ohio, and Wright's letters to her became more frequent and expansive. At the beginning of April 1950, Liberty traveled from Cleveland to spend the weekend at Kenyon with Wright, confirming their relationship to all his friends. Liberty had come to depend on him utterly. Her letters show her increasing anxiety; in her isolation, Wright had become her primary source of emotional support. The intense romantic longing that had once prompted Wright's letters to Susan Lamb he now transferred to his correspondence with Liberty, and the desire they shared to escape the Ohio Valley shaped a deep intimacy between them. Morosely self-conscious of his appearance, Wright had always believed that no woman would be attracted to him, and he welcomed Liberty's ardor and attention.

Liberty visited Wright again at Kenyon in November 1950, and at a college dance in the Great Hall, Wright befriended a freshman, Eugene Pugatch. They shared a passion for music, and Pugatch soon began his own study of German, swept up in Wright's excitement. As Nicholas Crome, a fellow German student, poet, and *Hika* staff member, recalled, "Jim loved classical music, and he loved singing. He was just irrepressible that way. He was not a happy person, mind you, but he had a tremendous *potential* for happiness." Wright delighted in jokes and invented obscene lyrics to popular songs. Though courteous with women, even old-fashioned, he enjoyed coarse humor, and often repeated the ribald jokes he heard others tell.

A kind of desperation shadowed Wright's laughter, however. A troubling letter from his mother in early December reminded him just how tenuous his place at Kenyon remained. "The big snow storm is finally over, and we have had a couple of rainy days. Now for the flood. Seems like life is just one damn thing after another. This war has me worried." The escalation of hostilities in Korea troubled Wright as well. Many of his classmates had transferred to schools with ROTC programs as a shelter from the draft, and the resulting financial shortfall at Kenyon led to the cancellation or postponement of scholarship money. Wright did not learn of the stipend supporting his final year at Kenyon until spring classes had already begun. His exceptional grades helped secure the award, and in March Wright celebrated his election to Phi Beta Kappa.

———

A young Methodist minister, Tony Stoneburner, took up his first appointment in Gambier in the spring of 1951, and he was soon drawn into the literary world of Kenyon at the barracks apartment of a poet named Lee Sutton, a friend of Wright's. The three men were adamant pacifists, and the Korean War was frequently on their minds. "Jim would be a part of the talk, but I also felt there was something like a *blocking* of talk," Stoneburner noted in his journal. When they debated literature, Wright remained distrustful of criticism, which he felt took the place of the poem. Stoneburner, for his part, objected to Wright's constant appeal to sincerity as a rhetorical strategy. "To me, that wasn't a sufficient argument, that I *feel* this—as though that removed the necessity for evidence or logic."

Nevertheless, Stoneburner grew close to Wright; he drove him to Cleveland to pick up Liberty when she visited Kenyon one weekend that April. When the couple found themselves alone at the Hanfmans' home, Wright finally proposed to her. A note of congratulation to Jim from his father dated April 17 makes it clear that he and Jessie were not surprised by the news. "He talked about her all the time," classmate Sy Weissman recalled. "He loved the sound of her name: *Liberty Kardules.*" It was a name she would be happy to give up. When *Hika* published a new issue that spring, it included two poems by Wright, a translation of Theodor Storm's "October" and a poem with his fiancée's given name, "Eleutheria."

Wright now boarded at the Hanfman home in Gambier and spent hours in conversation with his professor, translating German poetry and typing out pages of Nietzsche's prose. Roger Hecht observed how Wright translated "naturally," drafting versions of two or three poems each day. "Jim looked at the past as the present." Wright also had a seminar in German classical music inspired by lyric poetry, taught by Paul Schwartz, an Austrian professor. Wright became fascinated by descriptions of Vienna. "The Viennese atmosphere expresses delicacy, music, sensitivity," he wrote excitedly in his class notebook. An idea of Europe took form in Wright's imagination, with Vienna at its center. Even his spoken German took on an Austrian accent.

Wright studied with Ransom again that spring, reading English and American lyric poetry. In an essay dated April 1951, he makes a strong, personal statement defending the "hard-won simplicity" of Edward Thomas's poetry. Before his death in battle in France in 1917 at the age of thirty-nine, Thomas had written a few dozen sublime lyrics; for Wright, he was "one of the two or three greatest English poets of the first half of the twentieth century." Wright was especially moved by "this peculiar absence of sentimentality, this willingness to discover the natural world as it actually exists." He compares Thomas to "the great Japanese lyric poet Basho," and describes how Thomas and his friend Robert Frost were both "searching for the rhythm which will most closely approximate human speech." Ransom gave Wright's essay an A and noted: "This is an excellent paper. Its one fault comes also from its prime virtue, enthusiasm."

Though known on campus as a formidable scholar, Wright won greater fame as the college radio station's "authority on hillbilly music." Country music had been a constant presence in his childhood, and during his last two years at Kenyon, Wright hosted a weekly show of satire and country music that took as its name and theme song "The Great Speckled Bird" by Roy Acuff and his Smoky Mountain Boys. The program gained a following for its irreverence and humor, if not for the music. In a shrill Appalachian twang, "Warnock Jim Wright" led a group of his "New York bohemian" friends through surrealistic skits and ad-libbed commentary on current political and campus events, interspersed with music from the Grand Ole Opry. "Jim's was a boisterous, rebellious nature and he had a quick felicity of tongue," one cohort recalled, and the college soon realized the show "would do most anything to embarrass the Kenyon image." One acclaimed program aired on April 19, 1951, just hours after General Douglas MacArthur's address to Congress following his dismissal by President Truman as Commander in Chief of United Nations forces in Korea. Working from memory, Wright improvised a satirical re-creation of MacArthur's now legendary speech, which concluded: "Old soldiers never die; they just fade away." For all his defiant wit, however, Wright never showed contempt for country music. Doctorow believed that Wright's love for both country music and German lieder exposed the internal discord he constantly struggled with.

Wright abandoned a working manuscript of more than two hundred pages that spring; most were poems revised from his 1949 *Folio*. Of more significance are pages in Wright's class notebook dated April 27, 1951. As he began work on a translation of Theodor Storm's *novelle* "Paul the Puppet-Player," he jotted nine free-verse lines in a bottom margin, the conclusion to a poem he titled "Father." Within weeks, Ransom accepted the completed poem for *The Kenyon Review*, along with another titled "Lonely." Both poems had come to Wright without effort and with little need for revision; in a rare instance of pure inspiration, he had begun both after waking in the middle of the night. He had labored over hundreds of poems, but these two would mark Wright's debut in a national publication. After working tirelessly for years, his first success felt like a gift.

Lacking a set scheme of rhyme and meter, "Father" imagines the poet's own birth—literally coming into being—on the banks of a river, lifted from a ferryboat by his father. Its central lines read:

> And the wind began,
> Transfiguring my face from nothingness
> To tiny weeping eyes. And when my voice
> Grew real, there was a place
> Far, far below on earth. There was a tiny man—
>
> It was my father wandering round the waters at the wharf.

Wright's alertness to sensory details, his use of parallel syntax, and his kinetic turns of imagery are qualities found throughout his mature work.

In the final couplet—as first set down in his notebook—a shift in tone captures the "flat voice" Wright would later claim as his own:

> He drew me from the boat. I was asleep.
> And we went home together.

Wright traveled between Warnock and Gambier all that summer, returning to Kenyon's library for research on his Hardy thesis. He took a summer job with the Mount Vernon Bridge Company, painting primer on steel bridge beams, and returned to the library when his shift was over. Since Wright owned only one pair of shoes, the orange paint spots on his work boots became a kind of trademark. Classmates often came with him to the farm; Jack found Roger Hecht hard at work on a poem at their kitchen table, scratching at a sheet of butcher's paper Jessie had given him. Hecht and Wright often translated German poems together, including ballads by Heine and Bertolt Brecht. During his last three years at Kenyon, Wright drafted more than one hundred German translations, the work of sixteen different poets. As Hecht boarded a bus back to Gambier, Wright pressed his copy of Oscar Williams's *Little Treasury of Modern Poetry* into his hands, praising the book as his true introduction to poetry.

Liberty also visited the "sad little farm" in Warnock that summer and saw the laughter Wright shared with his mother as proof of their close bond. But Liberty already feared "losing him to his talent, [which] was too great to be confined by marriage." Ignoring her intuition, she "would not consider letting go of him."

———

Returning to campus in September, Wright shared a room on the fourth floor of the rebuilt Old Kenyon dormitory with Sy Weissman. Their large corner room on the top floor had a huge, round "bull's-eye" window, and it quickly became a gathering place. Weissman owned a large record collection and one of the few automobiles on campus—a fine new Chevy convertible in which he "chauffeured" his roommate. But Wright had first thought of rooming with him because they wore the same size clothes. "Jim was always dead broke. He didn't have a pot to piss in, just the money for his cigarettes. And he wore all my clothes."

Soon after classes began, Wright learned that a new poet had arrived on campus, a sixteen-year-old freshman by the name of Robert Mezey. He set out immediately to meet him.

I was at Kenyon, maybe the second or third day I was there, scared to death, and I was approached on Middle Path by this big, burly character dressed completely in army fatigues. He must have been about eight years older than I was at that time, but it might as well have been thirty, I mean, he was a man and I was a boy. And he came up to me and said: "You're a poet, kid. Listen to this," and launched into Hardy's lovely poem "To Lizbie Browne," which of course he had by heart, and which seemed to me one of the most beautiful things I had ever heard. That was the beginning of my thirty-year friendship with Jim and my lifelong passion for Thomas Hardy.

Mezey, for his part, impressed Wright from the first, and the two poets became inseparable; Wright could appear much like an older brother, and they recited Latin poems to each other and worked on translations together. Mezey learned that Wright translated in order to read poems he loved more carefully and deeply—the results were not that important. "The process of doing it was what mattered. He worked like a horse."

Wright's astonishing memory complemented this capacity for hard work. Rather than an eidetic, or "photographic," memory, Wright's ability has been called "phonographic"—a precise, auditory memory for sequences of sound patterns. He could recite Latin, German, or English poems interchangeably, and had a related gift for mimicry. Wright often used this talent to entertain, while at the same time keeping others at a distance. "It's as if he has a piano roll in his head," Weissman recalled. "Once you start pumping it up, it just rolls out by itself and it continues to play until it gets to the end of the roll—which might be a day and a half later."

———

Wright's first thesis advisor was the young, brilliant professor Denham Sutcliffe, who proved a lenient reader of Wright's effusive prose and exhaustive critical apparatus. But in the fall of 1951, Sutcliffe left to teach at Harvard and Charles Coffin, a more conservative academic, became

Wright's principal reader. By October, Wright's thesis had grown to more than 340 pages. Coffin balked at the length alone and demanded he rewrite it. When Wright resubmitted the paper in November, he had trimmed it by 100 pages. Dedicated "To my friend Edgar Doctorow," it was titled "The Will in the Thought and Art of Thomas Hardy" and included an extensive appendix of reference notes. Coffin returned this draft, still 245 pages long, too. Though he had read the essay closely and offered detailed comments, Wright was furious. He believed that Coffin's reproach denied him the chance to graduate with highest honors and he felt cheated. Wright became consumed with self-doubt, and suddenly his future seemed uncertain.

"Jim was just absolutely ready to commit suicide," Doctorow recalled. "I mean, he'd put so much of himself—he loved Hardy's work. We'd all studied Hardy with Ransom, and when Jim was asked to revise this thing, he felt it was a terrible kind of rejection." That same month, Doctorow traveled with Wright by bus to visit the farm in Warnock and hear a concert by the Wheeling Symphony; they then slept on the floor of Jim's aunt's house in Martins Ferry. Doctorow's friendship mattered more than any other to Wright, but Doctorow found it exhausting to spend that much time in Wright's company. "He couldn't be casual about anything. Everything was treated at a level of intensity that made him difficult to be around for very long. . . . There was nothing held back. He was always working all cylinders, always."

In December, Wright begrudgingly began to revise his thesis yet again, and completed other papers and reading for his comprehensive exams. He sat for hours at the typewriter in his dorm room in just his undershirt, working endlessly. Friends were astonished to see him consume an entire bottle of bourbon in the course of an evening, to no apparent effect. Just before classes ended, Wright gave the last of his annual readings of Dickens's *A Christmas Carol* before a small group of friends, mimicking the voice of Lionel Barrymore as Scrooge and inhabiting each character by turns.

Having just turned twenty-four, he still planned to marry Liberty but had no idea how or where they would live. Earlier that fall, he had confessed to Tony Stoneburner his grave doubts about marriage, acknowledging "the interplay of cowardice and of courage" he felt and his fear that the burden of a family would cancel his ambition as a poet. Wright suffered over the decision for months. On Christmas Eve, he stood with

Liberty at the crest of Riverview Cemetery and cast a Dantean curse on Martins Ferry, an image of his own fate stretched out below him.

Two days later, Wright phoned Liberty from Gambier. "I can't go through with it," he told her. "I can't get married. I'm sorry." From what she could make out, the reason was poetry. Since their engagement the previous spring, Wright had tried twice before to call off the wedding, but couldn't bear to see Liberty weeping. This time he phoned while she was on duty at the Martins Ferry hospital and quickly hung up.

For the next two weeks, Wright lived alone in his Old Kenyon dorm room, with just a chest of drawers, a small desk, and a cot. Without sheets or a blanket, he slept in his bathrobe. As John Schmitt observed, "one shirt was hanging on the chair, drying, and his other shirt was on him." In this monastic setting, Wright revised and retyped the final version of his Hardy thesis, "The Survival of the Beloved." It was now just sixty pages long. His approach to Hardy's work is philosophical as much as technical, and his clipped, spare sentences betray some of the rage he still felt. As he writes in conclusion:

> The nature in which Thomas Hardy is most frequently interested is the concrete reality in its richest and most subtle details. He is a dramatic writer, and his dramas are based on the struggle between concrete nature and certain human beings. . . . [O]ne of the dramatic motivations in Hardy's work is the attempt, conscious or unconscious, of his characters to find their way into some endurable relationship with concrete nature.

On a bitter cold night before New Year's Eve, Gene Pugatch returned to campus after the holiday break, exhausted from travel. Among the few students on campus he found John Schmitt in his dorm room in Old Kenyon, and he soon fell asleep on the bed. When he woke, Wright sat beside him, listening intently, over and over again, to the *Concerto Grosso for String Orchestra with Piano Obbligato* by Ernest Bloch. The final movement of the piece, which is structured as a fugue, fascinated him. "Jim said he didn't realize that modern composers were writing like that," Schmitt recalled. "He was surprised, with Bloch—it's modern, but it's controlled—it has a shape to it, a form, or a discipline." In the *Concerto*, Wright heard how Bloch had resolved a challenge he faced in his own poems. That the medium was music, not words, seemed incidental.

6

With the voice of
a resurrected blackbird

January 1952–September 1953

Everything about his future remained uncertain as Wright labored to pare down his thesis. With Hanfman's support, he had applied for a Fulbright grant to study Theodor Storm's work at the University of Vienna, but word of that decision would not come for months. After final exams at the end of January, he faced returning to his parents' farm in Warnock in the dead of winter and a melancholy seeped into Wright's truncated essay, as though he had become one of Hardy's disillusioned protagonists.

Two weeks after calling off his marriage, Wright phoned Liberty again at the Martins Ferry hospital. Asking her forgiveness, he promised once more to marry her. Liberty was overjoyed, but Wright remained troubled. He later described his decision by quoting Thoreau: "What is called resignation is confirmed desperation." The anxiety that hounded him is evident in a letter to his mother dated January 23, asking for a loan of twenty dollars to see him through the end of the month. More than his final exams, he worried about what would come after. He knew he could not work in the Ohio Valley or in a factory. "The Valley is more like hell than hell itself is; and work in a factory is, as far as I am concerned, distinctly worse than anything on earth." Wright believed that Liberty understood the intensity of his feelings.

She is going into this relationship with her eyes wide open. Life has been to a great extent a misery for both of us, though in different ways. We are trying very hard to give each other some consolation in the world, and a chance to live with at least a little dignity and fulfillment, instead of the animality and pointlessness which we have both largely known so far. We have hope.

Wright's indictment of his early life shows a startling openness with his mother; theatrically, he lays bare his deepest fears to her.

Two days later, in the middle of exams, a classmate presented a welcome opportunity. Tom Tenney's parents had started a small private boarding school for wealthy (albeit troubled) boys in Center Point, Texas, and they were suddenly in need of an English instructor and live-in dorm counselor. Although Wright had applied to graduate programs, he couldn't enroll before September, and Texas was a long way from Ohio. He gratefully accepted the teaching post, and after his last exam on January 31, he returned to Warnock and wrote friends of his imminent wedding and the couple's planned departure for Texas the following week. At the same time, in the days before they married on February 10, Liberty graduated from the School of Nursing in Martins Ferry.

During that harried, chaotic week, Wright shuttled back and forth between Warnock and Martins Ferry, finalizing plans for the ceremony and their trip south. On the eve of the service, he wrote Stoneburner, asking for a letter of recommendation for a potential fellowship at Princeton. Despite countless tasks and little sleep, Wright confessed he had spent the last few hours revising a long poem. He also completed a poem for Liberty in those early morning hours called "Villanelle: A Prayer on the Night Before My Wedding." Its opening line recurs throughout, sounding both urgent and despairing: "Dear God, be kind to her whom I so need."

The following day, Wright panicked again when the priest insisted the couple sign a declaration promising to raise their children in the Greek Orthodox faith. The ceremony was delayed for an hour as Liberty struggled to convince Wright the agreement held no weight. She would remember "the terrible tension between our families" that day. The lengthy service gave way to a spirited reception at the Kardules home on Pearl Street, where Liberty's father advised his new son-in-law that he should "get a good stick to make her behave." As Liberty later admitted, "Our marriage was doomed from the beginning, and I believe I knew it all along."

———

The four months Jim and Liberty spent in Texas proved an immediate trial. After a train journey of three days to San Antonio and hours more by car, they were put to work as soon as they arrived; Liberty served as both office secretary and resident nurse. The Tenney School stood at the edge of a broad, wooded mesa, where, as Jim wrote his parents, "a 165-foot cliff drops the eye to one of the softest and most resting horizons we have ever seen." But nineteen adolescents, all "rough Texans," boarded at the school, and nothing could have prepared the couple for the malice that animated "those vicious boys." All came from wealthy families, and many stabled horses on the grounds; most had been expelled from more prestigious boarding schools for good reason. They tormented the new arrivals with firecrackers tossed beneath their door; soon they were using live snakes. Wright even discovered a scorpion in the ceiling light fixture. After the first week, he carried a wooden paddle into the classroom.

In a bid to capture their interest, Wright tried teaching the King James Bible and found he enjoyed it. After hearing them read passages aloud from the story of David, he began a long narrative poem that obsessed him throughout the spring. Wright spent hours secluded in the couple's bedroom revising successive drafts of a dramatic monologue that swelled to more than a hundred pages of blank verse. The copy he mailed to Timberlake in May, titled *The Care of Phaltiel: A Tale in Ten Scenes*, filled seventy-three single-spaced pages. When the poem appeared in print five years later, all that remained were seven octaves of rhymed couplets titled "David."

Robert Mezey and Wright kept up an extensive correspondence for years after Wright left Kenyon. Long, discursive letters passed between them every week, full of gossip and opinions, as well as new translations and poems in progress. When Mezey appeared in Center Point at the end of March after hitchhiking from Gambier, the two poets went horseback riding and talked endlessly. Though a precocious seventeen-year-old at the time, Mezey recognized the friction already evident between Jim and Liberty, compounded by the nightmare of their students. Tenney's mother told her son she often heard them arguing. In one instance, Wright shouted, "Yes, we *are* going to have children!" to drown out Liberty's bitter protests. In May, after the Fulbright committee confirmed Wright's plan to study in Vienna, the couple gladly left "cowboy culture" and southern racial prejudices behind.

———

At ceremonies in Gambier on June 9, 1952, James Arlington Wright graduated from Kenyon College magna cum laude, with High Honors in English. Wright was also awarded the Robert Frost Poetry Prize, an honor bestowed jointly by Ransom, Coffin, and Timberlake. The prize itself was largely symbolic—a signed copy of Frost's poems—but for Wright the honor meant everything. When he had learned of the award that spring, he said a kind of prayer to himself in private. "Oh God, oh God. Am I going to get to be a poet? Just think, a poet, like Robert Frost or Ben Jonson. That would be the grandest thing." Wright's Fulbright scholarship to study at the University of Vienna had answered another furtive prayer. However, before the couple left in September they needed to make money. Following commencement, they boarded a train east for Mezey's hometown of Philadelphia.

Liberty soon found a nursing position at Temple University Hospital, while both Mezey and Wright took work on the night shift for Railway Express, "carrying and pushing large boxes around," Mezey recalled, "a real miserable job for shit wages." This was exactly the kind of work Wright had sworn he would never submit to, and he "conceived a particular hatred" for the foreman who harassed them through the hot, humid nights of that long summer. Once, as Wright rode in an open freight elevator, a huge barrel of fish slipped off the edge, falling two stories to land with an explosive crash right where the foreman had been standing. The mishap was easily explained as an accident, but Mezey couldn't be sure. "I never knew anybody whose rages were as monumental as Jim's, sometimes quite frightening."

———

By the first week in August, Wright and his wife had returned to Martins Ferry, where Liberty's mother lay gravely ill with cancer. After seven years, Wright's parents had finally given up on the Warnock farm, in part to help care for an ailing infant grandchild in the house that Ted had just finished building for his family near Zanesville. Marge knew that Jessie would never have willingly left the farm.

In a letter to Mezey in mid-August, Wright declared that his marriage couldn't last; both he and Liberty knew they were ill-suited for each other, but they had decided to stay together for the next year "as a matter of convenience." Quoting Yeats, he admitted to choosing his work over his life. Wright even sided with Liberty's father, who demanded she stay to care for her dying mother. Ereni Kardules wouldn't hear of it. She insisted that Liberty go with her husband, and was the first to recognize her daughter's pregnancy. Convinced this meant the end of his studies in Austria, Wright was inconsolable. But as Ereni chided them both, "women have been having babies in Europe, too."

The couple embarked from New York harbor on September 10, 1952. Doctorow went to see them off as they boarded the *Queen Mary*, and he recognized the same overalls and fatigue jacket Wright had worn at Kenyon. Among the other Fulbright scholars bound for Europe, Wright met Herbert Lindenberger, a graduate student in the new Comparative Literature Department at the University of Washington in Seattle. "Jim believed that if you didn't memorize poetry, you couldn't understand it completely," Lindenberger recalled, describing that first meeting. He felt drawn to Wright's unabashed enthusiasm, and during the crossing Wright began confiding in him, and confessed his feelings of apprehension and depression. He came to depend on Lindenberger, who was fluent in German and shared his passion for poetry.

After just one day in Paris, a small, close-knit group of Fulbright scholars boarded an overnight train to Vienna, arriving at the end of September in crisp, autumnal weather. The city had been devastated by the war and remained partitioned into five zones, with a shared international presence in the central, oldest section. Americans and those from Western Europe risked arrest if they crossed beyond posted city limits into the Russian zone. "Everybody looked bedraggled in Vienna in those days," Lindenberger recalled; throughout the city, empty, damaged buildings awaited demolition or repair. The Wrights took a third-floor apartment with two small rooms and a shared kitchen where Liberty cooked, frequenting the stall of a Greek grocer in the city's marketplace. When a bitter-cold winter set in, Lindenberger discovered it was cheaper to spend evenings at a theater or concert hall, rather than feed the wood-stove in his flat.

Wright had completed few poems in the previous year. Though he now wrote prolifically and worked to revise dozens of new pieces, nothing satisfied him. The importance of his study in Vienna did not become evident in his poetry for many years, the result of a fortuitous accident rather than diligence. Wright would vividly recall the first time he heard the poems of Georg Trakl, spoken "with the voice of a resurrected blackbird":

> In the autumn of 1952, I wandered into the wrong classroom at the University of Vienna. According to my instructions, the professor was supposed to be a German, whose name I forget. I also forget what course I had expected. But the lecturer who actually appeared was a short swarthy man; and he spoke soft, clear German, clinging to his Italian accent. His name was Professor Susini. The only other persons in that unheated room were a few old men, who resembled Bowery bums in America.

Wright had stumbled into the one course in modern poetry taught at the university; Eugene Susini, the French cultural attaché, was a visiting professor. Lindenberger joined Wright in Susini's weekly class, and the two constantly discussed Trakl's work, which had a lasting impact on them both. They returned to the half-light of that cold classroom all winter to hear Trakl's singular, image-based poems. Susini read beautifully, and as he explicated each piece in a careful, deliberate manner, his lectures "became downright luminous."

Trakl's work was not then widely known, although Martin Heidegger had recently lectured on his poetry in Vienna and published an essay the following year that helped draw attention to him. Austrian by birth, Trakl is a figure apart in early twentieth-century poetry. Traumatized by his service in the Austrian Medical Corps following the battle of Grodek, he took his own life in November 1914 at the age of twenty-seven. In the two years prior to his death, he wrote some one hundred poems and prose pieces using an idiosyncratic and restricted lexicon that invested certain nouns (such as *Nacht*, *Wald*, and *Schweigen*) with increasing personal resonance. Trakl's intimate observations of both internal and external landscapes possess a charged, hermetic quality.

While Trakl presents objects and images discernible to the senses, Lindenberger has suggested that "event" might better describe the fundamental ordering principle in his work, given the way that verbs anchor each structural unit. Inspired by Rimbaud's poetry, Trakl omits explicit semantic connections; he dramatizes states of consciousness by setting concrete images beside each other without commentary. Pointing to the suggestive power in objects themselves—a quality of French symbolism— is the innovation of Trakl's poetry that Rilke most admired. Trakl's late poem "Der Schlaf," or "Sleep," was one of many Wright began translating in Vienna and published ten years later in *Twenty Poems*, in collaboration with Robert Bly:

> Not your dark poisons again,
> White sleep!
> This fantastically strange garden
> Of trees in deepening twilight
> Fills up with serpents, nightmoths,
> Spiders, bats.
> Approaching stranger! Your abandoned shadow
> In the red of evening
> Is a dark pirate ship
> On the salty oceans of confusion.
> White birds from the outskirts of the night
> Flutter out over the shuddering cities
> Of steel.

In his introduction to these translations, Wright observes that the synesthetic quality of Trakl's imagination presents "a world where seeing and hearing are not two actions, but one." As Trakl himself once wrote, "all animated ear that I am, I lie in wait for the melodies which are within me and my winged eye dreams its pictures once again."

Wright shared the uncanny acuity that Trakl here describes. Though Wright's command of the spoken language remained weak, "he was very sensitive to the *sound* of German poetry." He worked at memorizing German poems to internalize their music, and while his study of Theodor Storm never progressed beyond scattered notes, Wright was "crazy" about Storm, Heine, and nineteenth-century German Romanticism. In a lyric tradition more intellectual and melancholy than its English counterpart, Wright identified with the image of the brooding hermit-poet.

Vienna—a partitioned city in ruins, run-down, and destitute— became the theater in which Wright first experienced Trakl's hauntingly prescient poems, written during the nightmare of the previous war. As winter descended and the narrow streets darkened with snow, Wright became absorbed by this stoic, visionary body of work. He saw the wreckage of war all around him, and Trakl's images evoked the same sense of loss and devastation.

———

Though Wright spent hours in Viennese coffeehouses—even scribbling lines of poetry on napkins that he later transcribed on his typewriter—he was rarely the lonely recluse he imagined himself to be. The small group of Fulbright students in Vienna often shared dinners or hikes in the wooded outskirts of the city, and attended opera, theater, and concert performances. They could live well on their monthly stipends. Wright heard music everywhere and became fascinated by Wagner's operas. Still, he often stood apart; rather than trying to master conversational German, he focused on translations and on his own poems.

Despite news of her mother's death in October, Liberty recalled the months of her pregnancy as a brief period of happiness in her marriage. Liberty had come to understand her husband, and learned to soothe his temper—especially when he'd been drinking. She saw him writing and reading extensively, immersed in the poetry of Rilke and Friedrich Hölderlin, absorbing their work in a profound way. "After a while it was difficult to know where Jim Wright was and Hölderlin. The boundaries were very, very diffuse."

In Vienna, Wright filled a black spring binder with three hundred pages of carefully typed fair copies of poems and translations. Even while surrounded by European culture, Wright was drawn back to Ohio. "On the Ohio River" begins with an epigraph from Blake: ". . . *the Ohio will wash me clean.*" It reads in part:

Here underneath the sulphurous moon
The rats return to find what they
May pick and choose from afternoon
Dropped in the waters. Green and gray

The trees along the river lean
And lip the waste with broken leaves,
And hoboes wipe their fingers clean
Like hoodlums tipping stones of graves.

The landscape of his childhood and images of the river rose almost un-
bidden to him. Many of his new poems from Vienna show this divergence
between memory and daily reality; they seem tentative yet labored and
are marked by a sense of restlessness. Wright abandoned many poems
after multiple drafts, only to begin again in a different meter and rhyme
scheme. As Keats had set himself the task of writing *Endymion* by se-
cluding himself to write two hundred lines each day, the sheer quantity
of work became a goal in itself for Wright.

On December 13, 1952, Wright turned twenty-five; as he well knew,
Keats had written all of his poetry by that age. In a long letter to Mezey
that day, he confessed his jealousy for the work of Keats and Heine, with
whom he shared a birthday. Though early translations of Trakl appear
scattered among Wright's typescripts and journals, Trakl's poetry had no
immediate influence. Instead, Wright continued to write sonnets—dozens
of them.

As spring arrived, his letters to Mezey filled with "ecstasies" over the
work of Storm and long passages transcribed from Hesse's *Steppenwolf*.
An entirely new theme inspired a number of poems, including one titled
"On the Birth of My Son in a Spring Morning." By the end of February,
Liberty and Jim had begun to worry about the lateness of the baby, and
made emergency plans as days dragged into weeks. They finally took a
trolley to the hospital and Liberty remained in labor for more than a day
before their first son, Franz Paul, was born on March 18, 1953. Wright
delighted in the newborn, whom he named for the Viennese composer
Franz Schubert.

Liberty returned to their apartment exhausted, but the baby's cries
made work at home impossible and Wright took refuge in cafés, music
halls, and theaters. In a letter to Mezey he described his "actual physical
hunger for music." With Lindenberger's guidance, Wright became fluent
in opera, fanatical about the works of Mozart and Strauss. Lindenberger
planned to return to the University of Washington in Seattle and persuaded Wright to apply. While he knew of Theodore Roethke's reputation as a poet and a teacher, Wright's memories of the Pacific Northwest
from his first weeks in the army were encouragement enough.

Wright loved the sounds his new son made as he began to vocalize,
and "he talked poetry to Franzy from the day he was born." Nevertheless,
Liberty soon noticed that "there were times Jim became irritable and
angrily pulled away and stayed away from us, sometimes for a few hours,

at other times, a day or more." That May, in a letter to Libby, Mezey counseled, "Don't worry yourself about Jim's moods and restlessness." The eighteen-year-old Mezey then tried to reassure Wright as well. "No, Jim, I don't think you're becoming an existentialist. I just think you're homesick." In response, Wright confessed that he longed for "some of that glorious barbarism, that gratifying bleakness and loneliness which is so much of America to me. There is no denying that the country America is crude and strange and frightening, but man I love it with my whole person. . . . I want to hear the people on the street spitting and snarling my own language." Mezey saw how the prospect of returning to the States had rejuvenated Wright, and encouraged him to cultivate that rage in his poetry. "Fury's your best mode."

———

The young family left Vienna at the beginning of June, "well stocked with diapers and baby food given to us by the Ambassador's wife." They traveled first to Germany and England, taking a boat up the Rhine to Cologne before continuing on to London. After two days they boarded a bus for Dorchester in a pilgrimage to Hardy country in the west of England. In a thatch-roofed cottage in Dorset, Wright engaged the care-taker at Hardy's birthplace in a long conversation, the inspiration for his masterful lyric "At Thomas Hardy's Birthplace, 1953."

After a turbulent weeklong crossing to New York on the steamer RMS *Mauretania*, the three stayed on in New York, visiting with Kenyon friends before returning to Ohio. Wright's parents were now living with Ted and Helen Wright in Chandlersville, outside of Zanesville, though Dudley kept a small room near the factory in South Wheeling during the week. Jim introduced Franz to his parents and siblings and prepared for the move to Seattle, where he had been accepted into the graduate programs in both advanced writing and English literature. All that sum-mer, Wright typed drafts and revisions to the poems and translations he had been gathering for a year and a half, submitting many to journals using his father-in-law's address on Pearl Street in Martins Ferry.

Wright's arrival home from Europe occasioned a vivid elegy for Biddy Lyons titled "My Grandmother's Ghost." On a staircase landing in the farmhouse in Chandlersville hung a framed photograph he had never seen before. When he asked his mother who the beautiful young woman was, Jessie teased him before saying, "Why, that's Grandma!" It startled him to realize that he had never imagined his grandmother as a young woman. The poem is a small masterpiece, Mezey has said, "where his ear is at its very best." Having written hundreds of sonnets over a dozen years, Wright shows complete command of the form. The poem's setting is the Weeks Cemetery, where Biddy lay buried and where, as a teenager, Wright had briefly worked one summer.

> She skimmed the yellow water like a moth,
> Trailing her feet across the shallow stream;
> She saw the berries, paused and sampled them
> Where a slight spider cleaned his narrow tooth.
> Light in the air, she fluttered up the path,
> So delicate to shun the leaves and damp,
> Like some young wife, holding a slender lamp
> To find her stray child, or the moon, or both.
>
> Even before she reached the empty house,
> She beat her wings ever so lightly, rose,
> Followed a bee where apples blew like snow;
> And then, forgetting what she wanted there,
> Too full of blossom and green light to care,
> She hurried to the ground, and slipped below.

Wright recited this poem more often than any other throughout his career and often told the story of its inspiration. His heartfelt connection to Biddy Lyons was tangled up with his conflicted feelings for Martins Ferry. Here, she becomes one of the significant ghost figures in Wright's work.

In early September, Wright and his family boarded a train to begin a three-day trip to Seattle. Before departing, Jim and Liberty brought their infant son to Martins Ferry to see her father, and they climbed once more to the hilltop cemetery overlooking town, where Liberty's mother now lay buried. Few of Wright's relatives remained in the Valley, and with relief he turned his back on the polluted, haunted shores of the Ohio River. He felt elated to be returning to the Pacific Northwest, repeating the journey he had taken at the age of eighteen.

7

To sing whatever is well-made

September 1953–August 1957

The teaching of poetry requires fanaticism.

—Theodore Roethke, from *Straw for the Fire*

Wright's study and—just as important—friendship with Theodore Roethke had a lasting impact on his life and work. Apart from the more erratic John Berryman, there was no better teacher of poetry in an American university; Wright adopted many of Roethke's methods and modeled his own rapport with students after Roethke's presence in the classroom. As a poet, Roethke appeared to match the paradigm of a troubled, hard-drinking explorer of dark psychic territories. Fortunately, he felt differently about his work. "In spite of all the muck and welter, the *dreck*, of [my] poems," Roethke said, "I count myself among the happy poets."

Roethke swept aside whatever conflict Wright still felt about pursuing a life of poetry. Born into a German immigrant family in Saginaw, Michigan, he shared Wright's working-class midwestern upbringing, in which literature and intellectual things were largely dismissed. Both men were burly and disheveled but passionate about the most delicate nuances of language and sensitive to the natural world. Roethke's restless, personal search, his mastery of craft and ardent lyricism impressed Wright as a poet's highest achievement.

In September 1953, Roethke's classroom gave Wright a delirious sense of liberation. He felt welcomed by his classmates, who included the poet

Carolyn Kizer. "He was our genius—we *knew* that. We were just stunned by the mastery of the work, even then, and I think Roethke was stunned by it, too." The Advanced Verse Writing students who gathered that fall in a high-ceilinged classroom in Parrington Hall were among the best Roethke ever taught. The poet Jack Gilbert was part of what Kizer called "that mad class," along with a seventy-year-old rabbi and a retired sea captain, older still. Roethke kept his class open to the public and chose the students he wanted. The catholicity of his tastes and his "pure delight" in language astounded Wright. "Roethke was wild," Lindenberger observed, "and they both saw kindred spirits in each other."

The Wrights found a cheap apartment near campus, and Liberty took a job at Doctors Hospital in the city. Wright's position as a teaching assistant paid for his tuition, but Liberty's work as a nurse supported the family. On his walk to campus—"with great enjoyment of song and conversation"—Wright dropped infant Franz off at day care. Liberty learned to drive on the steep hills of Seattle, leaving early each morning in the 1946 Ford Coupe they bought upon arriving. She recalled the long weekend drives they took to the Cascade Mountains and the Oregon coast as among the happiest times in their marriage. Wright never learned to drive, in part, he said, because he felt too easily distracted; he depended upon others and public transportation his whole life. But he loved to walk and considered Seattle the most beautiful place he had ever lived. He came to think of the University of Washington as the ideal intellectual environment.

When classes began on the last day of September, Wright became a first-year teaching assistant with multiple sections of basic freshman composition; he graded armloads of papers every week. He met Franz Schneider that first week, a fellow teaching assistant and graduate student from Germany. Schneider, who was himself a poet, studied with the noted scholar and translator Jackson Mathews in the fledgling Comparative Literature program. Wright shared an office with three other teaching assistants, each of them also a poet. He already knew Herb Lindenberger and Lloyd Parks, a Kenyon classmate. A third colleague, C. W. "Bill" Truesdale, recalled Wright distinctly. "Unlike the rest of us, he already seemed to know exactly who he was, as though he had sprung to life that way, fully-formed." Lindenberger agreed. "Jim was a force on campus—personally a force. He was voluble, and someone to be taken seriously."

Wright tested everything against his own sense and experience. In his notebooks on his first day in Roethke's class, he saw the disparity with Ransom's New Critical distance and innate reticence. "Honesty: This man is letting us see his own verse exercises. Imagine JCR's rage!" In the first weeks, Wright resisted Roethke's insistence that childhood memories were the source of a poet's art. "Childhood memories? Ohio valley? Hah! I'd like to forget that son-of-a-bitch." However, a poem he abandoned that first winter shows a potent new energy. "Winter Walk by a River" begins:

> I knew the river well enough,
> And all the river had to say
> Was *come*, and I would come,
> I had so well forgotten home.

Wright falls into an easy tetrameter line, and fills a page with descriptive recollections in rhymed couplets. But the poem takes a remarkable turn in the last stanza, as the speaker comes upon a hobo encampment beside the river:

> So may one soon blunder on God,
> His face covered with mud,
> His whiskers matted thick with thorn,
> His withered fingers labor-worn,
> Beer stained to his vest,
> His voice low as starving beast,
> His shoulder leaned against a rotted wall,
> And not so strong at all.

This startling conflation of the deity with a homeless drunk brings to mind dramatic occasions in E. A. Robinson's poems, while the repeated capitalized pronoun "His" echoes the cadence of the King James Bible. Wright's interest in social outcasts made for uncommon subject matter in the 1950s, despite the prominence of Robinson's verse in the first decades of the century. Like Robinson—and Roethke, too—Wright began to recognize the true material for his poems by the vitality of language they called up.

While Wright questioned many of Roethke's devotions and came to accept them only by degrees, he shared one of Roethke's passions from the first: "he believed very much in getting poems by heart in the old-fashioned way." Richard Hugo, who also studied with Roethke, saw how this was an essential facet of his teaching. "If a student wasn't a complete auditory clod, he could feel himself falling in love with the sound of words. To Roethke, that was the heart and soul of poetry."

Roethke's intellectual command was broad and associative, and even before his own poetry had an effect on Wright, his teaching methods and the poets he loved—Yeats, Hopkins, Auden, Dylan Thomas, Stanley Kunitz, Louise Bogan—began to influence Wright. Roethke often met his students in the bars along University Avenue and would come to their parties. At the age of forty-five, he was twenty years Wright's senior. But he, too, had recently married and had just returned from months of travel in Europe with his young bride, Beatrice O'Connell, a former student. The history of Roethke's manic-depressive illness was well-known on campus, and over the remaining decade of his life these episodes became more frequent. Roethke's devotion to poetry, however, was unshakable, and he worked continuously as a disciplined and committed craftsman.

After a month of classes, in the first week of November, word came of Dylan Thomas's sudden death. Roethke broke down in tears when he heard the news; within weeks, the shock and grief returned him to the hospital. Wright, too, was shaken, and began work on a poem titled "Rites to a Dead Magician." Like "Poem to Kathleen Ferrier"—written in memory of the celebrated contralto who had just died of cancer—the work Wright began publishing in journals and magazines was often elegiac. In February 1954, Karl Shapiro wrote to say that "The Resurrected" and "Elegy in a Firelit Room" would mark Wright's first appearance in *Poetry* magazine, beginning an astonishing run of publications. In the four-year span from 1955 through the end of 1958, more than 120 Wright poems would appear in magazines and journals.

Despite this early success, Wright was determined to earn his doctorate and make his living as a teacher. He wanted the security of a degree and a career, and his graduate coursework focused on English literature. Wright told Liberty he wanted to prove he could do it; she believed he needed the structure his classwork gave him. Either way, the graduate program was extremely tough. "The man was brilliant," Schneider recalled, "but he had the same kind of stresses and fears that we all had going through a demanding program. We had to work very, very hard."

In the winter of 1954, Wright studied Shakespeare and took a nineteenth-century literature course taught by Lawrence Zillman, a renowned scholar of Romantic poetry whose approach ran counter to the prevailing New Critical bias. Like Zillman, Wright believed that "a poem is never a poem until read aloud," and he reveled in the poetry of Shelley, a poet anathema to most of his colleagues. "Jim was a great critical mind, and he could explain why Shelley's language was interesting and experimental," Lindenberger said. "He was interested in what you could possibly do with language, and if it was working he didn't care how fashionable or unfashionable it was." Wright recited Shelley and argued for him without apology. Of more lasting importance, he became a passionate advocate for the poetry and novels of Hesse, whose work was not yet widely known in the United States.

"Jim never talked about getting groceries or going to the bank," Liberty recalled. "When he talked, he talked poetry. Whomever he was studying he would literally memorize." With Wright immersed in his studies, Libby was having a difficult time. She was left to care for the infant Franz after working long hours as a nursing supervisor at the hospital, where she was known as "a very tough nurse." Lindenberger saw trouble in the marriage the moment they arrived in Seattle. Jim began staying out drinking with friends, often bringing them home late at night, while Liberty left early each morning with increasing responsibility at her job. As the tensions between them went unresolved and the exhausting routine of her days wore her down, Liberty grew resentful. Meanwhile, Wright found nothing but encouragement in the Blue Moon Tavern and the coffee shops on University Avenue.

That spring, Wright took a second class with Roethke and a course in modern criticism with Jackson Mathews, who introduced him to the work of the French poet René Char. Roethke's new collection, *The Waking*, received the Pulitzer Prize in March, but his pleasure was muted by the loss of his mother just weeks before. Nonetheless, Roethke's passion in the classroom seemed undiminished. Kizer recalled the ecstatic look that would steal across Wright's face whenever Roethke recited Robert Herrick's love poems. "Ted was so open to raucousness and bombast—lowdown and dirty." When one student objected to Roethke's

critique of a poem and challenged him to define "spontaneity," Roethke
turned and leapt onto a narrow ledge outside the window of their second-
story classroom, disappearing from view. As he burst in through a different
window, he roared, "That's spontaneity, God dammit!"

"A course with Roethke was a course in very, very detailed and stren-
uous critical reading," Wright recalled. "Here was an assignment: he
wanted us to go to the library and find ten or maybe even twenty iambic
trimeter lines that had a caesura after the first syllable." Roethke also
assigned writing exercises, such as poems without any adjectives or
written entirely in Popeian couplets. Roethke himself enjoyed facility in
both open and metrical forms; he revered Yeats and the great Elizabethan plain stylists, poets whom he taught extensively. His students continued writing poems of their own, "and we all wrote over our heads,"
Kizer recalled. But "if anyone wrote a poem that was clearly influenced
by Ted, he would laugh them out of the room. He wouldn't have it. He
burlesqued and teased people out of being Roethke imitators." When
the student newspaper ran a tribute to Roethke, Wright said: "I consider
Roethke one of the greatest teachers of the world. He has the magical
ability to shock a student into being himself."

At the end of each quarter, Roethke's students submitted typed work-
books of the exercises, papers, and poems they completed, as well as the
notes they took in class. Students also typed out favorite poems and
passages of prose by other writers. Wright's work that spring included
a thirteen-page paper on the style of Dryden; a digression on the importance of Heine; and a study of meter and sound in the German of Trakl's
"Helian." Wright credits "that *spare richness* of Bogan" as a model more
immediately useful to him than "Trakl in his stony and glum little
elegiac poems about symbolic landscapes." And yet translations of Trakl
continued to appear among the hundreds of pages of drafts and revisions in Wright's papers from his years in Seattle. Wright abandoned
many dozens of his own poems after working through numerous drafts,
each carefully numbered to track successive versions. Alternating between
typed copies and longhand, he would often rewrite a poem entirely
"from mood & memory."

In the summer of 1954, Wright took an advanced course on Shakespeare and worked directly under Roethke's supervision to complete
his master's thesis. *Mr. Mould's Horses: Elegies and Occasional Poems, 1954*
gathered thirty-four pieces in the manuscript he submitted in support of

his degree that August. It included seven of the forty poems that would eventually appear in Wright's first collection, *The Green Wall*, in 1957.

———

David Wagoner, a former student of Roethke's from the University of Pennsylvania, joined the English faculty in Seattle in the fall of 1954. Wagoner had already heard of Wright, and when the two poets met, Wright surprised him by saying he was then reading only fiction, "to broaden his understanding of literature." Wagoner's recollection of Wright's "most remarkable memory" suggests the competitiveness that could flare up between them: "I remember stopping him on campus one day—he was on his way to class—and saying: 'Do you know "A Nocturne Upon St. Lucy's Day" by John Donne?' And he looked a little chagrined, and he said no, and I recited a couple of lines before he had to go. The next day we bumped into each other again and he recited the whole poem to me."

Wagoner was tall and slender, and physically the two poets made a stark contrast in appearance. But both had grown up in the Midwest, and their fathers still worked in factories there. Wright and Wagoner were among Roethke's close friends, and they became regular guests at parties hosted by Carolyn Kizer and other graduate students in the neighborhood surrounding the university campus.

Classmates also began gathering at Wright's rented home on Sunnyside Avenue that fall. Wright and his family had moved to three different apartments during their first year in Seattle before they found the run-down two-story clapboard house not far from campus where they lived for the next three years. The open first floor had a combined living room and dining room, making it ideal for parties. Amid the laughter and conversation, Wright's recitations amazed everyone: long passages from Dickens, Hardy, Chaucer, opera libretti, his friends' poems—and, always, German verse. As Wright became drunk, Kizer noticed that he turned to reciting German poetry and improvising translations. Drinking was an integral part of these gatherings, where staggering amounts of liquor were consumed.

As a woman in almost exclusively male company at places like the Blue Moon Tavern, Kizer was left at the fringe of conversation; she observed how Wright used his talent for recitation to deflect attention from himself, withdrawing even as he stood out in a crowd—hiding in plain sight. Franz Schneider also recognized his uneasiness among people. "Jim was a very shy person. He could be very voluble—he was a big guy—but he was also very, very shy, especially in a social situation where there were a lot of unfamiliar people around."

Wright's friendship with Schneider remained separate from his growing notoriety in the English Department as a poet appearing in prominent national journals. On a regular basis from the fall of 1954 until Wright left Seattle three years later, Liberty drove her husband to Schneider's home on Friday evenings to watch television. Wright came to see two programs in particular: a half-hour program of Catholic theology called *Life Is Worth Living*, hosted by Archbishop Fulton J. Sheen, followed by weekly professional boxing matches. Schneider remained puzzled by Wright's fascination with the television evangelist, but they did see "some fantastic fights—Carmen Basilio, Gene Fullmer, Sugar Ray Robinson." Often they spoke little, and drank little, before Libby returned.

> There is a gesture of his I still think about. When you started a conversation, he would lean in very close to you and then he would suddenly draw back. I still haven't figured out what that meant. It was something meditative—he seemed abstracted when he drew away. At first, he would look you in the eyes, but then he wouldn't, as though he was looking for something—trying to remember or to formulate something, because it was very important for him how he formulated something, whether it was a profound idea or whether it was a joke or a vulgarity.

Schneider shared Wright's love of German poetry, and they collaborated on a handful of translations. When he showed Wright an English version he had nearly completed of Rilke's "Orpheus. Eurydice. Hermes," he confessed that an image near the end had eluded him. "There was still this one line, which I just could not handle—*'und ausgeteilt wie hundertfacher Vorrat.'* And just like that Jim said: 'Scattered about like rich grain from a hoard.' It just blew my mind."

———

In December 1954, Wright responded to a request for poems from an editor at *The Paris Review*, initiating a lifelong correspondence with the poet Donald Hall. Raised in a prosperous Connecticut home, Hall had an ambitious nature that "attached itself to poetry" at an early age. Arriving at Harvard after studying at Exeter, Hall found himself in the company of many exceptional poets, including John Ashbery, Frank O'Hara, Robert Bly, and Adrienne Rich. The community of poets in the United States was then quite small, and Hall remembered reading Wright's first published poems. Hall accepted two poems for the *Review*, "To a Friend Condemned to Prison" and "A Complaint for George Doty in the Death House"—both displaying "that violent elegiac streak" in Wright's work that Hall identified with the poetry of Robinson. The initial formality between them soon faded, and the two began exchanging long letters and drafts of new poems.

Wright returned to Roethke's classroom in the spring of 1955 and absorbed his devotion to the poems of D. H. Lawrence. Wright's class notebook shows how closely he read Lawrence and how quickly he put his reading into practice: "Lawrence uses *one sentence* for the moonrise poem. *Try that*. Keep all the metaphysical corkscrews out. The one—try one of those sentences in Edmund Burke. And *hold to the symbol*. Just keep it down to *one*. Go on to the Trakl piece. Do the *scene* by the box-car in one sentence."

Wright shared his new poems with Kizer, Wagoner, and Hugo, with whom he felt a strong bond. But these friendships with classmates and colleagues exacerbated the stress in his marriage. As Kizer arrived to drive Wright to one of many nightly gatherings, she heard Liberty sneer, "Aren't you afraid you'll track shit on their expensive rugs?" "Liberty was jealous of all of us," Kizer allowed—perhaps of her most of all, since Kizer believed that "Jim was half in love with me." Ultimately, Wright's fidelity to poetry proved the true source of their discord.

When Roethke departed on a Fulbright grant to Italy for the 1955–56 school year, his close friend Stanley Kunitz arrived in Seattle to teach his classes. Kizer knew that the two shared poetic devotions—including Yeats—but where "Ted would discuss all the poems intuitively and instinctively, Stanley had read every book in Yeats's library." In contrast with Roethke, who communicated largely by "osmosis," Kunitz was very articulate and an excellent "poem doctor," attuned to individual students' needs. Wright benefited more directly from Kunitz's close reading of his work than from any of his other teachers.

Though Wagoner now taught at the university, he and Wright related as peers. It puzzled him that Wright showed no interest in writing fiction and yet devoted himself to studying and teaching literature; Wright wanted nothing to do with teaching creative writing. "I want my thesis work to be completely separate from my work in poetry," he told Lindenberger. He would always keep his writing at a distance from his teaching career. In preparation for his classes of freshmen, Wright copied out lecture notes, biographical data, bibliographies, and quotations. Nietzsche, Shakespeare, Cervantes, Coleridge, Fitzgerald, Burke, Swift, Dostoevsky, Tolstoy, Hardy—every writer or topic Wright took up in his English and humanities classes became part of his vast collection of hundreds of meticulously typed or handwritten index cards. His thesis research on Dickens also began in this way, a process overseen by the outspoken, iconoclastic critic and scholar Wayne Burns.

In the winter and spring of 1956, Wright began working closely with Burns, whose friendship over the next three years became as important to him as Roethke's. Burns was an unorthodox teacher who enjoyed spirited arguments with his students, and he often joined them in coffee shops after class. A dynamic, engaging thinker, Burns was also a keen listener. He saw little difference between a student and teacher, especially with a graduate student like Wright who reveled in Burns's "irreverent criticism." Wright also studied that spring with Maynard Mack, a visiting eighteenth-century scholar from Yale whose brilliance helped convince Wright to focus his doctoral work on the English novel. In notebooks for Mack's seminar, Wright rejected the standard judgments of poetic ranking. "The greatest poet of this period was *Swift*, not Pope—unless poetry is just metrics. What about the creative imagination? Swift is a great poet—a maker of new things."

Over the course of that winter, Wright had circulated a manuscript of sixty poems, asking for comments from trusted readers. In a letter to Hall in March, he held out little hope for the collection he had submitted to the Yale Series of Younger Poets, for which W. H. Auden served as judge. On May 17, 1956, however, Wright shot off two sentences to Hall—the briefest letter he ever wrote: "I've won the Yale Prize! Dear Don, I don't know what to say to you, I am so happy." The most prestigious competition in the country, whose recent volumes included first books by Ashbery, Rich, and W. S. Merwin, had now honored Wright's *The Green Wall*.

Before the official press announcement at the end of June, Wright saw one of his best sonnets, "My Grandmother's Ghost," in the June 9 edition of *The New Yorker*. That same week, he held a copy of the newly published bilingual collection of René Char's poems, *Hypnos Waking*, with three of his translations among versions by the book's editor, Jackson Mathews, William Carlos Williams, Richard Wilbur, and others. The book was widely praised in the following months, including an insightful review by Williams himself in *The New Republic*. In an essay on Char's work published later that year, Wright admits the difficulty of translating poetry, but argues that it "is the only way to read any great poet." Wright concluded his essay by quoting the last line of Rilke's "Archaic Torso of Apollo." One cannot engage the vision of any great artist "by staying as you are: '*Du musst dein Leben ändern.*'" You must change your life.

Wright's own life began to change as word of the Yale Prize spread. Though the book would not appear until the following April, he had become a celebrity. Liberty saw the difference in her husband that summer. "He just didn't know how to handle all that adulation—it's like he forgot that he had any commitments. Suddenly he got all this validation that he was a poet, and he could now believe it himself." She had been content to remain at the edge of conversation and his intense commitment to poetry, but the changes that attended this new notoriety distressed her. One morning Wright arrived home from a party at Kizer's just as Liberty was leaving for work at 6:00 a.m. Then, at a party in their own home, she chanced to see a woman with her arms around her husband's neck, kissing him. Enraged, Liberty declared that she was leaving, and flew to Ohio with three-year-old Franz later that week. Having won Wright's contrition, she soon returned, but she felt continually defied by his obsession with poetry. "I remembered his comment about not wanting to be a husband or a father. He wanted more out of life, and I did, too." More troubling than this rift, however, was Wright's now constant drinking. Alcohol had long been a way to ease his discomfort in social gatherings, but it had taken hold—not just part of Wright's public persona but a daily part of life.

At the beginning of July, Auden wrote from Italy. "May I take this opportunity of saying how impressed I am by your work: it is the best manuscript, I think, that I have read since I started being the judge for this series. It is, however, considerably too long, from a commercial point of view—and even from yours. I believe you will make a better impression upon your reader by giving them less." He left the choice to Wright;

among the seventeen poems Auden suggested he cut, a handful would appear in Wright's second book, including "At Thomas Hardy's Birthplace, 1953" and "In a Viennese Cemetery," an elegy for Hugo Wolf that Wright claimed to be "the only poem I salvaged from all the work I did in Vienna."

———

Looking back on his coursework in Seattle, Wright called David Fowler's classes in medieval literature—Chaucer, *Sir Gawain and the Green Knight*, Langland, and Malory—"the most exciting and the most useful courses I took." These were also the most difficult finals he faced, beginning in January 1957. After completing his doctoral exams in April, Wright sat in on a special humanities class, Classics of the Far East. Much of the reading centered on translations by the poet Arthur Waley, and included his *Three Ways of Thought in Ancient China* and a biography of the T'ang Dynasty poet Po Chu-i. Classical Chinese poetry—especially the work of Li Po, Tu Fu, and Po Chu-i—became a touchstone of Wright's poetry. He found the sheer variety of poetic occasions in Chinese poetry hugely liberating, as well as the patient, intimate attention devoted to the natural world. Taking Roethke's advice, Wright continued to type out poems and prose passages that inspired him, and this scattered personal anthology suggests the direction his imagination was turning. From the spring of 1957, among his own poem drafts and copies of Chinese translations, there is a typescript of Neruda's "Walking Around" translated by H. R. Hays, a poem Wright recited more often than any other from this time on. The drama of the poet's voice—"It so happens, I am sick of being a man"—thrilled him, and he shared the poem with anyone who hadn't heard it before.

At the end of March, even as Wright complained to Hall of the long wait for his first collection, Kunitz wrote from New York to say that his work had become a topic of conversation. "It's a good sign certainly that your name gets around, even before book-publication, in the small, fierce world of the poets!" A bibliography Wright typed that winter lists fifty-eight poems published over the preceding three years. More than half of the forty poems in *The Green Wall* had seen print, with three in *The New Yorker* and ten others in *Poetry*. When the book finally arrived in mid-April, it was widely praised.

Auden's foreword is both gracious and acute. Apart from Wright's "feelings of estrangement and nostalgia" about nature, he is fascinated that "the persons who have stimulated Mr. Wright's imagination" are all "social outsiders." Auden lists a murderer, a prostitute, and a lesbian, among others, and notes that none are the usual "romantic rebels" but rather "passive victims," denied status as "citizens." One sentence in particular is prescient: "He is anxious by necessity because at every moment he has to choose to become himself." From the outset, the elder poet glimpsed the restlessness that would characterize Wright's career.

Much to his regret, an offhand comment Wright made to a publicist at Yale University Press became the most commonly quoted statement on his work. As the dust jacket of *The Green Wall* quoted Wright: "I've tried very hard to write in the mode of Robert Frost and Edwin Arlington Robinson. I've wanted to make the poems say something humanly important instead of just showing off with language." These words dogged his heels throughout his life. Critics, reviewers, interviewers, and even poet colleagues discussing his work returned to these two sentences again and again, as if they stated a personal manifesto. His words embarrassed him—in part because of their sincerity.

Together with Auden's foreword, Wright's comments set the tone for much of the critical response to *The Green Wall*. Most gratifying, poets whom Wright admired found promise in the work. In her review in *The New Yorker*, Louise Bogan praised Wright for "the variety of his concerns" and for "dealing with them [in] the age-old manner of the lyric poet, who draws his thought and emotion so closely together that they fuse." His imaginative movement "toward haunted boundaries . . . gives his poetry an extra dimension, something quite rare at present but quite usual in Romanticism. In fact, Wright's poems on 'outsiders'—children, ghosts, the mad—are moving in the extreme." Bogan here anticipates directions Wright had only begun to explore; the ghost presences in his poetry become a compelling, insistent theme. The Romantic pull beneath his poems—evoking a personal, spiritual journey—stands in counterpoint to his classical temperament.

The essay Wright felt was "the best comment" on his book came from the poet Reed Whittemore, who dismissed his invocation of Robinson and Frost, and yet found important similarities among them. Wright shared their ultimately tragic worldview and felt drawn to the broad range of characters who inhabit their poems. But while *The Green Wall* consistently displays his ear for music in language, Wright comments more than he observes. Rarely does the personal pronoun appear, and the speaker seems to hold his subjects at arm's length.

———

In the middle of May, Wright traveled to the Pacific Coast Arts Festival, sponsored by Reed College in Portland, Oregon. The festival had intended to showcase Kenneth Rexroth, the singular poet, editor, and translator widely regarded as a guiding spirit to the loosely termed "Beat" writers—part of what Rexroth described as the San Francisco "renaissance." Rexroth, however, could not attend due to illness, giving Roethke pride of place; his reading on May 11 became the highlight of the three-day event. Wright, with Wagoner, Kizer, and others from Seattle, also participated in workshops, panel discussions, and readings. Events like these had a vital impact on poets and on their audience, for, as Gary Snyder recognized, they "reminded everybody that the excitement of poetry is a communal, social, human thing."

Wright mailed one of the first gift copies of *The Green Wall* to Philip Timberlake, now head of the English Department at Kenyon. "This is the real thing. I can't tell you how good it makes me feel to realize your achievement," Timberlake wrote back on April 29. But just one week later, Timberlake suffered a stroke from which he never regained consciousness; he died on May 11, 1957, at age sixty-one. Wright had not yet heard of Timberlake's death when the *Kenyon Alumni Newsletter* asked him to write an obituary. Wright was devastated; he phoned Roethke, who took Wright to a bar near his home that afternoon. Wright's tribute, published in August, recalled Timberlake as "the most gentle and the most sad of men . . . [who] taught us that the soul must be disciplined, and that, unless discipline comes from within, it is worthless."

Wright took these words to heart and channeled his grief into poetry; the elegy he wrote for Timberlake went through more drafts than any other poem in his life. Often, Wright abandoned one approach entirely and began again from scratch. A number of these false starts became separate poems, including "But Only Mine" and "What the Earth Asked Me." Months after Timberlake's death, in another season, Wright continued to mourn. As published in *Saint Judas*, "A Winter Day in Ohio" had endured endless revision; it had even been published in a dif-

ferent form as "What a Man Can Bear." It is an octave in the manner of
Robinson, sorrow distilled into eight lines, which concludes:

> . . . alone
> All afternoon, I take my time to mourn.
> I am too cold to cry against the snow
> Of roots and stars, drifting above your face.

That spring Wright had been offered an appointment as English instructor at the University of Minnesota in Minneapolis, a job coveted by
many of his classmates. The department director in Seattle, Robert Heilman, had personally supported Wright's candidacy. But Wright had
hoped instead that Heilman would make an exception, against long-
standing university policy, to allow him to remain in Seattle to teach, and
this hope grew into a desperate obsession. Throughout the summer, as
he prepared his fall coursework for the University of Minnesota, Wright
continued to imagine he would be granted a reprieve. However, the profound sense of unease that stalked him remained hidden from even
those closest to him. It appears most clearly in the letters he began to
write to a former student.

From the first, Wright loved to teach; having impressed his mentors
in Seattle, he had been given an Advanced Composition course for
exceptional new students. Among "the rising tide of freshmen" who had
arrived the previous fall was a gifted seventeen-year-old who remembered Wright distinctly. She had easily kept up with the heavy load of
reading and writing assignments he required, and though she took just
this one class with him, Sonjia Urseth was impressed by Wright's dedication and engaging manner. After completing her freshman year, Urseth
impulsively wrote to him, seeking encouragement for her writing.

Wright seized the chance to voice not just his wisdom as a teacher to
a talented student but also his private thoughts about his art and life.
On July 1, 1957, Wright typed a two-page, singled-spaced letter in response to Urseth's brief note. In a tone much like that of Rilke's *Letters
to a Young Poet*, he offers advice and recommends books she must read
by Henry Fielding and Sigmund Freud. But Wright's opening sentence
proves him more voluble than Rilke had ever been: "Is there an epistolary equivalent to the old saying about talking a person under the

table? If there is, you ought to be warned. . . . Let me hope now that you will continue to write me—punctually, and as fully or as briefly as you choose. Somehow I feel more myself with words that I can form on a page."

Wright remembered Urseth quite well; her alert intelligence and passion for literature had impressed him, as had her auburn red hair. A chance encounter on campus earlier that spring had inspired a sonnet, "To a Shy Girl," which he now enclosed to her, calling it "just a little ritual of fondness." It is a dreamlike poem set in a forest that identifies the figure of the girl—"your hair so near to fire"—with nature itself. The poem concludes, "I lean to touch you, but my fingers fail: / I cannot hold the mountain in my arms." Most striking is the likeness of the girl to a Muse figure—as well as her inaccessibility. Asking Urseth to write faithfully, Wright instructs her not to show his letters to anyone. "One more thing, my dear Sonjia: I wish to heaven you would address me as Jim. You were right to be hesitant about your name, for names have magic in them; but I take it we are friends now. Fondly, Jim."

By the time he left for Minneapolis at the end of August, Wright had mailed a dozen letters to Urseth at her parents' home in rural Washington. They were filled with passages from Keats, Hesse's *Steppenwolf*, and Yeats, as well as instructions to read Tolstoy, Graham Greene, and many others. Almost all of his letters included poems, both drafts and finished pieces. One he enclosed in his second letter, July 8, "is also about you—you form a kind of model for it, as a painter's model may do." Wright crafted the context and significance of their correspondence from the start. Flattered by Wright's attention, Urseth felt comfortable unburdening herself of feelings of "lonesomeness" and inadequacy, her "youth and ignorance," and seeking advice about becoming a writer.

At the end of July, Wright sounded harried. While carrying a full summer teaching load, he prepared for the move and for his fall classes. He also continued readings and research for his doctoral thesis. "Yet I need poetry very deeply; and it seems that the only time I have for it is the time that I have with you. Maybe we won't ever meet again," Wright worries, but "you are giving me an occasion to try, once more, to be true and beautiful to the deepest part of myself." For the first of many times in their extensive correspondence, he quotes a line of poetry by Sir Walter Raleigh that became an emblem of their friendship: "*I loved myself, because myself loved you.*" Wright then continues, "Yet we have nothing together but words."

In the first week of August, however, Urseth returned to Seattle to meet Wright briefly one afternoon. The idea troubled her parents, but they needn't have worried. "He was a very kind, caring man, and he was very solicitous of me," Urseth remembered; Wright never made her feel uncomfortable or made advances. But he confessed the truth to her a week later: "Forgive me, but restraint be hanged; I know that I should have held you in my arms before we parted. Abstinence saved me no despair." In Wright's imagination, a flesh-and-blood woman began to complicate his invocations of the Muse.

There are moments of privileged revelation throughout Wright's letters to Urseth, which he would later characterize as journal entries. On August 19, he writes: "I have never told you about the great weariness that comes over me sometimes—a curious hunted feeling, under the pressure of which I can neither read nor write. All I can do is walk the streets, as I have been doing this evening. This is an exhaustion of spirit that is strangely exciting. Perhaps it is hysteria. I don't know." The depressions Wright suffered did not have the pronounced, cyclical pattern—nor did Wright experience the prolonged "manic" episodes—that characterized Roethke's bipolar disorder. But Wright's drinking makes it difficult to get a clear understanding of his mental condition at any point in his life. Alcohol remained a staple of literary society; it was assumed that writers drank, and alcoholism was not widely understood as a disease until the 1960s. Wright, like Roethke, was an alcoholic, and however fine a model he served as a poet and a teacher, Roethke fulfilled the stereotype epitomized by his friend Dylan Thomas: a poet must indulge to excess in order to court the Muse. In America, the idea that the country was too massive and tough for a poet to survive reinforced the romantic figure of self-destructive genius.

But Wright and Roethke contradict common notions of what a poet must be. Both were children of working-class parents and tapped a wellspring of colloquial speech and idioms. They knew what it meant to work hard, and each felt driven to prove himself in the world of academia. With their roots in the Midwest, they shared a kinship and spoke to each other as though to family. As their friendship grew, Roethke treated Wright more and more as an equal; he asked for Wright's comments on his working manuscript for *Words for the Wind*, published in 1958. Roethke's distress over Wright's storm of difficulties in August 1958 led him to admit that Wright had become "more of an emotional symbol to me than I realized: a combination of student–younger brother—something like that." In reply, Wright insisted that he had never made a "papa" out of him, adopting Roethke's term from their discussions of poetic influence. He revealed, in spite of himself, how important a figure the older man had become. For each, the mystery presented by his father inspired deeply felt poems. Ultimately, Roethke's poetry mattered even more to Wright than his exemplary teaching. Roethke continually reimagined his work and pushed in new directions; in its sheer variety, Roethke's poetry remained a constant presence for Wright, long after he left Seattle in August 1957.

In the 1950s, a heavyweight boxing match was still a cultural event of the first order. Pete Rademacher had become a national hero after defeating a Soviet fighter at the 1956 Summer Olympics in Melbourne, Australia, inspiring promoters to back him as a challenger to the reigning champion, Floyd Patterson. In Seattle on August 22, 1957, Rademacher enjoyed a highly partisan hometown crowd but little else. Patterson knocked him down seven times after the second round; the fight was over in the sixth. Indistinguishable from the other seventeen thousand in attendance were two poets from the University of Washington. Roethke had decided this was the best way to celebrate Wright's graduation.

8

Sweating out an exile

September 1957–June 1958

Wright arrived in the vast industrial metropolis of Minneapolis in the fall of 1957, when the University of Minnesota boasted the largest student population in the country, with nearly one hundred thousand on campus. The school's academic standards were demanding and its faculty well regarded. At first, Wright shared an office with Allen Tate, a charter member of the New Critics and a close friend of John Crowe Ransom. A slender man of southern manners and charm, Tate had a strict sense of class and propriety. He showed Wright real kindness at the beginning of his teaching career, and Wright had great respect for him.

Though hired as a member of the English Department, Wright taught many of his classes in Humanities, which had gathered its own outstanding faculty. Though Robert Penn Warren had just left for a position at Yale, the poets John Berryman and Morgan Blum and the Latin scholar R. A. Swanson became Wright's colleagues. The department included the famed eighteenth-century scholar and critic Samuel Holt Monk; William Van O'Connor, the country's foremost authority on William Faulkner; and the American studies critic Brom Weber. Saul Bellow, who had taught at the university for two years before Wright's arrival, criticized the stubborn conservatism of the English Department, whose members distrusted creative writers, in contrast with the more open and supportive Humanities Department.

Upon arriving, the Wrights took the first apartment they saw, on the second floor of a house ten blocks north of campus, a mile from Wright's office and classrooms in Folwell Hall. The neighborhood on Fifth Avenue had a mix of residential and factory buildings that spread north along the eastern shore of the Mississippi River. In his first letter to Wayne Burns from Minneapolis, Wright confessed his anxieties about money, the beginning of classes, and the city itself, "a pretty tough-looking town."

To Sonjia Urseth he admitted that the physical distance between them "is about the best arrangement that could possibly be made for us," given the growing intensity of his feelings for her. His letters to Sonjia, then beginning her sophomore year, are full of humor and a careful, engaging courtesy. However, Wright had already begun associating his poetry and productivity with her, and many of his new poems were intended for her. "I can only give you what I always shall, and that is the poems that I write." Over the coming months, Wright's letters to her are rich with detail, describing his arrival and coming to terms with the city and the university.

> This house at the moment is a long-eared, lupine fury of books, half-opened boxes and chair-legs, lengths of electric-train tracks, neighborhood children, running noses, evangelistical music, the philosophy of the Enlightenment, and the dirty-fronted skivvy shirt and faded denim overalls and two-days' growth of whiskers within which resides myself, deeply thrust into the sensuous consciousness of life, or, as Yeats called it, this preposterous pragmatical pig of a world.

When one class on Goethe, Santayana, and Tolstoy "came unusually alive" discussing the story of Faust, Wright tells Sonjia how the legend "moves me very deeply, almost desperately . . . the storming at life, the demand that by God one is going to wring it dry, to find out what it is, to face it down."

From Wright's first years at the university, hundreds of pages of lecture notes and countless typed index cards prove his diligence as a teacher and the hours he spent in preparation. In composition classes, Wright felt at ease with Orwell and Swift, but having to lecture on the Enlightenment that first September left him "frightened to death," facing a classroom of seventy students. "I know absolutely nothing about the subject," he confessed to Burns. "As if there weren't enough to do and to be confused with, I have been strucken by that annoying Muse; and it has been three weeks of truly appalling production."

He had, in fact, been turning out new work for many months. In September, at Wright's new address at the northern edge of Dinkytown, *The Hudson Review, Poetry,* and *The New Orleans Poetry Journal* all arrived featuring multiple poems. Significant reviews of *The Green Wall* also appeared, including Bogan's praise in *The New Yorker.* One of three poems in *The New Orleans Poetry Journal,* "A Note Left in Jimmy Leonard's Shack" is pure Robinson, with five stanzas of interlocking rhymes. Wright's confident vernacular diction creates a voice as vivid as its surroundings—from the river to the back alleys of his hometown. Published alongside it are an early version of the graveside elegy "Devotions" and the uncollected poem "Under a Streetlight in Skid Row," addressed to an aging, homeless man. "Old man, forgive me now," it begins, sounding a theme common to many other poems he was then gathering into a new manuscript. Wright often began revising poems as soon as he saw them in print, and in his copy of the journal he inserted the line: "I curse your name, old man, I curse my own."

Wright still believed that an exception would be made for him to return to Seattle to teach. "Not until we were in Minneapolis did I realize how deeply wounded he really was by the 'rejection' of the English Department" in Seattle, Liberty recalled. "He got attached to the university like he got attached to his family. He felt rejected, and he was bitterly angry that they would not hire him at Washington." Though she was happy in Minneapolis and enrolled in night classes at the university, Liberty felt dismayed to see her husband drinking heavily and growing more distant from her and Franz, then four and a half. Their arrival in Minneapolis, she believed, hastened the dissolution of their marriage.

Wright's "exile" from Seattle excited his hatred of Minneapolis. Together with the need to prove himself as a teacher came the increased responsibility of supporting his family, while Liberty pursued her own studies. Two weeks after arriving, Wright told Roethke, "I expect that my chief resources through a cold winter will be Dickens, footnotes, teaching, and whiskey—the last of which is moderately priced and easily available, thank God." As Wright confided to Sonjia in mid-October:

The amount of work I have to do, simply to keep up with my classes, would seem overwhelming, were it not for something

within me—something I have never understood or really tried to
understand—which makes me feel an endless and terrible vigor. . . .
The city here is all right, though I don't like it. The feeling of alienation continues. It deepens and it does not fade. The Midwest
was never my home, though I was born here. It is a place which I
hate, as Tolstoy says, with a pitiless and unforgiving hatred.

His letters to her became gradually more intimate and confessional,
addressing Sonjia alternately as the student she was and the Muse he
sought to make of her. Despite his efforts to sound casual or lighthearted,
Wright's feelings for her are marked by intensity. Sonjia, for her part,
offered condolence and encouragement, while pressing for his opinions
about books, about writing, even about God and theology. Her simple
assurance that they would see each other again became an article of
faith for Wright. He sent her letters three or four times a week throughout the fall, and she became emblematic of the place he had left behind,
an image fresh in his mind.

Many poems that Wright gathered in *Saint Judas* can be traced to
Sonjia's inspiration. "A Girl Walking into Shadow" is part of a group of
seven love poems in the book, and like many others it acknowledges the
distance between them. "Now old, I love you slowly through my sound,"
he writes, echoing Ransom's famed "Piazza Piece." "The Ghost" and
"The Alarm" locate the speaker at an in-between place, with "neither
the living nor the dead." A growing restlessness and dissatisfaction seem
to lie beneath the surface of Wright's new poems, many of which present scenes of estrangement and isolation.

Amid all the changes of place and circumstance, Wright woke early
and worked hard in the quiet of morning. Over his first fifteen months
in Minneapolis, Charles Dickens was never far from his mind. The
buoyant comedy in Dickens's first six novels—from *The Pickwick Papers*
through *Martin Chuzzlewit*—helped keep in check the desolate terms
in which Wright saw his own life. "I have a good time in those earlier
hours," he writes on November 3, "snorting to the birds outside the window." Wright also enjoyed his "Billy Sunday-like haranguing lectures" on
Edmund Burke and Rousseau in front of his Humanities class. Wright
soon mastered his classwork and could discourse passionately for hours,
merging biographical and historical facts, prominent criticism, and passages from memory into compelling performances.

By the end of November, however, the aversion Wright felt toward Minneapolis spilled over into all his letters. "I hate the whole God damned area," he tells Roethke, insisting he might try to get work at the Boeing aircraft plant in Seattle, like Hugo, simply "to get back to the Pacific Northwest somehow, by hook or by crook. . . . I really feel as if I were sweating out an exile." In a morose fever, he tells Sonjia on December 3 that he is "so dismally unhappy that I've passed even beyond unhappiness."

Two days later, everything changed. "I'm afraid I'll get hysterical with joy," he tells her, sharing news of a poetry fellowship from *The Kenyon Review* that would free him from a year's teaching. Ransom had contacted Wright some three weeks before and urged him to apply. "I can go anywhere I like, and I don't have to do anything (My God, just imagine) at all except write poetry." Immediately, Wright imagined returning to Seattle for six months, alone, to finish his thesis, before traveling to England with his family. "Strange as it may sound in relation to some of my other moods," he tells Sonjia, "I think I am beginning to believe in happiness again—its justness, its rightness, its possibility, and its hope." He asks her to allow him to "look sometimes on your face again," explaining how "poets for many ages have thanked life for its kindnesses by calling it the Muse." This sense of renewed hope prompted Wright to immediately approach the director of the English Department in Seattle, Robert Heilman, pleading once more for the chance to be considered for a teaching position at the university.

On his thirtieth birthday, a week later, however, Wright drafted "An Empty House and a Great Stone." It reveals the storm of emotions within him, concluding:

I must be dead. Yet still I stand.
Chained by the shadowing arms of trees.
Manacled to the spinning ground.

This motif of death in life, of entrapment in some middle point between the two that he feels powerless to escape, is evident throughout *Saint Judas*. Here, the heady, euphoric wanderlust he had reveled in has vanished. Liberty was pregnant again.

Throughout that fall, Liberty had felt her husband pulling away from her, and she decided they should have another child. Wright concealed the fear and depression this news prompted in him by convincing himself that they would have a daughter. The couple even began referring to the baby as "Marcella." At the same time, they adopted "a great black monstrous puppy"; then preparing for a class in Shakespeare, Wright insisted on naming the Labrador pup Duncan. On December 18, they piled into the Chevy for the long drive east to visit their families for the Christmas holidays "and revisit the idyllic scenes of childhood. I feel as if I had swallowed rat-poison, and were irresistibly seeking to quench my thirst at the fount of nectar, the Ohio River."

The prospect of returning to Martins Ferry had haunted Wright for years. But a surprising admission appears in a handwritten letter to Sonjia on December 23, while visiting Liberty's family in town.

> I was afraid I would become so depressed at the sight of the old place (I haven't even passed through it for five years) that it would take me six months to recover.
>
> Yet I feel peaceful. At the moment I am sitting with a cup of coffee in the living room of my wife's sister's home. It's on a steep hillside—just above a factory and, beyond the smoky towers, the huge and swollen river—and just below the vast Valley graveyard which, it has always seemed to me, hangs ominously and promisingly over the entire city. No matter where one goes in the city, the dead hover just within his vision—yet they are not the idealized dead of the great ages of thought or belief, the Greek or the Hebrew; they are only my friends and relatives, whose bones are scattered awkwardly askew and whose gravestones, like their lives, are broken.
>
> Yet I am peaceful.

Wright was relieved to find his father healthy, and the potent wine of his Greek in-laws, combined with the high spirits of his own "Dickensian relatives," helped him win a kind of truce with his past. Though he always returned there in his work, he would never again walk the streets of Martins Ferry.

———

On the first day of 1958, the Wrights headed back to Minneapolis, and on January 4, Wright returned to his desk, typing letters to Ransom,

Heilman, and Sonjia. He had visited Ransom at Christmas—an important part of making peace with Ohio and his hometown. "Walking off his
porch," Wright told Heilman, "I felt again the old passionate delight and
surprise at the very existence of my mind and body, and I wanted very
much to be a good writer and an honest man"—a paraphrase of James
Baldwin. Ransom had asked Wright to choose four poems to appear in
The Kenyon Review, to announce his receipt of the Kenyon fellowship.
As he later told Sonjia, she had been the inspiration for each of them.

Wright had returned home to find a letter from Heilman refusing
once more his plea for a job in Seattle, and with strained equanimity he
grants the wisdom of Heilman's decision. Wright allows that his longing
for Seattle is "merely a desire to return to a part of my life that is finished. We all hate to see the old worlds of our selves die, and we have a
right to the pathos of their loss."

Days later, however, such consolations meant nothing to him. Two
letters from Sonjia arrived in quick succession, putting an end to their
correspondence. Wright's frequent letters to her at her parents' home
during the Christmas break had alarmed them. They mistrusted this
former teacher's attachment to their daughter and demanded that the
letters stop. Wright's profuse apologies to Sonjia's parents describe the
Platonic nature of their friendship, comparing it to those he enjoyed with
teachers such as Timberlake.

Wright is more candid and openly wounded in a much longer letter
to Sonjia a week later, after she returned to campus. He assures her
that she has nothing to do with his failed marriage. "My wife and I discovered years ago that we had made a dismal mistake in getting married, and we know that we can't last much longer." Wright concludes by
pledging his devotion to Sonjia, quoting a passage from Whitman that
had become a refrain: "For I could not die till I once looked on you, / For
I feared I might afterward lose you." A sense of struggle bleeds through
this last letter; Wright strives to resurrect his role as a teacher, while the
loss of her friendship deprived him of the intimate, ideal reader he had
come to depend on.

Later that week, on January 21, Wright began another long letter addressed to Sonjia, unsure if he was "indeed writing only to myself." Feeling "ghostly and inarticulate," he wonders at the irony of "having written
several poems about you in which I spoke from the viewpoint of a ghost."
He alludes to the depression that had now overcome him. "My illness

continues in full force, with occasional abatements. My chief weapon against it, as always, is to rise at 5 o'clock in the morning and to read Dickens for three or four hours with almost murderous devotion." Writing to Wayne Burns later that day, he admits that his "arrogant confidence" comes back to him in those early hours; he turned his work into a means of survival.

To Wright's surprise, the Muse did not desert him. Poems came to him steadily throughout the spring, and work on his dissertation advanced even as the demands of teaching increased. Begun at the end of January, "The Alarm" became another compelling ghost-themed poem, part of the "Sequence of Love Poems" in *Saint Judas*. The poem remained a source of reassurance. "Some blind gigantic burst of health in me has saved my life," he wrote in his journal. "It was a poem. Or, rather, it was the act of writing verses." Beginning to fear another breakdown, Wright responded by plowing energy into his poetry and teaching. Among countless pages of lecture notes that winter, Wright transcribed long passages from Thomas Carlyle's *Past and Present*. Near the top of two pages of single-spaced type, in block capital letters, he scrawled: ALL TRUE WORK IS SACRED.

Liberty believed that the fall had been a happy time for them; she now watched as the ferocity of her husband's anger and black moods consumed him. Driving along Hennepin Avenue that winter with Franz in the back seat, she saw Wright suddenly open the passenger-side door, as though he meant to fall into traffic. "He could be so dark and so angry, so hating Minneapolis and hating the university—just like he would be going into a mill or something." At Liberty's insistence, Wright finally agreed to meet with a psychiatrist in the university hospital. In a long and rambling letter to Burns on February 1, Wright apologizes for his anxieties and discursiveness. "It must be this God damned catathymic compulsion I suffer from. (Yes, I found out its name. I used to think it was the Muse.)" A British physician, Dr. Lamb, had given this label to Wright's condition. For the next few months, Wright continued to see Lamb, who also prescribed medication for depression. In his view, the principal characteristic of Wright's nervous disorder was "perseveration"—the anxious compulsion to complete any kind of work once he'd started. Wright acknowledged the aptness of this description, for what little practical help it afforded.

Wright's reading for coursework that winter inspired digressions he later developed in his dissertation. In a temporary wooden classroom building perched above the steep eastern bank of the Mississippi, he often performed passages from the comedies of Dickens and Shakespeare for his Humanities classes. "Right now I'm going thru Dostoevsky with a toothless comb," he told Burns in a postcard written at 5:00 a.m. on March 7, delighted to find "places (in *Crime and Punishment*) where he surely displays the whole Dickens routine!" For Wright, literature was a timeless wealth shared by a community of writers. When he learned that Roethke had returned to the hospital that March, he wrote to assure his mentor of the permanence of his achievement. In his letter, Wright touches upon a deeply held conviction. "Do you know what I mean when I say that I always think of Ben Jonson, Thomas Hardy, and Catullus as my *contemporaries?*"

———

Now that Liberty was expecting their second child at the end of July, the couple looked to purchase a home. They found a small house on Como Avenue a mile east of campus, began making payments over the winter and spring, and moved there in May. By the beginning of March, the pressing need for money forced Wright to abandon his plans of living in Seattle that fall. Instead, he searched for readings and "hack reviews for money." In April, Wright traveled to Wayne State University in Detroit, where he appeared with Jerome Mazzaro, Anthony Hecht, and Donald Hall—his first meeting with Hall. Wright's bawdy humor and gift for storytelling surprised Mazzaro, who heard entire skits from the repertoire of W. C. Fields.

While also revising individual poems that spring, Wright compulsively reworked the ordering of his second collection. After holding on to it for many months, the publisher Harper & Bros. turned down one manuscript of forty poems centered on "the theme of human love as a kind of miraculous agony," as he described it to an editor there. Unfazed, he went back to work. Wright also began arranging his first extensive reading tour, planned for December in New York and New England, initiating a friendship with Elizabeth Kray that would last until the end of Wright's life. Kray was instrumental in booking this and many subsequent tours, and her practical advice and farsighted assistance proved invaluable. From the 1950s until her death in 1987, Betty Kray was the foremost advocate for poetry and American poets in the country. After managing reading tours for Auden and e.e. cummings, she created a model for poetry circuits across the country by uniting colleges and universities in a given region to share the cost of bringing poets in to read on campus.

In Wright, Kray recognized one of the finest readers of his generation; his rich tenor voice had a quality of passionate restraint with a trace of southern Ohioan. What's more, she came to realize, "he is part ham." Combining his own work with a wide-ranging store of literature, Wright's readings became captivating performances. He mastered a precise and expressive manner, modeling his reading style after Roethke. Some compared Wright to the great Welsh poet whose voice still haunted English-language poetry. "He read with the fire, the conviction, the compassion, and cosmic sadness of a Dylan Thomas."

Wright's first recorded reading of his own work, fifteen poems in all, took place without an audience at the University of Minnesota on May 25, 1958. In February, Randall Jarrell at the Library of Congress had requested "a good many" poems for their archives, praising *The Green Wall* and three new poems that had just appeared in *The Sewanee Review*. There is a measured, almost plaintive quality to Wright's voice, which makes him seem older than thirty, but it has an almost hypnotic musicality. "A Note Left in Jimmy Leonard's Shack" sparks to life when the speaker, a twelve-year-old boy, utters a brief, sharp obscenity, cursing the brother of the town drunk on the streets of Martins Ferry.

In a letter to Ransom the morning of his reading, Wright offers to review Robert Penn Warren's new book, *Promises*, for *The Kenyon Review*. The poem "Court Martial," he believed, had opened new ground for the poet. "I mean that there must come a time when, after a man has mastered the essentials of the craft, he must then crack and break and snarl his own smoothness, so that he can let his own voice come through his poems." Wright's critical reviews—and his thesis—helped him articulate what he wanted from his own work:

Dickens has shaken me to the very bottom of myself. I chose him to work on mainly because I liked him, but liking a writer and finding him to be one's own imaginative resource—one of those really terrifying people like Cervantes—are two different things. I've had so many poems begin after reading Dickens that I ought to send part of the payment to his Estate.

9

The Lamentation of Saint Judas

June 1958–February 1959

Wright had now established himself in the basement of his new home on Como Avenue, a small house whose second floor had peaked ceilings like an attic. The privacy of his makeshift studio, combined with the freedom from teaching granted by the Kenyon fellowship, made it possible for him to write more than he ever had before—not just his dissertation, but letters, poems, reviews, journal notes, and passages from his reading; in all, a terrific outpouring of ideas and originality. Summarizing his thesis at the end of June, he planned to give "a general definition of the Dickensian comic imagination as an *instrument of discovery*." As he told Burns, "I'm writing like bloody hell this summer, but I'm not tired. On the contrary, I feel like going into the ring." In the midst of this wild productivity, a crisis of doubt would incite him to declare "His Farewell to Poetry."

In the first week in July, Wright picked a fight with one of the heavyweight critics in the small world of American poetry, James Dickey. A prominent and outspoken reviewer for *The Sewanee Review*, Dickey was a man of large ambition, huge appetites, and self-importance. Older than Wright by four years, Dickey had seen active duty as an air force bombardier in the Second World War and in Korea. Though he had yet to publish a full-length collection of poems—working at the time as an advertising copywriter in Atlanta—his incisive and opinionated reviews were widely read.

Wright had just submitted a review of his own to *Sewanee* of six recent books, an essay that digressed into a belligerent challenge of Dickey's obstinacy. Wright claimed to be defending another poet from a recent "attack" by Dickey, but the critic had snubbed his poems as well. In a review of the anthology *New Poets of England and America*, Dickey had consigned Wright's work to the "School of Charm." Wright's caustic letter triggered Dickey's condescension, and two days before drafting "His Farewell to Poetry," Wright pleaded for forgiveness and confessed his lost hope in becoming a "minor" poet. His constant deference to Dickey is hard to fathom. Wright would persist in his extravagant admiration for Dickey, in spite of the critic's bluster and egotism, which set Wright's self-doubts in sharp relief.

That summer, Wright continued to quote from James Baldwin's "masterpiece" *Notes of a Native Son*, claiming Baldwin's succinct ambition: "I want to be a good writer and an honest man." In his apology to Dickey on July 20, Wright allows himself the consolation that, if he is merely "a versifier lacking in any talent, it may be possible for me to be a good teacher and an honest man." What bothered him most was the truth behind Dickey's barbs. Of the five poems of Wright's in the *New Poets* anthology, three were from *The Green Wall*, and much of his new manuscript was also in rhyme and meter. Wright recognized his own poetry as "too old-fashioned"—as *The Fifties* magazine made clear.

Robert Bly's poems had been in the *New Poets* anthology, too, and the cramped ambitions of the work gathered there had startled him. "God knows," Bly said when he saw the book, "my own poems looked dead enough to me." A tall, solitary man with a commanding presence and a wild bird's nest of reddish hair, Bly had been raised on a farm in western Minnesota, on prairie land near the South Dakota border. He had served in the navy and studied at St. Olaf College in Northfield, Minnesota, before transferring to Harvard. Later, Bly enrolled in the Iowa Writers' Workshop, but he chose not to publish any of his early poems. For years, he lived alone in New York City, reading widely and writing in solitude. In the fall of 1956 Bly traveled to Norway on a Fulbright grant and began translating both poetry and prose. He discovered a volume of Pablo Neruda's poetry in an Oslo library—a lucky accident that led to his lifelong devotion to the Chilean's work. Bly conceived of *The Fifties* as a way to publish translations of European and South American modernists like Neruda beside new work by his American contemporaries. For more than a decade, the magazine remained notorious for its brashness, satire, and sharp criticism.

To Bly, Wright's poetry was the same as any other academic versifier. As a challenge, Bly and his coeditor, William Duffy, sent copies of the first issue of their magazine to every poet included in the *New Poets* anthology. The arrival of *The Fifties* in Wright's faculty mailbox at Folwell Hall on July 22 threw Wright into a state approaching vertigo. The poems in the magazine and Bly's keynote essay seemed to confirm all of his misgivings about the "mere competence" of his own poetry.

The most striking part of Wright's response to both Dickey and Bly is the way he sees his personal crisis as one that other poets confronted as well. He had been willing to quit, trusting others to go on. Writing to Donald Hall two days after his first letter to Bly, he intuits this common struggle in the new poems by Hall, Louis Simpson, and W. D. Snodgrass included in *The Fifties*. Wright felt excited by the challenge of absorbing the work of Neruda, Trakl, and Lorca, and by the possibilities opening up for "so many of us." Snodgrass's innovative *Heart's Needle*, published in 1959 to great acclaim (including a Pulitzer Prize), presented a different way forward. Its idiom of personal revelation and private history, however, influenced Wright far less than the Spanish and German modernists he translated in the months ahead.

———

Wright's second son, Marshall John Wright, was born July 30, 1958, and arrived home at Como Avenue with his mother on August 4; the event is mentioned in passing in a letter to Ransom. Enclosing his essay on Warren's *Promises*, Wright tells Ransom that his "study of Warren's rhythm" has influenced his own new poems. Quoting Nietzsche, he praises the seminal nature of Warren's new work for its artistic "self-overcoming."

Wright now disappeared into his basement study for long hours every day, especially after Libby's younger sister arrived with her own five-year-old son for a stay of uncertain length. The strain Wright felt from the writing projects he had taken on, from his dissertation, and even from the press of new poems and correspondence was compounded by the increased demands of his family in a house that had already been too small. He wrote to Dickey that he was not much caught up in "the usual interesting adjustments" required by his newborn son. Instead, Wright talked of poetry, quoting a letter from Stanley Kunitz: "What other morality has the artist but to endure? The only ones who survive, I think, beyond the equally destructive temptations of self-praise and self-pity, are those whose ultimate discontent is with themselves. The fiercest hearts are in love with a wild perfection."

In his letter accepting Wright's "Farewell to Poetry" for the second issue of *The Fifties*, Bly repeated his invitation to come out to the farm in Madison, three hours west of Minneapolis. Though the farmhouse—newly christened "Odin House"—had no indoor plumbing, Wright prevailed upon an exhausted Liberty, who was nursing the month-old Marshall. At the end of August, she agreed to drive the family out for a long weekend.

Wright bore the signs of fatigue and depression he had spoken of in letters to Burns and Roethke that August. Their concern for him was well founded, as Bly recognized when Wright stepped from the car, his head bent and his broad shoulders hunched. Recalling his first impression of Wright, Bly thought of lines by César Vallejo: "Well, on the day I was born, / God was sick." Wright would always remember his arrival at the Bly farm as "a kind of eternal uncluttered moment, and I felt that, at last, after having really given up hope, I had met somebody of about my age who cared about poetry in a great way."

The farm stood about two miles south of Madison, a town shadowed by a huge grain elevator at its southern edge near the county fairgrounds. The landscape was broad and open; the slightly rolling, expansive prairies of South Dakota lay a few miles to the west. A row of box elder trees protected the north side of the property, with apple and ash trees in front. The barn and the chickenhouse—converted into a writing shed, with an oil stove, a desk, and a small cot—stood behind the small, steep-roofed house. The farm had been divided from acreage owned by Bly's father; Robert and his wife, Carol—a spirited, outspoken woman of sharp wit and intellect—kept a large garden for much of their food. For the next decade, their farm became an essential refuge for Wright.

On the day they first met, Bly and Wright sat down together at the kitchen table to collaborate on translations of Georg Trakl's poetry. Wright told Bly of enduring faculty parties at the university by getting drunk and offending his colleagues and their wives with his recitations of Trakl's poetry in German. In Bly he had found his ideal audience, but from the first there were conflicts of passion and temperament. The real qualities of Wright's character—his empathy, humor, and keen intelligence—were not instantly apparent to Carol, who wrote in her journal: "He is weak & ego-centric and I was so bored I was delighted to spend the whole weekend washing dishes."

For Wright, the encounter had been exhilarating. Over the next few days he sent Bly drafts of three new poems, and they exchanged versions of Trakl's great final poem, "Grodek." Wright was so impressed by Michael Hamburger's just-published study of modern German poetry, *Reason and Energy,* he typed out two copies of the entire chapter on Trakl for both Robert and Carol. Bly and Wright also shared a love for classical Chinese poetry; they each saw "the possibility, the excitement of *inventing* a kind of discourse that would allow the soul or transparency of the Chinese poems to come into English—which is so cluttered, in a way." Rexroth's *One Hundred Poems from the Chinese,* Robert Payne's anthology, *The White Pony,* and Arthur Waley's translations were essential books for them. In September, Wright also bought a "cheap little Spanish grammar," determined to gain fluency with "daily application."

Wright considered Bly "a genuine and natural-born *editor, critic,*" whose method entailed cutting everything that wasn't essential. As Bly told him, "You have to, like a good gambler, agree to stake everything on one throw, and agree to let only one of the images stand for the whole idea." Reading a twenty-four-line poem of Wright's, his comments in the margin include: "too many thoughts" and "more concentration—but *not* excitement." Bly then circles a handful of lines at the center—"Lovely!"— and discovers the entire poem Wright would then publish in *The Fifties* No. 2, "In Fear of Harvests":

> It has happened
> Before: nearby,
> The nostrils of slow horses
> Breathe evenly,
> And the brown bees drag their high garlands,
> Heavily,
> Toward hives of snow.

But as a *"propagandist for new ideas,"* Wright realized, Bly could be overbearing, "a genuine *fanatic.*" In the same letter that returned Wright's poems cross-hatched with comments, Bly chastised him for saying he was "very busy: Busy over what? You do not teach for a year, you have absolutely nothing to be busy about. You have nothing to *do*." He even suggests that Wright's "damned thesis" merely got in the way of his poetry. Wright's response, dated October 11, is one of the longest letters he ever wrote, defending his thesis as the only way to secure his job and provide for his family. He also reveals his struggles with catathymia and depression.

> I do indeed have something to *do*. What I have to *do* is to feed my animals—the quite painful stress of my nerves—and I do not understand the disease at all, only its effects—to feed on three or four clear and definable actions, tasks, commitments, or whatever one wishes to call them. One strange effect of my being thus "busy" (teaching, fixing things, writing long letters to two or three trusted friends, etc.) is that the business actually frees whatever is left of my nervous system for meditation on poetry.

On October 6, Wright received a telegram from Wesleyan University Press telling him they would publish *The Lamentation of Saint Judas*. Donald Hall, as an editor for the new poetry series launched by the press, had asked to see the manuscript back in June and had advocated for the book, which became the second title they published. Wright dissembled to Hall, describing the "deeply moving ceremony" Liberty had made of telling him the news. But what mattered most about the book's acceptance was utterly private. That same afternoon he wrote a long, two-page letter of supplication to Sonjia Urseth's mother, asking for permission to dedicate the book to her daughter. "She represents to me an image of the very best devotion I am capable of possessing as a teacher," Wright explains, and "was a kind friend to me when I needed one badly." He writes of the noble calling and devotion of his own professors, of his happy family and newborn son. Disingenuously, he declares, "I certainly do not have any intention whatever of entering into correspondence with your daughter again." But he was already planning to travel to Seattle in January to defend his dissertation, and the idea of seeing Sonjia—and of writing to her—grew into an obsession. After receiving a brief, cordial note of approval from Mrs. Urseth, who suggested that Sonjia might also write to thank him, Wright began his anxious anticipation of a letter from her.

Two weeks later, as he recovered from severe dental surgery, Wright traveled with his family to Ann Arbor to spend a long weekend with Hall. Liberty stopped frequently to nurse three-month-old Marshall; when their car broke down on the way, they had no choice but to buy another one, arriving in Michigan a day later than planned. To Hall, Wright seemed "exhausted" and "intensely nervous" as he embarked on an agitated monologue that lasted nearly three days. "His voice was like the sea, when you stand at the rail of a ship watching the waves all day." By Sunday evening, Wright's "affable—if unstoppable—tirade suddenly turned black." He conceived of some unnamed authority that "wanted him to go back to the mills" in Martins Ferry, and he railed against these imaginary persecutors. The next morning, Wright stood outside "and smoked Pall Malls for two hours" as Liberty prepared their restive boys to leave.

Back in Minneapolis, Wright quickly sent a letter of apology to Hall and his wife, Kirby. He regretted not warning them of his "nervous disorder," which might have prepared them for the "intense and unexpected" terror attack he had suffered. Many things had fueled his anxiety— including the reading he had given at the university upon arriving and Hall's ready supply of whiskey—but Wright knew that his true friends must pass this "ultimate test" of seeing him at his worst.

The day after the family returned to Como Avenue, Robert Mezey arrived from Iowa; his visit could not have come at a worse time. "Jim and Libby were at each other's throats, and it was frightening." After Liberty cursed her husband for dropping a plate in the sink, Wright methodically broke every dish he could reach as Mezey hurried Franz from the kitchen. "I was glad to get away from there. Much as I cared for Jim, it was just too horrible to watch." Liberty's sister and her son were still living in the house, but by mid-November they were gone. Wright wanted only the privacy of his study, where he could work on his dissertation and wait for a letter from Sonjia.

A brief note from her gave him the chance to reply. Wright describes how the image of her face in his mind had given him strength since her last letters in January. Sonjia's lively, delicate features remained vivid to him, and Wright begs her to get permission for them to correspond. To Sonjia's mother, he wrote to offer "the friendship of me and my family," enclosing a handwritten letter from Liberty assuring her that they had discussed "this matter of our friendship with students." Throughout

November, Wright waited for an answer, pouring his energy into long letters to Bly and Hall. As the days grew shorter and the vents to the basement furnace began rattling above his head, Wright's uneasiness increased.

After twelve days with no reply from either Sonjia or her mother, Wright began a long sequence of journal entries addressed to his former student; he waited at the door each day for the mailman. By November 20, as he prepared for his two-week reading tour on the East Coast, Wright gave up hope of hearing from Sonjia. He drafted a long letter of farewell, enclosing a reprint of the four recent poems from *The Kenyon Review* that he had written for her. Before concluding—"Goodbye, my dear child"—he quotes a passage from Sterne's *Tristram Shandy*, condemning "this scurvy and disastrous world."

Wright believed that loss and despair were his "bare deserving," and the possibility of happiness continually surprised him. On Wednesday, November 26, 1958, as he left the house to begin his trip east, he lingered for the mail, and then "like a possessed man I dropped my suitcase, and I ran to that mailman and demanded my letter." Sonjia's four-page letter, heavily creased and annotated by Wright, became a kind of talisman that he carried in his wallet. Her promise to him prompted an outpouring of new work: "I am and always will be what you want me to be, whatever that is." Traveling by train to New York, Wright posted his first extravagant letter of gratitude to Sonjia from Chicago and began his "Journal to Sonjia" at once, with a new entry every day.

Wright's reading tour was a great success. Appearing at nine locations in twelve days, with readings sometimes twice in a day, he was continually on a train or bus and became immersed in the social world of East Coast poetry. As became his custom, Wright began his readings with poems and prose by other writers; on this tour, he included poems by Emily Dickinson, Emily Brontë, and Vassar Miller, and often performed Mr. Pecksniff's hilarious "after-dinner speech" from Dickens's *Martin Chuzzlewit*. Stanley Kunitz gave him a warm introduction at Brandeis University, and following a reading by Ransom at nearby Tufts University, Wright fell into a long, animated conversation with Robert Lowell at the home of John Holmes. Lowell invited Wright to join him the next day at Boston University.

"In Boston I spent five beautiful hours with Robert Lowell, and taught his seminar," he later told Hall. When he wrote to thank Lowell, he insisted that Lowell's close attention had helped with final revisions to poems in *Saint Judas*, "making their locality clearer, more specific." Wright's passion impressed one of Lowell's students in particular, a talented aspiring poet named Anne Sexton, whose therapist had encouraged her to take her writing more seriously.

Exhausted yet exhilarated when he returned to Minneapolis, Wright descended to his study to finalize his thesis and plans for traveling to Seattle. Writing to Burns on December 16—three days after his thirty-first birthday—he is candid and clearly rattled. "I'm going nuts again. Higher than hell almost all the time, hideously depressed the remainder. But I'll live, by God." Again, Wright sought refuge in his work. He completed the final chapter of his Dickens study on December 19, and then completely revised the first chapter before year's end, cutting it from sixty-five pages to just nineteen. Wright's dissertation is distinctive in the traffic of Dickens criticism, with an original approach to the work. "Energy of imagination does not preclude precision," he argues. "Dickens is able to write a clear, sharp, straightforward expository prose. Moreover, his handling of the relation between places and characters is often both subtle and precise." Throughout the 317 pages of Wright's thesis are lucid observations on Dickens's techniques and his "'wandering' intelligence," with close readings of passages from the first six novels.

At this same time, Wright had begun a close reading of García Lorca in Spanish, "incomparably the greatest poet of this century in any language, greater than Yeats, greater than Rilke even." He was surprised at how much of his high school Spanish returned as he worked on translations, and his delight in modern Spanish poetry conveys an almost physical energy. "Oh, if I could only learn it! They have dropped all rhetoric and gone straight to the truth of the soul itself." Wright admires Lorca's fearlessness, and believes that his restored friendship with Sonjia is the source of the courage he now brings to his own poems.

Sonjia returned to Seattle on the last day of 1958 to find eight long letters from Wright. She was delighted by his expansive prose and rambling interior monologues, and flattered by his request to help choose the epigraphs for his new book. He had planned to quote from *Tristram Shandy* a passage addressed to Jenny "in which Sterne interrupts his own plot to announce one of his most despairingly personal feelings of love, after which he quite explicitly tells the reader and the whole world that they can go straight to hell. But I was bitter and lost then. I am not now."

———

In the first week of the new year, demands crowded in on Wright. On January 2, 1959, he wrote to Dickey, asking for close criticism of "At the Executed Murderer's Grave" as it had appeared in the August issue of *Poetry.* "I really want to make this poem stand as an attempt to do something real." While still revising both the thesis and his manuscript of poems, Wright learned that his review committee in Seattle would meet at the end of the month, accelerating his plans for departure. The thought of seeing Sonjia again unnerved him, and after writing a long letter to her on January 6, he drafted "A Prayer in My Sickness," the last poem added to the *Saint Judas* manuscript.

In the days before his departure, Wright found a kind of ecstatic energy anticipating the return to his "impossible Eden." But his relief and exhilaration dissolved as soon as he arrived in Seattle. Liberty phoned in distress, telling him of the nervous breakdown she had suffered and demanding his return. Though she was soon released from the hospital, her doctor—the same Dr. Lamb who had treated Wright a year before—immediately began a series of outpatient electroshock treatments. Liberty had experienced her first episode of depression at age fifteen, and she continued to endure depressive periods "about once every decade, sometimes for years." Wright knew that his departure and her disabling collapse were not a coincidence, and though he was consumed by worry for her and the boys, he needed to defend his doctoral candidacy and complete his book of poems, due at his publisher by the first week in February.

Wright's peers in Seattle—who hadn't seen him in more than a year—were puzzled by his dislike of Minneapolis. They saw him drinking more than ever, but knew nothing of Liberty's collapse or the stress he was under. Richard Hugo and his wife, Barbara, who hosted Wright, quickly tired of his obsession with a recording of Vaughan Williams's "Variations on a Theme of Thomas Tallis," which Wright played over and over on their stereo. "I'm going to break that record!" Barbara told a friend. "I can't stand it anymore!"

While at the Hugos or working on campus at a typewriter in Parrington Hall, Wright continued to revise his poems and his thesis; he also began a new series of translations of the Spanish Nobel laureate Juan Ramón Jiménez. On January 15, two days after he arrived, Wright sent Hall a draft titled "Rosebushes," one of the many Jiménez poems he translated while in Seattle. The classical, restrained gaiety of Jiménez, like the music of Vaughan Williams, became a place of refuge.

Wright had looked forward to talking with his mentor again, but Roethke had returned to the hospital, recovering from another breakdown. Wright and David Wagoner visited Roethke in the violent ward of a mental facility called Halcyon House, and they were both frightened to see the dangerous conditions he lived in. Roethke's psychiatrist told them that the poet was lobbying to win the Nobel Prize, but the doctor couldn't convince Roethke that this was just a symptom of his illness— he had just received the National Book Award and the Bollingen Prize in succession. It was the last time Wright ever saw Roethke.

All told, the trip to Seattle went nothing like he had hoped. Though Wright easily defended his doctoral candidacy on January 30, the four-week span had been choked by work and anxieties. All he would later recall of his time in Seattle were the moments he spent with Sonjia, which were poignant but disappointing. On each occasion, Sonjia's roommate accompanied her and they spoke little. Just before he left Seattle, Wright endured a difficult series of dental procedures, removing the last six teeth from his upper jaw and getting fitted for a permanent plate. Months later, Wright recalled his last meeting with Sonjia in its best light. "We read together (that blessed, that holy, that glorious afternoon that lives like a luminous golden sunlight in my memory) some poems by the two great Chinese poets Po Chu-i and Yuan Chen, who were such close friends and were forced to live apart most of the time."

But Wright had come away with a plan and a promise from her. In the spirit of Rilke's *Letters to a Young Poet*, he believed that Sonjia's future as a writer was his greatest concern, and he insisted they both keep daily journals that could pass between them—no matter what her parents might say about letters. Sonjia pledged to keep up her part. On the afternoon of Sunday, February 8, Wright boarded the Great Northern Empire Builder heading back east. Before the train left King Street Station, Wright had time to scratch out a two-page letter to Sonjia. "You know *all* of me now, and I need not fear that you'll idealize me. I, too, am now, and will always be, whatever you want. . . . You will never get rid of me either. My weaknesses are many and obvious. But my friendship is tenacious and stubborn. . . . My dear child, don't suffer—trust your life and my friendship."

Sonjia was grateful for Wright's attention and confidence; his criticism and advice exalted her struggles as a young writer. When they had parted, she had given him four new short stories to read, and Wright praised them on a postcard from the train. He told her the stories had inspired him to completely revise "my last poem in *St. J.*"—"At the Executed Murderer's Grave."

In his letters to Sonjia, Wright often refers to the "undeserved blessing" of her friendship. But this was no simple friendship, platonic or otherwise. Wright deliberately set about confusing the twenty-year-old college student Sonjia with a Muse figure of his own creation. In their final meeting in Seattle, he described his plan for their correspondence in great detail, inspired in part by Jonathan Swift's letters to his protégé, Stella. "He had intentions to use this writing," Sonjia recalled. "I don't think he was fixated on *me* at all. I think there was a larger purpose." Over the coming months and nearly one hundred letters, it is impossible to say where the woman Sonjia leaves off and the figure Wright makes of her begins. His intentions—at least at the beginning—were clear. She would sign her letters with the name he had given her, and he would use this name to address her in everything he wrote.

A year and a half before, Wright had concluded his first letter to Sonjia, on July 1, 1957: "You were right to be hesitant about your name, for names have magic in them." Upon returning to Minneapolis on February 11, 1959, Wright immediately began a new letter to her. "Dear Jenny, We can write again."

10

Journal of Shipwreck

February–June 1959

In thirty-one years, Wright had never lived alone but had always found solitude by walking. He now sought refuge on the winter streets of Minneapolis. Together with electroshock treatments, Liberty had begun private therapy sessions, confronting the anger she held against both her parents. Upon returning from Seattle, Wright insisted that they should separate, and Liberty not only supported the idea but encouraged it. Both he and Liberty agreed that they "ought never have been married," and they now worried only for their children. Wright would leave Como Avenue for the first time in early April, but Liberty's stubborn refusal to grant a divorce created bitter conflict over the next three years and scarred every member of the family.

The guilt and desperation that now seemed to stalk Wright can be felt in much of his writing from this time. Over the course of his two-day train trip back to Minneapolis, "At the Executed Murderer's Grave" had become an entirely different poem. Without Dickey's comments or a draft of the poem at hand, Wright worked from memory. Declaring his name in the opening line, he invokes a long tradition; the poem's seven sections maintain a ground beat of iambic meter, and many lines are end-rhymed. But the energy is unrestrained and the sense of immediacy is wholly new. The biblical landscape and cadence of language reflect Wright's childhood immersion in Christian orthodoxy; both George Doty and the poet stand condemned.

> My name is James A. Wright, and I was born
> Twenty-five miles from this infected grave,
> In Martins Ferry, Ohio, where one slave
> To Hazel-Atlas Glass became my father.

The poem sustains this oracular voice, and its dramatic urgency suggests the fever pitch Wright lived at in the winter and spring of 1959.

The journal Wright began to keep is both a chronicle and a catalyst for the changes in his life and work during these months. He finished typing the final manuscript for *Saint Judas* and mailed it to Wesleyan in his first week back in Minneapolis. With his Dickens work also behind him, Wright faced a blank page for the first time in years. He had written a few excellent poems in the "new style," which relied on sharp, evocative images, but the challenges were different and the risks greater. The sense of starting all over again made him restless and easily discouraged; it also brought back memories of his first devotion to poetry in adolescence.

Wright's letters to Jenny express his most private thoughts and feelings. Over the seven-month period leading up to the publication of *Saint Judas* in September, Wright mailed hundreds of pages to Sonjia: four-by-six-inch lined notebook sheets filled with single-spaced type, punched with six holes in the margin and hand-numbered at the top. He included draft translations and new poems; he copied poems and prose he loved; and he offered encouragement for Sonjia's writing and advice for "the game of survival" in the world of publishing. Returning her stories on February 18, Wright offered to help place them with a magazine. Quickly, however, the artifice of distance he had tried to build between them began to collapse.

The eleven closely typed pages addressed to Jenny between February 8 and 19 are the crucial beginning of this new correspondence, announcing Wright's conviction that he must commit himself absolutely to his poetry. With this declaration, Wright once again invoked Rilke, and his letters anchor this resolve and defend his decision to Jenny and to himself. "It is the struggle between my inner self (poetry, for which I apologized in order to *live*) and the horrible gray world of deterministic hopelessness where I was born and which I only partly escaped. I've got to escape." Like Whitman, Yeats, and Sherwood Anderson, he affirms, "I am going to make my move at last—my voyage into *my own self.*"

Wright saw the work of translation as a way to shore up his resolve. He translated more widely and intensively in 1959 than at any time in his life, and Spanish poetry, more than any other source, became associated with the chance for a new life, and for a rebirth in his work. While he continued drafting versions of Trakl, he also translated the poetry of Lorca, Neruda, Antonio Machado, Jorge Guillén, and César Vallejo. More than any of these, Wright found hope in the "gorgeous, reviving, happy poems of Jiménez that I have clung to in the middle of hell." When Wright discovered a new one-volume collection of Jiménez's poetry in the university library, he began many more translations. He enclosed one titled "Life" in a February 23 letter to Jenny:

What I used to regard as a glory shut in my face,
was a door, opening
toward this clarity:
        Country without a name:

Nothing can destroy it, this road
of doors, opening, one after another,
always toward reality:
        Life without calculation!

This dynamic sense of new possibilities set in relief the crushing anxiety he felt.

One snowy night at the end of February, Wright grew convinced he could no longer write. He left his house and walked "all over town in the bitter cold, carrying under my arm the collected poems of the great Peruvian poet César Vallejo." The following day, he began translating Vallejo's poems. In a letter to Jenny, inspired by Vallejo's single-mindedness and courage, he describes his plan to meet Neruda in Chile and to live in South America, Puerto Rico, or Mexico—to become fluent in Spanish and "to regain Whitman for my own tongue." Sonjia's reply is the first of many rebukes in the coming months, turning Wright's own advice back on him. His rash declarations strike her as fanatical and foolhardy. "Poetry's been keeping you alive for years, right? Well, now it's your turn to keep it alive. And for God's sake, give yourself time. You told me to be patient. You must be, too."

By the beginning of March, Wright realized that his ambitious plans required practical decisions. He secured two classes at the university that spring and a heavier course load for the summer, though he was still on sabbatical. In a year, perhaps, he could be ready to leave. Naming once more the writers whose dedication led them to solitude, his only regret was for his children. The repetitions and hyperbole in Wright's daily letters to Jenny are disturbing, as are his wild swings of emotion. One day he claims possession of "the holy gift of fire," but days later laments how this "genuine gift . . . is defeated and dead." When Wright reread this journal months later, he sealed it in an envelope on which he wrote: "Of possible interest to medical students. All others wd. do well to leave alone."

Along with those inspired by Sonjia, the sequence of love poems in *Saint Judas* includes "The Accusation," a strange, unsettling piece in lines of alternating rhyme that recalls a woman Wright knew in adolescence who bore a "disgusting scar" on her face. Her disappearance spurs the speaker's lasting regret:

How can I ever love another?
You had no right to banish me
From that scarred truth of wretchedness,
Your face, that I shall never see
Again, though I search every place.

In letters to Sonjia that winter, Wright likens this figure to Jenny, another "source of strength." Whatever she meant to him as a teenager in Martins Ferry, Wright's memories of this woman form part of the composite Muse-figure in his poems addressed to "Jenny."

———

Writing from New York, Robert Bly was thrilled to hear that Wright had begun translating Vallejo, and immediately proposed that they work together to bring out a selection for the Fifties Press—sparking the idea for a series of translations. Offering a group of his Jiménez versions to Mazzaro's journal *Fresco*, Wright insists he isn't writing poems of his own. "I have done nothing but study Spanish for—well, since forever, almost." An award from the American Institute of Arts and Letters and checks for poems in magazines helped Wright weather the costs of Liberty's medical care and his infant son, but by the middle of March, practical reality had won out over his plan to "light out for the Territory." Wright realized that his "South American obsession" would require support, such as a Guggenheim grant; he also applied for teaching positions in the Pacific Northwest. His only hesitation was the thought of leaving his sons.

Returning to teaching that spring had helped relieve his restlessness, but emotional extremes continued. "I *am* happy, in the deepest way," Wright tells Jenny on March 16, having seen a new poem he dedicated to her in *The New Yorker*. Two weeks later, however, he confides, "I am in hell." In a bizarre, apologetic letter to Robert Heilman in Seattle, he voices his determination, "come hell or high water . . . to say Farewell to the Happy Middle West forever. I served my time here as a child, and now I have got my stomach full of it."

Liberty's relentless verbal abuse had escalated at Como Avenue. After she struck him twice across the face in an argument, Wright felt compelled to move to a small, rented sleeping room in Dinkytown at the beginning of April. On the cover of a new notebook he wrote, "Journal of Shipwreck"; the first entry is a long passage from José Ortega y Gasset. Later he worries, "Since I have at least found enough courage and strength to make my decision in favor of my spirit's life, it now remains to be seen precisely what manner of physical suffering will occur in the lives of my children." Wright's separation from his sons became an ongoing torment, one that shadowed him the rest of his life. Franz, then six years old, would remember watching as his father, "towering a mile above the boy," bent down to lift his "massive suitcase" and turn toward the door, "leaving the boy . . . crying forever, in the weird mote-filled sunlight filling the room."

Wright often told Sonjia that the collapse of his "ill-conceived" marriage had nothing to do with her. However, her casual mention of "this boy who wants to marry me" derailed him. Reminding Sonjia of "that glorious afternoon" when they were last together in Seattle, he transcribes a poem by Po Chu-i to Yuan Chen—"The rivers of our souls spring from the same well!"—and comes close to proposing to her himself. The next day, Wright knows he has "exposed myself as a ridiculous fool," but he doesn't retract his plea and begs Jenny not to withdraw from him. Sonjia had never considered a romance with Wright, and recognized his devotion to his children. His battered sense of self-worth made this "a very miserable time for him," and Wright's need for constant reassurance remained a burden.

Now living in a "small, grim sleeping room," Wright submitted to the care of Dr. Lamb and began a new medication for severe depression. He found no relief, however; his close study of Kierkegaard's *Fear and Trembling* would not have helped. In his journal Wright records that his own most private prayers are like those of a tree for water, and repeats his supplication to the "Mother of roots," quoting lines from his own "Farewell to Poetry." In an echo of Roethke, he continues, "I feel like a blind root, cut off from the main tree of things but nevertheless somehow groping about in the darkness of earth for light and water."

With fearsome determination, he turned to the work of translation, hour upon hour, poem after poem. Wright seemed able to lose himself in the music of another language with religious dedication. In his journal he realizes that his "prolonged and intensive study of Spanish, not to mention my tenacious readings in García Lorca, Vallejo, and Jiménez, has taught me how to read Trakl—and also, and even more important, how to translate him." In the first six days after Wright left Como Avenue, he completed twenty-seven translations—from Lorca, Vallejo, Neruda, and Trakl—as well as three new poems of his own. He transcribed long passages from Hesse's *Journey to the East* and wrote three separate letters to Jenny in one day—the first so unhinged as to intimate thoughts of suicide in response to Sonjia's outright refusal to marry him. After a week of intense productivity, Wright acknowledged that this "excitement" was a symptom of his illness—a "dark spell." In a letter to Dickey on April 17, he sounds more resolute. "I have no more troubles, really, than other people have. It's time I got used to this fact and went on with my work."

Wright now kept a detailed record of daily expenses, a ledger that lists his every purchase in excruciating detail. Over a three-month period, Wright tried to live on less than twenty dollars a week; cigarettes and his eight-dollar weekly room fee were, by far, his greatest expenditures. He often spent little more than a dollar a day on food—"for Lib's sake," as he notes in the ledger—and his university paychecks went directly to her. Wright literally starved himself, in what appears to be a kind of penance. When Howard Moss, poetry editor at *The New Yorker*, sent him a check for eighty-four dollars on April 20, he made plans to live on the money for a month. In his journal, he declares, "I have never felt healthier, freer, more sure of what I am and what I can do."

Advance copies of the second issue of *The Fifties* arrived from Ireland near the end of April; the cost of printing in the States had been too high, and now the editors could almost break even. The new issue included the first of Wright's poems in what Bly calls "his new manner" and a fascinating condemnation of recent British poetry by Bly that refers to "the deep images of the unconscious." Critics would soon use the phrase "deep image" to contrive a school of poetry, attaching this peculiar, sardonic label to Bly, Wright, and many other poets.

As spring finally came after a hard winter, Wright began work on a series of translations from the Spanish of Jorge Guillén. He also continued reading Neruda and shared his poems at every opportunity. During intermission at a Minneapolis Symphony concert, Neil Myers, a new university colleague, encountered a group of friends clustered around Wright in the lobby. "He was transfixing and he was *transfixed*, reciting Neruda as if he had just discovered him, but it seemed like whole pages. He just didn't stop. It was just astonishing, hearing him recite these Neruda poems, which none of us were aware of. I can still hear his vocal rhythms and the intensity of his voice." Robert Bly has described how a translator has the experience of falling in love again and again, a quality evident in Wright's exaltation during these feverish months.

Wright shared in Sonjia's happiness when he told her that two of her stories would be published in the international journal *Botteghe Oscure*. On the heels of this good news, however, Liberty threatened to write to Sonjia in a fit of "vengeful hatred." Though each new blowup proved he must remain on his own, such living was not easy for Wright. As May ground on, he ate little and rarely slept. Instead, he began a study of the German mystic and theologian Meister Eckhart, transcribing long passages and reading his work slowly, as a discipline. "Reality is defeat; I am shipwrecked, genuinely lost," Wright confided in his journal.

In mid-May, a handwritten scrawl concedes, "God damn it, I'm getting sick again." Whenever he returned to Como Avenue, often simply to get something to eat, horrific arguments ensued. Liberty saw him counting his steps as he climbed stairs; his constant talking, she believed, became a way to control his anxiety. Wright knew he was sick, but seemed to accept this as part of his new life. "I've grown so accustomed to being depressed," he wrote in his journal on May 19, "that I hardly can imagine any other state of mind." He had heard a rumor on campus blaming him for Liberty's illness, since he had left her to go to Seattle. Though he had been invited to the awards ceremony in New York for the American Academy of Arts and Letters on May 20, Wright knew he must decline. Echoing a line of Vallejo's, he wrote, "This afternoon, in Minneapolis, it is raining, and I dissolve further and further into chaos."

At the end of May, Wright's lectures on Nietzsche became a recurring part of his journals and now daily letters to Jenny. On June 2, Wright claims to be "the custodian of a holy fire to which I was absolutely answerable"; the condescension he sensed from everyone around him put him in a rage. He begged Sonjia, who had grown weary of answering his letters, "not to begrudge me the little warmth of friendship." Before she left Seattle for the summer, she received a last staggering handful. Wright's reading for a graduate course in Modern American Poetry had reignited his internal quarrel between the poetries of Whitman and Robinson, and while fanatically preparing for this seminar he struggled with correcting the spring quarter's final exams. Wright also began a series of new translations of Guillén and an intensive study of philosophy: Meister Eckhart, Ortega y Gasset, Miguel de Unamuno, and Nicolas Berdyaev—all of whom he pressed upon Sonjia, typing out long passages. A desperate urgency radiates from his prose.

For more than five months, Wright's nerves seemed somehow exposed to air; he responded to everything around him with raw immediacy. A state of exhaustion now ran him to ground. On June 12, he wrote to Donald Hall from Glenwood Hills Hospital to tell him of his "mild crack-up." Wright seems bemused to recall, "When Dave Wagoner took me to visit Ted Roethke at his rest home in Washington last January, lo and behold! Theodore the Bear, squatting among the other accursed Huns in the violent ward, surveyed my middle fingers—for both hands were stained with nicotine—and quite sanely predicted my collapse. And here I am."

11

In the Minneapolis of graves

June–December 1959

Wright's admission to Glenwood Hills on the outskirts of Minneapolis forced him to concede just how sick he was. His hospitalization meant giving up the summer classes he had taken on to support his family, and medical bills now compounded his worries. Wright's physician, Dr. Lamb, was a clinical psychiatrist who treated his patients for a somatic illness, augmenting tranquilizers with electroshock therapy. He saw no use in psychoanalysis. Wright received two electroshock treatments in his first days at the hospital; he was subjected to seven over a three-week period. Despite the primitive state of such therapy, its efficacy could not be ignored. In his journal, a week after his arrival, Wright insisted, "I feel less depressed now than I have felt in years." He wanted to believe that a lasting cure was possible; at one point, Wright even considered dedicating his next book to Dr. Lamb.

After Wright's first weekend in the hospital, Liberty deliberately provoked his transfer to the restricted ward, where he suffered the brutality of hospital attendants. Concerned about the imminent deadline for his translations of Guillén, Wright had phoned his wife, asking her to bring his working notebook to the hospital. She knew he was forbidden to contact her, and immediately informed Wright's psychiatrist. When Bly and Bill Duffy visited Glenwood Hills a few days later, Duffy was alarmed to see bruises all over Wright's face and arms. He told Duffy the guards had "beat the hell out of him." John Berryman also visited

Wright, but arrived while Wright was still recuperating from electro-shock. "Why are you coming to see me?" Wright asked him. "I'm dead. Don't you understand that, John?"

Complicating his hope for recovery, Wright received a letter from Sonjia within days of his arrival at the hospital in which she cautiously asked for an end to their correspondence "for a while." Wright found consolation in a rare letter from his father and in a correspondence he had begun with Vassar Miller—a poet he never met but whose well-crafted, traditional verse he admired. Their brief, intense exchange inspired an explicit articulation of his spiritual search. On June 17 Miller wrote, "I've found in my own experience that writing poetry and praying are kindred acts," prompting Wright's joyful marginalia: "pure Unamuno! Vassar Miller is a great human being." In response, he transcribed a page from Unamuno's *Tragic Sense of Life*, one of the few books he had brought to the hospital and read again and again.

Later that day, challenged by Unamuno's exhortation to faith—"we believe that God exists by force of wishing that He may exist"—Wright makes a surprising declaration in the margin of this book. "This is the answer. My God! What time is it? 6:50. June 22, 1959. I believe in God. My God. What next? The windows are opening." Expanding his thoughts in pages he later sent to Jenny, he paraphrases Tolstoy's belief that to love life is to love God. "Whatever happens, I will struggle to be worthy of what I now know I am marked to be: a religious poet."

Wright goes on to tell Jenny of Bly's insistence that he should translate all of Jiménez's *Diario de Poeta y Mar*, which could then be published in a bilingual edition. Bly understood how Wright's devotion to poetry was a spiritual pursuit outside traditional Christian beliefs. "That's what he liked so much about Juan Ramón—and about Vallejo, whose way was much darker." Undermined by the constant pull of depression, however, the inspirations of faith and promising plans could slip away from one day to the next.

The most crucial letter Wright received in the hospital came from another poet he had yet to meet, John Logan, who enclosed a handful of new poems. He had even dedicated a new long poem, "A Trip to Four or Five Towns," to Wright, out of admiration for his work. The poem impressed Wright immensely, and he never forgot Logan's kindness.

After three weeks of treatment at Glenwood Hills, Wright's doctor decided he could continue his convalescence at home. Wright had not lived at Como Avenue in months, and going back meant acknowledging his helplessness and the failure of his ambitious plans from the spring. His journals meditate on "homesickness," but with memories of Martins Ferry came feelings of alienation. Nightmares had begun to plague Wright, as they would for weeks to come. In one recurring dream, he describes being pursued down the darkened streets and alleys of his hometown. "And here is yet another evil dream out of which I have to waken. Into what, then? God knows. . . . I can't free my mind of that ghost of Po Chu-i, stranded at the Chiu-kuo River, chanting to me over a thousand years." His continuing nightmares prompted quotations from Ortega y Gasset in his journal, and he typed out the French original of Apollinaire's late masterpiece "La Jolie Rousse." His rough, incomplete translation begins: "We long to explore the huge country of kindness, where everything is quiet."

All that year, Wright completed few poems of his own. The fallow period he often described resulted, in part, from seeing *Saint Judas* into print. Many fertile beginnings are scattered throughout his journals, however, and a handful of important new poems saw print. Published that fall, the uncollected "A Whisper to the Ghost Who Woke Me" anticipates the surrounding darkness and defiance of his later collection *Shall We Gather at the River*. Addressed to the woman with the scarred face from Wright's youth—the Muse figure he resurrected in "The Accusation"—it begins:

Once more, the moon.
Why do I grieve for your shadow?
The scarred splotch on your face, alive

Though she didn't respond, Wright continued his letters to Sonjia, with a strained equanimity and consideration he hadn't shown for months. After leaving the hospital, he enclosed a maple leaf, a symbol of a name he had given her, hoping to convince her that he was now fully recovered. He tried to sound cheerful, but Sonjia remained silent.

Wright's return to his family's home on Como Avenue coincided with Gene Pugatch's arrival in Minneapolis to begin an internship at the University Hospital. Pugatch found Wright in a state of distress and fragility. He refused to speak of the "wretched treatment" he'd suffered at Glenwood Hills, and would sit for hours listening to his small collection of records, with his ear almost pressed against the speaker. Wright's generosity toward Pugatch remained undiminished, but he treated Liberty with cold disdain. Pugatch stayed briefly with the Wrights while seeking an apartment nearby and felt he was witnessing the dissolution of their marriage. Liberty became livid upon learning that Wright had dedicated *Saint Judas* to Sonjia, believing this proved the two had had an affair. She wrote to Sonjia demanding the end of her letters to Wright—an offense Wright never forgave. His anger toward Liberty became ferocious at times; he told Sonjia that he and his wife "are to be legally separated quite soon."

———

Advance copies of *Saint Judas* arrived in July, and Wright felt especially proud of the cover's striking design: the book's blasphemous title scrawled in longhand across lines of scripture, as though written in black crayon on a page of the Bible. The design had so shocked and pleased Wright when he first saw it in March "that I suddenly realized the intensity of the theme." The title poem that concludes the book is among Wright's most expert—both dramatic monologue and flawless sonnet. Judas, cursed beyond salvation and alone in suicidal despair, impulsively acts to relieve a stranger's suffering. The closing sestet reads:

> Banished from heaven, I found this victim beaten,
> Stripped, kneed, and left to cry. Dropping my rope
> Aside, I ran, ignored the uniforms:
> Then I remembered bread my flesh had eaten,
> The kiss that ate my flesh. Flayed without hope,
> I held the man for nothing in my arms.

As in many poems in the book, elements of craft stand in contrast with the subjects Wright is drawn to. In the centerpiece of the collection, "At the Executed Murderer's Grave," a kind of ghost-pentameter sounds beneath the poem's free-verse lines. But its movement is accomplished through imagery, with phrases and line lengths based on patterns of speech rather than meter, suggesting a new direction in Wright's work.

Renewing correspondence that July with Elizabeth Willerton Esterly, Wright described his new collection as "a religious book . . . far more severe and lyrical, or subjective, in style, and far darker in spirit" than

The Green Wall. In 1972, Wright called *Saint Judas* his personal favorite among his books, describing it as an attempt to come to terms "with what I felt to be the truth of my own life, which is that of a man who wants very much to be happy, but who is not happy." Bly's insightful and influential essay on Wright's work that later appeared in *The Sixties* No. 8 describes the essential terms of Wright's conflict. "Two energies have been trying to get free in James Wright's work; the first is natural American speech, the second images," Bly observed. "Through *Saint Judas* one can see his determination to keep the modest syntax of Robinson, at least, and still bring in the living voice."

Wright faced a difficult recovery that summer, hindered by the loss of his most intimate correspondent. "Never have I felt so uprooted and alone," Wright confides in his journal July 17, the day after moving "into a single, reasonably pleasant sleeping-room near the university." Later that day he begged Jenny to write. "You are the one who taught me the blessed secret of having faith in life." In despair, he confesses again how much his image of her is bound up with his art. "I knew that my own Muse looked exactly like you, and indeed was you."

Wright soon asked his doctor if he could return to Glenwood Hills Hospital, after "a heavy burden of depression fell on me." In quick succession Wright then received letters from both Sonjia and her mother, demanding that their correspondence cease. "I don't and never shall regret our friendship," Sonjia assured him, "and I shall never consider it ended." Promising to keep his letters safe, and certain that "someday we shall meet or write again," she tries to reassure him of her constancy and gratitude. "Please, always believe in me," she concludes, "and know I'm always your friend, whether as Sonjia or as Jenny Mapleleaf."

Wright spent another two weeks in the hospital before returning to Como Avenue. When he was finally released on August 5, he felt a sense of aimlessness; trying again to focus on a new collection, he began a list of poems for a book he called *The Trees of Minnesota*, and continued to write to Sonjia of his oppressive solitude. Sonjia did write again on August 23, to thank him for a gift copy of *Saint Judas* and his generosity in dedicating the book to her. "You have made hope out of nothing," she declares; "it's tremendous—violent, but stable in its violence and hopeful in its despair." But she remains resolute in ending their correspondence, trusting his understanding "for what I must do." She thanks him particularly for his kindness when he wrote that his Muse "looks like me." In a handwritten postscript, she promises to find a maple leaf to send him; as she had done for months, she signed her letter: "Always. Jenny M."

Wright began a new journal after receiving Sonjia's letter and scrawled a kind of epitaph across his previous one, realizing it was "not much use." The preceding months had been "a period during which I was lost in the jungle of illness, personal disturbance, disagreement and misunderstanding with my wife, and hard labor." Consumed by uncertainty and struggling to find balance as the new school term closed in, he was oppressed by the expenses of his lost summer. "I am—for the first time in my life—really frightened by poverty."

At the end of August, Wright returned to the Blys' farm in Madison, Minnesota, in time to welcome the arrival of a horse that Bly named David. Battered by failure and haunted by a sense of loss, Wright took up their translations of Trakl in earnest, work that offered fulfillment "in a rooted, deeply illuminating way." He felt a kinship with the Chinese poet Lu Yu—whose book Bly had given him when he arrived—and copied out many of his poems by hand. The sense of release from despair that rises palpably from the pages of *The Branch Will Not Break* has its beginnings on these late summer afternoons, a few miles from the South Dakota border.

———

Back in his basement study after the long weekend with the Blys, Wright typed out final versions of ten translations from Jiménez, poems he had revised obsessively over the past year. He took great pride in them. "But such labor," he wrote in his journal, "devoted though it is, and pleasant, still is only an apprenticeship toward some understanding of the spirit that is still unclear to me."

When Wright brought his family out to Madison at the beginning of October, Carol recoiled from the constant discord between the couple. In private, Liberty revealed to her that she had married Wright to get out of Martins Ferry. Liberty grew resentful of her husband's friendship with the Blys and believed they encouraged him to seek a divorce. She had no interest in excited literary talk; left to care for two young boys, she felt excluded. After spending a night with the Wrights in Minneapolis at the end of October, Carol offered a glimpse of their hopeless marriage in her journal. "He is insane and almost dangerous. She, too, is both neurotic and too muddled to clear her life. How miserable they are, and their children suffer." That fall, Wright admitted in a letter to the Blys that he and Liberty "may have struck rock bottom, and begun to ascend. Certainly there was no other direction to move in."

For Wright, music remained a source of relief, and his friendship with Harry Weber helped him survive difficult months ahead. Wright had introduced himself to Weber after hearing him sing folk songs outside the student union in April on one of the first warm days of spring. A classics scholar in the Humanities Department, Weber had a thorough knowledge of Latin poetry, but he was also a folk music aficionado with a strong voice. Younger by ten years, Weber had always admired Wright's poetry, and he quickly grew attached to him. In the fall of 1959, Weber often brought his guitar and some friends with him to Wright's home to play music, among them a talented local singer and guitarist, "Spider" John Koerner. A skinny eighteen-year-old newly arrived from northern Minnesota often came with them. Gifted and ambitious, "with no other cares or interests besides folk music," he had been living in Dinkytown since June, singing harmony behind Koerner and Weber in student coffeehouses like the 10 O'Clock Scholar. He had already chosen the name Bob Dylan.

Koerner had introduced Dylan to Harry Weber, "a tweed wearing, old fashioned intellectual," and Weber taught Dylan many new songs and gave him his personal copy of Woody Guthrie's autobiography, *Bound for Glory*. Pugatch first met all three musicians in Wright's Como Avenue living room and befriended Dylan. Wright loved folk music and rural blues, and as the musicians began tuning their guitars, he always asked for the same ballad. "Could you play 'Delia' now so you'll have time to play it again later?"

Wright heard Dylan and others perform at coffeehouses like the Scholar in Dinkytown, while many also heard Wright reciting poems in barrooms and at student parties all around the university. He felt at ease among students, many of whom were attracted to his lack of pretension and rare combination of bawdy humor and moral seriousness. Of the many bars near campus, the East Hennepin Bar attracted the most diverse crowd of working-class locals, faculty intellectuals, and proto-bohemians. On weekends, musicians from the Minneapolis Symphony Orchestra converged there after evening performances downtown. That fall, Wright became a regular at the East Henn, a mile north of his

Folwell Hall office on University Avenue. A motley host of characters were there on any given night, and these drinking companions formed a loose extended family for him over the next six years.

———

One of the first letters of praise for Wright's new book came from his father. "Have read your new book St. *Judas* and there *sticks out the real people* you write about. All the people you write about are real in my mind." Anthony Hecht agreed, praising the craft in Wright's new book in *The Hudson Review* that fall, quoting the pitch-perfect dramatic monologue "A Note Left in Jimmy Leonard's Shack." By the time the book saw print, however, Wright felt "very numb" about *Saint Judas* and impatient with its "archaic style." When Mazzaro called the book "Wordsworthian and sentimental," Wright agreed, but pressed the distinction further. "It had struck me more as morbid than as sentimental, but I suppose that amounts to the same thing. What I would like is a poetry in our own language that is not so weighed down by guilt toward the past, which is able to contain images of what is real to us and belongs to us, and which is sometimes happy."

All that fall, Wright seemed to be caught in a kind of dark suckhole, unable to fight his way to either shore: living at Como Avenue out of necessity, and yet desperate to leave Minneapolis and the whole Midwest behind. Rereading Unamuno's *Tragic Sense of Life*, he came across his own marginalia written while in the hospital in June. Beneath the ecstatic declaration of his belief in God and his calling as "a religious poet," Wright appended an additional note of weariness: "Ah. But I am *now* writing on Oct. 16, 1959. And I am still in despair."

An article by Stanley Kunitz in the October issue of *Harper's Magazine* offered some encouragement. Kunitz's *Selected Poems* had earned the Pulitzer Prize earlier that year, and his essay, "American Poetry's Silver Age," named Wright among a handful of gifted young poets to support his claim that the quality of poetry in America was "higher today than ever before." In his journal, Wright endorses Kunitz's idea "that the 'moral stamina' of a poet is equated with his powers of endurance." The notion struck a chord; his life often felt like something to be endured. "Now I will study Spanish. Tomorrow I must undertake the idiotic, time-consuming, exhausting trip to New York in order to read bad old poems aloud."

As it happened, Wright's reading proved to be extraordinary, and the weekend unforgettable. He traveled east by car with the Blys, and the trip helped cement the lasting friendship between them. The couple was once again relocating to New York for the winter, subletting an apartment in Greenwich Village. Robert had befriended Galway Kinnell, who coordinated a series of poetry readings at New York University that had become, over the previous two years, "a howling success." When Kinnell left for Europe in the fall of 1959, Bly took over the NYU reading series and arranged a reading by Wright and James Dickey on November 13 that many called "magical."

The three poets shared a long weekend in spirited conversation—the first meeting between Wright and his former nemesis. Their enthusiasm spilled over into letters, with both Bly and Wright quoting with delight Dickey's ecstatic pronouncement, "We're not going to die tonight!" Wright would embellish memories of the weekend for years to come, making it into a kind of legend. His letter to Dickey upon returning to Minneapolis is filled with elaborate praise and hyperbole. "I could never really tell in a thousand years how much it meant to me to be with you and Bly last week," Wright declares. "I can't really describe what it meant to feel free to emerge into that tremendous, ample sunlight of noble and heroic men with whom I spent those three days, drinking the great green waters of the first and last seas. Maybe now I can just face the fact of my own alienation."

Though their separation was inevitable, Wright and Liberty continued to argue bitterly. Sonjia had written one last time in mid-November, and Wright delayed in answering. He typed a long, meandering letter on November 27, worried about Liberty's threat—made in "blind nastiness"—to name Sonjia in court as the cause of their failed marriage. Eleven days later, when this danger had passed, Wright finally posted his letter addressed to Jenny, conceding, "You have borne a lot of pain for the sake of knowing me."

At the end of 1959, Wright turned from new versions of the Spanish of Guillén and Vallejo to the German of Trakl, often on the same day. Bly planned to publish *Twenty Poems of Georg Trakl* with the Fifties Press, and they often exchanged drafts by mail. On December 13—his thirty-second birthday—Wright typed a long letter to Carol and Robert, enclosing new drafts of two of Trakl's prose poems and asking for Robert's help on a difficult stanza of Vallejo's. The poem, "Espergesia," became a lifelong favorite of Wright's; its opening lines read, "Well, on the day I was born, / God was sick."

Wright also began assisting Bly and Duffy with the editorial tasks of the magazine. The most notorious aspect of *The Fifties*—which became *The Sixties* at the turn of the decade—was its irreverent humor and abrasive satire aimed chiefly at the literary establishment. "Madame Tussaud's Wax Museum," a regular feature, excerpted ridiculous stanzas of academic verse, while the Order of the Blue Toad was awarded to writers and editors with blatantly regressive political views and aesthetics. The rancor incited by *The Fifties* spread more widely than the actual magazine. While Wright objected to attacks on Ransom and Yvor Winters, his own name became linked to Bly and his magazine. Two more of Wright's poems in his "new style" were published in *The Fifties* No. 3, which appeared in December 1959.

When Harry Weber arrived at Como Avenue on Christmas Day, he found Wright in a state of excitement. "My God, you've gotta hear this stuff!" he cried, brandishing a magazine with poems by Anne Sexton. The controlled emotional fury in her language and her subtlety of craft thrilled him. Even as he led Weber down the stairs to his study, he began reading poems that would soon appear in Sexton's first book, *To Bedlam and Part Way Back*. As they returned upstairs, a tall, vigorous man arrived, with windblown reddish hair "all which way, like he'd slept in it, but in a suit and tie—an old-fashioned, banker's grey flannel suit." Weber would come to know both poets well. "Robert more or less threw me out," Weber recalled; Bly wanted to talk with Wright in private. "He looked Harvard and he dressed Harvard, but by God, he didn't talk Harvard."

Bly's encouragement helped sustain Wright as the new decade began. "As for not writing poems now—that is a mirage. . . . It is a surprise not to write much, but that is not the same as not to write," Bly insisted. The most important correspondence Wright had known was at an end; he had identified his poems so closely with his vision of Jenny that her loss continually disturbed him. Though he tried off and on to make a home with his wife and sons, the marriage finally could not be saved. In the black twilight of midwinter in Minneapolis, Wright felt as though he held the end of a frayed rope, suspended hundreds of feet above the frozen Mississippi.

PART II

12

The Wreckage of the Moon

January–December 1960

As the new decade began, Wright felt trapped in a state of "baffled loneliness." Frustrated by his own poetry, he had made a meditative practice out of the work of translation, slowly turning out English versions from Spanish and German. Over the next few months, whether praising Thomas Hardy, Richard Hugo, or Georg Trakl, Wright named *patience* a primary artistic virtue. From the soil he had left fallow for months, many of his most celebrated poems would appear. Though the decade would be marked by hardship and rootlessness, the two major collections Wright published in the 1960s would answer Frost's idea of the poet's greatest ambition: "to lodge a few poems where they will be hard to get rid of."

When the editor and poet Paul Carroll first met Wright in the winter of 1960 at a party in the home of Allen Tate and Isabella Gardner, he was struck by the discrepancy between Wright's appearance and his passionate speech. "Stout, balding, bespectacled, Jim didn't look like the young poet of the lyrics I'd admired: he looked like a used-car salesman. But he sure didn't talk like one. I loved his talk immediately. It was the intensity, and the overwhelming love of poetry. Jim talked poetry as if he were an Early Christian in the catacombs, talking Christ Crucified."

Wright's immoderate opinions made many of his university colleagues uneasy, especially as the evening wore on and his drinking gave his appeals an edge of belligerence. Tate had returned to campus that fall after a yearlong sabbatical, and he gave Wright an earful about Bly and *The Fifties* at a faculty gathering on New Year's Eve. The news pleased Bly enormously. Tate had written Bly a disparaging letter after reading the first issue; he regretted seeing "another young poet choosing to follow the insane lead of William Carlos Williams." Tate soon felt the same disappointment in Wright.

Wright had already internalized the divisive quarrel Tate alluded to—what Wright had described as the pendulum swing of his allegiance between the traditional, rhymed and metered poetry of Robinson and the more expansive and expressive vision of Whitman. While he felt this conflict more acutely than most, American poets of Wright's generation all confronted this profound shift toward free verse over the course of the 1960s. Robert Lowell characterized the division in modern poetry in March 1960 while accepting the National Book Award for *Life Studies*: "Two poetries are now competing, a cooked and a raw." Though Lowell conceded his exaggeration, T. S. Eliot and Yeats had for decades been archetypal figures in a largely Anglocentric "cooked" recipe for American poetry. The San Francisco Beat poets, the New York avant-garde school, and an outpouring of new English translations of European and South American modernists now challenged this dominant aesthetic. Many poets began to question the fundamental elements of their craft, though W. S. Merwin, reflecting on the change in his poems from this time, said simply, "Whatever provides their form is less apparent."

W. C. Williams had always stood apart from "academic" poetry in the United States, grounding his work on the banks of the Passaic River in Paterson, New Jersey. After decades of relative neglect, the elderly Williams had come to be praised as the most important heir to Whitman's poetry in "the American idiom." Though diminished in speech and vitality by a number of strokes, Williams continued to welcome young poets into his home in Rutherford, New Jersey. In mid-January 1960, Denise Levertov brought Yves Bonnefoy out to meet Williams and his wife, Flossie, together with Carol and Robert Bly. Williams's openness, generosity, and enthusiasm for new poems amazed Bly. When Bonnefoy praised the poem "Complaint," Williams asked his wife for a copy from a locked cabinet nearby—part of her effort to keep him from giving away all his books. Bly later found Flossie in tears in the kitchen. "So many young poets come to see him now, but you don't know what it was like. How they hated us."

Wright arrived in New York later that week to receive a citation from the Poetry Society of America at a black-tie dinner at the Waldorf Astoria. For the first time, Wright rented a tuxedo and marveled at what Bly called "a forest" of poets, including Robert Frost, Robert Graves, Delmore Schwartz, W. D. Snodgrass, May Swenson, and, most impressive for Wright, Marianne Moore. The high point of his brief trip east, however, was visiting Williams "and the immortal Flossie" in New Jersey with Bly. In a letter to Dickey, Wright despaired of describing Williams, the intensely dark-eyed poet who "looks young men right in the eye as an equal."

Back in Minneapolis Wright "exploded into a lot of writing." Three weeks later, a letter to Dickey included drafts of sixteen new poems, six of which would appear in his next two books. Much of this new work arose from memories of Ohio, framed in the present tense, as though the speaker stood once more on the Ohio riverbank or on the streets of Martins Ferry. But in a letter to Bly, Wright was troubled by rumors that his publishing as a poet rather than as a Dickens scholar—even his citation from the Poetry Society of America—worked against his standing at the university. With two prominent poets, Berryman and Tate, already on the faculty, they had no need for another, and Wright's illness the previous summer had delayed his promotion as a professor. He began to realize that his position there had grown precarious.

On February 7, 1960, Wright drafted a new table of contents for his work in progress, another in a staggering number of such provisional manuscripts that preceded the publication of *The Branch Will Not Break* in 1963. Already, he listed sixty finished poems; over the next three years, he would consider twice that number for his new book. Wright often divided the work into sections; here, they are "Closed Poems," "Open Poems," and "Voices"—the latter a series inspired by Robinson's first-person narratives. As had been true of early versions of *Saint Judas*, each of these manuscripts also included a selection of translations. But new poems kept appearing in his journals, which made any sequence provisional.

On a Tuesday morning in the middle of February, as Wright crossed a Minneapolis street, he "stepped carefully over a puddle of ice," anxious to protect his one good pair of shoes. In this instant of self-awareness—at the mercy of the weather and anxious about money—Wright once again thought of Po Chu-i, with whom he seemed to share so much.

Working in his journal later that day, he drafted "Thinking of a Chinese Master, as Winter Starts to Break Up." Even in its first, rough form, the poem shows the qualities of fresh perception and plain diction that would distinguish *The Branch*, where the finished poem opens the book.

As I Step Over a Puddle at the End of Winter, I Think of an Ancient Chinese Governor

> *And how can I, born in evil days*
> *And fresh from failure, ask a kindness of Fate?*
> —Written A.D. 819

Po Chu-i, balding old politician,
What's the use?
I think of you,
Uneasily entering the gorges of the Yang-Tze,
When you were being towed up the rapids
Toward some political job or other
In the city of Chungshou.
You made it, I guess,
By dark.

But it is 1960, it is almost spring again,
And the tall rocks of Minneapolis
Build me my own black twilight
Of bamboo ropes and waters.
Where is Yuan Chen, the friend you loved?
Where is the sea, that once solved the whole loneliness
Of the Midwest? Where is Minneapolis? I can see nothing
But the great terrible oak tree darkening with winter.
Did you find the city of isolated men beyond mountains?
Or have you been holding the end of a frayed rope
For a thousand years?

The last three lines of Wright's first draft are identical to this final version. Knowing that his teaching position stood in jeopardy heightened his empathy for Po's struggles in his "worldly career." Still, the poem wrests a kind of hopefulness out of the image of the poet at the end of his rope, as though Wright had come to Po's rescue in the act of writing the poem. This hope for relief from despair as spring arrives would set the tone for the entire collection.

––––––––

Wright worked incessantly that winter, typing translations, new poems, journal entries, class notes, lectures, essays, and letters. He also began a new correspondence that would become, for a time, utterly crucial to him. On February 10, Anne Sexton impulsively wrote a fan letter to Wright, praising *Saint Judas* and initiating an exchange of what she later described as "several hundred 'faintly scarlet' letters," most written over the next eleven months. "I doubt you remember meeting me at Robert Lowell's class," Sexton wrote, recalling his visit to Boston in December 1958. "I think your book is as nearly perfect as any I have read."

Of course Wright did remember her, even before reading her new poems that December. Sexton made a striking impression: long-limbed and graceful, she had a beguiling beauty and a talent, she claimed, for making men fall in love with her. She had two young daughters—the oldest Franz's age—but Sexton's marriage to a salesman in an affluent Boston suburb was shaken repeatedly by her infidelities and hospitalizations for nervous collapse and attempted suicide. With little formal education, she had claimed her vocation as a poet three years before, partly as a discipline in therapy. Raised in prosperity, Sexton was just a year younger than Wright; like him she was an alcoholic and fought against depression.

Sexton had good luck in befriending Wright at this time, and he also felt blessed. For a year and more, each found in the other a kind of Muse, and the poems in Sexton's second book benefited from Wright's close reading and criticism. Though few letters survive from their extensive correspondence, it is clear they shared a deep intimacy for many months. Sexton was making up for lost time as a poet, and her impatience had a feverish intensity that Wright answered with compulsive, "warmheartedly pedantic" letters that acknowledged her gift.

Though Wright now had dozens of new poems and translations in progress, he felt he had lost an essential connection with his poetry. Mailing off three new translations of Guillén for the bilingual collection *Cántico*, he still chided himself to "get back to work." After renewed efforts, Wright gave up trying to reach an understanding with Liberty.

As he recited Yeats's "Lapis Lazuli" to her in the kitchen one evening—urgently trying to convey how *necessary* poetry was to him—Liberty cut him short, complaining about the dishes piled in the sink. Consumed by her own disappointment and despair, she grew spiteful. She cursed him bitterly as he left for class one morning, disparaging him as a husband and a teacher—just as Wright's mother had often abused Dudley.

In his journal, Wright clung to small emblems of hope as winter loosened its hold over Minneapolis. Beginning a series of poems that, like their Chinese models, freely admitted to his drinking, he took heart from the sight of a blue jay outside his office window on one of the first warm days of spring:

> In a pine tree,
> A few yards away from my window sill,
> A brilliant blue jay is springing up and down, up and down,
> On a branch.
> I laugh, as I see him abandon himself
> To entire delight, for he knows as well as I do
> That the branch will not break.

———

Just as the new semester began in April, Wright again traveled to New York to stay with the Blys and to read at a poetry festival at Wesleyan University in Middletown, Connecticut. He knew the trip put his promotion in jeopardy, even as he requested a week's leave from classes. But he found inspiration at every turn during these few days. The night he arrived, he had long talks with Kenneth Rexroth and Yves Bonnefoy, and while in New York visited Oscar Williams and Stanley Kunitz. He also met John Logan for the first time and finalized translations for his forthcoming Trakl book with Bly. Louis Simpson often joined them, planning a stay at the Bly farm in August. One poet Wright did not meet was Anne Sexton. He canceled a rendezvous with her at the last minute, spurred by feelings of guilt and love for his family.

Wright's reading on April 12 came early in a monthlong festival organized in part by the poet and translator Willis Barnstone. "I was an evangelist instigator," Barnstone recalled, "fervently singing the goodness of Spanish poetry." Wright hung on his every word. The two talked for hours in a bar as Barnstone shared his vast knowledge—including the tragic life of Miguel Hernández, whom Wright had begun translating. On a scrap of paper, Barnstone wrote out in Spanish the words Hernández had scratched into the plaster beside the prison hospital cot where he lay dying in 1942: *"Adiós, hermanos, camaradas, amigos / Despedidme del sol y de los trigos."* Beneath, Wright added his own translation: "Goodbye, brothers, comrades, friends / Take leave of the sun and of the wheat for me." This meeting with Barnstone struck Wright as "an immortal, great moment," and he carried this slip of paper in his wallet for years.

Over the previous four months, Wright had been revising a group of poem fragments that sprang from a single historical event. On December 21, 1959, President Eisenhower had made the first state visit to Spain since that country's fascist overthrow, giving Generalissimo Franco a propaganda triumph before his own country and the world. The two leaders embraced in the glare of floodlights and flashbulbs on an airfield outside Madrid, and Franco declared, "Now at last I have won the Civil War." After Wright's encounter with Barnstone, new drafts of "Eisenhower's Visit to Franco, 1959" over the coming weeks incorporate stanzas describing Hernández in his final days. More than a year later, Wright realized that two different poems existed side by side; at the center of *The Branch*, "In Memory of a Spanish Poet" follows "Eisenhower's Visit" in sequence, preserving an impression of its original, composite form. The anger in both poems becomes subsumed by grief, and their sense of human scale makes the crimes they depict even more unsettling.

———

Wright's relationship with Anne Sexton reached its peak in the summer of 1960 when they spent a week together at a poetry gathering on Long Island. Their brief affair was ill-fated from the start and plagued by guilt on both sides. Together they created an intricate knot of desire, instability, alcohol, and fantasy; separately they made poems out of it.

Between February and the end of July, when Sexton joined Wright on the Montauk estate of the financier and poet Hy Sobiloff, their mutual attachment had grown tremendously. By Sexton's account, they each wrote almost daily, sometimes two or three letters in a day. Praising Sexton's poems in a letter to Houghton Mifflin on July 3, Wright denied that his words had been solicited as "a mere blurb." He simply felt compelled to thank them "for publishing this noble book," *To Bedlam and Part Way Back*. "The book is a work of genius. It signifies a moment of major importance to American literature." Despite his protest (or perhaps as he intended), these two sentences would be used on the back of Sexton's second book, *All My Pretty Ones*—a title Wright had suggested to her. Arguably her best single collection, the poems prove what an excellent student Sexton could be. Wright appears in the book as both character and Muse, but Sexton remained true to her own voice and instincts and took what she needed from his spirited lectures. She basked in being treated as an equal, while in his journal Wright admitted uneasily that he felt "sharply jealous of the overwhelming, unmistakable authenticity of her poetry."

The most intriguing proof of their intimacy endures in the names they gave each other early in their correspondence, names they used long after their mutual passions had cooled. The dedication of the final section of Sexton's *All My Pretty Ones*—poems inspired by their relationship—disguises Wright's identity: "For Comfort / who was actually my grandfather." When they met at Sobiloff's home at the end of July, Wright gave Sexton his personal copy of Edward Thomas's *Collected Poems*, a treasured book from his years at Kenyon. His lengthy inscription begins with his private name for her: "Dear Blessing"; Wright often shortened this to "Bee." "I always (even in the worst times) hoped to be worthy of giving this book to somebody," he wrote. "Oh, I knew you would come." A year earlier in Glenwood Hills Hospital, Wright had considered sending Sonjia this same book.

Sobiloff's poetry salon gathered on his estate, where Wright had been invited to work over Sobiloff's third collection of poems—just as Tate and Conrad Aiken had edited his earlier books. Since both her psychiatrist and her husband were out of town, Sexton agreed to join Wright there. This world of privilege on Montauk was familiar to her, but Wright felt self-conscious and ill at ease. He remained indoors working on a manuscript, like other guests, while Sexton joined Sobiloff on his yacht for fishing, swimming, and martinis. But Wright and Sexton shared a motel room for most of a week—changing motels after realizing that a family of Sobiloff's guests had taken the room next door.

In a long, detailed letter to Sexton's psychiatrist, Wright later described six separate incidents of Sexton's disturbing trance states during their time together, including three on one night following a heated argument. Wright had demanded that she divorce her husband and marry him, but Sexton refused to leave her family. Lost in a self-pitying monologue, Wright did not notice at first that Sexton had passed out facedown on the bed. Fearing she might have poisoned herself, Wright held Sexton's limp body in his arms until she regained consciousness, talking softly to her for hours. When she opened her eyes, however, she didn't speak to him but to some threatening apparition, in a voice not her own. In the morning she remembered nothing of the night before.

On their final night together, Sexton once more fell into a trancelike state after an argument about money; unknown to Wright, her fainting spells had become a pattern of response to stress and rejection. Sexton believed that Wright had been "taking" her financially after learning of his five-hundred-dollar stipend for editing Sobiloff's book. To Wright, Sexton seemed fabulously wealthy, but in truth she always felt pressed for money, and believed Wright held her class background against her. She had paid for their joint expenses, while Wright—with little practical sense about money—assumed that Sobiloff would cover everything. After Sexton told Sobiloff of Wright's precarious mental health, Sobiloff insisted that Wright visit a psychiatrist he knew in Minneapolis and offered to pay for his first sessions. That fall, Wright began seeing Dr. Marvin Sukov, whose patients included John Berryman. For many months, Wright met with Sukov as often as three times a week, believing that Sobiloff continued to fund his ongoing treatment.

On the morning of her departure Sexton drafted one of her many love poems to Wright, "Letter Written on a Ferry While Crossing Long Island Sound." For his part, Wright's "Lazy on a Saturday Morning" commemorates more than a shared fishing trip. On the copy he later sent her, Wright added in pencil: "As long as the sea lasts, it will remember us." Their brief time together—and their ongoing exchange of letters— proved an even greater spur to Sexton, who continued to write poems to "Comfort." She had learned that Wright, like Rilke, appeared at his best through the medium of words alone. When they said goodbye, they "parted with the indescribably painful determination to *get well*"—each for the sake of their writing.

Passing through New York City after leaving Montauk, Wright purchased a new book of poems by Gary Snyder, *Myths & Texts*, and during his flight home he filled the margins with annotations. He was struck by Snyder's "enormous patient silences" and his "strength of imagination," already sketching ideas for an essay on the poet's work. Wright was moved by the honesty and clarity in the poems, and he recognized a quality he aspired to: "The unselfish kindness of that rare creature, a grown man." In his journal, Wright declared another moment of rebirth: *My life is changed. I refuse to go on dying every day.* That's all."

Back in Minneapolis, however, nothing was so simple. Part of his "determination to get well" meant demanding a divorce from Liberty; she gave him "blistering hell" when she learned that Sexton had been one of Sobiloff's guests. Routinely now, Liberty hounded him with guilt when he descended the stairs to his study. Wright struggled to accept the blame he felt was his due, but the cycle of censure and recrimination was relentless. On August 12, he wrote a long letter to Liberty, begging her forgiveness, as he played Sibelius's Fifth Symphony over and over on the phonograph, "in order to keep from going out of my mind."

By contrast, Wright's letters to Sexton reveal the consolation he found once more in a singular, devoted correspondence. "My beautiful kind Blessing, my discovered love," he wrote four days later, "I survive by sitting and thinking of you." With Sibelius playing once more, he typed out Hays's translation of Neruda's "Walking Around," with a sharp, humorous explication, and offered close line edits to a new poem of Sexton's. His advice led her to pare down adjectives and to find the beginnings of two separate poems in the draft she had sent. Both would appear in her next book.

————

Bill Duffy recognized how Wright's visits to the Bly farm and his work with them on *The Sixties* magazine were like "a breath of fresh air for Jim, outside of the stuffy halls of academia—like letting an animal loose from a cage." During the last two weeks of August, Louis Simpson and his family stayed with the Blys in Madison, and Wright often joined them there. The poets spent time writing, reading, and critiquing one another's work, reciting poems long into the night. They went fishing on a nearby river, and shared the farmwork, repairing the derelict windmill that helped draw well water for the house.

Wright's continuous drinking troubled Simpson deeply; he saw Wright consume a fifth of whiskey to little effect. One night, after Wright read his new poem dedicated to Hernández and lamented the poet's tragic life, Simpson became enraged. "I don't want to hear about this poet who died and how sorry you are for him when you're killing yourself with whiskey," he shouted. Bly pulled Simpson aside, trying to defuse the confrontation. Looking back on this incident and the friendship between Wright and Bly, Simpson said: "Robert had sort of a father relationship to Jim. Jim was essentially an innocent. I don't care how many spoiled lives Jim wrote about, he was essentially himself a very pure spirit. And when you touched Jim, you knew that you were in touch with that. And he gave Robert something—moments of imagery and *seeing* things that were tremendously useful to Robert." Simpson believed that Wright *lived* poetry in a way that few poets ever could. "He was a visionary."

This intense, revitalizing sequence of events—from his meeting with Sexton on Long Island to the convergence of Bly and Simpson at Odin House—inspired a surge of new work. In September, after completing a new version of Vallejo's "Espergesia," three of Wright's most enduring poems took shape in his notebooks: "Autumn Begins in Martins Ferry, Ohio," "Lying in a Hammock at William Duffy's Farm in Pine Island, Minnesota," and "A Blessing."

At the end of August, Wright brought his family out to the Bly farm before the Simpsons departed; with so many new poems in progress, he wanted Robert's response. Bly has described how "we used to help each other by 'cutting the tails off' of poems"—emulating the concision of Chinese masters. A draft of Wright's "Autumn Begins" dated September 3 shows where he took Bly's advice—deleting an additional three lines from the poem—and where he ignored it, keeping other lines intact.

Bly also appears in two other poems Wright drafted in early September, if only as a figure in the background. Duffy's farm in Pine Island had been the editorial home of the first three issues of *The Fifties*, but when Duffy seized the chance to teach in Tangier, his sudden departure left Bly as sole editor. Duffy had not had time to close up his farmhouse for the winter and asked Robert to handle all the work he had left undone. Bly drove there with Wright on September 7, and while he and a carpenter drained the plumbing and built a new cellar door, among other chores, Wright retreated to a green hammock that hung between two maple trees at a distance from the house.

Lying in a Hammock at William Duffy's Farm in
Pine Island, Minnesota

Over my head, I see the bronze butterfly,
Asleep on the black trunk,

Blowing like a leaf in green shadow.
Down the ravine behind the empty house,
The cowbells follow one another
Into the distances of the afternoon.
To my right,
In a field of sunlight between two pines,
The droppings of last year's horses
Blaze up into golden stones.
I lean back, as the evening darkens and comes on.
A chicken hawk floats over, looking for home.
I have wasted my life.

The startling impression originally made by this poem is hard to recapture, now that its sensibility and strategies have been so widely assimilated. The objective description of nature in clear, straightforward syntax and language, followed by a simple statement of feeling, is the model offered by Chinese poetry. Wright always said as much; the lengthy, place-specific title calls attention to this source of inspiration. As in many of the poems in *The Branch*, he wanted to capture a particular instance of perception, a precise moment of thought and feeling. Some readers could see only puritanical moralizing or self-castigating despair, but Wright always insisted that the poem was simply descriptive. If he regretted anything, it was not spending more time in hammocks.

But Wright knew what he was doing. As has often been observed, the poem's abrupt concluding line echoes Rilke's "Archaic Torso of Apollo," a sonnet Wright had translated at Kenyon. Its last line—"You must change your life"—has a comparable sense of drama, using a poetic technique that Wright knew well from translating the poems of Heine and Trakl. But Wright is more faithful to Rilke's poem than this. Robert Hass has described "Archaic Torso of Apollo" as a poem that "seems absolutely given over to the moment of its making." Wright's "Lying in a Hammock" creates this same effect.

Returning from Duffy's farm one afternoon that same week in September, as Bly relocated *The Sixties* magazine to Odin House in Madison, he again had Wright's company driving back to Minneapolis. Wright insisted they pull off the highway and cross a barbed-wire fence into a field where he saw two horses in the shade of some willow trees.

When they returned to the car, Bly watched as Wright began scratching in his notebook; Bly later joked that he always had to drive while Wright could smoke and write as he pleased. As he revised "A Blessing" over the next few days, Wright crafted one of his most affecting poems, the enjambment in the final two lines balanced perfectly:

Suddenly I realize
That if I stepped out of my body I would break
Into blossom.

The intensity of the poet's longing is transferred to the horses—especially "the slenderer one." As emblems of passion and desire, horses appear often in Wright's poems; the cover illustration of *The Branch* would depict a horse's head in silhouette. In "A Blessing," Wright's clear physical description of "those two Indian ponies" prepares for the poem's final epiphany—a vision that acknowledges its impossibility. This rustic mysticism echoes an epigram by Meister Eckhart that Wright considered for the title page of his new manuscript: "If you would have the kernel, you must break the shell."

Wright's concluding image also points to his affinity with the work of the Spanish poet Antonio Machado, whom he had translated the previous fall. W. S. Merwin recognized "a temperamental sympathy between them," and Philip Levine agreed, noting how the poems of both Machado and Wright possess the "clarity of an almost static vision, something that feels rooted in a landscape." In November 1959, Wright translated a poem from Machado's early sequence "Del Camino" (or "On the Road") that celebrates the return of song after a passing storm. His first version of Machado's opening lines read: "On the naked earth of the road / The hour breaks into blossom."

————

As classes began at the end of September, Wright once more moved out of Como Avenue and took a small room off campus. "Nothing is 'solved,' and I don't really believe that anything will ever be solved," he wrote in his journal, in despair over his marriage. When Wright spent a weekend with the Blys in early October, he recounted Liberty's bitter remark as he left: "They think you're something, but they don't know you like I do."

In a blind rage, she had struck him repeatedly with the steel handlebar from a broken bicycle. That November, Liberty finally agreed to speak to her priest about a divorce.

Wright now worked in his office in Folwell Hall, preparing for classes and revising poems and translations. Harry Weber began to look after him as he grew increasingly uprooted. Beginning that fall of 1960 and continuing until the fall of 1963, Wright often took refuge at Weber's apartment on the edge of Dinkytown, halfway between Wright's office and his family on Como Avenue. Wright had begun drinking hard, Weber recalled, and seemed eager for company, but preferred the relative quiet and squalor of Weber's apartment to the raucous scene at the East Hennepin Bar. Arriving with an armful of records, he might lie for hours on the floor of the living room, playing the same songs repeatedly, whether Schubert lieder or folk ballads, and singing to himself. He favored Beethoven, Brahms, and Wagner, with whom he argued out loud even as he listened, muttering "Wagner, you fascist!" "You could sometimes see him sit down and just watch the tension drain out of him," Weber recalled. "And it was not that neat a sight—I mean, he just looked whipped. Being James Wright was a real job, and life was hard for him." Nonetheless, Weber insisted that Wright had "a talent for joy": "He could get it from his own work; he could get it from other people's work. He could get it from *music*. . . . He tried hard to be a good man, and I'm afraid if that were to get in the way of being a good poet, he'd choose the poet, because he had to."

Wright became more involved with *The Sixties* after Duffy's departure, and the anarchic humor he shared with Carol and Robert helped sustain the magazine. "We got so sick of seeing our own names in print that we undertook many pseudonyms," Wright recalled. "We were always serious, but not always sober." In *The Sixties* No. 4, which arrived that November, Wright's translations of Lorca were credited to "J. A. Cottonwood," while the poem "Rain"—his clearest homage to Trakl— was attributed to "Benjamin Clemenson." Bly's Machado translation is the work of "Charles Reynolds." *The Sixties* and Bly's name had begun to stir up animosity; as "Charles Reynolds," Bly published poems in the same magazines that had rejected them when he used his own name. Carol began using the name "Anne Reynolds" when she submitted stories.

Carol's sense of mischief inspired a long-standing practical joke with Wright, exchanging a battered copy of Charles Olson's *Maximus Poems*.

Wright harbored a peculiar rage against Olson's work, despite the fact that poets he admired, such as Robert Creeley and Paul Blackburn, praised Olson. When Wright arrived at the farm in mid-November, Robert noticed that all he had in his suitcase was a bottle of Jim Beam bourbon and a history of boxing called *The Saga of Sock*. But when Wright got back to Minneapolis, he found a copy of *The Maximus Poems* inside. Over the coming months, he and Carol each went to great lengths to surprise the other with the book's sudden appearance. After hiding the book in dirty laundry at the farm, Wright paid a bus driver to leave it on Carol's porch. In return, she had a friend in Salt Lake City mail the book to Wright, hidden beneath a fruitcake.

———

At the end of November, after receiving "harsh, acute criticism by Sarah Youngblood," his English Department colleague and cotranslator of Rilke, Wright listed sixty-one finished poems in his journal, though even published poems were subject to revision. John Frederick Nims, the editor of *Poetry* magazine, insisted on publishing "The Blessing" as Wright first submitted it rather than concede to his subsequent changes. Worried about the tone of sentimentality, Wright had deleted seven of the poem's twenty-four lines, erasing the emotions ascribed to the horses. In the last sentence, "Suddenly I realize" had become "I think." Wright agreed to see how the poem looked in print and ultimately accepted its original version.

The inevitability of divorce and separation from his sons disturbed Wright continually. Once classes ended, he spent a week on the Blys' farm and wrote a long, rambling letter to Dickey, able to celebrate the solitude of the chickenhouse and the poems of Gérard de Nerval. But his own poem "Having Lost My Sons, I Confront the Wreckage of the Moon: Christmas, 1960" gives a more sober accounting. A haunted, primordial loneliness stalks the speaker "Near the South Dakota border . . . / lost in the beautiful white ruins / Of America." The moon no longer promises the ghost-return of lost love; instead it has become an "inhuman fire."

Anne Sexton was one of the first to see this new poem, and she was thrilled to hear from Wright again after a lapse in his letters. He apologized for being out of touch, telling her that his new poems were now "the only writing I can do." Sexton answered with four brief letters in quick succession, including drafts of two new poems. "Things are going rather poorly for me lately," she confessed. "But then . . . one writes to literally avoid madness and still it has to be good otherwise why breathe? But, in truth, when I can work, the dogged hard tough work of making a poem, I feel good even if I am not. I know that you too understand this and experience it." The intensity of their correspondence had fallen off, but Sexton pressed Wright for renewed attention. When he finally replied in early January—with edits marked on a draft of "Death Wish"— Sexton was overjoyed. She invoked their private names for each other and begged Wright to restore their regular exchange of letters.

In mid-February 1961, however, Wright turned away. In a cool and distanced letter, Wright declared that he was "terrified by the stalking ghosts of work" and cataloged the demands on his time ("in order to support my family") that made it impossible for him to write to her. He scolded Sexton for her obsession about prizes—"You know that they don't mean a damned thing except temporary flattery"—and concluded by savaging a new poem she had sent. Though Sexton would again win Wright's attention when *All My Pretty Ones* appeared in the summer of 1962, their brief, passionate friendship had run its course. By ending his letters to Sexton, Wright no longer had a single, intimate correspondent. He turned this energy toward his poetry and his journals.

13

The amenities of stone are done

January–September 1961

Soon after Sonjia Urseth graduated from the University of Washington in June 1960, she sent a note to Wright telling him of her engagement to a fellow student. Richard Hugo later approached her on the street in Seattle and handed her a letter from Wright, "a diatribe," she recalled, declaring his anger and disappointment. Stunned by the fury of his response, Sonjia never wrote to him again.

In a sequence of poems begun in mid-November 1960 and revised repeatedly in January and early February 1961, Wright invented a strange fiction to account for his sense of loss. "Three Letters in One Evening" recounts the sudden, bizarre death of his friend Jenny, in separate poems addressed as letters to her mother, to her sister, and to her. The second of these poems describes the accident: while standing on a ladder, hanging curtains in her new home, Jenny paused to light a cigarette and suddenly became engulfed in flames. The poem's epigraph from Tolstoy's *The Death of Ivan Ilych*—a book Wright taught that fall—proves the source for his fantasy. The odd tone of condolence and suppressed grief in the first two poems recalls the dramatic monologues Wright first attempted at Kenyon, imitating Frost. The third poem, addressed to Jenny, is entirely different. In a series of brief images, Wright pictures faces he remembers or imagines—his father's "chiseled a hundred times / Out of its life"; factory workers leaving blast furnaces beside the river; Catullus "lost / In the loud streets of Alexandria"; and old Chinese poets "Starved on the bad wine of barbarians." Jenny's death has left him homeless. "This is not my country!" the speaker cries, "This is a strange / Moon's desolation, a disastrous place. / This is a stone my body rolls upon." The emotional landscape of this letter-poem becomes identical to the contemporaneous "Having Lost My Sons." The lyric intensity reaches its peak at the poem's conclusion:

> Now the amenities of stone are done,
> God damn me if I care whether or not
> Anyone reads this book, now you will not.

Throughout these "letters," he conceals Jenny's name with four periods following her capitalized initial. Wright continually revised this third "Letter" and kept it in his new manuscript in a section of "Fictitious Voices." He called it "His Farewell to Old Poetry."

In the arctic cold of another Minneapolis winter, Wright imagined his life as one of permanent exile, prompting him to think of Tu Fu. "I feel like a whole army after a defeat, running through strange forests in wild disorder, complete confusion." The warmth and companionship he found with the Blys meant everything. He sometimes brought Franz for the weekend, and in mid-January Wright took his seven-year-old hunting with Robert. Franz appreciated Carol's kindness and the freedom he had to roam the farm. "I was on my own most of the time because they never stopped talking about poetry." Wright enjoyed his son's company; his unconditional love for Franz was one of the few things he felt sure of.

By the end of February, Wright was at loose ends. Classes had resumed; he had fallen out of touch with trusted friends and ended his correspondence with Sexton. And now that divorce proceedings were finally under way, Liberty swore she would separate him from Franz and Marshall. "Everything I know of is dust and ashes," he wrote in his journal.

At the same time, the March 1961 issue of *Poetry* magazine appeared with five of Wright's recent poems, including "The Blessing," "Miners," and "Just Before a Thunder Shower." Readers could now see the startling shift in craft and intention that distinguished his new work. Given the notoriety of Wright's early career, these poems attracted attention. In tone and diction, they stood in contrast to the anguished, personal drama that was widely admired in Sylvia Plath's and Robert Lowell's latest work. In May, when *Harper's Magazine* published "As I Step Over a Puddle at the End of Winter, I Think of an Ancient Chinese Governor," the model of Chinese quietism confounded expectations still further.

Wright had not anticipated the skepticism that confronted his new work, or the disturbing effect these poems could have. "The strangest thing happened," Wright told Bly, describing a literary party in New York later that year. "Two or three poets I've known all my life came up and started to attack me with real viciousness for those poems. You know, sometimes when you say something that's calm and relaxed, some people get completely enraged."

Wright's new poems encouraged the misconception that he had renounced the rhymed, metrical verse that had first won him recognition. Critics had counted Wright among the most stylistically formal poets of his generation—qualities Auden had praised. Wright's image-based, free-verse poems *appeared* to be entirely different. But as Wright later described them, these new poems have a "definite but extremely difficult rhythm. . . . They are a combination of several rhythms that come from other languages, of a rhythm which I devised myself, and they all in their sounds cluster around a kind of secret heart of silences." The greatest difficulty Wright had in assembling his new manuscript was finding a way to include *both* the new and the old-style, metrical poems in one book.

Wright still felt that pendulum-swing of his allegiances. On March 29 in the old Guthrie Theater at the Minneapolis Institute of Arts, he organized "Voices: a Program of Poetry by Edwin Arlington Robinson and James Wright." He began by reading his own iambic narrative poems spoken in the voices of fictional characters—all among the most formal poems he ever wrote. In the program's second half, two other poets joined Wright to read Robinson's poems. "What stands out now is the *passion* that he felt he had to bring to it," Neil Myers recalled more than fifty years later. "This says a lot, I think, about what went into Jim's subsequent work."

In the spring of 1961, Harry Weber became Wright's teaching assistant in his Humanities class on eighteenth-century literature and the Enlightenment; they spent many hours working together on the third floor of Folwell Hall. Wright pushed his students hard, but they revered him. "When he got into class, he was wonderful—lucid and easygoing and when I say entertaining, he made it fun. His students learned a lot, but there's one caveat to that—*when* he was there." Wright's drinking had overtaken his life. More often now he didn't show up for classes or, unable to teach, sat chain-smoking in the back of the room, letting Weber take over.

Wright began spending more time at Weber's apartment and remained a regular at the East Hennepin Bar, where Roland Flint, a young graduate student and poet from the English Department, introduced himself. "Roland was a marvelous storyteller, an excellent talker," Weber recalled. "It would have been hard for either of them to resist the other." Flint soon became a trusted friend of Wright's. While many English Department professors were alcoholic (Tate among them), Wright ignored their unspoken rule: never drink with students. Had Wright known of Saul Bellow's experience with John Clarke, the English Department chair, he may have realized how tenuous his job truly was. After months of equivocating, Clarke had refused to rehire Bellow—despite the enthusiasm of Bellow's graduate students and many faculty members— "because I am *scandalous*," Bellow told Ralph Ross, the Humanities chair. "It seems a shame this poor sonofabitch should be merely head of the English Department. In the great Republic of the immortals he would be doing the laundry service for a chain of brothels."

————

As spring arrived in Minnesota, Wright sent a rambling and lyrical letter to Donald Hall from the Bly farm saying he felt ready to submit his new manuscript to Wesleyan University Press. His regular psychiatric visits with the "shrinker" have made him "long to throw off the terrible burden of ambition."

> I want to ask you if it is all right if I send my book to you now. It consists of three sections: academic (or, perhaps, formal or traditional) poems; some three or four monologues etc. which I call "fictitious voices"; and then a number of new poems, which perhaps I will call Explorations, or Experiments, or Open Poems . . . a set of little things at the end that pretend to be nothing except moments of happiness. Perhaps the idea of the book is the attempt to recognize and acknowledge vanity and then to shed

it. . . . It is long enough, and I may as well submit, without getting
melodramatic about it. It is, really, just a collection of some poems.

Considering the many successive manuscripts and painstaking effort
that would attend the book he finally published as *The Branch Will Not
Break*, his nonchalance at the outset is striking.

The sojourn that Wright's book survived on its way to publication
over the next two years helps chart his stylistic evolution. Its beginning
dates to the previous fall, with a collection of seventy-seven poems
organized in seven sections that he titled *Now I Am Awakened*. In
May 1961, Wesleyan accepted a new manuscript from Wright, with plans
to publish the book in January 1962; this is the one he described to Hall,
after cutting many poems and adding new ones. Wright already had
misgivings about the manuscript he called *Amenities of Stone*; he began
reworking the collection under a title he borrowed from Rilke: *New
Poems*. In March, Wright had begun to realize that two different books
were at odds in the same manuscript, and he also continued to weigh
the possibility of including a selection of translations. Still, he felt no
sense of urgency. "I want to discover what true thing I am capable of,
and I want to be faithful to it," he wrote in his journal in early May. At
this same time, Wright began making notes for an essay on Whitman, a
talk he would give in September. As his new book continued to evolve
over the summer, much of Wright's reading and thinking returned to
Whitman.

That same week in May, Wright learned that *The Kenyon Review* had
accepted "President Harding's Tomb in Ohio"—a poem in rhyme and
meter that would remain as one of two formal poems in *The Branch*. In
a letter to the editor thanking him for accepting the poem, Wright included another, the rewritten "letter" to Jenny now titled "His Farewell
to Old Poetry." He describes this long blank-verse poem as a "quiet lament for Philip Timberlake, that noble man," but then offers a gloss on
the woman he addresses throughout the poem. "I use the name Jenny to
stand for a kind of secret Muse, as Sterne uses it, in part, in *Tristram
Shandy* (the source of the phrase I use as epigraph): 'Time wastes too
fast; the days and hours of it, more precious, my dear Jenny, than the
rubies about thy neck, are flying over our heads like light clouds of a
windy day, never to return more.'" Though the poem remained part of

Wright's evolving manuscript for many months, it never appeared in print. The figure of Wright's "secret Muse" became ever more buried in the texture and depths of his poetry; her attributes became more various and earthbound. Earlier that week, scrawled in his journal while drunk one night at Weber's apartment, Wright had considered a one-word dedication for his new book: "Mapleleaf."

———

After living alone for many months, Wright was again forced to return to the house on Como Avenue to cut down on expenses over the summer, even as divorce proceedings went forward. His brother Jack, now an "overpaid scientist" in California, offered to help if the divorce left Jim destitute. Desperate for additional income, Wright sent a letter to Edgar Doctorow, now an editor at New American Library, asking if he could translate a selection of short stories and novellas by Theodor Storm. Doctorow agreed at once.

Though Wright remained distant, Anne Sexton never quite let go of the hope he would restore the intimacy between them and continued to write to him. In May, she thanked Wright for his gift of "*my beautiful Rilke*" and asked for more translations and, as always, advice on her poems. The following month, *The New Yorker* published one of Sexton's love poems to Wright, "Letter Written on a Ferry While Crossing Long Island Sound." But Wright rarely answered Sexton's letters, absorbed in his own writing and the demands of teaching.

During the first five-week summer session, Wright lectured twice a day, five days a week, teaching classes on the English novel and Shakespeare. When one of his new students, Erik Storlie, showed him a paper titled "Quixotic Elements in *The Great Gatsby* and *Tender Is the Night*," Wright was thrilled and encouraged Storlie to expand the piece into a scholarly article. It mattered nothing to Wright that their class was in the eighteenth-century English novel. Hunched over the battered oak desk in his office and chain-smoking, Wright grew wildly enthusiastic and filled the margins of Storlie's copy of *The Last Tycoon* with extensive notes on Fitzgerald's clear correspondences with Cervantes.

Many of Wright's students benefited from this generosity. Returning from a weekend at the Blys' farm that summer, Wright ran into Weber in a Dinkytown restaurant with a young poet he had never met. At the mention of Bly's name, the grad student cursed *The Sixties* magazine; he had submitted a poem months before and gotten no reply. After asking his name, Wright began reciting his poem from memory, praising lines he especially admired. Wright now assisted Bly in reading through the many hundreds of poems that poured in to the magazine. "He could see gold where a lot of people couldn't," Weber recalled.

When Hall and Simpson visited the Blys' farm in late June with their families, Wright had all three poets read his new manuscript. He then altered the sequence of the poems and deleted many before resubmitting the book to Wesleyan in early July. Two weeks later, however, Wright told his editor, José de la Torre Bueno, that he had revised the manuscript further still. "[I] swear that I will launch the final version of my manuscript to you very soon"—an interim collection that Wright never sent titled *New Poems*.

Wright now abandoned the idea of publishing the traditional, iambic work together with his new poems in open forms. He hoped that the interest shown in England for a *Selected Poems* volume that spring would give him a chance to publish the iambic and formal poems that continued to fall away from his working manuscript. Corresponding with Michael Hamburger at Longman Press, Wright envisioned a selection of his recent work in meter combined with poems from *The Green Wall* and *Saint Judas* as a separate, unified book. Emboldened by this idea, Wright now focused on making an entire collection of his more recent image-based poems. The Blys' windswept farm continued to prove fertile ground, and new work in his journal bolstered Wright's confidence. First drafts of "Milkweed" and "A Dream of Burial"—the concluding poems in *The Branch Will Not Break*—were written in quick succession at the end of July.

Before the month was out, however, Wright had signed the divorce agreement naming him as defendant in proceedings initiated by his wife. Liberty would keep everything they owned, including the house, and was awarded "permanent exclusive custody and control" of their sons. Wright faced monthly alimony and childcare payments of $240; when classes at the university were in session, his take-home pay totaled less than $280 a month. What's more, Wright shouldered all of the attorneys' fees and court costs for the settlement. He kept only his clothes, books, and records. It would be another year before the divorce was finalized, coinciding with Liberty's graduation from nursing classes at the university. Hemmed in by financial obligations, Wright continued to live off and on at Como Avenue—"Alone, lost, in my basement cell."

Wright's alcoholism continued to fuel the ongoing sense of shipwreck in his family, and the anger that spilled out from the marriage took its toll on the two boys. Weber witnessed much of this firsthand; he knew Wright was afflicted with "the worst kind of alcoholic craving—when it hit him, there was nothing he could do." At a Humanities Department party where no liquor was served, he found Wright drinking wine vinegar in the kitchen. Though Wright's temper would flare, Weber never saw him turn upon his sons. Rather, it was Liberty who would strike the boys, even in public. "Libby would get blazing angry," Weber recalled, lashing out at Franz or Marshall; the two were admittedly "a handful." The pain that was part of the marriage from the beginning was aggravated by Wright's drinking, and the whole family suffered.

————

The East Henn claimed a large clientele as one of the closest bars to the university campus, but this quickly changed in the summer of 1961 when the owner refused to serve a black man who sat down with his white girlfriend. A few of the regulars located a new home in the neighborhood of Seven Corners, across the Mississippi River from the main campus. As Wright came to feel more and more isolated from his family and the faculty at the university—and as his drinking grew more compulsive—the Mixers bar became a welcoming community, including students, professors, Korean War veterans, itinerant railroad workers, Native American construction crews, transients, bums, pensioners, petty criminals, raconteurs, aging boxers, bohemians, and proto-beatniks. The bar stood at the center of the Gateway District anchoring one end of Washington Avenue that ran to the center of Minneapolis, a skid-row neighborhood where many streets converged. An encampment of homeless and migrant workers lived on the flats of the river beneath the Washington Avenue Bridge that connected the neighborhood with the university; there were flophouses, whorehouses, music clubs, strip joints, and more than a dozen bars within a few dilapidated blocks—the equivalent of the Bowery in Manhattan at the time. The Mixers became the focal point of an unending scrim of conversation, cigarette smoke, alcohol, laughter, music, poetry, literature, and political debate from morning until closing time every night, with an occasional fistfight thrown in. As part of this miscellaneous, disreputable mob, Wright was "just in the swim," simply another guy drinking at the bar. "Jim had a real fondness for characters," Weber knew, and at the Mixers, "Everybody was a fuckin' character."

Over the next four years, before he left the Twin Cities for good in June 1965, the Seven Corners landscape became a key part of Wright's poetry. Urban renewal initiatives in Minneapolis had begun to demolish entire city blocks, and Wright witnessed the human cost on men and women he knew personally. Just as he had once prowled the banks of the Ohio River, he walked for hours along the Mississippi, which is shadowed by steep cliffs on either side. Bly once phoned Wright that fall to say he was coming to Minneapolis and needed to see him. Wright told him to look not in his office but down under the bridge. He had some friends there he wanted Bly to meet.

Wright shuttled between Seven Corners and the prairies of western Minnesota all that summer. He had become a family member at the farm, with the converted chickenhouse reserved for him; Carol even installed a rudimentary air conditioner. The intense heat that summer inspired one of her best practical jokes. As often happened when Wright stayed there in winter, he mishandled the oil stove settings when falling asleep in the shack, only to be awakened later by the wind and subzero temperatures. The previous winter, Wright had come into the farmhouse kitchen one bitter cold morning with his dentures frozen in a coffee mug he kept by the bed; as Robert quipped, it gave them an hour of blissful quiet. When Wright returned during a brutal heat wave that July, Carol snuck out late at night to filch the mug. "It spent six hours in our deep-freeze along with the plastic boxes of our garden beans. At eight in the morning we snuck the coffee mug back onto Jim's bedside table. We heard him growling, 'I won't believe it!' when we went to wake him later." Wright warned friends against staying with the Blys, saying, "Don't go there—they'll freeze your teeth!"

For weeks Wright had tried to finalize the manuscript he now called *New Poems*, but by August 22 he had resolved to withdraw his new book from Wesleyan. He realized that the two sections of his book—the first "composed in a classical iambic style" and the second in the newer open forms—"were so different from each other in style and tone as to break the book in half," he told Hamburger in England. "I also saw that in a few months I could certainly expand and strengthen those newer poems into a genuinely new book, one which would be more truly unified." In Wright's letter explaining his decision to his editor at Wesleyan, a fascinating simile suggests how the collection had taken on a life of its own. "It is actually re-shaping itself—and doing so with such energy that I am astounded. When I work on the manuscript, I have the feeling one gets on horseback: I just give the book its head: and it is cantering off into very strange places that I hadn't seen before." Wright now began the most radical reduction and rethinking of the book, focused solely on his new poems.

Since he had first seen the news photograph of Eisenhower shaking hands with Franco on an airfield in Spain in December 1959, Wright had tried to capture the profound sorrow of that moment. The circumstances of Miguel Hernández's death in prison had been folded into his original drafts, and when Wright returned to the poem—"suddenly fell into it and drowned"—at the end of August, he realized he had two distinct poems. In "Eisenhower's Visit to Franco, 1959," Wright strove to balance images of darkness and light to let small, significant details and gestures convey grief. Working separately on "In Memory of a Spanish Poet," Wright removed five lines from an early draft and gave them the title "Trying to Pray"—discovering a third poem that would appear in *The Branch*. Work had come easily to him for months, but as he told Roland Flint that summer, the book "just isn't good enough, and I should be over the vulgar thrill of seeing my name in print by now." When *The Branch* took its final form a year later, more than eighty-five poems had been discarded from successive manuscripts.

14

The seven corners / Of Hell, 14, Minnesota

September 1961–December 1962

Wright spent a week in New York at the beginning of September 1961, attending a four-day conference at Columbia University. Of all his critical prose, Wright was especially proud of the talk he presented, having worked on the essay all summer. In "The Delicacy of Walt Whitman," he emphasizes the "powers of restraint, clarity, and wholeness, all of which taken together embody that deep spiritual inwardness, that fertile strength, which I take to be the most beautiful power of [his] poetry." Quoting poems from memory, Wright highlighted Whitman's profound influence on poets writing in Spanish, and noted the "wave of translation" that had overtaken American poetry. He concluded by praising the work of current American poets such as Simpson and Levertov, and recited entire poems by Bly and David Ignatow. "Whitman dares, like Nietzsche, to challenge not only what he dislikes but also what he *values*," he writes, deriding the formlessness he saw in many Beat poets who claimed to be Whitman's followers. Implicitly, Wright offers a defense for the new direction his own poetry had taken and describes key principles of composition he shares with his great ancestor: "For he uses parallelism not as a device of repetition but as an occasion for development. . . . Form, in Whitman, is a principle of growth: one image or scene or sound grows out of another. . . . [It] is a principle of imagination: the proliferating of images out of one unifying vision."

Anne Sexton came to New York to meet Wright that September, and the two went to dinner with Roger Hecht. He remembered "Anne almost but not quite leaning into Jim as they walked in Greenwich Village" and Wright's aloofness, resisting her. More than once, Hecht heard him say, "Stop bugging me, Anne." To Hecht, Wright's discomfort seemed puzzling; he drank continuously, and Sexton couldn't understand why he withdrew from her. Four months later, she added one last poem to her new collection, the book Wright had figured in so decisively. "Dearest, / where are your letters?" she implores in "Letter Written During a January Northeaster," the concluding poem in the sequence dedicated to Wright. Again conflating the poet with her grandfather, she writes, "Now he is gone / as you are gone. / But he belongs to me like lost baggage." This disturbing quality of loss, marked paradoxically by a sense of possession, mourns the absence of Wright's letters, the words that should be hers alone.

The Sixties No. 5 appeared that fall, featuring translations of fourteen French poets, including a version by Wright of a poem by Gérard de Nerval. On September 19, 1961, *The New York Times* published Wright's "In a Warm Chickenhouse," a poem he had written the previous December lamenting Nerval's imprisonment a century before. Ironically, at the time Wright's poem appeared, Carol and Robert had resorted to locking him into that same writing shack until he finished his long-promised essay on the poetry of Gary Snyder. Wright's guest appearance as the magazine's resident reviewer, Crunk, was the only thing holding up *The Sixties* No. 6, which was due at the printers.

Wright had been studying Snyder's poems closely for more than a year; the "superior sensitivity" and "meditative power and privacy" of his work set him apart from the Beat poets. Snyder's poems, as part of a tradition of western and midwestern American writers, are filled "with concrete details of the lives of nonintellectual people" and a physical, sensuous alertness to the world. Wright goes on to praise the "interior" influence of Japanese and Chinese models, as evidenced by Snyder's "desire to overcome vanity and ambition." When Snyder read the essay the following spring, he wrote to Bly to say that Crunk had in fact been too nice.

Wright's new poems began showing up everywhere in the fall of 1961; *The Hudson Review* published five and the *Quarterly Review of Literature* included eight more. At the end of October, Wright embarked on a reading tour of colleges across Michigan, with ten readings in as many days. He often began by saying a series of "tiny poems"—by Jiménez, Machado, Tu Fu, Issa, and both Charles and Anne Reynolds. But Wright withheld the poets' names; he wanted his audience to hear the poems without distraction. He also chafed at being compared to Bly, and even briefly considered reinstating many of the "iambic dramas and songs in my new book, in spite of Robert's bullying. I have to be myself. If I am old-fashioned, so be it." Wright was grateful when the poet Michael Benedikt wrote to praise Wright's new poems for their kinship with the earlier work. "Well, it's a heartening relief to see that *someone* noticed the continuity."

At one stop on his "outrageous poetry-reading safari throughout the entire province of Michigan," Snodgrass and Mazzaro hosted Wright at Wayne State University in Detroit. They made the mistake of bringing him to a Greek belly-dancing restaurant—where Wright began drinking heavily—before driving to Snodgrass's cabin in the country. After a phone call from Robert Lowell, who asked whether divorcing his wife might free him from writer's block, Wright launched into a long narrative of his own tormented marriage. Though "still terribly torn about leaving his family," he called his decision to marry Liberty "a rescue operation," knowing the abuse she had suffered at her father's hand.

Wright began work in earnest on his commission to translate Storm's fiction that November. He noted in his journal that he felt pleased to have drafted one and a half pages after four hours of concentrated work one evening. But his progress had been won at the cost of disappointing his sons by his absence. "As for the writing, I just can't help it," he conceded, refusing to apologize even to himself. Strangely, Wright's journal writing grew more sporadic following this entry; there are frequent gaps of many months, a pattern of inconsistency that persists for the next eight years. What's more, he wrote few letters until the spring of 1964, when he began restoring correspondence with close friends.

In December, Wright completed another semester at the university, with exams and papers due in his classes on Shakespeare, the English novel, and the Enlightenment. At the same time, he was also preparing to resubmit his manuscript to Wesleyan. His letter to Willard Lockwood, the director of the Press, on December 22 opens with holiday greetings meant to brush aside his five months of silence. "This morning I placed in the mail the completed manuscript (typescript rather) of my new book. It is entitled simply *The Blessing*," Wright tells Lockwood. "I want to assure and reassure you, as emphatically as possible, that *this* version of the book is definitely and irrevocably finished, as far as I am concerned." Knowing this new manuscript would need the approval of the poetry board, Wright insists that it's simply a revision of the one they had already accepted—twice. He had added just three short lyrics but deleted many more, mainly from the first section of longer "academic" poems.

Three weeks later Wright's new book once again met with unanimous approval. At the end of January—when the original *Amenities of Stone* had been scheduled for publication—Lockwood wrote to inform Wright that he was absolutely bound to an August 1 deadline for submitting the final version of *The Blessing*. Over the course of those seven months, Wright added seventeen new poems to the book and removed many others. When it finally appeared in the summer of 1963, *The Branch Will Not Break* included forty-five poems, winnowed from three times that number written over a period of four years. The book became one of the early successes for the Wesleyan Poetry Series and would remain Wright's most celebrated book.

———

The winter of 1962 was the worst Wright had known in Minneapolis; on January 10 he noted the temperature at thirty-one degrees below zero. In the middle of May, it was still cold enough in Minneapolis to see a dusting of snow. Years later, Wright threatened an audience in Buffalo with "atrocity stories about the snow" in Minnesota. "The snow really does assume strange shapes, not only in itself, but after you've endured the snow for a long, long time, you yourself start to assume strange shapes. You meet yourself coming around corners."

Though still living in the basement at Como Avenue, Wright spent more and more time at Weber's apartment and with the crowd at the Mixers; he was also seen—and heard—at student parties in Seven Corners and Dinkytown. At one such gathering that winter, Wright, who'd been drinking before he arrived, began to recite poems by Robinson to a group gathered in the kitchen. He hadn't paused to take off his coat, and became so intent upon the words that he didn't realize he had backed up against a lit stove, igniting his coat. As a friend doused his smoldering coat with beer, Wright went on with the poem and "never missed a beat."

That winter, Wright still considered reinserting a section of translations in his new manuscript under the title "Apprenticeships." The work continued to sustain him; along with Storm, Wright translated fourteen of Rilke's poems that winter (together with Sarah Youngblood) and still more by Guillén for the collection *Cántico*. "At a bad, dark time," he wrote three years later, "I stayed alive by working at length at six of those poems, and they all, all in the book, shine from within."

His collaborations with Bly on *Twenty Poems* of Trakl had finally appeared that fall, and together with the poet John Knoepfle, Bly and Wright had now completed translations for *Twenty Poems* by César Vallejo. In January, Wright drafted a brief introductory note as Bly prepared the manuscript for the printers. In this first draft, he writes that Vallejo had a kind of spiritual courage that enabled him to face harsh realities with the strength of his imagination, through "the reality of the spirit, of what Meister Eckhart calls the inner man."

> I think he is one of the very greatest poets in any language I know of. There is not a single poem in which any human being is treated with irreverence. There are a great many poems in which death is hated and fought. And it is fought back, not by some vague "spiritual value." It is fought back by César Vallejo, lying sick in a charity hospital, dying of hunger and fury. . . . As a poet, he perpetually took a direct part in the creation of his own identity. He turned his back on the market-place; he denied the popular press's right, and the academic community's right, to judge the imagination by standards that have been comfortably dead for a hundred years; he was true to his inner self. He was a dangerously religious man.

The most striking illustration of Wright's dedication to Vallejo is a seven-line lyric in *The Branch* titled "The Jewel." In March 1962, the poem appears among drafts that Wright considered adding to his new book. With minor changes over the next few months, the poem is an ideal example of his new style:

There is this cave
In the air behind my body
That nobody is going to touch:
A cloister, a silence
Closing around a blossom of fire.
When I stand upright in the wind,
My bones turn to dark emeralds.

Wright had completed his translation of Vallejo's "Espergesia" a year and a half earlier, and its third stanza is the primary source for all but the final couplet of Wright's poem. The affinity between the two poets is undeniable. As Bly wrote following Wright's death, "I've never known any man who was closer in his inner despair and inner courage to Vallejo than James was. Vallejo made him aware that it was not wrong to try to go deep, even when you found down there immense grief and injustice. And I think Vallejo suggested the value of 'free verse' for that descent."

Even as he worked to complete his new book, the seeds for his subsequent volume began appearing in manuscripts and journal pages. Another of Wright's translations of Rilke, "Orpheus. Eurydice. Hermes," suggests the narrative arc of his next collection. *Shall We Gather at the River*—Wright's most carefully constructed book—begins and ends on the Ohio River shore; both its opening and its concluding poems appear in early drafts dated February 9, 1962. "To the Ohioan Muse" is already a poem of direct address, here to an "old hag . . . who used to live at 23rd & Water by the Vinegar Works"—the red-light district in Wheeling. "Now I have lost all others from my arms; / You alone, you, are always born again." The myth of Orpheus that guides the unfolding of Wright's next collection has already begun to surface.

———

Despite a number of commissioned essays published in the winter and spring, the need for money remained. Compelled to teach all summer, Wright canceled plans to serve as a "professional consultant and lecturer" for the U.S. Embassy at a literary conference in New Delhi, India. He instead retreated to the Blys' farm whenever he could. One Saturday morning in April, Wright joined in one of their elaborate practical jokes, dressed as an Easter bunny in costumes Carol made from Robert's navy uniforms. Together with Robert, Bill Duffy, and Robert's cousin

Orrin, Wright gave out colored eggs to delighted children in downtown Madison. After Robert furthered his feud with a local store owner by dropping a rotten egg on his counter, they all disappeared in a borrowed car. "And no one ever *did* find out who those Easter bunnies were!" Bly laughed while recounting the prank. "They talked about it for weeks!"

Wright considered each new poem he wrote for his still-evolving manuscript; that spring he even debated including a new iambic poem. Asked to stand as godfather for the Blys' first child, Wright composed a poem for her that he had printed as a broadside—a gift to those who gathered at the Faith Lutheran Church in Madison on the Sunday of her baptism. "Mary Bly" became one of the poems Wright added to his manuscript. As the August deadline approached, he knew his new book had become stronger and more cohesive. "It is not a 'great' book; but it might yet be a true book," he notes in his journal. "I've kept it hidden—fallow . . . there are times when it's necessary to let the book grow alone." Wright's journal reveals his solitary life. Though he often slept in the basement at Como Avenue, weathering Liberty's abuse and worrying about his sons, the Bly farm became the closest thing he had to a home.

At this unsettled time, while staying with the Blys one weekend that spring, Wright chanced to speak with an elderly aunt of Robert's who mentioned the town where Sonjia had lived. This "very strange and totally unexpected thing" inspired Wright to type one last undated letter to her. He never mentions Sonjia by name, but confesses his astonishment "to feel rising in myself the old sacred delight at the Muse's face." Despite "the harsh realities of life," Wright's long, four-page letter is contemplative and self-assured—or tries to sound so. "I have passed into another world of the spirit," he writes.

> I live alone, I teach with coherence and sometimes with a temporary and surprised joy, and my new book (which has been with me for months) has finished itself and then grown further and then changed shape and then finished itself yet again, several times over. I have cast off all previous ways of writing, and therefore I have deliberately undermined my previous quite comfortable reputation; readers can be tyrannical, with the best will in the world; they subtly resent your refusal to repeat yourself; but I do not want to repeat myself, I only want to grow.

He goes on to quote a passage from Hesse's *Steppenwolf*: "we have to stumble through so much humbug before we reach home. And we have no one to guide us. We have nothing but our homesickness." This idea—that the longing for home can serve as a kind of lodestar—informs the sense of spiritual search in Wright's poetry. Enclosing five recent poems, he ends the letter by invoking his private name for her: Jenny.

That spring, Wright also drafted an introduction to the collection of Hy Sobiloff's poems he had helped revise two years before on Montauk. The book was now complete, and Wright received a huge sum for the piece and a final critique of the poems. His essay, "The Quest for the Child Within," includes Wright's most sustained consideration of John Keats, one of the "heroes on the earth, whose heroism consisted in their willingness to face the facts of pain . . . [and] the tousled dusk of sorrowing human faces." Wright returns to Hesse's motif in *Steppenwolf*—the desire to find one's way home—and quotes a Rilke poem he had recently translated. By embracing the child within, the poet can "come home to himself at last. 'Every door in me opens,' said Rilke, 'and my whole childhood stands all around me.'" Nested within this essay is a cluster of key themes and obsessions, including Wright's faith in poetry as the means "to front life openly and live it fully," and of the journey home made possible by the poet's "power of reverence for himself." This essential self-forgiveness can tap "the springs of true feeling" that Wright identified with childhood and the source for poetry.

In March, responding to news from Roger Hecht that Wright was "going through a rough time," Anne Sexton wrote a poignant letter to Wright, pleading for his response. "I have loved you so long and so deeply. Almost as I love my two children or my own book, I love you. If I think of you, I am dwelling on something that is part of me, my own bone." Wright's response, if any, does not survive.

Almost four months later, however, Wright did thank Sexton for an advance copy of *All My Pretty Ones*. "My dear Bee," he began, "whatever either of us happens to be going through at any given moment, we are still totally unafraid and unguilty about saying or writing or phoning absolutely anything to each other." Despite his praise and promises, Wright did not renew his once steady stream of letters. Yet this brief note was a tremendous boon to Sexton, who shared it with her therapist. "He

gives me so many gifts, but with both of us it's a 'weird abundance.' . . .
He's not strong on responsibility—he's a genius—he makes me want to
write."

———

Though Liberty could have continued graduate studies in Minneapolis,
she chose a mental health care program at the University of California
in San Francisco. When she received her bachelor's degree in nursing
from the University of Minnesota on July 12, 1962, Wright attended
the ceremony, making a gift of Kierkegaard's *Works of Love*. The day
before, the two had received the final divorce decree, which left Wright
with the heavy burdens of monthly child-care and alimony payments.
Liberty took all of their furniture and joint possessions; she drove west
with a trailer on the back of a 1956 Chevrolet sedan. She knew no one in
San Francisco and spent the first night in the city sleeping in the car with
the boys. But Liberty had made good on her threat to separate Wright
from his children.

Without enough work available at the university that summer, Wright
accepted a last-minute offer to teach at Moorhead State College in
northwestern Minnesota, across the Red River from the larger city of
Fargo, North Dakota. In the middle of July, after an eight-hour bus trip,
Wright found himself in a familiar landscape, though hours north of the
Blys' farm. The wide expanse of prairie sky spread out above a convergence of railroad lines from all directions. The cities of Fargo and Moorhead were a major midwestern hub for the Burlington-Northern and
Santa Fe lines, with huge depots and mile-long strings of boxcars thread-
ing through both towns all day and night. There were also dozens of bars
amid the constant shuttle of rail traffic.

Wright shared an office with a former graduate student from the
University of Minnesota, Allan Hanna, who had told him of the job.
Hanna's wife, Mary Ann, grew alarmed when Wright first came to their
home for cocktails. "He drank us out of our whole liquor cabinet. He
didn't stay with just one kind—when one bottle went dry, he went on to
whatever else was there." But decades later she still recalled "the lyrical
quality to his voice" that evening as Wright recited poems for them by
heart.

Wright taught in a five-week session, with two literature classes and
one in composition meeting five days a week. His austere campus room

proved reason enough to seek out the bars in Moorhead and Fargo. Wright also walked for miles into the prairies that stretched south of town. Liberty had sold the Como Avenue house, and Wright's homesickness now bore the deep sorrow of losing his sons. The extreme solitude that shadowed him can be felt in one of the many poems he wrote in this landscape of railroads and open sky, "Outside Fargo, North Dakota":

> Along the sprawled body of the derailed Great Northern
>   freight car,
> I strike a match slowly and lift it slowly.
> No wind.
>
> Beyond town, three heavy white horses
> Wade all the way to their shoulders
> In a silo shadow.
>
> Suddenly the freight car lurches.
> The door slams back, a man with a flashlight
> Calls me good evening.
> I nod as I write down good evening, lonely
> And sick for home.

The poem exists in a kind of eternal present, unfolding for the reader in the same moment the poet is writing in his notebook. This immediacy helps convey the depth of the poet's isolation, as mirrored by the details in the landscape. The match flame is as tenuous as the anonymous human gestures exchanged with the watchman. The language is lean and clear, with an intensity of emotion sketched by understatement. Robert Hass saw in Wright's "absolute clarity of feeling" a way in which sensibility could become "something as lucid and alert as intelligence."

Wright's editor at Wesleyan received the final version of his new book on August 2, postmarked from Moorhead. By this point, Bueno was surely beyond surprise; the manuscript had again been completely revised. "You'll notice at once," Wright warned, "that I've changed the title from *The Blessing* to *The Branch Will Not Break*." At last, the book had the integrity and wholeness Wright had struggled to find for more than three years.

Upon returning to Minneapolis, Wright lived in a series of cheap furnished rooms, a way of life that would continue for the next four years. With most of his books stored at the Blys' farm, he had few possessions and little clothing. He found refuge at Weber's apartment in Dinkytown, at the Mixers, and at Erik Storlie's apartment, which was across the street from the bar and widely known as Ground Zero. Wright met many of the Seven Corners crowd there and often slept on the couch after the bars closed. The painter John Beauchamp had a studio on the ground floor, and when Storlie left for graduate study at Berkeley in September, a tough, blue-collar Irishman from St. Paul named James "Red" Nelson moved in. He was nearer to Wright in age and background than many others in their group, and the two men formed a close bond.

Wright remained part of the diverse and animated crowd at the Mixers; he could be heard reciting poetry or W. C. Fields, arguing politics and literature, or praising movies, plays, and architecture. He brought his own intensity to the scene. At closing time one night, Wright convinced three of his drinking companions to drive south from Minneapolis to find a building designed by the famed Chicago architect Louis Sullivan. His friends had no idea who Sullivan was. "We ended up around dawn in a small town in southern Minnesota, outside this building he wanted to see. He was just enthralled with it, except you couldn't see anything 'cuz it was dark." At other times, "he would become progressively more pugnacious" and argumentative at the end of a long night of drinking, picking fights with men twice his size. After one such fight, Wright was arrested in Seven Corners and spent the night in the drunk tank.

To those who didn't know him well, Wright appeared "to be veering along out of control, fiercely and relentlessly self-destructive." Alcohol had become essential for him to function at all, but in the classroom he could still be the same brilliant and devoted teacher. One of his students that fall, Garrison Keillor, recalled Wright vividly, trailed by a cloud of cigarette smoke. "He was a beautiful lecturer who spoke off the cuff in whole paragraphs. And he had—especially for the reading of poetry, whether his own or other peoples'—the most beautifully modulated voice, with nothing false or actorly about it. . . . He did not hand out praise like pieces of candy. James praised you by paying attention."

Inspired by Wright's "Lying in a Hammock at William Duffy's Farm in Pine Island, Minnesota," the Sixties Press published a chapbook in

September 1962 titled *The Lion's Tail and Eyes: Poems Written out of Laziness and Silence*, with ten poems each by Wright, Bly, and Duffy. It brought together the first substantial selections from both *The Branch* and Bly's first book, *Silence in the Snowy Fields*. Bly's collection (published by Wesleyan later that fall) preceded Wright's by a year, making it seem as though Wright had tried to emulate Bly. The prolonged delay in finalizing *The Branch* encouraged the misguided idea that Wright had become a mere disciple of Bly and turned his back on rhymed and metered verse. But Wright's work had influenced Bly's poetry just as much— as Bly readily acknowledged.

The two remained very different poets. For one thing, Bly knew that Wright would never be found at a meditation retreat. Wright's anger at encountering a small book titled *Sayings of Sri Ramakrishna* on the desk in the chickenhouse in early October inspired "A Prayer to the Lord Ramakrishna," which concludes, "You have nothing to do with us. / Sleep on." The finished poem mutes Wright's initial response. "I hate your goddamn Ramakrishna! I hate that!" he had shouted, enraged by the idea of Eastern saints who escape the body's pain and the mind's anguish. The extremity of his anger shocked Bly, who realized Wright felt threatened by the demands of spirituality; alcohol and his drinking companions became a way to avoid this realm.

Soon after his encounter with Ramakrishna's book, however, Wright began an intensive study of the Christian Universalist philosopher Nicolas Berdyaev. Wright's pursuit of a spiritual ground is the struggle of a man in doubt, troubled by the possibility of faith as a way to confront human suffering. Bly has described Wright's poetry as "God-haunted"; what troubled Wright was not so much the absence of the divine but rather its *almost presence*, like the image of a place he could never reach. Wright's translation of "Three Stanzas from Goethe" fits seamlessly among the poems in *The Branch*, where the poet stands blind to "the thousand fountains / So near him, dying of thirst / In his own desert."

The demands of daily life often left Wright baffled, and he found women to help him; some simply gave him home-cooked meals. His most significant companion, Barbara Thompson, was a former student whom Wright began seeing in the spring of 1962. She often traveled with him to readings or to the Blys' farm; she typed poems, cooked, and cared for him.

In December, Wright arranged poetry readings in San Francisco and Berkeley, California, as a way to visit his sons at Christmas. As he struggled to make sense of his new solitude in Minneapolis, enduring what he later called the worst year of his life, the seeds of new poems continued to appear in his journals. Some would take years to revise, but poems such as "Youth" and "The River Down Home"—central pieces in his next book—have their beginning with lines jotted down in November. Many other new poems also return to Martins Ferry; the material becomes more personal, with more at stake. As he remembers the face of a friend who "drowned in a suckhole" in the Ohio River, he looks out the window into the street, where "Minneapolis, / Drowns, dark. / It is dark. / I have no life." In some occult way, the Ohio had swollen the banks of the Mississippi.

15

To rebuild from scratch

January 1963–December 1964

In the winter of 1963, Robert Bly published a rambling, exasperating, and important essay in *Choice* magazine titled "A Wrong Turning in American Poetry," in which he declared, "The best thought in this century moves inward." His insight came from translating the richness of imagery and "abundant, clear thought" found in the modern poetries of Europe and Latin America. By comparison, he argued, "American poetry is marked by its fundamental absence of spiritual life." Together with his essay writing and political activism, *The Sixties* magazine worked to pull Bly onto the public stage. In his own poetry, he began to move away from the interiority he praised in this essay, a quality captured so well by the poems in *Silence in the Snowy Fields*. As John Logan, the editor of *Choice*, realized, the five new poems of Wright's that appeared in the same issue—including "A Prayer to the Lord Ramakrishna" and "The River Down Home"—exemplified the kind of poetry Bly wanted from his American contemporaries.

At the end of January, Robert Frost died at the age of eighty-eight and Allen Tate invited Wright to take part in a memorial reading for the poet at the university. Quoting from a eulogy by Roger Kahn in *The Nation*, Wright recited from memory the Frost poems that had "occurred" to him when he first read the piece. Tate continued to treat Wright warmly and often invited him to his home, where Wright became close with Tate's wife, Isabella Gardner. But Wright had been missing more classes, and gossip about his conduct outside the classroom infuriated Tate, who remained angry with him for his allegiance to Bly and William Carlos Williams. Though Wright believed in Tate's friendship—even acknowledging him in *The Branch*—Tate made certain Wright would not be granted tenure at the university.

Had the opinions of Wright's students been considered, the result would have been different. Many called him the best teacher in the English Department. One student remembered Wright's frustration in an English novel class that spring, when the importance of the novel *Adam Bede* had escaped his students' grasp. "He leaned forward on the podium, stared into space for what seemed far too long, and said: 'Well, *you* know George Eliot. She was one of *us*.' That was the clue I needed. . . . He tried to connect with us on a feeling level, not just through academic information. When he was 'on' he was brilliant, profound, funny." But Wright wasn't always "on." Students adopted a "ten-minute rule," leaving class if he hadn't yet appeared. One morning, Wright ducked his head in the room at the last minute and said, in a voice of mock-cheerfulness, "Hey gang, why don't we all go down to the drugstore for a Coke?" He waved and walked off, leaving them to file out in bewilderment.

Somehow Wright's poetry survived his drinking. The page proofs for *The Branch* show he read them closely, correcting spacing, spelling, and punctuation. "We are absolutely bidden to do our work," he told the painter John Beauchamp. At the end of April Wright revised poems begun in Fargo, and in early May his curse upon the city of Minneapolis started to take shape in his journal. But just as he began to find his balance, he learned the university had fired him. On the day the tenure committee met, Wright was appearing before an "old and distinguished literary society" at Cornell University. His poetry, however, had become a liability at Minnesota; his growing fame as a poet bred resentment. To compound his anguish, the entire campus learned of Wright's dismissal before he did.

In a bizarre personal letter to Wright meant to preempt "the twisted news of the grapevine," Tate admitted to voting against him, but not for the reports of his drinking with students. He condemned Wright's method of teaching, though he admits, perversely, "I have never heard you in the classroom. But I have heard you speak publicly, that is extemporaneously; and I have spent long evenings with you. It seems to me that it is almost impossible for you, unless you have a written text, to adhere to the subject, or deal with it concretely." Tate admits that he "leaned over backwards in severity" in his judgment of Wright. "If you were not a poet and a fine one," he concluded, "I should probably have been less hard on you in the voting."

When Wright met the following day with the English Department chair, John Clarke, his psychiatrist advised Barbara Thompson to accompany him. Clarke detailed a list of justifications for Wright's dismissal, including allegations of his drinking with students. Clarke, like Tate and others on the committee, was an alcoholic, and his condescension was infuriating. He referred to Wright as "damaged merchandise" and refused to recommend him to other schools.

Henry Parker, a colleague from the Humanities Department, encountered Wright late that night as he crossed the Washington Avenue Bridge into Seven Corners. "His head was down, he was bitter, violently angry, and crushed. . . . He said, 'Henry, the bastards on my committee didn't even know that I have a Ph.D. They voted me out because of *excessive drinking.*'" The hypocrisy shown by the English Department became widely criticized. A petition circulated by students quickly gained sixty-four signatures protesting Wright's dismissal. As Berryman wrote in condolence, a "poisonous atmosphere" hung over the entire "medieval" department.

It now seemed fortuitous that Wright had agreed to serve as a visiting lecturer at Macalester College in St. Paul for the coming school year. Anxious about his tenuous position at the university, Wright had agreed to the temporary appointment just weeks before his dismissal. Still pressed for money, Wright strangely offered to teach, as a favor, an advanced class in American poetry that summer, "a course ordinarily taught by my friend, Mr. Tate." It was the last time Wright taught at the University of Minnesota. In August, after learning that Roethke had died suddenly of a heart attack, Wright spent the entire hour and a half of the class reciting Roethke's poetry.

Wright made frequent trips to the farm in Madison that summer, though after his move to St. Paul in September he saw less of the Blys; their second child, Bridget, or "Biddy," had been born in April. After Doctorow's "miraculously heartening assurance" that they would still publish Wright's translations of Storm's *novellen*, the work became the "one connection with reality" left to him. Night after night, Red Nelson saw Wright hunched over the kitchen table at Ground Zero, laboring at those stories and reading passages aloud. Months later, in a letter thanking Doctorow, Wright told him, "In fact, the chance to work on the Storm translation was, more than once, the chance to go on living, almost the one chance."

Just when Wright felt most defeated, *The Branch Will Not Break* appeared in bookstores, together with the first reviews. Though some critics disparaged his turn toward free verse, the book gathered widespread praise. After reading an advance copy at the end of May, Bly offered an insightful appraisal in a letter: "Jim Wright's book is about an environment that *divides*: namely, the steel mining district of Ohio. The connection with solitude is deceptive; underlying it is a kind of social anguish."

When one of the first admiring reviews of *The Branch* appeared, Bly wrote immediately. "How right it was to wait till the book became all one thing! As he says it is a 'fresh start'—for everybody." After the critical success of Wright's first two books, however, the absence of traditional forms and meters was often perceived as a kind of betrayal. Some critics, like Thom Gunn, insisted that Wright's intention had been mere novelty; Gunn believed that "the operation of the discursive reason is deliberately excluded" from the poems in *The Branch*. Alarmed exaggerations like this suggest why Tate and others were so unnerved by Wright's new work.

Other critics did a better job of reading the actual poems. Alert to the subtlety and concision Wright had now mastered, one writer likened the poem "In Fear of Harvests" to Hardy's "In the Time of the Breaking of Nations." In his introduction to a new anthology, Donald Hall set aside issues of diction and technique to focus on what seemed "genuinely new": the quality of imagination in the poems. "There is an inwardness to these images, a profound subjectivity," Hall wrote, likening the effect to expressionist paintings. In a similar way, John Logan's review of *The Branch* published in August praised Wright's deft handling of "images where what is imaged is a gesture of the inner life of man." But even Logan grew impatient with a certain thematic sameness; there were "too many moons in his poetry, and too many horses." Recognizing the influence of Spanish poets such as Lorca, he warned that the horse "must not be allowed to multiply grotesquely like a rabbit."

For a generation of poets coming of age in the 1960s, Wright's new work was "an explosive discovery." As C. K. Williams recalled, *"The Branch Will Not Break*, for me, was just a thunderous book, it was just amazing. That book was a liberation for me." Philip Levine, an exact contemporary of Wright's, was impressed by his total command of free verse. "Jim seems to have just [*finger snap*] leaped into it and done it *extremely* well." When Levine introduced his students to the book, he saw the effect immediately. But not only younger poets acknowledged the influence. Brief lyrics in *The Branch* like "The Jewel" inspired a number of the poems in Galway Kinnell's 1967 collection, *Body Rags.*

Though heartened by the praise, Wright never really doubted the value of his poetry, even in the face of harsh criticism. His dismissal from the university, however, left him devastated; he felt hounded by the opinions and hearsay that followed him from Minneapolis to St. Paul. Determined to "rebuild myself as a teacher, rebuild literally from scratch," in his first classes at Macalester that fall Wright "labored more intensely than I've done on scholarship since I studied Latin in high school." He came to depend on the help of two old friends: Ray Livingston and Bill Truesdale.

Wright had met Livingston and his wife, Claire, a poet, soon after he arrived in Minneapolis, while Truesdale had been a fellow graduate student in Seattle. The Truesdale home became a haven for Wright, notwithstanding his drunken impositions and unvarying poverty. At the first staff meeting of the semester in September 1963, Wright was assigned two classes of freshman English and two literature classes. He made a good impression on his colleagues: easygoing, articulate, soft-spoken. It was the last staff meeting he ever attended at Macalester.

Few doubted Wright's commitment to teaching, which he proved in the face of physical and emotional distress. Truesdale believed that Wright never forgave Tate for what amounted to a betrayal of friendship and of poetry. His idealization of teachers like Ransom intensified the guilt and despair that came with losing his job. On the heels of his failed marriage, Wright felt a confusion of anger, resentment, anxiety, and remorse. Even with the best intentions, he was rarely at his best at Macalester. "Wright was seldom a truly happy man," Truesdale recalled. "His sense of responsibility toward his teaching and above all toward his students, though sorely tried and at times irregular, was as singular and real as his teaching could be extraordinary. Almost as much as literature itself, teaching was a necessity to him, something he craved, something that he also clung to in hard times."

Wright attracted a following of students at Macalester whose loyalty helped bolster his self-esteem. He continued his relationship with Barbara Thompson, even after she took a job in northern Minnesota; he often traveled to see her on weekends. One of the few times that Wright seemed happy that fall was on Halloween, dressed up in a Goldilocks wig and a dress borrowed from Truesdale's wife, Joan. With Bill wearing a red jumpsuit and menacing a pitchfork, the two men terrified children wherever they went.

Meanwhile, Wright's friends came to his aid, led by Betty Kray in New York. She coordinated his application for a Guggenheim Foundation fellowship, securing a letter of recommendation from Robert Lowell and even mailing Wright the stamped return envelopes for his signed forms. The praise for his new work that mattered most continued to arrive. Tom McGrath wrote from Fargo, saying, "I keep reading at your book and it keeps being very good." On the same day, Wright received a letter from a young Ohioan poet traveling in England who had ordered a copy of *The Branch* from America. "Tonight, in a room the size of a cupboard, I am broke, I am getting a cold, intermittently I am thinking of someone who never comes anymore, and nothing really matters. I am radiant with happiness because James Wright exists." Her letter is the first in the long correspondence Wright had with Mary Oliver.

Wright's friendship with Roland Flint remained essential to him. On November 22, as news spread of President John F. Kennedy's assassination in Dallas, Wright called Flint to ask if he could stay the night with him and his wife. The next morning, as they took a long walk together, Wright's thoughts turned to Roethke, who had died three months before. He said many of his poems by heart, and though Flint had then read little of Roethke's poetry, he soon decided to write his doctoral thesis on his work. Hearing that Roethke's body had been cremated, Wright said, "Fair enough. The old master always seemed about to burst into flames with life."

Wright felt very much alone in St. Paul. In December, he returned to read at the College of St. Teresa in Winona without pay, just for the company of the Catholic nuns and their students. The following day— his thirty-sixth birthday—he received a note of thanks and motherly advice. "When you first walked down the platform I was struck by what

I recognized later was sadness," Sister Bernetta Quinn wrote, encouraging him to "fight this tendency to depression." Wright's demeanor felt at odds with the "new serenity" of the poems he read. She cautioned him to never let that "gentle seriousness . . . sink into solemnity, lest the ghost of Theodore Roethke haunt you."

The possibility that Macalester might dismiss him intensified Wright's depression. A series of missed deadlines for administrative paperwork—as well as missed classes—prompted Livingston, the English Department chair, to rebuke him in a tone of cold contempt, insisting that he was "obviously repeating the pattern" that had cost him his job at the university. Wright typed a long letter of apology and self-defense "for the sake of friendship," admitting his failures but pleading to remain at Macalester. "I am shipwrecked, yes; but I must exert my own arms in order to stay afloat and find my way back to shore." But Wright continued to struggle with the demands of ordinary life. When a colleague at Macalester drove him back to the furnished room he rented in the attic of a house, Wright invited him in for a drink. "Come up with me and I'll show you my shirts." On a horizontal pole at shoulder height hung two dozen identical white shirts.

When Wright arrived in Ohio to visit his parents and siblings that Christmas, his brother's wife, Helen, didn't recognize him at first. "When he came to the house, he almost looked like a tramp, because none of his clothes fit him right and his topcoat was almost to the ground." Wright had adopted his father's old green overcoat with the soot of the mills and the smell of the factory still in it.

> Clothes didn't mean anything to him. In his raggedy old suitcase were all those symphony records. When we'd get through eating, and we would all go in the living room and start yakking, he'd say, "Would you mind if I go out and sit by the window here?"—and he started writing. Perspiration would just fall all over his face. That symphony music was all we heard that weekend, but that would ease his mind as he was writing.

A new portrait of Dudley was published that month in *The Hudson Review*, the poem "Youth." His father appears in each of Wright's books, most vividly in *Shall We Gather at the River*. In "Two Postures Beside a Fire," the first of two ten-line stanzas is in rhymed iambic meter and shows the gentleness and devotion found in Vallejo's poems about his family. The second stanza, in free verse, turns back upon the speaker, whose lined face and nervous hands accentuate the difference and the distance between them, a distance he realizes cannot be bridged. But the poem "Youth" depicts precisely this figurative communion. For Wright, "His song remains secret"; his father's anger and frustration at a life of hard labor were hidden from his son. As memory drifts back to childhood—"He came home as quiet as the evening"—past and future seem to converge in the word "home." In death, "his ghost will drift home / To the Ohio River." The poem's concluding lines dissolve time: "The waters flow past, older, younger / Than he is, or I am."

In January 1964, Wright fought off another bitter cold Minnesota winter by teaching a class called "The Spirit of Comedy" during Macalester's brief interim term. He assigned readings from Dickens, Fielding, Cervantes, and Twain, but ranged further, to works by Nathanael West, Ring Lardner, and Flannery O'Connor. The class met every afternoon for several hours, and Wright brought in guest speakers such as John Berryman, whose laughter merged with Wright's at the back of the room when they projected Chaplin's early films. Roland Flint joined Wright in a class devoted to a fellow Ohioan, the comedian Jonathan Winters, who inspired a comic routine that Wright became famous for. "He really would execute, unexpectedly, a surprisingly nimble dance step, hold his hands slightly aloft in an oddly if awkwardly expressive gesture and say, 'A butcher by day, by night—*a fabulous tap dancer!*'"

In the spring semester, Wright welcomed Freya Manfred, the daughter of the novelist Fred Manfred, into his classes on Shakespeare and twentieth-century literature. Wright had first read her poetry when she was thirteen. "I always felt an immediate connection with him," she remembered, "because he had this utterly vulnerable but powerful quality." Wright appeared to know all of *Anna Karenina* by heart, along with great swaths of Dostoevsky and Conrad. In his Shakespeare class, Manfred had the same impression: Wright spoke without notes and quoted passages from *Hamlet* and *Othello* at will. He loved the character of Iago—"the devil in the guise of man"—and instructed them to *"pretend in this play that everything he says is the opposite of what he means."* For Manfred, this opened up "the whole magic of Shakespeare," and showed Wright's effort to treat his students as equals. But his methods and demeanor in the classroom felt threatening to many of his fellow professors.

Wright worked to regain his faith in his abilities as a teacher and the trust of his colleagues by redoubling his efforts that spring. From February through May, in separate loose-leaf notebooks just four by seven inches, Wright typed hundreds of pages of lectures. Ten pages dated February 28, for example, bear the heading: "Kafka: The Few Blessed Facts of a Commercial Failure." Dostoevsky, John Stuart Mill, Freud, Ortega y Gasset, Unamuno, Fitzgerald, Eugene O'Neill, Willa Cather—whatever he taught that spring is elucidated by these notes, with biographical and critical sources mixed with quotations and personal reflections.

As Wright introduced his students to the character of Iago that February, he began a new poem in his journal that became a centerpiece in his new manuscript. After typing out a sequence of nine short poems by Tu Fu, he wrote the following lines by hand:

> I try my best, but I can discover no evil
> In that girl's beautiful face,
> In the cashier's window.

The chance juxtaposition in Wright's journal of Tu Fu's lyrics with these new lines of his own is preserved in the final version of "Before a Cashier's Window in a Department Store." In this first handwritten draft, the cashier's face rises like the moon over the shoulder of the young store manager who confronts the destitute poet. In the final version, the penultimate stanza borrows images from Tu Fu's "Traveling Northward," in which the poet crosses a battlefield in moonlight. Another handwritten draft on the reverse side of this journal page, "Reaching for Yuan Chen," would become, after months of revision, one of the "Poems to a Brown Cricket." Throughout the spring of 1964, Wright's journal filled with passages from T'ang Dynasty poets, from Rumi, Hafez, and the Christian mystic Jakob Boehme. These spiritual sources were like driftwood he reached for to keep afloat.

Wright lived in a series of furnished rooms throughout his time in St. Paul, in suburban neighborhoods not far from F. Scott Fitzgerald's childhood home. When Susan Lamb visited Minneapolis in March,

Wright insisted on meeting her, and the two talked for hours at a restaurant. She could see he was in a bad way: heavier and unkempt, "sort of a sad character." He railed against "the man who had fired him" from the university, prompted, Wright told her, by disapproval of Wright's new poems. But the most tenacious cause of his depression was getting "cut out" from his two sons. Lamb recognized the same intensity in him she had known in high school, and his tendency to do everything to excess. She never forgot the brown tobacco stains on Wright's fingers. Inscribing a gift copy of *The Branch*, he chose a line in Latin from Virgil's Third *Georgic*: "The best days are the first to flee." Lamb picked up the check for their meal, but when they parted, Wright still needed bus fare back to St. Paul.

————

Just before giving a talk at a student honors society gathering at Macalester on March 9, Wright learned by chance of the sudden death of his Kenyon professor Denham Sutcliffe, whom he spoke of as "the most magnificent teacher I ever had." His talk that evening had a heartfelt and forceful intensity, and the next day Wright received a letter of praise from Macalester's president, Dr. Harvey Rice, effectively inviting him to return to teach the following year. This recognition had a profound effect on Wright; he refers to it in letters months later. His talk on "The Art of Translation" coincided with the completion of his collection of Storm's prose, which he mailed to Doctorow that week. When he learned in April he'd been awarded the Guggenheim fellowship to begin in the fall, his good fortune began to seem unreal. "My conviction is that hopeful things don't happen to me, and so to hell with them," Wright told Liberty. He finally requested a year's postponement of the grant, both in gratitude to Macalester and to preserve the feeling of sanctuary he had found there. After months of failure and discouragement, Wright began to allow the possibility of hope, "that perhaps I need only try to follow the voice out of the many voices, that bids me stand and live."

At the end of winter, Wright enjoyed an ecstatic, drunken reunion with James Dickey in Minneapolis before traveling to New York to read at the Guggenheim Museum with Robert Bly. The audience greeted Wright warmly, and he responded with a confident, dynamic reading of poems both old and very new, concluding with an untitled draft of "Old Age Compensation" that he read from his journal. As always, he began by saying other poets' work, and introduced a new sequence of his own called "Poems to a Brown Cricket" by reciting Tu Fu's celebrated poem "The Cricket." To Wright's astonishment, Bly had just read a new poem of his own addressed to this same cricket, a fellow lodger in the chicken-house on the farm.

Wright visited friends during his brief stay in New York, including Doctorow, Kunitz, and Roger Hecht, who all praised his new work. *The Sixties* No. 7 also appeared that winter, with three of Wright's best translations: part of Neruda's "Heights of Macchu Picchu" and his "Some Beasts," as well as Vallejo's "Eternal Dice." His translations of Rilke, however, remained unknown during Wright's lifetime. In the spring of 1964, he returned to eight poems he had abandoned a year be-fore, even though the Rilke estate continued to prohibit new English translations. Among various drafts in a black spring binder are revisions to versions of the "Sixth Duino Elegy" and "Departure of the Prodigal Son"—a parable at the heart of Jakob Boehme's teachings.

> To take all this on oneself and in vain perhaps
> To give up what one possessed, in exchange for
> Dying alone, not knowing why—
>
> Is this the entrance to a new life?

This idea of rebirth appears often in Wright's letters and journals that spring; his ongoing fascination with Boehme is rooted in this imagery.

———

In April, Wright again spoke on the art of translation, giving a talk called "The Surprising Joy of the Translator" at a Catholic women's college in Duluth—traveling hundreds of miles for little more than the cost of the bus ticket. The translator, he wrote, "is not a hack, but an *apprentice*, who at some point inevitably discovers that he is performing an *anon-ymous* act of devotion, & is shocked to find himself freely, wonderfully *happy*." The success of his versions of Storm's stories shored up Wright's self-esteem; by fulfilling a promise to himself, his spirits be-gan to lift.

Wright also found encouragement from a young Swedish poet who had translated two of his poems from *The Branch*. Tomas Tranströmer's letter arrived in care of the Sixties Press on the same day that Bly had driven into Minneapolis to find Tranströmer's book *The Half-Finished Heaven* in the university library. "There was an instant kind of communion" among the three poets, Bly later wrote; Tranströmer said he felt closer to the two Americans than he did to Swedish poets of his own generation. He soon began a lifelong correspondence with Bly, as they set about translating each other's work. The readership for Tranströmer's work grew steadily over the next four decades, culminating in his receiving the Nobel Prize in 2011. At the time, his letter proved that the poems of Bly and Wright—and *The Sixties* magazine—had begun to win an audience in Europe.

Two important new poems appeared in typescript in late March and early April: "Homage to Little Crow" and "Rip." The eight lines Wright deleted from the opening of the latter poem reveal how the two poems began close in conception:

America? Oh,
What kind of lost heaven on earth is this for a ghost
To rise from the dead to?
But I thought I was born here; I thought this was my place.
My life! This shrivelling scar,
This healed grave whose door glides easily open
And does not make a sound.
America?

The poem's title, "Rip," fits multiple meanings, including a scar or tear; a dissolute vagrant or worn-out horse; a series of oaths; the letters carved on a tombstone; and the turbulence of a suckhole in a river. It also calls up Rip Van Winkle, as the poet wanders along the shore of a river, merging the Ohio with the Mississippi and denying "the passage of time." The landscape then turns inward: "Close by a big river, I am alive in my own country, / I am home again." Wright's personal ghosts find company with those that haunt American history. On a sheet of his therapist's stationery that spring, Wright began a poem inspired by Lorca's "Ode to Walt Whitman" whose title captures a dominant theme of his work in the mid-sixties: "The Presences of the Dead in America." Describing Wright's new poems to Tranströmer, Bly observed how they were "made of mingled streams of savagery and tranquility."

Wright was living at a fever pitch. He drank constantly and his emotions remained always near the surface. He had grown dependent upon Barbara Thompson but still lived alone, moving from one shabbily furnished room to another, all within a mile of the Macalester campus. Writing to good friends after years of silence became part of his struggle against loneliness. In congratulating Louis Simpson on receiving the Pulitzer Prize for *At the End of the Open Road*, Wright admits that his letter is, in part, an effort to restore his sanity and overcome "the weird dumbness and paralysis of will and heart that lay on me like a black cloud for month after month after month during the past year."

As the spring term drew to a close, Wright became caught up in "a kind of fury of ecstatic writing." In mid-June, Wright began correcting page proofs for his Storm translations, with the book slated to appear in August. He tells his brother Jack, "I am astounded at it. I worked through hell for 2½ years on it, and I was afraid it would sound like hell. It doesn't. It sounds like Storm." Storm's lyricism had a subtle, persistent influence on Wright's poems. In his foreword to *The Rider on the White Horse, and Other Stories*, Wright describes the quality of Storm's prose that proved so important to Thomas Mann and others, using the German term *stimmung*: "a certain luminosity of descriptive language intended to express the author's emotional attachment to the objects and the persons described." Many of the poems in *The Branch*—including "Milkweed" and "To the Evening Star: Central Minnesota"—achieve this effect. Wright's affinity with the melancholy spirit of German Romanticism made him an ideal translator for Storm. "I find myself strangely troubled by the thought of the loneliness and homesickness that haunt his stories"—a quality of feeling that later drew him to translate the work of Hesse. Wright's letter to his brother that June ends with a poignant exclamation: "Dear God, I want to go home."

———

Nearly two years after their divorce, friends of Jim and Liberty from Seattle, Franz Schneider and his wife, "fairly naïvely thought we could get the two together again." They invited them to their home in Spokane at the end of June. Marshall and Franz Wright, now ages five and eleven, traveled by bus with their mother from San Francisco for the longest visit they had had with their father since the divorce. Though he and Liberty spent long hours in conversation, the Schneiders quickly abandoned hope for a reconciliation. And as often happened, Wright made himself at home in the comfort of another family. "Jim would stay up late and drink and listen to Beethoven or whoever was uppermost in his mind. At the same time he was reading the galley proofs for Theodor Storm's *Schimmelreiter* novellas. It began to drive my wife crazy because he didn't just listen to music, he had it turned up to the *n*th degree." Schneider was familiar with Wright's fanatical obsession with music, but the enormity of Wright's drinking shocked him. Their stay lasted almost a week and was punctuated by long hours when the two friends would recite poems together in German.

After two weeks back in St. Paul, Wright again traveled north, returning to Moorhead State College to teach for five weeks in the second summer session. As in the summer of 1962, the intense five-day schedule included both literature and composition classes, but Wright felt welcome there. Living just off campus, he resumed his long, solitary walks into the prairies south of Fargo and revisited the trackside blue-collar bars. From Moorhead, Wright sent a letter to his son Marshall for his sixth birthday and included the gift of a poem, "For the Marsh's Birthday." It presents an odd variation on Wright's poem "Father," again imagining a child's consciousness before birth. Addressing his son directly, it begins, "I was alone once, waiting / For you, what you might be." Both the letter and poem suggest how difficult it was for Wright to relate to his sons when they were young; he felt more at ease with them as they got older. As Marshall recalled, "We understood that we were cared for, and deeply loved and deeply missed." But Wright had little talent for parenting and no real presence in their lives.

Wright faced two large classes in twentieth-century literature and another in freshman English when the new semester began at Macalester in September; dreading the start of the new term, he seemed to somehow intuit an approaching collapse. When Barbara Thompson forced an end to their relationship, Wright returned to psychiatric care—his first hospital stay since August 1959. He spent time in three separate hospitals over the next six weeks and admitted to thoughts of suicide. In a letter to Robert Mezey dated November 17, two months after his breakdown, Wright is still plagued by "unspeakable demons of agony and despair." In losing Thompson's practical support—she was known to bring him lunch and wash his clothes when he taught at Macalester—Wright fell into a state of helplessness. He even asked Truesdale and his wife,

Joan, if he could take a room in their house, though the couple had three young children. "My family life was, in his quite naïve view, a picture of the emotional stability he longed for and idealized," Truesdale recalled. Wright did stay in their home on occasion that fall, Joan allowed. "That was a very black period in Jim's life." A poem he drafted in the hospital in October shows an odd mix of surrender and resilience. It concludes:

As for me, I am strolling with Walt Whitman
Between two ugly and shattered galaxies
Of blinded mallards, looking for Issa's footprints
Among the glazed feathers and ruins of the dead,
Where the branch broke after all.

With the Blys traveling in Europe, others offered help, including Berryman, who taught a few of Wright's classes while he was ill. When Wright resumed teaching at the end of October, Ray Livingston shuttled him back and forth from the hospital to meet his classes. As Wright told Mezey, his lectures were sometimes marked by "a kind of ferocious brilliance" meant to thwart his deep depression. When John Beauchamp visited him one evening in "the nuthouse," as Wright called it, they drove to Berryman's home, where the two poets drank continuously into the early morning, immersed in a discussion of Lowell's translations of Baudelaire.

Wright improvised a kind of therapy by initiating two separate, obsessive exchanges of letters with much younger women. Prairie Dern, an aspiring actress, had been a student of his at the University of Minnesota; he had met "Deanna" in the hospital. He posted dozens of letters to them both in November and December, many resembling those he had written to Jenny five years earlier, affirming his love and resolving to make his life over to one of prayer. Wright copied out passages from Yeats, Raleigh, Dickinson, Jiménez, Hafez, and others, the books that continued to absorb him. Toward Deanna he shows a sense of responsibility for her well-being, as though keeping a promise to her. As a gift to Dern, he typed out "Lazy on a Saturday Morning"—the poem inspired by his brief romance with Sexton. "My new book is blossoming!" he wrote to Dern in October. He had started working in earnest to organize his new manuscript, "and now I know where to give it—oh, that is for the book's sake everything."

Once out of the hospital, Wright faced recurring periods of severe depression. An enraged letter to his therapist in mid-November describes his break with Thompson and includes quotations from the Book of Job. Wright resurrects a fantasy of traveling to India to find a guru who will teach him how to pray. "From that instant, I will absolutely renounce everything that I have known as 'life' on the earth so far. I am heartsick at my life, and I just do not want to live it any longer." He details a scheme that will allow him to continue child support payments as a hack writer for magazines. With a tone of finality, Wright ends by thanking Sukov for his efforts to help him.

Within days of his letter to Sukov, Wright received a postcard from Bill Knott—a poet he had never met, who wrote of his utter loneliness in Chicago. Wright responded by pledging to visit him on the weekend after Thanksgiving in the company of two pretty girls and a bunch of fresh bananas. He then made good on his promise. The meanness of Wright's existence matched Knott's own at the time; the two shared a commitment to poetry that led them both into a kind of monastic extremity. When Knott wrote to thank Wright for his generosity, he confessed, "I think your visit upset and frightened me somewhat. I had never come in such close, continuous contact with one as devoted and dedicated to poetry."

Wright struggled to keep his balance as the year drew to a close and the demands of teaching increased at semester's end. Upon returning from Chicago, Wright began revising the poem "Rip" and a companion piece he called his "Casida cursing the city of Minneapolis on my eternal departure therefrom." It had been inspired by Lorca's *Poet in New York*, particularly his "Ode to Walt Whitman," which Wright was then translating. He titled a new draft, dated December 2, 1964, "An Ode Written in Honor of the New Municipal Expansion Program in the City of Minneapolis." Half a dozen complete revisions followed in quick succession, each draft gradually closer to the cornerstone of *Shall We Gather at the River*, "The Minneapolis Poem."

After grading papers, Wright flew back to Ohio to spend Christmas with his parents in New Concord, together with his brothers, his sister, and their families. He arrived before his siblings and, after talking with his parents, claimed some "essential solitude." As twilight lingered into evening, he wrote one of his most lyrical letters—addressed to a young woman, a former student at Macalester. Wright describes a man he knew in childhood who attended every funeral in town, and who remained behind with the sexton after all the others had gone and night fell in the hilltop graveyard above Martins Ferry. The image of them together makes him glad—personifications of "the sociable twilight, and the night with a spade on its shoulder." Wright had recently been astounded to learn that the Hindu deity Shiva, known to Westerners in his aspect as the Destroyer, was revered for his abundance and good faith.

Sometimes he can be found at crossroads when they are deserted by all save the loneliest of persons, who stand at their own crossroads, amazed, as if just that moment wakened while sleepwalking, wondering where to turn. I have myself wakened thus, a couple of times. Shiva (the pious say) knows where to turn. That, you will agree, is a useful thing to know. He is the deity of regeneration.

I am glad that night has fallen and that it is still twilight in Ohio.

16

The rootlessness of things

January 1965–April 1966

At the end of December 1964, Wright spent a long afternoon talking with the seventy-six-year-old John Crowe Ransom in Gambier. As he wrote to his parents upon returning to St. Paul, he had felt "happier than I have in years" while in Ohio. Determined to leave Minnesota at the end of the school year before his Guggenheim fellowship commenced, Wright began saying goodbye to friends from Seven Corners that winter. He presented Erik Storlie with his personal copy of William Hung's biography and translations of Tu Fu. The nomadic life of the poet held little romance for Wright, who had no idea where he would go at the end of his exile in the Midwest.

In January, Liberty made an impulsive decision that proved damaging to her two young sons. After considering a handful of suitors from a San Francisco dating service, she met a Hungarian refugee named Miklos "Michael" Kovacs; five weeks later, the two drove all night to Reno, Nevada, to be married. Within four months, Liberty and the boys were living in Walnut Creek, an hour west of San Francisco, in a house with Kovacs's mother. A soldier in the German army in the Second World War, Kovacs had little interest in the boys and punished them severely.

Wright did not learn of the abuse his sons endured until years later; at the time of his ex-wife's remarriage, he was absorbed by the anxieties of his own life. "Plainly I sit at a crossroads," Wright worried on March 18.

Betty Kray—not given to sitting for long—continued to find practical solutions to his difficulties. He needed a teaching job and he needed money, so Kray arranged Wright's first extensive reading tour in four years—eleven colleges in California over a span of two weeks in late April and early May. Wright encouraged the idea as a chance to see Franz and Marshall; his role as a father had now been reduced to his feeling of missing them.

Dylan Thomas created a kind of template for the arduous tours of consecutive readings that became part of Wright's life as a poet. "I never seem to sleep in a bed any more," Thomas once wrote his wife from Kenyon, "only on planes & trains. I'm hardly living; I'm just a voice on wheels." Like Thomas, Wright sustained himself with alcohol, and at every reading he captivated his audience. At UC Berkeley on April 23, Wright ranged among the work of two dozen poets: Tagore, Rilke, Chesterton, Hardy, Surrey, Roethke, nursery rhymes, and old Irish curse poems. Defending poets he felt were unjustly neglected, his voice grew urgent and impassioned. As at his other stops, Wright said more poems by others than he did of his own, a generosity of spirit reinforced by the humor and animation of a gifted storyteller.

The readings were well attended and drew wide praise. Briefly reunited with his sons at San Francisco State University on April 26, Wright began with a poem translated from the Gaelic by Thomas MacDonagh called "The Yellow Bittern"—his favorite apologia for a drunken poet. Poems by Whitman, Robinson, Ransom, and Neruda followed; he concluded with "A Blessing." Seamless and compelling, the reading showed him utterly assured and at his best. It astonished many that Wright could perform so well so often, given the quantities of alcohol he consumed during those two weeks. At Fresno State College on April 27, Philip Levine was amazed he could stand at the podium.

> I had to wake him up to take him because he'd been drinking in the morning and the reading was in the afternoon. When I woke him he said, "I need a book." And I said, "I've got your books here, let's see, they're in my . . ." He said, "No, no, I don't need *my* books. *A* book, without a book jacket." So I handed him a thin book of poetry and, of course, he recited all the poems from memory. He faked it! He'd turn the pages, and then recite a poem, holding his hand over the cover.

Wright spent three days with Levine and his family, and the poets stayed up late talking and drinking. He had just visited with his sons, and Levine saw how shaken the experience had left him. "He was stocky and strong, but I felt emotionally he was not nearly as steady as I was. At times I thought he was close to tears."

Herbert Lindenberger had arranged Wright's April 30 reading on the UC campus at Riverside, east of Los Angeles. He greeted the poet warmly at the airport, but by the time he drove Wright to his brother Jack's the next day, he was afraid to be alone in the car with him. Upon first arriving at Lindenberger's home, Wright took a bottle of bourbon from the cupboard and announced, "I don't drink for the taste, I drink for the effect." To Lindenberger's wife, Claire, he later declared: "I'm not an alcoholic, I'm a drunk." "That distinction was very important to him," she recalled, "and I think it was a matter of class identity." Wright drank all through lunch; after Lindenberger woke him that afternoon for his reading, Wright spiked his coffee with vodka. As he then approached the podium, Wright made a bizarre, prayer-like gesture, grasping his shoulders and forcing his eyes closed, his body swaying. Lindenberger saw this as part of his performance, announcing to the audience that he was drunk—as Roethke or Dylan Thomas might do. And like them, he gave a magnificent reading.

While staying with his brother Jack in Venice, Wright read at UCLA and spent a night drinking with James Dickey; he concluded the tour with readings at UC Davis and Stanford University. Henry and Elizabeth Esterly greeted him at the end of his final reading, and when they invited him to stay with them in Cupertino that summer, Wright gratefully accepted. He returned briefly to St. Paul to store his few belongings. Most of his books were already at the Bly farm; many others were now scattered among friends. At the Truesdales he stored boxes of dirty shirts and a collection of small owl figurines.

———

Exhausted, Wright arrived in early June and spent more than two months with the Esterlys in Cupertino, in the foothills of the Santa Cruz Mountains west of San Jose. He soon began helping with gardening chores on the property, "tossing heavy sacks of feed around like a gentleman-stevedore" or picking apricots. In San Francisco he attended classical music concerts and met up with John Logan and an old Seven

Corners friend, Lyle Tollefson. But his new poems became Wright's main preoccupation. On July 6 he wrote, "I have now shaken my head clear and gone back into my book, which is of course a dark book. It is going to be called *Washed Up By Winter*. I am ashamed of myself, but I am not ashamed of my book."

Wright spent the early hours of July 15 composing a "long grieving letter" to Prairie Dern. Upon hearing Maurice Ravel's "Le Tombeau de Couperin" on the radio—that "glittering, sad, flawless composition"—Wright describes his rituals of self-discipline at Kenyon, when he was haunted by "the terror of poverty and defeat." Taking stock of the years in between, he refuses to be a victim of self-pity or despair. Wright's Guggenheim fellowship, releasing him from teaching for a year, was reason enough for hope. In addition, three consecutive issues of *The New Yorker*, from the end of June into early July, carried a new Wright poem, including his "Poems to a Brown Cricket" and "For the Marsh's Birthday." The publication of Marshall's poem coincided with his son's birthday at the end of July, and Wright spent "two good weeks" with his sons that summer.

Robert Bly wrote a long letter in July, describing his first meeting with Tomas Tranströmer in Sweden and inviting Wright to stay on the farm in September when the Blys returned from Europe. For Wright, restoring correspondence with old friends became a kind of ritual. "Writing to you again is something like rising from the dead," he told Donald Hall, "and I don't know how to apologize for being dead." Faced with the official beginning of his fellowship term on September 1, Wright confessed to his brother Jack a feeling of desperation. "This God damned Guggenheim, which apparently would be a blessing to many others, seems so far to be a grim matter to me; that is, I am still trying to clear my head enough to determine exactly where to go and what to do."

Wright flew back to Minnesota on September 12 and arrived at the farm during a visit from the poet Paul Zweig, with "several days of discussion, disquisition, and intellectual exploration that can only be called blistering in its intensity, lavish in its excitement." When Wright spoke of traveling to England in the fall, Zweig invited Wright to stay with him in Paris. Feeling more confident, Wright sent off for a copy of the birth certificate he needed for a new passport and happily returned to the chickenhouse to revise his new poems. On the whole, his new book continued to be "pretty jagged and difficult going." The uncertainty of his plans magnified his anxiety. At the conclusion of a plaintive letter to Hall at the end of September, he wrote, "I am sick of being so rootless and unsettled and alone. I feel like a hobo in the thirties."

In October, Wright received a letter from Hardie St. Martin in Barcelona with poems by the Spanish poet Pedro Salinas that St. Martin wanted Wright to translate. Philip Levine had traveled to Spain with his family that fall and, with St. Martin's help, he also began working on translations. They both looked forward to hosting Wright when he arrived in Europe that winter.

Before making final plans, however, Wright returned to his parents' home in New Concord. He spent two months with them at the end of the year, his last stay in Ohio of such length. He invited Bly to join him there to meet Dudley and Jessie. After a journey by bus from Minneapolis to Washington, D.C., with nearly a hundred others to attend one of the first mass protests against the Vietnam War, Bly came to Ohio for a series of readings and stayed with Wright and his parents at the end of November. Wright had warned Bly about Jessie—she kept Trotsky's *Collected Works* in the living room and talked back to the television—but the two got on famously. "She was a very energetic woman, with a lot of goodwill and a tremendous amount of humor," Bly recalled. "Immediately you could see that a lot of Jim's humor came directly from her." He understood how Jessie had once dominated her family and saw the strong bond Wright had with this intensely verbal woman.

In a letter to Tranströmer from New Concord on December 1, Bly wrote, "Jim feels very strong now, and very happy about poetry. I am too. How wonderful to be able to live in a time when something fresh can be written!" But as the march on Washington made evident, the mood of the country was darkening as it slipped deeper into the conflict in Southeast Asia. Wright's desire to travel abroad grew in part from his disgust with the escalation of U.S. involvement in Vietnam.

Before leaving for Europe, however, Wright wanted to secure a teaching position for the following year. Nothing came of numerous interviews at Ann Arbor, where Hall taught; many knew Wright's reputation as a drinker, which defeated his chances of working there. With the encouragement of Roger Hecht and Betty Kray, Wright resolved to live in New York that winter. Kray even welcomed him to stay with her while he looked for a job. For Wright, "Minneapolis" had become another name for hell on earth. "I have had so many failures there," he told Carol Bly in

January, "failures of every kind imaginable, and so many wounds, and so many defeats, that I just came to realize that the city has become, to me, a city of horrors. If only I could find some other place to live, I think I could be well again."

———

Though meant as a stopover before leaving for England and Europe, New York City offered the possibility of teaching at dozens of colleges and universities, and Wright had many friends there. In January, he stayed briefly with Kray and her husband, the composer Vladimir Ussachevsky, in their apartment in Morningside Heights near the Columbia University campus. Wright talked for hours with Dimir, who had a vast collection of classical records and three different reel-to-reel tape recorders in his living room, which he used in his process of composition.

Betty Kray had become the executive director of the Academy of American Poets after resigning from the 92nd Street Y's Poetry Center in protest over an act of censorship in 1962. At the Academy, she worked alongside its founder, the formidable Marie Bullock. Kray's Poets-in-the-Schools initiative, introduced in New York in 1966, would become a nationwide program funded by the National Endowment for the Arts. In myriad ways, Kray put her shrewdness and energy to work on behalf of poets, who she knew must "live by their wits," connecting them with readings, with jobs, even with apartments. "She was the center of the poetry universe at the time, certainly in New York City," the poet Gigi Bradford recalled. "She knew everybody." Kray arranged two reading tours for Wright during his first months in New York, and he had use of an office at the Academy whenever he needed a typewriter and privacy to work.

At the end of January, Wright interviewed at Sarah Lawrence College, where the poet Jane Cooper met him in the main hall to escort him to the president's office. Years earlier, Wright had praised her by name—and one poem in particular—in a review he'd written of an anthology. "When he saw me, he flopped down on his knees, looked soulfully upward, and announced, 'Is this the author of "The Faithful" that I see before me?' Of course, I burst out laughing, but I have to confess I was awfully pleased." The college, however, was looking for a creative writing instructor, and Wright insisted on teaching literature; it always surprised people to learn of his doctoral degree.

In a letter from the farm on February 7, Bly begged Wright for a proper address to forward his mail and urged him to seek out Galway Kinnell in Greenwich Village. A tall, striking Irishman with an expressive voice and tremendous memory for verse, Kinnell had long admired Wright's work and welcomed his friendship. He had published two celebrated books of poems and translations of François Villon; he had also traveled throughout Europe and the Middle East and took an active role in the civil rights movement. With Kray's help, Kinnell made his living as an itinerant poet, traveling constantly for readings and guest teaching stints at colleges.

In the winter of 1966, Wright often arrived at Kinnell's Bethune Street apartment without notice late at night, carrying an armful of records. He always brought the album *Many a Mile*, by a young Native Canadian folk singer named Buffy Sainte-Marie. Over and over again, he would play the song "Until It's Time for You to Go"—at high volume, no matter the time of night. Wright seemed to respond to a quality of emotional yearning in her voice. "I understood something about him from his obsession with that song," Kinnell recalled. "One thing that struck me was the pain that one felt so clearly in his presence. I wouldn't exactly say that he *suffered*; I would say, more precisely, that he *hurt*. There was something so immediate and visible and *with cause* about it. It was as though he had no skin and whatever painful thing there was that came into his ken, just caused him an immediate hurt." Wright's fixations could be understood as an "obsessive *joy* that he was taking in," Kinnell believed. "Jim was remarkably capable of enthusiasm, much more so than perhaps anybody I knew, or had ever met."

Wright gave a reading with Denise Levertov at the University of Chicago at the end of February and was hosted by Paul Carroll, who recalled his "electric, all but unbearable intensities." Carroll described Wright's public persona as compounded of "wretchedness and grandeur"; in private, this demeanor was enlivened by "an infectious, bubbling, lopsided humor."

Early one Sunday morning in 1966 after a long, exuberant dinner party in his honor—during which Wright delighted everybody by his spirited recitations from memory of what was literally an anthology of Irish pub and curse songs, American Indian runes, Housman lyrics, and impersonations of Wilkins Micawber and other Dickensian characters—I was awakened by the sound of his voice reciting aloud to himself in the hallway between his guest room and our bedroom the entire sonnet by Allen Tate: "Ah, Christ, I love you rings to the wild sky." I was astonished: it was as if poetry were the air he breathed, the dreams he had dreamt.

It is ironic that Tate's poem figures among those that Wright recited to himself that winter. In April, after Tate learned that Bly had circulated copies of his bizarre letter to Wright defending his decision to have him fired, Tate blamed Wright for the embarrassment. Wright replied with the same groveling, abject tone he had once used to placate another southern aristocrat, James Dickey. His deference suggests he felt somehow inferior to them in class, that despite his doctoral degree he might still track mud across expensive carpets.

––––––

Wright walked all over Manhattan. In what he always considered a stroke of good luck, he found a room on the eighteenth floor of the Hotel Regent at 104th Street and Broadway on the Upper West Side, ten blocks south of Columbia University. His single room on the hotel's top floor had a closet, a kitchenette with a small refrigerator, "and a real honest-to-god bathroom," at a cost of $27.50 a week. Though warned that the neighborhood—largely black, with many Haitian and Puerto Rican immigrants—could be dangerous, Wright soon felt at home. With trees barren of leaves, looking west across Broadway he could glimpse the Hudson River a few blocks away.

His nomadic wandering over the previous eight months had left him feeling exhausted, and Wright grew uncertain of his plans to travel to England. Writing to a former student from his hotel room, he admits to being "temporarily settled" in New York. "In my own way, I grieve for the rootlessness of things, and of myself especially." His struggle with his new book of poems—already three years in the making—was "perhaps most agitating of all."

Wright's apprehension corresponded with the growing sense of unrest in the country. Following an uncertain series of events in the Gulf of Tonkin in August 1964, President Johnson had declared war on North Vietnam. Many thousands of American servicemen had already been deployed into the jungles of Vietnam—two hundred thousand in each of the years 1965 and 1966. By early 1968, more than half a million U.S. troops would be stationed there. Following the march on Washington in November 1965, Robert Bly and David Ray began planning a nationwide series of readings to protest the war. Working with Carol Bly, they gathered dozens of writers from around the country for antiwar "read-ins" on college campuses, beginning in March and continuing throughout the spring, under the banner American Writers Against the Vietnam War. The readings in March 1966 were the first of their kind.

When Bly phoned Wright from Portland, Oregon, on March 1, asking him to fly out to participate, he promptly "dropped everything" and arrived in time for the first readings, held at Portland State College on March 4 and Reed College on March 5. The first Portland reading drew an overflow crowd of five hundred. The second night, at Reed, featured an expanded roster of ten poets, including Lawrence Ferlinghetti, George Hitchcock, John Logan, and Louis Simpson. A writer from *The New York Times* noted how Wright's reading of "Autumn Begins in Martins Ferry, Ohio" moved some in the audience to tears, while Bly later called the three-hour Reed College event the most inspiring reading he had ever heard.

Bly noticed something strange at the first Portland reading that held true for other antiwar events where he appeared with Wright. The crowds were often tense and restless, but "when Jim Wright walked onstage, he would stand there for two or three seconds and the audience would become completely still. They didn't know who he was, but there was something in the body—some connection of soul and feeling in the body. Everyone just stopped, to hear what he had to say." Mark Strand, who first heard Wright read in the late 1960s, agreed. "I don't think there was any other poet who had that kind of power over an audience."

Following a third read-in on March 6 at the University of Washington in Seattle, Wright returned to New York to begin his own tour of colleges in Pennsylvania. Reading "circuits" remained a vital source of income; with seven appearances over a span of two weeks, Wright made almost seven hundred dollars after travel expenses. "Jim was among the all-time great performers of poetry," recalled John Haag, a professor at Penn State University and a friend of Wright's from Seattle. In his readings, Wright sustained a sense of counterpoint between the poems' metrical patterns and the natural rhythms of speech, articulating the craft that enriched his work. Wright spent three days with Haag, who saw what the intervening decade had cost the poet. Wright drank steadily and hardly slept. When he discovered Buffy Sainte-Marie's first record in Haag's collection, he played it incessantly, once declaring her "our greatest poet." Haag made a gift of the album, "hoping he'd spare it a little, but no luck."

After returning briefly to New York, Wright joined Bly at readings in Chicago and Milwaukee in mid-April, and at six other read-ins on East Coast campuses in early May. In a span of twelve weeks that spring, Wright took part in more than two dozen readings. He found relief in traveling, and made himself at home with the families of friends. When he stayed with Edgar Doctorow that spring in New Rochelle, New York, his host woke to find Wright sitting in his ribbed T-shirt at the kitchen table with "a tumbler of bourbon and a Pall Mall," reciting poetry to Doctorow's three young children. The eldest, named Jenny, prompted Leigh Hunt's poem "Jenny Kissed Me," before Wright "came up in history through Browning and Tennyson, and eventually got to Trakl, the German poet, and recited, as I blinked and drank my coffee, a poem about German decadence, and it was not yet eight o'clock in the morning."

Meanwhile, Betty Kray and Jane Cooper were trying to find a teaching position for Wright. Cooper alerted her friend Allen Mandelbaum, an acclaimed translator and Italian scholar teaching at Hunter College; with Kray's encouragement, Mandelbaum brought Wright to the attention of the English Department chair, David Stevenson. Wright interviewed at Hunter at the end of March, and a week later received an offer to teach at their uptown Bronx campus the coming fall. Wright called Bly to share the news, pleased to remain in New York, "to which he has taken an enormous liking," Bly wrote to Tranströmer. "He'll never get to Europe at all this year."

17

A real New Yorker

April–December 1966

In April 1966, following protest readings in Milwaukee and Chicago, Wright returned to New York to hear the poet Josephine Miles at the Poetry Center of the 92nd Street Y. His new colleague at Hunter David Stevenson and his wife, Joan, hosted a party for Miles afterward in their townhouse. Wright felt at ease and recited from his store of Irish poems, Roethke poems, and many others. Among the small group of two dozen, he noticed a slim, attractive woman in a blue skirt and white silk blouse. Before the party ended, Wright had discovered who she was. At the end of the night, when only one cab turned up for all of those standing at the curb, Edith Anne Runk found herself sitting in James Wright's lap. "I was so impressed by his phenomenal memory for poetry. I was in awe of him because he seemed so intelligent. I thought that, as a nursery school teacher, I couldn't be very stimulating to him. I knew something of poetry, but it stopped with Robert Frost."

Anne, too, had just learned Wright's name that night; she was glad to give him her phone number. However, Wright didn't call. Within days, he had left the city and came back infrequently in the weeks ahead. But as he later confessed, he recalled their first meeting in great detail, down to the Band-Aid she wore on her knee. Anne had taught with Joan Stevenson at the Walden School before becoming director of a Head Start program in Manhattan; in June, she returned to the South to resume civil rights work. She kept thinking about "this sort of rumpled teddy

bear reciting poem after poem after poem." Before she left the city for
the summer, Anne found an anthology of Irish poetry, "in case I ever
saw him again." She searched libraries and bookstores, but couldn't find
any poems by "Theodore Retkey."

In addition to readings, Wright also left New York every week that
spring to teach a modern poetry class at Franklin & Marshall College,
outside of Philadelphia. Robert Mezey was recovering from an illness, and
for many weeks Wright traveled by train to Lancaster, Pennsylvania,
and stayed overnight. Trading poems from memory, Mezey was one of
the few who could keep pace with Wright.

> When I felt better, I sat in on a couple of classes, and they were
> kind of marvelous, but very weird. Jim was reciting Dickens to
> them. It had nothing to do with modern poetry, but they were
> entranced, and so was I. Probably none of these kids had ever
> read Dickens, had only heard of him, and Jim was reciting page
> after page, chapter after chapter, doing all the voices, and it was a
> wonderful performance.

Bly and Kinnell had arranged more than a dozen antiwar readings
across the Northeast in a span of ten days at the beginning of May. For
readings in upstate New York, "Jim Wright, and Galway and I go by
airplane, hopping about like World War I aviators," Bly told Tranströmer.
At Cornell, Denise Levertov and the Jesuit priest, poet, and antiwar ac-
tivist Daniel Berrigan joined them onstage. A capacity crowd of 1,400
gathered in Oberlin College's Finney Chapel on May 7 to hear Bly,
Wright, and others. The next day, at the University of Pennsylvania in
Philadelphia, sixteen writers—including Allen Ginsberg and Susan
Sontag—appeared before another large audience. Wright's restraint and
self-possession made a sharp contrast with Bly's "Jeremiah-like" dia-
tribes against the coercive forces of mass culture.

———

Apart from a thorough and sympathetic essay by Ralph J. Mills, Jr.,
that the poet himself admired, critics had not stepped back to consider
Wright's decade-long career. Crunk now leapt to the task with an inspired, opinionated essay in *The Sixties* No. 8, which appeared late in

the spring of 1966. Bly's impressions arise as much from Wright's physical presence in a room as from his poems on the page. He admires *Saint Judas* for the way it "expresses a fierce, almost ferocious, will to survive," and praises Wright's recent poems for their patience and alertness, and a kind of modesty. "Mr. Wright's poems embody a calm conviction that his self is significant and worthwhile, which he affirms quietly. This conviction becomes one of the deepest emotions in *The Branch Will Not Break*." Bly also admires the "remarkable and rare goodwill" his poems show, a quality found in "the best Chinese poetry." But what impresses him most is Wright's "extremely powerful intellectual energy."

His personality as a man drives forward, disregarding the consequences. Deep in his personality is the plower who does not look back. Everyone recognizes this in his work instinctively, and it is probably one reason for the great affection people have for his work. His instinct is to push everything to extremes, to twist away and go farther. It is obvious that out of devotion to poetry, he would leave any job in the world, with no notice, or live in any way.

In June, Wright completed another important poem in his evolving manuscript, declaring in its opening lines: "To speak in a flat voice / Is all that I can do." Earlier that spring, Wright had called it "A Psalm of Degrees"; in five stanzas of eight lines each, the poem calls to mind the limping meters of the King James Psalms. Finally titled "Speak," the poem sustains a loose sequence of off rhymes in alternating lines, but the pattern breaks in the third stanza and the poet complicates his prayer by invoking an old love:

And Jenny, oh my Jenny
Whom I love, rhyme be damned,
Has broken her spare beauty
In a whorehouse old.
She left her new baby
In a bus-station can,
And sprightly danced away
Through Jacksontown.

The complex, composite figure that bears the name of Wright's Muse has taken on strange depths. Freed from any one identity, Wright can access more grief, more darkness, and more reality through the figure, expanding the range of his materials. "Jenny" gathers into herself many women—young and old, real and imagined. She becomes one of the ghost figures in *Shall We Gather at the River*, a kind of genius of place, invoked in the book's dedication as well as in its concluding poem, "To the Muse."

———

Before quitting the city for the summer, Wright joined Bly and three other translator-poets at the 92nd Street Y's Poetry Center, where Pablo Neruda gave his first reading in New York in more than two decades. In robust health and at the height of his powers, Neruda "at sixty-one, pours out poems, topical or introspective, as unselfconsciously as a troubadour," the poet and critic Selden Rodman wrote at the time. A thunderous standing ovation greeted Neruda when he appeared on the Poetry Center stage on June 11, 1966. Introduced as "a great American poet" by Archibald MacLeish, Neruda told the audience he had purchased yet another copy of Whitman's *Leaves of Grass* just that morning, "this book which I have bought so many times." Quoting lines he had turned to at random, Neruda concluded, "I am proud to be an obscure, small, faraway follower of Walt Whitman, a lover of everything that is done by reasoning men." H. R. Hays, Ben Belitt, Clayton Eshleman, and Bly then alternated with Wright, reading English versions prior to Neruda's bravura recitations in Spanish, with gusts of applause following each poem.

Wright gladly took up the Blys' invitation to come out to the farm at the beginning of July—his last lengthy stay in Madison. Mary was then four years old and Biddy, two. "Jim is fine as a guest," Bly wrote to Tranströmer on July 11. "He just broods silently, and wanders around like a rock with hair." He remained a member of the Bly family. Despite their disagreements, Wright's friendship with Bly was "very close, unbreakable," Kinnell observed.

They're very different people. James is always much more sober, in a way, and grave in his utterances. Things *impinged* upon him and he took them hard so he was often in a defensive position

with regard to the world. Things hurt him as if he had no protec-
tion at all. And Robert wasn't like that. Robert was very much on
top of things, and so he was a very good friend for James to have.
You know, Bly has basically a comic vision of life and James a
tragic vision.

Soon after Wright arrived at the farm, Louis Simpson joined them,
determined to "talk about poetry for a week." The leisure and ardent
conversation spurred Wright to finish two new poems along with six
translations of Miguel Hernández, part of a feature to appear in *The
Sixties* No. 9. When a long letter arrived from Hardie St. Martin with
detailed comments and line edits on translations of Neruda, Hernández, Lorca, and Vallejo, Bly and Wright fell back to work at the kitchen
table. Bly marveled at Wright's facility. "He has an incredible gift for
language and is surely the best translator of poetry in the United States,"
Bly told an interviewer that spring, praising Wright's ability to catch "the
emotional tone" of the original poet.

After visiting friends in St. Paul and Chicago, Wright took a bus to
New Concord, Ohio, at the end of August, reuniting with his sons at
their grandparents' home. Jessie and Dudley had not seen the boys, now
ages thirteen and eight, in more than four years. With great pride, Wright
told them of the reading he would give at the Library of Congress that
December.

Back in New York on September 1, Wright returned to the Hotel
Regent, overjoyed to secure the same eighteenth-floor apartment he had
rented in the spring. But living alone never got easier for him; he alternated among three dress shirts, and shuttled back and forth to the
cleaners. That month Wright began teaching at what was then known
as Hunter Uptown in a northwestern part of the Bronx. While the student body presented great ethnic diversity, many freshmen struggled
with English language skills. Wright carried a heavy course load, and
his largest classes were in English literature and in composition. But he
soon adapted to his daily subway commute, and phoned his brother Ted
in Ohio to boast excitedly of having his pocket picked—an initiation
that made him "a real New Yorker."

Wright had not forgotten the woman he had met back in April. When
he learned that she had asked about him, he set aside tickets for the
Stevensons to his upcoming reading at the Poetry Center of the 92nd

Street Y—along with "one for your friend, Miss Runk." On the Monday
before Thanksgiving, Wright read with Isabella Gardner, introduced by
John Logan. After praising Wright as "a man of letters in the ancient
sense," Logan impishly revealed that Wright carried the manuscript for
his new book in a paper sack. There was nothing provisional about
Wright's reading, though. Of the dozen poems he read, half were from
his collection of new work, heard in public for the first time. Miss Runk
was astonished. "I thought his poetry was unbelievable, fantastic. And
when he read, 'I have wasted my life,' I thought, 'I've got to do something
about that!'" When she arrived at her second literary party, she found
Wright in a huge armchair holding a large glass of bourbon. "He
greeted me and pulled me down on the arm of the chair, opened his
wallet and showed me a picture of his two sons. And we just talked for
the rest of the evening."

Anne Runk did not realize at first how significant it was for Wright
to share that photo. She was a year younger than him, tall and willowy
with shoulder-length brown hair. Her green eyes became mischievous
when she laughed, which she did easily. She was hungry for literature
and good conversation; her gaiety and refined social grace captivated
the poet. Anne was now teaching at the Westside Community Nursery
School in Manhattan, having spent the summer in Georgia as the director of a new Head Start school—part of the push for integration. The
previous summer, in 1965, she'd helped lead day-care workshops for local
black women and spent four days in jail in Newton, Georgia, after her
arrest at a biracial march in support of voter registration.

Like Wright, Anne had been deeply attached to her maternal grandmother, though the fortunes of those matriarchs were poles apart. When
Edith Hoyt Smith married Eugene McKibbon Froment in 1904, they
united two distinguished lines of New York society. Their daughter
Louise, Anne's mother, was a bright but troubled child in a prominent
and wealthy family; there is no record of her social debut. She fell in love
with the handsome, profligate William North Runk, the exuberant son
of another wealthy family who summered on Nantucket. Anne's parents
married in June 1927 and lived near Bill's mother in Greenwich, Connecticut, where Edith Anne was born on February 23, 1929.

Until her late adolescence—and throughout the Depression—Anne
did not want for anything. By the age of seven she was the oldest of three
daughters who were cared for by a live-in maid. Her father worked for a

Manhattan jewelry firm, and he and his wife enjoyed hosting cocktail parties in Greenwich, parading their girls in front of guests before the maid put them to bed. Outwardly, their lives appeared idyllic. But Anne's mother suffered from a bipolar disorder; in manic phases, she became entirely absent from her children. As a teenager, Anne took on more of the care of her sisters, Jane and Louise. In 1942, her father started his own jewelry business in Washington, D.C., where Anne completed high school. But William Runk's drinking and the stress of caring for his wife combined to ruin his health and brought hardship to his family. Runk died in 1960 at the age of sixty following surgery on his diseased liver. Anne's mother and father remained distant figures for her, and their fall from prosperity made her prudent and careful about money. As a young woman, she came to depend on her mother's parents, the Froments. "My grandparents saved my life—I mean, they were really my parents."

Anne attended Wheelock College, an all-women teachers' college outside of Boston, majoring in early childhood education. She traveled for two months in Europe in the summer of 1952, spending much of that time in Italy, where damage from the war was still evident throughout the country. Captivated by Italy and France, she returned to teach there, living first in Rome and then in Paris over the course of three years, from 1954 until 1957. Back in the States, Anne joined Granny Froment on the Upper East Side of Manhattan and lived with her for seven years before taking her own apartment on Eighty-fifth Street near York Avenue. She taught first at the Chapin School—an exclusive private girls' school—and then at Walden. Though she dated and once considered marriage, Anne had shied away from serious relationships—until she met Wright.

Wright asked Anne out to dinner a week after his November reading. When he first arrived at her apartment, he was struck by the way her face appeared from behind the door at the end of the dark hallway. Wright's poem "The Lights in the Hallway" had its beginnings on that first date. After escorting her home, Wright remembered a poem by Rabindranath Tagore, and wrote to share it with Anne. It concludes:

Oh my only friend, my best beloved,
The gates are open at my house.
Do not pass by,
Like a dream.

Wright added a disarming handwritten postscript at the top of his letter
that owes a debt to *Huckleberry Finn*: "P.S. I don't have the text here, so
I may have lied, here & there. But not all that much." On their third
date, Anne cooked dinner at home, and Jim arrived with a bouquet of
roses and a paper bag with copies of his three books. She spent the next
morning reading them in bed, moved especially by poems in *The Branch
Will Not Break*. Anne found it all hard to resist. "He had such a deep,
rich voice, and every time he'd call and say, 'This is James Wright,' my
heart would flutter."

Anne was impressed to learn of Wright's reading in the Coolidge Auditorium of the Library of Congress in Washington, D.C., on December 5,
and Wright felt honored by the invitation. Recently named Consultant
in Poetry to the library, James Dickey served as moderator for Wright's
appearance with Louis Simpson in the first of a series of dual readings
that Dickey established during his contentious term as consultant.
Wright's opening comments had a defiant edge, refuting the simplistic idea
that he had given up writing poems in meter and rhyme. Referring indi-
rectly to his long-standing argument with Bly, Wright insisted that forms
in poetry are just different kinds of music, each appropriate depending
on the poem at hand. He disliked the phrase "free verse," but saw the
need for "a more precise way of dealing with the music of our own
American language." Wright's voice grew increasingly emphatic. "But
I love the English forms, too, and the conclusion that I've come to—as
far as I, myself, am concerned—is that I want *everything*. And I mean
to *have* it."

When Dickey asked about his unusual identification with "what
Dostoevsky called 'the insulted and injured'"—a stock response to his
poetry—Wright denied any mere "mechanical concern for these people.
But I feel like them. I think that, finally, America is a very lonely place.
And the relation between those of us who are sort of on top of it at any
moment and those who are on the bottom at any moment is somehow
likely to change very quickly." Wright then gave a reading of "Before a
Cashier's Window in a Department Store" that left Simpson speechless.
But Dickey again questioned Wright's interest in the poor—in Dickey's
words, those "intimidated" by the forces of commerce. Wright spoke
instead about why he wrote the poem, which goes to the heart of his effort as a writer. "I think it's an attempt to grow up, too. I think that a lot
of the suffering, or the desolation, are either going to end up in self-pity

or . . . some ability to realize what it *feels* like. Everybody's going to go under, one way or another. This is what I hope for: I would like to be a grown man." Wright had never stated his poetic ambition so directly.

Wright couldn't help his love for metrical verse and "the echoes that words make to one another," and back in New York he found sympathy with W. S. Merwin. The two met often that winter while Merwin oversaw the production of a Lorca play he had translated, a two-month run of *Yerma* at the Vivian Beaumont Theater of Lincoln Center. He became another of Wright's companions for long evenings of poetry and drink; they shared a fondness for Thomas Hardy's poems. "We used to sit and talk about poems late into the night sometimes. I did it out of love of James and out of love of poetry—and as a way of trying to keep him from drinking so much, too. He was drinking a lot in those days . . . [but] he was more interested in the poetry than in the drinking."

———

Before leaving New York to spend Christmas in Ohio with his parents, Wright received copies of a new collection of "tiny poems" that Bly had edited called *The Sea and the Honeycomb*. Wright gave one as "a kind of Christmas card" to Anne. Bly's letter dated December 14 shows keen interest in Wright's manuscript. "You have some magnificent new poems, and it'll be a strong, shining book. You have a lot to give— you have the most talent of anyone in our generation, there's no doubt about that, and you are just at the right age to use it!" Wright had just turned thirty-nine.

The dark landscape of Wright's new poems gave off its own strange light, but always with a glimmer of hope. The collection he had titled *Dark Water* was briefly called *Northern Pike*; his new working title was *Winter*. Wright borrowed a typewriter at his parents' home in Ohio and, in the days following Christmas, completed the concluding poem for his new book.

"To the Muse" had its beginnings more than a decade before. In 1955, Wright drafted "A Moan for Pauline Flitch," which began: "Fathers of moonlight, now must I begin / To spend this dark in mourning for a whore?" Two years later, these lines survived as the opening couplet of a different poem, "At a Girl's Grave in Ohio," published in the spring of 1957. Wright marked extensive revisions in the margins of that journal in August 1960. He then returned to these penciled changes and marginalia to seed a new poem in March 1964; after months of revision, it became "In Response to a Rumor That the Oldest Whorehouse in Wheeling, West Virginia, Has Been Condemned." But the version in Wright's journal dated March 5, 1964, is twice as long and uses the form of direct address—"I am yours now, poor haggard angel"—that distinguishes "To the Muse." In this and other ways, "In Response to a Rumor" belongs to the scattered sequence of poems addressed to Jenny, a motley figure composed of many different women Wright had known along the shores of the Ohio.

After numerous drafts, Wright had abandoned another attempt to speak to his Muse in February 1962; it begins by calling out to "You old hag," or "You harridan." The final two-page version of that long-lined poem wanders from the Warnock farm to the strip mines and pool halls of Martins Ferry—plaintive, guilt-ridden, and unfocused. Only the poem's concluding line seems truly touched by grief, when he commands his Muse to "Give me back my life."

Wright's new poem had flared into being in mid-September on the back of a torn scrap of envelope; these opening lines were then added to other rough stanzas handwritten on a sheet of yellow lined paper. On December 26 and 27, "To the Muse" went through multiple drafts, becoming a singular, visionary mixture of grief, longing, apology, and supplication. The journey of Orpheus into the underworld to reclaim Eurydice shadows the poem, as the speaker stands at an entrance to Hell on the banks of the Ohio across from Wheeling, West Virginia. Unlike other renderings of this myth (including Rilke's), this encounter is solely between the poet and his Muse. He addresses her directly, the divinity, "Face down in the unbelievable silk of spring" at the bottom of the Ohio River—the woman he calls "Jenny."

It is all right. All they do
Is go in by dividing
One rib from another. I wouldn't
Lie to you. It hurts
Like nothing I know. All they do
Is burn their way in with a wire.
It forks in and out a little like the tongue
Of that frightened garter snake we caught

At Cloverfield, you and me, Jenny
So long ago.

I would lie to you
If I could.
But the only way I can get you to come up
Out of the suckhole, the south face
Of the Powhatan pit, is to tell you
What you know:

You come up after dark, you poise alone
With me on the shore.
I lead you back to this world.

Three lady doctors in Wheeling open
Their offices at night.
I don't have to call them, they are always there.
But they only have to put the knife once
Under your breast.
Then they hang their contraption.
And you bear it.

It's awkward a while. Still, it lets you
Walk about on tiptoe if you don't
Jiggle the needle.
It might stab your heart, you see.
The blade hangs in your lung and the tube
Keeps it draining.
That way they only have to stab you
Once. Oh Jenny,
I wish to God I had made this world, this scurvy
And disastrous place. I
Didn't, I can't bear it
Either, I don't blame you, sleeping down there
Face down in the unbelievable silk of spring,
Muse of black sand,
Alone.

I don't blame you, I know
The place where you lie.
I admit everything. But look at me.
How can I live without you?
Come up to me, love,
Out of the river, or I will
Come down to you.

In the penultimate stanza the speaker echoes *Tristram Shandy* as he despairs of the world, "this scurvy / And disastrous place." And like Sterne's Muse, Wright's "Jenny" is a literary creation—extremely important and very real to the poet, but a creation nonetheless. Wright understood that the only Muse that could sustain him must be true to the reality and the place he knew, with all its pain and desolation. Here, she becomes a drowned suicide, likely a prostitute. Rooted to American soil and language, Jenny embodies what Lorca called *duende*—the terrifying, vitalizing awareness of death, the essential shadow figure and source of inspiration that Bly and others have called the *daemon*.

The entire poem is a terrible gamble and proof of enormous confidence. Spoken directly to the Muse and somehow overheard by the reader, its immediacy is chilling, with a visceral intensity that casts a powerful spell. Roger Hecht believed that Wright is best understood as a dramatic poet, and Sonjia Urseth agreed. She dismissed any simple identification of herself with the figure of "Jenny." "He didn't imply that that was *me*. This is a poem. Remember—in everything he did, there was a bit of drama and theater about it." Franz Wright saw the poem as "another way of talking about southern Ohio" and the "industrial horror of the Depression." Though he had escaped from it, his father "felt a responsibility to say something in their name, all the people that sort of drowned in that life."

"Speak," a companion poem Wright had completed months before, echoes Horace's plea in his Ode "To the Muses," which begs the deities to "Come down from heaven." In the despairing conclusion of Wright's new poem, that prayer is reversed:

Come up to me, love,
Out of the river, or I will
Come down to you.

The poet declares his allegiance to the place of his birth, but he can't be sure the Muse will answer him. As death-haunted as the poem can seem, there is a complexity of emotion and a range of tones, not least the stubborn will to survive. "I've gone for a long time in a kind of compromise with despair, not conscious of having written much, just conscious of several kinds of defeat," Wright had told Hall in a letter at the end of November. "And yet, somehow, the poems have appeared now and then, accumulating in a darkness."

18

Dark Waters

January 1967–September 1968

In January 1967, as he completed his first semester at Hunter Uptown, Wright's courtship with Anne moved to the center of his life. In a note apologizing for arriving late for dinner, he asks her to "accept my gratitude for your grace to me, which I care for as I care for, even now, the appearance of the trilliums in the Spring on the Ohioan cliffs of my childhood. Hanging there, dark purple, between Andromeda and the strip mines." Anne couldn't resist the charm and old-fashioned manners of this "gardener of weeds" with his uncommon gift for language. They often spoke on the phone and went to the movies; best of all, they laughed together. "He loved to joke around, and there was a great deal of playfulness," Anne remembered. "But it was his fantastic mind. I mean, I was in awe of it."

Wright often said poems as they walked in Manhattan—frequently Neruda's "Walking Around." When he sent Anne a copy of his love poem "The Lights in the Hallway," she kept it in her purse to read each morning on the crosstown bus to work. Her nursery school occupied a storefront on Columbus Avenue, a few blocks south of Wright's hotel room, and he became a frequent visitor, determined to charm sixteen four-year-olds. "He figured I wouldn't have a chance after that." One child in particular—a bright, melancholy boy named Garnie Braxton—grew very attached to the poet. Wright once appeared at Anne's apartment that winter with a button in his hand, asking, "What should I do with this?" Later, she discovered that "the button had just been wrenched from his overcoat outside the door. It was all an ingenious plot to win me over."

The key obstacle between them went unacknowledged for many weeks: Wright's alcoholism. "I knew he had a drinking problem, but I was not able to put *alcoholic* to it for a long time. That seemed to be such a taboo word in those days—or it was to me." When Wright asked her to marry him, Anne waited for him to confess to his drinking. She had seen the effects on her father and her family, but she believed she could make the difference for Wright. Though he finally admitted to his struggle with alcohol, he then refused to speak of it further. Instead, Wright gave her a copy of *As It Was*, the memoirs of Edward Thomas's widow, Helen, so she would "know what it's like living with a poet."

Paired with William Stafford, Wright gave an excellent reading at the Guggenheim Museum on March 9, 1967. Merwin approached him afterward and made him promise to title his next book after one of the new poems he had read: "In Response to a Rumor That the Oldest Whorehouse in Wheeling, West Virginia, Has Been Condemned." Also in the audience were Anne's friends Sheila and her husband, Nazri Ráshed, an eminent Pakistani poet who worked at the U.N. Sheila had taught with Anne at the Overseas School in Rome and shared an apartment with her for two years. Nazri was astonished by Wright's wide reading in Middle Eastern and Indian poetic traditions, and if Anne had wanted her friends' approval, it came immediately. The following day, she accepted Wright's proposal. After securing the blessing of Granny Froment on a trip to Westerly, Rhode Island, they decided to marry at the end of April. When Wright phoned the Blys to share the news, Robert confided to Anne, "He is *the* poet."

A few days before their wedding, Wright gave up his room at the Hotel Regent and Anne gave up her privacy. The couple now shared her ground-floor apartment on East Eighty-fifth Street, half a block from Carl Schurz Park along the East River. It was a long, narrow tenement flat, but they could climb out the kitchen window into a sizable back-yard, where Anne kept a small garden. The kitchen had a water closet at one end—the only bathroom—and at the other a tin shower stall. But the neighbors were friendly and the apartment rent-controlled; the two now shared forty-eight dollars in monthly rent. At the time, Wright alternated between two suits, wearing one for a week before exchanging it for one at the cleaners. "I thought it a bit strange," Anne admitted, "that the large suitcase he brought over from the hotel should be the one containing books and papers, and the small one clothes."

The interdenominational Riverside Church at 122nd Street and Riverside Drive had been the Froment family's church, and its history featured a long line of progressive Baptist ministers. Earlier that month, on April 4, 1967, the couple heard the Rev. Dr. Martin Luther King, Jr.'s historic speech in the main sanctuary opposing the war in Vietnam. With sixteen guests attending, they were married in Riverside's Spanish chapel on April 29, 1967—a year and a day after they had met. In a photo taken afterward on the church steps, the bride and her nine-year-old niece, Laura Lee, appear equally delighted. The groom seems poised between youth and middle age, stepping warily out into sunshine. From this day on, Anne became known as Annie—a coinage of her husband—and Jim became, at her insistence, James.*

Anne's marriage to James surprised some of her close friends; the news also startled Wright's two sons and Liberty. She and Miklos now had a child of their own, a son named Andy. As a result, Wright's boys suffered more at the hands of their stepfather. Miklos's "periodic rages and paranoia were terrifying and very traumatic for them," Liberty later admitted. After bouts of heavy drinking, he "turned his brutal vindictiveness first on Franz and Marshall, then on me." Franz had just turned fourteen, and after he refused to cut his hair, his stepfather wrestled him to the ground and hacked it off with a pair of scissors. Franz felt only "humiliation and terror" at home and was often afraid to return there after school. He began to experience periods of depression, and he and Marshall drifted apart. Liberty did not protect her sons from their stepfather's physical abuse, and neither she nor his sons spoke of it to Wright.

In New York that spring, Galway and Inés Kinnell and their new daughter, Maud, were living close by and the two couples saw each other often. The newlyweds also visited with the Rásheds, who would leave New York in the fall when Nazri took up a diplomatic post in Iran. Sheila recalled that Anne "would sit and listen and drink in everything James

---

*The name "Anne" is used throughout, except in quotations from Wright's poems, letters, and journals, and in instances where "Annie" is meant to distinguish the figure Wright created in the context of his poetry. Wright briefly adopted the name "James" following his marriage, but reverted to signing his name "Jim," which is how friends and relatives always knew him. The use of "James" became more common following his death.

said." She had the social graces he lacked, and insisted upon accepting invitations and having guests come for dinner. Wright could be oblivious to the cigarette ashes on his shirt, but Anne quickly took over and bought new clothes for him. She had hoped he would take charge of their shared finances, but though Wright helped with household chores, he was glad to have someone bring order to his life. At first he spoke of having a child with her, but Anne insisted they wait a year, and they soon abandoned the idea.

Anne could never be certain where or when her husband started drinking in the day, and could not know when he would stop. Unwilling to confront him directly, she trusted that he would, in time, find a way to quit. Wright rarely spoke of his private struggles. Soon after they were married, he told Anne of a dream in which he invited old friends to see where he was living now, to prove how much better he was doing. They gathered outside and started throwing mud at his house.

Wright could be just as capable of consciously tearing himself down. Robert Mezey was then editing a new anthology called *Naked Poetry*, intended to show the diversity of free verse being written in the United States. He solicited prose statements from each poet, and the long, single-spaced page Wright submitted was "heartbreaking . . . the whole statement, from beginning to end, was a savage disavowal of everything he had written." Mezey refused to publish it. The only poems of Wright's to appear that spring came in *The Sixties* No. 9, which included six of his translations of Hernández and one of his best new poems, "In Memory of Leopardi."

This same issue of *The Sixties*—the first significant attention paid to the poetry of Hernández in the United States—included Bly's incendiary review of Dickey's *Buckdancer's Choice*, which had been highly praised in the press. "The Collapse of James Dickey" mourned the "catastrophic" decline of his poetry in a brief span of years, condemning the poet's careerist verse and public stance as a "toady" for the war in Vietnam, "a sort of Georgia cracker Kipling." The public feud that had grown between Bly and Dickey now escalated beyond repair.

———

The Wrights traveled to Westerly, Rhode Island, in mid-June to see Granny Froment. They also visited Betty Kray at her home in nearby Shannock, a two-hundred-year-old farmhouse she was restoring with her husband.

Over the next decade the Wrights often returned to Atlantic beaches near Westerly in the summer. At the end of the month, they flew to Milwaukee, where Wright taught a class called Developments in Modern Poetry in a monthlong summer term at the University of Wisconsin. He enjoyed the students and the school so much that he returned to teach there the following summer. In an interview with the city newspaper, the reporter seems grateful that Wright's "intensely serious" poems were "brightened by wit and warmed by humor. He acknowledges, rather cheerfully, that he takes a tragic view of life." His enthusiasm and good spirits in Milwaukee helped keep his drinking under control. "We drank together," Anne recalled, "but I had one drink and he'd finish the bottle."

Anne began to observe her husband's writing habits, amazed to see how "he wrote on the fly, all the time"—on scraps of paper, even on napkins. He carried small, wire-bound notebooks in his pocket, held tight by rubber bands that he slipped onto his left wrist as he wrote; she grew accustomed to seeing the marks left there. Anne sat in on Wright's class that summer, which centered on close readings of poems by Hardy, Lawrence, Robinson, Frost, and W. C. Williams. As had been true for Roethke, Lawrence's poetry became more and more crucial to Wright. He understood what was at stake for Lawrence: "Admitting & recording his true feelings in his poems, he is freeing himself to be a whole man."

————

The Blys had invited the couple to the farm for a belated honeymoon, but Wright became sullen and anxious as he prepared to return to Minnesota; the unrest growing in the country encouraged his despondency. The Wrights boarded a plane for Minneapolis on July 17—the fourth day of rioting in the inner city of Newark, New Jersey. Prompted by widespread violence against blacks, including incidents of police brutality, urban communities across the nation witnessed the worst rioting in American history in the summer of 1967. By the end of July, outbreaks in Detroit had left forty-three dead and more than a thousand injured. Each day brought news of Johnson's escalation of the war in Vietnam and, more often, increasing public resistance.

The Wrights arrived in Minnesota during a brutal heat wave, which remained unbroken for weeks. Staying with Roland Flint and his wife at Isabella Gardner's home in Minneapolis, Wright took Anne to McCosh's

bookstore in Dinkytown and introduced her to old friends. Wright's colleague from Macalester, Ray Livingston, had taken his own life in May,
and the couple visited his widow, Claire, and their eleven-year-old son.
Livingston had helped Wright endure a breakdown, even shuttling him
to his classes from the hospital, but had never spoken of his own deep
depression. His suicide enraged Wright—just one of the spurs to his
heavy drinking while in Minneapolis. Though Tate seemed excluded,
Wright began cursing "the people around Tate" who had fired him. Everywhere he saw reminders of his defeat, and he angrily turned upon his
wife one night at a party. "Take it easy," Flint counseled, pulling him aside.
"I mean, Annie is the center after all." Wright shot back, "No. *Poetry* is
the center."

When Bly arrived to bring the couple out to the country, Flint persuaded Wright and Bly to record a conversation at the university radio
station, where he hosted a weekly program on contemporary poetry. For
more than an hour the three poets shared their enthusiasms and traded
impassioned readings of poems by Whitman, Yeats, Goethe, and Roethke.
After reciting haiku by Issa and praising the same "affection for life"
found in Lawrence, their talk turned political. Wright recited Wilfred
Owen's "Dulce et Decorum Est" and his own "Autumn Begins in Martins Ferry, Ohio," and the program concluded with four of Bly's fer-
vent antiwar poems from *The Light Around the Body*, his forthcoming
collection.

The Wrights stayed for two weeks on the Blys' farm, with its bright
red farmhouse and Norwegian flag. Bly had purchased an old one-room
schoolhouse and moved it into a grove of maples, fitting it out with an
antique wooden bed and a writing desk for the couple's honeymoon cabin.
To fight the heat, they often went swimming at the town pool with the
girls, Mary and Biddy, but the evenings were full of talk and poetry. Anne
saw her husband chafe at some of Robert's opinions, but what impressed
her most was Wright's love for Carol. The two sat for hours in the kitchen
talking with complete ease. The cabin's new outhouse featured a copy of
Charles Olson's *Maximus Poems*.

While on the farm, Wright finalized the order of his new manuscript,
now titled *Shall We Gather at the River*. Galway Kinnell had returned a
working copy at the end of June with comments and suggestions, and
Wright went through his edits carefully, revising the final stanza of "Rip"
extensively. A handwritten table of contents dated August 11 is identical

to the published version; with the later restoration of the proemial "A Christmas Greeting," the manuscript included thirty-seven poems. It is Wright's most carefully conceived and painstaking collection, a disturbing masterpiece, as he well knew. "It hangs together on the string of a cold black music, and the opening image fulfills itself in the last phrase of the book." Wesleyan had received the manuscript in June; in his cover letter Wright asks his editor, José de la Torre Bueno, to publish the book as quickly as they can. "I have got to get it off my back. . . . It is a terrible book, but it is the best book I have ever written." John Berryman had encouraged his own publisher, Farrar, Straus and Giroux, to solicit the manuscript, but Wright declined their invitation. His friendship with Bueno and the patience Wesleyan had shown him for years delayed Wright's move to the more prestigious publisher.

Hardie St. Martin arrived from Barcelona near the end of the Wrights' stay at the farm, and the three poets worked together on Spanish translations. The fastidious, solitary St. Martin bore himself with "quiet dignity," despite the endless teasing and poking he endured at the hands of the two Bly girls, then ages three and five. One night, Robert took both Anne and James for a walk after midnight and they lay down at the side of the road "so we could hear the animals running in the field," Anne recalled. "It was very romantic." But as they prepared to leave for Ohio, Wright's drinking got worse. On the morning of their departure, Anne hid all the liquor from the Blys' cabinet, forcing Wright to endure the long journey sober, fuming silently. But they both avoided confronting the matter head-on. When Wright's drinking came up, "he'd say, 'Oh, I'll give it up'—but he couldn't."

Wright's parents welcomed Jim and his new bride. Dudley seemed particularly glad to see his son again, and Jessie talked endlessly, telling family stories, tall tales, and gossip. Jessie tended a vegetable garden, rosebushes, and sunflowers; she and Jim laughed easily together. Toward Dudley, however, Jessie was still sharp-tongued and domineering, which visibly troubled Wright. His father seemed immune to her restless, unappeasable nature. Anne found him a "very gentle and saintly man," a true innocent. Anne and Jim returned to New Concord the following summer and at Christmas for years to come. Every year they would find that Jessie had rearranged the furniture throughout the house.

The most significant ritual the couple established in the first months of their marriage began after their return to New York. Before classes resumed for them both, they impulsively decided to escape to a lakeside resort for four days in the Shawangunk Mountains outside of New Paltz, New York. This proved to be the first of twenty-eight separate stays at Wildmere House overlooking Lake Minnewaska, a deep, glacial lake between granite cliffs surrounded by forests of chestnut, oak, and hemlock pine. The seclusion and altitude contributed to an old-world atmosphere at two enormous Victorian guest hotels beginning to fall into disrepair on the shore of the lake. Much cooler than the city, the grounds prohibited cars and offered hiking trails, swimming, and canoeing; the land was located along a major flyway, and there were songbirds and migratory flocks. The rooms had private balconies with views of the lake, and the staff was cheerful and attentive. The place felt timeless and vaguely European; they paid for meals in advance and ate in a common dining room. The peace and fresh air of the surrounding forest were rejuvenating, and the couple took long walks. They returned to Lake Minnewaska at every opportunity.

Revisiting Minneapolis had been painful for Wright. "He rarely talked about his first marriage, but the last years in Minnesota were just a nightmare to him." The rage took Anne by surprise, as did the true extent of his alcoholism. She couldn't make out a pattern or trigger to his drinking bouts; the struggle "was going on in his mind all the time—like fighting demons." More than once that fall, when Wright had been drinking heavily, he phoned the Mixers in Minneapolis, asking to speak to any of his old friends there. The bartender would shout, "Does anyone here know a James Wright?" before passing the phone down the bar.

––––––

As Wright began his second year at Hunter Uptown, he borrowed from Roethke at every turn. In his Poetics course, he instructed his students to keep a commonplace book, where passages from poems and writing exercises were recorded beside personal notes on class readings. Teaching—and teaching well—helped Wright keep his bearings, and finding Anne had made it possible "to create sense" out of the chaos of his life. In September, he felt relieved to hear from Bly, who had "savagely criticized" his new book at the farm but now praised it. "It has a sting and a darkness about it," Wright told Sister Bernetta Quinn that month, "but I want it to have the Herrick-like (maybe Stevens-like) music, for the music is the theme."

Wright traveled alone to Buffalo in November, invited by John Logan to give two readings at the university, including an afternoon talk in Logan's Modern Poetry class. That evening before a large audience, Wright gave a superb performance, composed entirely of poems from *Shall We Gather at the River*. "It's taken me a long time to write it," he said of his new book, "and I wrote it many times." Seven years had passed since the first of these poems had been written, and many of them he insisted were just descriptions, including "Before a Cashier's Window in a Department Store." "It's sort of a Chinese-like poem, I hope. Again, it's just a description. And I've been trying to learn, again and again, how to write a real description. If one can only get down what actually happens, all the feeling would be there." A rapt audience heard the first eleven poems from the book in sequence and three others, ending with "To the Muse." The effect was mesmerizing. Introducing the "very literary poem" that concluded his new collection, Wright said, "Well, this is to the Muse, trying to tell her what it's like in the world as we know it, and calling her up out of the river—the Ohio River, what else?"

The last poem added to the new manuscript became the first in the book, published in italics with the title "A Christmas Greeting." A handwritten draft dated December 18 is in free verse, titled "Suicides: Part 2." Wright tried different metrical forms in many drafts, searching for the right tone and diction for his encounter with the ghost of a suicide-drunk from childhood. The final version is not only in iambic pentameter but also in heroic couplets. Wright had been lecturing on Alexander Pope—a master of the form—just days before reworking the poem. As John Haag observed, "Out of what should produce a clash of content and form he creates unbearable tensions. The candor and the power of image and language make clear that virtuosity was the least of his concerns." The poem helps establish the overriding tenor of the book, declaring the kinship the poet feels with those living at the bare margins of the American Dream.

––––––––

There is a characteristic gesture in Wright's letters from the early years of his second marriage: after recounting a brief history of his hardships, he declares how much better his life is now and then introduces Annie. She begins to show up in poems as well—in significant ways, a figure distinct from the woman he married. As "Annie" appears in his poetry, she is his creation—as is Jenny. Both aspects of Wright's Muse inhabit separate poems for years to come.

As soon as he sent off his final manuscript to Wesleyan, Wright began sketching new work in his journal. Over the coming years, fewer interim drafts precede the final versions of poems; the classical poise that distinguishes his language seems more casual. In accessing childhood memories, he often exploits the vivid idioms and diction he knew in southern Ohio. A draft of "Trouble," dated February 2, 1968, includes snatches of dialogue and vernacular phrases. In claiming these linguistic resources, new possibilities constantly appeared.

The entire Bly family came to New York that winter, renting an apartment in Manhattan for five months before traveling to Sweden in June. Biddy and Mary Bly attended classes at the Westside Community Nursery School, where Anne Wright taught and served as director. Robert and Jim saw each other often. Their collaboration on *Twenty Poems of Neruda* would finally come out in June, and in the fall both poets would publish new collections.

In the first week of April, *The New Yorker* carried Wright's sorrowful, unsettling poem "Speak," a centerpiece of his new book that the poet described as "a prayer and a hymn." The issue reached newsstands as the world learned of the assassination of Rev. Dr. Martin Luther King, Jr., in Memphis on April 4. The final stanza begins:

I have gone forward with
Some, a few lonely some.
They have fallen to death.
I die with them.

Four days later, Wright and his wife attended a memorial service for Dr. King at Riverside Church. The crush of national events intensified as the year went on. News reports tallied the mounting loss of life in Vietnam and described the escalation of carpet-bombing and chemical deforestation. The antiwar readings that Bly and Wright had helped organize more than two years before were now a common part of campus protests across the country.

Wright and Anne traveled to California for a week in mid-April to visit with his two sons. Upon his arrival, Wright gave a powerful reading at the Poetry Center of San Francisco State University; by the end, applause followed after each poem. Introducing the second of "Two Poems About President Harding," Wright revealed the emotional identification he felt with the inhabitants of Martins Ferry: "If you were born in Ohio, somehow all these people belong to you. You belong to them. It's a strange place." The concluding poem, "Before a Cashier's Window in a Department Store," transfixed the audience. Wright delivered the final lines with a melancholy shrewdness, as though shrugging his shoulders:

> I am hungry. In two more days
> It will be spring. So this
> Is what it feels like.

Applause continued for many minutes after Wright left the podium.

When Liberty brought Franz and Marshall into the city for a day of sightseeing with their father, she saw Wright make a nervous, absent-minded gesture, prodding his dentures with a finger, and pounced. "I see you're still having problems with your teeth." These were the first words Anne ever heard her speak. The boys had already met Anne at Thanksgiving when they had spent a week in New York. She found nine-year-old Marshall to be a "warm, slightly immature boy, very outgoing," while Franz, at fifteen, was "apt to be sullen and withdrawn." Anxious in her new role as stepmother, Anne tried hard to win the boys' approval, but Wright, too, felt uneasy as a parent and struggled to build a sense of trust and intimacy with his sons.

———

When Wesleyan University Press, then setting type for his new book, asked Wright about publishing his *Collected Poems*, he agreed at once. The thought of choosing poems for a *Selected* volume intimidated him, and a *Collected* would let him include a book-length section of new poems. A brief list Wright made in his journal that June already shows many of the best of these, including "Northern Pike" and "A Centenary Ode: Inscribed to Little Crow, Leader of the Sioux Rebellion in Minnesota, 1862." Wright had wanted to publish translations in every one of his books, and the *Collected* also gave him the chance to gather his best work from Spanish and German. Grouped modestly as *Some Translations* between *Saint Judas* and *The Branch Will Not Break*, Wright's apprenticeship in other languages would now become clear to readers and enrich the critical appreciation of his work.

The Sixties Press brought out the bilingual *Twenty Poems of Neruda* that he and Bly had translated in the same month Wright published an essay on Neruda in the June issue of *Poetry*. In recommending Nathaniel Tarn's new version of Neruda's *Heights of Macchu Picchu*, Wright's meditation on Neruda's genius inspired something of a personal manifesto.

> But a great poet is a disturbance. If poetry means anything, it means heart, liver, and soul. If great poetry means anything, anything at all, it means disturbance, secret disturbance. . . . It is bad enough to be miserable; but to be happy, how far beyond shock it is. To be alive, with all one's unexpected senses, and yet to face the fact of unhappiness. . . . I want poetry to make me happy, but the poetry I want should deal with the hell of our lives or else it leaves me cold.

He praises other translations by Kenneth Rexroth and H. R. Hays, and hardly troubles with Tarn's skill or shortcomings. Wright wants only to convey Neruda's great "abundance."

Returning to Milwaukee for the summer, Wright had a rare chance to discuss the work of his contemporaries in a class he called Poetry & Pity. As a way to introduce poems by Allen Ginsberg, John Logan, and Galway Kinnell, Wright began with lectures on Wilfred Owen and D. H. Lawrence. To the astonishment of his students (including Anne, who again sat in), he recited long passages of Lawrence's critical prose from memory, followed by a wide range of his poems. The class concluded with a study of Kinnell's just-published *Body Rags*, including his ambitious, disjunctive meditation on race, "The Last River."

When the summer session ended, the couple flew to California to spend three weeks with Henry and Elizabeth Esterly in Cupertino. They also visited with Wright's sons and had dinner with Rexroth and his family at their home in San Francisco. The two poets talked for hours about Chinese poetry and Rexroth's life in Japan. Chinese poetry remained close to Wright's heart; he had found a new copy of *The White Pony* that spring and carried it with him, inspired by the exuberance and deep interiority of Tao Yuan-Ming's "Drinking Songs."

Wright kept his own drinking more private, however, and when he wrote to friends after a lapse of years he often declared his sobriety. In a letter to Gene Pugatch he breathes an almost audible sigh of relief. Pugatch was considering a move to New York City, and after effusive encouragements, Wright praised Annie for his rejuvenation:

> So many things have happened during the past few years—so many struggles and searches, failures and false starts and defeats and new beginnings—and now I feel I'm finding my way, that I'm once again capable of being the serious friend that I used to be, before my life began to fall to pieces. Annie has been so good to me. I have never been so happy with people and with my work.

Wright had rebuilt his life, and sitting outdoors on a summer morning in the foothills of the Santa Cruz Mountains, he even believed he could stop drinking.

Then he and Anne flew back to Ohio. Wright's sister, Marge, was recuperating from surgery in a Wheeling hospital, and they traveled by bus from Ted's home outside Zanesville to visit her. This was as close as Wright ever came to returning to Martins Ferry in the last decades of his life. They wandered around Wheeling and visited the cigar store on Market Street where he had worked in high school. Despite a huge decline in population, it all looked much the same; the streets of Wheeling unnerved him. As they crossed back over the Ohio River heading west, suspended above the dark water, Wright gestured in an abstracted way out the bus window to the north—toward Martins Ferry—and turned his head away.

19

The shape of one's own life

September 1968–June 1970

In September 1968, when Wright began teaching at the Hunter College campus in midtown Manhattan, the move aggravated the stress he always felt at the start of a school year. Overcrowding among both students and faculty would remain a chronic problem. At Hunter Uptown (which now became Lehman College), Wright had enjoyed a smaller campus and fewer students. Hunter's midtown location took up an entire block between Park Avenue and Lexington at Sixty-eighth Street, and the college attracted students from all over the city. The move eased Wright's commute, but in his new office Anne saw that "a large number of people shared a room the size of a broom closet, where it wasn't safe to leave an overcoat or a briefcase."

The official publication date for *Shall We Gather at the River*, September 19, coincided with the start of classes at Hunter that fall. When Wright received the first copies of the book, Anne became curious about the one-word dedication: "Jenny." "I'm not telling anyone!" he growled impatiently when she asked who it was. After a long silence, in a different tone, he said, "If we ever have a daughter, I want to name her Jenny." All she would ever learn about the name was that it came from *Tristram Shandy*.

Shall We Gather at the River marks the culmination of a major arc in Wright's career. Beginning with the poems in *The Green Wall* that first "started to call up a kind of darkness," he had worked to master different poetic forms to help articulate the rage, joy, anguish, and longing he experienced. Robert Mezey called *The River* Wright's greatest work. Roger Hecht agreed; in completing the book, Wright's "anger and self-conflicts had exhausted themselves." Hecht called the work that followed "a resurrection into something different."

————

Whatever self-confidence Wright gained by the positive reception that greeted his new book was undermined by a bizarre public embarrassment that took months to shake off. On the night before the presidential election that pitted the Minnesotan Hubert Humphrey against Richard Nixon, Wright introduced two young poets at the Poetry Center of the 92nd Street Y. Marge Piercy and Michael Benedikt had both published their first books in the Wesleyan Poetry Series that year. Piercy taught at Columbia University and many of her students attended the reading; the large crowd seemed tense and agitated before the elections. Some mistook Wright's decorum and civility for conservatism, and his subtle humor went misunderstood.

After the poets each read, Wright tried to engage them in an open discussion—an experiment, they told the audience. Though he praised the "extraordinarily beautiful" poems and songs of Bob Dylan, Wright couldn't resist making a joke about his singing voice, prompting loud boos and hisses. Surprised and shaken by the animosity, he became unnerved. When Piercy grew quarrelsome, one audience member cheered her as "a revolutionary." Another shouted, "The point is that the moderator is a fatuous ass!" Enraged, Wright commanded the man to stand and identify himself. After Benedikt and Piercy each read a final poem, Wright struggled to keep his temper in check before closing the evening from the podium with a vehement threat. "Don't come near me after the reading tonight, *buster*, or I'll take you apart."

The next day, the country elected Richard M. Nixon its thirty-seventh president. Though he had promised to end U.S. involvement in the Vietnam War, Nixon meant to decrease the presence of American soldiers by expanding the massive bombing campaign in Indochina. As Wright knew, it was "a very dark moment in the history of this country." That Saturday, Bill Truesdale invited the Wrights to a dinner party at his new home in Manhattan. He had moved his family there to promote his writing career, and already felt dissatisfied by how little Wright was doing to help him. Wright was still infuriated by the heckling incident, which he considered "a supremely personal attack on himself." He fixated on another guest, one of the glib "social redeemers and utopians" who embodied "all that youthful rebelliousness he so despised. He strode over to him and literally cursed him: 'I think you are the scum of the earth.'"

Anne recalled how the night turned sour after Wright spoke with fondness of his days in the army, baiting the prejudices of the "callow youth," who began taunting him. In other versions, Wright looms above the cowering man and points a menacing finger before uttering his curse. Wright's rage arose from a complex moral dilemma that grew into a subject for his poetry: he felt patriotic devotion but hated what his country was doing. Truesdale believed that Wright "did not fit this age at all. He never did make his peace with it. It did not belong to him." In Anne's view, "the anger was always close to the surface."

Wright could now choose among offers to read on college campuses, and on December 13—his forty-first birthday—he and Anne traveled to Montreal for a reading at Sir George Williams University. The night brought a heavy snowstorm to the city, but an enthusiastic audience heard a generous reading. "I have a very strong classical streak in me," Wright began; admitting his preference for "poems that are passionately intellectual," the first poem he read was Ben Jonson's "On My First Son." After a Lorca poem and a pair of Irish ones, he recited an uncollected Rilke poem, first in German before improvising an English version on the spot. "You can't say that I'm translating it by sight—but perhaps by ear." Introducing "Before a Cashier's Window," Wright likened his own experience with poverty to that of Orwell's in *Down and Out in Paris and London*. Wright's epiphany in a Minneapolis department store gave him awareness he could not have gotten any other way. "I realized something that I had never realized before, but I am content simply to think about it. I don't want it to happen to me again. I thought, 'Jesus Christ, there are millions of people in this country who are treated like *things*, every single intimate moment of their lives.'"

As 1969 began, Wright fought his troubles to a stalemate, buoyed by praise for his new collection and yet weighed down by depression and alcohol. Anne encouraged him to seek private counseling to help him stop drinking, and Wright quickly established a close rapport with Dr. Irving Silver, a colleague of Anne's own psychiatrist. Silver grew convinced that Wright did not suffer from a bipolar illness, but that his periods of depression—some of long duration—were "situational" or "responsive," triggered by stressful events or circumstances. Drug therapies, however, were complicated by Wright's constant drinking.

That winter, unqualified successes were undermined by setbacks, even thoughts of suicide. This struggle can be felt in poems begun and abandoned in his journal. He continues to rage against the "gang of punks in the audience [who] hissed, insulted, & made a fool of me" back in November, and even declares that he is leaving New York for good. The figure of Jenny appears in a number of dark, despairing fragments; in others, Annie becomes a kind of savior, her presence a product of "Grace, not Deserving."

The River continued to receive widespread notice, with many reviewers calling it his strongest work. At the end of January, Wright's photo appeared in *Time* magazine and he was named one of "a crop of poets who cannot be pigeonholed in schools or academies." This new prominence encouraged Wright's innate cautiousness; after his marriage to Anne, all his letters are more deliberate and restrained. His journals, however, retain their intimacy and ragged eloquence; glimpses of redemption are met in quick succession by moments of hopelessness. With a nod to Sappho, Wright swears to Annie that he will "write a poem that will make men remember and love your name." Days later, he drafted "My Epitaph, If I Have Enough to Pay for It," lines of pure despair dedicated to Jenny that he later reworked into the poem "October Ghosts."

In February, Wright gave a reading at the Guggenheim Museum that proved a great success. "The voice of a major poet is instantly recognizable," David Ignatow began, praising Wright's devotion to the Midwest and comparing his work to that of Sherwood Anderson and Theodore Dreiser. The audience welcomed him and the reading went well; later that night, however, Wright swore he would never read in public again. Addressing both Jenny and his "Little brown notebook," he writes, "I don't know why, / But I can't bear it." In this handwritten entry dated February 25, his journal becomes a kind of surrogate presence. The poem's last stanza quotes again from Hesse's *Steppenwolf*:

Jenny, I have nobody,
And I have nothing
To help me
But my homesickness.
Nobody else to lead me home,
Nobody but you,
You dead.

Ever since Wright began believing that Jenny was dead—"Out of the reach of change"—his Muse had become more malleable, able to assume whatever form he wished.

———

Robert Bly had agreed to accept the National Book Award for *The Light Around the Body* if he was allowed to speak freely in front of the illustrious writers and publishers who gathered on the night of the ceremony. Wright joined David Ignatow, Paul Zweig, Saul Galin, and Bly in the hours before his appearance, working together to revise his defiant speech. At Philharmonic Hall in Lincoln Center on March 6, 1969, Bly denounced the Vietnam War, as well as those in the audience who had kept silent. He called a student member of the War Resisters League onto the stage and handed him the thousand-dollar check, encouraging him to defy the draft and to help others do so. Congress had recently declared these acts to be criminal offenses. As scattered applause grew louder at the end of Bly's address, Ignatow saw federal agents leaving the auditorium.

Wright's drinking continually pushed his marriage into crisis and he confesses to thoughts of suicide in his journal. Following a bitter argument with Anne, a handwritten prose passage titled "Not the East River" details his plans to finalize a will and return to Ohio. "I am going to drown in my *own* river: right at Bare-Ass Beach in Aetnaville, where I was born." The main purpose of his will is to assure his burial beside Grandma Lyons, "to spend my eternity in Hell" with her. He marvels at being granted two years of happiness in his marriage, and despairs at the thought that "I very nearly succeeded in becoming a good and loving man." It is hard to gauge Wright's sincerity in the drunken hours before "this bleak and somehow final dawn of my life." He insists he means all of it, "fully and in cold blood," but even as he's writing he thinks of revising these lines. The entire passage becomes marked with line breaks and edits, eventually comprising the second section of the uneven assemblage titled "Many of Our Waters."

At the same time, the "stubborn, manly honesty" of *Shall We Gather at the River* continued to win widespread praise. In March, Robert Penn Warren wrote to say he found it "a book of beauty and power. There aren't many of them." Ignatow published one of the most prominent— and admiring—appraisals in *The New York Times Book Review*. "This is the poetry of a man in control of his art," he declared, "the most personal and affecting" of Wright's four books. *The River* gained such notoriety that Wright was invited to appear on a PBS television series devoted to poetry called *Critique*, where he read from his new work and was interviewed by the critic and editor for *The New Republic* Stanley Kauffmann and a panel that included Richard Gilman, John Hollander, and Arthur Gregor. Franz and Marshall were visiting from California when the program was recorded in April, and they joined Anne to watch their father in the studio. Then sixteen years old, Franz had been writing poems for years but had yet to show any to his father. "He was such a brilliant talker and, my God, I got my whole education just sitting and listening to him talk. And when he was drinking, he was radiant. It was like listening to Bach or something." Wright had begun to feel more at ease with Franz and often spoke to him more as a peer than as a parent.

A week later, after his sons returned to California, Wright traveled to a reading in Ann Arbor. Earlier that year, he had discovered a slim volume of prose and poetry by the Harlem Renaissance writer Jean Toomer, a novel called *Cane* first published in 1923 and returned to print after decades of neglect. Wright began his reading on April 11 with two long passages from this "unique masterpiece." Toomer's command of southern idiomatic speech became a point of inspiration for the use of dialect in the poems Wright was then drafting. Speaking of his own "complicated" ancestry as he introduced "The Minneapolis Poem," Wright focused on the lasting rift caused by the Civil War. "I sometimes think that since that terrible war started, there's been an awful, suicidal impulse in American life for us all to secede from one another. And I hope we can check that and realize that despair is very easily sunken into, as Jean Toomer wrote a long time ago. And we can't live without one another. We just can't do it."

Wright also considered using a passage from *Cane* in the sermon he was then writing. While visiting Orrin Bly and his wife in the Hudson Valley that spring, he and Anne had attended services with them at the United Methodist Church in Old Chatham, New York. The pastor invited Wright to give a sermon, and the poet was thrilled. "I would give a straight Protestant Christian sermon, and I would like to choose the hymns to be sung. Old Methodist hymns that I loved as a child, & still love." At the end of April, Wright began by reciting verses from the ninth chapter of Saint John, "the dark lyric poet of the Gospels." He based his talk on the miracle of the man blind from birth whom Jesus cured, quoting from the King James version of the parable the same lines reproduced on the cover of *Saint Judas*: "And they answered and said unto him, 'Thou wast altogether born in sin, and dost thou teach us?' And they cast him out." Wright was earnest, even pious, as he stood in the pulpit, clearly delighted by the occasion. As he later told the critic Richard Howard, "I know of no poem of mine that hasn't come out of the King James Bible."

Wright kept his promise to Anne that he wouldn't drink before his appearance as a preacher in Old Chatham. Two weeks later, however, when they traveled to Fort Collins, Colorado, he was rarely sober. Nick Crome, his classmate from Kenyon who had arranged his reading at Colorado State University, was stunned. "I'd never seen him drink like that. I don't know that I ever saw *anybody* drinking that way." Nonetheless, Wright's inspired reading, paired with a student seminar he led the next morning, captures an eloquent meditation on the forms of poetry and the sanctity of human life. "The most powerfully subversive force in this country is poetry, but by poetry I don't mean a scheme of metrics, I mean the realization that one's own life is irrevocably precious," he told the class, "a precious and irreducible and irrevocable spirit." Quoting widely from his store of poetry and prose, he circled back to the question he had asked at the beginning of his reading the night before—"What is the form of poetry?" All told, Wright spent more than three hours offering an answer. "It really goes beyond the rhetoric into the discovery, I suppose, of the shape of one's own life. And if one can discover the shape of one's own life, then one is dealing with poetry. He's discovered, or has started to discover, the true shape of poetry."

———

At the end of June 1969, Wright began a summer teaching appointment at the State University of New York at Buffalo. The weather was fine and the city shaded by "cathedrals of elms." Leslie Fiedler and Nathaniel Tarn joined him on campus that summer, as did the novelist John Barth; better still, Wright's old friend Jerry Mazzaro had the office next door. "Jim was happy in Buffalo," he recalled—the students appreciated him and his drinking was under control. Wright seemed at ease and "very much in love" with Anne. They first stayed in the home of Morgan and Carolyn Epes near Forest Lawn Cemetery. "Mickey" Epes had been a classmate of Anne's at Wheelock College, and the two couples became close. The Wrights moved on as "house-sitters" to two other homes nearby during their three-month stay. He taught two courses in Buffalo, devoting himself to a graduate-level seminar called Modern Poetry from Hardy to the Present, with readings in Robinson Jeffers, Frost, Robinson, Lawrence, and Williams.

Wright now faced deadlines with two different publishers: his *Collected* with Wesleyan and Hesse's *Selected Poems* for Farrar, Straus and Giroux. A year before, an editor at FSG, Michael di Capua, had invited him to translate a selection of poems by Hesse, whose novels enjoyed enormous popularity. Wright made progress that summer on the translations—reading through all six hundred pages of Hesse's poetry in German—but felt stymied by his own collection, particularly the gathering of new poems meant to conclude the book. Though Wright spoke excitedly with Mazzaro about his recent work, and felt he was "breaking new ground," he asked Wesleyan to postpone his *Collected* for a year. He knew he had reached "the end of a road" with the poems he'd published in what he still called "the Dark Waters book." Regarding his own new poems, Wright quoted a passage from Williams's 1920 *Kora in Hell: Improvisations*, which he read aloud to his graduate students that July: "There is nothing sacred about literature, it is damned from one end to the other. There is nothing in literature but change and change is mockery. I'll write whatever I damn please . . . and it'll be good if the authentic spirit of change is on it."

Wright began another in his series of American elegies when he encountered the grave of the Native American Seneca chief Red Jacket while walking in the extensive grounds of Forest Lawn Cemetery. Beginning as a meditation on the First World War dead buried there, the poem expands into a lament for the anonymous black laborers who dug the graves and "hugged the stones / Into the ground"—another effort to name those who are forgotten. The poet trying to break new ground himself imagines the calluses on the gravediggers' hands. Experimenting with tone and diction, Wright left some of his new poems sounding jagged and unfinished. The line breaks in "Red Jacket's Grave" appear willful, as though he deliberately sought to alter the "sentence sounds" that were a key formal element in his free-verse poems. But many other excellent new poems, including "Small Frogs Killed on the Highway," published in August in the *New American Review*, still show Wright's keen sense of music.

Wright repeatedly came back to Roethke's poetry and teaching when he gave his most candid, far-reaching interview that August, a conversation recorded by Allen DeLoach in the company of another summer-session poet, Anselm Hollo. Their discussion ranges over the writing process, Elizabethan poetics, Virgil, Ginsberg, and working-class story-telling, with Wright unrestrained at center stage. In a fascinating discourse near the end of their two-hour talk, he condemns the frontier mentality that keeps the United States "very, very far from being, in any good sense, a civilized country." Wright praises Lawrence's *Studies in Classic American Literature*, underscoring the guilt that haunts the country following its decimation of the indigenous North American peoples. "Lawrence says that we're not going to be able to really become anything like a civilization until we recognize that we've got to shed somehow all this death. But it's very hard to shed your guilt. You've got to face it first."

For Wright, his relationship with his sons continued to be an acute source of guilt. That summer, however, his correspondence with Franz grew more frequent and substantial. In July, Franz mailed his father a sheaf of writing that turned their exchange into a mentorship. "I confess that I knew it was coming," Wright tells his son on July 20, encouraging Franz to sharpen his prose. "Instead of giving you a harangue about the art, let me do what good craftsmen—I am a good craftsman, no small thing—have always done: let me turn you to the men who know how to do it." He then lists Faulkner's *Pylon*, Hemingway's *In Our Time*, and Fitzgerald's *The Great Gatsby* and *The Crack-Up*. Wright asks if he can show Franz's work—anonymously—"to two or three of the best and most ruthless critics I know" and then transcribes a poem from Anna Akhmatova's sequence "Requiem." Following his father's death, Franz would turn the conclusion of this letter into a curse, in spite of Wright's clear intention to praise his son's determination. "Franz, I am non-plussed; I'll be damned. You can write. What should I say? Welcome to Hell, / Dad." Wright had recently confided as much in his journal, consoling himself: "Real writing is hell."

––––––––

As a teacher, Wright desired the respect of his peers, and with Anne's help he was determined to look the part. John Knoepfle, Wright's fellow translator of Vallejo, also taught at Buffalo and ferried him to his classes all summer in a decrepit Volkswagen bus with "gasoline sloshing somewhere under the seat." He recalled Wright's strict formality, which won out over the severe heat. "Jim was maybe one of two people wearing coats on campus that summer." At the end of July, Wright began growing a beard, which, as he told Anne, he thought of as a kind of tribute to the astronauts landing on the moon. He would wear one for the rest of his life.

Back at Hunter in September, Wright appreciated the seriousness of his students and colleagues; the more impersonal atmosphere at the college suited him. He felt welcomed and accepted, and yet could easily avoid the pressure of social obligations. When Wright returned home after work, however, Anne could never be sure if he'd already been drinking; he had become more adept at concealing it from her. She had seen this behavior in her father. Though she felt uneasy confronting her husband, Anne discouraged him from seeing some of his old drinking cohorts from Minnesota, like Bill Truesdale.

She did, however, entertain one old friend of Wright's with whom he had shared more than a few drinks. That September, Anne Sexton was living in Manhattan, overseeing rehearsals of her play *Mercy Street*, which debuted Off-Broadway at the American Place Theatre in early October. Sexton and her companion, Lois Ames, were staying at the Algonquin Hotel, a short walk from where the play was being staged. The night before the Wrights attended a preview performance, they invited Sexton and Ames for dinner at their apartment. Though the two poets had spoken on the phone and exchanged a few letters, they hadn't seen each other in eight years. In that time, Sexton had become one of the most famous writers in America, winning the Pulitzer Prize in 1967 for her collection *Live or Die*. Anne Wright found Sexton's manner imperious, but she had to admit that the poet was "very attractive." She served an elaborate dish of osso buco, and as she cleared the plates she saw Sexton lean toward her husband and whisper theatrically, "I wish I had a wife like Annie."

Wright's teaching demanded so much of his time that fall that he managed little work in his journal; together with two undergraduate classes, he taught a graduate course on Dickens and completed final versions of Hesse's poems. Two of his best translations that fall, however, were not from German or Spanish but from Portuguese. At a dinner party, Betty Kray introduced Wright to the Brazilian poet Emanuel Brasil, then working at the United Nations. Within days, Wright completed a version of João Cabral de Melo Neto's poem "The End of the World," and by the time of a bilingual reading of Melo Neto's work two weeks later, he had also translated "Education by Stone." W. S. Merwin, Jane Cooper, Galway Kinnell, and Louis Simpson took part as well in this celebration at the Guggenheim Museum on October 21, where Melo Neto's brother read the Portuguese originals.

When Franz sent his father two "superb" new poems in October, Wright responded with warmth and enthusiasm. Though Franz's technical mastery of verse is "hair-raising," Wright encourages the sixteen-year-old to "wait a little while before you publish anything" and recommends Fitzgerald's discussions of the writer's craft, especially in his letters. To impress upon Franz his complete belief in his son's work, Wright drops his guard. "Modesty be damned: I am one of the best poetic craftsmen of my generation, and one of the most acute readers of poetry. Out of this knowledge, I can tell you that beyond question you have a thrilling poetic gift." Franz could not have doubted his father's praise of his poetry, which Wright found to be "marvelously alive." Their relationship had shifted decisively in the course of three months.

At the time, Wright also struck up a correspondence with the brilliant poet and critic Hayden Carruth. A unique figure in American poetry, Carruth was a solitary poet of great range and fluency who, wholly devoted to the art, lived outside the margins of literary life in northern Vermont. Nevertheless, he exerted a salutary force as one of the most clear-minded critics and reviewers of poetry in America. Wright had written to thank Carruth, the poetry editor at *The Hudson Review*, for his suggested revisions to a number of poems that Wright had submitted in the spring. "I think it's very much a mark of the kind of man Jim Wright was, he wrote me back a letter in which he was very grateful for my interest, for my help. He accepted most of the recommendations I'd made."

Carruth rarely wrote personal letters to contributors, but the two poets immediately found common ground. Wright "was always very pleased that he was a professional scholar, and not a teacher of creative writing," Carruth recalled. "He made that point with a certain kind of shy pride." Carruth wrote book reviews for periodicals such as *The Nation*, *The New Republic*, and *Poetry*—often as many as fifteen a week, each characterized by discrimination and honesty. "I worked hard on the reviews, because I had to. They were the only cash living I had when I was up in the country. I wrote book reviews every night, when it got too dark to work outdoors." It would be years before Wright met Carruth in person, but their correspondence became crucial to him.

That fall, Gibbons Ruark invited Wright to read on the Newark campus of the University of Delaware in November. A gifted poet fourteen years Wright's junior, Ruark had been a graduate student of Joseph Langland's at the University of Massachusetts in Amherst, and Ruark shared Wright's Irish heritage and love of Irish verse. He had been teaching at Delaware for just a year when he met Wright's train on Friday, November 14. An enormous crowd filled the station, protesters heading to Washington for what became the largest antiwar demonstration in American history. When the two poets finally spotted each other, Wright greeted Ruark warmly, saying, "It takes one to know one." After his reading, the two stayed up drinking, reciting poems, and singing Irish songs. They shared an immediate and lasting rapport.

Wright looked forward to some welcome time off in the new year, thanks to a Rockefeller Foundation award meant to allow him a break from teaching. Due to a misunderstanding with Hunter College, however, the grant actually made life more difficult over the next few months. The Wrights planned to take the summer off, but the grant required Wright to take a full semester, not just a summer term; the foundation assumed that Hunter would provide matching funds. Hunter permitted Wright's absence that spring, but without pay, leaving the couple short of money while still hoping to travel to Europe in June.

Still, Wright rejoiced in a break from teaching, and his spirits lifted as the year drew to a close. Hesse's *Selected Poems* was ready for the printer when he began work on another book of translations for Farrar, Straus and Giroux: a selection of journal entries Hesse had titled

Wandering, "a strange and haunting little book made out of his note-books during the few years leading up to 1920." Wright planned the work as a collaboration: he would draft versions of Hesse's prose, while the book's ten poems would be translated by Franz.

On December 5, 1969, Wright appeared at the Phi Beta Kappa induction ceremony at the College of William & Mary in Williamsburg, Virginia, debuting a long, "scattering" poem in seven parts with the awkward title "Many of Our Waters: Variations on a Poem by a Black Child." Wright treated the honor with solemnity; at least, the poem is the longest he would ever publish. Meeting Wright for the first time that evening, the poet Dave Smith recalled how he "seemed distracted, as anyone might, but smelled of alcohol." The poem he read often seemed to match his state of inebriation. Exactly three years before, Wright had tried to articulate his ambition as a writer to Simpson and Dickey at the Library of Congress. In lines often quoted from this new poem, he makes another attempt:

> The kind of poetry I want to write is
> The poetry of a grown man.
> The young poets of New York come to me with
> Their mangled figures of speech,
> But they have little pity
> For the pure clear word.

Wright's insistence upon "the pure clear word" marks his kinship with Horace, a model he invoked continually. At the end of December, while spending Christmas in Ohio, the kernel of narrative that inspired Wright's own "Ars Poetica" sprang to life in his journal. The poem would join the long tradition of poems about poetry that Horace initiated in 13 B.C.E. As with so many Wright poems, it also served as an elegy, a portrait of his aunt Agnes Lyons.

––––––

When he and Anne escaped to Lake Minnewaska in the first week of January 1970, the lake was frozen solid and a thick mist hung over the surface. With the months ahead open to him, Wright turned to finishing the work at hand—his *Collected Poems* for Wesleyan and final corrections to Hesse's *Poems.* He wrote little in his journals in the first half of the year, and began few new poems before leaving for Europe in June. The couple went ahead with travel plans, despite losing Wright's Hunter salary for the spring semester. At the end of April, they were relieved to learn that he would receive a grant from the Ingram Merrill Foundation, ostensibly to help complete his two book projects.

Wright delivered Hesse's *Poems* on February 4, and the book appeared three months later. The bilingual collection included just thirty-one poems, limited to those that "deal with the single theme of homesickness." Wright quotes the long passage from *Steppenwolf* that he used as a "guide"—the same one he had often included in his letters. Both Hesse and Wright use the word *Heimweh*—homesickness—to describe a passionate, spiritual aspiration. Wright chose poems Hesse had written between 1899 and 1921, with many drawn from the early years of the First World War, when horrific images of war were inescapable. The idea of *homesickness* thus includes the sense of loss that pervaded the era, when nineteenth-century trust in civilization, culture, and progress became meaningless. Renewed interest in the Nobel laureate's work—especially among younger readers—had inspired the idea to translate Hesse's poems, and Wright knew he spoke to many thousands of conscription-age students confronted by violence and death on a large scale. For Wright, the idea of homesickness encompassed a recognition of the sanctity of life.

In early February, Wright received a despondent letter from Franz, who threatened to drop out of high school. Wright responded with empathy and affirmation. "It is our lot to work hard in the darkness," he wrote, assuring his son that he knew "the despair you speak of. I have come to understand that the confrontation with despair is the source of art and life. And there is only one way to confront despair; and that is through work." Franz remained in school; he sought his father's advice more often now, and their letters show a growing warmth and intimacy.

Wright felt that the choices his students—and his son—now faced made the era "the hardest time in American history, for young men and women." A draft lottery had been instituted in December 1969, dictating the sequence of induction into the armed forces based on dates of birth. Though not immediately threatened by conscription, Franz grew anxious. On March 11, Wright discouraged Franz's plan to renounce his U.S. citizenship and leave for Canada. Believing that a thorough physical exam might disqualify Franz from service, Wright told him to contact Gene Pugatch, now a respected physician. The U.S. medical staff had proven their incompetence to Wright when he had needed to argue his way *into* the army in 1946.

Later that month, Wright traveled to the University of Massachusetts in Amherst to join in the March Moratorium Poetry Festival organized by Joseph Langland. More than forty visiting and local poets appeared over the course of six days, and Wright arrived for the festival's final event on Saturday, March 14, appearing with Bly and Robert Creeley. When he called Bly out of the audience to say a poem they had translated together, Bly climbed over the seats in the crowded auditorium, reciting even before he reached the stage. Bly then asked Wright for a poem, but taunted him when he finished: "You never were good at that one. Let me say it." The two then recited each other's poems, with boisterous parodies and impersonations.

Ten days later, the Wrights made their last visit together to the Bly farm in Minnesota, after flying first to Los Angeles to see Jack Wright and meet his fiancée, Elizabeth. During their brief stay in Minnesota as spring came to the prairie, Wright had the sense of leisure that had largely eluded him all winter. At Carol's instigation, however, he again found himself in front of students when every ninth-grader in town filled the Madison High cafeteria. Carol had promised an engaging talk on Dickens, calling Jim an "actor and ham as well as poet." But Wright began with a respectful, slightly pompous lecture, detailing dates, names, and historical background. Carol grew discouraged, sharing in the puzzlement she saw on the teenagers' faces.

> Then suddenly it was there. Literally as if a windowpane had blown smash into the room, Jim began to give his gift. . . . For twenty minutes Jim Wright *presented* in a one-man show to 107 fourteen-year-old Minnesotans just how cruel, just how absolutely unscrupulously avaricious, Anglo-Saxon adults with authority over anyone—especially over children—can be. . . . [These] kids hadn't even thought, before, how much a good man, Charles Dickens or James Wright, can hate human cruelty. You could see them trying it for size while they listened to Jim, saying to themselves, should I hate cruelty? Will I hate cruelty? They were very interested.

As they had countless times before, Wright and Bly fell to work at the kitchen table in the farmhouse, returning to the poems of Vallejo and Neruda for an expanded selection of translations for the Beacon Press. Some of the additions to their original *Twenty Poems* collections came from drafts abandoned a decade earlier, and they worked over each one with notes and criticism from Hardie St. Martin. They continued to exchange successive drafts by mail, determined to include more from Vallejo's difficult masterpiece *Trilce* and his posthumous *Poemas Humanos*.

———

While the Ingram Merrill grant salvaged their plans to travel in Europe that summer, Wright learned that his former benefactor Hy Sobiloff had not paid for all of Wright's therapy bills with Dr. Marvin Sukov, his psychiatrist in Minneapolis. Realizing he still owed a considerable sum, Wright agreed to an intense series of readings on the Ohio college circuit for three weeks in early May, traveling alone. By trying to pay for past treatment, he pushed himself almost to a breaking point. After lecturing at Syracuse University for three days, Wright continued on to Ohio, already troubled by news that his mother had been hospitalized for acute diabetes.

On Thursday, April 30, President Nixon appeared on television to announce the "Cambodian Incursion" by U.S. combat forces, widening the war in Southeast Asia. That weekend, violent protests at Kent State University in northeastern Ohio prompted the state's governor to send National Guard troops to the campus. On Monday, May 4, the guardsmen opened fire on student demonstrators who had refused to disperse; four students were killed and nine others wounded. In the wake of the shootings, a nationwide student-led strike quickly engaged more than four million students, leading to the closure of hundreds of colleges, universities, and high schools. The Kent State campus remained closed for six weeks. On May 9, the Saturday following the student killings, more than a hundred thousand marched in Washington, D.C., to protest the deaths and escalation of the war—a crucial turning point in the public debate over the United States' role in Vietnam. This was the Ohio that Wright returned to at the beginning of May 1970, the heart of a nation at war with itself.

Martins Ferry, Ohio, facing southeast toward Wheeling, West Virginia, from Riverview Cemetery, April 1984. The Terminal Bridge is visible in the center of the photo. (Photograph by Madeline Zulauf)

Dudley and Jessie
Wright, circa 1925
(Courtesy of Andersen
Library Archives, University
of Minnesota, Minneapolis)

Ted, Jim, and Marge Wright,
Martins Ferry, circa 1928
(Courtesy of Anne Wright)

Elizabeth (Biddy) Lyons,
Jessie's mother, in Martins
Ferry, with a granddaughter,
circa 1930 (Courtesy of Penny
Wright Monroe)

Ted and Jim Wright,
Martins Ferry,
Christmas 1932
(Courtesy of Anne Wright)

James Wright, Shreve High School
graduation portrait, Martins Ferry,
June 1946 (Courtesy of Anne Wright)

Allen Tate, John Crowe Ransom, and Philip Blair Rice, the School of English at Kenyon College, summer 1948 (Courtesy of Kenyon College Library, Greenslade Archives)

Hika literary magazine staff, fall 1951: (Clockwise from lower left) Evan Lottman; Ed Doctorow; Wright; Sy Weissman; Nicholas Crome; George Geasey (Courtesy of Kenyon College Library, Greenslade Archives)

Wright, Liberty, and infant Franz, Vienna, May 1953 (Courtesy of Liberty Kovacs)

Theodore Roethke portrait, 1952 (Photograph by James O. Sneddon, University of Washington Libraries, Special Collections)

Dudley and Franz Wright, Chandlersville, Ohio, September 1953 (Photograph by Liberty
Kovacs)

Wright with Marshall and Franz, Como Avenue, Minneapolis, March 1959 (Photograph by Liberty Kovacs)

Oscar Williams and Wright, New York City, April 1960 (Courtesy of Andersen Library Archives)

Wright and Anne Sexton, Montauk, New York, August 1960 (Photograph by Oscar Williams, the Lilly Library, Indiana University, Bloomington, courtesy of the Williams Estate)

Louis Simpson, Wright, and Robert Bly, Bly farm, Madison, Minnesota, August 1960 (Photograph by Carol Bly)

Roger Hecht and Wright, New York City, circa winter 1960 (Courtesy of Wade Newman)

Wright in his basement study, Como Avenue, Minneapolis, circa summer 1960 (Photograph by Liberty Kovacs)

Carol Bly with the family dog, Simon, Bly farm, circa 1960 (Photograph by Robert Bly)

Wright, Bly farm, August 1962 (Photograph by Carol Bly)

Franz and Marshall Wright, circa 1962 (Courtesy of Liberty Kovacs)

Wright, James Dickey, and Louis Simpson, Library of Congress reading, Washington, D.C., December 5, 1966 (Courtesy of Anne Wright)

Wright and Anne after their wedding, with Laura Lee, Riverside Church, New York City, April 29, 1967 (Photograph by Jane Lee)

John Logan, Robert and Mary Bly, New York City, February 1968 (Photograph by Carol Bly)

Wright with Garnie Braxton (embracing him) and siblings, New York City, winter 1970 (Photograph by Anne Wright)

Wright, Indiana University at Bloomington, spring 1970 (Photograph by Richard Pflum)

Dudley, Jessie, Marge, Wright, Jack, and Ted Wright at the wedding of Ted's daughter Penny, Zanesville, Ohio, June 19, 1971 (Photograph by Helen Wright)

Wright and Marshall, Montreal, Canada, July 1971 (Photograph by Anne Wright)

Anne Wright, Hotel Wildmere, Lake Minnewaska, New York, August 1971 (Photograph by Orrin Bly)

Wright, Hotel Wildmere, August 1971 (Photograph by Orrin Bly)

Wright, Anghiari, Italy, August 2, 1972 (Photograph by Anne Wright)

Anne and Wright in front of Notre-Dame, Paris, August 1972
(Photograph by Laura Lee DeCinque)

Wright at Max Jacob's grave, Saint-Benoît-sur-Loire, France, July
1973 (Photograph by Anne Wright)

Wright and W. S. Merwin, Hawaii, August 1976 (Photograph by Anne Wright)

Leslie Marmon Silko, Idle Hour Ranch, Tucson, 1982 (Photograph by Anne Wright)

Wright with Maud and Galway Kinnell, Nice, France, January 1979 (Photograph by Anne Wright)

Anne and James Wright, near San Gimignano, Italy, July 1979 (Photograph by Jane Lee)

View from Wright's study window in the Higgins apartment, showing Sacré Coeur, Paris (Photograph by Jonathan Blunk)

Hosted by James Reiss at Miami University in Oxford, Ohio, Wright's reading on May 4 went on as planned even as word spread of the shootings earlier that day. Anne had not yet heard the news when Wright called to assure her he was safe. "His evening reading wasn't well attended," Reiss recalled, "and I could feel a pall when I introduced him to a smattering of students and faculty members. In his antics Jim appeared dazed, unaware of Kent State." Thus began the most troubled reading tour of Wright's career. His appearance at Kent State was canceled, as were other readings. Wright felt uncomfortable appearing as a distinguished writer in the midst of such palpable grief and uncertainty, and he instead resorted to reading poems by others and inviting audience members onstage to read—infuriating the school sponsors who had paid to hear his work.

As the tour ground on, Wright's drinking grew more pronounced. At the University of Ohio in Athens, he balked at the long-standing rule that drinks could not be carried from the bar to the dining room. "You could tell that that exasperated him. So he just finished his martini in a gulp. But the indignation, and compliance—if you could combine them in a single gesture, you'd call it ballet." At Kenyon on May 8, Wright's reading went so poorly that college administrators swore they would never invite him back. Following Ransom's generous introduction, Wright announced that he couldn't go on during such awful times, and "therefore let us read poems to one another." Some scurried to find poems to read, simply to fill the silence in the auditorium. When his next reading was canceled, Wright remained in Gambier for two days longer than planned and emptied his host's liquor cabinet.

As Tony Stoneburner observed, Wright had been "stirred by the outward disturbance to an inward one" that triggered an unrelenting drinking binge. At Denison University, Wright had seemed "garrulous perhaps, compulsively loquacious," but not disabled. By the time he arrived at Oberlin College on May 11, however, the poet and professor David Young could see that Wright "was on a real bender." While Oberlin did not experience the violence that sprang up elsewhere, classes had been suspended and faculty looked to Wright's reading as a chance to connect with students. But again, Wright declined to say his own poems and invited others to take the stage. As he backed away from the podium's spotlight, he took with him a jar filled with bourbon. "You really couldn't have a conversation with him," Young recalled. "He'd get excited and recite the first chapter of *Great Expectations* or some Horace, but he really wouldn't converse. It was partly because he was in such bad shape and just not *able* to converse."

Wright did not share with anyone the news that his mother had suffered a heart attack while in the hospital. Leaving Oberlin, he anxiously hoped to see both his parents later that afternoon. Jessie had recovered, though she remained noticeably weaker. Her newfound religious faith struck many as more remarkable than her resiliency. To Marge she revealed that Jesus had visited her in the hospital; she now spoke with mild propriety. Having listened to Jessie curse for more than fifty years, Marge could not believe it. "I never, ever heard my mother refrain from swearing in my life, because she *loved* to shock the preachers." Weeks later, Jessie returned to ignoring restrictions on her diet, but she now kept a civil tongue.

Reassured about his mother's health, Wright felt relieved to get back to New York after three long weeks of travel. With Anne he attended Gene Pugatch's wedding and recited "A Blessing" at the couple's reception. "He really loved New York," recalled Pugatch, who joined Wright at all manner of musical events, from opera to chamber music recitals, throughout the city. "I think whatever deeply felt religious experiences he had clearly came through music." Wright felt at home in the city, bemused that he was never accepted as a "New York poet." He betrayed his true allegiance in the heat of an argument with Anne. When she declared, "If you don't like it, you can just leave!" Wright shot back, with more mischief than anger, "What? And leave a forty-eight-dollar-a-month apartment in Manhattan?"

Having Betty Kray's help was reason enough to stay in New York. When she heard that Wright needed a typist to help complete his *Collected Poems*, she offered her own assistant, the writer Kathleen Norris. Betty and Anne then colluded to delay her in completing the task, knowing that anxiety would consume Wright once the manuscript was done. On June 3, 1970, as the couple began packing for Europe, Wright mailed the *Collected Poems* manuscript to Wesleyan and made the first entry in his journal in months.

This afternoon I completed, with Annie's indispensable life and help, *Collected Poems, 1970*. In a few moments we are going to take it, with some copies of the Hesse translation, to the post office.

I didn't want this terrible and heavy book to be completed in pain.

Will I never learn?

Everything that is created is created in pain.

I live in the hope that she will love the book when it appears.

As with his previous collection, the dedication bore only one name; this time it was: "Annie."

20

A certain high summer

June 1970–August 1971

The Wrights spent a few days at Lake Minnewaska before flying to Paris—the first of six European sojourns over the next decade. Their trip was ambitious: in just ten weeks, they traveled from Paris through the South of France to Italy—including Tuscany and Venice—and on to Vienna for three weeks with Franz and Marshall; their final week would find them in Yugoslavia. Wright felt a sense of relief and rejuvenation in Paris, where he had longed to return for eighteen years, ever since he passed through during his Fulbright year. They felt welcome in the "slightly shabby and inexpensive" Hotel Lenox on the Left Bank on the rue de l'Université, three blocks from the Seine near Boulevard Saint-Germain. Decades before, James Joyce and T. S. Eliot had been guests at the hotel, and an air of threadbare grandeur survived, with red velvet curtains and elegant ironwork in the windows.

The first café the couple entered after they arrived was the small, family-owned Café Bizuth on rue du Pré aux Clercs and Boulevard Saint-Germain, and it became a second home for Wright in Paris. As he and Anne left that first afternoon, they noticed a plaque on the wall outside commemorating the building as one of the last homes of Apollinaire, who had lived there with his young wife, Jacqueline Kolb—"La Jolie Rousse." Wright returned to Café Bizuth as often as he could. Anne frequented a separate café farther down the boulevard, knowing her husband might sit writing for hours. "Surprisingly," Wright later reflected, "all sorts of poems began to appear in my mind."

Wright's expatriation seemed to lift a weight from his shoulders. Among the "New Poems" in his *Collected*, he had included a translation of Apollinaire's "The Pretty Redhead," which seeks to reconcile the "long quarrel between tradition and imagination"—what Wright once conceived as the opposite poles of Robinson and Whitman. Paris helped ease an old argument Wright had with himself. A steady flow of new work appeared in his journal all summer, the first sustained period of writing he'd enjoyed in years. The couple discovered the street market on rue Mouffetard and established a routine of shopping for a picnic lunch each morning, then choosing a destination: a museum, a church, the Tuileries, the Luxembourg Gardens. The human scale of the city, the river, the sycamores, and the rain put him at ease, and Wright began to shape a personal rapport with Paris in his journal.

When they left, the couple traveled to Orléans and Saint-Benoît-sur-Loire before continuing south; more than a dozen poems in Wright's next book could be arranged to show their itinerary that summer, from "Hotel Lenox" to "Afternoon and Evening at Ohrid." Among his first prose pieces is an elegy to the poet Max Jacob, written at his gravesite in Fleury-sur-Loire. A plaque in the basilica in Saint-Benoît said simply that Jacob had prayed there, but Wright became intrigued and sought out his grave. Published in couplets in *Two Citizens*, much of "The Snail's Road" is identical to the initial prose version in Wright's journal. It stood as the concluding poem of his new manuscript until its final arrangement. Jacob, who died in a deportation camp in 1944 at the age of sixty-seven, was a master of the prose poem, and Wright returned to Jacob's work now with a new interest in the lyrical prose form.

Wright's prose in his journal that summer is by turns taut and expansive, rooted in detailed observations. The urgency and the restlessness that define the poems in *Shall We Gather at the River* are less in evidence. Instead, Wright relaxes into the flexibility of sentence structures; even in line-break poems, the sentence is the primary formal element. His description of the city of Orléans has the immediacy felt throughout his travel journals. "We arrived somewhat weary and frazzled last evening, after a whole day by train, to discover this refreshingly lemon-colored city." Absorbed by the quality of light, Wright focuses on the scene before him. "What sunlight it is. Not the heavy old gold of certain autumn [days] that we love in America, but something newly-minted, some lightness to the fingers, a certain high summer that doesn't pass away, the fresh light flashing quickly from the children's faces into the very wine we drink." Their stay in the "mysterious and melancholy" town of Arles found Wright casually counting the shades of green in the trees and searching for the bridge Van Gogh had painted there. Before leaving for Avignon and Nice, Wright drafted one of his best new poems, "The Old Dog in the Ruins of the Graves at Arles," granting to "one stray mutt . . . almost indistinguishable from the dust" the "lonely wisdom [that] graves last longer than men." The poem appears in *Two Citizens* exactly as he first wrote it down. This rich fluency arose in part from relative sobriety; traveling with Anne in Europe, he was able to keep his drinking in check.

———

Anne's familiarity with French and Italian helped negotiate their travels, but they trusted to luck on this first trip and didn't book hotels in advance. They arrived in Bologna by train from Nice on a Sunday afternoon and chose the Pensione Farini from a list on a wall in the station house. Their spacious room had a painted ceiling and two balconies; when they wandered out the next day they found themselves in the heart of the market district. "Bologna: A Poem About Gold," the first of many ekphrastic poems written on his European travels, describes the St. Cecilia Altarpiece by Raphael in the National Painting Gallery. In his journal, the poem began as a description of the city itself, as seen "from the hilltop church of San Michele in Bosco. Roofs, towers, and buildings alike are a kind of golden rust, interspersed with a varied and rich green. A stone city, which has nevertheless encouraged its trees, vines, and flowers. It is a poem about gold." Wright delighted in the food and was charmed by the warmth and friendliness of the Italian people. The entire country quickly claimed his affection and proved as generous in inspiration as southern Ohio could be in memory.

While staying in Arezzo, Wright was astounded by the frescoes of Piero della Francesca in the Basilica of San Francesco; the couple soon made a day trip to San Sepulcro to see Piero's *Resurrection*. The work of the Early Renaissance master left a profound impression, and Wright made many pilgrimages to his paintings, captivated by Piero's calm, res-

onant humanism. He and Anne made a day trip to Siena as well, but
they arrived on an election day and found much of the city closed. As
with their overnight stay in Florence, they consoled themselves with plans
to return. If Wright ever "quested" after anything, Anne believed, it was
simply to get back to Italy as often as he could.

The couple passed through Ravenna on their way to Venice, where
they stayed for five days at the pensione La Calcina on the Giudecca
Canal, across from the Church of the Redentore. They took a second-
floor room that had a writing desk and a balcony facing the canal—a
room they would always return to. Wright's first visit to the city, however,
became shadowed by depression. His journals reveal this struggle and
his means of combating it: more writing, whatever the cost. Though Anne
reassured him they had plenty of money, small difficulties fed his anxiety.
Wright sympathized with Lawrence's troubled first impressions of Venice, which he called an "[a]bhorrent, green, slippery city."

As they boarded a train to Vienna, Anne believed that her husband
would now take on the task of guiding their way in German. Wright
shrugged her off, saying only, "I hope you're not serious." Afraid of embarrassment, he continued to depend on Anne and was even shy of asking for bread or a newspaper. Soon after they arrived at the beginning of
August, the couple took up a vigil at the train station, meeting every
train from Frankfurt in expectation of Wright's two sons. Liberty had
told them the date but never said which train. When the boys finally appeared, they were sleepless and hungry after an overnight journey.

Marshall, who had just turned twelve, recalled how Franz "took on
the role of the Scout leader" during the long ordeal. The brothers shared
a room in the Hotel Alderhof in Old Vienna, with windows that looked
out on the dome of the Greek Orthodox Church where Franz had been
baptized. Marshall was overjoyed to spend three weeks with their
father. "Dad was the freedom giver, the release giver, the providential
repairer of the experience with Mike. He spoiled us." Marshall loved the
bumper car races, horse-drawn carriage rides, and the Riesenrad Ferris
Wheel. They visited homes where Beethoven had lived, as well as Jim
and Liberty's old apartment, and frequented concerts in the Stadtpark.

His sons grew accustomed, however, to seeing Wright disappear into
a café for hours at a time to work in his journal. "We knew his greatness
from the beginning," Marshall recalled, "and we never doubted it. I always assumed that he was one of the most creative persons who'd ever

lived." Franz agreed. "Just to be in the same room with him was all I required—and that was very hard for him." While Franz, then seventeen, was excited to see the city where he had been born, what he wanted most was simply to be with his father. Years later, Franz recalled an afternoon they spent in a small café in Vienna, when he had "wept like a child" to hear his father's careful criticism of his new poems. "The thing is, you told me the truth," Franz wrote his father in August 1979. "So that now, if you tell me a poem of mine has moved you, or strikes you as true to the world, it's possible for me to believe you are telling me the truth, and take heart and go on."

Months earlier, Wright had been invited by the Macedonian Writers' Union to participate in the Struga Poetry Festival, together with other American and international poets. The final week of the Wrights' European trip took them to Belgrade, where they boarded a charter plane to a newly opened luxury hotel on the shore of Lake Ohrid in the mountains of south-central Yugoslavia. One of forty invited poets, Wright joined the mayor and other dignitaries for a lavish meal in the city; the showcase reading drew many hundreds of local townspeople and writers from around the country. Actors read translations of the foreign poets' work after each spoke, from a stage set on the span of an ancient stone bridge lit by burning torches.

Against the wishes of their hosts, the Wrights took to exploring. "The place was so spectacularly beautiful that we started to avoid the literary conferences between the Russians and the Communists from Morocco and the rest, and accepting the spirit of the Yugoslavians, who are very beautiful, very independent people, we wandered around on our own. We didn't know the language." The very foreignness of Serbo-Croatian set the music of their words in relief and inspired "Afternoon and Evening at Ohrid," one of the many love poems in Wright's evolving manuscript. With only his knowledge of French, German, and Italian to assist him, the poet felt cast in the role of primordial Adam, naming the flowers and birds he discovered with Annie in that mountainous paradise.

———

When Wright resumed teaching in the fall, Hunter College had become an altogether different place. Protests led by black and Puerto Rican students the previous year—including the occupation of buildings on many campuses—had demanded the full integration of the City Univer-

sity of New York. In September 1970, CUNY schools began implement-
ing an open admissions policy, accepting all high school graduates from
the five boroughs, regardless of their academic preparedness. At the same
time, the colleges offered free tuition, and the two initiatives brought a
staggering increase in student enrollment. The matriculating freshman
class nearly doubled in size throughout the city that fall, and included
three times the number of black, Hispanic, and international immigrant
students. Teachers like Wright welcomed this diversity, but they now
faced overcrowded classrooms where remedial instruction became a
primary focus. Hunter had long been noted for its academic rigor, but
the character of the school changed dramatically. Wright responded by
working harder, trying to maintain the open dialogue with students that
distinguished his classes.

In late September, Wright was invited to read at SUNY Brockport,
and also sat for a videotaped interview the next day with the poets Jerome
Mazzaro and William Heyen. His reading included a dozen poems
from his "new book"—the sequence of "New Poems" from his *Collected*
volume, due to be published in the spring. He concluded with "Northern Pike," and as the applause faded, John Logan called out for a poem
from *The Branch*, prompting others to do the same. Wright continued
with poems by Trakl and Vallejo, but his translation of Apollinaire's "The
Pretty Redhead" marked the emotional center of the evening.

After a brief sketch of the French poet's life, Wright said, "this poem
means a great deal to me, for personal reasons—as well as literary reasons." In the middle of his impassioned reading, he stopped and spoke
softly, as though to himself. Wright let silence gather following the line
"All we want is to explore kindness the enormous country where everything is silent." Looking out at the crowd, he then whispered earnestly,
"Christ, I'd rather have written that than go to heaven." As the writer
Charles Baxter, then a graduate student at Buffalo, vividly recalled, "It
was an astounding moment. Everybody knew from his tone of voice that
he wasn't kidding, that he meant every word of what he had just said."
Despite Wright's willingness to strike this Faustian bargain, there is a
curious irony in his confession. He *had*, in a real sense, written the line
he so admired, having created in English a masterful version of Apollinaire's poem.

On the morning after his reading, the recorded interview shows Heyen
and Mazzaro jostling nervously to steer the conversation; with care and

conviction, Wright says every poem they ask for—all from his first three books. Their talk ranges widely, from his Kenyon education to the spirit of Dickens, from Laurel and Hardy's slapstick to Roethke's poetic achievement—"one of the chosen ones, I think." Repeatedly, however, the questions return to Wright's supposed repudiation of formal verse with the publication of *The Branch* seven years earlier. Wright had hoped that idea had already been put to rest.

> There wasn't a truly radical change taking place between the books *Saint Judas* and *The Branch Will Not Break*. But it was just that I hadn't previously tried to subject myself to the discipline of writing real, good free verse. I thought it was about time to do that. I wanted to—and I continue to try to—listen to as many kinds of music in our language as I could.

Anne and James each learned separately that fall that their apartment building had been sold to the Horace Mann School, raising the risk that they might lose their home on East Eighty-fifth Street. Neither one spoke of it, however, to protect the other from bad news. The gloom cast by the Vietnam War on "the spiritual weather of so much of America" troubled them both, and they returned to Lake Minnewaska twice that autumn.

When Wright heard that Allen Tate would read at the Morgan Library in New York in December, he saw an opportunity to redeem himself in Tate's eyes by introducing him to Anne. Though Tate had actually written in support of Wright's job at Hunter, Wright still associated him with the humiliation he had suffered at the University of Minnesota. Kray's Academy of American Poets sponsored extravagant black-tie affairs at the Morgan, and Wright rented a tuxedo, determined to prove to Tate that he had turned his life around. After the reading, as Wright approached with Anne on his arm, he was stunned to realize that Tate didn't recognize him. "It was appalling," Anne remembered. Tate turned away and scarcely acknowledged him.

Wright made plans to welcome his sons at Christmas as the holidays drew near. Preparing to send his final corrections to Bly for their expanded collection of Neruda and Vallejo translations, he asked Hardie St. Martin, who was in New York that December, to approve last-minute

changes. "Jim looks better than I've ever seen him," St. Martin wrote to
Bly, "and seemed to be drinking much less. Said something about
Europe having done him a lot of good." With his *Collected Poems* due out
in the spring, Wright again began assembling new work and sketching
provisional sequences for his next collection. Back in June 1965, he had
called his growing manuscript *Washed Up by Winter*—the book that
became *Shall We Gather at the River*. By contrast, many of his new poems
found inspiration in European sunlight rather than midwestern shadows. "I'm getting sort of tired of the darkness," he had told Heyen and
Mazzaro in September. "There is something to be said for the light, also,
after all." The prospect of returning to Europe shored up Wright's optimism; as he weathered another New York winter, he thought of calling
his next book *The Beginning of Summer*.

Turning from his first tentative ordering of new poems—most written
while in Europe—Wright began work in earnest on the new Hesse translations following Franz's stay in December. Over the coming year, Franz
worked on versions of the ten poems Hesse had included among the
prose pieces in *Wandering*. He exchanged drafts with his father, observing firsthand Wright's particular genius for translation. "He would
make these uncannily inspired suggestions that were just so wonderful in
English. They weren't just literally accurate, they were inspired images
or lines in English." A translator considers many alternatives of rhythm,
sense, and music before choosing the best words, and this process of
composition will influence the poet's own work. But a poet doesn't begin
a translation to get a finished product. "One thing my dad said that's
absolutely true is that it's simply the best way to *read* a poem in a language that's not your own, because you end up thinking about every
single word and comma, and every single thing that goes into making it.
You get inside of it and read it much more closely than you ever could read
a poem in your own language."

Wright was an excellent translator for Hesse, as his editor Michael di
Capua realized. "I felt, while reading what you've done so far, that I was
hearing Hesse's authentic voice." Wright subtitled his translation "Notes
and Sketches," referring to the plein air watercolors Hesse had included
in his book. These short prose meditations—impressions arising from
carefully observed landscapes—are another significant model for Wright's
own prose pieces, which, like Hesse's, were "mined from his casual
writings" in journals. As Wright noted in a description for his publisher,

"[Hesse's] pure prose, his old-fashioned lyricism, and his remarkable eye for the old earth and its places that renew themselves—all sing and see together in this lovely little book."

Just before the first classes of the spring semester at Hunter, Wright learned of his appointment to full professorship—a recognition that had long eluded him. In Anne's view, "the experience of being fired from Minnesota haunted him until his death, and he was never sure of himself—even when he got tenure." But as far as Hunter was concerned, Wright was "a superb teacher"; one colleague called him "the best I have seen in my years of official observation." Many praised Wright's astonishing memory and his lack of pretension with students. "His originality in the classroom somehow seemed to make his students more original than they were likely to be in other classes." In truth, Wright needed to teach. The daily structure the work demanded, his engagement with favorite writers, and the inspiration he drew from his students helped keep him in touch with his own strengths.

––––––

In March 1971, *The New Yorker* published two of Wright's "New Poems" in separate issues, anticipating the appearance of his *Collected Poems* in April. Both are examples of Wright's capacious form of historical elegy: "Red Jacket's Grave" and "A Secret Gratitude," a tribute to Edna St. Vincent Millay and her husband. Stanley Plumly recognized the work that Wright began publishing in "New Poems" and *Two Citizens* as something new in American poetry, where the poet's presence becomes "more than a transparency. It's as if the *I* had entered the other," not just empathized with them, while avoiding self-indulgence or sentimentality. Wright had learned Rilke's lesson of observing something so closely that one becomes nearly inseparable from it—like the fish he celebrates in "Northern Pike."

The first major review of *Collected Poems* appeared in the middle of May on a full page of *The New York Times Book Review*. The reviewer, Peter Stitt, began by declaring Wright to be "emphatically" among "the best poets of our age." He admired Wright's compassion and, as evidenced by the poems in *The Branch*, his courage "in assuming his new style . . . partially based on a loosening of form." *Collected Poems* "has the authority that only the best books have," the review concludes; "it forces on us the recognition that James Wright is among the masters of our day." Wright could not have wanted more fulsome praise.

Wright's relationship with Torre Bueno, his editor at Wesleyan, made it a difficult decision for him to publish his next book with Farrar, Straus and Giroux. Responding to a letter from Bueno, Wright tried to dismiss the *Times* review—no matter how much it must have pleased Wesleyan. "I care more about poetry and friendship than I care about an accidental twitch of flattery in brief print," Wright told Bueno. "I feel like the guy Ben Jonson wrote about: today I live forever, and tomorrow somebody will use my book to wrap a fish in." As FSG drafted a contract for Wright's next book, the poet considered dedicating *Two Citizens* to Bueno and his wife.

That same week in May, Wright continued revising one of the center-pieces of his new manuscript, "Prayer to the Good Poet," a poem for both Wright's father and the Latin poet Horace. From its earliest draft, Wright uses a loose, eleven-beat measure adapted from the hendecasyllabic line used by Catullus. Horace and Dudley become merged in his imagination, the two "loving fathers" who helped guide him into adulthood in Martins Ferry. Wright longs to reconcile with them both—"by Tiber, by Ohio"—and also with his son, whom he welcomes as "another poet." In Franz he recognized something of himself when he first left home in 1946 to serve in the army. The poem attempts a kind of awkward embrace.

Franz graduated from high school in June and soon left for Europe, living with a family in Belgium as an exchange student. Wright also left the country that summer, teaching for two months in Montreal at Sir George Williams University. With Anne, Wright welcomed Marshall for two months, and they celebrated his thirteenth birthday at the end of July. Anne's niece Karin East also joined them in the "big, nutty, eleven-room house" they rented in the city's leafy suburbs.

Though Wright's salary could scarcely pay for the cost of the trip up from New York, his students were among the best he ever taught; his evening class included many teachers pursuing advanced degrees. Teaching his Comic Spirit course, Wright felt inspired by his students' maturity and dedication. In addition, the Dante scholar John Freccero and Irving Massey from the University at Buffalo proved fine companions. "That was one of the happiest times he had teaching in the summer," Anne recalled—and the best time Wright ever shared with his younger son. They were together more that summer than at any time since Marshall was a toddler. They visited the old parts of Montreal and the fairgrounds of the 1967 World's Fair, and frequented a neighborhood pool all summer. As Wright told the Blys, Marsh was "splendid company—humorous, affectionate, adventurous, musical."

But friction grew between Anne and Marshall, in step with his increasing defiance. When Karin, a year older than Marshall, arrived in August, she witnessed more disturbing behavior and much that eluded his father and stepmother, including physical displays of anger and depression. Spurred by the cruelty of teenage boys killing grasshoppers at the pool, Marshall threw himself in a rage at the small gang, but succeeded only in getting himself thrown out by the lifeguard.

When John Logan and Daniela Gioseffi visited Wright in Montreal, they were startled by his continuing fury at a recent article in *Time* magazine. In a long, sneering attack supposedly based on interviews with "scores of collegiate poets and critics," the *Time* writer insisted that American poets could be "rudely divided into five groups," each category more disparaging than the next. Blaming "the depressed state" of poetry in America on "a closed mutual-admiration society" of established poets, the mean-spirited piece concluded with a wholesale dismissal: "Today's intentionally unmemorable, flatted verse seems an unnecessary and misguided burden upon the ear and the imagination." Wright grew apoplectic, seeing such ill-conceived malice condoned by the country's largest weekly magazine.

Wright's violent reaction was not provoked simply by one critic's stupidity. The whole business of categorizing American poets set Wright's teeth on edge, and the diversity of work being published made such an effort almost meaningless by the end of the 1960s. The decade had seen an enormous growth in the art, multiplying both the numbers of those writing it and their readership. Poetry had begun to thrive in cities and colleges across the country, and the impact of international poetry in translation gave younger poets a profusion of new models. Wright's work exemplifies the eclecticism that poets now take for granted; his decision to use prose, free verse, or rhyme and meter depended on the poem at hand. "As for the different kinds of form," he said that October, "I call it just a continuous exploration."

What angered Wright most was how poorly America treated her poets; to Logan he swore he would stay in Canada. His discontent with America became a major theme in the poems he gathered in *Two Citizens*, and the poet's combative stance would provoke even the most sympathetic critics. The book's new title first appears on a table of contents in mid-August, where Wright also jots down the epigraph he would use from Hemingway's short story "The Killers"—seven lines of dialogue, beginning "'Well, bright boy,' Max said, looking into the mirror, 'why don't you say something?'" With twenty-eight poems in various stages of revision, he divides them beneath two columns: "America the Past" and "Europe the Tragic." His translation of Virgil's Third *Georgic* still needs work, he notes; he never would complete it. Added later in a large, hand-written scrawl is another possible epigraph for the book: "To turn on the dead in fury, and be damned."

While living in Montreal that summer, Wright saw reviews of *Collected Poems* appearing everywhere. "The presiding genius loci here is midwestern," Babette Deutsch began her review in *The New Republic*, highlighting "the note of sad serenity" that Wright shared with "those old Chinese poems" and with Virgil as well. In *The Nation*, Roger Hecht agreed, suggesting that the poet "has in his own way continued the stories of Sherwood Anderson." Hayden Carruth included *Collected Poems* in a wide-ranging *Hudson Review* essay, and chose the first stanza of "A Prayer to the Lord Ramakrishna" to show Wright at his best:

The anguish of a naked body is more terrible
To bear than God.
And the rain goes on falling.

"Hard, clear, simple, abiding; the tragic sense carried forward in classic wholeness."

In another omnibus review published in *The New York Review of Books* on July 22, 1971, Stephen Spender devoted most of his energy and prose to a new book by Ted Hughes, *Crow*, and paid scant attention to Wright's *Collected*. The most fascinating part of Spender's review appears only in the margins of Wright's copy of it. Shrugging off Spender's condescension, he suddenly saw a way to shape his growing manuscript: "I respect this review, & learn: the next step is to flood the *second half* of 2 *Citizens* with love poems. Because Agnes is the tragic reality, & Annie is the reality of resurrection. *End* the book with *The Snail's Road*. Begin it with *Ars Poetica*. Jenny in the middle, the strange Muse."

Wright's poem about his aunt Agnes, "Ars Poetica: Some Recent Criticism," became the first in the book, a bitter, unforgiving outburst of anger and grief. He grouped love poems to Annie in the second half of *Two Citizens*, and included two significant new poems to Jenny.

21

It is all we have,
just each other

August 1971–January 1973

Despite the welcome his *Collected Poems* had received, Wright felt uneasy about returning to the States. "America is so gloomy and exhausting
these days," he told the Blys, weeks after the tirade in *Time* magazine.
The Wrights left Montreal on August 27 and dropped their luggage on
East Eighty-fifth Street and fled to the mountains. They stayed at Hotel
Wildmere for more than a week before confronting New York and the
new school year.

Wright returned to Hunter's teeming classrooms and, unexpectedly,
a crowded apartment as well. After traveling all summer through France,
Italy, and Yugoslavia, Franz became overwhelmed by depression just as
the school semester began in Brussels. Abruptly leaving Europe, he arrived in New York at the end of September, planning to stay with his
father indefinitely. There simply wasn't room. The apartment afforded no
privacy: the bathroom and shower stall stood beside the narrow kitchen,
and the single bedroom was the only room with a door. For three weeks,
before he returned to California, Franz slept on the living room couch
with his suitcase on the floor. Wright was appalled to finally learn of the
abuse his sons had suffered at the hand of their stepfather, and he now
understood a root cause of Franz's recurrent anger. Accepted by Oberlin
College in Ohio, Franz pressed to be admitted at midterm in January, so
he could leave California for good.

When "October Ghosts" came out in *The New Yorker* on October 2, 1971, the figure of Jenny made one of her last appearances in print. A central poem in *Two Citizens*, it exemplifies Wright's unique form of love poem–elegy, here addressed to the Muse, "Jenny cold, Jenny darkness":

> I will walk with you and Callimachus
> Into the gorges
> Of Ohio, where the miners
> Are dead with us.

The poem combines a visionary reach with an almost occult sense of intimacy, recalling the affection Wright had once poured into his letters to Sonjia Urseth. But in "October Ghosts," Jenny is more than a lost love; she survives as a kind of folk legend—the "fat blossoming grand-mother of the dead" rooted in the hills of Appalachia.

Wright had struck a rich vein of imagery from his childhood that would continue to nourish his poems. For all of its rough edges and defi-ance, *Two Citizens* marks a stylistic turn almost as significant as *The Branch*, though Wright shook off suggestions of this kind. Speaking with the Canadian poet Michael André in early October, Wright dis-couraged any attempt to trace "development" in his work. "I wouldn't look for it. I think I knew pretty well what I was going to do from the beginning. I was just trying to find out ways to do it."

Throughout his interview with André, published the following spring in the journal *Unmuzzled Ox*, Wright underscores the continuity of his work. As he had at Kenyon, Wright names Edward Thomas his favorite poet: "He's able to write about nature with a sense of the religious value of things, the life of the spirit." With Po Chu-i and John Keats, Thomas is "one of the secret spirits who help keep us alive. . . . I'm not saying that Edward Thomas is a great poet. He's not Aeschylus, he's not Shake-speare, he's not Neruda. Well, neither am I. Who is? And there's a sense in which one ought to be able to say, who *has* to be? We should be able to listen to people's music for its own sake."

———

In mid-October, William Matthews organized an exceptional series of readings at Cornell University, "a sort of minor festival." Joining Bly, Logan,

Kinnell, and Wright, Tomas Tranströmer arrived from Sweden at the start of a fall tour of the United States. Robert Morgan, at the beginning of a distinguished career in the English Department, called that October weekend "one of the most remarkable" series ever held on campus. Logan quickly won over the audience; his engaging, conversational manner made it difficult to know when he had started saying a poem. Wright read with more care and reflection—what Morgan recognized as the reticence common to men "from our part of the world," linking Wright's Alleghenies with his own Blue Ridge Mountains.

Wright felt more relaxed at the farmhouse of the poet Anselm Parlatore outside of Ithaca. Excited to be together with Bly and Tranströmer, Wright kept them up late talking, long after other guests had left. He and Anne went walking through the surrounding fields the next day "hand in hand, only to come back with some large sunflowers, both so happy and child-like in their exuberance and delight," Parlatore recalled. "They seemed very much in love."

Wright continued to add new poems to his growing manuscript that fall, and a new elegy to Philip Timberlake is shot through with the affection more common to a love poem. As he finalized "At the Grave" at the end of November, he admitted to his old professor, "I am not among the English poets." Three weeks later, however, he had reason to believe he might be among the American ones. Marie Bullock phoned before Christmas to confirm that he would receive the prestigious Fellowship of the Academy of American Poets, with an award of ten thousand dollars. With Anne in his arms, Wright danced around their kitchen when he heard the news. They began planning a long sabbatical in Europe, to begin in June 1973.

Though Wright often fought off depression in winter, this December was different. He enjoyed dressing up as Santa Claus for Anne's students at the Downstate Medical School Co-op Nursery in Brooklyn, where she had been teaching since September. The couple traveled to Ohio to see Wright's parents at Christmas and then welcomed his sons to New York the following week. "It was just exhilaration—childish ease, and fun," Marshall recalled; for him, these brief stays with his father were true holidays.

Wright received the Academy Fellowship award at a Donnell Library ceremony in New York on January 25, 1972, at which he read to an overflow audience. The recognition amplified the discomfort he always felt in public, and triggered a night of heavy drinking. What was worse, John Berryman—one of the Academy chancellors who voted for Wright's election—had thrown himself from the Washington Avenue Bridge in Minneapolis just two weeks before. Wright felt profound gratitude toward Berryman; the two poets had shared a deeply empathic imagination, and Berryman's suicide troubled Wright for months.

At the reception at Bullock's Fifth Avenue apartment following his reading, Wright "was pretty much in his cups," telling a circle of by-standers how he suffered more than other people. Anne overheard this and interjected, "No, James, you *drink* more than other people." Doctorow knew that "the court circling about Jim was a different cast of characters" than those at Kenyon, but he worried to see that same self-indulgence in Wright, who had always trusted the more critical voices among his friends "in order to stay honest." Considering how much Wright was drinking, Doctorow saw the poet "affecting a kind of martyrdom."

———

Franz had been accepted to Oberlin College while still in New York the previous October, and in January 1972 he joined a group of serious, tal-ented student writers there. He was attracted to Oberlin's outstanding academic reputation, especially in literature and languages. Franz had also read the first issues of *Field* magazine, already a significant journal for poetry in the United States. David Young, one of the editors of *Field*, became a crucial mentor to Franz. For a young writer besotted with poetry, there was no better place in the country at the time. Franz's pro-fessors recognized his talent immediately. As Young recalled, "Already as a student he was writing poems that I can remember, and I could think, *that's a really good poem.*" Wright knew Oberlin's reputation as well, which included student drinking and drug use; for a long time the thought of Franz at Oberlin made him anxious. But he understood that his son's devotion to poetry was in earnest. Knowing the high cost of tuition, Wright arranged for all of the royalty payments for their just-published Hesse book, *Wandering*, to go to Franz.

In mid-February Wright traveled to Buffalo to read on two succes-sive evenings as a major snowstorm descended across New York State and the Northeast. As snow continued to fall the day after his reading on the university campus, Wright joined a benefit reading for a local school that became a tribute to John Logan, who was stranded in the Detroit airport. In his absence, William Matthews, Al Poulin, Robert Hass, and Leslie Fiedler each read favorite poems by Logan following their own work. The evening culminated with Wright's bravura recitation of "A Trip to Four or Five Towns"—the long, numbered poem Logan had dedicated to him in 1959.

Hass, who rode with Wright to a dinner party afterward, had read a poem of his own that mentioned Thomas Hobbes, and Wright was intrigued. After Hass sputtered praise for Hobbes's prose, Wright launched into a half-hour recitation from *The Leviathan* as they crawled across town in a blizzard. "It was totally magical to be riding through this heavy, wet, fluffy snow of the Great Lakes, like a St. Petersburg white night, inching along in this car with Wright reciting—it must have been five or six pages, leading up to the passage about how the life of man is 'nasty, brutish, and short.'"

In New York City that winter, Wright hosted five advanced students in his narrow railroad apartment for a weekly honors seminar called Some Americans. Along with the poetry of Whitman and Robinson, the class read short works by Hawthorne, Henry James, Sherwood Anderson, and—subversively—Rexroth's *One Hundred Poems from the Chinese*. Roger Hecht often joined them, and the living room quickly filled with smoke; while swept up in talk, Wright lit cigarettes with theatrical flair, each time puzzled to find one already burning in the ashtray.

———

Wright's name appeared once more beside Robert Bly's that spring in what was to be the final issue of the magazine that had first brought them together, now called *The Seventies*. Their joint translation of "Poem to Be Read and Sung" demonstrates Vallejo's genius for what Bly called "Leaping Poetry"—the theme that united all the poems in the issue. A great work of art often shows a leap of swift association between unconscious sources and more familiar, rational material, Bly argued, and he praised Neruda's poetry as exemplary of "Spanish leaping." The previous fall, the Nobel Prize in Literature had honored Neruda, and in April 1972 he returned to New York to address the PEN American Center. On the Sunday before his appearance, Wright spent the whole day with him. They traveled by car with Anne and Neruda's wife, Matilde, for a luncheon in Scarsdale, New York, together with Fernando Alegría, a Chilean poet. Wright and Neruda felt at ease together, and that afternoon the three poets collaborated on an English translation of Neruda's "To My North American Friend." Years later, in attempting to describe the morning sunlight of San Gimignano in late autumn, Wright would remember: "And once I spent an entire day of my life (my life!) talking with Pablo Neruda and looking into his face."

The next evening, April 10, Neruda addressed the PEN gathering on the occasion of its fiftieth anniversary. As an ambassador for the Allende government, Neruda had just taken part in negotiations to restructure Chile's national debt. He titled his remarks "The Murdered Albatross," and his reference to Coleridge was clear: if you destroy us, we will be the albatross around your neck. But Neruda insisted upon his gratitude to North America. "As for myself, now a man of almost seventy, I was barely fifteen when I discovered Walt Whitman, my primary creditor. I stand here among you today still owing this marvelous debt that has helped me live." At a reading that week at the 92nd Street Y's Poetry Center, Wright joined five other translators, alternating English versions with Neruda's Spanish. After H. R. Hays read his translation of "Walking Around," Bly revealed that Wright had recited the poem backstage to give Hays a copy to read from. Days later, when Wright traveled to Newark, Delaware, for a reading, he was "repeatedly amazed to have been in the same room with Neruda. It was all he could talk about."

Back home in New York City, Anne persuaded her husband to accept an invitation from the Poetry Society of America, who wanted him to accept the Melville Cane Award at their annual awards dinner held at the Plaza Hotel. This was a lavish black-tie affair, and though Anne delayed their arrival to curb his drinking, Wright soon held a large martini. Galway Kinnell and Donald Justice joined Wright at the table of honorees, and the speeches and awards commenced after dinner. When Kinnell saw Wright put his head down on the table from boredom, he pulled Anne from the crowd, hoping she could intervene. At the podium, Wright defended Neruda, who had been censured for his Communist views after receiving the Nobel Prize. Wildly drunk, Wright would have come to blows with a waiter if other guests had not restrained him.

What became Wright's best-known interview began the following afternoon, though three years would pass before it saw print. Over the course of two days, Wright spoke candidly of his own work and of the writers who mattered most to him as part of the prominent "Art of Poetry" series featured in *The Paris Review*. With fine weather coinciding with the interview, Wright often turns to figures of spring and renewal. He speaks of Horace's work as his ideal. "I regard myself primarily as a craftsman, as a Horatian," he says, though his need to write poetry has always been "a kind of curse. I've thought that many a time. Why the hell couldn't I have been a carpenter or a handyman?" When the interviewer, Peter Stitt, praises *Shall We Gather at the River* for its integrity and coherence, Wright makes a startling admission:

> I know damn well that that book is perfectly constructed, and I knew exactly what I was doing from the very first syllable to the very last one. . . . I was trying to move from death to resurrection and death again, and challenge death finally. Well, if I must tell you, I was trying to write about a girl I was in love with who has been dead for a long time. I tried to sing with her in that book. Not to recreate her; you can't recreate anybody, at least I can't. But I thought maybe I could come to terms with that feeling which has hung on in my heart for so long. The book has been damned because it is so carefully dreamed.

———

A week later, Wright suffered a shock of good fortune it took him months to recover from. On Monday, May 1, Anne returned home from work to find her husband on the phone to Wesleyan University Press, trying to confirm a rumor that he had won the Pulitzer Prize. The telegram arrived an hour later confirming that his *Collected Poems* would receive the Poetry Prize for 1972. The next day the awards made front-page news. "He handled it very badly," Anne remembered. "He was not celebrating. He was not even talking about it—he was almost angry." They made no effort to phone friends, but congratulatory calls kept coming in. "James never stopped feeling vulnerable," Anne believed; he felt he didn't deserve the recognition. The award from the academy had been different because he respected the chancellors, and he trusted Kray. But the Pulitzer seemed to come out of the blue and was accompanied by overwhelming publicity. Talking with his parents on the phone the next day, all he could say was "Well, it will look good on my résumé."

Though Anne no longer taught on the west side of Manhattan, the Wrights still made a point of seeing her student Garnie Braxton and his three siblings. Taking the thousand-dollar award that accompanied the prize, Wright insisted on dividing the money in four equal amounts and opening a savings account for each of them. Giving the money away helped ease his anxiety, but Anne couldn't tell if Wright's drinking kept getting worse; at the time, his "drinking was *always* a problem."

In the weeks after the award, Wright tried to get back to his new manuscript, while completing the semester's final exams and papers. He told a Hunter College newspaper reporter that he would rather be known as a great teacher than a great poet, repeating his desire to achieve "pure, clear classicism in language." Only to Kray did he betray something other than bewilderment concerning the Pulitzer, asking her, "Aren't you a little bit proud of me, Betty?"

Wright felt more at ease accepting another honor that month when he traveled to Seattle on his own to give the Theodore Roethke Memorial Reading on May 25. On the way, he stopped in Missoula, Montana, for a reading and a chance to see Richard Hugo. The two shared a night of heavy drinking, and it set a precedent for Wright's time in Seattle—even though he stayed with William Matchett, an imposing, robust Quaker. Wright had deputized Matchett to write a letter to Sonjia Urseth, asking her to come to his reading, but as Urseth recalled, "I just knew I didn't dare. I just couldn't do it. I was afraid. . . . I really think that [our friendship] was not always a good thing." Urseth still believed she had played a part in ruining Wright's first marriage and "wrecking his life."

Though he drank continually, Wright appeared voluble and attentive when he first arrived. Irv Broughton, filming a documentary on Richard Eberhart, captured the two poets in conversation and was struck by the "uncanny richness to Wright's speech."

> I sensed at the time the power of this man, and that I had met more people in one person in him than in anyone I had known. James Wright was too much, and not enough. He was the proverbial wise-guy; the orator; the comic; the tragedian; the brilliant scholar; the old shoe; he was the quickest to follow the updraft of one's words; and a most thoughtful and quiet listener.

Throughout their conversation, Wright deferred to Eberhart, whom he greatly admired, and recited many of Eberhart's poems from memory.

In two separate interviews published the day of his reading, Wright described the uneasiness that troubled him since winning the Pulitzer, repeating that he didn't think he deserved the attention. The media presence surrounding the dedication of the Roethke Auditorium prior to Wright's reading only fueled his distress. David Wagoner hosted him that afternoon and was astonished to hear Wright recount in great detail an argument they once had in the Blue Moon Tavern seventeen years earlier. Wagoner had reconciled a bitter exchange between them by declaring his abiding love for Wright and his work, something Wright "was still thinking about." Hoping to keep him relatively sober, Wagoner offered a double-shot of whiskey. Offended, Wright seized the bottle and downed a tumbler at one go.

On what would have been Roethke's sixty-fourth birthday, Wright gave "a marvelous performance," moving between thunderous grandeur and moments of delicacy—often within the same poem. Wright knew the importance of the occasion. Following the dedication of the auditorium in Roethke's name and Wagoner's brief words, Wright recited Roethke's poem "The Wraith," from the sequence "Four for Sir John Davies." The grave pacing of the poem cast an immediate spell. He followed Roethke's poem with Wagoner's "Halcyon Days," recounting their hospital visit to Roethke, and Stanley Kunitz's early masterpiece "Open the Gates"—each said from memory with brooding intensity.

Turning to poems of his own, Wright began with a prose piece he had typed out that afternoon. With no word from Urseth, he half-believed she might be somewhere in the audience. Wright asks forgiveness of an unnamed black man who overheard an offensive joke he told the day before. But the poem pleads for a more encompassing mercy, linking his Muse with his native country: "Sometimes, poor old America, I get scared that not even forgiveness is enough. It is all we have, just each other. Jenny, my only Jenny, I have no idea at all where you may be, but I know you hear me, and I beg your pardon, too. I tried to walk on water. I sank. I beg your pardon. I wish this were a poem. If only it were."

While in Seattle, Wright worked incessantly on the final typescript of *Two Citizens*, determined to submit his manuscript to Farrar, Straus and Giroux before leaving for Europe in June. He welcomed the offer from an old friend, Rae Tufts, to use her spacious studio, and Tufts was glad to shuttle him back and forth across the city in her red convertible. But the night before Wright flew back to New York, he suffered a nosebleed in Tufts's car as they were leaving a farewell dinner party. Back at the Matchetts, Wright tried to shrug off the incident, but even with ice and towels, the hemorrhaging didn't stop for hours. Wright refused to go to the hospital, anxious about missing his flight. By the time his plane landed in New York, however, his nosebleed had returned. Anne took him to the emergency room at Mount Sinai Hospital the next day, the Sunday of a long Memorial Day weekend. After waiting for hours in a hallway on a gurney, Wright grew incoherent from loss of blood. It took Anne's urgent plea to a passing doctor for him to get immediate care.

Wright's hospitalization at the age of forty-four became a turning point in his fight to get sober. Dr. Robert Segal, after testing for cirrhosis of the liver, spoke unequivocally: "If you don't stop drinking, you'll be dead in ten years." For the next three months—throughout their time in Europe that summer—Wright quit drinking. Dr. Silver, Wright's psychiatrist, began prescribing Valium, in part to treat the stress that continued long after the Pulitzer award. Silver even encouraged Wright's obsession with television—"anything to let him relax."

———

Their European trip came at a perfect time. Days before the couple flew to Paris, Michael di Capua sent a copy of the *Two Citizens* manuscript, ready for the printers. Wright felt relieved to put the work behind him as they left for France and Italy. When they arrived at the Hotel Lenox on June 19, 1972, the joy of travel overtook them once more. And after weeks of silence, Wright again picked up his journal, a small black six-ring notebook with lined paper just four inches by seven. On his second day in Paris he wrote, "We both feel as if we had shed about 50 pounds of darkness from our spines."

In June, the Wrights went from Paris to Saint-Benoît and on to Rome—Wright's first visit to the city. They spent sixteen days there, and it took time for him to get over his discomfort. As Wright lamented in a poem about leaving "the beloved," Paris, behind, "Any traveler toward Rome who has learned his Latin along the Ohio River knows loneliness and fear and the apprehension of disaster." Wright felt as Rilke had, observing how Rome "makes one feel stifled with sadness for the first few days: through the gloomy and lifeless museum-atmosphere that it exhales, through the abundance of its pasts."

Wright began to make peace with the city when he first saw a green lizard cross his path. Describing "children at the top of a tall natural cascade" outside the gardens of the Villa d'Este in Tivoli, "thrashing out family laundry," his prose becomes more relaxed and at the same time more spacious. "Maybe the green lizard is the presiding genius of mountain children who wash clothes outside the walls," Wright reflects. This "patient god" becomes "the key to the door of homesickness" and "the wandering American's last friend on the earth." As with Hardy and Roethke, Wright's imagination springs to life when small animals seize his attention. This same quickening can be felt in his memories of Martins Ferry; the Roman people and their cobbled streets brought vivid images back to him. Sitting at a wobbly café table in the shadow of the Colosseum, the "antiquity of the railed streetcars" reminded him of those in his childhood, "with their wicker-woven seats and the dull headlights whose yellow color itself seemed to rattle aloud through the slow summer dark."

With costs still low in Europe, the Wrights traveled in modest luxury: in Rome they had a small suite at the Hotel Portuguese near the Piazza Navona. They ate breakfast in their room and had dinner at the same small restaurant every night. Even more than the Colosseum and the Forum, Wright wanted to see the grave of John Keats in the Protestant Cemetery. The pilgrimage inspired a journal piece about Martins Ferry, and helped dispel his ambivalence toward Rome.

In mid-July the couple traveled to Assisi, where an old friend of Anne's, Rachel Evans, joined them from England. Rachel and Anne had taught at the American School in Rome and explored Venice together in the mid-1950s; after Assisi the three met up again in Urbino and Arezzo. In the interim, the Wrights traveled to a town on the Adriatic coast that Anne had found mentioned in an old cookbook, intrigued by a photo of the Roman arch built by Augustus at the beginning of the ancient road inland. Fano quickly became a beloved place, a kind of secret the couple guarded between them. Largely free of foreign tourists, the town thrived on its fishing trade, with busy dockyards to the south of a broad swimming beach. Two-story stone houses and linden trees shaded the town's narrow streets. Fano reminded Anne of the Italy she had known decades before, with its wide central piazza and outdoor market. Wright watched fishermen mending seining nets along the causeway near the docks and studied the Roman history of the town, named for the goddess Fortuna. They took a room at the beachside Hotel Astoria and dined there each night, family-style with other guests.

In Urbino, the Wrights reunited with Rachel and also met up with Alfredo Rizzardi—a friend to both Eugenio Montale and Isabella Gardner—and Leslie Fiedler, a colleague from Buffalo who, like Rizzardi, was taking part in a summer conference at the university. While staying in the walled city, Wright began a long prose piece titled "Silence," continuing his meditations on St. Francis, Jesus, and Thoreau. "It occurs to me that I have sometimes felt very happy in the midst of a solitude I have fought for, walled up, and won. It is a cave in the air."

With Rachel, the Wrights arrived in Arezzo by train and, after leaving their bags at the hotel, continued uphill to the church of San Francesco to revisit Piero della Francesca's cycle of frescoes depicting the Legend of the True Cross. Piero's uncanny portraits and command of perspective captivated Wright, and the three resolved to take a bus the next day to the village of Monterchi to find one of Piero's most profound works, the *Madonna del Parto*. This magnificent fresco of a blue-gowned Mary pregnant with the Christ child was still sheltered in a small cemetery chapel in a field below the town, sought out by only the most determined travelers. "Names in Monterchi: To Rachel" recalls this first visit; they had the cool shadows of the chapel to themselves before hiking more than a mile to find a different bus back to Arezzo.

After parting with Rachel, the Wrights passed through Florence before returning to San Sepulcro, Piero's birthplace, and its small museum with his paintings. The following night they stayed in nearby Anghiari, a medieval walled town built on the edge of a steep cliff overlooking the Tiber Valley on the border between Tuscany and Umbria. Anghiari had intrigued Wright since he had first glimpsed it from a bus window two years before. In the morning they climbed up a road above the town leading out into the countryside, which appeared to be close at hand. "There was just the dirt road and fields of wildflowers," Anne remembered. They stopped along the roadside to spread out the picnic they'd brought, and in the wild brush beside the road, Wright discovered a splendid spider's web. In Nice a week later, Wright scrawled a brief poem in his journal titled "Spider in Anghiari":

Your dark joists unhinged
by a single medieval summer,
the wild sweetpea petal seems older

than the cracked face
of Christ down the hill.

Behind this poem, eventually titled "The Journey," is the sorrowful face
of Christ stepping from the tomb in Piero's *Resurrection*, the celebrated
fresco in the Museo Civico in San Sepulcro—"down the hill" from Anghiari. On the day before he found the spider's web in the wind, along a
dirt road in the Tuscan hills, Wright had stood for a long time in front of
Piero's painting.

The Wrights arrived in Nice by way of Pisa, and stayed a week before
stopping in Avignon on their way back to Paris. In Nice they welcomed
Anne's two nieces, Laura Lee and Karin East, both fifteen years old and
elated to be in Europe for the first time. They remembered how their
uncle gestured with his hands as he spoke—"almost like a ballet," and
always with a cigarette. He wore the same light blue shirts every day, his
journal and a pen in one breast pocket and a pack of Pall Malls in the
other. Uncle James, who was "very creative with his swearing" and "used
it elegantly," admired the French curse words the girls soon picked up
from teenage boys on the street. They traveled together for three weeks,
and Wright felt blessed. In Nice he wrote, "Laura & Karin arrived yester-
day, and, with Annie, they are so startling in their beauty that I feel like
a man who has just faded the house in a Riviera crap game." In a new
poem begun in Paris, Wright begged forgiveness from Marcel Dupré,
the celebrated organist, for arriving late to San Sulpice because "The
fates have changed their names again" and his three beautiful companions had been leisurely in brushing their hair.

Although diffuse and tentative at times, the prose in Wright's journal
points to a major formal breakthrough. In readings and interviews he
insisted on calling these paragraphs "prose pieces," and the work has the
miscellaneous nature the name implies; they began variously as journal
entries, poem drafts, or travel letters mailed back to the States. Hesse's
prose passages in *Wandering* offered one clear inspiration for the form.
In early pieces, Wright even adopted Hesse's persona: a traveler with no
destination, a chance observer of the present moment.

————

The Wrights arrived back in the United States on the last day of August
and headed to Lake Minnewaska for the long holiday weekend, avoiding

a full reckoning with New York City. Wright taught three classes at Hunter that fall, including a graduate seminar on the nineteenth-century novel. Despite his new notoriety at the college, he still thought of himself primarily as a teacher. Wright's colleagues never doubted his dedication. "Jim always wore a suit and tie when he was teaching—although at times his sartorial jacket seemed to be coming apart a bit at the seams," the English Department chair, Richard Barickman, remembered. Wright's sabbatical would begin in January, but daily pressures increased—not only teaching but also managing a heavier schedule of readings, now handled through a booking agency. Social events with friends and colleagues brought alcohol within easy reach, and a glass of wine at a birthday party put a sudden end to months of sobriety.

In Wright's poems, it matters where the speaker is standing, where the poem takes place. For Wright, the names of people mattered, too. When *The New Yorker* insisted that he use a fictional name for a childhood friend before it would publish "Prayer to the Good Poet," he scrawled a satirical new poem in the margin of the editor's letter and swore to use the actual name in his new book. Wright wanted authentic details, to keep the poem true to his experience. "Prayer to the Good Poet"—a stunning tour de force—finally appeared in mid-October. As in the best poems in *Two Citizens*, Marilyn Hacker saw how Wright, like Adrienne Rich, was breaking new ground, not only by modifying traditional prosody and classical meters to enlarge what poetry can say, but also through his vision of a broader audience for poetry. Wright's invocations of Horace—"my good secret"—are more than shorthand for his devotion to poetic craft. In Wright's view, Horace shared something essential with William Carlos Williams: an ear for the rhythms of spoken language.

Like many others, Wright was disheartened by Richard Nixon's landslide reelection that November. When pressed by an interviewer, he admitted he felt disturbed, but not hopeless, about the country's myopia and callous self-interest. "People feel I may be against America," Wright said, "but I love it too much. Maybe I ought to be *more* upset over some of the things that are happening." Even after the Watergate break-in and cover-up were exposed over the coming months, he pointedly declared his patriotism at readings—a conviction as strong as any for Wright. In a letter to Gibbons Ruark in December, he wrote of "the America which I still love," and thanked Ruark for a poem he had written about his father, which "brought finally to a focus my own wanderings about my own father, and that is what turned me to my Latin again, for some reason, and my beautiful Horace." Wright tells him of his poem in *The New Republic*, "The Old WPA Swimming Pool in Martins Ferry, Ohio," which captures the complicated range of emotions the poet feels toward his father, his uncles, and the strangers of his childhood.

Ever since the Academy fellowship award the previous December, Wright had been anticipating the start of his yearlong sabbatical that January; he and Anne would leave for a seven-month stay in Europe in June 1973. Dudley and Jessie were both in failing health, and the family knew that this Christmas would likely be the last they would all spend together. After a few days in New York, Marshall traveled with his father and Anne to Zanesville, Ohio, where Franz joined them from Oberlin. Surrounded by talented peers, Franz had found his way at the college and was becoming an accomplished writer. Marshall worshipped his brother and grew silent when Franz and his father started talking about books and poetry. "He talked to Franz as a pupil, or as an equal—as a fellow artist," Marshall recalled, "and he was nurturing his skills."

Marshall, however, had become unmoored in high school. He had suffered a traumatic summer trip to Texas in the company of a teacher who told Liberty that her son would be taking summer classes. Instead, the two had lived in a trailer. While learning to drive a car, Marshall had suffered a concussion when he lost control and crashed. He had watched a boy die after diving off a bridge where they often went swimming. In August, Marshall had returned alone to California by bus, in a deep depression. He now admitted to his father that marijuana was everywhere at his school and "gambling under the trees" nearby had become "a way of life." Wright grieved to see how Marsh, now fourteen, had lost the innocence he had shown just a year before, but deep love endured between them.

Even Franz was surprised by his brother's troubled life in high school, and felt guilty for leaving him alone in their stepfather's house. But the boys enjoyed a warm reunion with their father that Christmas; it had been two years since they had all been together. The visit with their grandparents was even more rare. As Franz recalled, Dudley "would always take me aside and say, 'Always remember that we love you.' That was very important to him, to say that to me. And I didn't know what to make of that then, but it means a lot to me now." The family gathering was joyous, with the three Wright brothers laughing together at stories from childhood. Taking Anne aside, Jessie told her that she blessed the day that she and Jim had married.

Back in May, when a reporter called with the news that their son had won the Pulitzer Prize, Jessie told him that Jim was "preparing to write a book about his parents, which will be titled, 'Two Citizens—Jessie and Dudley.'" Though Wright never confirmed his intentions regarding the book's title, kinship and citizenship are its central themes. Jessie and Dudley had lived together for fifty-six years, raising four children and teaching them, by example, the fortitude to endure hardship. After this festive Christmas gathering in December 1972, Wright would not see either of his parents again.

PART III

PART IV

22

I have torn myself out of many bitter places / In America

January 1973–January 1974

Monday morning in Jan., 73:

Every poet ought to visit the grave of John Keats at the Protestant Cemetery in Rome.

I don't mean for Keats's sake, for Christ's sake, I mean for the poet's sake. Whatever may have happened to you in the past, and whoever you are, and however you hope to go on living, you take forever to find the grave, that doesn't even have Keats's name on it.

The tough little bastard got his work done. Never mind his work. You don't mind it when you stand there and know he is in the ground. You know that the best thing to do is to get your work done. You are going to die, too. Just like John Keats.

I don't know why it is. I have nothing flowery to say about the graveyard. Shelley is there, and Goethe's son, and all kinds of professional Italians. What I like best is the café just across the street from the phony pyramid of Cestius, where at least you can get a cheap cup of tea.

I don't want to die, not even just like John Keats. I want to live my own life, though, just as he did, the little Cockney hell-raiser.

This entry in a new journal is a kind of invocation. It fills one side of the small lined loose-leaf pages Wright slipped into his typewriter; his prose entries often reach the end of just one page. Wright's travel letters—tissue-thin, single-sheet aerograms—show this same compression, as though his imagination could wander more freely when aware of a boundary. Over the next seven years, his journal moved to the center of his life and work.

Relieved of teaching for the coming year and with page proofs due for his new book, Wright felt unrestrained as 1973 began. He resumed correspondence with many writers that winter and completed a long-promised essay on Richard Hugo's work along with other critical prose. Writing to Mary Oliver in January, Wright could boast, "This spring, thank Christ, I don't have to teach. All I am doing is fooling around in my new notebook, working on an essay, and letting myself be delighted." However, Wright had agreed to a heavy schedule of readings throughout the spring; he wrote only sporadically in his journal before leaving for Europe in June. And without the responsibility of teaching, little remained to curb his drinking. At a favorite local bar on Eighty-fifth Street and York Avenue called Loftis—much like an Irish pub—Wright became known as "the Professor" among the regulars.

On the last day of January, Anne Sexton sent Wright an entire manuscript of thirty-nine poems written over the course of twenty days, "with two days out for despair and three days out in a mental hospital." This would become Sexton's posthumous book *The Awful Rowing Toward God*, a collection she had resolved to dedicate, in part, to Wright. Sexton implored him to give the poems the kind of close, honest reading he had once lavished on her work, and she closed her affectionate letter with the private name Wright had given her more than a decade before: Bee. Without remorse, Wright filled the margins of her poems with brutal, passionate annotations, insisting that stanzas and even whole poems be deleted or rewritten. "Strip the language and shackle accidents," he demanded; "*listen, listen*; trust your own strange voice." Returning her letter together with the poems, Wright scratched in the bottom margin, "I have no intention of excusing your bad verse and your bad prose. There are some poems here that I think are fine. There are some that I think are junk. The choice between them is yours.—C." Wright cut short even Sexton's old endearment—Comfort.

Maxine Kumin, whose encouragement helped restore Sexton's poems and self-confidence, recalled how devastating this exchange was for Sexton. At heart, it was a question of craft that roused Wright's anger; it upset him to see poets publish too soon and too often, and Sexton had come to rely on her raw talent and notoriety. She had sent work just pulled from her typewriter, and might have anticipated his harsh response. But Sexton's poems had also arrived just when Wright received the page proofs for his own new collection, and he already had doubts about the work. For the first time, he had not shown the manuscript to trusted readers before publishing it.

Individual poems from *Two Citizens* began to appear in magazines and journals before the book came out in April. The poet and editor Michael Cuddihy wrote in February to praise "The Young Good Man," published in *Harper's*. He found it "plain and direct, as though the poem were an act whose intention went beyond itself. No self-concern or self-pity. Concern for another. Tender and tough, how well they go together sometimes." Cuddihy intuited a major new current in Wright's work: "How moving, even beautiful, almost anything can be if we regard it with enough attention." These brief, spontaneous comments say more about *Two Citizens* than many columns of print would over the coming months.

Wright embarked on another reading tour in mid-February, appearing with John Logan and Denise Levertov at Florida Tech as part of an inaugural Poetry Festival. Wright gave an extended introduction to "The Minneapolis Poem," in part to praise Logan's insights that had helped him revise the poem. Wright had wanted to curse the city, but Logan believed the poem to be a kind of benediction. "If you can only be true enough, somehow, to your own feeling," Wright realized, "you'll end up blessing it."

That same week, after reading in Oklahoma, Wright traveled with Anne to the University of Arizona in Tucson. Their stay became a reunion for the three Wright brothers. Ted and Helen Wright were visiting their son, Ted Jr., at a nearby air force base, and Jack and Elizabeth drove from California to join them. The three fell in together "as if no time had passed," and the talk among them always turned back to Martins Ferry and stories of their mother. James and Anne stayed at the Poet's Cottage on campus, hosted by Richard and Lois Shelton. After a week of constant travel and his brothers' arrival, Wright felt anxious before the reading, but the audience in the packed auditorium gave him an enthusiastic reception, responding warmly to the poet's humorous detours. He gave a generous reading; though guarded at first, Wright relaxed more with each poem, reading mainly from page proofs of *Two Citizens*. The reading included a revelatory debut of "The Old WPA Swimming

Pool in Martins Ferry, Ohio." Acknowledging his brother Ted from the stage, Wright introduced an early poem, "To a Defeated Savior," by telling the story of Ted's failed attempt to rescue a boy who drowned in a suckhole in the Ohio River when they were young. Ted had never heard the poem before and was startled to learn that Jim even knew about the event.

While Wright kept his drinking under control throughout their stay in Tucson—especially around his brothers—his abstinence and the exhaustion of travel left him feeling vulnerable. Anne and others recalled a joyful reunion, but Richard Shelton wrote of how distraught Wright became after talking with his brothers one evening about their childhood. Once Ted and Jack had left, the Sheltons and their teenage son took Anne and James for a long walk in the desert. The astonishing landscape—"an earth strangely familiar"—spurred an outpouring of work, and by early summer three separate poems would appear in print. Shelton had encouraged Wright to stand beneath the unusual, downstretched arms of a saguaro cactus that formed a kind of circle—"an incredible force field," Shelton believed. After a few moments, Wright was overcome by emotion, as glimpsed in the last stanza of "To the Saguaro Cactus Tree in the Desert Rain":

> Your green arms lower and gather me.
> I am an elf owl's shadow, a secret
> Member of your family.

In a rambling, irregular poem called "Redemption" begun two days later, the poet travels from New York to the desert before returning to the cemetery high above Martins Ferry where he wandered as a teenager, even at night:

> All I wanted to do was walk in spring
> Among the brief green things,
> The weeds before they got killed.
> But I assure you friends they don't want nobody walking
> In the graves of southern Ohio
> At night, nobody lover of the green dead.

The adjective "green"—beloved by Spanish poets such as Jiménez and Lorca for its wealth of meanings—is at the heart of Wright's poetic vocabulary. The broad experimenting he had done in "New Poems" and *Two Citizens* made childhood and adolescent experiences somehow more vivid and accessible to his imagination.

————

Back in New York, Wright tried to keep pace with the heavy reading schedule his agency had arranged for him, with appearances almost every week. Mark Strand recalled a reading Wright gave at Brooklyn College at which the audience sat "stunned and wide-eyed" at the edge of their seats. "There was something so emotionally raw about those readings that created a tremendously powerful presence." Wright traveled to Pennsylvania, North Carolina, Maryland, Massachusetts, Ohio, and Illinois that spring, an arduous series of engagements that made his departure for Europe in June seem too far away.

Returning home one afternoon at the end of March, he realized that the Blys had finally made good on their threat to return the books he had stored on the farm for more than a decade. Wright found thirty-four boxes filled with his books and papers stacked along the sidewalk outside their apartment building. They had arrived in an eighteen-wheel trailer, piled six feet high and strapped to a shipping pallet. Anne had convinced the driver to help her untie the boxes and unload them, learning later that Carol Bly had overseen their shipment from Madison, where the boxes had been packaged and weighed on cattle scales. The books were then stored in disused coal bins in the basement, since their apartment had no room for Wright's library.

Wright regretted the harsh tone he'd taken with Sexton that winter, as evidenced by a handwritten poem dated April 5 in short-lined couplets titled "To Bee, for her Book." It begins, "All I keep thinking about / Is your long slim lovely lines"—echoing the tone their letters once shared. Wright praises her for the "nerve" he lacks; "And most of what I want / Is this courage, this book, / And never mind the rest." Wright cancels his earlier disdain in favor of the genuine daring shown by Sexton's new poems.

Later that April Wright met Maxine Kumin when they joined James Merrill as judges for the Glascock Intercollegiate Poetry Contest at Mount Holyoke College. At a joint reading, Wright grew unnerved by the presence of Merrill and Kumin—"two natural aristocrats"—and had Anne ask Kumin if he could read first. He later admitted to Kumin that he now gave so many readings he no longer enjoyed them. Days later, back in New York, Sexton called to ask why he agreed to readings he didn't want to give—"why let people push you into it?" Wright was furious, both with Sexton and with Kumin for betraying his confidence. But he finally conceded to his own exhaustion. He canceled a trip to Ohio in May and resigned from his booking agency, declaring the entire experiment "a fiasco."

The Wrights sublet their railroad apartment on East Eighty-fifth Street for the next seven months to Kathleen Norris and her future husband, who assumed care of the willow tree and garden outside the ground-floor kitchen window. Anne had resigned from her job in Brooklyn and looked forward to a full year off from teaching. They flew to London on June 18, 1973, and spent five days in Rachel Evans's flat overlooking Norland Square. Traveling by bus to Dorchester, Wright made his second pilgrimage to Hardy country after exactly twenty years. The first of many prose pieces from this extended journey, "The Moorhen and Her Eight Young," appeared in Wright's journal after his return to the thatched cottage where Hardy was born. The couple stayed in Eype, a tiny village on the Dorset coast, before traveling to Fowey in Cornwall. After ten days in the country, they returned to London to meet Marshall, who joined them for the next three weeks. Together they took the boat train to Paris and returned to the Hotel Lenox on the Left Bank and the daily rituals of the Café Bizuth.

On their last day in London, Wright found a copy of Geoffrey Hill's new book, a collection of thirty numbered prose poems titled *Mercian Hymns*. He recognized that these short paragraphs offered examples of the lyrical compression he had been searching for in his own prose pieces. Hill's condensed, hermetic prose interweaves the poet's childhood with the present and the ancient past, and Wright admired Hill's daring and imagination. "This beautiful and strange book will require further and further exploration," he wrote in his journal. "I will keep it by my side during the coming months." He praised the book in a letter to Donald Hall two months later, having read it "at least twenty times." Inspired by the book's formal inventiveness, Wright looked for new ways to suspend and collapse time in his own short prose. But he avoided Hill's elevated literary style. He wanted the sense of an actual person thinking and talking.

The Wrights stayed at the Hotel Lenox for three weeks, through the first week in August, but a sharp increase in prices over the previous year already threatened their budget. Still, they kept up a modest café life, in the shade of the sycamore trees along Saint-Germain-des-Prés. Wright worked daily in his journal, and they walked all over the city with Marshall. Returning to Saint-Benoît-sur-Loire for a long weekend, they followed the towpaths along the canal to the tiny village of Port. When Anne made a brief trip back to London to visit Sheila Ráshed, she left Wright and Marshall to celebrate his fifteenth birthday on their own in Paris. After a boat ride on the Seine, Wright took his son to "the magnificent Folies Bergère. I have seldom seen Marsh so thoroughly enchanted." They often returned to Café Bizuth and talked for hours; it was a time of great tenderness between the two, and Wright learned the full extent of the abuse Marshall had suffered. Over the past year, Marshall had been in open conflict with his stepfather and had once run away from home.

Marshall never doubted his father's affection, but their time together was always too short. When Marshall left Paris he was anxious and depressed. Bizarrely, Liberty sent him back to Texas, trusting the same teacher who had put him at risk the summer before. Marshall spent only a few weeks in Texas before returning, once more on his own, to his stepfather's house in California.

A letter from Helen Wright had warned of Dudley's failing health when the Wrights first arrived in Paris; soon after Marshall's departure Wright learned that his father had died. Dudley Wright's obituary identified him as a "50-year employee of Hazel-Atlas Glass Co., Wheeling"; his occupation was described as "machinist." In his journal, Wright makes no mention of his father's death for many weeks. Returning to Paris four years later, however, he and Anne "stepped all unknowing into Notre Dame and found ourselves embraced by music," an experience of sudden joy that brought Dudley to mind. "Notre Dame always makes me think of my father," he reflects. After learning of his death, "I walked alone down the Seine and lit a candle for the old man in the cathedral," recalling how, when he was a boy, his father had once made a gift of an owl's feather.

At the beginning of August the Wrights traveled by train to Milan, passing through Burgundy and along the shore of Lake Geneva. They then
spent a week outside Torri del Benaco on the eastern shore of Lake
Garda, in an old villa surrounded by an untended olive orchard. They
often went swimming in early morning and again under moonlight. One
of Wright's most perfect love poems describes a vision of Annie framed
by their window. As published, "A Small Grove in Torri del Benaco" is
virtually identical to his first handwritten draft. Wright borrows an image
from Lawrence, who described the slender cypress trees surrounding
the town as "candles of darkness."

While in Paris, Wright had bought another copy of Lawrence's *Twilight in Italy*, and he reread it on the lakeshore where much of it was
written. The couple passed the book back and forth all summer. Lawrence's lyrical prose is another model for Wright's experiments in form,
most noticeably in his travel writing. He drafted another new prose
piece as they traveled south across Lake Garda, borrowing the title from
Lawrence: "Poetry of the Present Moment."

After arriving in Verona by train, Wright immediately fell in love
with the city. In the kindness of the cabdriver who took them to their
hotel he recognized the native hospitality of the Veronesi, and Wright
claimed the Café Dante on Piazza dei Signori as his own. Seated at an
outdoor table, Anne began to read from her guidebook, naming the classical figures carved in relief above the central statue of Dante, but she
soon realized that her husband knew them all by sight. From their
breakfast table in the Hotel Aurora, they watched wooden carts bringing produce to the Piazza delle Erbe, where fruit stalls appeared each
morning. The city felt vibrant with life. Verona's narrow streets sometimes opened, surprisingly, on the river Adige—it all seemed somehow
familiar to Wright. They wandered all over the city and attended a performance of *La Bohème* at the Arena, the beautifully preserved Roman
amphitheatre. Just before the music began, the pink marble of the grand
oval began to glow, lit by thousands of candles. A neighbor explained
that this was always done, in honor of Puccini, and gave her own candle
to Anne. The couple decided then to book another stay in Verona that
October.

The couple returned to Venice for the next two weeks, taking the same room in La Calcina hotel, filled with morning sunlight and the sounds of the Giudecca Canal below their balcony. They woke early to walk in the neighborhood, venturing as far as Santa Maria della Salute before returning along the Zattere. They stopped in the same bar each morning, joining working-class Venetians for a first cappuccino.

As they traveled, Wright's journals filled with new work. He wrote at leisure at the antique desk set between two large windows, with a view of La Giudecca island, the sounds of boat engines, voices, and seagulls, and the sunlight off the canal reflected on the ceiling. Wright used a compact traveling typewriter to transfer his handwritten jottings from the small wire-bound notebooks he carried everywhere into his larger journal. The prose piece "Under the Canals" would remain unchanged from the version Wright typed at his desk on August 28, 1973. But in a letter to Logan the following day, he demurred about his work that summer. "I've been writing a good deal of prose in a notebook, but not much else."

The Wrights often returned to a favorite café in the Campo San Barnaba in the afternoon, and this is where they learned of the United States–backed overthrow of the Chilean government on September 11. Protests sprang up around the city, and placards in the square declared "The CIA Murdered Allende." An air of melancholy hangs over a new poem Wright sketched out the following day, "Fresh Wind in Venice"; on the reverse side of this journal page is his first attempt at an elegy for Neruda. It is highly probable that Neruda was murdered in a hospital twelve days after the military coup—one day before he planned to leave the country.

From Venice the couple returned to the Hotel Alderhof in Vienna, staying in Udine and Grado on their way north. Just as he had half a lifetime before, Wright relished the chance to hear operas—an extravagance he rarely allowed himself in New York—and by delaying their departure they heard a performance of *Der Rosenkavalier*. When W. H. Auden died in his sleep in nearby Kirchstetten on September 28, 1973, Wright began work on an elegy that mourned not only Auden but Neruda and his own father as well. As he lights a candle in one of the oldest churches in the city, his grief widens to include "A dead girl I lay with / And Jesus Christ, another / Who did not understand."

———

The Wrights spent almost a month in Vienna, with trips to the forests and villages on the outskirts of the city. As he had done so often in the past, Wright sent an animated and candid letter to Robert Mezey. Describing a trip to the village of Perchtoldsdorf, he wrote, "It is so golden in its autumn, that one of the disappointments of the world is the absence of Keats in that place." Even days of glorious sunshine, however, could provoke the despair Wright had felt when he first walked the streets of Vienna. In words remarkably like those he had written to Mezey as a twenty-five-year-old expatriate, he confessed, "I am dreadfully homesick for America. I am revoltingly homesick for my own heart."

Returning to Verona helped rejuvenate Wright, and on a day trip to Mantua on October 22, next to a train schedule jotted hastily in his small notepad, he began a new poem:

The first thing I saw in the morning
Was a huge golden bee ploughing
His burly right shoulder into the belly
Of a sleek yellow pear
Low on a bough.

This first handwritten draft would become the beginning of the poem published as "The First Days"; its concluding lines were added later:

The best days are the first
To flee, sang the lovely
Musician born in this town
So like my own.
I let the bee go
Among the gasworks at the edge of Mantua.

Wright felt a kinship with Virgil when he saw the industrial landscape on the outskirts of Mantua, the poet's birthplace. Back in Verona that afternoon, they sat at an outdoor café table watching two workmen lifting out one of the huge floor stones of pink marble the Romans had laid in the piazza, and Wright amazed Anne by naming each of the tools they used in their difficult and exacting task. In one continuous journal entry, Wright sketched out both "The First Days" and a poem he later titled separately "The Best Days." The epigraph for both—a line from Virgil's Third *Georgic* that Wright had first read in high school, *optima dies prima fugit*—becomes a refrain as well: "the best days are the first to flee."

The mild, sunny autumn weather continued throughout November as the Wrights continued south to Rome. They traveled to Ferrara and spent a week in Bologna, where they again visited with Alfredo Rizzardi and his family; the two poets even talked of translating each other's work. Anne's sister Jane joined them in Rome, and after a week in the city they rented a car and began a tour of Tuscany. After Assisi, Florence, and Pisa, the three found their way to the small, medieval hilltop town of San Gimignano, arriving after dark one evening and waking the next morning to the startling beauty of the landscape stretched out below them. Their charmed whirlwind tour continued back through Siena to Piero's frescoes in Arezzo and Monterchi. The three spent Thanksgiving in Venice, where Wright returned to work at his desk at La Calcina for five days. The Wrights parted with Jane back in Rome and then spent the first week of December in Florence. With the streets closed to traffic on their last day in Italy, they wandered the city in bright sunshine, became swept up in a street parade, and viewed the Duomo and Michelangelo's *David* without crowds or car exhaust. As they prepared to leave, "two shepherds from the Abruzzi went past us on the Ponte Vecchio," Anne recalled, "dressed in sheepskin and playing old carols on a goatskin bagpipe."

During their last month in Europe—at the Hotel Lenox in Paris— Wright took stock of the work he'd begun in his journals. He also drafted an elegy for his father, "Winter, Bassano del Grappa." He had spent just a few hours there in September, on a tour of villas in the Vicenza region northwest of Venice. Straddling the River Brenta, Bassano del Grappa— like many other Italian places—brought Martins Ferry back to him. "Underground, the hair / Of the old man is growing / Golden again," this short lyric begins. But more compelling than his father's restored youth is the turn at the poem's conclusion, where the evening:

Shows the old
Man a moment, casting
Light on a girl's face.

She carries a little
Basket of willow
Slowly home.

Months after his father's death, Wright is able to approach the old man in the half-light of a winter evening. The figure of a girl reflects Dudley's quietness and assurance; her direction is everything: home. She has the gait of a lingering twilight. This young female figure would appear in different forms in Wright's journals and poems whenever he returned to Europe.

The couple had long planned to attend Christmas Eve mass at Chartres Cathedral that December. In their hotel room they trimmed a huge branch of mistletoe with ornaments from Vienna. They spent the night in Chartres, where a children's choir sang carols high up in a cathedral loft and a small group of musicians played Renaissance period instruments. Walking back to their hotel, they saw that the crèche manger, empty that evening, now held the infant, as the tower bells rang out at midnight. They stayed on in Paris for another two weeks, but New York City—left behind for seven months—cast a long shadow across the new year.

23

Apologia for the Ohioan Tongue

January–September 1974

Back in the States on January 21, 1974, the Wrights again retreated to Lake Minnewaska before braving New York's winter streets. Anne began looking for a new teaching position for the fall and, more pressingly, a new apartment. Wright braced for a full semester at Hunter. Open admissions had changed the character of the college, with many more students coming to study English as a second language. During Wright's career, Hunter increasingly became a cross section of New York City. Most students also held jobs while pursuing a degree, but they were eager to learn, and Hunter remained a premier undergraduate college in the CUNY system.

In addition to a freshman seminar, Wright taught the two classes he enjoyed most: The Comic Vision and a graduate-level course on Dickens. Richard Barickman, himself a Dickens scholar, understood why Wright's class was so popular. "Dickens wrote, in *Our Mutual Friend*, 'He do the Police in different voices'—well, Jim Wright could do *Dickens* in many voices." Donna Masini took every class Wright taught at Hunter and, though she was writing her own poems, had no idea of Wright's reputation when she first encountered him as a professor. "He took us seriously," and his thoughtfulness and sensitivity affected her deeply. "Mostly I wanted to listen to him—the way he read, the way he recited poems was just amazing to me. They would just come alive." Wright kept a sense of formality in his classroom, standing outside the door to greet each student as they arrived. "He was a real performer, in a very rich, classical way," recalled Kathy Purcell, as likely to quote Sophocles as a passage from Raymond Chandler.

All that winter, Wright worried about Anne's search for a new apartment and his mother's declining health. He also began to suspect that he never should have published *Two Citizens*, realizing in February, "It doesn't say what I want to say." While Wright had anticipated an uneven critical response, the vicious attacks his book provoked took him by surprise. In the Spring issue of *The Georgia Review*, a critic named Edward Butscher published the most strident condemnation of Wright's career ever to see print. Claiming to trace a steady "decline into mawkishness," the critic dismissed Wright's *Collected Poems* and his Pulitzer Prize. The "almost total failure" of *Two Citizens* was beneath comment, proof that Wright's "art is no longer viable." As though standing with a shovel over the poet's grave, Butscher declares that "time and good taste" will side with him. Reviews such as this had a devastating effect on Wright; eventually, he disowned *Two Citizens* and refused to read poems from it, saying, "That book was a mistake."

Some granted the ambitions of *Two Citizens* while still faulting its excesses. Alan Williamson, writing in *Shenandoah*, suggested that Wright's "emotional exclamatoriness" in the book "is part of the American speech that Wright, as much as Williams, wants to speak: a vocal violence needed to break the *macho* barrier against uttering feeling at all in our culture." In *The Southern Review*, Edward Engelberg agreed, calling the collection, for all its flaws, "straight, honest, unpretentious work, accessible to anyone who cares." The book opened ground for the work that followed, but its "mannerism of sentimental toughness" obscures Wright's experiments with spoken language. Mazzaro talked extensively with Wright about *Two Citizens* and saw Hemingway and Twain as models behind the work. "I think Jim concentrated on language because that was his *distinctive* voice." By the spring of 1974, however, Wright wanted to forget *Two Citizens*; he regretted not showing the manuscript to poet friends two years before. In his journal he declared, "No more readings. No more prizes."

One brief rebuke of *Two Citizens* in an omnibus review published in *The Hudson Review* while Wright was in Europe became an obsessive wound—a gratuitous sneer, in an issue of the journal that included two of Wright's new poems. Under the title "Poetry Matters," the critic William H. Pritchard dispensed with seventeen books in as many pages, including collections by Wilbur, Hugo, Rich, Nemerov, and Hollander, three by Lowell, and an Oxford anthology. He gave 250 words to Wright's *Two Citizens*, quoting lines from "To the Creature of the Creation" for the sake of a dull joke. Pritchard's arrogance betrayed his class superiority, which Wright found unforgivable.

Wright's rage infected a new poem at the end of February; in lines he later deleted, he cursed the critic by name. At the top of the page, in place of a title, he typed: "I will call it Hook." As if a decade's time were erased, the poet stands on a street corner in Minneapolis in the dead of winter. It is thirty-five degrees below zero,

Too cold for the snow to fall
Anymore. I don't
Have to be told
Any more somebody
Hates us.

Giving his anger free rein, Wright accesses a range of other emotions—including compassion. The original second stanza he typed on February 27, 1974, would remain unchanged:

I was only a young man
In those days. On that evening
The cold was so God damned
Bitter there was nothing.
Nothing. I was in trouble
With a woman, and there was nothing
There but me and dead snow.

The appearance of the young, disfigured Sioux, looming over him on a frigid winter night, is a signature moment in Wright's poetry. The speaker's recognition of their common struggles with poverty and loss—"his scars / Were just my age"—is transformative, an instance of true sympathy, of shared feeling *with*, not pity *for*, another human being. The poet's acceptance of the man's gesture of help confers dignity on them both.

Did you ever feel a man hold
Sixty-five cents
In a hook,
And place it
Gently
In your freezing hand?

I took it.
It wasn't the money I needed.
But I took it.

This intimate, direct address to the reader builds dramatic tension, while the poem's flexible line lengths create a sense of falling, down through the poem. The sentences are clipped, and heavy with Old English words: *dead / stood / lashed / pit / hunting / loomed / hook / took.* As Stephen Yenser observed when Wright's next collection appeared, "'Hook' conveys a desolate scene in language so stark that it spurns even realism as frivolous embellishment. It has the economy of dream." Wright crafted the title poem of the book, "To a Blossoming Pear Tree," out of stanzas removed from his initial draft of "Hook."

In October, while Wright was in Europe, Jessie had been hospitalized for advanced arteriosclerosis, and she had been living in a nursing home since her release. Wright had not seen his mother in more than a year when news came from Ohio on March 2 that she had died—just seven months after her husband. Back in New York after Jessie's funeral in Ohio, Wright set aside an elegy for her to type a letter to Marshall, inviting him to come to New York to live with them. He and Anne searched for a new apartment with two bedrooms, scouring the neighborhood where she had lived for more than a decade. By luck, they found a fourth-floor apartment directly across the street, on the north side of Eighty-fifth Street, with tall ceilings and a spacious living room, a galley kitchen, and a separate bathroom with a full bathtub. The south-facing windows gave the living room an open, airy feel, and Wright finally had a separate study. In the end, their plans to have Marshall join them came to nothing. He resisted leaving his high school and friends in California, and the couple shared his ambivalence, uncertain if they could handle the fifteen-year-old.

That spring, Franz took time off from Oberlin to study for a semester with Charles Simic at the University of New Hampshire. While living in Ohio, he worked odd jobs, painting houses or, during one summer, exterminating mosquitoes. When Franz wasn't enrolled in classes at Oberlin, David Young felt free to publish his poems in *Field*, and the Spring 1974 issue included three of Franz's poems and two by his father (early versions of "The Best Days" and "The First Days"), marking their first appearance together in a magazine.

Wright returned to Ohio at the end of April, as a special guest of Kenyon College at their Honors Day Convocation, and his brothers and their wives joined him in Gambier. Ransom introduced Wright at the ceremony, and Wright then honored his teacher by saying Ransom's "Winter Remembered" from memory. It was the last time the two poets would meet; Ransom died two months later at the age of eighty-six. However, the occasion proved more significant than Wright could have imagined. Kenyon's president, William Caples, who presented him with an honorary doctorate, welcomed Wright to the podium with these words: "You have brilliantly fulfilled the promise of your youth and the hopes of your friends and teachers." The words startled Wright; he thought, *No, I haven't, because I'm still drinking*. From that moment, his battle with alcohol changed radically.

When the siblings returned to New Concord to begin cleaning out their parents' home, Wright told them he was leaving, insisting that his Hunter classes demanded it. Anne stayed behind to help out but felt anxious after Wright left for New York alone; they had just completed their move across the street and everything but the furniture remained in boxes at the new apartment. Waking there alone the day after his return, "it struck me like lightning," he told Bly. "I had to stop drinking; and I had to have help in stopping." After consulting with his therapist and his physician, Wright checked himself into Doctors Hospital, a few blocks from his apartment, and spent three days there. He began a regimen of Antabuse, a therapy that induces nausea, headaches, and severe discomfort when even a small quantity of alcohol is consumed. "I quit cold turkey," he said later, but the stress from his withdrawal grew steadily that summer. Becoming ever more reclusive, Wright suffered from anxiety, depression, and the physical effects of detoxification. Anne, feeling increasingly shut out, could only watch as each day became more difficult for him over the next four months.

At their new apartment, the previous tenants had left behind an antique wooden desk that Wright claimed for his new study, and he re-established a routine of rising early to work in his journal. He'd rescued many hundreds of his books from the coal bins in the basement of their old apartment, and these boxes were joined by others from Ohio. Anne recalled how glad he was to lift out each book in turn, sitting on the floor of their living room. They had built floor-to-ceiling bookshelves along one entire wall, and at the age of forty-six, Wright had a home for his library at last.

Wright now chose either his students or solitude; he avoided readings and public events if he could. On May 22, sitting beside Walker Evans afforded him the only pleasure at the ceremony honoring his induction to the National Institute of Arts and Letters. In a letter to *The American Poetry Review*, Wright spoke of an acquaintance approaching him after a recent reading who wanted to commiserate about the "wretched bad writing" in *Two Citizens*. Wright announced that he would "retire from such readings indefinitely," and jokingly asked for donations from the magazine's readers. Months later, after checks were forwarded to him by the editors at *APR*, he formally retracted his request and acknowledged his failed attempt at humor.

At the end of May, Wright received a letter in the form of a free-verse poem from his childhood friend Tom Hodge, now a doctor in California. Though the letter would go unanswered for five years, Wright carried it with him and read it often. With sharp, telling details, Hodge recalled the "tired gray house" where Wright lived on Broadway near the Martins Ferry town dump, and the boy "Who would rather read under the streetlight / Than raid the grape arbor down the alley on Pearl." This sudden, surprising voice spoke powerfully to Wright, and it echoes in a childhood memoir he then drafted in his journal, titled "The Infidel."

Wright worked intensely at the beginning of June, also drafting prose tributes to the poets Richard Hugo and Bill Knott. He had promised a selection of his prose for a new anthology and began to focus a frantic energy on his work. Days after making a spirited list of his favorite writings about poetry, Wright sent a new prose statement to Robert Mezey for his *Naked Poetry* anthology—a digressive monologue compelled by bitterness that consigned his own poetry to the trash heap. After three dense pages of self-contempt and cynical wit, he concludes: "I care about a few things and a few people, but I can assure you they are damned few."

————

While *Two Citizens* continued to weather criticism, Wright's newest poems were indebted to the experiments he had made in that book. At the end of June, just as Wright and Anne arrived in Buffalo for the summer, his new poem "Redwings" appeared in *The Nation*. It points to a subtle yet significant shift in Wright's poetry. The "benevolence and grace" that Jerome Mazzaro identifies as characteristic of Wright's late work is already evident in "Redwings." Mazzaro talked with Wright often that summer and felt that the strained emotional tenor of *Two Citizens* resulted from a kind of willed optimism. "But he begins to speak of a *we*, which is a much more potent force in his last books." The love poems in *Two Citizens* imply the presence of Annie or, less often, the figure of Jenny. More important, Wright begins to use "we" to include others, such as the townspeople in "The Old WPA Swimming Pool in Martins Ferry, Ohio." "Redwings" goes further, gathering into that pronoun the poet's relatives, "The skinny girl I fell in love with down home," a hobo from Wright's youth, the redwing blackbirds—and the reader.

> Somebody is on the wing, somebody
> Is wondering right at this moment
> How to get rid of us, while we sleep.
>
> Together among the dead gorges
> Of highway construction, we flare
> Across highways and drive
> Motorists crazy, we fly
> Down home to the river.

Joel Lipman, a graduate student at Buffalo, became Wright's teaching assistant and chauffeur that summer. At age thirty-two, he was fourteen years younger than Wright but older than most other students, having already taught for four years. Lipman was a single parent, raising his four-year-old son while shuttling Wright to classes and helping him in any way he could. A poet himself and a midwesterner from Wisconsin,

Lipman had come to Buffalo to study with John Logan and Robert Creeley. Wright became a mentor for him, sharing openly not only his knowledge but also his anxieties and his hopes for the coming year. "It was like my own private seminar," Lipman recalled, "and I didn't have to say a word, because he loved to talk."

Picking up Wright each morning, working with him in the classroom, and driving him home, Lipman saw the difficult, ongoing effects of Wright's withdrawal from alcohol. Antabuse was "clearly a hellish drug to be on," he observed. "I remember the kind of look—it wasn't a grimace, it was a look of deep pain about the illness that the drug impacted upon him if he consumed alcohol." Wright showed signs of depression and fought constantly to control his emotions, especially in front of his students. "He was intense. I could see him just exploding at some point, or not being able to maintain that state of encapsulated energy." Both Anne and Mazzaro witnessed bizarre, inexplicable outbursts of rage that summer. "All this time I knew he was upset and depressed," Anne later reflected, "but I never realized to what extent."

Wright poured this pent-up energy into his teaching and his journals. Along with a graduate seminar, he taught a prose composition course for undergraduates that met at 8:15 each morning for more than two hours. The course demanded frequent writing assignments from sixteen students, but Wright insisted on reading and grading every paper and exam. Lipman observed every one of Wright's classes, and it changed his whole approach to teaching. "Wright was most attentive to the truly needy student rather than to the best prepared," Lipman recalled, describing his commitment to a young Latino student who struggled with English. Wright practically taught the class to him alone. "I know that you are thinking about the question deeply, but what you're writing doesn't do justice to what you're thinking," Wright finally said to him. "It doesn't let your mind be revealed in what you've written. And you don't want to be trapped like that!" The young man became tearful with gratitude.

Wright's manner put students at ease, a courtly demeanor set off ironically by his appearance. "He had a good, rumpled, wooly herringbone sort of style about him, and it wasn't polished in any way," Lipman said. "In fact, it was haggard and worn and kind of beaten down and resurrected. I just sort of felt that he had taken the fall and climbed back up." Wright fought to reach students who might otherwise hold back; many were disarmed by his fondness for quoting unlikely authorities, including Mae West and Groucho Marx. But his quotations were not just empty display or entertainment. Wright's extemporaneous performances revealed what Lipman called "the stitching between ideas," when Wright focused his memory and attention on making a clear and significant point in the classroom. He didn't care how he got an idea across, whether with Sappho or W. C. Fields—or both together.

Wright's graduate-level Modern Poetry class asked even more of him—and benefited more from the barely contained energy that coursed through his thinking and writing that summer. Beginning with Hardy, Wright focused on six early modernists, including Robinson, Lawrence, Frost, Jeffers, and Williams. His passion for each poet's work spilled over into his own writing as well as that of his students. Lawrence, in particular, seemed foremost in his thoughts, while Catullus, Shakespeare, Rimbaud, Christopher Smart, and "jaunty renditions of Medieval and Renaissance songs" also figured into the "stitching" of his improvised lectures.

As Lipman observed in both classes, Wright's incantatory voice— "that drawing *up* of sound"—was startling; students were impressed by his "great affection for the sounds of words" and the attention he gave to language. Discussing Williams's *Kora in Hell: Improvisations*, Wright defended the use of prose lines in longer poetic forms to contrast moments of heightened imaginative intensity; this relaxation of rhythm resulted in poems that were "neither narrative nor song." He believed that true emotion could surface more naturally in this way. As models, Wright recited prose poems in French, as well as several of Lawrence's lyrics, such as "The Snake," which he called an ideal instance of "illumination combined with contemplation." In his own work, he spoke of wanting the patience to "listen more," to let the music and movement of his language find its own form.

———

After a full week of teaching, Wright told Franz, "My work here has been furiously busy, but all right." Days later, he wrote to Bly, sharing news of his sudden sobriety. Wright wanted his opinion on the prose pieces he enclosed and praised Bly's own *Point Reyes* poems. "I am having a most joyful time writing in my notebooks, where all sorts of things are coming out." He credits the inspiration of Lake Garda and Lawrence's

Twilight in Italy for his recent work in prose, "something new and strange" that had begun "to flower up every once in a while." Tacitly admitting the havoc that alcohol had wreaked on his poetry, Wright says, "I got lost somewhere, as you know, but something seems to be trying to lead me back to the true path."

His struggle continued, however, even from one hour to the next. On the same day he wrote to Bly, he and Anne attended a Fourth of July party, where Mazzaro recognized the burden of depression that Wright endured. Aware of his own instability, Wright often spoke by phone with his doctors that summer. The continuing revelations surrounding the Watergate cover-up and the televised atrocities from the war in Vietnam contributed to a feeling of ongoing crisis. Working fifteen hours a day on his summer courses, Wright had lost more than twenty pounds. By July 20, he and Anne had decided to return to Italy for three weeks in August, "primarily for me to regain strength," he admitted. Wright also began treatment for hypertension, a condition exacerbated by his alcoholism.

At the end of July, Wright turned back to his notebooks with redoubled intensity; entries throughout the month of August reveal his staggering productivity. But the poems came at a huge cost and often show the sharp mental anguish he faced without alcohol's anesthetic effects. Years earlier in Minneapolis, Wright's doctor had described his "catathymic" condition, characterized by "perseveration"—the compulsive need to see something through to completion. The accuracy of this diagnosis appears undeniable. Well over a hundred separate poems, epigrams, prose pieces, and prayers can be dated to August 1974, and a great many found their way into print. Some are vivid recollections of Martins Ferry; together with Latin and German poets—all "the voices of my dead"— who kept crowding into his mind, the pressure of Wright's memory and imagination is almost palpable. He revisits moments of his life with awful clarity and feeling, while the present is marked by grief and fear. Having withdrawn so deeply into himself, he seems compelled to devise atonements for every bitter memory. As Wright later admitted, he turned to his poetry to forestall the breakdown he sensed might overtake him.

Wright's Modern Poetry seminar had developed a unique bond, and in their final class Wright presented his students with "A Horatian Ode and Prayer at the End of Summer for My Buffalo Friends"—an effusion of fifty-two lines of rhymed couplets blessing eighteen different students and colleagues by name. He had shown a keen interest in classical poets all summer, reciting Catullus, Sappho, and Horace in both English and Latin. His "Horatian Ode" betrays the "willed optimism" that Mazzaro had first recognized in the poems of *Two Citizens*; Wright declares that the worst is past and that the trip to Italy will heal him.

A compulsive series of epigrams in Wright's journal varies in subject and quality, including harsh curses directed at critics and intimate personal "Prayers." Many other poems return to his childhood; there are six numbered index cards of densely typed prose titled "Apologia for the Ohioan Tongue." The most chilling of these dark poems are two prose pieces that touch upon the deaths of his parents. In one, he laments that he is "still as far away from home as I always was," and remembers his father "smiling with weariness into my mother's insane rage." In a separate typescript titled simply "My Mother," Wright can find no forgiveness. "God damn all candles and a cold wind blast her black grave," he cries. "How she hated me." Day by day, the raw emotion becomes more corrosive and ungovernable.

Leaving Buffalo, the Wrights returned to New York before heading for Europe, largely to confer with Wright's doctors. They had chosen an ideal time to leave America behind, if only briefly; as they taxied onto the runway for their flight to London on August 8, they heard the evening news broadcast of Nixon's resignation. With any luck, Wright missed seeing the excoriation of *Two Citizens* published in *The New York Times Book Review* that Sunday. They hoped the vacation would be restorative, but things went awry from the start; flying into Milan, their suitcase was lost, and as the week progressed, Wright retreated into a solitude Anne couldn't reach. During his first days in Italy he addresses separate poems to Anne Sexton and to Jenny. "All I want is to live with peace and be with my dead. . . . pay her no mind, Jenny my underworld." A handwritten prose piece drafted the next day suggests that he would even welcome death if he could find the grave of "Jenny my darkness in secret, Jenny my chill spring," to mourn for her.

After three days in Milan, the Wrights boarded a crowded train for Torri del Benaco, planning to stay for a week in the same hotel that had welcomed them exactly one year before. Their disappointment grew when they were turned away and forced to take a room elsewhere. Nothing slowed the writing, however, as Wright filled two separate notebooks with daily entries. In Torri del Benaco, Wright jotted down the second stanza of Storm's poem "Hyacinthen"—lines inextricably linked to memories of Sonjia. In a new prose piece, he writes, "She is dead"—as though reminding himself; the poem addresses a reader who stands beside him. The insular, private world he once shared with Sonjia in correspondence opens before him again, but this time in utter solitude. The following day he writes, "I am alone. / I am falling. / Not even Rilke in his Autumn can comfort me now." Passages of urgent prayer appear often. Recalling a dream in which he felt like Caliban, unable to make his words understood, Wright remembers plummeting into darkness. "I have been falling through this very same space so many times, that if I had a twin brother his name would be Loss."

––––––––

Wright had brought just one book with him to Italy, "a book that I had for ten years given up for lost"—a small, compact edition of *The Cloud of Unknowing*, the anonymous fourteenth-century mystical Christian book of devotion and contemplation. He turned to it constantly and transcribed long passages into his journal. On the flyleaf, Wright inscribed a quote from Tolstoy: "The flesh rages and riots, and the spirit follows it helpless and miserable." Wright worked furiously in Italy, and, surprisingly often, the poems were nearly flawless. During his first three days in Torri del Benaco, he drafted "Piccolini," "The Flying Eagles of Troop 62," and "The Wheeling Gospel Tabernacle," among numerous other poems and prose pieces.

The Wrights traveled from Lake Garda to San Alessio outside of Lucca near Italy's western coast, where they stayed as guests of Louis Simpson at his mother's villa. Wright sustained a monologue for hours beside the pool, even though Simpson's mother and her husband had no idea what he was saying. On the train from Florence to Padua, Wright drafted one of his finest prose pieces, "The Lambs on the Boulder," recounting how the Florentine painter Cimabue discovered a young shepherd boy scratching the faces of his sheep on a stone. This was Giotto, who became his pupil at the advent of the Italian Renaissance. The sensitive, penetrating faces of Giotto's figures affected Wright deeply, especially the masterful fresco cycle in the Scrovegni Chapel in Padua.

Lost in his own work, Wright found a reprieve; the moments of stillness and peace were real—as long as he was writing—and marked by
an intense clarity of vision. Sitting in the sunlight at an outdoor café the
next morning for an early breakfast on Padua's Piazza della Frutta, he
and Anne watched the marketplace and fruit stalls open and crowds
beginning to gather in the vast square. "The Fruits of the Season" captures a singular moment in late summer with precise and sensual details. It, too, stands with Wright's best work in prose.

While in Padua, Wright became convinced that a chance discovery in
a local bookstore was, in fact, "an herb of healing, a balsam, and a sign."
He had found a pocket-size German pamphlet of a story by Theodor
Storm, "Paul the Puppet-Player," the first he had tried to translate while
at Kenyon. On the flyleaf he inscribed the stanza from "Hyacinthen"—
Storm's obsessive imagining of a lost love—that he had recalled nine
days before when summoning all "the voices of my dead." Coming across
Storm's book, Wright felt as if Jenny had appeared to him again; only
hours before, he had searched for her as he leaned against the city's
Ponte della Morte—the Bridge of Death.

Wright withdrew into solitude for hours on end. Anne saw how his
work had become a means to cope with abstinence; he remained sober
all summer. Though in public Wright could "force cheerfulness into my
face with anybody," by the end of their trip he rarely spoke to his wife
and spent much of each day entirely alone. Wright still believed he could
will himself into health, and he later remembered only his days in
Verona, at the end of their brief stay in Italy, as truly restful. Hearing
Verdi's *Requiem* in the ancient Arena, he wrote an homage to the city
and a lone cricket "trying to sing himself to sleep among the warm darkened stones" on the opposite side of the enormous amphitheatre—the
prose piece "Magnificence."

On the day before they left, Wright drafted two poems that show he
no longer felt a stranger in Verona. On the back of a gaudy, oversized
postcard showing a retouched photo of Romeo climbing the famed balcony of Juliet, Wright began a letter that he quickly appropriated for a
new poem: "Written on a Big Cheap Postcard from Verona." Beside it in
his journal, "One Last Look at the Adige River in Verona" marks a shift
of allegiance away from the shores of the Ohio. Taking his leave reluc-
tantly, the poet addresses the river directly:

A half-witted angel drawling Ohioan
In the warm Italian rain.

In the middle of my own life
I woke up and found myself
Dying, fair enough, still
Alive in the friendly city
Of my body, my secret Verona . . .

Wright's allusions to Dante's *Inferno* and the brief, full life of Catullus—
"He left home and went straight / To hell in Rome"—call on the city's
poets to bless his departure. Wright had chosen Verona as his home,
and leaving it behind was a jagged sorrow—like the broken chip of pink
marble from the Arena that he worried in his pocket.

The overcrowded Italian trains made Wright anxious, so when they
left Verona they boarded a bus in the Piazza Bra. In one last prose piece
written in Verona, "The Silent Angel," he sees or imagines a musician
waving him goodbye from the shadows of "one of the pink marble arches
at the base of the great Roman Arena." He gritted his teeth to think of
returning to New York; in the days ahead a sense of falling overwhelmed
him. On the eight-hour plane flight from Heathrow to Kennedy, Wright
filled the last pages of two small notebooks. One numbered sequence of
prose pieces titled "America for Me" begins: "In about five more hours
we will land in New York City. Verona is far behind me. I am so wretch-
edly homesick I can hardly bear it. But Verona is a long way off. I was
born in America, and so I am lost."

24

The Road Back

September 1974–January 1976

> I had no idea
> How far down I was.
> —"Hell"

Debilitated by depression, Wright returned to New York only a week before classes resumed at Hunter. The crowds and subways were oppressive, and the sense of responsibility for his students troubled him. Rereading Graham Greene's essay "The Young Dickens" in preparation for his seminar, Wright drew heavy lines beneath Dickens's description of "the cold wet shelterless midnight streets of London" and Greene's insistence that the Manichean world that Dickens creates "is a world without God." While preparing for classes, he turned to the hundreds of new pages in his journals, typing fair copies of dozens of prose pieces and poems and sorting them for submission to various magazines. Within weeks his new work began appearing in *The American Poetry Review*, *The Ohio Review*, and elsewhere.

Wright's letter to Franz on September 12 shows his anxiety for his son, who remained on leave from Oberlin and unemployed. "My own classes have begun, and the disorganization at Hunter has been very confusing and disheartening." Since the beginning of open admissions four years before, class sizes had swollen; Wright's Dickens seminar had a third more students—thirty-eight in all. But Donna Masini saw nothing in his manner to suggest that Wright felt uneasy. "He seemed very balanced, moving around the room continually with such incredible grace—like a sort of slow-motion ballet. You got the sense he could feel the rhythms of what he was seeing and talking about, and he was expressing them both with his voice and with his body."

In mid-September, however, a feeling of profound discouragement consumed Wright. He confessed to Anne that he had been hearing voices since their return from Italy. Restless and yet weary, he found that simply facing his students became more difficult. On Friday, September 20, Anne returned home from her first day at a new job to find her husband immobilized by depression. Wright was admitted to the psychiatric care unit of Mount Sinai Hospital and remained there for a month. Hypertension and exhaustion had precipitated his breakdown; the mental and physical pressures of withdrawal from alcohol—magnified by grief at his parents' deaths—had finally overwhelmed him. "I'm letting myself move slowly," he wrote to Franz a week later. "Within me there is certainly something healthy that will heal me if I give it a chance."

Knowing how fragile he remained, his wife was reluctant to tell Wright about Anne Sexton's suicide on October 4; she asked a doctor to break the news. With Maxine Kumin's help, Sexton had finished correcting the galley proofs of her new book on the day she took her own life. *The Awful Rowing Toward God* would appear in the spring bearing a dedication to Wright. The act of suicide always enraged him, but he was also furious with himself for turning away from Sexton.

Wright's struggle to regain his equilibrium can be felt in a letter to Frederick Morgan at *The Hudson Review*, thanking the editor for *rejecting* three new poems. On October 19, he jotted down his first new journal entry in more than a month, a modest, one-sentence prose piece:

Saying Dante Aloud

You can feel the muscles and veins rippling in widening and
    rising circles, like a bird in flight under your tongue.

The day after his discharge from Mount Sinai on October 22, Wright sent a long letter to Bly detailing the events that led to his breakdown.

"I feel more whole and healthy inside myself—in my soul, really—than I can recall ever having felt before in my entire life," he insisted, aware of his own tendency "to go to extremes in attempting to describe a feeling." Glad to reestablish their correspondence, Wright enclosed a new prose piece. "I am somewhat tired. But I am refreshed. I feel a vast richness within me."

Relieved from teaching, Wright read widely and impulsively over the next three months, surprised by the prospect of genuine rest for the first time in years. Preparing for a spring class in Cervantes and the English Novel gave him an excuse to reread the raunchy, hilarious, and "utterly fearless" novelists of the eighteenth century. He submitted a chapbook-length sequence of prose poems to David R. Godine, a publisher of letterpress editions in Boston, and—more carefully than he had in September—sent off handfuls of poems to journals and magazines. His letters show a resolute self-confidence, but when Bly visited at the end of November, Wright appeared remarkably frail. More than thirty pounds lighter than Bly had ever seen him, he had so little energy it seemed "as if he had turned into his own father."

Wright joined Helen Vendler and Louis Simpson as a judge for the Pulitzer Prize that fall and read all sixty-seven nominated books, taking detailed notes on each one. He lobbied for Gary Snyder's new collection, *Turtle Island*, which went on to receive the award. Wright stood by his praise for Snyder; as Crunk had written in *The Sixties* a dozen years before, Snyder's poems are "powerfully located—sown, rooted—in the landscape of the Western states." From the first time he saw the Pacific Northwest as an eighteen-year-old soldier, this was a landscape Wright felt at home in.

In December, for his forty-seventh birthday, Anne made a gift of the two-volume *Complete Poems of D. H. Lawrence*, which joined the small shelf of treasured books Wright kept beside his reading chair in the living room with works by Orwell, Forster, Mencken, and Twain. Now that Wright's parents were gone, he and Anne stayed in New York that Christmas, and Franz traveled from Ohio to be with them. "He never stopped being a lecturer," Franz remembered. "You don't really converse with him so much as listen to him lecture—and they were beautiful lectures. . . . There was nothing that excited me more in my life than being around him. We were very, very close, and we talked when we were alone in a way I didn't see him talk with anybody else." This intimacy can be felt in Wright's letters to Franz, which are often his most candid and expressive.

————

Anne realized that her husband had started drinking again sometime in the winter of 1975. It's unclear what triggered his relapse, though the pressure of returning to the classroom at the end of January played some part. Philip Levine saw Wright often in New York and recognized the enormous effort it took for him to quit. "I felt that a lot of energy was going into that, to keep himself going. I had this sense that Jim was really *holding* himself together."

One clue to Wright's drinking appears in a letter to Carolee Coombs-Stacy, a composer who had set a handful of poems from *The Branch* to music. When she wrote of suffering severe bouts of depression, he responded in kind. "My own attacks—a strong word, but an accurate one—of unhappiness come in the form of an awful, perhaps indescribable loneliness. It is not a loneliness of the body—there are plenty of people around, in New York especially—but a loneliness of the soul, in which I feel an appalling sense of abandonment and loss." Coombs-Stacy also admitted to the shame she felt for a birthmark, prompting Wright to tell her about the woman with a scar whom he had loved in high school. This early model for his Muse had shown him "some of her soul, and had opened to me a world of books and music that gave me a vision of the beauty that I hungered for."

The same day he wrote Coombs-Stacy on January 10, Wright drafted a new poem titled "To Bee, Who Is Dead." Addressing Sexton, he regrets she did not call on him in the end. Rather than dissuade her, he insists he would have joined her, baring his own breast to the "horn beak" of the "great bird . . . Hunting cold to kill." The poem ends:

And now, God damn it,
I have to go alone.

They thought I loved them, but they were crazy.
I loved you, alone,
And I wanted to go
With you, alone.

This seems close in spirit to Sexton's work, striving in voice and imagery to call her back. The poem reveals his feelings of guilt and loss following Sexton's death and exposes a chafed, unsteady mind.

The volume of mail he received from importuning writers and admirers had multiplied in recent years. Wright answered a steady stream of requests for support from friends and students pursuing fellowships or graduate school. He also encouraged young poets to send him their work; if a student pressed poems on him, he rarely said no. Jeanne Foster Hill, one of his summer students in Buffalo, had sent poems to him while he was still in the hospital in October. They maintained a correspondence for the next two years. When David Ignatow asked Wright to select "a folio of favorite poets" for *The American Poetry Review*, he included Hill among the ten he chose. He selected poets without regard for age or reputation; some he knew personally, like Gibbons Ruark and Joel Lipman, while others, such as Marilyn Hacker, Louis Jenkins, and Thomas Lux, were simply poets whose work he admired. Ignatow had stressed *APR*'s urgent deadline, but to Wright's ongoing embarrassment the portfolio was continually postponed.

Returning to Hunter in January, Wright taught an upper-level class on satire that included readings in Swift and Fielding, but it began, as so many of his classes did, with *Don Quixote*. Masini recalled the "sense of camaraderie" that characterized his fondness for authors such as Cervantes, Hardy, Robinson, and Frost. "There was always this sense of simultaneity, that they were all part of this one huge community."

In April 1975, Wright finally conceded that Alcoholics Anonymous might help him stay sober, and he and Anne attended an initial meeting together. In front of that first gathering, he confessed that his desire to quit drinking had been triggered by the comments of Kenyon's president a year before, when he declared that Wright had achieved the promise of his youth. His full commitment to AA took some time, however; he didn't attend meetings regularly for more than a year. Michael Graves, a student of Wright's who also joined AA that spring, knew that he despised the sanctimony shown by many members.

At the end of April, Wright traveled with Anne to Ohio for a poetry festival at Case Western Reserve University in Cleveland, his first public reading in almost two years. James Dickey, though invited as another featured reader, merely introduced a showing of the recent movie based on his novel, *Deliverance*, and bragged of his rapport with Burt Reynolds and others on location during filming. While staying at the same hotel, Dickey happily told Anne of his Oberlin reading earlier that week; he had watched Franz consume a fifth of bourbon at a party afterward. She begged him not to tell her husband, but when Wright joined them in the lobby Dickey immediately began embellishing his story. Anne then realized that Dickey was wearing the winter coat they had given Franz at Christmas.

Philip Levine recognized "a kind of ambient jealousy" among Wright's colleagues—some also heavy drinkers—who were made uneasy by his abstinence. Like Dickey, many of them blamed Anne for suppressing the exuberant, unrestrained poet they had known. But it was Wright's decision to get sober, and his struggle alone.

————

Wright often sent letters to poets whose work he esteemed, whether he knew them personally or not. Back in January he had praised Michael S. Harper's new collection, *Nightmare Begins Responsibility*, and singled out the poem "Kin" for a quality of language he also found in Keats's work. Harper then persuaded Wright to give a reading at Brown University before a small gathering of students. He knew that Wright had not been reading often in public and had the foresight to record the event, feeling "that there was going to be some magic." On a Friday afternoon in early May, they gathered in the intimate Crystal Room on Brown's Pembroke campus, with windows open to warm spring weather. Wright felt relaxed and expansive; as always, he began with poems by others—Allen Tate, Edna St. Vincent Millay, and two Irish poets. "I used to say, 'I wish I'd written that poem,'" he admitted. "Now, 'I'm very glad somebody wrote these poems.'" When he turned to read half a dozen of his own, "he was in a storytelling mode," Harper recalled, and introduced each one with personal, elegiac recollections, as though reacquainting himself with the poems.

As his Brown reading suggests, Wright's self-confidence—and his memory—slowly returned as he fought to stay sober. But without teaching or travel to absorb him that summer, he slipped back into drinking. Proof came with the monthly phone bill, detailing his compulsive late-night calls to friends around the country. Wright's drinking fueled ongoing friction with Anne, and in early June a conflict arose between them. Anne had confided in Betty Kray about their outstanding debts from his fall hospitalization, and Kray had then solicited a grant on Wright's behalf from the Mark Rothko Foundation—an award he had assumed was meant to honor his poetry. On June 6, after learning of Anne's indiscretion, Wright typed eight pages filled with rage, describing his plan to commit suicide in the Pacific Ocean after setting his affairs in order and visiting the grave of "my poor Jenny."

Later that day, however, Wright began a separate diary he called a "Daily Record of *Der Weg Zurück*," or "The Road Back," meticulously recording his AA meetings and days of "Total sobriety." Though this notebook breaks off a month later, it shows his determination to quit drinking and repair his marriage. The daily entries express his fears and his despair; he notes feeling that the apartment belongs to Anne, not to them both, and that he is merely "a house-guest who outstayed his welcome." More often, though, Wright records the relief he finds in the company of others at AA meetings—which he often attended twice a day—and moments when "I felt I really belonged among those good people."

Wright's recurrent depression caused him to doubt his own poetry, and the ongoing critical censure of *Two Citizens*—still appearing two years after the book's publication—prompted him to consider writing an anonymous review himself, "to condemn this book with absolutely murderous finality." At this same time, the summer issue of *The Paris Review* featured the interview Wright had given more than three years before. *Two Citizens* had yet to be published when the interview was recorded in April 1972, and Wright shows a muted enthusiasm for the book—or at least for "what lies behind it, because it grew directly out of my new life" with Anne and their travels in Europe. Throughout, the interview gives evidence of a poet profoundly committed to his craft and to his work as a teacher; these two aspects of his life are equally important to him. Wright is forceful and articulate. As he extemporizes criticism and quotes poems and prose at will, his intellectual agility is undeniable.

But *The Paris Review* also published a portfolio of ten new poems, which included eight prose pieces and two others that mixed prose passages with verse. These new pieces seem even more unfinished than the most discursive poems in *Two Citizens*. The majority were journal fragments; stanzas in varied end-rhymes are extended skillfully, but the effect and the emotion feel contrived. Taken together, the poems make sincerity look like an act of will—and a lot of work. Most were products of his feverish output the previous August, and Wright never reprinted them. The last poem in the sequence, "Dawn Prayer in Cold Darkness to My Secret Ghost," includes stanzas of rhymed pentameter that Wright claims to have "[t]ranslated from an anonymous Latin author." He invokes both Horace and "my lovely ghost," Jenny, who is now "nothing but a leaf of grass." Though she would return again in Wright's journals, this poem marks the last time her name appeared in print: "God save me in my darkness where I go, / Where Jenny walked before me, long ago."

Anne remembered that summer as the most troubled time in their marriage. "He seemed so distant," she recalled, "and I couldn't get through to him. He was pulling away." In desperation, she contacted Irving Silver, her husband's therapist and a close colleague of her own psychiatrist. The two analysts consulted by phone and worked together to save the Wrights' marriage. A turning point in the couple's impasse came during a stay at the end of June at Lake Minnewaska, where they tried to rebuild a sense of trust with long walks and frank exchanges.

After returning from Minnewaska—a reprieve that had "melted the ice in me"—Wright traveled alone to Michigan for ten days. Together with Galway Kinnell and Robert Bly, Wright was a featured participant in the inaugural National Poetry Festival sponsored by Grand Valley State Colleges in Allendale, on the western edge of the state bordering Lake Michigan. While the evening reading series drew large crowds, the paying audience for the daytime seminars and manuscript review sessions remained small. An outstanding roster of poets had come, however, including Robert Creeley, John Woods, and Etheridge Knight.

The festival gave Wright the chance to share long, open days with Bly and Kinnell, and the three poets reestablished close bonds. Mary Bly, now thirteen, had accompanied her father, and Wright was delighted to see his goddaughter again. Throughout the conference, Wright called upon his vast store of literature and carried a notebook to which he added favorite poems by others; when he said poems in German, he improvised translations. In a seminar he led with Kinnell, they spent two hours saying poems they loved, and encouraged the audience to join them. Wright recited a long passage from Shakespeare's *King Lear* to show how "the vast swings of Lear's emotion could be captured in blank verse." Kinnell then said Wright's poem "Rip" by heart, counting it among his own favorites.

Jeanne Hill, whom Wright had invited to the festival, noticed how protective Kinnell acted toward Wright, aware of his fight to keep sober. To many, Hill appeared to be the one "sort of shepherding him around." As one of the few with a car, she drove Wright to AA meetings during those ten days. "He was very much convinced that it was because of AA that he was able to get sober," she recalled, and he felt open and relaxed among the other members. Over the previous months, Wright had come to trust in Hill, whom he often called late at night after he'd been drinking. On the phone and in occasional letters, Wright treated her as "a confidante," maintaining an element of secrecy in their calls and correspondence. Wright continued to phone and write to Hill well into the following spring, when he stayed in Buffalo for a few days with Hill and her boyfriend and secured a reading for her at the Cooper Union in New York.

Wright's fragile state seemed apparent to many at the festival, even some who barely knew him, an impression reinforced by the constant presence of Hill at his side. A large audience gathered for Wright's dynamic evening reading, which received a standing ovation. He said poems from throughout his career and made a lasting impression on many poets in the audience. "Wright's poetry had a profound effect on the work of all of us at the conference," recalled Leslie Marmon Silko.

———

After just ten days back in New York City, Wright and Anne settled into a cottage in Misquamicut, Rhode Island, a modest beach town not far from the more elegant Watch Hill on the western border of the state near Connecticut. The couple spent the month of August there, close to a secluded, mile-long stretch of beach on the Atlantic Ocean, with a saltwater pond separated by dunes. They arrived "kind of battered," Anne remembered, but after many long talks, "things started to get better." Kray was nearby and they saw a lot of her that month. Wright attended AA meetings, and during long afternoons on the beach they passed a copy of Doctorow's new novel, *Ragtime*, between them. The vacation strengthened a process of healing in their troubled marriage.

Back at Hunter, Wright's classwork consumed him that fall. The financial crisis in New York City had diminished the number of full-time faculty, and class sizes continued to increase; composition and literature courses had as many as forty students. There was also wide-spread frustration with administrative bureaucracy, not just at Hunter but throughout the CUNY system. And day by day, Wright's struggle with alcohol persisted. Continuing with the twelve steps of the Alcoholics Anonymous program, he phoned Kray, "in his post-summer mood of confidence," to admit to the pain he had caused others because of his drinking. "Jim's sense of form gives his telephone calls an inexorable continuity," Kray wrote in a brief prose memoir; if she interrupted him at any point he would begin all over again.

Wright still felt haunted by the public failure of *Two Citizens*; the book now represented the damage drinking had done to his poetry. There were moments when he felt "painfully low and depressed . . . really and truly beginning to suspect . . . that I am not a real poet after all." These feelings alternated with the hopefulness that autumn always brought. The gift of a British edition of Edward Thomas's *Collected Prose* inspired a fascinating inscription, evidence of the optimism Wright worked to sustain. Rereading the book after many years, he sensed the distance he had come since his days in Minnesota. Dated October 7, 1975, Wright's cramped scrawl on the book's front endpaper concludes:

> I think I have shed a lot of dead skin. I dreaded starting all over again—all that heavy labor, all over again.
>
> I am totally surprised to realize that I feel as light and quick as a new moth, fluttering in the darkness, rising or falling as the darkness pleases, in the good darkness.
>
> "My youth is spent, and yet I am not old."

Wright had named Thomas "one of the secret spirits who help keep us alive," and for him this may have been literally true. Five days after he inscribed Thomas's book, a half-page typescript titled "Words of Practical Interest" reveals the great swings of emotion that still plagued him. In what seems to be a straightforward bequest—almost a suicide note—Wright gives all his books to Franz and assigns "Dr. Jerome Mazzaro" the task of seeing his last book into print. Wright asks to be buried "at the Weeks Cemetery near Colerain, Ohio, as near to my grandmother's grave as can be arranged," and asks for two lines to be carved on his tombstone:

VERGIEB MIR MEINE FREUDE.
I had my heart's desire.

The line beneath the German ("Forgive me my joy") echoes a poem by Edward Thomas. In a postscript written by hand, this brief note concludes:

> I have inflicted a good deal of pain on others and on myself during my lifetime. But God knows I have suffered inwardly quite enough hell to pay for it.
> So I see no reason for apologizing to anyone for my life or my death.
> I wish to say good-night to my friends, who know who they are.

On the same day that Wright recorded this despairing passage, the editor of Dryad Press, Merrill Leffler, posted a letter inviting him to submit a chapbook manuscript. Leffler had recently published collections by Roland Flint and John Logan, and the quality and physical beauty of the books had impressed Wright. This welcome idea helped lift his spirits as he traveled to Michigan for a brief reading tour in mid-October, visiting Donald Hall in Ann Arbor and appearing at two other colleges. The glorious fall weather helped restore a sense of promise; that same week, *The Nation* featured one of his most significant new poems, "To a Blossoming Pear Tree." At Eastern Michigan University in Ypsilanti, Wright recited "just about every poem any lover of his work could hope to hear," recalled Peter Serchuk. "I can still see him, grey beard and ash-marked pants, almost singing the final lines to 'A Blessing.'"

By the end of October, Wright and Anne had begun planning a trip to Hawaii the following summer, where he had finally agreed to teach a course in creative writing at the University of Hawaii at Honolulu. They invited Marshall to join them, to celebrate his eighteenth birthday there. Wright had just learned that Marsh was in the hospital, which Liberty blamed on his "drug abuse." In fact, Marshall had suffered a violent psychotic break and physically attacked his stepfather, but for some reason Liberty withheld the truth about his condition from Wright. Doctors now believed that Marshall suffered from a manic-depressive disorder and prescribed a series of drugs, including lithium. He spent the next year and a half in various residential programs for adolescents; forbidden to return home, he graduated from high school while living on his own. But Wright and Anne believed that Marshall's troubles had been wholly a consequence of drug abuse. They were not told about his diagnosis and ongoing treatment.

Wright had been thinking about a chapbook-length collection of prose pieces for more than a year. Feeling unready to finalize a full manuscript, he told Leffler on November 2 that the chance to publish with Dryad Press came "at just the right time." Wright had already chosen a selection of fifteen pieces "written in (or about) certain places in Italy" and imagined including illustrations with them. "I am still learning about this kind of poem, so thrillingly new to me even though I can now see it has been sleeping in me for a long time." Wright's travel letters already show him testing the lyrical possibilities of prose. His evolving use of the short prose form gave him room to experiment with narrative pace and interior digressions of thought and memory. Wright insisted on calling the work "prose sketches." "Every one of those poems is set in a place," Leffler realized, "but it's not only a moment in that place, it's a moment in the mind, ranging and letting anything in." He was thrilled to publish a book by Wright.

Jane Cooper joined Wright in his apartment later that day to share the poems they would read the following Sunday in a program dedicated to neglected American poets of the nineteenth century. Cooper had discovered a trove of suppressed nursery rhymes and a number of overlooked women poets, while Wright, not surprisingly, returned to the work of Edwin Arlington Robinson. Darkness fell outside the book-lined living room on Eighty-fifth Street while he recited dozens of Robinson's poems by heart. "As the afternoon wore on and wore on, his voice became a kind of enchantment."

The week after his reading with Cooper, Wright was scheduled to appear at the Poetry Center of the 92nd Street Y, to read his own poems in New York for the first time in years. The evening before, however, he was overcome by stomach pains and admitted to the emergency ward at Mount Sinai for three days of tests. Wright began treatment for acute gastritis, a common side effect of alcoholism. With only a few hours' notice, three good friends agreed to read on his behalf, each choosing their own favorite Wright poems: Robert Mezey, Grace Schulman, and Louis Simpson.

In his journal three days later, Wright seems finally able to make peace with the open wound that *Two Citizens* had become. He acknowledges the risks he had taken in the poems and the courage that required. Wright even anticipates revising the collection, knowing that "the classical *idea* of the book remains sound." While some writers praised the poems, the whole effort of weighing success and failure had grown tiresome. "The main thing is to learn from errors and to go on living, thinking and feeling and writing actively."

25

Redwings and Solitaries

January–December 1976

The Winter 1976 issue of *The Hudson Review* featured Wright's poem "Hook," which the magazine's poetry editor, Hayden Carruth, had praised for its sharp sympathy, rich internal music, and emotional openness. In the same issue, Carruth published an essay titled "The Question of Poetic Form," which proved to be crucial for Wright. Carruth wanted to defuse the antagonism that still endured between "academic" formalists, such as Allen Tate, and the advocates of free-verse expression in a common language, like Williams. All poetic forms exist as a range of possibilities, Carruth reasons; if a poem succeeds, formal elements are beside the point. "The classification of poems, old or new, is a hurtful, false endeavor. Let the warring cease."

Wright spent the first weeks in January rearranging a sequence of eighteen prose pieces for his chapbook, work that led to a new round of revisions. When questioned about the shambling group of prose pieces that *The Paris Review* had printed months before, Wright seemed to shrug off his new focus on prose. On January 16 he wrote, "I have never known how to write prose, and I felt it was about time I tried to find out." After he extensively revised many of the pieces that month, *Moments of the Italian Summer* included just fourteen poems. Wright mailed the final selection to Leffler on January 19, including photos he hoped might inspire the book's illustrations. "Once I discovered the proper order of this sequence of prose pieces, I took wing for a while, and worked for long hours, writing them all out again in longhand and trying to prune and purify the language," he told the editor. Already adopting Carruth's terms to describe a poem's formal character, Wright says, "It has made me happy to put these pieces together, and to discover their inner form."

Moments of the Italian Summer shares something with the poems in *The Branch*: the rediscovery of happiness, as Wright noticed himself in arranging the chapbook. But while images of darkness hold sway in *The Branch*, these new prose pieces are suffused with "the light of the river Adige." The conception and the landscapes of the chapbook bear striking similarities to *Wandering*, the prose sketches Hesse had interspersed with watercolors and poems. Leffler and Wright agreed on an unusual, eight-inch-square page size, to accommodate the long lines, with elegant typography, paper stock, and illustrations. Though they had hoped to bring the book out by late spring, it took longer to secure the work of the illustrator, Joan Root; it would be late in the fall before *Moments of the Italian Summer* appeared. The physical book, a limited pressing, shows all the care that went into it. So does Wright's relaxed prose, free from any sense of struggle. "I don't see how this could be any better," Robert Hass marveled when he first read "The Lambs on the Boulder." "The poem feels intricate with thought."

Wright was also arranging a full manuscript, and in January he wrote a long autobiographical letter to Helen McNeely Sheriff, his high school Latin teacher, asking to dedicate the book to her—then titled *Redwings and the Secret of Light*. As in other letters from this time, Wright depicts himself on firmer ground; he admits to difficult years in the past but looks ahead with confidence. He tells Sheriff of a public ceremony in his honor to be held in Martins Ferry at the end of June, but he writes again weeks later to tell her that he has canceled his homecoming, infuriated by "the nine (!) public ceremonies within a mere two days" that the mayor had planned for him—some of them "transparently political."

At Hunter that spring, Wright taught an advanced course on the British Comic Novel and another called the Comic Vision; both classes began with *Don Quixote*. Wright found Cervantes's understanding of human life, with its tangle of comedy and tragedy, endlessly fascinating as well as instructive for his students. "He was a man who had a large and generous capacity for experience, and nothing was lost on him," Wright told them, paraphrasing Henry James's advice to young writers.

Wright's letters to a teenage poet in Minnesota, Janice Thurn, show the kind of respect and openness that characterized his classroom. Thurn had first written to him the previous spring—enclosing two poems in a letter mailed to Macalester College—and they now corresponded regularly. In his journal writing and letters, Wright's prose often shows a casual grace and fluid lyricism. On May 4, 1976, his description to Thurn of walking in the park along the East River becomes a reverie recalling a long, slow walk in Rome, "all the way to the Garden of the Vestal Virgins in the Forum, where there is a nice girl with a flawed face, still, still."

An anthology called *American Poets in 1976* appeared in May, the first substantial gathering of Wright's work in prose. William Heyen had solicited new prose work from "twenty-nine contemporaries writing on their own lives and work," and Wright's entries present the most imaginative approach to the idea of self-portraiture. He chose three travel letters and a dozen other miscellaneous pieces: memoir-like essays on Richard Hugo and Bill Knott, journal passages, and a handful of new prose poems. Wright valued the prose piece "A Letter to Franz Wright" so highly that it long stood as the first poem in his new manuscript. The tone of his letters to Franz can sound like a cautious master instructing a volatile student, but Wright's prose is often inspired. Just as his father had done as an undergraduate, Franz was translating Rilke, including the sequence "The Life of Mary" that Wright praised in a letter that May. Though their poetry is strikingly different, both father and son understood Rilke's "Christ's Descent into Hell" to be emblematic of the poet's task.

At the end of May, John Logan sent an ecstatic letter, astounded by Wright's work in the *American Poets in 1976* volume, in which Logan also appeared. "The sheer beauty of your description of places you love sent my mind reeling to scenes like Camus writing about Algiers," Logan enthused. "These are absolute jewels of American language and letters." After *Moments of the Italian Summer* appeared, Logan's brief essay on Wright's prose went further. "I know of no other writer since Dante whose love imagery is so linked with light." Wright valued Logan's "uncluttered vision," which avoided the fruitless "technical nitpicking about the 'prose poem'" that distracted other critics. "All I am trying to do is to learn how to write old-fashioned prose, and I hope it is plain. Of course, what I really mean is that I am trying to balance language itself with my experience of the intractable world and, in that balance, ring a kind of chime."

After classes at Hunter ended, Wright began preparing his course for Hawaii and gathering the writing he had done since *Two Citizens*. At Lake Minnewaska that June he began new poems as well, including "Goodbye to Ohio," inspired by his refusal to return to Martins Ferry. As with so many Ohio poems, a portrait of Wright's father is at its center. "He was a worn-out hillbilly who lived his life / At the dead end of the Appalachians." On the reverse side of a typescript draft, Wright's hand-written revision of the poem concludes:

> My old man is dead. The Ohio River is dead.
> You can have my share of it.
> I hope you make money.

While Wright remained bitter about his canceled trip to Martins Ferry, Anne and others believed that he chose to stay away for the sake of his poetry. "He had a Martins Ferry in his mind that he didn't want to disturb."

The two months Wright spent in Hawaii mark a significant step in his fight for sobriety; at the same time, his marriage returned to firmer ground. Simply traveling together helped, as did the overwhelming natural beauty of the islands. Even after Marshall joined them at the end of July and troubles multiplied, Wright avoided drink. The pressures of living and teaching in New York made it much more difficult to stay sober back home. "All the news that comes to me from NYC makes the place seem damned somehow. When I think of Hunter, I shudder: all the increased workload, the necessity of pouring so much energy into a task that is largely hopeless; the loss of one's very self in the human wave," he told the poet Ann Sanfedele. "I wish I could stay here permanently." Apart from brief lapses over the next two years, Wright avoided drink, and his memories of Hawaii—like those of Verona—helped sustain him. His journal writing also grew into an active means of staying sober.

W. S. Merwin, who was then building a house on Maui with his companion, Dana, greeted the Wrights at the airport when they arrived on July 1, and the two couples met often throughout the summer. Merwin drove them to different beaches to swim, and exchanged new poems with Wright; it was the most time the two poets ever spent together. The

Wrights stayed in a friend's apartment that overlooked the beach, and Anne recalled that the first weeks of their stay were idyllic. "Every morning there was a rainbow in the sky. We loved Honolulu." Wright had always avoided creative writing courses and taught this one much as he would his modern poetry course, with close readings and discussions of Williams, Hardy, and Lawrence.

Marshall arrived as planned at the end of July for a three-week visit to celebrate his eighteenth birthday. He told them of his difficult times over the past ten months, shuttling between the hospital and halfway houses, and of his doctors' diagnosis of manic depression. The seriousness of Marshall's illness and the setbacks he had suffered, including dropping out of high school, upset his father. Unaware that Marshall had stopped taking his prescribed medications, Wright became convinced that his son's condition was debilitating—or had become so because of marijuana and other drugs, the only concerns Liberty had warned them about. Marshall's behavior became increasingly erratic, and neither Wright nor Anne could distinguish the symptoms of his illness from the effects of drug abuse or withdrawal. Wright also felt ill at ease as a parent of a teenager. When he lectured Marshall, worried that he was destroying his life, his son responded with characteristic optimism, "I'll be fine!"

It fell to Anne to care for Marshall, who made the task difficult. "I deliberately chose to disavow her in the role of my mother," he recalled. He might sit in the dark with a book held upside down or stare at an empty television screen; at the beach or other public places, he seemed always eager to wander off. On his final day in Hawaii, Marshall begged his father to take him to Waikiki Beach, where he quickly disappeared for more than an hour. After looking everywhere, Wright found his son standing in a men's room with thirty dollars in his hand, trying to buy drugs. Wright was frightened by the incident and furious. "If I ever find out who started you on drugs, I will kill them with my bare hands," Wright swore, clutching his fists in frustration. He and Anne walked with Marshall to the gate for his plane back to San Francisco, having asked the flight attendants in confidence to look after him. The image of Marshall crossing the tarmac and climbing the stairs into the airplane would be the last glimpse Wright ever had of his son.

Throughout these difficult weeks, Wright completed his classwork at the university and pored over comments on his new poems from Bly and

Kinnell; a detailed letter from Hall awaited him in New York upon his return. Wright consistently trusted Kinnell's brief comments, deleting lines or removing entire poems from the manuscript. Bly returned Wright's poems in batches throughout his time in Hawaii, including a detailed letter dated July 24 with seventeen poems he felt strongly should be left out of the book. Grateful for their close readings, Wright knew he had asked for responses at the right time.

In their final week there, Wright and Anne had Hawaii to themselves. "Our five days at Lahaina on Maui, and at Hana Bay, and up at Haleakala, are so far beyond descriptions, that I am writing poems about them," he told Merwin a month later. The pristine beauty of Maui remained vivid for him. As they packed on their last morning in Honolulu, Wright was reluctant to leave, "seeing the sun streaming above the rainclouds in Manoa Valley."

On their way back to New York, the couple stopped off to see Jack and Elizabeth Wright in Venice, California, and the talk between the two brothers returned once more to their childhood. Wright jotted down fragments of their conversation in his journal, alert to idioms they both remembered from their youth. After a brief stop in New York, he and Anne left once more for Lake Minnewaska, a "necessary" place that had become "a kind of spring for us, a resource." A handful of revisions and new poems found their way into Wright's journal before work at Hunter began in earnest in September.

———

Wright kept the letters from Bly, Kinnell, and Hall at the front of his manuscript, referring to their comments as he revised individual poems. Only a few of the prose pieces had won praise from all three, but Wright wanted the book to alternate between prose and verse. On September 21, Wright asked Hall for more detailed comments on poems Bly had insisted on cutting from the manuscript; he felt many could be saved through revision. Wright praised Hall's own new work without reservation, poems Hall would soon gather into his volume *Kicking the Leaves*.

Working in his journal a week later, Wright turned to redraft a prose piece he had begun years before in Rome; "A Lament for the Martyrs" would soon appear in *Moments of the Italian Summer*. Bly's critique of it suggested that a new approach to the poem might be more successful: "I don't feel the imagination really engaging in this poem, so as to fuse the curious details from Ohio with the Coliseum. In another mood it would have all fused—this time it did not." Wright decided to start over from scratch. Handwritten changes and line breaks marked on the first of two new prose paragraphs then carve out a different poem, with a new title: "Beautiful Ohio."

At the top of this new prose piece Wright had typed, and then emphatically crossed out: FOR REVISION OF LAMENT FOR THE MARTYRS. After setting the scene outside the Colosseum, the piece moves in a wholly new direction, although his meditation on the interplay between shadows and light continues. The piece begins: "Sitting comfortably here in Rome, sipping my cool mineral water that consoles me and allows me to feel at home with the summer heat, I can see something sinister in the light of those big stones. I can feel again a special horror I felt long ago the first time I learned that the word Ohio was an Indian word that meant Beautiful River." In the margin at this point on the page, he wrote: "Begin here. Type it out in couplets." With slash marks designating line breaks across the next seven sentences, the resulting poem became the last major addition to his new manuscript and the concluding poem to the book.

> Those old Winnebago men
> Knew what they were singing.
> All summer long and all alone,
> I had found a way
> To sit on a railroad tie
> Above the sewer main.
> It spilled a shining waterfall out of a pipe
> Somebody had gouged through the slanted earth.
> Sixteen thousand and five hundred more or less people
> In Martins Ferry, my home, my native country,
> Quickened the river
> With the speed of light.
> And the light caught there
> The solid speed of their lives
> In the instant of that waterfall.
> I know what we call it
> Most of the time.
> But I have my own song for it,

And sometimes, even today,
I call it beauty.

On the same afternoon Wright completed this new poem, he and
Anne rode to New Jersey with the poet Sander Zulauf for Wright's reading
at the County College of Morris, where Zulauf taught. Smoking continuously in the back of Zulauf's aged Ford Galaxy, Wright leaned
forward to ask if anything would be different about that night's reading
from one he had given at the college two years earlier. When Zulauf reminded him that the reading would be videotaped, Wright slumped
back in his seat, muttering, "Christ have mercy."

Wright gave a measured but captivating reading—one of very few
documents of the poet on film. Dressed in a wool suit jacket and tie, his
beard trim and head balding, Wright leaned forward into the microphone
at intervals, clasping his hands behind his back in cautious formality.
As he grew more relaxed, his hands began to make delicate gestures to
accent his words, eyebrows darting above horn-rimmed glasses at moments of sardonic humor. His appearance that September 30 before a
large, attentive audience came just a month before national elections—
part of a bicentennial reading series—and he began with poems about
"two political figures": Po Chu-i and Warren G. Harding. After four of
his own poems, he read his translation of Pedro Salinas's "Not in Marble
Palaces." "He means so much to me," Wright confesses; he also speaks
movingly about Catullus, introducing "Picollini" from a folder of new
work by quoting lines in flawless Latin. As he concludes the reading
with his new poem "Hook," his eyes are closed when he lifts his head
from the manuscript—swept up in the music of the words.

Carruth was impressed by the assurance and musicality in Wright's
voice when they finally met in mid-October at Kinnell's home in Shef-
field, Vermont. "Everything Jim had to say was either funny or important,"
Carruth marveled, alert to the Appalachian inflections that lingered in
his speech and the twinkle in his eyes. "He was a true poet. He was a real
poet because he was an *amateur*. He was a *lover* of poetry—he couldn't
help it." Waking in the unheated house after an overnight snowfall, the
three poets huddled around the fireplace, talking for hours. "Jim was a
good talker," but not a dominating one; he listened intently and often
paused "to catch exactly the right word that he wanted." Two weeks later,
Wright asked if he could read some of Carruth's new work at his own

upcoming appearance at the 92nd Street Y's Poetry Center, knowing
that Carruth then had trouble reading in public. Carruth agreed that they
shared a "similar sense of the 'music' you speak of, in spite of our different backgrounds and regional accents; perhaps it comes from Herrick."

Planning an advanced seminar on comic fiction for the spring, Wright
again returned to Orwell's work; his letters and journal entries show
how deeply he reread him that fall. "I care about Orwell," Wright mused,
in part because his writing opens important themes and discussions.
"Maybe that's why he means so much: it's impossible to read Orwell
alone." As Franz observed, Wright's sobriety made him see how isolated
from others he had become. His father revered Orwell not only for his
matchless prose style but also because Orwell "had so thoroughly immersed himself in a real dedication to other human beings. I think he
felt sort of cut off from that." In November, Wright marked a passage in
his copy of Orwell's novel *Coming Up for Air* as a possible epigraph for
his new book.

As always, Wright considered many different epigraphs as the book
took shape, including a couplet by Ben Jonson and another by Horace:
"Sharp winter relaxes with the welcome change to spring and the west
wind, and the cables haul the dry keels of ships." At the time, Wright
referred to the collection as *Hook: Sketches and Verses*, and began the
sequence with "A Letter to Franz Wright" printed in italics, calling attention to its formal resemblance to a Petrarchan sonnet. In December,
he still had fifty poems under consideration, but was "prepared to delete
15 poems that I love. (I wouldn't have said this truly when I was a young
man. But I am not a young man now.)"

Wright felt optimistic as the year drew to a close. He shared copies
of his chapbook *Moments of the Italian Summer*, and saw his work included in an international anthology on the prose poem edited by Michael
Benedikt—an important collection for decades to come. Wright also
traveled to Brandeis University, outside of Boston, to interview for a
Distinguished Faculty Chair appointment. Though a job offer did not
follow, his growing self-confidence made it possible to think of teaching
somewhere other than in Hunter's overcrowded classrooms.

On December 10, Wright gave an excellent reading on the Brandeis
campus, introduced by J. V. Cunningham with extravagant praise. When
the poet Fran Quinn later joked with Bly that Wright's double-breasted
pinstripe suit made him look like an undertaker, Bly quipped, "Since he's

stopped drinking, he thinks he *is* an undertaker." Some noticed this new reticence in Wright's public manner, now that he was sober. "It was as if a sheet of clear glass or plastic descended between him and us," Carolyn Kizer insisted, though she admitted that in private he showed the same warmth she'd known when they first met.

Early in the new year, Wright sent his entire collection of revised poems off to Bly, confessing that he had "finally reached the point of near-exhaustion with my manuscript." He felt confident in the book, and considered it his best work. As he had told Carruth in November, the effort to write well "is, at last, the only thing that matters at all."

26

To cultivate the art of listening

January–December 1977

In January, with more than a month before classes resumed, the fatigue from teaching lingered. Impatient to return to Europe, the Wrights began planning a trip that would take them back to France and Italy in the summer. Wright carried a heavy course load again that spring, teaching advanced classes on Dickens, poetry, comic fiction, and expository writing, in addition to his work on English Department committees. Wright also returned to Chinese poetry in earnest, preparing for a conference in New York in April organized by Kray. Amid everything else, he attended weekly AA meetings and furthered work in his journal.

Franz completed his final semester at Oberlin that spring and wrote to his father often, but Wright had heard little from Marshall since he'd left Hawaii in August. Impulsively, he had enlisted in the navy at the end of January, only to be discharged five weeks later from a base in San Diego, unable to adapt to the discipline and responsibilities. Having witnessed his trouble coping with simple daily routines in Hawaii, it did not surprise Wright that Marshall had been discharged, but he feared that his son would have even more trouble living on his own. He wrote to Marshall on March 11, and also separately to Liberty, promising to help financially and to support her if she felt their son again required hospitalization.

At the end of March, Wright gave a revelatory talk, sharing the authors who mattered most to him, as part of a series of conversations Kray had organized for the Academy of American Poets. It surprised Wright himself "to realize that most of them are writers of prose." Apart from a passage by Shakespeare, his talk focused on prose stylists: Twain, Forster, Tolstoy, and "my old favorite, the journalist H. L. Mencken."

These are the things that come back to me. They are the books I care most about. It isn't just the author's tone of voice and style; it seems to me if he's any good he'll try to reach beyond that, and cultivate the art of listening. I think that there is something not only artistically beautiful, but something very healing about the author who can step back and let other voices come out. . . . The idea that comes to me from the prose I like is that possibility of varying one's own voice through listening in a poem.

On April 1, Bly returned a manuscript of fifty poems that Wright had sent in early February, cutting the number to just twenty-nine. Wright set about restoring half a dozen poems to the book, but he now abandoned a plan to divide it into two sections. As Bly had argued, "I found that the Italian poems need—very much—Ohio poems in between them," and Wright adopted this strategy. After rejecting numerous other titles, he finally decided to call his book *To a Blossoming Pear Tree.*

Two weeks later, Wright and Bly took part in a symposium sponsored by the academy called "Chinese Poetry and the American Imagination." Kray credited Wright for giving her the idea for the conference, and with the help of the translator and scholar David Lattimore, she gathered not just American poets but also Chinese poets, calligraphers, and musicians in New York. Kunitz, Rexroth, Snyder, and many other poets and translators took part in panels and readings scheduled over the course of three days. Kray asked Wright to read the English versions of poems under discussion. Wright found a sense of "endless abundance" in classical Chinese poems, joined with an "uncluttered" quality that he cherished. He admired the Chinese poets' ability "to record vivid human personality" but, more than this, their "capacity to *feel*—to experience human emotion, whether the occasion of that emotion be a great public event, a disaster, or the most intimate private event or scene." Wright then quoted Wordsworth, who knew how essential it is "to keep human feeling alive" when faced with the constant onslaught of "gross and violent stimulants."

The chance to talk with Snyder, Rexroth, Ignatow, Bly, and others came at an auspicious time for Wright. As he wrote to Kray on April 26, the conference had been "the finest discussion of poetry I have ever attended." Wright had thanked her publicly on behalf of all the participants, but also wrote to share his personal gratitude. "You are one of the noblest people alive, and your friendship makes me feel that it is a fine thing to live and be at my best." The exhilaration generated by the conference, he writes, had helped him complete work on *To a Blossoming Pear Tree*; he submitted the final manuscript to his editor the following day.

Wright decided on two epigraphs for the book: a prose passage from 1945 by Richard Aldington lamenting the damage to San Gimignano during World War II; and five lines excerpted from a poem by Sherwood Anderson, "American Spring Song," written in 1918:

No one knew that I knelt in the mud beneath the bridge
In the city of Chicago. . . .
And then, you see, it was spring
And soft sunlight came through the cracks of the bridge.
I had been long alone in a strange place where no gods came.

Both passages had been written "at the end of a war," and link Italy with the American Midwest, anticipating themes and shifting tones of voice in the poems. Wright here acknowledges Anderson, whose work Stanley Plumly has called Wright's "greatest source."

Almost as soon as he dispatched the book to his publisher, Wright began to enjoy some heartening critical attention, beginning with a special feature in *The Ohio Review*. "Beautiful Ohio" and three other new poems preceded an insightful essay by William Matthews, a tribute poem by Bly, and a review of *Moments of the Italian Summer* by Wayne Dodd. "Wright recognizes that it is a long and intricate enterprise to forge a personal relationship to literary tradition," Matthews observes, dismissing his supposed "conversion" to free verse. Dodd admires "the old dark knowledge" that Lorca called *duende* that can be felt throughout Wright's work, even in his new Italian prose pieces. "But mostly the book affirms, accepts, rejoices."

Logan also wrote to praise Wright's new manuscript that spring. As he cautiously admitted in reply, Wright believed he had finally written the book he had always wanted to write. The first entry in Wright's travel journal, recorded in Paris on June 16, shares in this uncertain optimism. "I am still praying for the patience to waken from my body's bad dream of desolation."

Following a brief trip to Ohio at the end of May to attend Franz's graduation from Oberlin College, the Wrights left for Europe and an eleven-week sojourn through southern France and northern Italy, returning to Paris for the whole month of August. They traveled by train to Auxerre and Avallon, en route to Dijon in Burgundy, and Wright's journals once again sprang to life with new poems and prose pieces. After drafting a sonnet, "Remembering Owen," in memory of the English poet, he considered reworking the poem in prose—now a common strategy in his process of composition. In the leisure of August in Paris, after many drafts, Wright would finalize the poem in free verse: "Dawn near an Old Battlefield, in a Time of Peace." Wright never forgot the feeling of unusual abundance he enjoyed during these two weeks in Burgundy, fully engaged once more with his work.

Wright often returned to the novels of Graham Greene, V. S. Naipaul, and Evelyn Waugh while traveling in Europe. He reread two of Waugh's novels that summer, *Officers and Gentlemen* and *Men at Arms*. Allowing for an element of chance (he found these copies while browsing bookstores in Paris and Florence), his choices were far from accidental. Before leaving Dijon for Milan, he noted in his journal:

> I must listen as closely as I can to the movement of Waugh's prose. The image is of water: the long sentence and the short. Try a long simple sentence followed by a short complex sentence. Try it as *Waters*: lake, ocean, roadside rivulet, puddle, overflowing curb, fountain, mist, rain, cloud, foggy breath, my human body, and the twilight falling across the valley of diamonds behind my face.

The open hours spent on a train or a bus encouraged an attitude of experiment and speculation, and Wright's journals show enormous variety in language and feeling.

It had been three years since the Wrights had been in Italy, and they returned to Milan, Lake Garda, and Verona, as they had during their brief three-week trip in the summer of 1974. Though Italy remained much the same, Wright felt changed by the intervening years, sober and more at ease. The desperate, agitated productivity of those other summer days gave way to a leisurely, meditative prose. In Milan, he notes, "There is something in the air of this workers' city that I can breathe and feel at home in."

The Wrights arrived in Sirmione on Lake Garda on July 1. "This morning the little gray haze in the sky is riddled with swallows. They've been up for hours, evidently determined to find the sun." Before returning to Verona, they traveled by boat to Limone, hoping to glimpse D. H. Lawrence's house. Returning to the Albergo Aurora on the Piazza delle Erbe in Verona on July 8, they quickly decided to stay for a full week instead of just three days. "After a long still visit to the Giusti Garden where Goethe walked" on their first afternoon back, Wright recorded a dream in which he sat beside "a silent golden lizard on a hillside. We both gazed out over the red roofs, over the curving Adige. My delight was so great, I woke up, and suddenly I began to struggle to bear the truth: I am in Verona." Lizards populate the banks along the river, and he found a café with a terrace that looked out over the Adige from the shade of linden trees—not unlike those in the East River park near the Wrights' apartment in New York.

They made a day trip to Padua to revisit the Giotto chapel, and by luck heard a performance of Gounod's *Romeo and Juliet* in the Arena on their last night in Verona. The couple then traveled by train to Arezzo, where they spent ten days. Piero's frescoes in the basilica were an endless source of wonder. Wright used the same manuscript folder to gather and arrange each of his last two books; on the cover, he had taped a postcard of Piero's *Madonna del Parto*, the painting sheltered in a small cemetery chapel in Monterchi.

In Arezzo, Wright collected the mail that had gathered for the past month and steeled himself "to begin dealing with the tasks of reality." He had little reason to complain. Wright posted two letters on July 17, one to his editor at Farrar, Straus and Giroux, who hoped to send proofs for his new book to Paris, and another to Michael Cuddihy, the editor of the journal *Ironwood*, who was preparing a special issue devoted to Wright's poetry. To Cuddihy, he enclosed two just-completed poems to join a selection of new work. "In Memory of Mayor Richard Daley" begins in Martins Ferry, but its true landscape is an interior one, as common as the outskirts of any industrial town in America or Italy, outside Mantua or Milan. The poem's first stanza reads:

When you get down to it,
It, which is the edge of town,
You find a slab of gritstone
Face down in the burned stubble, the stinkweed,
The sumac, the elderberry.
Everything has gone out of the blossoms except the breath
Of rust from the railroad tracks.

"One is never so alone as one can be in such places," Louis Simpson later wrote about this poem, praising Wright's essential courage.

From Arezzo they took day trips to nearby Tuscan towns, including Florence, Cortona, and Poppi. Wherever they traveled, they resumed their ritual of purchasing food each morning at open markets for an afternoon picnic—bread, cheese, fruit, and prosciutto. They returned to Arezzo each night, eating at the same restaurant near their hotel and often seeing a movie at the theater across the street. After ten days in the "strange golden light" of Arezzo, they stayed at the Pensione Palazzo Ravizza in Siena, in a suite of rooms that overlooked the southern wall of the city near the Porto San Marco. A classically beautiful Tuscan landscape stretched out below them, with a small, wooded cemetery across a ravine filled with olive trees. Wright enjoyed working for hours in his journal at café tables in Il Campo, Siena's central, sloping piazza. After five days there, the couple traveled to Volterra and San Gimignano before returning to Paris.

Anne could see how relaxed her husband felt in Italy, which set in relief the tenor of their life in America. "You know, he was a different person in Italy. Somehow, he felt freer to be himself." Months before, at the end of a long New York winter and anticipating days of Italian sunlight, Wright had typed a brief prose piece, just one sentence, in his journal. He titled it "On American Poetry": "I would rather be dead in Italy than immortal in Ohio."

———

Upon leaving Italy on July 31, the Wrights made their home in a neighborhood new to them in Paris. They moved into a top-floor apartment in the 14th Arrondissement in the southern part of the city, not far from the Luxembourg Gardens and one block from the market stalls along the rue Daguerre. Robert and Claude Higgins—friends of Gene Pugatch and his wife, Vera—had offered their apartment to the Wrights for the month of August while the family left town on vacation, and the couple quickly felt at home in the congenial warren of rooms. The windows faced northeast across the city, and the sounds from the busy market street drifted up throughout the day. Dr. Higgins's small, garret-like study became Wright's ideal workspace. Just ten feet square with a low, seven-foot ceiling and walls lined with cork, the room resembled nothing so much as a ship's cabin; it even held a compact captain's desk. Bookshelves lined two walls, and glass doors opened onto a small terrace with flowering plants. A single bed filled one corner, with a tiny six-inch-square window above it like a portal. A larger window, facing north on the same wall, framed a view of Montmartre in the distance, hovering above a landscape of mansard roofs and chimney pots in terra cotta and beige, "this immense, welcoming skyline of Paris." The study is "a dream of comfort and freedom," Wright rejoiced on August 1. He immediately set to work, culling from his journals the poems and fragments he'd begun over the past six weeks.

The most significant poem launched in earnest that summer became one of Wright's finest elegies, honoring a figure from Martins Ferry held in awe by the townspeople, the river diver John Shunk—"the one they called for" when a swimmer went missing. Two decades before, in Seattle, Wright had published "an imitation" of a German poem that included a portrait of the diver with his grappling hook. The idea of a poem for Shunk had troubled him for more than five years, and fragmentary stanzas appeared in a span of ten days that August. "It has been hounding me day and night," Wright grouses on August 23. "I wonder what it would sound like in prose." For days, he worries that he still cannot "hear" it. "Few lines are written down so far," he confesses, "and yet phrases sing in and out of my head like the voices of flying fish. What labors do they undergo there under the surface?"

Before heading back to the States, the Wrights made an overnight visit to the town of Moret-sur-Loing, staying in a hotel beside the river that Alfred Sisley had often painted at the end of his life. Wright had affection for Sisley's paintings (in part due to the artist's reputation as a "minor" Impressionist), and the couple wandered beneath the poplars that shaded the towpaths beside the Loing, searching out the landscapes Sisley had painted. The town's medieval stone architecture and quiet streets made it seem removed from contemporary life.

In this the town was like Lake Minnewaska—where they returned in early September. Continuing work in his journals there, Wright realized how this daily ritual had helped him "indescribably to keep my balance in France and Italy this past summer." His elegy for Shunk obsessed him in the days before classes resumed at Hunter. Wright revised the poem continually as multiple typescripts and complete, handwritten revisions piled up. One draft dated September 7, 1977, begins with the poet walking for miles along the Ohio shore, searching for the diver's home just as Shunk did for lost bodies. A week later, an entirely new poem addresses Shunk as the undeclared mayor of Martins Ferry.

―――――

When Wright returned to his classes at Hunter, he was determined to arrange a full year's sabbatical to begin the following fall. In the middle of October, Gibbons Ruark invited him to give another reading at the University of Delaware in Newark, and his appearance so impressed the faculty that they invited him to serve as Distinguished Guest Professor the next fall, teaching just two classes. He accepted at once and began planning to return to Europe for an eight-month stay after his semester's appointment in Delaware.

On October 24, Wright appeared with Richard Eberhart at the Poetry Center of the 92nd Street Y in New York and read exclusively from *Pear Tree*, which would arrive in bookstores a month later. Introducing the poets, Frank MacShane, biographer of Raymond Chandler and professor at Columbia, compared Wright to "his predecessor Sherwood Anderson," calling him "a realist who is also an idealist." Wright responded by reciting the epigraphs to his new book, including the lines from Anderson's poem. His introduction to "Hook," the last of the eight poems he read, ends with a fine example of his deadpan humor: "I spent eight years of my life living in Minneapolis, and when you and I die, other things being equal, I'll be eight years ahead of you." Though he now disliked giving readings—and even the sound of his own voice—Wright later admitted to Carruth that the Y event had gone "really all right."

A marathon reading by Eberhart followed Wright's own that night, and at the book signing afterward, a young woman named Betsy Fogelman rushed up to Wright, desperate to have him sign her copy of *Two Citizens* before she caught the last train back to Philadelphia. A junior at Temple University, Fogelman was studying Wright's poems in a workshop with C. K. Williams, and her first letter to him a week later began an extensive correspondence. "You are to me, *my* poet. The one who says all I want to say, nearly perfectly," she told Wright. "I just wanted you to know that you *help* me." Her letter arrived at a welcome time, following "weeks of soaking, gloomy, neurotic weather" that Wright described as "Viennese."

Wright's letters remained central to his working process, and those he wrote to Franz are among his most lyrical. On October 30, 1977, after praising a pair of new poems Franz had sent, Wright is carried back to a dirt road in Tuscany more than five years before.

I specially value the startling one about the wolf-spider. Did I ever tell you about the spider I found on a country road, just outside the very very old town of Anghiari in Italy? The town itself is medieval, sloping down a very steep hill and suddenly sweeping out to the edge of a steep cliff at the bottom of the town. Annie and I had climbed the hill behind the town, and found ourselves in strange Tuscan countryside. Wind had been blowing across hilltops for days, and everything was covered with dust— everything, including several small children whom we met along the road, strolling along and carrying a little caged bird. We sat to rest in some dusty brushwood by the roadside, and I looked into a spiderweb between bushes. It positively sagged with dust. And as I watched, a slim, brilliantly yellow spider stepped out of her doorway in the center of the web. In all that dust she was amazing: she was totally untouched by the smallest speck, as though she had just gone inside and taken a shower.

The letter becomes an initial draft for the centerpiece of his final collection, "The Journey," capturing the poem's narrative pace and much of its exact language. The poem had been in Wright's mind since he first encountered the spider in 1972; he would add a concluding stanza months after this letter. "The Journey" took shape in tandem with his elegy for John Shunk, and he recognized a "subterranean" connection between them. Wright would revise drafts of both poems in the spring of 1978 and return to them that August.

In early November, Wright received copies of the *Ironwood* issue devoted to his work, including fourteen essays and memoirs, four tribute poems, and a handful of photographs. The feature had been planned for more than a year and it represented, as he told Cuddihy, "the most serious and extended work anybody has ever done on my books, and the most truly presented." Robert and Carol Bly each wrote separate recollections of the days Wright spent at Odin House in Minnesota; Ignatow and Logan offered brief essays; and Hugo and Penn Warren dedicated poems to Wright. Also included were seven new poems by Wright and four uncollected ones from the spring of 1964, poems left out of *Shall We Gather at the River*. "It gave me odd feelings to reread those old poems," Wright admitted. "My, what a life I led during those years. It's a wonder I didn't get killed. No, that's melodramatic. It's a wonder I'm alive now."

The pivotal work of criticism, written by Robert Hass, begins, "I have been worrying the bone of this essay for days because, in an issue of *Ironwood* honoring James Wright, I want to say some things against his poems." The essay had troubled Cuddihy when he first read it, because he had promised Wright that the issue would include no "outside gun" disparaging his poetry. "You can't *not* print this," Hass argued, "because it's full of admiration for his work." He convinced Cuddihy to print the piece without revisions, despite its barbed criticism pointing to "a sentimentality in his writing, which is connected to identification with victims." Wright later thanked Hass, calling his essay "the soundest and truest thing anyone has ever, to my knowledge, written about my books."

Even more than his correspondence during this time, Wright's journals sustained his most essential ritual. He continually reworked lines and sentences in his head before sitting down to write, and his sense of craft thus remained always engaged—one reason so many late poems required little revision. In the pages of his journal, he recognized an image of himself at his best. "I want to return to my notebook—to that center of myself. I will try to find myself—or, rather, that inner companion who can help me through the world." Sounding beneath his words is a poem by Jiménez that Wright knew by heart:

I am not I.

    I am this one
walking beside me whom I do not see;

whom at times I manage to visit,
and whom at other times I forget;
who remains calm and silent while I talk
and forgives, gently, when I hate,
who walks where I am not,
who will remain standing when I die.

27

A river flowing underground

January–December 1978

By the first days of January 1978, Wright had settled plans to return to Europe following his appointment in Delaware in the fall. He already imagined another August in Paris at Dr. Higgins's desk. "I had my coffee, my Perrier, and my notebook, and my God I was happy," he wrote to Donald Hall. "I felt like Thoreau and e. e. cummings rolled into one fat Ohioan." After a week spent grading exams, Wright read and reread Carruth's just-completed book *Brothers, I Loved You All*, filling pages in his journal with comments on the poems. In a note he shared with Carruth's publisher, Wright praises the clear, Lucretian intelligence "in this poet's cold and compassionate reading of the world," especially the "long, grieving poem" that concludes the book, "Paragraphs."

Wright took part in a unique celebration of the eighteenth-century English poet Christopher Smart that Kray and Kinnell organized in February, as one of two dozen poets reading Smart's poem *Jubilate Agno*. Surprisingly, a crowd of more than a thousand gathered to hear the long, free-verse, religious meditation, with many left standing outside the door of the Episcopal Church of the Transfiguration on lower Fifth Avenue. Allen Ginsberg, Philip Levine, Grace Paley, Paul Zweig, Etheridge Knight, and many others took part, while Wright was given the honor of saying the most famous section of the poem, dedicated to Smart's cat, Jeoffry. "We all wanted to read that," Gerald Stern recalled, "and it was just lovely. Jim was beautiful!"

When Gib and Kay Ruark came to New York for a weekend that month, Wright and Anne arranged to meet them. Wright arrived late, however; he was "deeply disturbed" by a prominent review of *To a Blossoming Pear Tree* that would appear the following day in *The New York Times Book Review*, and had spent all the money he had with him on a half-bottle of wine. The critic Hugh Kenner seemed bent on dismissing the new directions Wright's recent work had taken. He called the collection "an unexpectedly weak book," describing the poem "Hook," for example, as simply "anecdotal matter with nostalgic auras."

But most other reviewers celebrated the book. In the *Saturday Review*, Robert Pinsky likened individual pieces in *Pear Tree* to poems by William Carlos Williams and concluded by quoting from "Beautiful Ohio." Richard Howard, writing in *New York Arts Journal*, recommended the book without reservation, recognizing how Wright "has put away any bitterness." Perhaps the most discerning review came from Carruth in *Harper's Magazine*, in which he recognized the prevailing tone of grief in the collection, in spite of the light that flooded so many of the poems written in Italy. The book was indispensable, Carruth declared, "perhaps better poems than he has ever written before: poems chiefly of sorrow for the damage done to this world." Quoting in full the masterful, loosely rhymed "In Defense of Late Summer," Carruth notes the compression and unexpectedness that are characteristic of Wright. "Its very deliberateness establishes its urgency," he wrote, praising the "passionate voice" at the heart of all true works of art.

More than the critical reception for his new book, Wright worried about Marshall and their broken relationship. His anger at his son's drug use clouded his understanding of Marshall's mental health and the challenges he faced. Wright learned from Liberty that Marshall had changed his name to "Mark Kovacs," adopting his stepfather's surname. Though he had managed to work for eight months in California's Job Corps, he was forced to quit after instigating conflicts with his peers. In mid-February, Wright pleaded with his son to respond to his letters; it had been more than a year since he'd been in touch. But Marshall continued to ignore his father, leaving him in a "confusion of grief and loss." In a letter to Liberty, Wright admitted that his absence during Marshall's early years had contributed to their son's troubles and told her he would wait to hear from Marsh before writing to him again. "I will just have to live with my own unqualified love for him." Though Marshall didn't realize it, Wright continued to help pay for his expenses.

In what came as another emotional shock, Robert Bly wrote at the end of February to say that he and Carol would soon be divorced. Both were Wright's close friends, of course, and their separation was devastating. Concern for their four children had long delayed the couple's decision, and Robert now strived to arrange joint custody. Wright may have barely noticed Bly's praise in the same letter for the poems in *Pear Tree* and their "true serene music."

Wright turned to his teaching as a means to weather his anxieties. In a front-page feature interview in Hunter College's *Envoy* magazine that February, he insisted that teaching was a greater art than poetry. But he defended his own worth as a "minor poet," quoting Yvor Winters's comment that "Robert Herrick is not so great a poet as Shakespeare, but God willing, he will live as long." For himself, Wright simply wanted to teach and to write as well as he could, admitting he would always write poems. "I'll stop when I'm dead," he allowed as the interview concluded, pausing a moment before adding, "I suppose."

In mid-March, Wright received word of a Guggenheim grant for the coming year, a windfall that confirmed the breadth of the plans that he and Anne had made to travel in Europe. Together with the well-paid appointment in Delaware in the fall, he could feel relieved about money and free to take the summer off from teaching. A relaxed sigh can be heard in an autobiographical letter Wright sent to Diane Wakoski on March 20, recalling "the dog days of August, 1943," and the work he found on a Sears loading dock after his breakdown at age fifteen, when he "began to rise from the dead." The prospect of standing in Chartres Cathedral once more to hear Christmas Eve mass seemed to relieve the sense of constriction imposed by his teaching and life in New York City. For the next eighteen months, until Wright came back from Europe in September 1979, a rare, almost classical facility distinguishes his letters, poems, and journal writing.

Wright had returned to a habit of waking early to work in his journal as light grew in the tall windows of their living room. Often he prepared for classes—his Comic Fiction seminar that spring included Byron, Fielding, and *Don Quixote*—or read the new books that arrived almost daily in the mail. On March 21, the first day of spring, Wright began to organize the manuscript that filled his black spring binder with Piero's *Madonna* on the cover. He wanted the still-unfinished elegy for John Shunk to conclude his new collection and reminded himself, "Write out that spider from Anghiari." A month later, after returning from a trip to Ohio, Wright fully revised both poems. A prose piece dated April 22 uses his letter to Franz from October to frame "Getting Out of Town Before It's Too Late," though Wright scrawled on it in frustration, START OVER. Days later, a new attempt at the Shunk poem, "Goodnight to John Shunk," becomes a different poem entirely: "Wishes for My Son," which Wright kept in his manuscript.

Wright had just returned from a reading in Ohio when he threw himself back into these poems in earnest. On Miami University's Oxford campus, a two-day Festival of Ohio Poets had brought him together with William Matthews, Stanley Plumly, Rita Dove, and Alberta Turner. The festival's organizer, James Reiss, recalled how different Wright seemed from his appearance on campus eight years before, the week of the Kent State shootings. No longer the "middle-aged roaring boy" fueled by alcohol, he now appeared sober in every way and "taciturn as a church," with Anne always at his side. Plumly, too, recalled how Wright seemed "very oddly decorous and polite," but his poems came across powerfully in his reading. Though he had the work at hand, he often closed his eyes, squeezing them tight as if recalling the words took effort. "You felt it was coming out of the whole face, the whole head, and constantly with a cigarette in one hand and the book in the other. It was like there would be an imbalance otherwise."

It happened that another group on campus had invited Robert Bly to read that weekend, and the two poets embraced warmly when they met. Unknown to Wright, however, Anne approached Bly separately, troubled by his divorce from Carol and the breakup of their family. "We don't approve of what you've done, Robert, but we still love you," Anne told him— implying that she spoke for her husband. As the difficulties in Bly's life multiplied over the coming year, he neglected Wright's letters, causing Wright to worry he had somehow angered Bly. After working to reestablish their correspondence, it disturbed Wright to see their exchange lapse once more. Bly later insisted that his withdrawal had more to do with the "general chaos" of his life at the time, but the divorce caused a rift between Bly and Hall as well, and Wright's concern proved justified.

Following exams at Hunter on June 1, the Wrights left New York for a full week at Lake Minnewaska. Their century-old hotel, Wright admitted to Janice Thurn, was "getting ramshackle more and more all the time," but the casual tranquility and outdated charm of the place appealed to them. The months before the couple left for Europe felt at times like a period of waiting, with weeks of unaccustomed leisure in New York; both had taken a year's leave of absence from their jobs. They traveled for a week in early July to Buffalo, where Wright drafted a long, free-verse poem in homage to the Greek lyric poet Anacreon titled after one of his odes, "To the Cicada." Its first stanza confuses the narrator's perspective with that of the cicada and the setting recalls Wright's days of poverty in Minneapolis; even the tone echoes his "Poems to a Brown Cricket." But Wright's destination is the Warnock farm, "the dry dirt, the southern barrenness, / The Ohio hillside twenty-five miles lost / Away from the river." The countryside appears in sharp detail, rising like the dust in a barn doorway as evening comes on, "Twilight, that belongs to you." The poem shows the same "strange gentleness" Wright had praised in the poems of Tu Mu months before. Capacious and lucid, Wright's late, meditative lyrics unfold in an unhurried way. When he returned in memory to Ohio, a fluid sense of time recurs, the distant past appropriated as the present.

———

The most significant event of that summer went unrecorded, though the date became clearly fixed in Wright's mind. In the middle of July, Wright took his last drink. During the month of August, he and Anne rented a house a short walk from the ocean in Misquamicut, and Wright felt relaxed enough that he rarely attended the local AA meetings. Rhode Island was "absolutely marvelous," Anne recalled, with frequent visits to Kray's farmhouse and daily walks along the beach; the couple even rented bicycles. Wright worked steadily at his typewriter, turning out poems, journal pages, and letters. On August 2, he tells Betsy Fogelman, "We're going soon to an immense farm-market, for corn, squash, sausage, and all those things that force me to confess what a startlingly sensuous person I am. I can't help it." Writing to Carol Bly, he describes the "simple, old-fashioned joy" he has found in a new hobby: baking bread.

Betty Kray had press-ganged Wright into a presentation of poems by
Neruda and Vallejo that summer, and their work was again on his mind
when he returned to his drafts of two twinned poems. "Perhaps the brilliant fresh face of that yellow spider rinsing and unfolding herself out of
the dusty countryside road on the farther side of Anghiari was the momentary face of John Shunk, the one important face in my life that I
have never seen," he mused on the back of one typescript. He spent
many hours trying to bring these two poems—uniting Ohio and Italy by
a "river flowing underground"—to completion. On August 10, he drafted
the last stanza of the poem he would title "The Journey":

> ~~The secret~~
> Many men
> Have searched all over Tuscany and never found
> What I found there, the heart of the light
> Itself shelled and leaved, balancing
> On filaments among roots. The secret
> Of this journey is to let the wind
> Blow its dust all over your bones,
> ~~And not to care.~~
> To let it go on blowing, to step all the way through
> The ruins, and not to care.

The overwhelming feeling of a burden lifted—the "lightness" by which
he had addressed a cicada—persists throughout. The poem's final version
is more emphatic, merging images of visual light ("the heart of the light")
with the lifting of weight and an attitude of graciousness.

> The secret
> Of this journey is to let the wind
> Blow its dust all over your body,
> To let it go on blowing, to step lightly, lightly
> All the way through your ruins, and not to lose
> Any sleep over the dead, who surely
> Will bury their own, don't worry.

In quoting Jesus' admonition, Wright roughens the poem's diction, translating the Gospels into southern Ohioan. What began as a letter to Franz

passed back and forth between drafts in prose and free verse before Wright finalized the poem in February 1979. His facility and self-assurance made the borderline between prose and poetry enormously fluid. This is a distinguishing quality of the last great period in his writing life.

On August 23, Wright posted a letter to Carol Bly, belatedly thanking her for her memoir in *Ironwood* the previous fall. He writes of the autobiographical sketch he had just completed for an Ohio library pamphlet celebrating his work. Wright felt odd recording memories about his early days in Ohio. "I kept getting the feeling of a kind of swelling abundance. My God, the old details of one's life rise up like bread." Shunk appears again in Wright's brief "Childhood Sketch," and he refers to his elegy for this mystifying man. The poem Wright finally published, "A Flower Passage," does not include a single line from countless previous drafts.

––––––

In a letter to Robert Hass praising his first book, *Field Guide*, Wright notes that he brought just two other books of poetry with him to Rhode Island—Edward Lear, and David Schubert's collection *Initial A*. A New York City poet not widely known, Schubert had died at the age of thirty-three in 1946. Wright filled seven pages of his journal with notes on Schubert's poems that August, drafting what would be his final piece of critical prose. In his unaccustomed freedom that month, Wright also became captivated by the work of a young Native American poet, Leslie Marmon Silko, whose celebrated first novel, *Ceremony*, had appeared the previous year. They had met briefly at the poetry festival in Michigan three summers before, where Silko had read a section from the novel in draft. Wright typed a long passage from the book into his journal, and his first letter to Silko, dated August 28, 1978, initiated the last crucial correspondence of his life. "I am very happy you are alive and writing books," he concludes his brief letter, telling Silko that his attempts to praise her novel all fell short.

While Wright's relationship with Silko evolved entirely through letters, his closeness with Gibbons Ruark grew from their daily contact over the coming weeks and months in Delaware; the two became inseparable. Ruark drove up from Delaware to bring the Wrights to the Newark campus, and Ruark's wife, Kay, and their two young daughters welcomed them warmly, sharing dinners, picnics, and family life. "He spoke in beautiful periodic sentences, just in conversation," Ruark recalled, "and he was just thinking out loud." Ruark also knew "he had a very playful, childlike streak." Within days of their arrival, walking past a bicycle shop, Wright turned to Anne and said how wonderful it would be to have bicycles while they were there. They purchased them on the spot and rode them back to the house they were renting for the fall. "Here I am, fifty years old, and at last I have my own bicycle."

The responsibilities of Wright's appointment were fairly light, and he was endlessly amused by his grandiose title as "Distinguished Visiting Professor." He gave a reading and a public lecture, and taught two upper-level classes in the English Department: a course in Poetics and—since he had been invited as a poet—a writing workshop. Wright enjoyed leading his large group of graduate students through the history of English prosody, thrilled to have "an attentive class who really do care about pondering the fantastic movements of a fiercely original master like the Earl of Surrey." In a letter to Carruth in his first weeks in Delaware, he confessed how the regular schedule of teaching afforded him a kind of comfort. "Such a routine is one of my deepest needs, and all my life I have had a desperate time trying to find it." A week later, still feeling "scattered," he reminds himself in his journal to practice Meister Eckhart's way toward leading an orderly life: simply, *to do the next thing*.

Sobriety made all the difference. In his time in Minnesota in the early 1960s, alcohol had undermined Wright's life and provoked a crippling sense of anxiety. As he types notes for his talk on David Schubert's poems, his refusal to address the poet's poverty leads directly into autobiography and a detailed recollection of standing "Before a Cashier's Window in a Department Store." He seems compelled to confront once more that poem's awful epiphany.

They stood not more than two feet away from me. They whispered together. Their communion seemed to me more intimate than love. And when they spoke of me, they spoke of me in the third person. I was gone, as far as they were concerned. Dead. I was dead, and knew it. I had the inconvenience of death, and none of its blessing. Socrates sang in vain for me. I had at that moment my quick glimpse of a life lived every day, all day, by people who owe money to just about everyone they meet; and every time they meet someone, that person speaks of them in the third person, so their absence deepens and deepens.

In trying to imagine Schubert's suffering, Wright returned to his own frightening experience of poverty, an emotional fact he could recall with unnerving accuracy. The entry ends: "One can feel for a moment a wind puffed in between the stars, like a breath that freezes the instant it touches the window glass; so one wanders through the empty house, looking for a hand to touch."

———

Before presenting his talk on Schubert in Delaware, Wright traveled with Anne to New Orleans at the beginning of October, where he gave a reading at Loyola University to a capacity crowd. His well-received appearance offered a range of poems, both early and recent, including "Written on a Big Cheap Postcard from Verona," one of the few he embellished with introductory remarks. He paused, head bowed, after each poem, commanding a hush over the audience. "Unlike most speakers, Wright was not afraid of silence," a student reviewer marveled in the campus paper. To Bruce Henricksen, who hosted Wright's visit, his serious demeanor onstage had more to do with nervousness. Since he now gave readings infrequently, each appearance became more significant to him.

Following his Friday reading, the Wrights spent two days wandering the French Quarter and Garden District of New Orleans. The quality of light in the city fascinated him, as well as its echoes of Europe, and the food inspired worshipful descriptions in his letters. Many of the things he talked about with Henricksen that Saturday afternoon as they walked the city's streets returned the following day when Wright consented to an interview. He spoke at length about Ortega's *The Revolt of the Masses* and decried the collapse of the American public education system, a victim of the self-interested cry for smaller government and less taxes, "some madness in the air." The importance of teaching each student the value of an orderly life, "a life of disciplined hope," Wright believed, is essential to a democracy.

"Many things in our marriage give me great pleasure," he confided to Fogelman upon returning with Anne from New Orleans, "and one of the finest of these is the fact that she and I are such good friends." Wright now wrote with candor to both Fogelman and Silko; a paternal quality enters into his correspondence with Fogelman, but with Silko the conversation is between peers. In her reply to his first letter, Silko recalls the "sheer tenacity" of the poems she had heard him read in Michigan three years before. "Your directness and leanness I could understand in the way that the old people at home talked." With disarming assurance and telling details of her life on a desert ranch outside of Tucson, Silko's second letter opens onto a world where stories and memories are of a piece with the surrounding land. Her long, spontaneous description of a malicious pet rooster—"the rooster out of all the rooster stories my grandmother ever told me"—introduced a recurring character in her letters, joined later by an inquisitive roadrunner. With her October 3 letter Silko enclosed her book of poems, *Laguna Woman*, a sheaf of recent poems, and a short story, "Storyteller." The desert landscape had left a strong impression on Wright years before, and he admired Silko's alert prose and narrative authority. He sent her a copy of *Pear Tree* and they continued to exchange new work.

Wright's letter to her on October 12 already shows greater intimacy than is found in his other correspondence, a trust that deepened over the last eighteen months of his life. "I am closer to finding the proper ceremony for my life now," he tells Silko. "I hope you'll forgive me for appropriating that word 'ceremony' but it is a true word, and I need it. My ceremony is to rise early. It is in the early hours that I feel most at home with myself." Part of the closeness between them goes unspoken, a ground of common experience: alcoholism, divorce, and devotion to language.

From the beginning, a sense of gratitude characterizes both sides of their correspondence. In subtle ways, Native American traditions of narrative begin to affect Wright's strategies of storytelling in the poems and prose pieces he would gather into his final collection. Silko understood that stories arise from a specific place and forever remain a part of it; she tells Wright that *Ceremony* resulted from her attempt to remake the Laguna country for herself, having been separated from it for so long. "I am extremely glad, and, in a way, *relieved*, that you exist," Wright says, recognizing in Silko an "abundance . . . as the seasons themselves are abundant." In his journals and letters, Wright presses to describe this feeling; it is this same sense of *abundance*, a store of emotions and sensations, that sends him back to the shore of the Ohio River and memories of Martins Ferry.

In Wright's talk on the poems of David Schubert on October 17, he again tries to describe this quality of abundance. "Attentiveness is also a fullness," he insists, praising the courage and clear-sightedness evident in Schubert's poems. Admired by both Frost and Williams, Schubert had died while readying his first book for publication; he had known poverty since childhood. Wright wanted to avoid speaking of the difficulties of Schubert's life, and his talk begins with a digression condemning "the prying biographer" who claims the right to ransack an artist's privacy. Quoting Faulkner and Santayana, he defends the importance of focusing solely on the poems, "surely the part of his life which matters most." Nevertheless, what fascinates Wright most is the "noble gaiety" he finds in Schubert's triumph over hardships and despair.

Wright calls his talk "A Master of Silence," and he praises Schubert's "power of gathering and preserving silence in the midst of noise," most notably in poems inspired by life in New York City. These reflections show how closely Wright continued to read *The World of Silence*, by the Swiss theologian Max Picard; he carried the book with him that fall and copied passages into his journals. This quasi-devotional text, a kind of extended prose poem, absorbed him, and he continually returned to it.

———

Three days after Wright's talk, he received a phone call from Marshall— the first time he'd heard from his son in a year and a half. In "a long and terrifying speech, barely coherent, full of anger and confusion," it became clear that the twenty-year-old had opened a letter addressed to Liberty in which his father had shared his "desperate concern" about his sons, including "some rather severe—and honest—things about Franz." Wright responded immediately, sending a letter to Marshall and pleading with him to reply. When he did, Marshall addressed his letter "To Mr. James Wright"—five handwritten pages that proved devastating, "repetitive, confused, circumlocutory." Marshall had shared Wright's letter with Franz and insisted that neither of them wanted any more contact with him. Marshall did not want Wright disturbing "our happy home"; most painfully, he wrote, "remember you are not after all my father." He returned Wright's letter and signed his own "Mark Kovacs."

Wright sent off letters to Liberty, Franz, and Jack Wright but otherwise kept this heartbreak private, struggling to come to terms with Marshall's denial of him. Wright's letter to Franz received no reply; in phone calls with Liberty he learned that his older son had just gotten married. Three weeks after Marshall's letter, he still felt raw with sorrow, but even in this emotional crisis he resisted the temptation to drink and remained "fairly good-humored and strong." Though he continued to help with his younger son's expenses, and sought news of him through Liberty and Franz, Marshall's rejection struck a lasting wound.

While staying with Anne's relatives in Pennsylvania for Thanksgiving, a feature article on Wright appeared in the Philadelphia *Evening Bulletin* with the curious title "Poet's Life at Odds with Verse." The interviewer seems confused by Wright's humility and his insistence that teaching mattered more to him than his poetry. "I've been able to write badly even as I grow old," he confesses wryly. "I have been trying all my life to say what I have to say clearly and to write simply." Pressed to give his reasons for writing, he suggests that the impulse comes "from a need to share a feeling, but I'm never sure I'll succeed in doing it."

Days later, Wright gave his final reading in New York at the Guggenheim Museum. Introducing Wright, Mark Strand praised the "rare sincerity" of his poems, "in which the shape of feeling becomes the dominant formal property of the voice." The reading was one of Wright's best, focused and self-assured, with work drawn entirely from *Pear Tree*. The speaker in these poems is open and inquisitive, and admits his uncertainties. In Wright's reading of "The Wheeling Gospel Tabernacle," the phrase "For all I know" becomes a kind of musical refrain.

As they packed for nine months of travel in Europe, Anne asked her husband to lay out on the bed what he needed for the trip. Beside his Olivetti portable typewriter in its compact blue case—a Spanish model with additional keys—she found his journals, folders of poem drafts, and letters waiting to be answered. Wright chose only one book to bring: *The Cloud of Unknowing*. He had taken it with him to Italy before, in the ill-starred summer of 1974. On the inside cover he had written Tolstoy's words: "The flesh rages and riots, and the spirit follows it, helpless and miserable." In September 1961, this had been the epigraph to his unpublished manuscript, *Now I Am Awakened*. But Wright felt no such anguish in December 1978. After all, he would soon be in Paris.

28

The silence of all the light

December 1978–May 1979

I have spent the day well just looking and looking. It is the same in art as in life. The deeper one penetrates, the broader grows the view.

—Goethe, *Italian Journey*, October 19, 1786

Simone [Weil] says that one of the principal truths of Christianity, "a truth which goes almost unrecognized today, is that the looking is what saves us."

—Herbert Read, "The Cult of Sincerity," spring 1968

In a corner of the vast square in front of the Church of Saint-Sulpice, the quiet and elegant Hotel Recamier, shaded by sycamores, had become the Wrights' preferred retreat in Paris. When Wright opened the windows to their fifth-floor room upon arriving on December 22, 1978, the bells in the church began to ring. Saint-Sulpice was his favorite church in the city; he loved the celebrated Delacroix mural of Jacob wrestling the Angel, and he stood beneath the painting feeling stronger than when he left Paris a year and a half before. Wright made daily entries in his journal for the next thirteen months. "These are the loveliest of moments in the notebook, for they expand," he wrote the day after he arrived, sitting beside the Seine. "The very words I set down here are like the roots underground in winter. They look a little skimpy on this page, but they carry secret pages in them."

Wright recorded at least one complete sentence in his journal every day, a modest promise to himself that sustained seven months of stunning productivity. He wanted to finish at least thirty new poems by the time he returned to New York—the central work for a new book. Already he had twenty pieces in his manuscript folder. He carried his small looseleaf, four-ring notebook everywhere, numbering each page meticulously at the top and recording the date and place. When he had a desk, Wright mined this notebook for poems, typing drafts on full-size sheets for his working manuscript. He made lists of essays and book reviews for his projected volume of critical prose—a book first conceived in 1969—as well as reminders of daily tasks and correspondence. He copied passages from his letters into his notebooks as well.

The couple took a train to Chartres on Christmas Eve and stayed overnight, attending midnight mass as they had five years before. Near the end of the service, the small statue of the Christ child was once more slipped secretly into the crèche manger. On Christmas Day, they returned to the Higginses' apartment, glad to accept their invitation to stay for the week while the family was away, and Wright fell to work in that ship's cabin of a study. On December 30, he typed a new prose piece he later titled "Come, Look Quietly," a delicate sketch of a small bird scavenging the Higginses' discarded Christmas tree in a landscape of Parisian rooftops. The poem took its final form after Wright deleted a paragraph of bitter recollection, in which he stood once more at the edge of the Martins Ferry town dump. A handwritten note on his first draft cautions, "Stop cursing. Find another way."

Wright typed a letter to Robert Bly early in the morning on the last day of the year. He had sent a Christmas gift of Arthur Waley's *Life of Po Chu-I*, and now invoked Rilke, reminding Bly of the marvelous object poems that Rilke had written in the nearby Luxembourg Gardens. Bly's silence troubled him, and he implored Robert to write in care of Galway Kinnell, whom he and Anne would soon join in the South of France. Gib Ruark had arrived in Paris the day before, and he stayed with the Wrights on rue de Cresson. As a cold rain turned to snow, they spent New Year's Eve wandering the city. Just as they stepped inside Notre-Dame Cathedral that evening, Bach's "Jesu, Joy of Man's Desiring" began to fill the vaulted, resonant space. Wright's face lit up with a kind of ecstatic bemusement; catching Ruark's eye, he gestured casually toward the choir, as though one could take such wonders for granted in Paris.

Snow was still on the rooftops on January 5 as the Wrights boarded a train for Nice, where Kinnell had been teaching for a term at the university as a Fulbright professor. Wright wanted to see for himself "the legendary winter of the blue coast" on the Mediterranean that he had imagined from the work of Albert Camus. At the window of their hotel room, he stood amazed to see an orange tree bearing fruit in the garden below. "Right at the dead center of winter, the clouds suddenly blew out to sea," Wright marvels. "The sky is a startling blue. Down a small street below our window a gate just opened. School children at recess are dancing and jumping and shouting with relief and delight."

The following day, Kinnell drove Wright and Anne up into the hills near Vence, where he and his family were living "in an old, rambling, strange house on a winding road up a mountainside that looked over a huge valley to a beautiful mountain beyond." They spent the weekend with Galway, his wife, Inés, and their two children, Maud and Fergus. On Sunday morning, they attended early mass at the nearby Matisse Chapel. "The chapel is astonishing: pure, simple, uncluttered, a living prayer of light. My own prayer began earlier. I rose before daylight, sat outside on the hillside, and watched the dawn over the Mediterranean. The silence of all the light."

Later that day, in a postcard to Carruth, Wright recognized the strength of a phrase he then copied into his journal: "The rest of Europe is under the snow; but we are all sitting here strangely on top of the sunlight." "A Winter Daybreak Above Vence" is quickened by the past week's sense of renewal—from the children bursting into spring weather to the purity of the chapel and the warm southern winds. Kinnell knew firsthand the surprising and vivid accuracy of the poem's images and came to feel that Wright had surpassed the need for the "magical transformations of some of his early poems because there's a sense that—why bother, the earth is already magic."

Wright had once imagined the release of stepping outside "my poor brother my body," hoping he might "break / Into blossom." The fraternal pact he now makes is not about escape:

> How can I feel so warm
> Here in the dead center of January? I can
> Scarcely believe it, and yet I have to, this is
> The only life I have. I get up from the stone.

My body mumbles something unseemly
And follows me. Now we are all sitting here strangely
On top of the sunlight.

As in so many of the poems that appear in his journals in these weeks, the act of paying attention—"without any irritable reaching after fact and reason," as Keats observed—presents an occasion for poetry, a small moment that seems like a gift. "He was more present to other people, I think, than at any other time I had ever seen him," Kinnell remembered.

The Wrights drifted back to Paris by way of Nîmes, Arles, Toulouse, and Albi, where they decided to stay on for a few days. Wandering the ruins of the Roman temple of Diana inspired the two bookend poems to Wright's final collection. The first, "Entering the Temple in Nîmes," appears in type dated January 20; the second is written by hand the following day, with line breaks indicated by slash marks due to the narrow width of the pages. This necessity encouraged his now common strategy of revision, alternating between prose and line-break drafts of new poems. He typed prose pieces in verse so he could "listen to what happens."

"This is one of those times when I have a sense of the abundance of things, of actually lived life," Wright told Fogelman while still in Nîmes. He realizes he has been in France exactly a month, a time blessed by the "same quality of incorruptible endurance" that had marked his two weeks in Burgundy two summers before. In "Leaving the Temple in Nîmes," Wright's impressions of the goddess Diana become mingled with "an American girl" back home, with Ausonius (a poet from the Bordeaux region), and with Whitman, "The old man rooted in an ugly place / Pure with his lovingkindness." Wright praises the poet with a word he used to describe Jenny two decades before.

———

The Wrights' itinerary remained flexible. From Toulouse and Albi they made day trips to surrounding towns, including Cordes-sur-Ciel, Moissac, and Carcassonne. After a brief stay in Paris, the Wrights headed to England, back into severe winter weather and days of continual snowfall. They visited with Anne's friends Rachel Evans in London and Sheila Ráshed farther north in the snowbound midlands. Nazri Ráshed, the poet and diplomat with whom Wright had quickly formed a bond, had died suddenly of a heart attack in October 1975, and Sheila was now raising their son, Nazeil, on her own. Wrapped in snow flurries and raw, gray weather, Wright's imagination leapt ahead to imagine spring coming to Verona, "a city I love so much it makes my heart ache just to think about it, just to hear or read the name." He had planned to make a pilgrimage to Husum, Germany—Theodor Storm's hometown near the Danish border—but the fierce weather across northern Europe canceled the excursion. After two months of traveling, Wright already felt the strain, and questioned the frantic pace they had kept up.

Arriving in Amsterdam, Wright grew more relaxed, charmed by the city, the Dutch people, and the muttering dog in their hotel. He sat with Anne in silence one morning in front of four of Vermeer's canvases in the Rijksmuseum, stunned by "the incredible purity of light." Leaving the Van Gogh Museum the following afternoon, they paused on one of the city's countless small bridges to watch "crowds of fathers and children skating vigorously and hilariously far along the canal." To Roger Hecht, he confessed that the drawings and ink sketches of Rembrandt impressed him most deeply. "I wonder if any other human being has ever seen things and places and people quite so clearly and drawn them with such accuracy." Amsterdam's narrow streets and small squares transported him back to Martins Ferry. "The place took me startlingly back to my childhood and the shocking realization that some of that childhood was beautiful."

Trusting an ever more battered copy of *Europe on $15 a Day*, the couple traveled by train from Amsterdam to Brussels and on to Bruges, which Wright found "unutterably beautiful." In a marvelous letter to Silko, he describes their walk into town from the train station in a heavy, enveloping fog, when "only a dim tower or two would reveal part of itself from time to time as the mist parted." The next morning, Wright shared an ecstatic dream with Anne, in which the Northern Renaissance painter Hans Memling had appeared in a long green velvet robe to show him around the city. After visiting Memling's home later that day—a museum with many of his paintings—the couple wandered the markets in Bruges and chose exquisite lace handkerchiefs as gifts. Enclosing one in a letter to Silko for her birthday, Wright remembers the brutal wars that laid waste to Belgium, miseries outlasted by the fragile and enduring craft of lacemaking.

Leaving the cold rains of Holland and Belgium, they returned to Paris as signs of spring appeared across the city in the first week of March.

Settled once more in the Hotel Recamier, Wright felt relieved to see "the sun of early spring beginning to warm the honey stones of the bell tower of tall Saint Sulpice." They made an overnight stay in Moret-sur-Loing, an hour south of Paris by train, where the season had taken hold in the countryside and the branches of poplar trees along the river Loing were tipped with deep red buds. For the sake of his book, however, Wright remained impatient to settle in Verona and press forward.

Back in August 1972, Wright's journal had first described "the fresh yellow spider in the accumulated dust of Anghiari," but despite numerous attempts, the poem had eluded him; he drafted a prose version that February before the poem took final form in verse. From Paris he sent "The Journey" and "Entering the Temple in Nîmes" to Howard Moss at *The New Yorker*, who quickly accepted them. Further encouragement came from Carruth, who assured him he would gladly read and comment on Wright's new manuscript. "As poets you and I belong to a company, naturally joined and comparatively small, of equals," Carruth told him. "That's one of the blessings, to offset the difficulties of a poet's life."

After two months in Europe, Wright worried that he hadn't completed enough work, but a change in plans brought a change in mood. He and Anne decided not to travel to Greece, choosing instead to spend the entire month of June in Sirmione; a feeling of hopefulness prompted a rush of new poems. "Blessed peace! Blessed work!" he celebrated in his journal. Boarding a train early on a Sunday morning, March 11, the couple passed through Burgundy, Switzerland, and Milan on the day-long trip, reaching Verona at dusk. Spring weather had arrived before them. From a table outside the Café Dante or on the patio of the Hotel Aurora overlooking the Piazza delle Erbe, Wright disappeared into his notebooks for the next two weeks. Despite the dim, cramped confines of their hotel room, he set up his typewriter on a small red table and worked through successive fair copies of new poems.

On a day trip to Sirmione, the Wrights booked the month of June at Albergo Grifone on the shore of Lake Garda. Wright's letter to Silko about their stay in Bruges is dated the following day from Verona. He joins her in lamenting the loss of her vicious pet rooster to coyotes in the Sonoran desert. The two poets shared a kind of spiritual awareness of animal presences; Wright drafted "A Dark Moor Bird" later that week, a keenly observed poem set on the banks of the Adige. As a continuous passage in prose, the first typed version fits the dimensions of one journal page exactly.

During their second week in Verona, Wright and Anne took two long walks above the city, crossing the Adige and climbing the steep surrounding hills to follow the ancient battlement walls leading to the Fort of San Pietro. They saw cherry, peach, and pear trees in bloom, and the first violets and lizards emerging from between the warm stones. High above the church of San Fermo Maggiore, Wright jotted lines for a new poem on the shifting seasons, imagery that moves from "a black snowdrift / In Ohio" into "the warm Italian sunlight." In his journal, a revised draft of "Above San Fermo" is preceded by a prose piece about his father's friendship with the town junkman in Martins Ferry, one Felix Jacoby. Spurned by the townspeople, the man had been known by the mocking perversion of his name: "Jabicoe." Over the next two months, Wright tried to find his way to a finished poem about him without success. This first attempt, however, offers an illuminating glimpse of Dudley:

> I asked my father how he could sit down with Jabicoe in his yard. It stank. "Oh, I know," he would say, "I know all about it, I know it stinks. The man works hard."
> Work, to my father, was a holy thing.

As Wright prepared to take leave of Verona once more, he recorded a quiet epiphany that struck him as he stood far above the city. "I felt at home as I am ever likely to feel on this earth till I am inside it." This entry on the last day of their stay continues as a prose draft of the poem he eventually titled "Yes, But," with handwritten marks to indicate line breaks. Believing Verona "must be a good place to die in"—as opposed to Ohio—his meditation goes further:

> Even if it were true,
> Even if I were dead and buried in Verona,
> I believe I would come out and wash my face
> In the chill spring.

The published poem begins at this middle point of his longer meditation, as the poet imagines himself somehow already beyond death, in

communion with "the plump lizards along the Adige" in the afternoon sun.

————

Arriving in Florence on a Sunday mobbed with tourists, the couple was
glad to see spring rains dispersing the crowds over the next week. Though
Wright felt encouraged by the wealth of new work in his journals, he
still had doubts about organizing his new book. "I have foundered my
way halfway deep in Spring," he worried. Wright found his footing once
more in Rome, in spite of its "literally insane" traffic and ungodly noise;
within an hour of their arrival on April 1 they decided to stay there a full
two weeks. The Roman sunshine sparked a rush of work, with many
new poems and a host of letters that came "comfortably and easily." The
spring weather and "weirdly silent places" in Rome came as a relief,
"the sense of very ancient time in immediate touch with the present," as
he wrote to Carruth upon arriving.

In five days, Wright drafted a series of five different poems inspired
by images of transformation. "Reading a 1979 Inscription on Belli's Monument" is a Petrarchan sonnet, virtually identical to its final version.
The unpublished "Daphne" draws upon imagery in a recent letter from
Silko describing the cholla cactus; the following day, he returned to the
idea of metamorphosis in the masterful lyric "The Vestal in the Forum."
With casual assurance, Wright presents a doubled transformation of the
human becoming stone and a statue taking on human presence. Though
the poem is elegiac, the poet refuses despair. "The slow wind and the
slow roses / Are ruining" a solitary, anonymous statue in the Roman
Forum, one of the strange refuges of silence that Wright found at the
center of the city.

> But in this little while
> Before she is gone, her very haggardness
> Amazes me. A dissolving
> Stone, she seems to change from stone to something
> Frail, to someone I can know, someone
> I can almost name.

The Wrights arrived in Naples on the Monday after Easter, where
celebrations continued in the narrow streets and made the long taxi ride

to their hotel high above the city longer still. From a terrace outside their room, they had a stunning view of the bay and of Mount Vesuvius, which they visited on a day trip to Pompeii. At first, Naples seemed serene in contrast with Rome, but Wright realized his mistake during their week-long stay. "Every time you turn around somebody is trying to sell you stolen goods or to steal from you. It is a happy-go-lucky, tap-dancing menace." This same journal entry, dated April 21, admits another reason for his disquiet: "A particularly vigorous phase of writing in this note-book appears to have fallen into rest." He turned instead to revising the dozens of new pieces he had begun over the previous four months.

After a daylong train journey, the Wrights reached Taranto, in Apulia on the inner coastline of southeastern Italy, just as harbor lights began to illuminate the bay. Their large, high-ceilinged room in the Albergo Miremare had a balcony view of the Mare Piccolo and the old part of the town; even better, it also had a large wooden desk. Wright insisted on unpacking his typewriter and beginning a new journal entry before they left for dinner. It concludes:

We are now settled in Taranto, on the Ionian sea. All across southern Italy we saw strange pale cities placed with great care on the tips of green mountains. The country is wilder and greener down here than I had imagined it.

Taranto: Plato came here to visit. We will walk where he walked.

The Wrights stayed nine days in Taranto, "whose old city is a small island set perfectly between two peninsulas" in the wide bay that forms the instep of the Italian boot. They made day trips to towns along the Apulian coast, including Metaponto, where Pythagoras and Cicero had passed between the columns of the temple to Apollo; Wright leaned down and reverently touched the fallen stones. "We walked for miles through unbelievable masses of wildflowers: scarlet poppies so thick they con-cealed the green of their own leaves; wild brilliant yellow camomila flowers that look like daisies with aristocratic jaundice; and too many other varieties to count, much less name," he told Franz. "It was healing to see and feel the creation still being created there."

Many rural peasants and villagers in southern Italy lived in abject poverty, as Wright witnessed from train windows across the southern peninsula, images not unlike those filmed by Francesco Rosi in his new movie, *Christ Stopped at Eboli*. The film is based on a memoir by Carlo Levi, which Wright reread that spring. Having already seen the movie twice, Wright encouraged others in letters back to the States to seek out both the film and the book. "Not all the naturalistic novelists who ever lived, including Dreiser and Zola, gave a truer account of the lives of poor people." Wright's journal often reflects the qualities of the land and its people. In Lecce, near the Adriatic coast, he describes a city of pale gold limestone "where the very houses seem made of sunlight." From Lecce they made trips to Otranto and to Gallipoli on the western shore of the peninsula. In the prose pieces "In Memory of the Ottomans" and "Camomilla," for example, and the poems "Apollo" and "In a Field near Metaponto," his language has a mournful spareness, presenting vivid depictions of the sun-blanched countryside and the fortitude of the townspeople and fishermen of southern Italy.

Turning north, the couple had planned a lengthy stay in the Adriatic port of Bari, where Wright hoped to work steadily again. When they arrived on May 9, the intense street noise and traffic outside their hotel forced them to find lodging closer to the sea. Resettled in a quiet neighborhood with fish market stalls and small stretches of beach, Anne wrote excitedly in her journal: "There is a festive air in Old Bari on Sundays. Quite different from the melancholy Taranto, the stillness of Otranto and the quiet desperation in Gallipoli." There were, however, two distinct cities: the old, even ancient part, and the new Bari plagued by unemployment and urban decay. With national elections less than a month away, political unrest and violence had spread throughout Italy—especially in the cities, as the Wrights soon learned.

As they walked to dinner along a quiet, block-long side street in the modern section of Bari, a young man leapt out from between two parked cars, trying to grab Anne's purse and pushing her to the ground. As she yelled for help, the empty-handed thief jumped on the back of an accomplice's scooter and disappeared. The incident troubled the couple for days afterward, prompting a new wariness and lingering unease. Wright felt he should have done more to protect his wife and detain the thugs; both he and Anne remained frustrated by "the futility of our anger."

The day following the attempted purse-snatching, they went to a museum but found it unaccountably shuttered; walking along the beach instead, they came upon the corpse of a dead calf below the seawall. They finally cut short their stay in Bari and decided to return to the fishing village and resort of Fano, the ancient Roman town they had discovered seven years earlier. The Wrights had first stayed in Fano on a whim in July 1972, and the town remained just as they remembered it. After the harsh realities of Bari, the couple ascribed healing properties to the modest seaport with its bronze statue of Fortuna in the central piazza. With five days of marvelous weather, they took long walks into the fields and farmland to the north, among wildflowers, olive trees, and vineyards, never quite reaching the steep headlands they could see from the beach. The quiet of the town, the green shade of linden trees in the piazzas, and the Adriatic breeze combined to cast a spell. "It is old, old, old as sunlight," and has "somehow so far kept itself alive" in a "spiritually battered world . . . greedy for its own ruin."

In Fano, the north–south train line to Venice separates the beachside hotels and fishing marinas from the old part of the town, which occupies a higher plateau to the west—geography not unlike Martins Ferry, with its train lines along the Ohio River. While there, Wright drafted a vivid prose piece shaded with humor in memory of "Old Bud" Romick, an obese old man falling asleep in a porch swing "as the twilight comes down Pearl Street in Martins Ferry, Ohio." As in so many Ohio poems, he casts memory in the present tense; he makes a refrain of the phrase "I don't know"—at ease in a state of reverie.

On Sunday, May 27—the first full day at his desk in Sirmione—Wright typed the prose piece "The Sumac in Ohio." It begins: "Toward the end of May, the air in southern Ohio is filling with fragrances, and I am a long way from home." The poet stands once more beside the Ohio River, where sumac trees grow in profusion in a gully cut parallel to the riverbank, and "right before my eyes, the tough leaf branches turn a bewildering scarlet." As with Ohio and her people, he admires the tenacity of sumac bark. "You cannot even carve a girl's name on the sumac. It is viciously determined to live and die alone, and you can go straight to hell."

29

To gaze as deeply as I can

May–September 1979

I seemed all the while I was here to be, as it were, upon a journey, and
from home. —from *Robinson Crusoe*, by Daniel Defoe, from a passage
transcribed by Wright into his journal, August 9, 1979,
as a possible epigraph for *This Journey*

Anne felt reluctant to leave Fano until Wright reminded her that they
would soon be in Sirmione. The month they spent on Lake Garda would
prove enormously fruitful, a *mensis mirabilis* during which he revised
and arranged the bulk of his new manuscript. When they arrived at the
train station in Verona, Wright argued for the extravagance of a taxi to
their hotel, some twenty-five miles to the west. As they approached the
lake in late afternoon sunlight, the Garda Mountains appeared to
the north, above the vineyards, olive groves, and orchards that lined the
road. The medieval Castello Scaligero stands beside Il Grifone hotel on
the lakeshore, with swallowtail crenellations along the castle walls and
swans circling the moat. The oleander, bougainvillea, and honeysuckle
were just beginning to bloom, bright and fragrant beneath the silver
shadows of the pines and sycamores that lined the footpaths and dirt
roads, with brittle grasses bleached nearly white and a faint smell of
rosemary. The pebbled shore below their hotel window and the cicadas
filled the silences at night, after the swallows returned to their nests.

The town remained off the beaten track for most tourists, particularly this early in the season; snowcaps could still be seen on the peaks of the southern foothills of the Alps. The lizards, however, had already begun to appear in the afternoon sun on the stone walls and on the cliff face at the northern edge of the peninsula near the Grotto di Cattullo. They both felt immediately at home, Anne recalled; it was "perhaps the happiest time of our lives."

The first letter Wright mailed from Sirmione went to Leslie Silko. She had found a copy of *Moments of the Italian Summer* in a used bookstore in Tucson and "The Language of the Present Moment" became a favorite poem, with its prayer for the ghost of Catullus to return to Sirmione while lemon trees were in blossom. Silko had been reading Wright's prose to her classes that spring. "I talk with my students about narrative writing instead of separating poetry from fiction exactly," she wrote, at ease with the prose pieces that were now central to his work. "Much of that little book was written right here where I am sitting and writing to you now," Wright replied, marveling at the "truly violent" poems that Catullus had written in Rome and the refuge he had found in Sirmione. "He must have been an odd kind of guy. But my God, he could sing like a bird." Wright would compliment Silko with this same phrase two months later.

Catullus's famous poem about Sirmione, a place he calls *paene insularum*, "almost an island" and, strangely, "the eye of all islands," had impressed Wright since he first read it in high school. Catullus remained a presiding spirit—together with the lizards. The peninsula is uniquely subject to the vagaries of weather, which Wright observed closely. Many of the pieces he began in his notebook that month—his last sustained period of new work—are focused on Sirmione and other lakeshore towns. His descriptions of the peninsula and of Lake Garda in a letter to his brother Jack pleased him so much he thought of including the letter in his evolving manuscript of selected prose.

At a desk set in front of his hotel room window, Wright worked for a few hours each morning and again in the afternoon, a disciplined round of letters, notebook work, and revisions of poems. Sending a group of six to Frederick Morgan at *The Hudson Review* (including three in rhyme and meter), Wright sounds relieved, "after a good deal of wandering and a lot of work in my notebook," to finally bring some new poems to completion.

In his journal that summer, Wright returned to meditations inspired by Max Picard's *The World of Silence*. "I wonder where words are before anybody speaks them," he mused on June 4, describing the landscape and songbirds outside his window. The next day, he continues this reverie in a prose piece dedicated to Robert Bly, "A True Voice." He asked Louis Simpson for news of Bly, who had not answered a letter from him in more than a year. "I want and need to be in touch with the people I know best and respect the most."

On Friday, June 8, Wright typed three letters in one day. To Janice Thurn, he described the songbirds throughout the peninsula that, "scarcely able to believe their good luck in their home," can even be heard to "sing indecently in their sleep." Reaching out once more to Bly, he included a draft of the new prose piece dedicated to him, and gratefully acknowledged the example of Bly's "gift for solitude," which he now felt able to cultivate in his own life. And Wright finally responded to a letter he had carried with him for five years from his high school classmate Thomas Hodge, who had recounted their adolescence in Martins Ferry in long free-verse lines. "The years are awfully heavy, but this evening I feel like shaking them off," Wright affirmed, reminding Hodge of Catullus's poem about Sirmione from their old Latin textbook. In the simple act of writing to Hodge, he seems able to forgive himself and his hometown a weight of grievances.

The following day, Wright drafted a provisional table of contents for his new manuscript, beginning a process that continued intermittently throughout the summer and fall. His final collection has a vital sense of wholeness, a product of his careful sequencing and the "inner relations that exist in the individual poems." For example, the prose piece "May Morning," when printed as verse, shows it to be a near-perfect sonnet. In the sequence of *This Journey*, it precedes his tribute poem to Bly, making a sly joke of their long-standing argument about traditional English forms.

———

Often that month, the couple took a picnic lunch to the fields near the Grotto di Cattullo on the peninsula's northern point, where a cliff rises above Lake Garda. They swam every day, moving to a more secluded beach when tourists began to arrive in mid-June. By boat, they traveled to towns along the lakeshore, including Desanzano and Garda. On June 13

Wright notes, "All I am doing at the window is opening my eyes on a fine morning"—a gesture that suggests the ease with which he worked all month. At midday they disembarked in Gargnano, on the lake's western shore, and walked up into the hills on narrow cobbled paths. Olive trees in blossom surrounded them, so many pale yellow flowers falling that "to find a way to sit down, we had to lean over and scoop away whole handfulls of them, like snow." They found the Church of San Tommaso perched high above the port in dazzling sunlight—the same convent that had lured D. H. Lawrence by the sound of its tower bells. Back at his desk, Wright drafted a prose piece, "Flowering Olives," that begins: "It is futile to pretend I am looking at something else. In fact, I am doing my best to gaze as deeply as I can into the crevice of a single olive blossom." His meticulous observations show an uncommon patience and empathy. The piece concludes, "The whole mile of this mountain road high above tiny golden Gargnano gleams right now in a momentary noon of olive flowers, and I am the only darkness alive in the Alps."

In Sirmione, Wright's revisions from his notebooks yielded thirty new poems by the middle of June, which joined an equal number already gathered in his manuscript folder. "Now they will have to lie there by themselves for a while until they change," he told Silko, trusting the poems to "ripen" naturally; with time, he would bring new insights and discrimination to the work. This is a process markedly different from Wright's early poems, many of which can be traced through dozens of successive drafts. Now, before turning a new sheet of paper into his typewriter, he already heard the rhythm of words from which he began. A richness of internal rhyme sustains a new kind of lyricism while the sense of improvisation opens the poems to curiosity and discovery. His journal, he believed, helped make this work possible; in Sirmione he even drafted a new lyric titled "My Notebook."

"I no longer think of Verona as an Eden from which we are finally banished," Wright realized on his final visit there. "The city is the best of man. It is like a girl bringing you a cup of water drawn from a great pure natural spring." He and Anne spent Saturday, June 23, walking all over Verona and ascending the Lombard Tower to see the red tile roofs of the city spread out beneath them. They visited Castelvecchio once more and crossed the Adige to walk along its banks. "It is the human city," he reflected, back at his desk in Sirmione, "embattled many times, and scarred and bombed, yet able through prayer and labor (these are one: *laborare est orare*) to rise and offer bread, water, and flowers to the wanderer." Wright took leave of Verona "without regret and with no bitterness in my heart." He trusted in the creatures that represented the spirit of the place: "I saw my one lizard along the Adige, blazing on white stone under the swallowtail walls, and I am content."

———

Moments of contentment such as this would become more rare in the coming weeks and months, and fewer new poems appeared in Wright's notebooks. Arriving in Venice by train on June 27, Anne described the city as "hot, humid, and crowded." Though they took their same hotel room at La Calcina on the Zattere along the Giudecca Canal—a productive haven in the past—Wright already longed for Tuscany. "It is brutally hot in this oozing city, and I am exhausted," he noted on June 28—the first entry to mention the fatigue that would shadow him for the last two months in Europe and into the fall.

When Anne's sister Jane joined them, they rented a car for a two-week excursion south. They arrived in Siena two days before Il Palio, one of the annual horse races to circle the Piazza del Campo in competitions among the seventeen local *contrades*, with bareback riders dressed in the colors and insignia of the city's various wards. Their hotel's location in the southwestern section of Siena inspired the couple's loyalty to the district known as the Contrada of the Snail. They took the same suite of rooms in the Palazzo Ravizza with a view of the small cemetery in an olive grove beyond the city walls, bordered by cypress trees. Rows of small lights came on in the cemetery after dark; there were fireflies and the sound of crickets. "By God, when I die let me be buried there," Wright told Anne on their first evening back in Siena. "How safe, how good to be there." Church bells woke them on the morning of the race, and they joined the crowd outside the local chapel where the horse and rider were blessed, the streets nearby decorated in brilliant red and yellow flags emblazoned with the insignia of the snail. The Wrights later joined the parade in celebration of their victorious *contrada*, and saw their colors flown throughout Siena for the rest of their stay.

"It is the day of the Palio, the great medieval pageant, and curiously I have Ohio on my mind," Wright reflected in his journal, "and my bitterly heartbreaking cousin Dave, who is dead." His melancholy ran counter to the city's festive atmosphere, and he typed a fragmentary elegy recalling his childhood companion. When rain scattered the crowds in Il Campo the following day, Wright secretly rejoiced in "triumph for the dry weeds by the railroad tracks in Ohio." This feeling of unease—of standing apart—grew stronger each day.

Frank MacShane had seen the Wrights in Rome that spring, and they had dinner in Venice at the end of June after meeting by chance along the Zattere. As luck would have it, they crossed paths again in Siena and the Wrights joined MacShane one afternoon in the twelfth-century Tuscan house where he was staying that summer. In Rome, MacShane had noticed how Wright seemed to tire easily, and though "he seemed to dominate the long narrow dining room" where they gathered for lunch, "he was nevertheless curiously fragile or delicate, somewhat tentative and unsure of himself" before taking his place at the head of the table.

We talked about John O'Hara, Sherwood Anderson, and Theodore Dreiser. Distance from home seemed to exhilarate Jim's passion for America, and he quoted long paragraphs from H. L. Mencken. . . . His anger at the betrayal of America, especially by the politicians who were pledged to protect and preserve it, was the other side of a sensibility that was deeply moved by the miseries of the anonymous poor and rejected whose lives were always marginal.

After a week in Siena, the Wrights drove with Jane to San Gimignano, and then to Passignano on Lake Trasimeno and on to Assisi. In Arezzo, "golden as ever," they spent three days, returning to view Piero's frescoes once more. On a visit to Florence, however, Wright feared the city had become "an inescapable instance of contemporary degeneracy." His patience spent, he renders Dante's city as a modern-day Inferno. "We seem not even to be dead any more, but to have come out in a region of Hell at once ugly and ridiculous." On Friday, July 13, the three left Arezzo and drove through Sansepolcro and Urbino to the coast and north toward Venice. In his journal, Wright again notes his exhaustion. "I will be glad to get back to Paris, where I think it will be possible to get some rest before we have to return to America." The months of travel had taken a toll. "It is odd to feel worn out in such a beautiful place as Italy."

They arrived back in Venice during the annual Festa del Redentore, a celebration that featured fireworks and a temporary pontoon bridge stretching across the Giudecca Canal from the Zattere to the island and the majestic sixteenth-century Church of the Redeemer designed by Andrea Palladio. Along with thousands of others, Venetians and tourists alike, the three made the pilgrimage across the canal to the cathedral. By sunset on Sunday, the canal and Saint Mark's basin were filled with all manner of boats, festooned with balloons and garlands, waiting for the grand fireworks display. Though still in good spirits, Wright had become edgy and irritable in Venice, "in a way that he'd never been before," sensitive to any disturbance and noticeably more fatigued. "This town is so noisy the various rackets nearly cancel each other out," he grumbled in his notebook. "Venice is strange and beautiful in its way, but I am very tired of scuttering about, distracted by noise and other agitations." He wanted nothing but the quiet of Higgins's study, where he could work again. "I am bone sick of travel of this kind."

Wright moved the small antique desk in their hotel room between the windows looking out on the canal and answered letters from Leslie Silko that had finally caught up with him in Venice. She had written twice in June, telling him of her return to Laguna, New Mexico, where she lost a custody battle over her two sons, "and you, dear friend, are the only person I am able to correspond with these days." Her brief mention of this grief affected Wright keenly. His response, dated July 18, recounts his estrangement from his own son and the letter Marshall had sent the previous October "in which, with great verbal confusion, he told me that I was not his father." This is the only time Wright spoke of this loss, "my worst pain," outside his family, confessing to Silko how, since the break, he had "mainly clung to my books, my writing." The intimacy of their friendship is nowhere more apparent than in this exchange. "I am deeply moved by the letter you sent," Silko wrote in reply, "and want you to know that I will always cherish and guard its story."

———

During their last week in Italy, after Anne's sister departed, the couple made a day trip to Padua, intent upon seeing Giotto's fresco cycle in the Scrovegni Chapel once more. As Wright gazed up at the paintings he felt a hand on his shoulder and turned to greet Anthony Hecht, whom they then joined for dinner with his family. But the joys of Italy could not dispel the "exhaustion of spirit" he felt. To Janice Thurn he wrote of the solace he found in rising very early, "for I love the daybreak," a time when Venice seemed more at peace.

Only a few local Italians, the tool-knowing Venetians, were awake, and their tempers shed their foulness and surliness as we stepped into one or another café to have an early coffee, standing up at the bar with the fruit-vendors, street-sweepers, paint-chippers, admirals of garbage-scows, avid and slinky gondoliere, whores, pimps, and assorted sons-of-bitches of one profession or another.

The Wrights flew to Paris on July 23, but their stay in the Higginses' apartment was delayed and they decided to spend four days in Moret-sur-Loing. From a window overlooking the river there, Wright drafted a new prose piece, joining two successive notebook entries to make "The Sunlight Falling at Peace in Moret-sur-Loing." On its surface it seems a delicate, elegiac meditation on summer mosquitoes "deep in the light" above the river, "exposed and defenseless." But the poem was inspired by a conversation with friends of Anne's who had visited in Sirmione. They had talked of the profound naiveté of young men in the first days of World War I who arrived in taxis at the front lines along the Marne River, some still dressed in tuxedos. Wright often brooded over the elaborate monuments to the dead from that war in the center of every French village, and the poem's concluding sentence refers to this obliquely, as the Loing river's "fate guides it . . . downstream, to enter the dark red waters of the Marne."

Finally settled in their top-floor apartment in Paris and the welcome seclusion and quiet of Higgins's study, Wright turned back to his book. Despite a heat wave that lasted ten days and the weariness that oppressed him, he made daily progress on notebook entries and revisions, organizing completed poems in his manuscript binder. He sent eight new poems to *Antaeus* on the same day he learned that *The Hudson Review* had accepted others. With many shops already closing for August on the rue Daguerre, Paris began to take on its relaxed summer character. They rode the subway into the city and took leisurely walks, returning to the terrace of their apartment to watch lights flicker on across the rooftop landscape. As the white domes of Sacré Coeur reflected the sunset, Wright put Erik Satie's piano music on the turntable, beginning with

Trois Gymnopédies. Over cups of chamomile tea, the couple often sat without speaking.

As they had done in 1977, they hosted Anne's friend Sheila Ráshed and her son, Nazeil, for a week in early August, but the couple soon returned to their shared privacies, gathering energy for the return to New York and the burdens they had escaped for more than a year. In a letter to Silko, Wright prayed for reconciliation with Marshall and struggled to shake off the sadness he felt. "I can't—or won't—be indifferent to life, and yet when I turn my face toward it, how sorrowful it seems." After acknowledging Virgil's wisdom—"these are the tears of things"—he thanks Silko for her description of an owl perched on a saguaro that had watched as she played cards with her son. "This year I've written a good deal about the non-human presences that, in some message of the spirit, come and sit with us and keep us alive."

"It has been a good year for us," he reflected in the middle of August, "and my work is certainly not done yet, but I feel slow and sort of empty. I don't feel exactly barren, but sort of weary and lost." Though prompted by his awareness of the difficulties in returning to America, this entry betrays a deeper sense of unease. Anne's journal from this same time reveals what Wright never refers to directly:

> During these Paris days we both feel a strain of sadness. We feel subdued under our pleasure, a little weary. I feel more rested after the first week but James continues to be exhausted. He gets a sore throat that won't go away. I think our trouble may be the thought of returning to New York, a city no longer beautiful, where we have to live and work. We do not speak of these things often.

While in Paris, the couple began work on a joint chapbook of the prose they had written while in Europe. Wright felt enthusiastic when Anne showed him passages from the journal she had kept, and they worked together choosing and arranging the work. A new poem he began in Paris, however, shows his hidden agitation. "To the Adriatic Wind, Becalmed" is a plea for the wind to return and "do beloved Venice a kindness": to "blow it down, / All the way into the water / Where the towers belong." A terrifying calm calls up images of ruin and flood.

On August 18, Wright turned to composing two difficult letters: one to Donald Hall concerning Bly's continuing silence and another to Franz, who had finally written to his father after many months. "This morning in Paris it is raining (that sounds a little like an echo of Vallejo: *esta tarde llueve como nunca* . . .)," Wright began. "But I love the rain in this gray city, the smoky August that blows through the great spaces of the parks and squares." Though he worried about Franz, who had no steady work and still lived in Oberlin, he felt proud of his son's genuine talent. "Your own devotion to poetry—to the life of the spirit—is unmistakably true," he wrote. "You are writing beautifully, and your work improves all the time." Franz turned aside any help finding his way in the world, a stubbornness his father would recognize.

Wright's apprehension grew as their departure neared. "I am weary of Europe and even of Paris," he confessed in his journal. "Come hell or high water, I have to go back and face the complex difficulties of life, of teaching [students] who have no interest in the written language." He tried to throw off worry during their last days there, but finally conceded, "I'm like a man waiting to go into battle." Wright always kept working, however. He invented a couple of lively Greek epigrams in his journal and paid tribute to François Villon and the rats along the Seine. A dramatic concision marks many late prose pieces, so straightforward in their language and syntax and yet shot through with visionary imagery. "Beside the Tour Magne in Nîmes"—one of the last poems he drafted in Europe—encloses an inexplicable image, a kernel of weird beauty, within a simple, prosaic form. Gazing up at the tower, his imagination takes flight: "Not even the doctors of history, with their fine hands sifting the skeletons of ancient leaves away from the branches of lost children's hands, can find on the great tower the slightest scar that can tell who built it here and left it for someone finally to approach and leave alone." This breakthrough, merging a lyric voice with prosaic directness, enriches Wright's late work.

On Sunday, September 2, the couple returned to the Hotel Recamier for their final two days in Paris, and Wright put off work on a number of new poems. He wanted to be alone; he made lists of the chores that awaited him in New York. Caught in a rain shower in front of Saint-Sulpice, he longed to remain behind with the waterlogged sparrows clinging to sycamore branches. "But first I have to return to America, and resume my journey through the only life I have." This last sentence, part of a handwritten entry, shows the phrase "through ugliness and despair" crossed out two separate times.

For more than eight months, Wright had kept his promise to work every day in his notebook; his final entry in Paris appears on page 424 in the third of his small loose-leaf notebooks. Written by hand in the hotel as he prepared to leave for the airport on Tuesday, September 4, it reads:

It is the last day in Paris—in fact, the last day in Europe for some while. Well. A few minutes ago I returned to the Recamier from the Church of St. Sulpice, where I had spent some time, praying and lighting a candle down at the dark far end behind the altar, and finally standing in silence—a bright silence—and saying goodbye to Delacroix's great fresco of Jacob wrestling with the angel.

Now we fly home to New York. In a way I will be glad to get home. But my only real hope is to move with a kind of grim and clenched-teeth orderliness through a life that—whatever its appearances and pretenses may be—is in cold fact a series of ordeals: struggle, confusion, loneliness, and despair. This is the truth, my true Ohio: all I have to build on.

30

My true Ohio

September 1979–January 1980

> Pleasure is oft a visitant, but pain
> Clings cruelly to us.
> —Keats, *Endymion*, Book I, line 906

Arriving back in New York after the long flight from Paris on September 4, Wright found "a pile of busy mail" awaiting him—more than a hundred letters demanding attention, from page proofs to requests for interviews and readings. But among the chores and the clutter, Wright found a letter from Robert Bly, the first in almost a year and a half. "It is good to write you at last," Bly began, admitting that he felt more settled now that his divorce had been sorted. He and Carol shared custody of the children, "with a lot of going back and forth in between and an easy feeling about it." To bolster her resistance to the idea, Carol had often quoted the Wrights' disapproval, which Robert resented. "I was angry with both of you for taking part in it," he scolded. Though his long silence could now be explained, the easy flow of letters between Bly and Wright didn't return.

Wright's correspondence with Leslie Silko, however, continued to thrive, in some ways taking the place of his once vital exchange with Bly. From Paris, he had sent her six of his new poems, in "gratitude for the inspiration that your friendship never fails to provide." Silko found encouragement for her own work in them. "You are fearless of the language

America speaks and you love it," she responded. "With your poems behind me I can speak confidently now about a beauty which is purely from the American heart." In the poem "Wherever Home Is," Wright bids "Goodbye to Leonardo, good riddance," and Silko praises his keen ear and the expressiveness of his native idiom: "That Ohio country gives us your voice."

It had been more than a year since he and Anne had lived in their apartment, and they slowly began "getting accustomed to the spirit of the place again." They both returned to work on September 14, and Anne began a job at New York University's program for young adults with learning disabilities. With the crush of responsibilities and pressures that seemed part of the very air in New York, Wright gratefully returned to weekly AA meetings and continued his daily journal work. Waking before dawn became part of his strategy to stay engaged with his poetry as he returned to teaching; he now drafted lines for poems in his head before working in his notebook. On September 10, he wrote, "I must learn how to remain in the rhythm of active language while I am acting on other things."

Wright revised the prose piece "Camomilla" the following day, an unsettling meditation on war by way of an intimate look at camomilla leaves in a field in Apulia, a part of southern Italy ravaged over centuries. "They hid as long as they could beneath the white flowers," he says of the fallen leaves. "They were like the faces of frightened people in a war," superimposing images of the plants with the faces of local victims. "Just like such brutally ransacked people, the camomilla leaves turn their faces away." His empathy for the place and its people exposes his own profound need for solitude. "The faces of camomilla leaves would wish me away again, wish me back into the sea again, wish me to leave them alone in peace."

Wright taught three courses that fall: an intro to literature class, a freshman composition class, and an upper-level course on the eighteenth-century English novel. Weekends became consumed by teaching chores, which overshadowed his three separate writing projects: his new manuscript of poems, the collected prose volume, and the joint chapbook of prose pieces with Anne. As consolation, the literature classes returned Wright to *Huckleberry Finn*, Defoe, Fielding, Smollett, Austen, and, as always, Cervantes. "I want to read *Don Quixote* again, the country that ought to be familiar to me by now, I have gone there so often in the past." Wright realized the work's genius anew, how "at any moment there the commonplace creatures reveal their true strangeness, and reading his book is as though I had never lived my own life yet."

Reaching out to Hall, Carruth, and Hugo, Wright was determined "to stay sober and continue to work, as I've been able to do during the past year with a pleasure and a good will that I've never, truly, felt so fully before." Throughout that fall, he tried to revive poems that had eluded him for months, while beginning a few new prose pieces that would also remain unfinished. Despite everything, he kept up with his journal. Wright's daily entries include random speculations, prose passages and poems by others, and reflections on the work at hand. "Sometimes I think that writing for a while in this notebook is like tossing a single line into water without especially hoping to catch anything."

On the last day of September, a Sunday, Wright submitted to an interview—a ritual he had come to detest. He had agreed to talk with Dave Smith on the condition that Gib Ruark take part as well. Smith was gathering a book of critical essays on Wright's work, inspired by the special *Ironwood* issue from the fall of 1977, and the interview would be featured in the new collection. Wright had asked to see a list of questions Smith wanted to ask, and it arrived three days before they met. The six-page list, including some sixty questions, alarmed Wright—particularly Smith's interest in family history and his sons. It took Ruark's persuasion to convince him to go through with it.

The interview begins biographically, as Wright recalls the communal occasion and ceremony of football in the Ohio River Valley and admits his "peculiar kind of devotion to Martins Ferry." A poem can begin anywhere, Wright reasons, "as long as the poet is willing to approach that location with the appropriate reverence. Even very ugly places." He then expands upon Lawrence's idea of "the spirit of place" and considers the violent legacy of American history. The figure of George Doty fascinated Smith, and the most extensive discussion of Wright's poetry centers on "At the Executed Murderer's Grave." Encapsulating his own preoccupation with Doty, his crime, and his punishment, Wright says, "It startled me for a while, the whole notion of how little we human beings understand one another." Wright's talk ranges widely, from his teaching methods to his love of Dickens, from the "genuinely subversive" joys of *Huckleberry Finn* to his devotion to Horace, Robert Herrick, and Edward Thomas. He insists on the term "prose pieces" to describe his own work in the form and praises Mencken and Forster. "I don't think that, in any deep sense, it makes a damn bit of difference whether or not one is writing in prose or in verse, just so he's trying to be imaginative and true to what he is hearing." Despite his initial resistance, he felt satisfied with the interview. "I spoke more freely than I had thought I might," he reflected in his journal. "I'm surprised that I got to say as much as I did about the actual physical labor, the craft of writing."

————

In the first week of October, Wright joined Betsy Fogelman for a picnic lunch in the city. She had recently moved to New York, and though many letters had passed between them, they hadn't met in more than a year. He brought small gifts from Europe, including a lace handkerchief from Bruges, and the two shared an easy familiarity. In a letter to her that evening, Wright describes a quality he had noticed in her from the first, "something totally unpretentious and unaffected" that reminded him of F. Scott Fitzgerald's "poignant, heart-aching phrase about America: he said that America is not really a place, nor a time; it is 'A willingness of the heart.'" Teaching *The Great Gatsby* again, Wright became absorbed by Fitzgerald's work throughout that fall and read widely in his short stories and other writings.

The two resort hotels on the shore of Lake Minnewaska had been in their prime in the 1920s, the decade of Fitzgerald's great success. An air of old-fashioned grandeur had been part of the appeal whenever the Wrights escaped to the Wildmere Hotel on the lake's eastern shore. The building's twin, the older Cliff House, had been abandoned in 1972 and burnt to the ground in the winter of 1978. They had seen the wreckage that June, the last time they had come. At the time, there had been plans to renovate Wildmere. On the afternoon of Friday, October 5, the couple arrived for a three-day stay they hoped might cure Wright's lingering sore throat. Instead, they learned they had come on the hotel's final weekend. Signs of deterioration were everywhere; large bowls were set out to catch the rain leaking from the ceiling of the once majestic dining room. A cold, driving rain continued without letup, making even a short walk impossible. They left the next morning. "It was devastating," Anne recalled. She believed that weekend marked a turning point; his therapist later told her that Wright had felt the same way. "We are like an army in defeat, driven out by the abomination of desolation," he wrote in his notebook, quoting in Latin a sober lament by Horace.

Wright's health became a pressing concern; despite penicillin treatment prescribed by his doctor, the unrelenting soreness in his throat now made it difficult to eat, and he grew weak. Both he and Anne felt disoriented by their return to America, clouding their awareness of how serious his condition might be. Anne continued to believe that her husband's symptoms were psychosomatic. "He was very private about it, and didn't let me know how sick he felt, so I couldn't understand, sometimes, the way he was behaving. He seemed very distant, very aloof. It was such a shock—a shock being back in the country."

Wright had first spoken of his need to "keep faith" with his journals in a letter to Bly in July 1974, and the phrase recurred often as a private encouragement and promise to himself. Now that he had returned to New York, Wright realized that this effort "might make it possible for me finally to touch this city with my imagination as well as with my hands." But Wright disguised his growing anxiety even in his notebooks; his planned trip to Harvard University for a reading seemed merely a nuisance to him, more of the distracting "clutter" that annoyed him day after day. "I reckon I'll read things about Ohio, mostly," he reflected. "I wonder what, if anything, the Harvards will make of Ohio, my Ohio."

Most of the poems Wright chose did return to Ohio in a career-spanning reading, among the finest he ever gave. Anne's teaching prevented her from going, so Wright asked Roger Hecht to fly with him to Boston for the afternoon reading on Thursday, October 11. The renowned poet and translator Robert Fitzgerald introduced Wright, praising him as "an explorer and a poet of what Williams called 'the American grain,'" before adding with a sly smile, "and lately I think he has ventured in European grains as well." To begin his reading, as he so often did, Wright chose to say another poet's work, this time in memory of Elizabeth Bishop, who had died suddenly in Boston just five days before at age sixty-eight.

Thinking about Elizabeth Bishop this afternoon, as I was lying down for a few minutes, it suddenly appeared in my mind the way things will sometimes, just by themselves, the old poem of Yeats about poetry. It's a very beautiful poem, and it's an *ars poetica*, a poem about poetry, and I would like to say it, thinking about Elizabeth Bishop. It's "Adam's Curse." Everybody knows it, but it doesn't hurt to sing it again.

From this opening recitation of Yeats, Wright captivated his audience for more than an hour, giving a measured, thoughtful reading that ranged from his early sonnet "My Grandmother's Ghost" to a playful ballade in the manner of Villon that would soon appear in *The Hudson Review*. Joking about the two new sonnets about Rome that would accompany it, he admitted the "great, sort of criminal pleasure" he took from the reactions he expected to his publishing formal verse. "I have friends all over the place who are going to say, 'What's happening to him? He's getting senile.'" Wright seems finally at ease with his own traditional temperament. Significantly, every line of verse he ever published begins with a capital letter, a convention he followed without fail.

Apollinaire's "The Pretty Redhead" again marks the emotional center of his reading, set between "The Minneapolis Poem" and "A Blessing." As it had for Apollinaire at the end of his life, the poem represents Wright's coming to terms with the pull of his poetic allegiances—caught between Robinson and Whitman—that had once threatened to tear him apart. The poet asks his readers for understanding, in a gesture matched by self-forgiveness. The poem had also come to shelter a private memory; hidden behind "the lovely appearance / Of an adorable redhead" is the Muse, Jenny, who had once taken that form.

The concluding poem, "A Farewell to the Mayor of Toulouse," is a curse upon the town that Wright had drafted at the end of January. Introducing his "cracked ballade," he admitted, "After a few days, I kind of liked the place, but the poem was started by then." In the recording, his Ohioan accent is still evident, but at times he sounds short of breath, as though troubled by a cold. None whom he met—not even Hecht—suspected the constant pain he endured. In his journal that evening, Wright admired the graciousness of his hosts; after two decades of public appearances, it startled him to think that Harvard had been "the pleasantest place of all."

———

Wright's patience grew more brittle as the pain in his throat wore him down; he felt more discouraged by his classes at Hunter than ever before. Lacking assistance, he realized that the problems with collecting his critical prose were "so monstrous that I have put the whole thing to one side of my mind." As Wright's discomfort and apprehension increased, his journal betrays moments of rage and exhaustion. A throat specialist, Dr. Blaugrund, who examined him on October 18, could find nothing wrong; his exorbitant fee and a "prescription for some stuff that I'm supposed to gargle" infuriated Wright. He looked for relief in his work and exchanged short prose pieces with Anne for their chapbook. The passages she had revised from her European journal delighted him.

The poem he returned to most often that fall was a lyric titled "With the Gift of a Fresh New Notebook I Found in Florence," the penultimate poem in his manuscript. He had given the small red-bound notebook to Gib Ruark the weekend of their interview in New York but continued to revise the poem meant to accompany the gift. Wright captures both the concrete and the evanescent by varying the poem's diction and tone in flexible free-verse lines. The precision of detail—describing the exact location of the stationer's store—balances the inward-focused energy of the poem. The notebook's blank pages offer a sense of promise:

Nobody yet has walked across and sat down
At the edge under a pear tree
To savor the air of the natural blossoms and leave them
Alone, and leave the heavy place alone.

Without a dominant metrical pattern, each line carries a sense of possibility and surprise; the space surrounding the lines has an air of solitude. Even the formal occasion of the poem—presenting the journal as a gift—underscores the importance to him of his own notebooks.

Wright clung to routines that had made their European days so relaxed and productive, including a *passeggiata* with Anne, walking in their neighborhood after dinner. In Carl Schurz Park along the East River, the couple watched neon signs flashing on the opposite shore and tugboats making steady progress against the current. The roiling waters of that tidal estuary to the Atlantic often absorbed him in reverie.

When I hear Shakespeare's phrase about "the dark backward and abysm of time," I think how deep the Ohio River seemed in the evening, thoroughly bottomless as it never seemed in the full of daylight, and old Beenie Maag, my mother's strange friend, standing on the porch of her houseboat below the great cracks of the mud-flats, turning her big-boned face away from the shore, and humming her nutty old West Virginia songs, fragments of bewilderment and tenderness.

———

The Wrights traveled to Delaware at the end of October to visit the Ruarks, and though he complained of a sore throat Wright was otherwise "in good form." Back at Hunter on October 31, his journal recounts an arduous sequence of classes and meetings, after first waking at 4:30 a.m. to make progress on his own work. The following evening, after being asked to lead his AA group, it surprised him to realize it had gone remarkably well. "It was a good solid meeting, and I have to call it, without exaggeration, one of the happiest experiences I have ever had." Even as his health deteriorated, Wright stayed sober, an accomplishment made more exceptional by the difficulties that life in "workaday New York City" brought with it. By his estimation, three months of sobriety there "is the equivalent of a whole year anywhere else."

Wright worked on his poems whenever he could, and made a list of more than sixty different prose pieces from his European notebooks. After writing in support of Mary Oliver's application for a Guggenheim fellowship, he assured her that her new collection, *Twelve Moons*, was her best, "immediate, clear, and positively soaked with life, real life. . . . I sometimes idly wonder," he concluded, "if and when you and I will ever actually meet—though, in a way, we seem to have known each other since childhood." Oliver later recalled how important their correspondence had been to her as a young poet. "I felt, as he expressed, that we did know each other, deeply and for a long time. That feeling was very strong." Oliver had discovered *The Branch Will Not Break* at a crucial early point in her career, and she described how Wright went on to merge "the exquisite and the narrative together" in his poems, with a subtlety of American diction that rivals William Carlos Williams.

What progress Wright made with his work seemed small and the moments of peace few; he rarely mentioned the constant pain in his throat to Anne and reminded himself to avoid complaining in his journal. In mid-November he wrote a letter to Liberty about their sons, whose lives felt ever more distant. Franz had visited New York when Wright first returned in September, but he remained unemployed in Ohio at the age of twenty-six, which drove his father to distraction. Marshall, now twenty-one, had phoned that fall, and once tried to apologize for his brutal, rejecting letter. The calls came collect, long-distance, but they troubled his father less for their extravagance than for their disjointedness and confusion.

Returning to his study on Friday, November 16, after four hours of teaching, Wright found himself "literally summoning up enough physical strength to push my fingers against the typewriter keys." The following day, though he managed to revise two prose pieces and type a final list of ten titles for his chapbook with Anne, he admitted how tension had become the "basic condition of life these days," a feeling that nagged at him like his aching throat. Writing to Silko, he admitted that his intense daily schedule left him "struggling hard," but said nothing about his health. He believed he was just one of many "in danger of being suffocated by busywork." Wright took pride in his notebooks, "but I certainly feel driven," he told her. A jubilant note had also come from Robert Bly—the first since his reproachful letter in August—with the idea of making corrections together on their Trakl book. It was a clear effort to rekindle their friendship. In an interview that same week, Bly spoke at length about Wright's poetry, and what they had learned from each other.

But as the days grew shorter that fall, Wright's health worsened. In a letter to Robert Mezey on November 19, Wright admitted that he and Anne had both been "working frantically at school and at home—much more desperately than we can remember having ever done before." The following day he confessed in his journal, "I feel so sick that it is physically difficult for me to draw the breath in and out of my lungs." They canceled plans to spend Thanksgiving in Pennsylvania with Anne's sister after scheduling an overnight hospital stay for that week.

Wright had sent two poems to Carruth from Rome in April, welcoming his advice, and in mid-November Carruth responded with detailed edits—"Suggestions only"—and his enthusiastic acceptance of "A Winter Daybreak Above Vence" for Harper's. In the days leading up to Thanksgiving, Wright significantly revised both poems and working on the revisions helped lift his spirits. "I see how necessary it is for me to shake off despair, somehow, and to live on faith." But he now worried that he wouldn't have the energy to finish the semester. "It is an exceedingly odd moment. I don't even know what to pray for."

Suspecting the truth about his condition, Wright struggled to keep his composure among his colleagues and to meet his classes. The day before entering Mount Sinai, he recorded a disturbing vision:

> No matter which way I turn, or what window I look out of or hallway I stare down, trying to catch a glimpse of something in the light, the dark man appears there. . . . I looked out the window and saw him under a tree, made of leaves and twine. Down the hallway he appeared only for a moment. He turned his face in my direction and just as suddenly he was gone, leaving nothing but a ring of gold around the light.

This is the only time "the dark man" appears in Wright's journal, though a sense of foreboding is evident on every page from this point on.

After waiting six hours for a bed, Wright was finally admitted to the hospital at 9:00 p.m. on Thanksgiving Day, November 29, for an examination and biopsy of his throat. He waited another seven hours the next day before anesthesia granted him relief. Writing by hand, he managed to make an entry in his journal. "It is a grim time, quite as bad as any I've ever had to face—and I've faced some bad ones." After the procedure was further delayed, Wright remained in Mount Sinai over Friday night; having spent an entire day free from pain, he dreaded his eventual discharge. He depended completely on Anne's company, their hours together now more precious and "oddly beautiful."

Wright left the hospital almost certain of what Dr. Blaugrund's "final verdict" would be, and yet it took almost a week for the test results to arrive. He now worried about the time he needed to finish the work he had in progress. "I believe that in two or three months I could complete the manuscripts of the book of critical prose and the book of poems. Before I lose the ability to function," he reflected the day after returning home. "Death is a nuisance." The delay in receiving final word became its own nightmare. "Really the only thing worse than this pain, which sings, and I mean sings in my nerves, is the uncertainty." His physical weakness made the world around him seem ghostly and dreamlike. On Wednesday, December 5, with still no word from his doctor, Wright imagined himself in the cemetery above Martins Ferry, looking downriver toward the state penitentiary. "M. E. Ketchum the Warden from Moundsville throws his shadow, and the shadows of all the silent and bleeding years, back up the hill where I sit in the wind, above the river, waiting for the wind to die down, waiting to go down, to the river."

On Friday afternoon, December 7, Dr. Blaugrund finally phoned, glad to have reached Anne rather than her husband. The biopsy confirmed a malignant tumor at the base of Wright's tongue; the doctor asked to see the couple the following morning to schedule surgery and discuss further treatment. Though he wanted to guide his notebook away from his illness, Wright couldn't help dwelling on just how much time he had left. In plain, blunt sentences, he confronted the realities of cancer and a painful death; he placed little hope in his supposed recovery.

Three months after Anne Sexton's suicide in 1974, Wright had addressed a poem to her that imagined a figure of death, a raptor with a "horn beak," a "great bird . . . / Hunting cold to kill." His journal entry on December 7, 1979, concludes by recalling the first six lines of a different poem, one that he had drafted months earlier in Paris. He typed its title in block letters: TO THE SEA WIND:

> Come on.
> Shift your wings a little.
> You have plenty of strength left in your shoulders,
> Your pure beak glittering like a scimitar,
> Your hawk mouth that does not care,
> Proud as moonlight.

The conclusion of his first draft of this poem asks the Adriatic wind to blow the sagging city of Venice "All the way into the water":

> Now is the time
> To do beloved Venice a kindness.
> Come, blow it the rest of the way
> Down.

The next morning, Wright listened with Anne as Dr. Blaugrund explained at length how he could survive the complicated series of radiation and chemo treatments that would both precede and follow radical surgery to remove the tumor. The prospect that the operation would permanently damage his voice left Wright distraught. Though he now faced the hope of getting better, he knew that the weakness and pain would get worse; over the previous two months, he had already lost twenty-five pounds. But Wright tried to put a brave face on his diagnosis, telling Roland Flint, "I'm gonna beat this thing."

———

Wright focused his energy on his Hunter classes and, when he felt able, gathered finished poems to send off to magazines. Over the next four weeks, he grew obsessed with completing a series of ten prose pieces intended for the editor Stephen Berg at *The American Poetry Review*; he worked on the sequence until the last days at his desk in January. Revising individual poems helped distract him from his key concern: the fate of his final manuscript. Though he first considered asking Donald Hall, he decided that Hayden Carruth should be the editor of what he began to call *Last Poems*. Wright trusted Michael di Capua at Farrar, Straus and Giroux to edit and publish his *Collected Prose*.

Even just reading or typing fair copies, however, left Wright exhausted; after an hour's work at his desk, his eyesight grew blurred. Seeking a second opinion regarding treatment, he met with a specialist who gave him "a 50/50 chance" of surviving, a judgment spoken "in the tone of a man who was about to offer me a discount coffin from a little business his brother-in-law runs on the side." Trying to imagine his life without use of his voice, Wright realized, "to my fascination, that I am simply not interested in such a life. Or any life at all, thus. Odd: the thought doesn't even depress me. Life is simply over. That is all." Throughout December, his journal often shows this chilling composure, fostered by unbroken weariness. "And so good night. How strange. After all this fuss." The one entry to admit some hope comes on December 14—the day after his fifty-second birthday. He had spent five hours with students that day and writes, "I was only sorry we did not have (as I said to them) that large peace and leisureliness to do justice to our subject. . . . Maybe I'll survive. Maybe."

The need to inform his friends and family, including Hunter colleagues, about his illness becoming its own tiresome chore. "It is like sending out invitations for something." Wright welcomed a heartfelt call from Franz in Ohio, and knew he must tell those with whom he felt closest. On December 18, he wrote his final letters to Robert Bly and to Leslie Silko. "I want to share the worst of this news with a very few people whom I admire and value the most," Wright told Silko, "and it is interesting to me that you stand very high in my mind among those—the people, I mean, who strike me as embodying in their own lives and work something—some value, some spirit—that I absolutely care about and believe in." Wright often spoke of his faith in an enduring community of writers. "One of the best things I have is my knowledge that you exist and that you are going on living and working."

Wright's doctors planned a series of twenty radiation treatments to try to shrink the tumor at the base of his tongue prior to surgery, which they scheduled for the end of January. "Enter these nazis into my insides," he despaired on December 20. "I could go crazy." The fatigue, pain, and nausea he had borne for weeks grew worse. With the days that remained to him at his desk, Wright returned to his journal, anxiously trying to complete the sequence of prose pieces he intended for *APR* and to finalize his manuscript. That fall, he had also begun work on a piece of fiction. Wright's therapist had heard him speak hesitantly of a novel, and Silver asked Anne after Wright's death if she had seen it. She recalled a folder with drafts and notes her husband had shown her, but she searched for it without success. Before entering the hospital, Wright destroyed many unfinished drafts and letters, leaving his briefcase almost empty.

Even when he found time to himself, classwork chores and unrelieved pain distracted him. He recalled "the wise, despairing, funny and hopeless old words" of Schopenhauer, who lamented the incursions of noise on anyone trying to do real thinking. Months earlier, in Venice, this same essay on "Noise" had been constantly on his mind; he had come to think of silence as a kind of sanctuary—a place apart from words, which now seemed to fail him. "Well, in any event, the silences are not impaired, and I am certainly working—a singing and moving—over in those places I can only call silences." Wright kept Picard's *World of Silence* close at hand. He had first written about Picard and Schopenhauer in his journal in May 1977, recognizing that "[w]e live in the world of silence while we die in the world of noise."

Three days before Christmas, Wright traveled with Anne to Lititz in eastern Pennsylvania, to stay with her sister Jane's family for the holiday. He attended an evening of carol singing at the local Moravian Church and enjoyed the company of his niece Laura and the quiet of the open countryside, "a glimpse of this gentle town on the other side of pain." He could eat little and felt terribly weak, but he found some peace while he was there. For Christmas, Wright gave Anne a gift from Holland he had kept hidden for months, a small decorative pin depicting a lizard, which he presented to her with a new poem titled "Yes, But." Begun in Verona in March, the poem is spoken to Annie and shares the potent energy and foreknowledge of death that can be felt in Keats's ode "To Autumn."

By late December, Wright had entered the same veiled territory that Keats traveled in the final months of his life, aware of the physical suffering that lay ahead of him. He felt cursed to spend "entire day[s] of sunlight" in the waiting rooms of doctors' offices. "Can anyone doubt that the City is reality itself, in all its delay, its smell, and its pain?" Surrounded by others afflicted by pain and uncertainty, beauty seemed held away from him, kept at a distance. In a quiet moment in their living room, Anne heard him say, "We really have a beautiful home"—as though seeing it for the first time.

On December 30, a Sunday, Gib and Kay Ruark came to New York and spent the afternoon with the Wrights at their apartment on Eighty-fifth Street. The couples even took a brief walk in the park beside the East River, and Wright recited his poem for Ruark, "With the Gift of a Fresh New Notebook I Found in Florence"—the last poem he brought to completion. "There wasn't a sense of leave-taking," Ruark recalled, despite the enormous concern they all shared. As he and Wright talked of a writer's responsibility to his readers, Wright reached for Edmund Wilson's *The Shores of Light* from the small shelf of books beside his chair and read from Wilson's acerbic essay "The Literary Worker's Polonius." Before they parted, Wright reminded Ruark of words attributed to Mozart as he lay dying, words that kept coming back to him: "And now I must go, when I have only just learned to live quietly."

———

On the last day of the year, as Wright sat for hours awaiting treatment, he confronted the fact of death in his journal. Back at his desk, he finally answered Galway Kinnell's letter from Hawaii. "From that first day when you walked into our Bethune Street apartment in 1965," Kinnell had written, "I felt a brotherhood with you." For Wright, too, Kinnell was "like a natural brother," as he told him in the last letter he ever wrote. "I've been working hard on something," Wright closes, "and if it turns out all right, I'll send it to you."

In early December, an invitation had come from Rosalynn and Jimmy Carter for a reception at the White House honoring American poets on

January 3, and Wright's doctors delayed his admission to the hospital until after the event. But insomnia and nausea compounded Wright's physical weakness; he could barely swallow and Anne now put all his food in a blender. The day before traveling to Washington, he again spent hours awaiting radiation treatment. In his journal—his handwriting more and more illegible—he despaired: "I am becoming one gray barnacle among the others here, as we shrink and shrink, each into his own pain. There is no doubt about the state I am in, and somehow I have always known that it existed. It [is] the place where all pain is, and no escape from any pain, and the worst of all things, and all the veils and illusions gone."

Wright tried to preserve his energy for the White House reception, an honor that meant a great deal to him. After flying to Washington, he and Anne met Roland Flint, who remained at Wright's side. More than five hundred poets and guests attended the reception and readings hosted by Rosalynn Carter in the final days of her husband's presidency, the first gathering of its kind at the White House. Twenty-one poets read from their work, and the Wrights joined the large audience in the East Room that evening to hear Stanley Kunitz, Josephine Jacobsen, and Robert Hayden. Wright and seventy-five other American poets were honored and shook hands with the president and first lady. To Grace Schulman, the Wrights appeared in good spirits, "even though he had a cloud over him." His appearance startled many who hadn't seen him in months. Wright told only a handful of close friends about the cancer, "but one look at him and people knew," Anne admitted.

One old friend whom he greeted recoiled from him, furious that Wright had come to spoil the occasion. James Dickey, one of the featured readers, walked quickly away from Wright and never spoke to him again. Philip Levine and Richard Hugo embraced Wright warmly, but after he was gone Hugo broke down in tears. "There are just three of us," he told Levine, acknowledging a kinship their poetry shared, a working-class ethos. "And now are we going to lose Jim?" Levine tried to reassure Hugo, convinced that Wright appeared strong and determined to fight the illness.

"It struck me that some of the very best poets present were those most conventional and old-fashioned in their appearance and behavior," Wright reflected in his journal that night after returning to New York. "Nobody read aloud more beautifully than Robert Hayden, and with greater dignity." The honor of attending the White House reception moved Wright deeply; Gib Ruark knew "he had a kind of boyish pride and awe in being there." At one point Wright turned and whispered to Anne, "If only my parents could see me now."

Following their return to New York, Wright was near collapse. Dawn still found him in the living room as light grew slowly above the East River, but it became harder for him to stand on his own. Anne focused solely on his care as they waited for a room to open up at Mount Sinai. Wright continued to be amazed by his wife's forbearance. The day after their trip to Washington, his reflections turned to Roethke's love poems.

> I can understand more clearly these days the impulse that led
> T. Roethke to the discovery of his great sequence of love poems,
> "Four for Sir John Davies," and some others that grew out of
> them. There in fact ought to be a separate publishing of the love
> poems of Roethke. They don't contain everything he had to say,
> but they contain a good deal of it, and they bring it to a very clear
> focus, and a clear music.
>
> What I've always owed to TR was sure, but difficult to state. . . .
>
> I really do hope that I make it through these current troubles,
> and go on writing about Annie. She is honest to God one of the
> great themes.

Wright struggled to finish reading a last batch of student term papers during his final weekend at home and lingered over his chapbook with Anne one more time. Upon returning from Washington, Wright had given up smoking—for the first time in more than thirty-seven years. He knew "it is the cause of most, if not all, of the trouble" and yet questioned his own resolve—in a future he could still believe in. Leslie Silko, in her letter responding to Wright's bitter news, grasped better than anyone how the loss of his voice distressed him as he imagined recovering from surgery. Looking past her own sorrow, Silko tried to shore up Wright's courage, but in his journal later that day he confessed how helpless and disoriented he felt. His tongue had become so swollen he could no longer drink a glass of water.

Before composing his last letter to Kinnell on December 31, Wright had been reading the proofs of Kinnell's new collection, *Mortal Acts, Mortal Words*. He noted in his journal how they shared "a certain very dark and almost speechless knowledge of death and pain," something "we have both been struggling through all our books to understand." In his letter, Wright despaired of explaining this to Kinnell, but he tried just the same. "For the truth is there is something terrible, almost unspeakably terrible, in our lives, and it demands respect, and, for some reason that seems to me quite insane, it doesn't hate us." On January 9, in his last journal entry—marred by crossed-out words, as his handwriting seemed to slur—Wright tried once more to articulate this strange, "almost speechless" understanding. "There must be a way to write down this simple truth, without being frivolous and morbid, that these phases of severe illnesses are life itself . . ." Like the words on the page, his thought and syntax begin to drift. He added two sentences later that day:

> Everything—object, person, idea—seems conspired to distract my attention. It is terrible upsetting—to lose

31

These are my hopes

January 12–March 25, 1980

. . . and in a real dark night of the soul it is always three o'clock in the morning, day after day.   —F. Scott Fitzgerald, *The Crack-Up*

On Saturday, January 12, 1980, Wright took a cab to the hospital, aided by his wife and a neighbor. He could no longer get out of bed without help. An examination of Wright's throat revealed that radiation, rather than shrinking the tumor, had caused it to swell, making surgery impossible. A young intern let slip to Anne the truth of her husband's condition before doctors spoke to them both the following day: at best, he might live six months. Wright understood that removing the tumor had been the one chance of saving his life.

Wright spent the next three days in intensive care, recuperating from a tracheotomy that made breathing easier but disabled his speech. At last, in the hospital, he received medication for the excruciating pain he had endured for weeks. As a consequence, however, Wright found it more difficult to focus on brief conversations or, on good days, periods of reading. Of three books he brought with him, only Orwell's *Collection of Essays* held his attention; he knew much of it by heart. After Carruth learned of Wright's hospitalization, he wrote every day, sometimes just a postcard. Wright received a heartfelt letter from Bly with a new poem, asking for his comments and suggestions. Bly tells him he is trying to learn from Wright's "ability to touch on grief, land on grief, settle on grief, like a heron on a shore, without being spooked by it." Bly's first poems about his father resulted from this new focus. "Our friendship and brotherhood has meant so much to me; I felt so lonely in the literary world until I met you, and you came out to the farm, and we had the chance to brood over horse-poems and Trakl poems together." Bly's sorrow is deepened by regret for the silence he had let stand between them.

The conditions at Mount Sinai proved bleak and, at times, distressing; the rooms were ill lit and dirty. Seeing her husband recovering from surgery without adequate care, Anne arranged for a private nurse to attend to him around the clock. Wright felt disoriented by his surroundings, with three other patients sharing a sixth-floor room partitioned by curtains. Though one west-facing window offered a glimpse of Central Park, patients could not see it from their beds. Losing the ability to speak oppressed Wright, and what little sleep he found was troubled by nightmares. Reduced to guttural, one-word responses, he now wrote brief messages on a lined pad of yellow paper. "It's far worse than I expected," he told Anne on January 15, three days after entering the hospital. In an unsteady hand, he asked for something to ease the pain; he repeated these requests almost every day. The couple comforted each other with the fiction of traveling to Italy once Wright could leave the hospital. In a letter to Hall, however, Anne made clear that her husband would not live long.

––––––

A succession of friends, family, and fellow poets came to Mount Sinai over the next two months. Gene Pugatch visited often, as did his wife, Vera; they encouraged Anne to keep her husband in the company of others, instead of seeking a private room. On the wall above his bed Anne tacked photos of Wright's sons and of their friends' children, and when visitors came he often rallied. Greeting Mark Strand and Philip Levine when they arrived on January 18, Wright scrawled a phrase W. C. Fields had intended for his epitaph: "I'd rather be in Philadelphia." When Edgar Doctorow entered the room a few days later, Wright printed four words in block capital letters on his pad, a satirical joke Doctorow had made of Romantic poets one autumn day at Kenyon thirty years before. "I could feel his eyes as he watched my face for my reaction. I read in the same round grade-school hand I remembered: 'The leaves are falling.'" Overwhelmed by the sight of his old friend, Doctorow offered to help Anne with the mounting medical costs.

Wright's brothers and their wives came to New York to see him at the end of January. Both Jack and Ted visited often during their brief stay, but Wright slept for hours on end, recuperating from the first of a series of chemotherapy treatments. To them he confided that it was "as truly horrible as any pain I've ever had. It's frightening." Self-conscious about his appearance and "old-fashioned" in his sense of decorum, Wright felt uncomfortable with women visiting him, yet Betty Kray and the poets Jean Valentine and Jane Cooper prevailed, and made a ritual of joining Anne every Friday morning at a coffee shop near the hospital.

As a week of bitter-cold weather set in, two poet visitors arrived on the first day of February. In perfume and furs, Carolyn Kizer brushed aside any objection and spent an hour with Wright, recalling their days in Seattle with Roethke and keeping up "a stream of jokes and reminiscences." To Kizer, Wright's haggard face and "shapely thin grey beard" made him look "phenomenally like Li Po." Later that day Robert Bly entered the room quietly and embraced Wright without speaking. Bly had not seen him in almost two years and understood the gravity of his illness. No rancor or misunderstanding remained between them that afternoon. Fighting off exhaustion, Wright was "alive and alert in a way he hadn't been for weeks and he never was again," Anne recalled. That evening, he confessed his gratitude for Bly's visit. "I was afraid Robert was gone for good, and I'm so relieved he's not." As Anne left, he added, "Today was good. I love you."

Leslie Silko's arrival on February 6 had a similar, heartening effect. Three decades later, Silko recalled Wright vividly: "a warmth, a kindness, and humanity—a gentleness and love for the world and its beings." Her visit calmed and encouraged him as he began a new stage of treatment. Administered with other chemotherapies, platinum injections made directly into the tumor were intended to shrink it, but the procedure proved more painful than any he had yet undergone. Roger Hecht—who visited often—witnessed Wright's distress following the first of these injections; the swelling in his throat made it difficult for him to breathe. After two weeks, Wright refused the treatments.

In the midst of this crisis, Janice Thurn arrived at the hospital to meet Wright for the first time, though they had corresponded for five years. Now twenty-three, Thurn had traveled from Minnesota to visit him. Of his new manuscript he wrote, "I had to leave the book way up in the middle of the air, and it may never have finished itself." Wright still considered keeping only forty poems in the book out of more than eighty he had gathered in typescript. He had asked Anne to bring his note-books and manuscript from home, and though he could rarely focus his thoughts, the book continued to obsess him.

Wright had asked to see Betsy Fogelman, who "tried to make New York sound glamorous and vital for him." She couldn't believe the pain and con-fusion he endured. Trying to buoy her husband's spirits, Anne proposed a series of fantastic plans for traveling in Italy and France later that spring. When Galway Kinnell arrived on February 15 from Hawaii, he read aloud the poems Wright chose from his "big green Madonna manuscript"—including "A Winter Daybreak Above Vence," in which Kinnell appears. Reading "Yes, But" for the first time, he immediately recognized "one of the great love poems of the twentieth century." Wright told Kinnell of his "beautiful visit" with Bly, who "spoke with great longing of his lost friendship with you, & his hope for a reconciliation. Personally, it would mean very much to me," he wrote, a gesture that helped reunite them.

Franz Wright arrived in New York in mid-February and visited with his father eleven times over the next three weeks. Nearly destitute and still living in Ohio, he welcomed Valentine's offer to stay in her apart-ment while she was out of town. "[Franz] seemed to get sharply angry when I told him of my illness," Wright had confided to Bly. "I'm sure it must scare him." When Franz recalled his visits to the hospital years later, the scene reminded him of his father's "To the Muse": the poem's images "horribly prefigure the kind of experience he had when he was dying himself." Once, as Franz rose to leave Wright's bedside, Ann San-fedele arrived and heard him say, "Dad, you're immortal, like Auden or Yeats." To her, Franz appeared numb, as if in a state of shock.

Wright wanted to see his sons, but he felt ashamed of his debility and appearance. Anne had pleaded with him to welcome Franz, but the sud-den arrival of Marshall from California distressed her. Marshall's phone calls that fall had always left Wright in anguish, and she refused to let Marshall see his father until both he and Franz spoke with Wright's psychiatrist. Marshall then agreed with the doctor that the meeting could prove disastrous. Apart from the impact on Wright, Silver worried about the effect on Marshall of seeing his father. Having neglected his medications since boarding a bus the week before, Marshall himself recognized the beginning of a manic episode in the cycle of his disorder. Anne insisted that the decision to prevent him from seeing his father was hers alone—Wright never knew that Marshall had come to New

York. When Franz visited his father on February 29, Wright asked him to look after his brother. "Be sure to keep in touch with Marsh. Have you heard anything at all of him?"

———

Wright's poem "The Journey" appeared in *The New Yorker* dated February 25, 1980—the last of his poems he saw in print. By this time, Anne and Wright's doctors had begun discussing his transfer to Calvary Hospital in the Bronx for hospice care, a recent alternative for patients with terminal illnesses. "As the days bleed past, it is clearer that a vacation (Sirmione) is going to be out of the question," he told Anne. "At least, I don't want to hope for one." He believed his transfer to Calvary was months away; once there, he imagined being able to work on his book. When Hall visited at the end of February, he sat at Wright's bedside reading poem after poem from the new manuscript silently to himself. Wright insisted that the book still needed "2 or 3 strippings" and asked Hall to phone di Capua to learn his plans for its publication.

The first week in March brought the coldest days of a long New York winter. When Frank MacShane visited the poet on Sunday, March 2, Wright recalled a phrase from Fitzgerald's *The Crack-Up* that Anne transcribed on his writing pad: "in a real dark night of the soul it is always three o'clock in the morning, day after day." But MacShane wanted to hear about his new poems; when they had met in Siena in July, he had heard of Wright's month of brilliant productivity in Sirmione. MacShane praised "The Journey," which he'd seen in *The New Yorker*, and asked, "Well, what do you think you'll call the book, Jim?" Suddenly, Wright knew the answer. "Isn't it becoming CLEAR that the title of the new book should be *This Journey*?" he jotted on his pad. "It takes in the whole book, unusually large, & its specific moment—*this* journey." The title's inclusiveness would allow the book to remain as it was, in all its abundance, permitting a diversity of forms and subjects. The moment came as a great relief.

But Wright remained anxious about his unfinished work. Michael di Capua refused to consider publishing the chapbook he had made with Anne as a separate volume. Though Anne pleaded with him in private to simply *tell* Wright he would do it, di Capua was obstinate. Anticipating his reluctance, Wright had thought of offering the collection to Stanley Moss's Sheep Meadow Press. When Moss heard of di Capua's rejection, he came to Mount Sinai to assure Wright he would publish the smaller book. Wright now worried only about his full collection. "I must complete the book," he told Anne on March 7, "if God wills it. And so I do believe it."

The next day Wright received a visit from a strikingly tall, young black man whom he hadn't seen in years; in fact, Garnie Braxton hadn't been half so tall the last time they had met. Now seventeen, Garnie entered the room, brushed aside the curtain, and embraced Wright without a word—much as Bly had done a month before. Braxton was one of the few people Wright had asked to see. "You're the only one who'll ever know what the sight of Garnie did for me," he told Anne that evening. "They were kindred souls," Anne believed, with "this strange humor and this dreadful sadness."

Despite medication and heavy fatigue, Wright continued to have trouble sleeping at night and came to fear the long hours of darkness. He asked the night nurse on duty to bring his book of Orwell's essays and to check on him often. Following surgery to attach a feeding tube shunt to his stomach, Wright begged her for "a plain old-fashioned tranquilizer." Wright allowed few visitors during his final days at Mount Sinai, and when Anne's nieces Karin and Laura arrived, he asked his wife to "prepare them" for his appearance. Though he no longer remained tethered to an intravenous drip, he had lost a shocking amount of weight.

On March 16, Kinnell came to Mount Sinai one last time before returning to Hawaii. Declaring his book "more or less done," Wright asked Kinnell to read the manuscript and send it on to Hall and Carruth. He remained apprehensive about showing it to Bly, given Bly's ruthless criticism in the past. He also shared the dedication he'd chosen for the book: "To the city of Fano / Where we got well / From Annie and me." The very name of the place had become invested with healing properties, after the shock of modern Bari the previous spring. For weeks Wright and Anne had fantasized together about returning to Fano, Verona, Sirmione, and Paris. When a nurse tried to learn his wishes concerning transfer into hospice care, she asked, "What would you like to do, Mr. Wright?" He took her question literally: "I'd like to go back to Italy." In private, without Anne present, Wright was more direct: "I would like to come to honorable terms with pain & death—these are surely distinct possibilities."

These words appear in Wright's hand on March 18, the day his son Franz turned twenty-seven. After learning of his father's transfer to hospice care three days later, Franz realized he must return to New York from Oberlin immediately. He appeared at David Young's home in distress, telling him he had no money for the long drive from Ohio. Though Young handed Franz his gasoline credit card, Franz did not make the trip in time to see his father again.

Anne arrived at Mount Sinai on the morning of March 21 to travel with her husband by ambulance to Calvary Hospital in the Bronx. To her, Mount Sinai seemed "dingier than ever." The day proved to be the windiest day of an already tempestuous month, with gusts over sixty miles per hour. Almost certainly, Wright contracted the pneumonia that hastened his death during his transfer between hospitals. Thankfully, Calvary could not have been more different from Mount Sinai; a nurse greeted them before they even stepped from the ambulance. When Anne entered the clean, brightly lit room after doctors had examined Wright, he smiled and wrote, "They didn't hurt me." It was the first time anyone else had combed his hair in more than two months, and Wright finally seemed relaxed. The doctor in charge of his care asked Anne for copies of Wright's books, telling her he wanted to know him as a person and not just a patient.

"Am I likely to die here?" Wright asked his doctor later that evening. "I am simply trying to meet reality. I want to finish my book, & I want my wife to be provided for. These are my hopes." The next day, as he sat alone in silence with Anne, he suddenly said: "Well, this is it"—as if to acknowledge what had gone unspoken between them. But at that moment a nurse entered and abruptly pulled the curtain back, cutting him short. While a succession of clergy—a priest, a rabbi, and a Protestant minister—came to his bedside at Calvary, Wright never asked for a Bible or showed concern over these visitations. Strangely, the one book he asked Anne to bring him was a critical treatise on tragic drama he had used in his Humanities classes at the University of Minnesota. When he rose into consciousness out of medicated sleep, he seemed adrift in time. Among the last entries in Wright's hand on his writing pad declares, in block capital letters: NERUDA FINEST SPANISH POET!

Only two visitors came to Calvary during Wright's last days: Donald Hall and Anne's niece Karin, who both arrived on a Saturday afternoon, March 22. "It was a relief to see him there after the squalor of Mt. Sinai," Hall later recalled. "Jim stared continually at Annie as if he memorized her to take her with him." Hall presented Wright with a new edition of his prose collection *String Too Short to Be Saved*, a book Wright admired as some of Hall's best writing. He insisted that both Hall and Karin sign their names on the title page of the book, a request that mystified them.

Wright then added his own inscription: "Don, talking to me about this book is like talking to someone about the fourteenth Chapter of Saint John. I love it that much.—Jim." Anne had brought to the hospital photocopied sets of Wright's manuscript that he wanted to send to the poet friends he trusted to finalize the work. With Hall present, Wright "improvised a small ritual" as he gave over a copy of his book. On the cover of the envelope he wrote, "I can do no more," adding the date beneath.

———

In his final days, Wright asked only for sleep, for "something stronger" to silence the unending pain. As he drifted in and out of consciousness in New York on Sunday, March 23, a small group gathered in the Martins Ferry Public Library to listen to his poems, most unaware that the poet lay gravely ill. Organized by the head librarian, John Storck, who had corresponded with Wright, the event inaugurated an annual poetry festival in Wright's honor. Dudley Wright's sister, Lillian Renzler, rose to defend her nephew's poems against claims that he had disparaged and disowned Martins Ferry. "Nobody loved the town more than Jim did. He was quiet as a boy. He often stood back and listened."

This sense of active, intense *listening* is evident throughout Wright's poetry, nowhere more than in the poem "Beginning." As he prepared to leave the Twin Cities and Minnesota for good on March 23, 1965—exactly fifteen years before his aunt spoke in Martins Ferry—Wright came across an old notebook from three years before, a time when he often visited the Blys' farm. He then began a new entry on one of the journal's blank pages. In successive entries dated April 30, 1962, he had written out initial drafts of three separate poems that would all appear in *The Branch Will Not Break*: "The Jewel," "To the Evening Star," and a poem completely unchanged from its first draft, "Beginning."

> The moon drops one or two feathers into the field.
> The dark wheat listens.
> Be still.
> Now.
> There they are, the moon's young, trying
> Their wings.
> Between trees, a slender woman lifts up the lovely shadow
> Of her face, and now she steps into the air, now she is gone

Wholly, into the air.
I stand alone by an elder tree, I do not dare breathe
Or move.
I listen.
The wheat leans back toward its own darkness,
And I lean toward mine.

To Wright the poem represented "the special intervention by the Muses"—a gift. Looking back at this sequence of poems—a day's work in his journal—Wright realized the importance of the notebook itself. "I suppose the notebook with its poems wasn't enough to save, much less justify, my life—my solitary and (as always) incommunicable disaster. But my little notebook was all I had."

Later that spring morning in 1965, Wright transcribed this long notebook passage into a letter of farewell to a woman he left behind in Minnesota. At the end of the letter he appended a new translation from the Spanish of Juan Ramón Jiménez titled "El viaje definitivo." Wright had translated the poem as a way of "asking the blessing of that great man" as he stood at a crossroads, beginning a period of wandering and uncertainty. He called his version "The True Journey at Last"; it begins: "And I shall depart. And the birds will remain, / Singing."

With the title of his final collection, *This Journey*, Wright asked one last blessing of Jiménez. The title appealed to him for many reasons, not least the permission it gave him to make a generous book. The words "journal" and "journey" derive from the Latin *diurnal*; they connote the daily act of writing, and the distance traveled in a day. The root word indicates the span of daylight, the present moment, and a day's work. In glass factories like the one Wright's father had worked in, a cycle of labor converting a quantity of glass into its finished product was called a "journey." The word also once referred to a military battle, particularly to a siege.

James Wright died of cancer of the tongue—hastened by pneumonia—on March 25, 1980, at 9:30 a.m. After weeks of gray weather and near-constant rain, the day broke fair. The doctor on duty that morning discovered Wright up and out of bed at dawn, walking around his room in an agitated state. "My book, my book," Wright kept repeating. Spring sunlight filled the windows and he could hear birds singing. He had always found daybreak the best time for writing.

One Last Look at the Adige:
Verona in the Rain

On Tuesday, March 25, 1980, the headline of the evening *Times-Leader* newspaper in Martins Ferry read: FERRY-BORN POET SUCCUMBS. When *The New York Times* printed Wright's obituary two days later, both "A Blessing" and "Two Hangovers" appeared in full. Calling Wright "an experimenter, an artist who was not afraid to change his ways of making poems," the *Times* writer credited the "sustained intensity" and "life-affirming quality of his work" that marked it "among the finest lyric poetry written since World War II."

That afternoon, March 27, Wright's funeral service was held at Riverside Church, in the same chapel where he and Anne had been married almost thirteen years before. "It was an astonishing outpouring," Sander Zulauf recalled; like so many others, he had not known the severity of Wright's illness, and his death was devastating. Following the ceremony, Betty Kray hosted a gathering at her apartment, a short walk from the church. News of Wright's death spread quickly through the community of American poets, a loss so sudden and unsettling that over the next few years many dozens of elegies appeared in magazines and books. Few American poets have been memorialized in verse as movingly or as often.

The poems written during his last months in Europe began to appear everywhere that summer, work Wright had submitted the previous fall from New York. In *Poetry, The Georgia Review, Harper's,* and *The*

Hudson Review, a dozen poems appeared, with many more featured in other journals over the coming months. In its May/June issue, *The American Poetry Review* finally published Wright's portfolio of nine poets he had asked to contribute more than five years before. The interview conducted by Dave Smith with Gibbons Ruark the previous September also appeared there for the first time. A feature on C. K. Williams's new poems from his forthcoming collection *Tar* included "On Learning of a Friend's Illness, for James Wright," one of the most heartfelt elegies to confront Wright's death in the first months after his passing.

In July 1980, Anne Wright joined Donald Hall at Galway Kinnell's home in Vermont to finalize the contents and sequence for Wright's last book. They also had comments on the manuscript from Robert Bly, Hayden Carruth, and Robert Mezey. "We left it as it was as much as possible," Anne recalled, though the ordering altered slightly and a handful of poems were removed from Wright's arrangement of the book. As published, *This Journey* included seventy-one poems and prose pieces from the last three years of his career, though some, like the title poem and "A Flower Passage," had been finding their form over the past decade.

After Anne submitted the manuscript to Michael di Capua in the fall of 1980, he held on to the book for more than eight months without comment. It took a call to Robert Giroux by Frank MacShane to finally get a reply. Di Capua offered such a meager advance that Anne withdrew the book from Farrar, Straus and Giroux. Philip Levine then approached Harry Ford about publishing Wright's posthumous collection, walking to Atheneum's offices immediately upon hearing of Anne's trouble with di Capua. After Ford declined the book, Levine contacted Jonathan Galassi, then an editor at Random House. Galassi welcomed the chance to publish *This Journey,* and the collection appeared in March 1982.

This Journey was embraced by a wide readership, and many reviewers offered assessments of Wright's entire career. "That sense of astonishment at being alive and at the way things disappear and change is one of the leitmotifs of the volume," Edward Hirsch recognized, writing in *The New York Times Book Review* in April 1982. That summer, Robert B. Shaw praised the book in *The Nation,* observing how "Wright achieved an elegiac tone as complex as Hardy's." Shaw marvels at how Wright felt so at ease in the old world of Europe. "Perhaps surprisingly, what comes through most vividly is the poet's sense of being at home. The stone vestal in the Forum, her shoulders 'pitted by winter,' turns on him a familiar face." Kathy Callaway, in a review for *Parnassus*, grasped the true originality evidenced by Wright's last poems and the direction his work was heading. "The solution is not elsewhere, or other, but in observation of the actual *with perfect attention*. This act is outside of time."

John Haag expands upon this insight in his memoir of Wright, responding to the poem "Inscription for the Tank." "Wright is not a confessional—ecstatics have little to confess—they celebrate this moment, this experience and its associations. It's not repetitions, it's impetus, the poet's energy flowing through the forms." The poems, as containers, not only convey a landscape or perception, but also hold to the deep intention of Wright's original feeling and experience. As Carruth observed, "Clarity of feeling was his mode of understanding." Marilyn Hacker, another poet interested in both metrical verse and open forms, praised "the expansive humanity" in Wright's poems, "an element of intelligent compassion—of noticing who the other person is, whoever that other person may happen to be—that is rare. I think the reader, herself or himself, in turn, feels recognized."

Hacker's perception helps explain the unique annual festival celebrating Wright's work that gathered every spring in Martins Ferry for twenty-seven years following his death. More than fifty distinguished poets took part in the James Wright Poetry Festival and many welcomed the chance to return, reading both Wright's work and their own before the hundreds who gathered in Martins Ferry each spring. In April 1990, as Farrar, Straus and Giroux, and Wesleyan University Press, published *Above the River*, Wright's complete poems, the tenth annual festival included more than a dozen poets in readings and seminars across four days. Stanley Kunitz spoke then of the enduring quality of Wright's poems.

> Behind all of them is the manifestation of his spirit, that psychic energy that flowed from him and that continues to flow from his poems. Jim Wright was a poet who was not putting on the page something for ornament or even for simple pleasure. He was writing in order to discover what he really believed in and what could save him. He was writing out of a primal need, and that distinguishes Jim from those who use poetry for technical or ornamental gratifications. It's a distinguishing characteristic. Poetry has to be a search for true values. It has to be an art of transformation and of transcendence.

The venue for the festival honored what Wright himself had cherished: his childhood place and her people. As Denise Levertov observed when she appeared in Martins Ferry for the fourth festival in 1984:

You can't separate the feeling for the place from the feeling of the lives of the people that live in the place—unfulfilled lives, twisted lives, oppressed lives. And that is very, very strong in his poetry. And it wouldn't be so strong and so passionate if you didn't feel his own roots in the place. He's not speaking about "them" or "you." He's speaking about "I" and "us" in his poems, of all Ohio, I think. And he's speaking with love and grief. *That's* what it is. Love and grief.

Gerald Stern, a featured reader at three different Wright Poetry Festivals, recognizes the importance of Wright's *voice*. "It's penetrating. It doesn't suffer fools. It's tolerant, and generous, but insistent on itself. It seems to me a continuance of Roethke's voice." But beyond the terror and the sadness in the poems, Stern believes that Wright held fast to an "affirmative view." Stern admires Wright's "extraordinary mind" and the intellectual power that underwrites every line in his poetry. Robert Bly, who has done more than any other poet to secure Wright's legacy, takes Stern's insight further. "Wright was born with a superb literary intelligence—that's the most amazing fact about him, I think—so fine that it cannot be distinguished from a musical intelligence."

"We hunger for neatness of pattern," Walter Jackson Bate wrote in his exemplary biography of John Keats. This human impulse suggests one reason many readers believe that Wright's posthumous poems are shadowed by his foreknowledge of death, as though this helps explain their elegiac tone and consummate mastery. But the facility and strength evidenced by the poems of *This Journey* had been won over a lifetime, four decades of devotion to his craft. "I do think the book after it would have been more wonderful still," Kinnell reflected. Wright had only just begun the next chapter in his work.

Anne Wright lived in the apartment she had shared with her husband on East Eighty-fifth Street for another thirty-six years. In May 2015, as she prepared to leave New York, she found Wright's leather wallet among the mementos and possessions of his she had kept. Folded within an inner pocket she discovered a letter from Sonjia Urseth dated April 30, 1959. This one-page note is a gesture of thanks; Urseth had just learned that two of her short stories would appear in an international journal—her first publications. It is a fascinating, candid expression of her conflicting reactions upon hearing the news, her self-doubt mingled with pure joy, what she describes as "this beautiful, unbelievable, divided emotion of fear and delight." Wright understood her confusion, and added his own words in the margin of her letter. "What a dazzling gift for conveying what the life of the emotions *really* is—a rich chaos of contradiction, insoluble in rationalistic terms, horrible in its agony, yet somehow fiercely precious beyond grief, or tears."

Notes

All of the interviews and transcriptions quoted herein are by the author, unless otherwise noted. A scholarly edition of this biography, with expanded content, footnotes, and citations, will be available in the Elmer L. Andersen Library, Literary Manuscripts/ Upper Midwest Literary Archives, at the University of Minnesota, Minneapolis, where Wright's personal papers are held. The collections of Robert Bly and Carol Bly are also part of the Andersen Library Archives.

All of Wright's poems and prose pieces referenced herein, unless otherwise noted, can be found in *Above the River: The Complete Poems* (New York: Farrar, Straus and Giroux; and Middletown, CT: University Press of New England, 1990).

James Wright: An Annotated Bibliography by William H. Roberson (Lanham, MD: Scarecrow Press, 1995), lists and annotates published writings by and about Wright. This work was subsequently corrected and expanded in "A James Wright Research Guide," a dissertation by William Todd Copeland (PhD dissertation, Texas A&M University, May 2000).

Abbreviations

Clear Word *The Pure Clear Word: Essays on the Poetry of James Wright*, ed. Dave Smith (Urbana: University of Illinois Press, 1982).

CP James Wright, *Collected Prose*, ed. Anne Wright (Ann Arbor: University of Michigan Press, 1983).

Delicacy *The Delicacy and Strength of Lace: Letters Between Leslie Marmon Silko and James Wright*, ed. Anne Wright (Minneapolis: Graywolf, 2009). Graywolf first published this collection in 1986.

HotL *James Wright: The Heart of the Light*, ed. Peter Stitt and Frank Graziano (Ann Arbor: University of Michigan Press, 1990). This collection of critical essays and reviews includes a select bibliography of secondary sources.

In Defense	James Wright, *In Defense Against This Exile: Letters to Wayne Burns*, ed. John R. Doheny (Seattle: Genitron Press, 1985).
JW	James Wright
LK memoir	Liberty Kovacs, *Liberty's Quest* (Bandon, OR: Robert D. Reed Publishers, 2008).
Maley	Saundra Rose Maley, *Solitary Apprenticeship: James Wright and German Poetry* (Lewiston, NY: Mellen University Press, 1996).
WP	James Wright, *A Wild Perfection: The Selected Letters of James Wright*, ed. by Anne Wright and Saundra Rose Maley, with Jonathan Blunk (New York: Farrar, Straus and Giroux, 2005).

Epigraph

vii *"We are not human"*: Robert J. Furey, *The Joy of Kindness* (New York: Crossroads, 1993), 138.

Prologue: At a point of beginning

3 *"Two huge molten"*: JW letter to Sonjia Urseth, November 16, 1958.

3 *"There is something"*: JW letter to Sonjia Urseth, July 29, 1957.

4 *"this crazily organized study"*: JW letter to Sonjia Urseth, December 21, 1958.

4 *"trapped by the very thing"*: JW letter to Theodore Roethke, August 5, 1958, in *WP*, 137.

4 *"denying the darker"*: JW letter to Donald Hall, July 25, 1958, in *WP*, 131.

4 *"ploddingly 'sincere'"*: James Dickey, "In the Presence of Anthologies," *The Sewanee Review* 66 (April–June 1958): 294–314.

4 *"generosity is not only"*: JW letter to James Dickey, July 6, 1958.

5 *"paranoid and . . . though minor"*: JW letter to James Dickey, July 20, 1958.

5 *"howling at me"*: JW letter to Donald Hall, January 15, 1959, in *WP*, 251.

5 *"absolutely fixed"*: JW letter to Robert Bly, July 22, 1958, in *WP*, 111.

6 *"the old tradition"*: *The Fifties* No. 1 (July 1958): 36. Bly's polemic served to announce the kinds of poems *The Fifties* would publish; the back cover listed two dozen writers in other languages whose work would appear in future issues, with original texts facing translations. Barbed satires and essays of criticism were also central to the magazine. In all, eleven issues of *The Fifties*—soon, *The Sixties*—appeared on an irregular basis over the next fourteen years. It became one of the most provocative and influential magazines of its time.

7 *"to build a genuine"*: JW letter to Robert Bly, July 23, 1958, in *WP*, 121.

7 *"failure . . . voice of oneself"*: JW letter to Hall, July 25, 1958, in *WP*, 131.

7 *"Thank you immensely"*: Robert Bly letter to JW, August 1, 1958. See "Robert Bly and James Wright: A Correspondence," *The Virginia Quarterly Review*, vol. 81, no. 1 (Winter 2005), 119. Robert Bly papers, Andersen Library Archives.

8 *"Your own phrase"*: JW letter to Robert Bly, August 6, 1958, in *WP*, 140.

8 *"shortened by about"*: JW letter to Robert Bly, August 26, 1958, in *WP*, 163.

9 *"I worry my can off"*: Theodore Roethke letter to JW, August 16, 1958. See *Selected Letters of Theodore Roethke*, ed. Ralph J. Mills Jr. (Seattle: University of Washington Press, 1968), 220.

9 *"take about two weeks . . . Shakespeare"*: JW letter to Theodore Roethke, August 18, 1958, in *WP*, 157.

9 *"everything exploded"*: JW letter to James Dickey, July 25, 1958, in *WP*, 124.

9 *"the courage to try"*: JW letter to James Dickey, August 25, 1958, in *WP*, 159.

9 *"perfection of the life"*: William Butler Yeats, "The Choice," in *Collected Poems* (New York: Macmillan, 1956), 242.

9 *"I said that I felt"*: JW to Robert Bly, August 26, 1958.

10 *"in the basement"*: JW letter to Donald Hall, August 15, 1958, in *WP*, 153.

1. That is my country, that river

13 *"That is my country, that river"*: JW reading, Colorado State University, Fort Collins, May 16, 1969. Printed in *Georgia Review* 55, no. 3 (Fall 2001): 432. Transcribed, edited, and introduced by the author.

13 *"[My parents] are sturdy"*: JW letter to Mary Oliver, September 16, 1965, in *WP*, 336.

13 *"the sense, the vista"*: JW, "Childhood Sketch," August 1978, in *CP*, 334.

13 *"among the brief"*: JW, "Redemption" (uncollected); *The American Poetry Review* 2, no. 4 (July/August 1973).

14 *"'Give up hope'"*: Interviews with Liberty Kovacs, June 13, 2001, and October 17, 2006.

14 *"peculiar kind"*: JW interview, September 30, 1979, in *CP*, 194.

14–15 *"I have done . . . scar."*: JW, draft typescript of "Childhood Sketch," August 1978.

15 *"I had lived"*: JW, "Childhood Sketch," in *CP*, 331. See interview with Stanley Kunitz, April 22, 1990. Kunitz understood Wright's acute sense of place. "It was enormously important to him, and just as he had a phenomenal memory for poems, he had an astonishing clarity of perception about the places he had occupied. They spoke to him."

15 *"beautiful"*: JW, "Beautiful Ohio." See Allan W. Eckert, *That Dark and Bloody River: Chronicles of the Ohio River Valley* (New York: Bantam, 1995).

16 *"River of Blood"*: Ibid.

16 *"a good waggon Road"*: Ibid. Quoting Zane's petition for support from the fledgling American Congress.

17 *By the 1870s . . . the western bank*: See Annie C. Tanks, ed., *A Town of Grandeur: Essays on the History of Martins Ferry, Ohio* (Martins Ferry, OH: Martins Ferry Public Library, 1987).

17 *"honest-to-God"*: JW, "Childhood Sketch," 331. Wright's mother, Jessie Lyons, spoke of her family's French and Native American ancestry, a common heritage in the northern Appalachians.

18 *Lyons's violent temper*: Wright's sister, Marge Wright Pyle, related a story of Rawley, in a rage, putting his son Willy's head on a chopping block before Biddy intervened. Marge Wright Pyle, interview recorded by Peter Stitt with Anne Wright, May 9, 1995. Original tape courtesy of Anne Wright, transcribed by the author.

18 *"slaved"*: JW, "Childhood Sketch," 332.

18 *"almost obscene gift"*: JW journal, February 19, 1969.

19 *James Arlington Wright*: Dudley named his second son after an uncle, while his middle name belonged to a family friend. Wright's kinship with Edwin Arlington Robinson thus began as pure coincidence. Robinson came to learn that his middle name had been literally pulled from a hat.

19 *"part of my spirit"*: JW reading, Florida Institute of Technology, Melbourne, FL, February 15, 1973. The Poetry Collection of the University Libraries, University at Buffalo, the State University of New York.

20 *"I was born"*: "Childhood Sketch," 330.

20 *"It was like hopscotch"*: Marge Wright Pyle, interviewed by Peter Stitt with Anne Wright, May 9, 1995. "By the time I was sixteen, I had lived in fifteen or sixteen houses." One evening, Dudley returned from work to find that Jessie had moved the family again; he had to ask his mother-in-law where they'd gone.

20 *portrait taken from life*: Interview with Jack Wright, June 21, 2001.

20 *"stopping to look"*: Interview with Anne Wright, May 28, 2003, quoting Jessie Wright.

21 *"hoboing and hopping"*: Interview with Paul Pyle, April 15, 2005.

21 *Vast neighborhoods*: Urban renewal initiatives leveled the area in the early 1960s, and it is hard to imagine the varied communities and buildings that once occupied this land. Churches, bars, restaurants, and tenement buildings were packed between foundries and factories, including two different rail lines and a streetcar track. A four-lane highway now separates the upper part of town from the river.

22 *"I have a reasonably"*: JW, "Epistle from the Amphitheatre."

22 *A friend of Wright's*: Interview with Lemoyne Krone, April 19, 2002.

22 *"children of the blast furnaces"*: JW, "Childhood Sketch," 333.

23 *"a kind of a poor-man's beach"*: Ted Wright, NPR phone interview conducted by Noah Adams, 1990. From "A Poet and His Hometown," first broadcast over National Public Radio in November 1990.

23 *"hideous Ohio phrase"*: JW interview, September 24, 1970, in *CP*, 153; see LK memoir, 108.

23 *Both Jim and Ted*: Marge Wright Pyle believed this contributed to Jim's nervous breakdown when he was fifteen. "I think just seeing something like that and not being able to do anything about it, it just knotted him up and he didn't know how to let that hard hurt out." Pyle, NPR interview, 1990. From "A Poet and His Hometown." See also JW, "Childhood Sketch," *CP*, 332; "To a Defeated Savior"; "The River Down Home."

24 *"up on the hill"*: Interview with Dr. Thomas Hodge, October 17, 2006. The farmer, named "Bluthardt," posted a sign on the fence surrounding his orchards: "Pray as you enter. Shotgun law."

24 *Wright "discovered"*: "A Sketch of the Life of James Wright," May 1946.

24 *"he could just go"*: Hodge, October 17, 2006. Wright gave Hodge credit for lending him Byron's *Complete Works*, but Hodge insisted that Wright chose books entirely on his own. Wright also borrowed collections of Greek and Roman myths. JW interview, September 30, 1979, *CP*, 197.

24 *even Jack*: Jack Wright, unpublished draft memoir, 2002.

24 *"One of the strangest"*: JW, "Contributor's Note," *The Fifties* No. 2 (1959). The second of two stanzas from William Blake's "Thames and Ohio" reads:

> Though born on the cheating banks of Thames,
> Though his waters bathed my infant limbs,
> The Ohio shall wash his stains from me:
> I was born a slave, but I go to be free.

For Blake, the Ohio signified the many utopian communities in the New World that were advertised and promoted throughout England in the early 1800s.

24 *"solitary and morose"*: JW, "Childhood sketch," *CP*, 333.

25 *His trouble began*: Elizabeth Starkey Lyons died on September 26, 1942, at the age of eighty.

25 *One was*: The Bible Unmasked: Joseph Lewis, *The Bible Unmasked* (New York: Freethought Press, 1926); Hodge, October 17, 2006.

25 *"When he came home"*: Interview with Helen Wright, April 21, 2002.

25 *She blamed another*: Sir James Hopwood Jeans, *The Mysterious Universe* (New York: Macmillan, 1932).

26 *"In about my fourteenth"*: JW application to Kenyon College; in Maley, 18.

26 *As Wright later confessed*: Kovacs, June 13, 2001.

26 *"He became possessed"*: JW, "A Sketch of the Life" (1946). In a draft of this auto-biography, Wright imitates Thomas Wolfe's "Young Faustus" section in the novel *Of Time and the River*. JW high school notebook, spring 1946.

26 *"where he met"*: Ibid.

26 *"a time when I"*: JW letter to Diane Wakoski, March 20, 1978, in *WP*, 496.

27 *"abominated the Ohio Valley"*: JW letter to Wayne Burns, November 30, 1957, in *In Defense*, 29, and *WP*, 71.

27 *"that unspeakable rat-hole"*: JW letter to Robert Bly, July 23, 1958, in *WP*, 113.

27 *Later in life*: Interview with Anne Wright, May 28, 2003. Charles Dickens was tormented by similar dreams long after his extraordinary success.

2. And I got out

29 *He stands at*: See Maggie Anderson, "The River Down Home: James Wright and My Hillbilly Father," *Ohioana Quarterly* 44, no. 1 (Spring 2001): 8. For Anderson, Wright's poem shows his awareness of close-knit Appalachian communities and uses the diction of a townsperson speaking in public, in front of strangers.

30 *Hanson would appear*: See, for example, "Sonnet—Peace"; appendix to *WP*, 556.

30 *"This was wartime"*: Interview with Richard Hodge, October 17, 2006.

30 *"a hardnosed, tough bunch"*: Interview with William Holbrook, April 22, 2002.

30 *With Wright as captain*: Interviews with Lemoyne Krone, April 19, 2002; Holbrook, April 22, 2002; Harley "Pete" Lannum, April 24, 2002. As Lannum recalled, a Bellaire opponent once made the mistake of punching Wright, trying to intimidate him. "After the next play that guy was out cold. I don't know what Jim did, but that guy didn't get up. He had a lot of sides to him, Jim did."

30 *"that the use of"*: JW, Ohioana Arts Award acceptance speech, October 1960.

30 *"I have never written"*: JW, "Childhood Sketch," *CP*, 334. The last collection of poems Wright saw into print—*To a Blossoming Pear Tree*—is dedicated, in part, to Sheriff, who learned of Wright's tribute before she died at the age of ninety in 1977.

30 *strategy for survival*: JW letter to Robert Bly, November 11, 1958, in *WP*, 179.

31 *"I was a good student"*: Interview with Susan Lamb, April 16, 2005.

31 *"I cannot write"*: Untitled sonnet, fall 1945. *Gettysburg Review* 3, no. 1 (Winter 1990): 27.

31 *"You made warm mention"*: JW, "Sonnet: Response," ibid., 31. See also "Lame Apollo" and "To Critics, and to Hell with Them," which Wright signed "J. Wolfing-ham Wright."

31 *"Fanny" as his inspiration*: See, for example, "Sleep and Music," a sonnet dated March 14, 1946.

32 *"a desire for . . . Nobody ever does"*: JW letter to Sonjia Urseth, July 8, 1957.

32 *"He was very intense"*: Lamb, April 16, 2005.

33 *"I could always tell"*: Interview with Annie Tanks, April 19, 2002.

33 *"Suicide Note"*: JW high school notebook, spring 1946.

33 *"A Sketch of the Life"*: JW high school notebook, spring 1946. A handwritten draft of this memoir is preceded by an outline of Thomas Wolfe's biography and synopses of his novels.

33 *"a beautiful Greek girl"*: Interview with Gladys Van Horne, April 20, 2002.

33–34 *"That's how we met . . . more than anything else"*: Interview with Liberty Kovacs, June 13, 2001.

34 *"a confident sunburst"*: Alan Natali, "Portrait of the Artist," *Ohio Magazine* 10 (May 1987): 44.

34 *The only celebration*: Gladys Van Horne, *Wheeling News-Register*, April 29, 1988.

34 *"serious reading bouts"*: Interview with Jack Wright, June 21, 2001.

34 *"Think of it!"*: JW letter to Susan Lamb, July 6, 1946.

3. Between the river and the rice fields

35 *"Between the river"*: JW letter to Lamb, August 9, 1949; *WP*, p. 19.

35 *"I had quite a time"*: Interview with Susan Lamb, April 16, 2005.

35 *"It seems that I pour"*: JW letter to Susan Lamb, September 3, 1946, in *WP*, 10.

36 *"But, being my mother"*: JW letter to Jessie Lyons Wright, August 5, 1946, in *WP*, 9.

36 *"I don't give a damn"*: JW letter to Susan Lamb, August 25, 1946.

36 *"I am not a useful citizen"*: JW letter to Susan Lamb, August 31, 1946.

36 *"I experienced some"*: JW to Lamb, September 3, 1946.

36 *"lofty visions"*: JW letter to Susan Lamb, August 19, 1946.

37 *"symbolic to me"*: JW to Lamb, September 3, 1946.

37 *"practical knowledge of"*: JW letter to Susan Lamb, October 4, 1946.

37 *"All my writings"*: JW letter to Susan Lamb, October 10, 1946.

37 *"to see my folks"*: JW letter to Susan Lamb, November 13, 1946.

37 *"the marvelously wild"*: JW letter to Susan Lamb, November 25, 1946.

37 *"I took the way"*: JW letter to Sonjia Urseth, June 2, 1959.

37 *"the melancholy ecstasy"*: JW application to Kenyon College; in Maley, 18.

38 *"Catullus is as dear"*: JW letter to Elizabeth Willerton, January 6, 1947, in *WP*, 14.

38 *"I still have a love"*: JW letter to Susan Lamb, January 7, 1947.

38 *"some hole in"*: JW letter to Susan Lamb, January 13, 1947.

38 *"I pitched over"*: JW letter to Mary McLean, June 5, 1974.

38 *"I am more utterly"*: JW letter to Susan Lamb, February 24, 1947.

38 *"the bleak barn-like"*: JW letter to Susan Lamb, February 28, 1947.

39 *"Wonderful ear"*: Marginalia in Wright's personal copy. James Joyce, *A Portrait of the Artist as a Young Man* (New York: Modern Library, 1944), 27.

39 *Oscar Williams published*: Oscar Williams, ed., *A Little Treasury of Modern Poetry* (New York: C. Scribner's Sons, 1946).

39 *"By God, I am"*: JW to Lamb, February 28, 1947.

39 *"unbelievably pleasant"*: JW letter to Susan Lamb, March 20, 1947.

40 *No matter how hard*: Jessie had kept a popular book of farm husbandry close at hand for a decade: M. G. Kains's *Five Acres and Independence—A Practical Guide to the Selection and Management of the Small Farm* (New York: Greenberg, 1935). But in choosing the site the Wrights made many of the common mistakes the book warned against.

40 *"It had lain fallow"*: JW letter to Susan Lamb, August 9, 1949, *WP*, 23.

40 *"That farm was just"*: Marge Wright Pyle, interviewed by Peter Stitt with Anne Wright, May 9, 1995.

41 *"the fates"*: JW letter to Susan Lamb, July 1949.

41 *"I am now situated"*: JW letter to Susan Lamb, December 4, 1947.

4. Bitterly hard, sincere work

42 *"Bitterly hard"*: JW letter to Lamb, July 1949. "I have to keep in mind that I am financially hanging by a string, and that the only compensation for not being a rich man's son is the production of hours of bitterly hard, sincere work."

42 *"a gathering place"*: Jack Furniss, *Kenyon Alumni Bulletin*, Spring 1982 (vol. 6, no. 2).

42 *"his grave, punctilious"*: Richard Lee Francis, letter to *Kenyon Alumni Bulletin*, April 6, 1980, in Maley, 32.

43 *"The faculty wanted"*: Interview with E. L. Doctorow, March 19, 2002.

43 *"were a little bit"*: Interview with Dr. Frank LeFever, January 30, 2003.

43 *"to bring literary"*: Thomas Daniel Young, *Gentleman in a Dustcoat: A Biography of John Crow Ransom* (Baton Rouge: Louisiana State Press, 1976), 386.

43 *"vigorously 'explicated' poems"*: George Lanning, *The Kenyon Collegian*, 1964, in Maley, 32.

43 *"with nothing in his makeup"*: Jack Furniss, quoted in D. Campbell, *The Columbus Citizen Journal*, May 31, 1980.

43 *"He had a lot of trouble"*: Doctorow, March 19, 2002.

44 *"experimental compositions"*: JW journal, July 1949.

45 *"I lived for his letters"*: LK memoir, 146.

45 *"He had a round face"*: E. L. Doctorow, "James Wright at Kenyon," in *Jack London, Hemingway, and the Constitution: Selected Essays, 1977–1992* (New York: Random House, 1993), 183.

46 *"blustering, Baron"*: Interview with Nicholas Crome, April 24, 1999.

46 *"the constant company"*: John Crowe Ransom, preface to *The World's Body*, quoted in Maley, 39.

46 *"It was not the classes"*: Robert Lowell, *Collected Prose* (New York: Farrar, Straus and Giroux, 1987), 18.

46 *Ransom found*: See Ian Hamilton, *Robert Lowell: A Biography* (New York: Random House, 1982), 56.

46 *"a certain crude energy"*: JW letter to Elizabeth Willerton Esterly, May 10, 1949, in WP, 16.

47 *"campus misfits"*: Edward Spievak, in Maley, 46.

47 *"We were all just shattered"*: Doctorow, March 19, 2002.

47 *"Sonnet"* and *"The Lover"*: Hika [Kenyon College student literary magazine] 14 (Commencement) [May 1949], 18.

48 *There are thousands*: Wright celebrated Baudelaire, Auden, Shelley, Hart Crane, Frost, Henry James, Pound, Keats, Dostoevsky, Basho, and Thomas Campion. There is a "Late Song for García Lorca" and a "Lament for Robinson Jeffers, Who Mourned Ossian." He also honors Grieg, Bach, Beethoven, Ravel, Tchaikovsky, and "Mozart in the Slag Heaps."

48 *Wright revered Patchen's poems*: See, for example, Patchen's "O Fiery River" and "May I Ask You a Question, Mr. Youngstown Sheet & Tube?" In "For the Mother of My Mother's Mother," Patchen writes (in 1943): "Jenny, my darling Jenny . . . /

Black are the leaves that fall / On your grave." Kenneth Patchen, *Selected Poems* (New York: New Directions, 1957), 14, 37, 43.

49 *"There is no reason"*: JW journal, September 1949.

49 *"with some measure"*: JW letter to Susan Lamb, August 9, 1949, in *WP*, 17.

49 *"big three-story house"*: JW letter to "Mrs. Urseth," Sonjia's mother, August 1, 1959.

50 *Wright also read the Spanish*: Sy Weissman, in Maley, 50. Wright had studied Spanish in his last two years of high school, his only formal training in the language.

50 *"a language was not"*: Doctorow, "James Wright at Kenyon."

50 *"You'd find him"*: Ibid.

50 *"They loved to make Jim laugh"*: Doctorow, March 19, 2002. "He was extremely generous with his friends, in terms of the attention he paid."

50 *"I'm so damned"*: JW letter to Susan Lamb, December 13, 1949.

50 *"At the present moment"*: JW letter to Susan Lamb, December 25, 1949.

5. Writing like a Dionysian maniac

51 *"Rilke is as musical"*: JW letter to Elizabeth Willerton Esterly, January 1, 1950, in *WP*, 27. JW's translation is of Rilke's "Herbst" ("Autumn").

51 *In one of Wright's notebooks*: See JW notebooks, June 1949.

52 *"We talked politics"*: Interview with E. L. Doctorow, March 19, 2002.

52 *"in a fit"*: *The Times Leader* (Martins Ferry), June 17, 1950. In a letter to John Nims dated October 15, 1979, Wright refers to Doty as "a distant family friend."

52 *"He studied hard"*: Marge Wright Pyle, interviewed by Peter Stitt with Anne Wright, May 9, 1995.

52 *"with pretty clear"*: JW letter to Jack Furniss, July 18, 1950.

52 *He also reread*: JW letter to Jack Furniss, August 1950, in *WP*, 35.

52 *"how beautiful Ohio"*: Interview with Jack Wright, June 21, 2001.

52 *"The most characteristic"*: JW letter to Al Herzing, August 8, 1950.

53 *Wright even attempted*: See Melvin LaFountaine letter to JW, September 18, 1950; and JW, "The Webs," August 1950.

53 *"Coffin's tastes"*: Roger Hecht, in Maley, 44.

53 *"I used to study"*: JW letter to Prairie Dern, July 15, 1965.

53 *"sitting in the fading"*: Richard Lee Francis, *Kenyon Alumni Bulletin* 4, no. 2 (Spring 1980).

54 *"responded with a luminous delight"*: JW, "Letter to Mr. Bromitch [*sic*, David Bromwich] on Mr. Frost" [typescript, unsent], January 1977.

54 *Her letters show*: Interview with Liberty Kovacs, October 17, 2006. "Emotionally, I was so distraught, and he was my lifeline. I couldn't go home. And he was the only one I had." Following her divorce from Wright and remarriage in February 1965, Kovacs destroyed all of Wright's letters to her.

54 *Wright befriended*: Interview with Dr. Eugene Pugatch, February 2, 2000. Pugatch matriculated in the last class of students recruited by Norris Rahming, who had encouraged ethnic and social diversity at Kenyon. As Kenyon's professor of art, Rahming focused his recruitment on Boston, New York, and Philadelphia, to afford him the chance to visit the first-rate museums in these cities.

54 *"Jim loved classical music"*: Interview with Nicholas Crome, April 24, 1999.

55 *"The big snow storm"*: Jessie Lyons Wright letter to JW, December 4, 1950.

55 *"Jim would be"*: Tony Stoneburner, private journal, spring 1951; and interview with Stoneburner, April 16, 2009.

55 *"He talked about her"*: Interview with Sy Weissman, May 4, 2005.

56 *translated "naturally"*: Roger Hecht, interviewed by Saundra Maley, August 24, 1989; transcribed by author from original tape recording. Hecht believed Wright did this work solely for himself, work reflected in the severe, classical discipline of his first two books.

56 *"The Viennese atmosphere"*: JW Kenyon class notebook, March 1951.

56 *"hard-won simplicity"*: JW essay, with Ransom's comments, April 1951.

56 *"Jim's was a boisterous"*: Eugene "Sam" Turner letter to Saundra Maley, July 27, 1992.

57 *For all his defiant wit*: Doctorow, March 19, 2002. "Jim loved Roy Acuff and that whole Grand Ole Opry culture. He was very ironic about this material but he loved the innocence of it, the kind of purity it had, and the naiveté. After all, he was a serious poet, and singing these lyrics—about the 'Great Speckled Bird' and the 'Wreck on the Highway'—was a constant font of good humor. . . . Depending on the mood, he loved to sing Roy Acuff songs, as much as he did Schubert lieder. The conflict he must have felt was expressed in this way—there are the polarities, right there. There's always a certain amount of guilt when you pull yourself up out of your origins."

57 *Wright abandoned*: On the cover, Wright scrawled: "for hart crane / or anybody, for that matter."

57 *Both poems had come*: JW interviewed by Doris B. Wiley, *The Bulletin* (Philadelphia), November 22, 1978. "Lonely" would later appear in *Saint Judas* with the title "Paul."

58 *sixteen different poets*: Including Rilke (forty), Heine, Storm, Hesse, Goethe, Hölderlin, Nietzsche, and Trakl. See Maley, 7.

58 *As Hecht boarded*: Maley, 66, no. 53.

58 *Liberty also visited . . . "letting go of him"*: LK memoir, 152, 162; and Kovacs, October 17, 2006.

58 *"Jim was always"*: Weissman, May 4, 2005.

59 *"I was at Kenyon"*: Interview with Robert Mezey, October 14, 1999. Like Wright's before, Mezey's admiration for Hardy's poetry was "quickly reinforced by John Crowe Ransom's course in modern poetry, who's probably the best critic Hardy has had."

59 *"The process of doing it"*: Ibid.

59 *Wright's astonishing memory*: In interviews, both Jack Wright and Jim's Kenyon classmate Frank LeFever separately used the phrase "phonographic memory" to characterize Wright's ability. Poetry had all the cues he needed: the modulation of consonants and vowels over a ground beat of rhythm with overlying emotional textures. See Aniruddh D. Patel, *Music, Language, and the Brain* (Cambridge, UK: Oxford University Press, 2008), 86: "Music and speech may have a substantial degree of overlap" in the brain.

59 *He could recite*: The charismatic English professor Denham Sutcliffe boasted of having memorized all of Milton's *Paradise Lost*. Wright loved to imitate *Sutcliffe* reciting Milton.

59 *"It's as if"*: Weissman, May 4, 2005.

60 *Wright was furious*: In a course notebook from mid-November, explosions of rage punctuate Wright's class notes during a lecture by Coffin. "Son of a bitch. I hate to be annihilated like that. I could cut a man's throat for doing that to me. . . . What the hell do I care for their stinking degrees?"

60 *"Jim was just absolutely"*: Doctorow, March 19, 2002.

60 *"He couldn't be casual"*: Ibid.

60 *Just before classes ended*: Interviews with Mezey, October 14, 1999; Weissman, May 4, 2005. William Goldhurst, in Maley, 48.

60 *"the interplay of"*: Stoneburner private journal, October 1951. Wright quoted Schopenhauer and Bernard Shaw to support breaking off his engagement, but he feared
his own conscience and what others would say.

61 *"I can't go through with it"*: Interview with Liberty Kovacs, June 13, 2001.

61 *"one shirt was hanging"*: Interview with John Schmitt, August 20, 2003.

61 *"The nature in which"*: JW honors thesis, Kenyon College, January 1952.

61 *When he woke*: Pugatch, February 2, 2000.

61 *"Jim said he didn't"*: Schmitt, August 20, 2003. Ernest Bloch, *Concerto Grosso
for String Orchestra with Piano Obbligato*, recording by the Chicago Symphony
Orchestra, conducted by Rafael Kubelík.

6. With the voice of a resurrected blackbird

62 *"What is called"*: JW letter to Sonjia Urseth, March 3, 1959, quoting Henry David
Thoreau, *Walden* (New York: Library of America, 1985), 329.

62 *"The Valley is more . . . We have hope"*: JW letter to Jessie Wright, January 23, 1952.

63 *Tom Tenney's parents*: Interview with Thomas Tenney, April 26, 2009.

63 *On the eve of*: JW letter to Tony Stoneburner, February 9, 1952. In his private journal,
Stoneburner gives a quick sketch of Wright in February 1952: "the fellow with the
rather chunky body and the almost innocent face and the never quite controlled hair
and the always disciplined soft distinct speech and the always efficient motion and
gesture. . . . Jim Wright is a farmboy from not too far from the farm. War weighs upon
him. He thinks that it is an absolute evil. And he pitches his life into that thought."

63 *"the terrible tension . . . all along"*: LK memoir, 166.

64 *"a 165-foot cliff"*: JW letter to Dudley and Jessie Wright, February [17], 1952.

64 *"rough Texans"*: Tenney, April 26, 2009.

64 *Tenney's mother*: Ibid.

65 *"Oh God, oh God"*: Interview with Roland Flint, October 28, 1999.

65 *"carrying and pushing . . . quite frightening"*: Interview with Robert Mezey, October 14, 1999.

66 *"as a matter of convenience"*: Robert Mezey letter to JW, August 16, 1952, quoting a
letter from JW.

66 *"women have been"*: Interview with Liberty Kovacs, June 13, 2001.

66 *"Jim believed"*: Interview with Herbert Lindenberger, August 29, 2008.

66 *"Everybody looked bedraggled"*: Ibid. Carol Reed's *The Third Man*, filmed in Vienna
in 1948 from a screenplay by Graham Greene, provides a vivid portrayal of the
postwar city.

67 *"with the voice of . . . bums in America"*: JW, "A Note on Trakl," in *CP*, 82.

67 *Lindenberger joined*: Lindenberger, August 29, 2008. "The poetry was a revelation.
I think this was the most important intellectual experience Jim had in Vienna. . . .
He was devoted to Rilke, but I'm certain that Trakl was the thing that unleashed
big things in Jim, so that understanding Trakl is to begin to understand Jim." Lin-
denberger wrote a doctoral thesis on the poet's work, published as *Georg Trakl*
(New York: Twayne, 1971).

67 *"became downright luminous"*: JW letter to Joseph McElrath, April 4, 1971.

67 *Trakl's work*: The German nouns: "night," "wood," and "silence." See Wayne Koestenbaum, public talk, "The Soul's Springtime: The Poetry of George Trakl," Poets
House, New York City, March 17, 2011.

68 *Pointing to*: Rilke argued for the ultimately affirmative nature of Trakl's work. "Trakl's poetry is to me an object of sublime existence . . . [in which] falling is the pretext for the most continuous ascension. In the history of the poem, Trakl's books are important contributions to the liberation of the poetic image." Rainer Maria Rilke letter to Erhard Buschbeck, February 22, 1917. Rilke, ed. Ruth Seiber-Rilke and Carl Seiber, *Briefe aus den Jahren 1914 bis 1921* (Leipzig: Insel Verlag, 1938), 126.

68 *"all animated ear"*: Maley, 480.

68 *"he was very sensitive"*: Lindenberger, August 29, 2008.

69 *Liberty had come*: As Herbert Lindenberger observed, "I knew then that alcohol did not go well with Jim; it brought out the manic in him." He became convinced that Wright's behavior "certainly manifested bipolar characteristics." Ibid.

69 *"After a while"*: Liberty Kovacs, interviewed in *James Wright's Ohio*, short film produced and directed by Larry Smith and Tom Koba, 1986.

70 *"actual physical"*: Robert Mezey letter to JW, May 8, 1953, quoting a letter from JW.

70 *"he talked poetry"*: Kovacs, June 13, 2001.

71 *"Don't worry"*: Robert Mezey letter to Liberty Wright, May 8, 1953.

71 *"No, Jim"*: Robert Mezey letter to JW, May 8, 1953.

71 *"some of that glorious"*: JW letter to Robert Mezey, May 1953, in *WP*, 50.

71 *"Fury's your best mode"*: Robert Mezey letter to JW, May 1953.

71 *"well stocked"*: Kovacs, June 13, 2001.

71 *"Why, that's Grandma!"*: JW reading, Brown University, Providence, RI, May 9, 1975.

72 *"where his ear"*: Mezey, October 14, 1999.

7. To sing whatever is well-made

73 *"To sing whatever"*: JW letter to Arnold Stein, April 8, 1964. *WP*, p. 295.

73 *"The teaching of poetry"*: David Wagoner, ed., *Straw for the Fire: From the Notebooks of Theodore Roethke* (Seattle: University of Washington Press, 1972), 231.

73 *"In spite of all"*: Edward Hirsch, ed., Introduction to *Theodore Roethke: Selected Poems* (New York: Library of America, 2005), xxv.

74 *"He was our genius"*: Carolyn Kizer, public talk, "Into Blossom," in conversation with Robert Bly and Marilyn Chin, Saratoga, CA, March 22, 1997.

74 *"that mad class"*: Interview with Carolyn Kizer, April 15, 2000; and Carolyn Kizer, "Theodore Roethke as Teacher," in *Picking and Choosing: Essays on Prose* (Cheney, WA: Eastern Washington University Press, 1995), 158.

74 *"Roethke was wild"*: Interview with Herbert Lindenberger, August 29, 2008.

74 *"with great enjoyment"*: JW journal, September 10, 1979.

74 *"Unlike the rest"*: C. W. Truesdale, "The Grain of Poetry: In Memory of Dr. James Wright"; *Milkweed Chronicle*, vol. 1, no. 2; Spring/Summer 1980.

74 *"Jim was a force"*: Lindenberger, August 29, 2008.

75 *"Honesty: This man"*: JW University of Washington class notes, October 1, 1953.

75 *"Childhood memories?"*: JW University of Washington class notes, November 1953.

76 *"he believed"*: JW interview, September 24, 1970, in *CP*, 155.

76 *"If a student"*: Richard Hugo, *The Triggering Town: Lectures and Essays on Poetry and Writing* (New York: W. W. Norton, 1979), 27.

76 *At the age of forty-five*: See Allan Seager, *The Glass House: The Life of Theodore Roethke* (Ann Arbor: University of Michigan Press, 1991), 217.
76 *In February 1954*: Karl Shapiro postcard to JW, February 14, 1954; and *Poetry* 84, no. 4 (July 1954).
76 *"The man was brilliant"*: Interview with Franz Schneider, October 20, 2006.
77 *"a poem is never"*: Obituary for Lawrence Zillman, *The Seattle Times*, September 8, 1990.
77 *"Jim was a great critical"*: Lindenberger, August 29, 2008.
77 *"Jim never talked"*: Liberty Kovacs, interviewed in *James Wright's Ohio*, short film produced and directed by Larry Smith and Tom Koba, 1986.
77 *"a very tough nurse"*: Lindenberger, August 29, 2008, quoting a doctor who worked with Liberty.
77 *Jackson Mathews*: Wright included Mathews in the dedication to *The Green Wall*, with Roethke and his brothers: "To two Teds and two Jacks."
77 *"Ted was so open"*: Kizer, public talk, Saratoga, CA, March 22, 1997.
77 *When one student objected*: JW, as told to Robert Bly, in conversation with Carolyn Kizer, who confirmed this anecdote, in ibid.
78 *"A course with Roethke"*: JW interview, September 30, 1979, in *CP*, 203.
78 *"and we all wrote"*: Kizer, "Roethke as Teacher."
78 *"I consider Roethke"*: JW interview, 1954, University of Washington, Seattle, *UW Daily* campus newspaper.
78 *"that* spare richness": JW essay for Theodore Roethke, spring 1954.
78 *"from mood & memory"*: JW marginalia on draft of sonnet "Judas," spring 1953.
78 Mr. Mould's Horses: JW's title is from Dickens's *Martin Chuzzlewit*.
79 *"to broaden his"*: Interview with David Wagoner, June 8, 1999. "He was already a better poet than a lot of others who were very well known—there was never any doubt about it. He could quote paragraphs of Goethe in English *and* German . . . or Tolstoy . . . oh, every damn poem I knew, he knew, too! I was considered a phenomenon, a walking anthology, but I was nothing compared to Jim Wright."
79 *Amid the laughter*: Kizer, April 15, 2000; and Kizer, "Roethke as Teacher."
80 *"Jim was a very shy person"*: Schneider, October 20, 2006.
80 *"There is a gesture . . . blew my mind"*: Ibid.
81 *"attached itself to poetry"*: Interview with Donald Hall, February 22, 1999.
81 *"Lawrence uses* one sentence": JW course notebook, University of Washington, May 24, 1955.
81 *"Aren't you afraid"*: Kizer, April 15, 2000.
81 *"Ted would discuss"*: Kizer, "Roethke as Teacher."
81 *"osmosis . . . poem doctor"*: Wagoner, June 8, 1999. "He probably got more direct, paraphrasable help from Kunitz than he did from Roethke."
82 *"I want my thesis"*: Lindenberger, August 29, 2008.
82 *"irreverent criticism"*: JW letter to Wayne Burns, June 25, 1958, in *In Defense*, 58; see Doheny, introduction to *In Defense*, 9.
82 *"The greatest poet"*: JW class notes for Maynard Mack's Eighteenth Century Literature, University of Washington, April 1956.
82 *"I've won"*: JW letter to Donald Hall, May 17, 1956, in *WP*, 65.
83 *The book was widely*: William Carlos Williams, *Something to Say* (New York: New Directions, 1985), 219. Char, Williams wrote, "is attached to the immediately-before-him, which he would investigate to its last *feeling*."

83 *"is the only way"*: JW, "Meditations on René Char," in *CP*, 63.

83 *"He just didn't know"*: Interview with Liberty Kovacs, June 13, 2001.

83 *Then, at a party*: Ibid. Also, interview with Rae Tufts, June 2, 1999.

83 *"I remembered"*: LK memoir, 189.

83 *"May I take this"*: W. H. Auden letter to JW, July 2, 1956.

84 *"the only poem"*: JW letter to Carolee Coombs-Stacy, November 25, 1974.

84 *"the most exciting"*: JW interview, September 30, 1979, in *CP*, 203.

84 *Neruda's "Walking Around"*: Appendix to *WP*, 572. The original title is in English.

84 *"It's a good sign"*: Stanley Kunitz letter to JW, March 31, 1957.

85 *"feelings of estrangement"*: W. H. Auden, foreword to *The Green Wall*, in *Clear Word*, 43; and *HotL*, 23.

85 *"I've tried very hard"*: Dust jacket of *The Green Wall* (New Haven, CT: Yale University Press, 1957); see also JW letter to James Dickey, July 25, 1958, in *WP*, 126. Wright admits the "humorless foolishness" of his statement and praises "the civil and salutary derision of Mr. Howard Nemerov (whose writings I admire very much), who commented that it 'sounded like being against sin.'"

85 *"the variety of . . . in the extreme"*: Louise Bogan, review of *The Green Wall*, in *The New Yorker*, September 14, 1957.

85 *"the best comment"*: JW letter to Donald Hall, November 12, 1958, in *WP*, 183.

86 *San Francisco "renaissance"*: Kenneth Rexroth, *Evergreen Review* 2, no. 6 (June 1957). That same month, *Time* magazine ran a feature profile of Rexroth, with the title "The Cool, Cool Bards."

86 *"reminded everybody"*: Gary Snyder, June 12, 1964, in *On Bread & Poetry: A Panel Discussion with Gary Snyder, Lew Welch & Philip Whelan* (Bolinas, CA: Grey Fox Press, 1977), 13.

86 *"This is the real"*: Philip Timberlake letter to JW, April 29, 1957.

86 *"the most gentle"*: JW obituary for Philip Timberlake, *Kenyon Alumni Newsletter*, August 1957.

86 *A number of these*: See JW to Hall, November 12, 1958. Multiple versions of this poem, showing its evolution, are included in *WP*, pp. 186, 189, and 192.

87 *"the rising tide"*: The phrase is Timberlake's, from a letter to JW, August 8, 1956.

87 *She had easily*: Interview with Sonjia Urseth, October 22, 2006.

87–88 *"Is there an epistolary . . . form on a page"*: JW's first letter to Sonjia Urseth, July 1, 1957.

88 *"To a Shy Girl"*: Uncollected, *The New Orleans Poetry Journal* 4 (January 1958).

88 *"is also about you"*: JW letter to Sonjia Urseth, July 8, 1957.

88 *"Yet I need poetry . . . but words"*: JW letter to Sonjia Urseth, July 29, 1957. The lines quoted are from Raleigh's "The Excuse."

89 *"He was a very kind"*: Urseth, October 22, 2006.

89 *"Forgive me"*: JW letter to Sonjia Urseth, August 15, 1957.

89 *"I have never told"*: JW letter to Sonjia Urseth, August 19, 1957.

89 *"more of an emotional"*: Theodore Roethke letter to JW, August 16, 1958. See *Selected Letters of Theodore Roethke*, ed. Ralph J. Mills Jr. (Seattle: University of Washington Press, 1968), 220.

90 *In the 1950s*: See David Margolick, "The Reader in the Ring," *New York Review of Books*, May 31, 2007, 46.

90 *Pete Rademacher . . . over in the sixth*: Alan H. Levy, *Floyd Patterson: A Boxer and a Gentleman* (Jefferson, NC: McFarland, 2008), 68.

90 *Roethke had decided*: See JW letter to Theodore Roethke, December 15, 1957, in *WP*, 76: "Allen Tate has been very kind to us. He certainly seems to think you're the Heavyweight Champion of contemporary American poetry."

8. Sweating out an exile

91 *Saul Bellow, who had taught*: As James Atlas noted, Minneapolis "gave perspective to the marginality of the literary enterprise." Atlas, *Bellow: A Biography* (New York: Random House, 2000), 252.

92 *"a pretty tough-looking town"*: JW letter to Wayne Burns, September 2, 1957, in *In Defense*, 21.

92 *"is about the best"*: JW letter to Sonjia Urseth, September 5, 1957.

92 *"I can only give"*: JW letter to Sonjia Urseth, September 12, 1957.

92 *"This house at the moment . . . face it down"*: JW letter to Sonjia Urseth, September 17, 1957.

92–93 *"frightened . . . appalling production"*: JW letter to Wayne Burns, September 22, 1957, in *In Defense*, 22. Wright had just completed "All the Beautiful Are Blameless" that day, one of seven new poems.

93 *"Not until we were"*: LK memoir, 193.

93 *"He got attached"*: Liberty Kovacs, interviewed in *James Wright's Ohio*, short film produced and directed by Larry Smith and Tom Koba, 1986.

93 *"I expect that"*: JW letter to Theodore Roethke, September 13, 1957, in *WP*, 68.

93 *"The amount of work"*: JW letter to Sonjia Urseth, October 10, 1957.

94 *"Piazza Piece"*: John Crowe Ransom, *American Poetry: The Twentieth Century*, Volume One (New York: Library of America, 2000), 805. Ransom's dialogue between "an old man" and "a lady young in beauty waiting" begins, "—I am a gentleman in a dustcoat trying / To make you hear."

94 *"I have a good time"*: JW letter to Sonjia Urseth, November 3, 1957.

95 *"I hate the whole"*: JW letter to Theodore Roethke, November 23, 1957.

95 *"so dismally unhappy"*: JW letter to Sonjia Urseth, December 3, 1957.

95 *"I'm afraid I'll get . . . the Muse"*: JW letter to Sonjia Urseth, December 8, 1957.

95 *Throughout that fall*: LK memoir, 193. "Oddly, in the midst of all the emotional turmoil that we were both experiencing, I felt the deep stirrings of a primal instinct. I felt the urge for another child."

96 *"a great black . . . Ohio River"*: JW letter to Lloyd Parks, December 17, 1957, in *WP*, 77.

96 *"I was afraid . . . Dickensian relatives"*: JW letter to Sonjia Urseth, December 13, 1957.

97 *"Walking off his porch"*: JW letter to Heilman, January 4, 1958. See James Baldwin, "Autobiographical Notes," from *Notes of a Native Son*, in *Collected Essays* (New York: Library of America, 1998), 5.

97 *As he later told*: "With the Gift of a Feather"; "A Girl Walking into a Shadow"; "All the Beautiful Are Blameless"; and "Safety" (uncollected) would finally appear in the Autumn 1958 issue of *The Kenyon Review* (vol. 20, no. 4).

97 *"merely a desire"*: JW letter to Robert Heilman, January 4, 1958.

97 *"My wife and I"*: JW letter to Sonjia Urseth, January 17, 1958.

97 *"For I could not die"*: Walt Whitman, "Out of the Rolling Ocean the Crowd," from *Poetry and Prose* (New York: Library of America, 1982), 263. Wright often quoted these lines in his letters to Urseth.

97–98 *"indeed writing only . . . murderous devotion"*: JW journal, January 21, 1958.

98 *"arrogant confidence"*: JW letter to Wayne Burns, January 21, 1958, in *In Defense*, 36.

98 *"Some blind gigantic burst"*: JW journal, January 28, 1958.

98 *"He could be so dark"*: Interview with Liberty Kovacs, October 17, 2006.

98 *"It must be this"*: JW letter to Wayne Burns, February 1, 1958, in *In Defense*, 44, and *WP*, 78. See also JW letter to Theodore Roethke, August 18, 1958, in *WP*, 158.

99 *"Right now I'm"*: JW postcard to Wayne Burns, March 7, 1958, in *In Defense*, 50.

99 *"Do you know what"*: JW letter to Theodore Roethke, March 12, 1958, in *WP*, 84.

99 *Wright's bawdy humor*: Interview with Jerome Mazzaro, February 6, 2003. Also per public talks by Roland Flint, April 8, 1993, and July 15, 1993: After Wright read in Rochester a few years later, Anthony Hecht recited Milton's "Lycidas" in the voice of Fields, reducing Wright to tears of laughter. Hecht lingered over particular lines, altering their meaning by inflection: "He must not float upon his watery bier . . . hmmm, watery bier."

99 *"the theme of"*: JW letter to Elizabeth Lawrence, Harper & Bros., April 7, 1958, in *WP*, 87.

99 *Elizabeth Kray*: See Kathleen Norris, *The Virgin of Bennington* (New York: Riverhead Books, 2001), 54. Meeting Kray in the early 1950s, Stanley Kunitz found her to be "down-to-earth, generous, buoyant, and simply mad about poetry." See also interview with Kathleen Norris, January 8, 2012.

100 *"he is part ham"*: Elizabeth Kray letter of recommendation for JW to A. Bower, Public Broadcast Laboratories, October 13, 1967, in Elizabeth D. Kray Papers, Poets House Archives, Poets House, New York, NY.

100 *"He read with the fire"*: Henry Parker, "Minnesota's Golden Age: A Tribute to Saul Bellow," *Poésie Première*, Paris, 2005. "When Wright opened his mouth, one could see in his eyes that he was not in the auditorium, but inside the world of the poem. As he spoke from another dimension, his voice was pure, rich, full, powerful, sometimes vociferous, and always melodious."

100 *"I mean that there must"*: JW letter to John Crowe Ransom, May 25, 1958, in *WP*, 92. See also "The Stiff Smile of Mr. Warren," in *CP*, 239.

100 *"Dickens has shaken me"*: JW letter to Wayne Burns, June 19, 1958, in *In Defense*, 56, and *WP*, 97.

9. The Lamentation of Saint Judas

101 *"a general definition . . . into the ring"*: JW letter to Wayne Burns, June 25, 1958, in *In Defense*, 58.

102 *"School of Charm"*: James Dickey, *The Sewanee Review* 66, no. 2 (April–June 1958). Dickey had savaged poems by Philip Booth.

102 *a "minor" poet*: JW letter to James Dickey, July 20, 1958.

102 *"I want to be"*: JW letter to Wayne Burns, July 17, 1958, in *In Defense*, 68.

102 *"a versifier lacking"*: JW letter to James Dickey, July 20, 1958.

102 *"God knows"*: Robert Bly letter to Donald Hall, June 1957, quoted in interview with Mark Gustafson, April 17, 2009.

103 *To Bly, Wright's poetry*: Interview with Donald Hall, February 22, 1999. In starting the magazine, Bly told Hall that "he didn't want to *know* poets. He said, just for *example*, 'I don't want to *know* James Wright.' It wasn't hostile to Jim—it was just an example." This exchange came more than a year before Bly first met Wright.

103 *"study of Warren's rhythm"*: JW letter to John Crowe Ransom, August 4, 1958.

103 *"self-overcoming"*: See Walter Kaufmann, on *Thus Spake Zarathustra*: "Yet this break is constructive only when accomplished not by one who wants to make things easy for himself, but by one who has previously subjected himself to the discipline of tradition. First comes the beast of burden, then the defiant lion, then creation." Preface (New York: Modern Library, 1995). In his letter to Hall on July 25, 1958, Wright's concept of the stages a poet must pass through to find "the truly shaped voice of one's self" owes a similar debt to *Zarathustra*.

103 *"the usual interesting adjustments"*: JW letter to James Dickey, August 12, 1958, in *WP*, 147.

104 *Recalling his first*: Interview with Robert Bly, April 7, 1990. Bly quotes JW's translation of César Vallejo, "Espergesia" ("Have You Anything to Say in Your Defense?"), in Bly, ed., *Neruda and Vallejo: Selected Poems* (Boston: Beacon Press, 1971; reissued 1993), 216.

104 *"a kind of eternal"*: JW letter to Kenneth Rexroth, May 7, 1960.

105 *"He is weak"*: Carol Bly, diary entry, September 1, 1958. Carol Bly papers, Andersen Library Archives.

105 *Wright was so impressed*: JW letters to Robert and Carol Bly, September 4, 1958, and October 16, 1958, in *WP*, 165 and 174; and Michael Hamburger, *Reason and Energy: Studies in German Literature* (New York: Grove Press, 1957), 246.

105 *"the possibility"*: Robert Bly, public talk, "A Celebration," University of Minnesota, Minneapolis, April 8, 1993.

105 *"cheap little Spanish grammar"*: JW letter to Robert and Carol Bly, September 25, 1958.

105 *"a genuine and"*: JW letter to Donald Hall, September 17, 1958, in *WP*, 167.

105 *"You have to"*: Robert Bly letter to JW, August 14, 1958.

105 *"In Fear of Harvests"*: Robert Bly's comments on a typescript draft, October 9, 1958.

105 *"propagandist for"*: JW letter to Donald Hall, September 17, 1958.

105 *"very busy: Busy"*: Robert Bly letter to JW, October 9, 1958.

106 *"I do indeed have"*: JW letter to Robert Bly, October 11, 1958 (with Bly's previous letter quoted), *New England Review* 25, no. 4 (Fall 2004): 20.

106 *"She represents to me"*: JW letter to "Mrs. Urseth," October 6, 1958.

107 *"exhausted . . . for two hours"*: Donald Hall, introduction to *Above the River: The Complete Poems* (New York: Farrar, Straus and Giroux; Middletown, CT: University Press of New England, 1990), xxx.

107 *"nervous disorder"*: JW letter to Donald Hall, October 30, 1958. See ibid., xxvii. Paraphrasing Wright's letter, Hall says, "Every now and then, he said, this madness flashed over him." Hall then allows, "Jim had been drinking over the weekend." His account mistakenly implies that Wright entered a mental hospital "[w]hen he returned to Minneapolis"—an event eight months in the future. Hall's comparisons of Wright's behavior to Roethke's wrongly suggest that Wright also suffered from manic depression. "On the whole we had bad luck in getting together," Hall admitted, but then, for him their friendship was always "partly based on rivalry." This three-day span was the longest period the two poets ever spent together. Interview with Donald Hall, February 22, 1999.

107 *"Jim and Libby"*: Interview with Robert Mezey, October 14, 1999.

107 *"the friendship of"*: JW letter to "Mrs. Urseth," November 4, 1958, enclosing a separate letter from Liberty Wright.

108 *"Goodbye, my dear child"*: JW letter to Sonjia Urseth, November 20, 1958.

108 *"this scurvy and"*: Laurence Sterne, *The Life and Opinions of Tristram Shandy, Gentleman* (New York: Modern Library, 2004), 9.

108 *"bare deserving"*: "The Slothful Brother's Prayer to the Muse" (uncollected). As late as March 1958, this poem had been intended as the dedicatory poem, set in italics, to open the collection *The Lamentation of Saint Judas*.

108 *"like a possessed man"*: JW letter to Sonjia Urseth, November 26, 1958.

108 *"I am and always"*: Sonjia Urseth letter to JW, November 24, 1958.

108 *"In Boston I spent"*: JW letter to Donald Hall, December 15, 1958, in *WP*, 188.

109 *"making their locality"*: JW letter to Robert Lowell, February 29, 1959, in *WP*, 204.

109 *"I'm going nuts again"*: JW letter to Wayne Burns, December 16, 1958, in *In Defense*, 110.

109 *"Energy of imagination"*: JW, "The Comic Imagination of the Young Dickens" (doctoral dissertation, University of Washington, Seattle, 1959), 18.

109 *"incomparably the greatest"*: JW letter to Sonjia Urseth, December 22, 1958. Wright was then translating Lorca's *Poema del Cante Jondo*; he includes a version of "Malagueña."

109 *"in which Sterne"*: JW letter to Sonjia Urseth, December 30, 1958.

110 *"I really want to"*: JW letter to James Dickey, January 2, 1959, in *WP*, 199.

110 *"impossible Eden"*: JW letter to Wayne Burns, January 7, 1959, in *In Defense*, 115; and JW letter to Theodore Roethke, February 11, 1958, in *WP*, 82.

110 *"about once every decade"*: LK memoir, 164. Both her mother and her father—"a moody, angry, and aggressive man"—had suffered from severe depression; so had Liberty's paternal grandfather and "several members of different generations" of her family. LK memoir, 52, 79.

110 *"I'm going to"*: Barbara Hugo, quoted in interview with Rae Tufts, June 2, 1999.

110–11 *Wright sent Hall*: JW letter to Donald Hall, January 15, 1959, in *WP*, 201.

111 *Roethke's psychiatrist*: Interview with David Wagoner, June 8, 1999. These awards honored Roethke's *Words for the Wind* (1958).

111 *"We read together"*: JW letter to Sonjia Urseth, April 7, 1959.

111 *"You know* all *of me"*: JW letter to Sonjia Urseth, February 8, 1959.

112 *"my last poem"*: JW postcard to Sonjia Urseth, February 9, 1959.

112 *"He had intentions"*: Interview with Sonjia Urseth, October 22, 2006. "I think he wanted sort of an anonymous name, and I was going to be 'Jenny.' I always thought that it was like a brand name, and that he might know many Jennys. So, it was his idea. I do not think that he wanted it to be private. Jonathan Swift had a correspondence with Stella, and he used that as an example of what our correspondence would be. . . . He expressly asked me to keep all our correspondence—he would keep mine, and I would keep his, and we'd put them in these little notebooks, the right size and everything, six-hole paper." In his journal, Wright refers to Sonjia as "Jenny Sterne" (April 26, 1959). In a letter to Urseth's mother in July 1959, he identifies the source of the name as Sterne's *Tristram Shandy*.

112 *"Dear Jenny"*: JW letter to Sonjia Urseth, February 11, 1958.

10. *Journal of Shipwreck*

113 *Upon returning*: There are many references to this mutual understanding in Wright's journal and in his letters to Sonjia Urseth. JW letter to Urseth, March 4, 1959: Liberty "understands, and advocates, our coming separation even more clearly and strongly than I do." In a letter to Urseth on May 6, 1959, Liberty writes of the amicable agreement they had reached regarding their separation.

113 *"ought never have been"*: JW letters to Sonjia Urseth, February 21 and 19, 1959.

113 *over the course*: Appendix to *WP*, 564. See also Jane Robinett, "Two Poems and Two Poets," in *HotL*, 49.

114 *The journal*: In a letter to Donald Hall on February 21, 1959, Wright refers obliquely to his correspondence with Sonjia Urseth as "a prose book not for publication."

114 *"the game of"*: JW letter to Sonjia Urseth, February 11, 1959.

114 *"It is the struggle"*: JW letter to Sonjia Urseth, February 16–17, 1959. See also Rainer Maria Rilke, first letter, February 17, 1903, in *Letters to a Young Poet*, trans. Stephen Mitchell (New York: Modern Library, 2001), 6.

114 *"I am going to"*: JW letter to Sonjia Urseth, February 25, 1959.

115 *"gorgeous, reviving"*: JW letter to Sonjia Urseth, February 23, 1959.

115 *"all over town . . . my own tongue"*: JW letter to Sonjia Urseth, February 27, 1959.

115 *"Poetry's been keeping you"*: Sonjia Urseth letter to JW, February 28, 1959.

116 *Naming once more*: JW letter to Sonjia Urseth, March 3, 1959. "One must choose. And, like Thoreau and Whitman and Anderson and Joyce, I have chosen."

116 *"the holy gift . . . source of strength"*: JW letters to Sonjia Urseth, February 27 and March 7, 1959.

116 *"I have done nothing"*: JW letter to Jerome Mazzaro, March 7, 1959.

117 *"light out for the Territory"*: Mark Twain, *Adventures of Huckleberry Finn*, in *Mississippi Writings* (New York: Library of America, 1982), 912.

117 *"South American obsession"*: JW marginalia, March 1959, to Mark Van Doren, *Edwin Arlington Robinson* (New York: Literary Guild of America, 1927), 72–74.

117 *"I am happy"*: JW letter to Sonjia Urseth, March 16, 1959; and "To a Young Girl on a Premature Spring Day" (uncollected), *The New Yorker*, March 14, 1959, 48.

117 *"I am in hell"*: JW journal, March 31, 1959.

117 *"come hell or high water"*: JW letter to Robert Heilman, March 29, 1959.

117 *After she struck him*: JW journal, March 31, 1959.

117 *"Since I have"*: JW journal, April 10, 1959.

117 *"towering a mile"*: "The Choice," an unpublished prose piece by Franz Wright contained in an e-mail to Jonathan Galassi, December 22, 2010.

117 *"this boy who"*: Sonjia Urseth letter to JW, April 1–4, 1959.

117 *"that glorious afternoon . . . a ridiculous fool"*: JW letters to Sonjia Urseth, April 1959.

117–18 *"a very miserable time"*: Interview with Sonjia Urseth, October 22, 2006.

118 *"small, grim"*: JW journal, April 10, 1959.

118 *"Mother of roots"*: JW journal, April 12, 1959.

118 *"prolonged and intensive"*: JW journal, April 14, 1959. In an essay titled "Bringing Blood to Trakl's Ghost," Mark Gustafson underscores the sense of liberation and release of creative energy that result from the work of translation. *Antioch Review* 72, no. 4 (Fall 2014): 636.

118 *"excitement . . . dark spell"*: JW letter to Sonjia Urseth, April 22, 1959.

118 *"I have no more"*: JW letter to James Dickey, April 17, 1959, in *WP*, 209.

119 *"I have never felt"*: JW journal, April 20, 1959.

119 *"the deep images"*: *The Fifties* No. 2 (April 1959): 56. This same issue included two Wright poems: "In the Hard Sun" and "In Fear of Harvests."

119 *"He was transfixing"*: Interview with Neil Myers, November 29, 2010. Wright recited many poems in Spanish and improvised translations.

119 *Robert Bly has described*: Robert Bly, public talk, CUNY Graduate Center, New York, NY, May 3, 2006.

119 *Wright shared in*: See JW letter to Sonjia Urseth, April 28, 1959, quoting the editor, Mme. Caetani, who said, "the girl is a born writer—no doubt of this."

119 *"vengeful hatred"*: JW letter to Sonjia Urseth, April 30, 1959.

119 *"Reality is defeat"*: JW journal, May 9, 1959.

119 *"God damn it"*: JW journal, May 14, 1959.

119 *Liberty saw him*: Interview with Liberty Kovacs, October 17, 2006.

119–20 *"I've grown so accustomed . . . into chaos"*: JW journal, May 20, 1959; and César Vallejo, "Down to the Dregs," translated by JW, in Robert Bly, ed., *Neruda and Vallejo: Selected Poems* (Boston: Beacon Press, 1971; reissued 1993), 191.

120 *"not to begrudge me"*: JW letter to Sonjia Urseth, June 2, 1959. "Jenny, I am more arrogant than you know. When I sound humble, I am so, not in relation to my contemporaries. I am not competing with our current punk lyric poets. In my mind, I am competing with Ben Jonson, Catullus, Sappho, Heine, Leopardi, Pushkin, and everyone. I am a hellish man."

120 *"mild crack-up . . . here I am"*: JW letter to Donald Hall, June 12, 1959, in *WP*, 216.

11. In the Minneapolis of graves

121 *"I feel less depressed"*: JW journal, in a letter to Sonjia Urseth, June 22, 1959.

121 *She knew*: JW journal, June 16, 1959.

121 *"beat the hell out of him"*: Interview with William Duffy, October 4, 2000.

122 *"Why are you"*: Interview with Robert Bly, April 7, 1990.

122 *"for a while"*: Sonjia Urseth letter to JW, June 18, 1959.

122 *"I've found . . . human being"*: Vassar Miller letter to JW, June 17, 1959; and JW's marginalia.

122 *"This is the answer"*: JW's marginalia in Miguel de Unamuno, *Tragic Sense of Life* (Mineola, NY: Dover Publications, 1954), 150.

122 *"Whatever happens"*: JW journal, June 22, 1959 (pages sent to Sonjia Urseth).

122 *"That's what he liked"*: Interview with Robert Bly, August 2, 2009. "'You mean a Christian can think like this?' This excited Jim very much."

122 *The most crucial*: John Logan letter to JW, June 27, 1959. In a postscript, Logan asked Wright to send the poems back to him when he could, since Logan had no other copies.

123 *"And here is yet another"*: JW journal, July 1 and 6, 1959. Wright refers to Arthur Waley's translation of Po Chu-i, "Kept Waiting in the Boat at Chiu-K'ou Ten Days by an Adverse Wind." Wright would later recite this poem in readings to introduce his own "As I Step Over a Puddle," which quotes Po's "Alarm at First Entering the Yang-Tze Gorges" in its epigraph. Both translations are by Arthur Waley, from *Chinese Poems* (London: George Allen & Unwin Ltd, 1946), 139 and 149, respectively.

123 *"La Jolie Rousse"*: JW journal, July 6, 1959.

123 *"wretched treatment"*: Interview with Dr. Eugene Pugatch, February 2, 2000.

124 *Liberty became livid*: Ibid. The chronology in Liberty Kovacs's memoir, *Liberty's Quest* (2008), is inaccurate, and the book is unreliable in points of fact. To give two examples, Kovacs recounts her discovery at this time of "a cardboard box . . . filled with letters addressed to Jim" by some unnamed woman. She describes feeling compelled to climb into an otherwise empty "attic" to search for the hidden box. The Como Avenue house, however, had no attic. Kovacs dates the arrival of her sister and nephew in Minneapolis to the summer of 1959 and writes

that the two never stayed at Como Avenue. In fact, they lived there for three months in the fall of 1958, arriving at the time of Marshall's birth.

124 *"are to be legally"*: JW letter to Sonjia Urseth, July 13, 1959.

124 *Advance copies*: In lines from the Gospel According to John, the Pharisees rebuke the man blind from birth whom Christ has healed. "They answered and said unto him, Thou wast altogether born in sin, and dost thou teach us? And they cast him out" (John 9:34).

124 *"that I suddenly realized"*: JW letter to Sonjia Urseth, March 24, 1959.

124 *"a religious book"*: JW letter to Elizabeth Willerton Esterly, July 7, 1959, in *WP*, 217.

125 *"with what I felt"*: JW interview, "The Art of Poetry XIX," *The Paris Review* 62 (Summer 1975). Reprinted in Peter Stitt, *The World's Hieroglyphic Beauty* (Athens: University of Georgia Press, 1985), 194.

125 *"Two energies"*: Robert Bly ("Crunk"), "Work of James Wright," *The Sixties* No. 8 (Spring 1966), in *Clear Word*, 78; *HotL*, 109.

125 *"Never have I felt"*: JW journal, July 17, 1959.

125 *"You are the one"*: JW letter to Sonjia Urseth, July 17, 1959.

125 *"a heavy burden"*: JW letter to Sonjia Urseth, July 21, 1959; and JW journal, July 22, 1959.

125 *"I don't and never shall"*: Sonjia Urseth letter to JW, July 20, 1959. Wright had first addressed Sonjia as "Jenny Mapleleaf" in May. The figure of "Jenny" in Wright's poetry is thus, from the first, linked to his figuration of trees, which often appear as forces of inspiration.

125 The Trees of Minnesota: Appendix to *WP*, 569; and JW letter to Sonjia Urseth, August 5, 1959.

125 *"You have made hope"*: Sonjia Urseth letter to JW, August 23, 1959.

126 *"a period during . . . poverty"*: JW journal, August 25 and 26, 1959.

126 *"in a rooted"*: JW journal, September 2, 1959.

126 *"But such labor"*: JW journal, September 8, 1959.

126 *In private, Liberty revealed*: Interview with Carol Bly, April 16, 2000.

126 *"He is insane"*: Carol Bly, diary entry, October 25, 1959. Carol Bly papers, Andersen Library Archives.

127 *"may have struck"*: JW letter to Robert and Carol Bly, November 18, 1959, in *WP*, 223.

127 *"with no other cares"*: Bob Dylan, *Chronicles: Volume One* (New York: Simon & Schuster, 2004), 236.

127 *"a tweed wearing"*: Ibid., 239.

127 *Weber taught Dylan*: Interviews with Eugene Pugatch, December 12, 2001, and with Harry Weber, January 12, 2005: "Pugatch caught on to who Dylan was before almost anybody else did around town. He saw what Dylan was going to become in a way that nobody else did."

127 *"Could you play 'Delia'"*: Pugatch, December 12, 2001.

128 *"Have read your new book"*: Dudley Wright letter to JW, October 7, 1959.

128 *"very numb . . . sometimes happy"*: JW letter to Jerome Mazzaro, November 24, 1959.

128 *"Ah. But I am now"*: JW's marginalia, October 16, 1959, in Unamuno, *Tragic Sense of Life*, 150.

128 *"higher today"*: Stanley Kunitz, "American Poetry's Silver Age," *Harper's Magazine*, October 1959.

128 *"Now I will study"*: JW journal, November 9, 1959.

129 *"a howling success"*: Interview with Galway Kinnell, January 30, 2002.

129 *"magical"*: Robert Bly letters to JW, November 16 and December 3, 1959.

129 *"I could never"*: JW letter to James Dickey, November 19, 1959, in *WP*, 224.

129 *"blind nastiness . . . knowing me'"*: JW letters to Sonjia Urseth, November 27 and December 8, 1959.

130 *Two more of Wright's poems*: "The Dream of the American Frontier" (uncollected) and an early version of "American Wedding," titled "On an American Girl's Marriage," *The Fifties* No. 2 (April 1959): 2, 6.

130 *"My God, you've gotta"*: Interviews with Harry Weber, July 29, 2003, and January 12, 2005.

130 *"all which way"*: Weber, July 29, 2003.

130 *"He looked Harvard"*: Weber, January 12, 2005, quoting Eddie Richer.

130 *"As for not writing"*: Robert Bly letter to JW, December 3, 1959.

12. The Wreckage of the Moon

133 *"baffled loneliness"*: JW letter to Sonjia Urseth, October 13, 1959.

133 *Wright named* patience: See, for example, JW, "An Afterword" to Thomas Hardy's *Far From the Madding Crowd*, drafted May 1960, in *CP*, 23; and JW, "A Note on Trakl," drafted June 1960, in *CP*, 82.

133 *"to lodge a few"*: Robert Frost, introduction to Edwin Arlington Robinson, *King Jasper*, in *Collected Poems, Prose, and Plays* (New York: Library of America, 1995), 744. "The utmost of ambition is to lodge a few poems where they will be hard to get rid of, to lodge a few irreducible bits where Robinson lodged more than his share."

133 *"Stout, balding"*: Paul Carroll, *Straight Poets I Have Known and Loved* (Boone, NC: Big Table Books, 1995), 75.

133 *edge of belligerence*: Interview with William Duffy, October 4, 2000; and JW letter to Robert Bly, December 13, 1959, in *WP*, 226.

134 *The news pleased Bly*: Carol Bly had been a favorite student of Tate's before her marriage to Robert, part of the bitter feud between the two poets.

134 *"another young poet"*: Robert Bly reading, University of Minnesota, Minneapolis, January 27, 1968. Recording courtesy of the Andersen Library Archives.

134 *"Two poetries"*: Robert Lowell, accepting the National Book Award, March 23, 1960, quoted in Ian Hamilton, *Robert Lowell: A Biography* (New York: Random House, 1982), 277.

134 *"whatever provides"*: W. S. Merwin, preface to *The Second Four Books of Poems* (Port Townsend, WA: Copper Canyon Press, 1993), 1.

134 *"the American idiom"*: William Carlos Williams, "Book V," *Paterson*. "We poets have to talk in a language which is not English. It is the American idiom." Marked in Wright's copy of *The William Carlos Williams Reader*. M. L. Rosenthal, ed., *Williams Reader* (New York: New Directions, 1966), 100.

134 *Williams's openness*: Robert Bly letter to JW, January 15, 1960. "I read him your two new poems from [*The Fifties*] #3, which he liked tremendously." Bly returned to Rutherford three days later to bring Williams and his wife into New York to see Ingmar Bergman's *Wild Strawberries*, "which he wants so much to see, and had given up all hope of seeing it."

134 *"So many young poets"*: Bly reading, January 27, 1968.

135 *"immortal Flossie"*: Tony Stoneburner private journal, May 5, 1970.

135 *"looks young men . . . a lot of writing"*: JW letter to James Dickey, February 13, 1960, in *WP*, 231.

135 *Three weeks later*: Ibid. See appendix to *WP* with uncollected poems, 574–83.

135 *Already, he listed*: Kevin Stein, *James Wright: The Poetry of a Grown Man* (Athens: Ohio University Press, 1989), 45.

136 *"Thinking of a Chinese Master"*: JW journal, February 16, 1960.

137 *"several hundred"*: Anne Sexton to Brother Dennis Farrell, January 22, 1963, Anne Sexton Papers, Harry Ransom Humanities Research Center, University of Texas at Austin. In a letter to Wright on February 6, 1964, Sexton calls their earlier correspondence "[a] funny out of time miracle, all those letters."

137 *"I doubt you remember"*: Anne Sexton letter to JW, February 10, 1960.

137 *Sexton had good luck*: Diane Wood Middlebrook, *Anne Sexton: A Biography* (Wilmington, MA: Houghton Mifflin, 1991), 128. As Sexton's biographer concludes her thumbnail sketch of Wright: "Quirkily learned, he was ardent about music and literature. He was also a natural storyteller; his long letters, like his talk, veered self-delightingly between pedantry and comedy. Like Sexton, Wright never lost the awe of a person given a second chance. He was, as Sexton put it, 'real.'"

137 *Though few letters*: At the time of Sexton's suicide in October 1974, almost all of the letters the two poets had exchanged disappeared from Sexton's papers. Wright told Anne Wright he had returned Sexton's letters to keep them safe after Liberty threatened to burn them. Interview with Anne Wright, April 10, 2012.

137 *"warmheartedly pedantic"*: Middlebrook, *Sexton*, 131. "But it was not so much Wright's practical advice as his acceptance of her as a peer that mattered to Sexton, helping her to internalize the identity she was rapidly acquiring in the professional world of poetry."

137 *"get back to work"*: JW journal, March 6–8, 1960; and Jorge Guillén, *Cántico: A Selection*, ed. Norman di Giovanni (New York: Little, Brown, 1965).

138 *As he recited*: JW journal, March 11, 1960.

138 *She cursed him*: Interview with Robert Bly, April 7, 1990; and interview with Carol Bly, April 16, 2000.

138 *Beginning a series*: JW journal, March 1960. With minor revisions, the poem became the second of "Two Hangovers." Introducing the poem at the State University of New York at Buffalo on February 18, 1972, Wright points out that it is part of a tradition. "I found out through reading many translations that the hangover has been almost like the villanelle in Chinese poetry."

138 *He canceled*: JW journal, April 3, 1960. "I love my family . . . I do not feel free."

138 *"I was an evangelist"*: Willis Barnstone e-mail to author, September 8, 2005.

139 *On a scrap of paper*: JW letter to Willis Barnstone, May 12, 1960, in *WP*, 243; and JW letter to Robert Bly, June 20, 1960, in *WP*, 245. See also Barnstone, "Talking with James Wright," in Ted Genoways, ed., *The Selected Poems of Miguel Hernández* (Chicago: University of Chicago Press, 2001), 277.

139 *"Now at last"*: Raymond Carr, "A Seemingly Ordinary Man," review of *Franco*, by Paul Preston, *New York Review of Books*, November 17, 1994.

139 *"a mere blurb"*: JW letter to Houghton Mifflin, New York, July 3, 1960.

140 *"sharply jealous"*: JW journal, July 30, 1960 (Montauk, Long Island, NY).

140 *"For Comfort"*: Anne Sexton, *All My Pretty Ones* (Boston: Houghton Mifflin, 1962), 53.

140 *"Dear Blessing"*: JW inscription to Anne Sexton, July 26, 1960, in *WP*, 246.

140 *In a long, detailed letter*: JW letter to Dr. Martin Orne, September 14, 1960.

141 *On their final night*: Middlebrook, *Sexton*, 44.

141 *After Sexton told*: JW journal, August 2, 1960, Montauk, NY.

141 *"Letter Written"*: Diane Wood Middlebrook and Diana Hume George, eds., *Selected Poems of Anne Sexton* (Boston: Houghton Mifflin, 1988), 65.

141 *"As long as"*: Middlebrook, *Sexton*, 133.

141 *She had learned*: See Sexton, "[I called him *Comfort*]," *Selected Poems*, 259. This undated Sexton poem published posthumously reveals the strange dynamic that existed between them at this time.

141 *"parted with the"*: JW journal, August 2, 1960, Montauk, NY.

141 *"enormous patient silences"*: See JW marginalia to Gary Snyder, *Myths & Texts* (New York: Corinth Books/Totem Press, 1960), 31.

142 "My life is changed": JW journal, August 5, 1960.

142 *"in order to keep"*: JW letter to Liberty Wright, August 12, 1960, in *WP*, 247.

142 *"My beautiful kind Blessing"*: Middlebrook, *Sexton*, 130.

142 *His advice led*: JW letter to Anne Sexton, August 16, 1960, with marginalia on her draft of "Refusal" (which became "The Truth the Dead Know" and "A Curse Against Elegies"), inspired by Sexton's impatience with the frequent appearance of ghosts and graveyards in Wright's poems.

142 *"a breath of fresh air"*: Duffy, October 4, 2000.

142–43 *"I don't want to hear . . . a visionary"*: Interview with Louis Simpson, February 15, 2000, in "The Sound That Comes from Character," *The Georgia Review* 55, no. 3 (Fall 2001): 473.

143 *"we used to help"*: Robert Bly, public talk, "Into Blossom," in conversation with Carolyn Kizer, Saratoga, CA, March 22, 1997.

144 *If he regretted*: JW interview, fall 1971, in *CP*, 138. Wright comments explicitly, and with some impatience: "The poem is only descriptive . . . it's an evocative poem. All I did was describe what I felt and what I saw lying there in the hammock. Shouldn't that be enough?" He credits the inspiration of Chinese poems translated by Waley and others.

144 *"seems absolutely"*: Robert Hass, introduction to Stephen Mitchell, ed. and trans., *The Selected Poetry of Rainer Maria Rilke* (New York: Vintage, 1989), xxiv. Saskia Hamilton has also noted how Wright's revision of the last line shows a deeper affinity with Rilke than merely echoing his language. Hamilton, "Listening to the Mourners," *The Kenyon Review* 29, no. 2 (Spring 2007).

145 *Bly later joked*: Interview with Robert Bly, August 3, 2003.

145 *"If you would"*: Meister Eckhart, *Sermons*. Quoted by JW as a possible epigraph on early cover page for *Now I Am Awakened*, fall 1961.See Sheldon Cheney, *Men Who Have Walked with God* (New York: Knopf, 1945).

145 *"a temperamental sympathy"*: Interview with W. S. Merwin, October 20, 1998. Merwin believed that Wright had discovered in Machado an affinity that released a new kind of energy and imagination in his poems.

145 *"clarity of an almost"*: Interview with Philip Levine, December 15, 2004. See also JW journal, November 19, 1959, from a sequence by Antonio Machado, "Del Camino" (XXIII), in *Soledades* (1899–1907).

145 *"Nothing is 'solved'"*: JW journal, September 26, 1960.

145 *"They think you're"*: Robert Bly, August 3, 2003.

146 *In a blind rage*: LK memoir, 204. No interviewees or sources represented that Wright had ever physically abused Liberty.

146 *"Wagner, you fascist! . . . because he had to"*: Interviews with Harry Weber, July 29, 2003, and January 12, 2005.

146 *"We got so sick"*: JW letter to Belle McMaster, September 21, 1970.

146 *In* The Sixties *No. 4*: The Contributor's Notes state that Clemenson "was born in Caldwell, NJ. He took a law degree, and is currently running for sheriff of Erie County, New York." See interview with Robert Bly, October 1, 2000.

147 *Wright harbored*: Interview with Robert Bly, April 7, 1990. Bly attributed Wright's "Depressed by a Book of Bad Poetry" to his first encounter with Olson's *Maximus Poems*. But Bly (April 8, 1993) also blamed Donald Allen's anthology, *The New American Poetry 1945–1960*. See JW, "The Few Poets of England and America," in *CP*, 268.

147 *After hiding the book*: Robert Bly, public talk, University of Minnesota, Minneapolis, April 8, 1993; and interview with Carol Bly, April 16, 2000.

147 *"harsh, acute criticism"*: JW journal, November 30, 1960.

147 *Worried about the tone*: JW, revised draft, December 13, 1960: "Just Off the Highway to Rochester, Minnesota."

147 *Once classes ended*: JW letter to James Dickey, December 18, 1960, in *WP*, 261.

147 *"Having Lost My Sons"*: Interview with Mark Strand, April 30, 2010. "You feel in some poems, like [this one], as though you're driving towards the kernel that is the center of the poem—the poem is in search of itself and always driving towards its own emotional center."

147 *"Near the South Dakota border"*: Introducing a reading of this poem at the State University of New York at Buffalo on July 2, 1969, Wright remarked how "the very place in America where the prairies proper begin seems to me to be a kind of haunting and haunted place." The Poetry Collection of the University Libraries, University at Buffalo, the State University of New York.

148 *"Things are going rather poorly"*: Anne Sexton letter to JW, December 29, 1960.

148 *She invoked*: Anne Sexton letter to JW, January 6, 1961. "Dear Comfort," Sexton concluded, writing by hand in huge, childlike letters, "Bee."

148 *"terrified by . . . temporary flattery"*: JW letter to Anne Sexton, February 15, 1961.

13. The amenities of stone are done

149 *"a diatribe"*: Interview with Sonjia Urseth, October 22, 2006.

149 *In a sequence*: Kevin Stein reproduces facsimiles of these poems in an appendix to *James Wright: The Poetry of a Grown Man* (Athens: Ohio University Press, 1989).

150 *"Now the amenities"*: The draft quoted is a fair copy typescript from late January 1961. The final lines of this version reappear in a 1971 poem, "October Ghosts": "We came so early, we thought to stay so long. / But it is already midnight, and we are gone."

150 *"I feel like a whole army"*: JW journal, January 19, 1961.

150 *"I was on my own"*: Interview with Franz Wright, May 23, 2001.

150 *"Everything I know"*: JW journal, February 25, 1961.

151 *"The strangest thing"*: Interview with Robert Bly, April 7, 1990. Bly felt there was "a kind of heroism" in Wright's determination to follow this new direction in his work. Bly, public talk, Saratoga, CA, March 22, 1997.

151 *"definite but extremely"*: JW letter to Carolee Coombs-Stacy, November 25, 1974.

151 *He began by reading*: Only two of these poems, "Mutterings over the Crib of a Deaf Child" and "A Song for the Middle of the Night," remain in his *Collected Poems*.

151 *In the program's*: Morgan Blum and a graduate student and actor, David Jones, joined Wright, who chose a sequence of sonnets and a passage from Robinson's

"Captain Craig" that he often included in his own readings. See *CP*, 233. In conclusion, all three poets performed the dramatic narrative "Isaac and Archibald."

151 *"What stands out now"*: Interview with Neil Myers, November 29, 2010. "There was a kind of anger in him, anger combined with vulnerability. . . . Jim didn't carry his own ideology or agenda. What he did was *react*—he was a reactor. That's what brought out his own deepest feeling."

151–52 *"When he got into class . . . resist the other"*: Interview with Harry Weber, January 12, 2005.

152 *"because I am* scandalous": James Atlas, *Bellow: A Biography* (New York: Random House, 2000), 302.

152–53 *"long to throw off . . . some poems"*: JW letter to Donald Hall, April 22, 1961, in *WP*, 267.

153 *Its beginning dates*: Briefly, the manuscript titled *Now I Am Awakened* on October 21, 1960, contained seventy-seven poems divided into seven sections; twenty-three of the forty-five poems eventually published in *The Branch* were already part of that original October 1960 manuscript. A later manuscript with the title *Amenities of Stone*, dated March 5, 1961, consisted of three sections of sixty-five poems total, forty-eight of them carried over from *Awakened*; five new poems had been added and a dozen others removed. As finally published, *The Branch* includes no divisions or titled sections. Over a span of nearly four years, between the fall of 1958 (when he finalized the contents of *Saint Judas*) and July 1962, Wright considered at least 113 different poems for inclusion in his next book. Of the poems Wright withheld, more than eighty-five—enough for two additional collections—never appeared in book form. See Stein, *Grown Man*, excerpt in *HotL*, 118. Also: Nicholas Gattuccio, "Now My Amenities of Stone Are Done: Some Notes on the Style of James Wright," *Scape: Seattle, New York*, no. 1 (1981), 31; reprinted in *Concerning Poetry* 15, no. 1 (1982), 61.

153 *In May 1961, Wesleyan*: Wright received a telegram of acceptance from José de la Torre Bueno, the managing editor of the Press, on May 22, 1961, one month to the day after he wrote to Hall.

153 *"I want to discover"*: JW journal, May 3, 1961.

153 *That same week*: Wright's "Two Poems on President Harding"—the first one in free verse—together suggest the kind of book he struggled to make for years.

153 *"quiet lament . . . return more'"*: JW letter to Mr. Macauley, editor of *The Kenyon Review*, May 16, 1961; and Laurence Sterne, *The Life and Opinions of Tristram Shandy, Gentleman* (New York: Modern Library, 2004), 635.

154 *"Mapleleaf"*: JW journal, May 9, 1961. The dedication for *Shall We Gather at the River* is one word: "Jenny."

154 *"overpaid scientist"*: Jack Wright letter to JW, June 3, 1961.

154 *"my beautiful Rilke"*: Anne Sexton letter to JW, May 4, 1961.

154 *Hunched over*: Interview with Erik Storlie, June 27, 2002. See also Erik Fraser Storlie, *Go Deep & Take Plenty of Root: A Prairie Norwegian Father, Rebellion in Minneapolis, Basement Zen, Growing Up, Growing Tender* (CreateSpace, 2013), 169.

155 *"He could see gold"*: Weber, January 12, 2005. Ted Blodgett was the student poet.

155 *"[I] swear that"*: JW letter to José de la Torre Bueno, July 19, 1961.

156 *"Alone, lost"*: JW journal, November 10, 1961.

156 *"the worst kind"*: Weber, January 12, 2005.

156 *"Libby would get"*: Ibid. "She had as bad a temper as I've ever seen in a woman," Weber recalled, while Franz and Marshall were "little hellions" (interview with Weber, July 29, 2003).

157 *"just in the swim"*: Storlie, June 27, 2002.

157 *"Jim had a real fondness"*: Weber, January 12, 2005.

157 *"Everybody was"*: Interview with Marv Davidov, July 30, 2003.

157 *The previous winter*: Interview with Robert Bly, August 3, 2003. See, for example, "In the Cold House."

157 *"It spent six hours"*: Carol Bly memoir, "James Wright's Visits to Odin House," *Ironwood* 10, vol. 5, no. 2 (1977), 33.

157 *"Don't go there"*: Carol Bly, public talk, Ninth Annual James Wright Poetry Festival, Martins Ferry, OH, April 8, 1989; and interview with Robert Bly, April 7, 1990.

157–58 *"composed in . . . truly unified"*: JW letter to Michael Hamburger, August 22, 1961, in *WP*, 274.

158 *"It is actually"*: JW letter to José de la Torre Bueno, August 22, 1961.

158 *"suddenly fell into it"*: JW letter to Carol and Robert Bly, August 30, 1961.

158 *"just isn't good enough"*: Roland Flint, public talks, University of Minnesota, Minneapolis, April 8, 1993, and Warren Wilson College MFA Program for Writers, Swannanoa, NC, July 15, 1993.

14. The seven corners / Of Hell, 14, Minnesota

159 *"The seven corners"*: "Larry."

159 *Of all his critical prose*: Interview with Harry Weber, January 12, 2005.

159 *"The Delicacy of Walt Whitman"*: in *CP*, 3ff.

160 *"Anne almost but"*: Diane Wood Middlebrook, *Anne Sexton: A Biography* (Wilmington, MA: Houghton Mifflin, 1991), 149.

160 *"In a Warm Chickenhouse"*: JW letter to James Dickey, December 18, 1960, in *WP*, 261; see also appendix to *WP*, 591; and *CP*, 310.

160 *Wright's guest appearance*: JW, "The Work of Gary Snyder," in *CP*, 105.

160 *When Snyder read*: Interview with Mark Gustafson, April 17, 2009.

161 *"iambic dramas and songs"*: JW journal, October 10, 1961. See also JW letter to Robert and Carol Bly, August 30, 1961.

161 *"Well, it's a heartening"*: Michael Benedikt letter to JW, November 7, 1961; and JW's marginalia.

161 *"outrageous poetry-reading"*: Roger Hecht letter to JW, quoting Wright, November 1961.

161 *"still terribly torn"*: Interview with Jerome Mazzaro, February 6, 2003.

161 *"As for the writing"*: JW journal, November 9, 1961.

162 *"This morning I placed"*: JW letter to Willard Lockwood, Wesleyan University Press, December 22, 1961.

162 *The winter of 1962*: JW's inscription on flyleaf of *The English Novel*, a textbook; and JW journal, May 15, 1962.

162 *"atrocity stories"*: JW, introducing "Snowstorm in the Midwest" at a reading in Buffalo, July 2, 1969. The Poetry Collection of the University Libraries, University at Buffalo, the State University of New York.

163 *"never missed a beat"*: Interview with William Breer, August 1, 2003.

163 *"Apprenticeships"*: JW note, January 5, 1962. See also Kevin Stein, *James Wright: The Poetry of a Grown Man*, excerpt in *HotL*, 134.

163 *"At a bad, dark time"*: JW marginalia, June 17, 1965, on draft translation of Guillén's "Ring" dated February 24, 1962.

163 *His collaborations with Bly*: A significant acknowledgment appears at the beginning of *Twenty Poems of César Vallejo* (Madison, MN: Sixties Press, 1962): "The translators would like to thank Hardie St. Martin for his generous criticism of these translations in manuscript." St. Martin—a native speaker, a fine poet, and a scholar of Spanish poetry—remained an essential resource for Wright as well as Bly, vetting all of their work in Spanish.

163 *"the reality of the spirit . . . religious man"*: Draft of "A Note on César Vallejo," January 1962. Wright revised the final version extensively; see *CP*, 85.

163 *"The Jewel"*: JW typescript, March 18, 1962; and "Espergesia," translated by JW, in Robert Bly, ed., *Neruda and Vallejo: Selected Poems* (Boston: Beacon Press, 1971; reissued 1993), 217.

164 *"I've never known"*: Robert Bly letter to the author, March 18, 1981.

164 *"To the Ohioan Muse"*: JW typescript, February 9, 1962.

164 *"professional consultant"*: JW letter to U.S. Education Foundation in India, March 30, 1962; and Department of State letter to JW, May 4, 1962.

165 *"And no one ever"*: Interview with Robert Bly, April 7, 1990; Carol Bly, public talk, University of Minnesota, Minneapolis, April 8, 1993; and interview with Anne Wright, November 13, 2016.

165 *"It is not a 'great' book"*: JW's marginalia on typescript of "Holding a Pearl in My Hand, April 1962," May 21, 1962. See Stein, *Grown Man*, excerpt in *HotL*, 134.

165 *Though he often slept*: Liberty referred to Wright as an "emotional cripple." JW journal, May 15, 1962.

165 *"very strange and . . . want to grow"*: Undated JW letter to Sonjia Urseth, spring 1962.

166 *"The Quest for the Child Within"*: JW, introduction to Hy Sobiloff, *Breathing of First Things* (New York: Dial Press, 1963), in Frank Graziano and Peter Stitt, eds., *James Wright: A Profile* (Durango, CO: Logbridge-Rhodes, 1988), 59.

166 *"'Every door in me'"*: JW and Sarah Youngblood, translation of Rilke, "Wenn die Uhren so nah . . ." ("When the clocks nearby"), in Maley, appendix C-5, 579.

166 *"going through a"*: Anne Sexton letter to JW, March 21, 1962.

166 *"My dear Bee"*: JW letter to Anne Sexton, July 11, 1962.

166–67 *"He gives me"*: Middlebrook, *Sexton*, 134.

167 *When she received*: LK memoir, 213.

167 *"He drank us out"*: Interview with Mary Ann Hanna, August 13, 2005.

168 *"absolute clarity"*: Robert Hass, "James Wright" (1977), in *Clear Word*, 196, *HotL*, 278.

168 *"You'll notice at once"*: JW letter to José de la Torre Bueno, July 30, 1962.

169 *He found refuge*: Interview with Erik Storlie, June 27, 2002; and Storlie letter to JW, September 14, 1962. See also Erik Fraser Storlie, *Go Deep & Take Plenty of Root: A Prairie Norwegian Father, Rebellion in Minneapolis, Basement Zen, Growing Up, Growing Tender* (CreateSpace, 2013), 135ff.

169 *The painter John Beauchamp*: Interview with James "Red" Nelson, July 1, 2002.

169 *"We ended up"*: Interview with Bruce Rubenstein, July 30, 2003. Wright convinced his companions to drive to Owatonna, Minnesota, sixty-five miles south of Minneapolis, to see Louis Sullivan's National Farmers' Bank building.

169 *"he would become"*: Interview with Bruce Rubenstein, August 1, 2003; and Nelson, July 1, 2002.

169 *After one such*: Interview with Erik Storlie, August 1, 2003, quoting Weber; and interview with Rubenstein, August 1, 2003. See "Inscription for the Tank."

169 *"to be veering along"*: James Breslin, "James Wright's *The Branch Will Not Break*," *American Poetry Review* 11, no. 2 (March/April 1982): 39–46.

169 *"He was a beautiful"*: Garrison Keillor, public talk, "A Tribute to James Wright," Teachers and Writers Collaborative, New York, NY, December 13, 2000.

170 *But Wright's work*: Robert Bly, public talk, University of Minnesota, Minneapolis, April 8, 1993. Bly pointed to "Snowbanks North of the House" as a poem directly influenced by Wright. "And the whole book of mine called *The Man in the Black Coat Turns* owes its somber tone to James's example." In an interview ten years later he spoke of Wright's influence on "Summer 1960, Minnesota" and "Laziness and Silence," among others. Interview with Bly, August 3, 2003.

170 *"I hate your goddamn"*: Robert Bly, April 7, 1990, and August 3, 2003.

170 *Nicolas Berdyaev*: Nicolas Berdyaev, *The Meaning of the Creative Act*, trans. Donald A. Lowrie (New York: Collier Books, 1962), inscribed November 8, 1962, and heavily annotated by JW.

170 *"God-haunted"*: Robert Bly, quoted by Galway Kinnell, public talk, Second Annual James Wright Poetry Festival, Martins Ferry, OH, May 9, 1982.

170 *His most significant*: For a period of nearly two years, Wright practically gave up writing letters, making it difficult to know the details of this relationship or of his day-to-day life.

171 *worst year*: Interview with Anne Wright, November 30, 2010, quoting JW.

171 *"Minneapolis, / Drowns"*: JW typescript draft, "The River Down Home," November 27, 1962.

15. To rebuild from scratch

172 *"A Wrong Turning"*: Robert Bly, in *Choice* 3 (1963), 33, reprinted in *American Poetry: Wildness and Domesticity* (New York: Harper & Row, 1990), 7.

172 *"occurred" to him*: JW reading, University of Minnesota, Minneapolis, February 22, 1963. Kahn's tribute in *The Nation*, February 9, 1963.

173 *"He leaned forward . . . for a Coke?"* Interview with Nancy Paddock, February 4, 2010.

173 *"We are absolutely"*: Interview with John Beauchamp, July 1, 2002.

173 *"old and distinguished"*: JW letter to Ray Livingston, December 7, 1963.

173 *before he did*: JW, as told to Anne Wright, quoted in Alan Natali, "Portrait of the Artist," *Ohio Magazine* 10 (May 1987).

173–74 *"the twisted news . . . the voting"*: Allen Tate letter to JW, May 19, 1963.

174 *"damaged merchandise"*: JW to Ray Livingston, December 7, 1963.

174 *"His head was down"*: Henry Parker, "Minnesota's Golden Age: A Tribute to Saul Bellow," *Poésie Première*, Paris, 2005.

174 *"poisonous atmosphere"*: John Berryman letter to JW, June 22, 1963.

174 *"my friend, Mr. Tate"*: Course description, University of Minnesota, Minneapolis, August 6, 1963.

174 *In August, after learning*: Interview with Peter Stitt, October 27, 1999, and Stitt, public talk, "A Celebration of James Wright," University of Minnesota, Minneapo-

lis, April 8, 1993. Roethke died suddenly of a heart attack on August 1, 1963, at age fifty-five.

174–75 *"miraculously heartening . . . the one chance"*: JW letter to E. L. Doctorow, March 13, 1964, in *WP*, 287.

175 *"Jim Wright's book"*: Robert Bly letter to Sister Bernetta Quinn, May 18, 1963. Robert Bly papers, Andersen Library Archives.

175 *"How right it was"*: Robert Bly letter to JW, May 22, 1963.

175 *"the operation of"*: Thom Gunn, spring 1964, quoted in *HotL*, 159.

175 *Alert to the subtlety*: Robin Skelton, *The Critical Survey* 1, no. 3 (Autumn 1963).

175 *"genuinely new"*: Donald Hall, ed., *Contemporary American Poetry* (London: Penguin, 1962), 32.

175 *"images where what is"*: John Logan, August 1963, reprinted in *A Ballet for the Ear: Interviews, Essays, and Reviews*, ed. A. Poulin, Jr. (Ann Arbor: University of Michigan Press, 1983), 228.

176 *"an explosive discovery"*: Interview with C. K. Williams, March 24, 2011.

176 *"Jim seems to have"*: Interview with Philip Levine, December 15, 2004.

176 *Brief lyrics in*: Interview with Galway Kinnell, January 30, 2002.

176 *"rebuild myself as"*: JW letter to Liberty Wright, May 28, 1964, in *WP*, 302.

176–77 *Truesdale believed . . . "in hard times"*: C. W. Truesdale, "The Grain of Poetry: In Memory of Dr. James Wright"; *Milkweed Chronicle*, vol. 1, no. 2; Spring/Summer 1980.

177 *She coordinated his*: Elizabeth Kray letter to JW, November 27, 1963. "Cal Lowell very much admires your work and was pleased to have the chance to express it."

177 *"I keep reading at"*: Tom McGrath letter to JW, November 15, 1963.

177 *"Tonight, in a room"*: Mary Oliver letter to JW, November 15, 1963.

177 *"Fair enough"*: Interview with Roland Flint, October 28, 1999; public talk by Flint, Warren Wilson College MFA Program for Writers, Swannanoa, NC, July 15, 1993.

177 *"When you first walked"*: Sister Bernetta Quinn letter to JW, December 13, 1963.

178 *"for the sake of"*: JW letter to Ray Livingston, December 7, 1963.

178 *"Come up with me"*: Interview with Howard Huelster, August 4, 2010, quoting Roger Blakely.

178 *"When he came to . . . he was writing"*: Interview with Helen Wright, April 21, 2002.

179 *Chaplin's early films*: Paul Mariani, *Dreamsong: The Life of John Berryman* (New York: William Morrow, 1990), 410.

179 *"He really would"*: Roland Flint, public talk, University of Minnesota, Minneapolis, April 8, 1993, and interview, October 28, 1999.

179 *"I always felt . . . magic of Shakespeare"*: Interview with Freya Manfred, October 1, 2000.

180 *"Traveling Northward"*: Wright knew Tu Fu's poem from both Kenneth Rexroth's *One Hundred Poems from the Chinese* (New York: New Directions, 1956), 10, and as "Journey to the North," part III, in Robert Payne's *The White Pony* (New York: George Allen & Unwin, Ltd, 1949), 209.

181 *"sort of a sad"*: Interview with Susan Lamb, April 16, 2005.

181 *"the most magnificent"*: JW typescript draft of talk, "The Art of Translation," March 9, 1964. Many of Wright's professors had by then died exceptionally young: Timberlake at sixty-two; Roethke at fifty-five; Coffin at fifty-two. Sutcliffe had been just fifty-one.

181 *"My conviction is that"*: JW letter to Liberty Wright, May 28, 1964, in *WP*, 302.

181 *"that perhaps I need"*: JW letter to Sister Bernetta Quinn, March 13, 1964, in *WP*, 287.

181 *The audience greeted*: JW reading, March 20, 1964, AAP recording; and JW letter to Paul Carroll, spring 1965, in *WP*, 330. Bly's poem to that same cricket is titled "Listening to a Hidden Cricket."

182 *"To take all this"*: Rainer Maria Rilke, "Departure of the Prodigal Son," JW draft, spring 1964. Working with Sarah Youngblood, Wright completed versions of more than two dozen poems by Rilke, many begun years before at Kenyon.

182 *"is not a hack"*: JW's marginalia to a letter from Sister Joselyn, College of St. Scholastica, Duluth, MN, April 1, 1964. Wright traveled there to speak on April 9 and 10, 1964.

182 *Wright also found*: "Eisenhower's Visit to Franco, 1959" and "Today I Was Happy, So I Wrote This Poem." Tranströmer had read Wright's poems in an English magazine, and wrote to ask permission to publish his translations. Tomas and Monica Tranströmer, letter to author, February 11, 2001.

183 *"There was an instant"*: Robert Bly letter to Torbjörn Schmidt, February 3, 2000, in *Airmail: The Letters of Robert Bly and Tomas Tranströmer* (Minneapolis: Graywolf, 2013), 417.

183 *"the passage of time"*: See JW letter to Jack Wright, June 11, 1964. Wright describes how revisions to "a poem about Rip Van Winkle, after months spent studying the works of the Sufi mystic Jallalu-d'in Rumi and the Egyptian fanatic Ibn al-Farid . . . turned out to be a Casida cursing the city of [Minneapolis] on my eternal departure therefrom." An interim draft of "Rip" bears the title "This Time, I Woke Near the Mississippi."

183 *"made of mingled"*: Robert Bly letter to Tomas Tranströmer, August 25, 1964, in *Airmail*, 8.

184 *"the weird dumbness"*: JW letter to Louis Simpson, May 11, 1964, in *WP*, 300.

184 *"a kind of fury"*: JW letter to Tomas Tranströmer, July 6, 1964, in *WP*, 316.

184 *"I am astounded"*: JW letter to Jack Wright, June 11, 1964. As Michael Ondaatje observed, "I think the title story is absolutely amazing and a masterpiece of translation." E-mail to author, March 17, 2014.

184 *"a certain luminosity . . . his stories"*: "Theodor Storm: Foreword," in *CP*, 71.

184–85 *"fairly naïvely thought . . . to the nth degree"*: Interview with Franz Schneider, October 20, 2006.

185 *"For the Marsh's Birthday"*: JW letter to Marshall Wright, July 28, 1964, in *WP*, 321.

185 *"We understood that"*: Interview with Marshall Wright, October 17, 2006.

185 *When Barbara Thompson*: Interview with C. W. Truesdale, October 4, 2000. Thompson "got involved with somebody else, and Jim couldn't take that. He fell apart completely." See also JW letter to Dr. Marvin Sukov, November 11, 1964. Wright tells his therapist that Thompson had accepted his proposal of marriage; they had been together "More than three years!"

185 *"unspeakable demons"*: JW letter to Robert Mezey, November 17, 1964, in *WP*, 322.

186 *"My family life"*: C. W. Truesdale, "The Grain of Poetry: In Memory of Dr. James Wright"; *Milkweed Chronicle*, vol. 1, no. 2; Spring/Summer 1980.

186 *"That was a"*: Interview with Joan Wurtele Truesdale, August 9, 2010.

186 *"As for me"*: JW journal, October 12, 1964 ("I Have Nothing to Do with This Poem").

186 *With the Blys*: JW letter to John Haffenden, February 19, 1974.

186 *"a kind of ferocious brilliance"*: JW letter to Robert Mezey, November 17, 1964, in *WP*, 322.

186 *"the nuthouse"*: Beauchamp, July 1, 2002.

186 *"My new book"*: JW letter to Prairie Dern, October 16, 1964.

187 *An enraged letter*: JW letter to Dr. Marvin Sukov, November 11, 1964.

187 *Within days of*: See JW, "On the Occasion of a Poem: Bill Knott," in *CP*, 310; and JW letter to Bill Knott, November 16, 1964.

187 *"I think your visit"*: Bill Knott letter to JW, spring 1965.

187 *"Casida cursing the city"*: JW letter to Jack Wright, June 11, 1964.

187 *It had been inspired*: A letter from Bly to Wright dated February 7, 1966, praises his new version of Lorca's "Ode to Walt Whitman," and notes how it bore a close affinity to Wright's own new work.

187–88 *"essential solitude . . . twilight in Ohio"*: JW letter to Susan Gardner, December 23, 1964, in *WP*, 328. Mary Ruefle (interviewed October 19, 2010), Saskia Hamilton ("Listening to the Mourners," *The Kenyon Review* 29, no. 2 [Spring 2007]: 177), and others have called this the most exceptional letter in *A Wild Perfection*.

16. The rootlessness of things

189 *"happier than I"*: JW letter to Dudley and Jessie Wright, January 22, 1965.

189 *In January, Liberty*: Interviews with Liberty Kovacs, June 13, 2001, and October 17, 2006; and interview with Franz Wright, May 23, 2001. See also LK memoir, 248. Liberty met Miklos Kovacs on January 15 and the two were married on February 20, 1965.

189 *Within four months*: While packing to move to her new home, Liberty Kovacs burned hundreds of letters that Wright had written to her during their courtship. LK memoir, 271–72.

189 *Wright did not learn*: Both boys suffered physical abuse from their stepfather, particularly Marshall, who was six years old at the time his mother remarried. Wright did not learn the extent of this abuse until Franz, age eighteen, stayed with his father in New York in September 1971. "[Kovacs] used to beat us up . . . He was incredibly brutal." Interview with Franz Wright, May 23, 2001.

189 *"Plainly I sit"*: JW letter to Prairie Dern, March 18, 1965.

190 *"I never seem to sleep"*: Paul Ferris, *Dylan Thomas* (New York: Dial Press, 1977), 243.

190 *Wright began with a poem*: The Poetry Center of San Francisco State University, April 26, 1965.

190 *"I had to wake him"*: Interview with Philip Levine, December 15, 2004.

191 *"I don't drink for"*: Interviews with Herbert and Claire Lindenberger, August 29, 2008.

191 *And like them*: Ibid. Claire Lindenberger agreed with her husband that Wright showed symptoms of a bipolar disorder.

191 *"tossing heavy sacks"*: JW letter to "Carol" [surname unknown], July 10, 1965.

192 *"I have now shaken"*: JW letter to "Carol" [surname unknown], July 6, 1965.

192 *"long grieving letter"*: JW letter to Prairie Dern, July 15, 1965.

192 *"two good weeks"*: JW letter to Mary Oliver, September 16, 1965, in *WP*, 337.

192 *Robert Bly wrote*: Robert Bly letter to JW, July 8, 1965. "[Tranströmer] was very touching—he knew entire poems of yours and mine by heart, and dozens & dozens

of lines, which he would come up with in conversation about a tree or something. He said that *Lion's Tail & Eyes*, even the subtitle Poems About Laziness and Silence, had taught him something incredibly rare—something about *how to live*. He'd bend his head and say this in a dogged way, so I can imagine the pressures in Sweden *against* laziness and *against* silence."

192 *"Writing to you"*: JW letter to Donald Hall, August 11, 1965.

192 *"This God damned"*: JW letter to Jack Wright, August 14, 1965.

192 *"several days of"*: JW letter to Elizabeth Willerton Esterly, September 16, 1965, in *WP*, 334.

192 *"pretty jagged"*: JW letter to Mary Oliver, July 10, 1965, in *WP*, 334.

193 *"I am sick of being"*: JW letter to Donald Hall, September 29, 1965, in *WP*, 338.

193 *In October, Wright*: St. Martin letter to JW, care of Bly, October 26, 1965. The translations St. Martin solicited from Wright, Levine, and many others eventually appeared in the landmark bilingual anthology *Roots and Wings: Poetry from Spain 1900–1975* (Harper & Row, NY: 1976).

193 *"She was a very"*: Robert Bly, public talk, Eleventh Annual James Wright Poetry Festival, Martins Ferry, OH, April 12, 1991.

193 *"Jim feels very strong"*: Robert Bly letter to Tomas Tranströmer, December 1, 1965, in *Airmail: The Letters of Robert Bly and Tomas Tranströmer* (Minneapolis: Graywolf, 2013), 23.

193 *"I have had so many"*: JW letter to Carol Bly, January 16, 1966, in *WP*, 342.

194 *Wright talked for hours*: Ussachevsky was a cofounder and director of the Columbia-Princeton Electronic Music Center. Miller Theatre archives, Columbia University Libraries, New York, NY.

194 *Betty Kray had become*: Frederick Seidel's first book of poetry had won a prize sponsored by the Poetry Center of the 92nd Street Y, which then rescinded the award after he refused to delete an instance of perceived libel. In protest, Kray and Stanley Kunitz both resigned their positions at the Poetry Center.

194 *"live by their wits"*: Galway Kinnell, eulogy, printed in Festschrift from Elizabeth Kray memorial service, November 25, 1987.

194 *"She was the center"*: Interview with Gigi Bradford, September 22, 2011. Kray excelled as an "arts administrator" before such a vocation existed.

194 *"When he saw me"*: Jane Cooper, "A Tribute to James Wright," Teachers and Writers Collaborative, New York, NY, December 13, 2000; and interview with Cooper, January 18, 2001. See also Jane Cooper, *The Flashboat: Poems Collected and Reclaimed* (New York: W. W. Norton, 2000), 28.

195 *"I understood something"*: Galway Kinnell, public talk, Kenyon College, Gambier, OH, March 26, 1983.

195 *"obsessive joy that he"*: Interview with Galway Kinnell, January 30, 2002.

195–96 *"electric, all but unbearable . . . he had dreamt"*: Paul Carroll, *Straight Poets I Have Known and Loved* (Boone, NC: Big Table Books, 1995), 75.

196 *"and a real"*: JW letter to Larry Lawrence, June 2, 1973.

196 *"temporarily settled"*: JW letter to "Miss Munro" [given name unknown], undated, late winter 1966.

196 *Many thousands*: Howard Zinn, *The Twentieth Century: A People's History* (New York: Harper Perennial, 2003), 221, 231.

197 *Working with Carol Bly*: Interview with Michael True, May 30, 2013.

197 *"dropped everything"*: Robert Bly letter to Sister Bernetta Quinn, March 11, 1966. Wright had just returned to New York from a reading in Chicago; he left for Oregon immediately after another appearance on March 3, 1966, at the Guggenheim Museum.

197 *A writer from*: *The New York Times*, "Poets Hold 'Read-In' in Oregon to Protest U.S. Role in Vietnam," March 6, 1966, 4; and Robert Bly, introduction to *A Poetry Reading Against the Vietnam War* (Madison, MN: Sixties Press, 1967), 9.

197 *"when Jim Wright walked"*: Robert Bly, public talk, Saratoga, CA, March 22, 1997.

197 *"I don't think there was"*: Interview with Mark Strand, April 30, 2010.

197 *"Jim was among"*: John Haag, "Beyond the Green Wall," AWP's *The Writer's Chronicle* 25, no. 4 (February 1993): 11–16. "He read his poems as though they were made up of sentences—as indeed they are—stressing the rhetorical timing (as we all do in natural speech) and he let the meter, that strong base, take care of itself, supporting the poem's music as a pianist's left hand supports the right."

198 *"our greatest poet . . . no luck"*: Ibid.

198 *"a tumbler of . . . in the morning"*: E. L. Doctorow, "Wright at Kenyon," in *Jack London, Hemingway, and the Constitution: Selected Essays, 1977–1992* (New York: Random House, 1993), 196.

198 *Wright interviewed*: Interview with Jane Cooper, January 18, 2001; and Alan Holder, "James Wright: Teacher–Poet," *The Hunter Magazine*, Winter 1988, 16. Holder quotes letters of recommendation submitted on Wright's behalf in April 1966 from John Crowe Ransom, Maynard Mack, and Allen Tate.

198 *"to which he has taken"*: Robert Bly letter to Tomas Tranströmer, April 10, 1966, in *Airmail*, 42.

17. A real New Yorker

199 *In April 1966 . . . Wright's lap*: Interviews with Anne Wright, June 25, 1990, and November 5, 2009; interview with Jane Cooper, January 18, 2001; and interview with Jean Valentine, March 20, 2000.

199 *"I was so impressed"*: Anne Wright, quoted in Alan Natali, "Portrait of the Artist," *Ohio Magazine* 10 (May 1987).

200 *"in case I ever"*: Interview with Anne Wright, September 18, 2001.

200 *"When I felt better"*: Interview with Robert Mezey, October 14, 1999.

200 *"Jim Wright, and Galway"*: Robert Bly letter to Tomas Tranströmer, April 29, 1966, in *Airmail: The Letters of Robert Bly and Tomas Tranströmer* (Minneapolis: Graywolf, 2013), 46. See also Galway Kinnell, August 1976, in *Walking Down the Stairs: Selections from Interviews* (Ann Arbor: University of Michigan Press, 1978), 110.

200 *"Jeremiah-like"*: Interview with Howard Nelson, April 17, 2009. See also Nelson, *Robert Bly: An Introduction* (New York: Columbia University Press, 1984).

200 *Apart from a thorough*: See Ralph J. Mills, Jr., *Contemporary American Poetry* (New York: Random House, 1965), quoted in *HotL*, 59.

201 *"expresses a fierce . . . live in any way"*: Robert Bly ("Crunk"), "The Work of James Wright," *The Sixties* No. 8 (Spring 1966), quoted in *Clear Word*, 98, *HotL*, 94.

202 *"at sixty-one"*: Selden Rodman, "A Day with Pablo Neruda," *Saturday Review*, July 9, 1966, 16.

202 *"a great American . . . reasoning men"*: Neruda reading, Poetry Center of the 92nd Street Y, June 11, 1966. Neruda quoted the first three lines of section seven of Whitman's "Song of the Exposition." Unterberg Poetry Center recording.

202 *"Jim is fine"*: Robert Bly letter to Tomas Tranströmer, July 11, 1966, in *Airmail*, 49.

202–203 *"very close . . . tragic vision"*: Interview with Galway Kinnell, January 30, 2002.

203 *"talk about poetry"*: Bly to Tranströmer, July 11, 1966.

203 *"He has an incredible"*: Robert Bly interview, spring 1966, in *Talking All Morning* (Ann Arbor: University of Michigan Press, 1980), 51.

203 *"a real New Yorker"*: Interview with Helen Wright, April 16, 2005; and JW letter to Larry Lawrence, June 2, 1973.

204 *"one for your friend"*: Interviews with Anne Wright, September 18, 2001, and May 28, 2003.

204 *"a man of letters"*: John Logan, introduction to JW reading, Unterberg Poetry Center recording, 92nd Street Y, New York, November 21, 1966,

204 *"I thought his poetry"*: Anne Wright, May 28, 2003. See the last line of "Lying in a Hammock."

204 *"He greeted me"*: Anne Wright, September 18, 2001, and May 28, 2003.

204 *Anne Runk . . . voter registration*: Interviews with Anne Wright, August 22, 2002, and Nancy Sayles-Evarts, September 16, 2008.

204–205 *Until her late . . . careful about money.* Interviews with Anne Wright, August 23, 2002, and Sayles-Evarts, September 16, 2008. See also Anne Wright, May 30, 2012 (interviewed by Chard deNiord), *American Poetry Review* 42, no. 4 (July/August 2013), 26ff.

205 *"My grandparents"*: Anne Wright, May 28, 2003.

205 *"Oh my only friend"*: JW letter to Edith Anne Runk, November 29, 1966, in *WP*, 350.

206 *"He had such a"*: Anne Wright, quoted in Natali, "Portrait of the Artist."

206–207 *"a more precise . . . grown man"*: JW reading, Coolidge Auditorium, Library of Congress, Washington, DC, with Louis Simpson, moderated by James Dickey, December 5, 1966. (See photograph.)

207 *"We used to sit"*: Interview with W. S. Merwin, October 20, 1998. "You'd be surprised at this, but one of the poets we both loved to read and recite was Alexander Pope. He adored Pope."

207 *"a kind of Christmas card"*: Anne Wright, September 18, 2001. Inscription by JW.

207 *"You have some"*: Robert Bly letter to JW, December 14, 1966.

207 *"At a Girl's Grave in Ohio"*: *Listen* 2, no. 2 (Spring 1957), East Yorkshire, England. The poem is end-rhymed, iambic pentameter. Wright's marginalia and revisions are inscribed August 11, 1960.

208 *"In Response to a Rumor"*: JW journal, March 5, 1964. Draft titled "To the Mayor of Aetnaville, O., 1964" (retitled "A Pondering of My Childhood").

208 *"You old hag . . . back my life"*: The poem had been titled "To the Ohioan Muse" and at times included a dedication to Robinson Jeffers. See multiple drafts, February 9, 1962.

210 *Wright's "Jenny"*: Interviews with Fran Quinn, June 11, 2013, and Roland Flint, October 28, 1999, and September 29, 2000. I am indebted to both poets for their insightful readings of this and many other Wright poems.

210 *Rooted to American*: Interview with Robert Bly, August 3, 2003. "I think that Lorca is very important [in "To the Muse"]. The word *Muse* is used incorrectly if it leaves out the *daemon* completely . . . [Wright was] aware of the connection of the Muse to the *daemon*."

210 *The entire poem . . . powerful spell*: Interview with Brooks Haxton, December 19, 2000.

210 *Roger Hecht believed*: Roger Hecht, interviewed by Saundra Maley, August 24, 1989.

210 *"He didn't imply"*: Interview with Sonjia Urseth, October 22, 2006. Wright spoke of a handicapped girl he knew in high school who figured in his conception of "Jenny." See JW letter, May 14, 1973, to an unnamed Japanese woman who had written to ask about "To the Muse." Wright explained that an early love had died of cancer, and described how three doctors had cut into her breast, trying to surgically remove the tumor with an electric wire. "She is buried in Weeks Cemetery, near Colerain, Ohio, a place you have never heard about."

210 *"another way of talking"*: Interview with Franz Wright, May 23, 2001.

210 *"Come down from heaven"*: David Ferry, *The Odes of Horace* (New York: Farrar, Straus and Giroux, 1997), iii.4, 169.

211 *"I've gone for a long time"*: JW letter to Donald Hall, November 25, 1966, in *WP*, 349.

18. *Dark Waters*

212 *"accept my gratitude"*: JW letter to Edith Anne Runk, January 6, 1967. "I did not bring you a mere half-dozen roses. I brought you three trilliums: my books."

212 *"He loved to joke"*: Interviews with Anne Wright, May 28, 2003, and December 31, 2006.

212 *"He figured I wouldn't"*: Anne Wright, public talk at Hunter College, November 4, 1987, published as "James Wright and Hunter College," *The Hunter Magazine*, Winter 1988, 19.

212 *One child in particular*: Interviews with Anne Wright, September 18, 2001, and October 31, 2003.

213 *"the button had just been"*: Anne Wright, quoted in Alan Natali, "Portrait of the Artist," *Ohio Magazine* 10 (May 1987).

213 *"I knew he had . . . living with a poet"*: Interviews with Anne Wright, August 23, 2002, and January 26, 2003.

213 *Merwin approached him*: Interview with W. S. Merwin, October 20, 1998.

213 *Nazri was astonished*: Interview with Sheila Ráshed, July 11, 2011. See Mahmood Jamal, ed., *The Penguin Book of Modern Urdu Poetry* (New York: Penguin, 1986), 42–57.

213 *"He is the poet"*: Anne Wright, September 18, 2001.

213 *A few days . . . monthly rent*: Anne Wright, May 28, 2003; and Kathleen Norris, *The Virgin of Bennington* (New York: Riverhead Books, 2001), 155. The address was 526 East Eighty-Fifth Street, Apt. 1W, between York and East End Avenues.

214 *"I thought it a bit"*: Anne Wright, public talk, Kenyon College, Gambier, OH, March 26, 1983.

214 *Earlier that month*: Dr. Martin Luther King, Jr., "A Time to Break the Silence," speech at Riverside Church, New York, April 4, 1967.

214 *"periodic rages"*: LK memoir, 23, 288, 290–294, 302.

214 *"humiliation and terror"*: Interview with Franz Wright, May 23, 2001.

214 *Liberty did not protect*: LK memoir, 409.

214 *"would sit and listen"*: Sheila Ráshed, July 11, 2011.

215 *Soon after they were*: Interview with Anne Wright, October 31, 2004.

215 *Robert Mezey was then editing*: Interview with Robert Mezey, October 14, 1999. Mezey later repudiated the anthology.

215 *"heartbreaking"*: Ibid. See JW letter to Robert Mezey, spring 1967, in *WP*, 352. Mezey had heard Wright rant in this way before, "but never with that kind of unmitigated hatred and disgust and totality. It was part of him." The letter in *WP* is a statement Wright sent to replace the first. Mezey, October 14, 1999.

215 *"catastrophic" decline*: Robert Bly, "The Collapse of James Dickey," *The Sixties* No. 9 (Spring 1967): 70; and interview with Mark Gustafson, April 17, 2009.

216 *"intensely serious"*: JW interviewed by Leslie Cross, "James Wright's Animals Are the McCoy," *The Milwaukee Journal*, July 2, 1967, part 5, 4.

216 *"We drank together"*: Anne Wright, October 31, 2003.

216 *"he wrote on the fly"*: Ibid.

216 *"Admitting & recording"*: Anne Wright class notes, June 28, 1967. See also the more detailed class notes recorded by Therese Vezeridis.

216 *Prompted by . . . public resistance*: Howard Zinn, *The Twentieth Century: A People's History* (New York: Harper Perennial, 2003), 203.

217 *"the people around Tate"*: Interview with Anne Wright, May 19, 2011.

217 *"Take it easy"*: Interviews with Roland Flint, October 28, 1999, and Anne Wright, January 15, 2013.

217 *"affection for life"*: JW and Robert Bly, readings, with Roland Flint, "The Language That Saves," two half-hour programs recorded at University of Minnesota, Minneapolis, KUOM studios, late July 1967.

217 *The cabin's new outhouse*: Interviews with Anne Wright, April 19, 2009, and Carol Bly, April 16, 2000.

218 *"It hangs together . . . have ever written"*: JW letter to José de la Torre Bueno, June 23, 1967.

218 *"quiet dignity"*: Interview with Anne Wright, August 22, 2002.

218 *"so we could hear"*: Anne Wright, October 31, 2003.

218 *"he'd say, 'Oh'"*: Ibid.

218 *"very gentle and saintly man"*: Interview with Anne Wright, March 23, 2000.

219 *They returned to*: See Anne Wright, "Many Waters," in Frank Graziano, ed., *James Wright: A Profile* (Durango, CO: Logbridge-Rhodes, 1988), 111. Anne's memoir offers detailed recollections of their stays at Lake Minnewaska.

219 *"He rarely talked"*: Interview with Anne Wright, May 28, 2003.

219 *"was going on in his mind"*: Ibid.

219 *The bartender would shout*: Interviews with Anne Wright, April 15, 2009, and Lyle Tollefson, April 15, 2009.

219 *"to create sense"*: JW letter to John Crowe Ransom, January 15, 1968, in *WP*, 356; and JW letter to Muriam Black, December 13, 1967, in *WP*, 354.

219 *"It has a sting"*: JW letter to Sister Bernetta Quinn, October 16, 1967.

220 *"It's taken me a long time . . . what else?"*: JW reading, State University of New York at Buffalo, November 15, 1967, The Poetry Collection of the University Libraries, University at Buffalo, the State University of New York

220 *"Out of what"*: John Haag, "Beyond the Green Wall," AWP's *The Writer's Chronicle* 25, no. 4 (February 1993). "Considering the impact, who will notice or give a damn about the form in the shock of first reading?"

221 *"a prayer and a hymn"*: JW reading, State University of New York at Buffalo, November 15, 1967.

222 *"If you were born"*: JW reading, San Francisco State University, CA, April 17, 1968, The Poetry Center and American Poetry Archives.

222 *"Before a Cashier's"*: Ibid. One inspiration for the poem's conclusion can be heard in lines from Robinson's "Captain Craig" that Wright often recited, in which the protagonist asks, "But what has this to do / With Spring?" See *CP*, 233.

222 *"I see you're still"*: Interviews with Anne Wright, October 13, 2008, and Marshall Wright, October 17, 2006.

222 *"warm, slightly immature"*: Anne Wright letter to Henry Esterly, February 20, 1982.

223 *"But a great poet"*: JW essay/review, "I Come to Speak for Your Dead Mouths," June 1968, in *CP*, 291.

224 *"So many things"*: JW letter to Eugene Pugatch, July 28, 1968. See also JW letter to Fred Hein, July 28, 1968, in *WP*, 358.

224 *Wright's sister, Marge . . . his head away.* Anne Wright, March 11, 2007.

19. The shape of one's own life

225 *"a large number"*: Anne Wright, public talk, November 4, 1987, published as "James Wright and Hunter College," *The Hunter Magazine*, Winter 1988.

225 *"I'm not telling anyone!"*: Interview with Anne Wright, March 21, 2004.

225 *"started to call up"*: JW reading, San Francisco State University, CA, April 17, 1968. The Poetry Center and American Poetry Archives.

226 *Robert Mezey called*: Interview with Robert Mezey, October 14, 1999.

226 *"anger and self-conflicts"*: Roger Hecht, interviewed by Saundra Maley, August 24, 1989.

226 *Marge Piercy and Michael Benedikt*: JW, moderator, Unterberg Poetry Center recording, 92nd Street Y, New York, November 4, 1968; interview with C. W. Truesdale and Anne Wright, October 4, 2000; and interview with Anne Wright, November 5, 2010.

226 *"a very dark moment"*: JW letter to Allen Tate, December 6, 1968, in *WP*, 362.

227 *"a supremely personal . . . of the earth'"*: C. W. Truesdale, "The Grain of Poetry: In Memory of Dr. James Wright"; *Milkweed Chronicle*, vol. 1, no. 2; Spring/Summer 1980; Truesdale, October 4, 2000; and interview with Charles Baxter, May 21, 2010.

227 *"callow youth"*: Truesdale (1986), quoting a letter by Anne Wright; footnote to "On Which Side of the Green Wall Were They Standing?," review of Leslie Marmon Silko and James Wright, *The Delicacy and Strength of Lace: Letters*, in *Abraxas* 34 (Fall 1986): 78.

227 *In other versions*: Truesdale, Anne Wright, October 4, 2000; and Baxter, May 21, 2010. Baxter's short story "The Cousins" dramatizes this scene with a character named Burroughs Hammond, who is based on Wright. *Gryphon: New and Selected Stories* (New York: Pantheon Books, 2011), 363.

227 *"did not fit this age"*: Truesdale, "The Grain of Poetry" (1980). In his review of *Delicacy*, "On Which Side" (1986), Truesdale noted, "The rage [Wright] felt and sometimes exercised toward those who did not share his beliefs was really Swiftean in its magnitude."

227 *"the anger was"*: Interview with Anne Wright, November 9, 2010.

227 *"I have a very strong . . . passionately intellectual"*: JW reading, Sir George Williams University, Montreal, Canada, December 13, 1968.

227 *Uncollected Rilke poem*: Wright recited Rilke's "Wenn die Uhren so nah" ("When the clocks nearby / Strike as if their own hearts were beating"), JW typescript circa 1960–61, working with Sarah Youngblood. See Maley, appendix C-5, 579.

228 *Silver grew convinced*: Dr. Irving Silver, as quoted in interviews with Anne Wright, September 18, 2001, and December 3, 2006.

228 *"gang of punks"*: JW journal, January 18, 1969.

228 *"Grace, not Deserving"*: JW marginalia to letter from Diane Wakoski, February 4, 1969.

228 *"a crop of poets"*: *Time*, "Combatting Society with Surrealism," January 24, 1969 (vol. 93, no. 4), 72–76. The article printed the first stanzas of "Inscription for the Tank," but the poem's bitter irony entirely escaped the reviewer.

228 *"write a poem"*: JW journal, February 19, 1969.

228 *"The voice of a major"*: David Ignatow, introducing JW reading, Guggenheim Museum, New York, February 25, 1969. See Ignatow, *The One in the Many: A Poet's Memoirs* (Middletown, CT: Wesleyan University Press, 1988), 141.

228–229 *"Little brown notebook . . . You dead"*: JW journal, "Another Phony Addition to the Book of Job," February 25, 1969.

229 *"Out of the reach of change"*: JW poem draft, undated, verso draft dated March 10, 1969.

229 *As scattered applause*: Ignatow, *The One in the Many*, 110.

229 *"Not the East River"*: JW handwritten draft, March 19, 1969. Wright's edits begin: "Call it: 'This is Not an Apology to the Muse.' Then revise the concluding lines thus . . .'"

230 *"stubborn, manly honesty"*: Laurence Lieberman (*Poetry*, April 1969), *HotL*, 186.

230 *"a book of beauty"*: Robert Penn Warren letter to JW, March 7, 1969.

230 *"This is the poetry"*: David Ignatow, *New York Times Book Review*, March 9, 1969, 31. Reprinted, titled "James Wright," in *Open Between Us* (Poets on Poetry), David Ignatow, ed. Ralph J. Mills, Jr. (Ann Arbor: University of Michigan Press, 1980), 252.

230 Critique: JW interview and reading, WNDT Educational Broadcasting Corp, April 1, 1969; and interview with Anne Wright, March 2, 2010.

230 *"He was such a brilliant"*: Interview with Franz Wright, May 23, 2001. "Once on the telephone when I was in high school he said, 'What are you reading in your English class?' And I said, '*Beowulf*,' and then he started reciting *Beowulf*—in *Old English*—off the top of his head for five minutes."

230 *"unique masterpiece"*: JW journal, February 19, 1969. Jean Toomer, *Cane* (New York: Perennial Classic, Harper & Row, 1969). Wright's teaching copy is heavily annotated; marginal notes include references to Rilke's *Notebooks of Malte Laurids Brigge*, Aristotle's *Poetics*, and southern Ohio vernacular street rhymes. He also notes parallel images and metaphors in Dickens and Rilke.

230 *"I sometimes think"*: JW reading, University of Michigan, Ann Arbor, April 11, 1969.

231 *"I would give"*: JW marginalia on Rev. Dilio E. Mariotti letter to JW, March 24, 1969. Wright gave his sermon at the United Methodist Church in Old Chatham, New York, on April 27, 1969.

231 *"the dark lyric poet"*: JW, "Of Things Invisible," in *CP*, 126.

231 *"I know of no"*: JW letter to Richard Howard, November 30, 1970; *WP*, 367. See Richard Howard, ed., *Preferences* (New York: Viking Press, 1974), 321. For Howard's anthology, Wright paired "To Flood Stage Again" with a passage from *Ecclesiastes* (IX, 11, 12), to suggest a source of influence.

231 *"I'd never seen him"*: Interview with Nicholas Crome, April 24, 1999.

231 *"The most powerfully"*: JW reading, Colorado State University, Fort Collins, May 16, 1969. Printed in *Georgia Review* 55, no. 3 (Fall 2001): 420. Transcribed, edited, and introduced by the author.

232 *"cathedrals of elms"*: John Knoepfle (memoir), "A *Green Snake* Interview: 'In the Picture'" (a self-interview; from unpublished manuscript).

232 *"Jim was happy in Buffalo"*: Interview with Jerome Mazzaro, February 6, 2003.

232 *"breaking new ground"*: Ibid.

232 *"There is nothing sacred"*: William Carlos Williams, from Prologue to *Kora in Hell: Improvisations*, in *Imaginations* (New York: New Directions, 1970), 13; quoted in M. L. Rosenthal, ed., *The William Carlos Williams Reader* (New York: New Directions, 1966), xv. In Wright's teaching copy of *The WCW Reader*, these lines are underscored, with the marginal comment: "read aloud." In his introduction, Rosenthal misquotes Williams's text, deleting "whenever I damn please and as I damn please" at the point marked with ellipsis.

233 *"very, very far"*: JW interview, with Allen DeLoach and Anselm Hollo, Buffalo, New York, August 12, 1969, The Poetry Collection of the University Libraries, University at Buffalo, the State University of New York.

233–34 *"I confess that I knew . . . Welcome to Hell, / Dad."* JW letter to Franz Wright, July 20, 1969.

234 *"Real writing is hell"*: JW journal, February 25, 1969.

234 *"gasoline sloshing"*: Knoepfle, memoir.

234 *At the end of July*: Interview with Anne Wright, February 29, 2016.

234 *That September, Anne Sexton*: Diane Wood Middlebrook, *Anne Sexton: A Biography* (Wilmington, MA: Houghton Mifflin, 1991), 328, 336.

234 *"very attractive"*: Interview with Anne Wright, May 28, 2003.

235 *"I wish I had"*: Anne Sexton, quoted by Anne Wright, ibid.

235 *"The End of the World"*: Both of Wright's translations of Melo Neto (including "Education by Stone") were chosen for the bilingual anthology *Twentieth Century Brazilian Poetry*, edited by Elizabeth Bishop and Emanuel Brasil (Middletown, CT: Wesleyan University Press, 1972).

235 *"superb . . . marvelously alive"*: JW letter to Franz Wright, October 16, 1969.

235 *A unique figure*: Born in 1921, Carruth wrote about the hardships of rural poverty and explored many languages and forms of poetry. He shared Wright's struggles with alcohol and mental illness. Carruth's anthology, *The Voice That Is Great Within Us: American Poetry of the Twentieth Century* (New York: Bantam Books, 1971), remains one of the best collections of its kind.

235–36 *"I think it's very much . . . kind of shy pride"*: Hayden Carruth, public talk, Fourth Annual James Wright Poetry Festival, Martins Ferry, OH, May 4, 1984.

236 *"I worked hard"*: Interview with Hayden Carruth, December 19, 2000.

236 *"It takes one to know one"*: Interview with Gibbons Ruark, October 29, 1999.

237 *"a strange and haunting"*: JW letter to Galway Kinnell, August 12, 1969.

237 *"seemed distracted"*: Interview with Dave Smith, March 25, 2010.

238 *"deal with the single"*: JW, "Translator's Note on Herman Hesse," in *CP*, 87.

238 *Wright chose poems*: See Maley, 9, 382. Wright had drafted versions of four of the thirty-one Hesse *Poems* while at Kenyon.

238 *"It is our lot . . . men and women"*: JW letter to Franz Wright, February 6, 1970.

239 *More than forty*: JW reading, University of Massachusetts, Amherst, March 14, 1970; see *The Massachusetts Daily Collegian*, March 16, 1970, 2. Robert Francis,

Michael Harper, David Ignatow, Donald Hall, Denise Levertov, John Logan, and many others appeared.

239 *"You never were good"*: Robert Bly, at ibid., as told to Fran Quinn by Joseph Langland, interviewed August 27, 2013, and others.

239 *"actor and ham . . . very interested"*: Carol Bly memoir, "James Wright's Visits to Odin House," *Ironwood* 10, vol. 5, no. 2 (1977), 33.

240 *On Thursday, April 30*: Howard Zinn, *The Twentieth Century: A People's History* (New York: Harper Perennial, 2003), 240.

241 *"His evening reading"*: Interview with James Reiss, December 5, 2011.

241 *"You could tell"*: Interview with Tony Stoneburner, April 16, 2009.

241 *"therefore let us read"*: Tony Stoneburner, private journal, May 1970, quoting Robert Daniel, Kenneth Marshall, and others. Wright stayed at the home of the English Department chair, Robert Daniel.

241 *"garrulous perhaps"*: Stoneburner, April 16, 2009.

241 *"was on a real bender"*: Interview with David Young, September 3, 2013.

242 *"I never, ever heard"*: Marge Wright Pyle, interviewed by Peter Stitt with Anne Wright, May 9, 1995.

242 *"He really loved New York"*: Interviews with Eugene Pugatch, February 2, 2000, and with Pugatch, Robert Mezey, and Anne Wright, December 12, 2001.

242 *"If you don't like it"*: Interview with Anne Wright, November 23, 2003.

242 *Betty and Anne*: Interview with Kathleen Norris, January 8, 2012; and Kathleen Norris, *The Virgin of Bennington* (New York: Riverhead Books, 2001), 150.

242 *"This afternoon I completed"*: JW journal, June 3, 1970.

20. A certain high summer

244 *"slightly shabby and inexpensive"*: Anne Wright, unpublished "Paris Walks" memoir.

245 *"Surprisingly, all sorts"*: JW interview, September 24, 1970, in *CP*, 162.

245 *Among his first*: JW journal, June 28, 1970, and interview with Anne Wright, July 11, 2011.

245 *"We arrived somewhat weary"*: JW journal, July 4, 1970.

246 *"mysterious and melancholy"*: JW journal, July 10, 1970.

246 *"Bologna: A Poem About Gold"*: JW journal, July 14, 1970; and interview with Anne Wright, August 22, 2002.

247 *If Wright ever "quested"*: Interview with Anne Wright, February 15, 2011.

247 *His journals reveal*: JW journal, July 29, 1970.

247 *"[a]bhorrent, green"*: D. H. Lawrence, "Pomegranate"; *The Complete Poems*, ed. Pinto and Roberts (New York: Viking Press, 1964), 278. See JW, "Two Moments in Venice," 307.

247 *"I hope you're not serious"*: JW, quoted in interview with Anne Wright, April 13, 2003.

247–48 *"took on the role . . . who'd ever lived"*: Interview with Marshall Wright, October 17, 2006.

248 *"Just to be in"*: Interview with Franz Wright, May 23, 2001.

248 *"wept like a child . . . and go on"*: Franz Wright letter to JW, August 6, 1979.

248 *"The place was so"*: JW reading, Poetry Center of the University of Arizona, Tucson, February 21, 1973.

249 *In September 1970*: JW letter to Jack Wright, September 25, 1976, in *WP*, 457, and interview with Richard Barickman, May 20, 2005.

249 *His reading included*: JW reading, State University of New York, Brockport, September 23, 1970, The Poetry Collection of the University Libraries, University at Buffalo, the State University of New York.

249 *"All we want is"*: Ibid. Wright considered using this line as the epigraph for *The River* when the manuscript was still called *Dark Water* in December 1965.

249 *"It was an astounding moment"*: Interviews with Charles Baxter, May 21, 2010, and August 8, 2010. See also Baxter, "Writers and the Bottle," PowellsBooks.Blog, January 30, 2015.

249 *He had, in a real sense*: Paul Auster, ed., *Random House Book of Twentieth Century French Poetry* (New York: Random House, 1982), 27.

250 *"one of the chosen . . . as I could"*: JW interview, September 24, 1970, in *CP*, 155.

250 *"the spiritual weather"*: JW letter to Franz Wright, September 26, 1970.

250 *"It was appalling"*: Interview with Anne Wright, January 18, 2001. The reading took place December 9, 1970.

251 *"Jim looks better"*: Hardie St. Martin letter to Robert Bly, December 22, 1970. Robert Bly papers, Andersen Library Archives.

251 *"I'm getting sort of tired"*: JW interview, September 24, 1970, in *CP*, 158.

251 *"He would make . . . your own language"*: Franz Wright, May 23, 2001.

251 *"I felt, while reading"*: Michael di Capua letter to JW, June 1, 1971.

251–52 *"mined from his . . . lovely little book"*: JW, "Blurb on Hesse's *Wanderung*," April 14, 1971.

252 *"the experience of being"*: Anne Wright, January 18, 2001.

252 *"His originality in the classroom"*: Alan Holder, "James Wright: Teacher–Poet"; *The Hunter Magazine*, Winter 1988, 16.

252 *In truth, Wright*: Interview with Jane Giles McClung, June 1, 2009.

252 *"more than a transparency"*: Interview with Stanley Plumly, October 15, 2002. "That was when, for me, Jim Wright elevated to greatness as a poet," Plumly said, recalling the first time he read these new poems. In the arc of Wright's career, "it's a transforming moment."

252 *"emphatically . . . of our day"*: Peter Stitt, *New York Times Book Review*, May 16, 1971, in *HotL*, 239.

253 *"I care more about"*: JW letter to José de la Torre Bueno, May 24, 1971.

253 *"big, nutty"*: JW letter to Karin East, June 2, 1971; and interview with Howard Fink, March 27, 2007.

253 *"That was one of the happiest"*: Interview with Anne Wright, November 1, 2002.

254 *"splendid company"*: JW letter to Robert and Carol Bly, August 5, 1971, in *WP*, 370.

254 *Spurred by the cruelty*: Interviews with Anne Wright, March 11, 2007, and Karin East Marvin, January 22, 2011.

254 *"scores of collegiate . . . the imagination"*: A. T. Baker, "Poetry Today: Low Profile, Flatted Voice," *Time*, July 12, 1971. Sylvia Plath is named the "Virgin Mary" of the "Confessional Sufferers," who "have their enshrined god in Lowell." Robert Bly is bizarrely paired with Gregory Corso as a "Polemical Roarer," beholden to their "guru," Allen Ginsberg. Galway Kinnell and Wright are incongruously joined with Robert Creeley and Charles Olson's "Tiny Imagists."

254 *"As for the different kinds"*: JW interview, October 1971, in *CP*, 133.

254–55 *The book's new title . . . "be damned"*: JW typescript table of contents, August 13, 1971.

255 *"Well, bright boy,'"*: Ernest Hemingway, "The Killers," from *The Complete Short Stories* (The Finca Vigia Edition) (New York: Scribner, 1987), 217.

255 *"The presiding genius"*: Babette Deutsch, "A 'Fashionable' Poet?," *The New Republic*, July 17, 1971. Wright's marginalia reads: "N.B.: for 2 *Citizens*: remember Vergil, *Georgics*, III: 'Optima dies prima fugit,' etc."

255 *"has in his own way"*: Roger Hecht, review of *Collected Poems* in *The Nation*, August 2, 1971.

255 *"Hard, clear, simple"*: Hayden Carruth, review of *Collected Poems* in *The Hudson Review* 24, no. 2 (Summer 1971): 331.

255 *"I respect this review"*: JW marginalia to Stephen Spender, review of *Collected Poems* in *The New York Review of Books*, July 22, 1971.

21. It is all we have, just each other

256 *"America is so gloomy"*: JW letter to Robert and Carol Bly, August 5, 1971, in *WP*, 370.

257 *"October Ghosts"*: See Robert Hass, "James Wright" (1977), in *Clear Word*, 218; *HotL*, 302; and interview with Stanley Plumly, October 15, 2002. Plumly characterizes Wright's "love poem–elegy" as his "essential emotional stance toward the world."

257 *"I wouldn't look for . . . its own sake"*: JW interview, fall 1971, in *CP*, 145.

257 *"a sort of minor festival"*: Robert Bly letter to Tomas Tranströmer, September 3, 1971, in *Airmail: The Letters of Robert Bly and Tomas Tranströmer* (Minneapolis: Graywolf, 2013), 205. The photograph of Bly, Wright, and Anne Wright used as the frontispiece to Wright's *Selected Poems* (Farrar, Straus and Giroux, 2005) was taken by Katherine Saltonstall Dewart at this event, October 15–17, 1971.

258 *"one of the most . . . of the world"*: Interview with Robert Morgan, September 10, 2012.

258 *"hand in hand"*: Anselm Parlatore, e-mail to author, February 9, 2012.

258 *"It was just exhilaration"*: Interview with Marshall Wright, October 17, 2006.

259 *"was pretty much . . . than other people"*: Plumly, October 15, 2002; and quoting Anne Wright.

259 *"the court circling . . . martyrdom"*: Interview with E. L. Doctorow, March 19, 2002.

259 *"Already as a student"*: Interview with David Young, September 3, 2013.

259 *Wright knew Oberlin's reputation*: See LK memoir, 318. Liberty Kovacs writes, "Franz became addicted to alcohol and drugs at Oberlin, and he graduated in 1977." Also interview with Anne Wright, March 19, 2013.

259 *In mid-February*: JW readings, Buffalo, New York, February 18 and 19, 1972, The Poetry Collection of the University Libraries, University at Buffalo, the State University of New York.

260 *"It was totally magical"*: Interview with Robert Hass, June 18, 2001. Hass recognized this "act of showmanship" as a form of self-protection—not shyness so much as "a way of just leaving his private life out, of not having to deal with questions and answers and small talk."

260 *In New York City*: Anne Wright, public talk, November 4, 1987, published as "James Wright and Hunter College," *The Hunter Magazine*, Winter 1988, 19, quoting Douglas Henderson, a student; and interview with Jane Giles McClung, June 1, 2009.

260 *"Spanish leaping"*: Republished as Robert Bly, ed., *Leaping Poetry: An Idea with Poems and Translations* (Boston: Beacon Press, 1975).

261 *"And once I spent"*: JW, "A Letter to Franz Wright." See JW letter to Franz Wright, November 27, 1973, in *WP*, 399; and JW journal, November 14, 1976.

261 *"As for myself"*: Pablo Neruda, "The Murdered Albatross," trans. M. S. Peden, 1983, in Neruda, *Passions and Impressions* (New York: Farrar, Straus and Giroux, 1983), 375; and Adam Feinstein, *Pablo Neruda: A Passion for Life* (New York: Bloomsbury, 2004), 386.

261 *After H. R. Hays*: Neruda reading, with JW, Unterberg Poetry Center recording, 92nd Street Y, New York, April 12, 1972. Bly, Hays, Ben Belitt, Nathaniel Tarn, and Donald Walsh also took part.

261 *"repeatedly amazed"*: Interviews with Gibbons Ruark, October 29, 1999, and June 25, 2011.

262 *"I regard myself . . . carefully dreamed"*: JW, interviewed by Peter Stitt, April 21 and 22, 1972, "Art of Poetry" interview for *The Paris Review*, vol. 16, no. 62 (Summer 1975): 34, reprinted in Peter Stitt, *The World's Hieroglyphic Beauty: Five American Poets* (Athens: University of Georgia Press, 1985).

262 *"He handled it . . . vulnerable"*: Interview with Anne Wright, January 28, 2014.

262 *"Well, it will look"*: JW, to his parents, quoted in interview with Anne Wright, Febraury 4, 2014.

263 *"drinking was always a problem"*: Interview with Anne Wright, October 31, 2003.

263 *"pure, clear classicism"*: JW interview, *Envoy*, Hunter College, May 12, 1972.

263 *"Aren't you a little bit"*: JW to Elizabeth Kray, quoted in interview with Jean Valentine, March 20, 2000.

263 *"I just knew"*: Interview with Sonjia Urseth, October 22, 2006. When Diane Wood Middlebrook published her biography of Anne Sexton in 1991, Urseth discovered with relief that she had little to do with Wright's troubles and unhappy marriage. In May 1972, she was still convinced that she had "broken his heart."

263 *"uncanny richness . . . quiet listener"*: Irv Broughton, "Pastiche from an Afternoon with James Wright," *Copula* 1, no. 2 (1980), 50.

264 *"was still thinking about"*: Interview with David Wagoner, June 8, 1999.

264 *"a marvelous performance"*: Ibid., and JW reading, University of Washington, Seattle, May 25, 1972, Special Collections, University Library Archives.

264 *"Sometimes, poor old America"*: JW, untitled prose typescript, May 25, 1972.

264 *While in Seattle*: Interview with Rae Tufts, June 2, 1999.

265 *Anne took him*: Interview with Anne Wright, August 23, 2006. Wright suffered from a rare type of hemophilia—the same condition that led to Franz's dismissal from military service. Interview with Dr. Eugene Pugatch, January 23, 2004.

265 *"If you don't stop"*: Interviews with Dr. Robert Segal, March 22, 2010, and Anne Wright, November 17, 2009.

265 *Silver even encouraged*: Dr. Irving Silver, quoted in interview with Anne Wright, November 1, 2002.

265 *"We both feel"*: JW journal, Paris, June 20, 1972.

265 *"Any traveler toward"*: JW, "The Last Day in Paris," *The Paris Review* 16, no. 62 (Summer 1975): 65.

265 *"makes one feel"*: Rainer Maria Rilke, *Letters to a Young Poet*, no. 5, October 29, 1903, from Rome, trans. Stephen Mitchell (New York: Modern Library, 1984), 46.

265 *"children at the top . . . on the earth"*: JW journal, Rome, July 5, 1972. See also "The Snail's Road."

266 *"antiquity of . . . summer dark"*: JW journal, "Martyrdom," Rome, July 8, 1972. See "A Lament for the Martyrs," in *Moments of the Italian Summer* (Washington, DC: Dryad Press, 1976), 16, and the edited piece published in *Pear Tree*: "A Lament for the Shadows in the Ditches," 287.

266 *With costs still low*: Interviews with Anne Wright, November 20, 1999, and July 7, 2004.

266 *The pilgrimage inspired*: JW journal, "At the Tomb of Cestius, Near the Protestant Cemetery in Rome," July 9, 1972.

266 *Fano quickly became*: Interview with Anne Wright, Fano, July 13, 2004.

267 *"It occurs to me"*: JW journal, Urbino, July 24, 1972. The image echoes Wright's translation of Vallejo, adapted as "The Jewel"; variations on this theme recur in his journals. See, e.g., JW journal, July 15, 1979, and December 21, 1979.

267 *"There was just the dirt"*: Interview with Anne Wright, Anghiari, July 7, 2004.

267 *"Spider in Anghiari"*: JW journal, Nice, France, August 10, 1972.

268 *"almost like a ballet"*: Interview with Laura Lee DeCinque, January 22, 2011.

268 *"very creative with"*: Interview with Karin East Marvin, January 22, 2011.

268 *"Laura & Karin"*: JW journal, Nice, France, August 9, 1972.

268 *"The fates have changed"*: JW, "To Marcel Dupré, Organist of San Sulpice," *The Hudson Review* 26, no. 3 (Autumn 1973): 507.

269 *"Jim always wore"*: Interview with Richard Barickman, May 20, 2005.

269 *When* The New Yorker: "On a Correction, For Money," marginalia on letter from *New Yorker* editor, September 11, 1972.

269 *As in the best*: Interview with Marilyn Hacker, December 15, 2000.

269 *"People feel I may"*: JW, quoted in "Capturing of Images Secret, Pulitzer Prize Poet Says Here," *The Pittsburgh Press*, November 18, 1972.

269 *"the America which I still love"*: JW letter to Gibbons Ruark, December 6, 1972. Wright refers to Ruark's poem "Night Fishing." Ruark, *Passing Through Customs: New and Selected Poems* (Baton Rouge: Louisiana State University Press, 1999), 3.

270 *"He talked to Franz"*: Marshall Wright, October 17, 2006.

270 *"gambling under the trees"*: Ibid.; Anne Wright, November 1, 2002; and LK memoir, 307.

270 *"would always take me aside"*: Interview with Franz Wright, May 23, 2001.

271 *"preparing to write a book"*: "Pulitzer Prize Winner's Family Lives in County," *The Times-Recorder* (Zanesville, Ohio), May 3, 1972.

22. I have torn myself out of many bitter places / In America

275 *"I have torn myself out"*: JW, "To the Saguaro Cactus Tree in the Desert Rain."

275 *"Every poet ought to visit"*: JW journal, January 15, 1973 (complete entry).

276 *"This spring, thank Christ"*: JW letter to Mary Oliver, January 24, 1973.

276 *"the Professor"*: Interview with Anne Wright, March 11, 2014.

276 *"with two days out"*: Diane Wood Middlebrook, *Anne Sexton: A Biography* (Wilmington, MA: Houghton Mifflin, 1991), 366.

276 *"Strip the language"*: Ibid., 367.

276 *Maxine Kumin*: Interview with Maxine Kumin, October 28, 2008. Other critics would echo Wright's judgments when the book appeared after Sexton's death, but by then the poems had already benefited from Wright's detailed comments. Ibid., 368.

277 *"plain and direct . . . with enough attention"*: Michael Cuddihy letter to JW, February 9, 1973.

277 *"If you can only be"*: JW reading, Florida Institute of Technology, Melbourne, FL, February 15, 1973, The Poetry Collection of the University Libraries, University at Buffalo, the State University of New York.

277 *"as if no time"*: Interview with Anne Wright, April 3, 2012.

277 *He gave a generous*: JW reading, Poetry Center of the University of Arizona, Tucson, February 21, 1973; Poetry Center recording.

278 *Acknowledging his brother*: Interviews with Helen Wright, April 21, 2002, and Michael S. Harper, September 19, 2001.

278 *Anne and others*: See Richard Shelton letter to Tony Stoneburner, Stoneburner private journal, February 1973.

278 *"an incredible force field"*: Richard Shelton, memorial reading for JW, Poetry Center of the University of Arizona, Tucson, April 2, 1980.

278 *"Redemption"*: JW journal, February 25, 1973; *APR*, July/August 1973; vol. 2, no. 4; 35 (uncollected).

279 *"stunned and wide-eyed"*: Interview with Mark Strand, April 30, 2010.

279 *Returning home one afternoon*: Interviews with Anne Wright, December 17, 2009, and Carol Bly, April 16, 2000.

279 *"To Bee, for her Book"*: JW journal, April 5, 1973.

279 *"two natural aristocrats"*: JW letter to Sarah Youngblood, May 2, 1973; interviews with Anne Wright, March 11, 2014, and Maxine Kumin, October 28, 2008.

280 *"why let people push"*: JW, as told to Anne Wright, interviewed October 11, 2008.

280 *"a fiasco"*: Anne Wright notes; and interview with Anne Wright, March 11, 2014. See also JW letter to Sarah Youngblood, June 8, 1973.

280 Mercian Hymns: Geoffrey Hill, *Selected Poems* (New Haven, CT: Yale University Press, 2006), 59. The sequence refers to the historical King Offa, who ruled in eighth-century Britain, and his figurative appearance as "the presiding genius of the West Midlands." JW journal, July 14, 1973.

280 *"This beautiful and strange book"*: JW journal, July 25, 1973.

280 *"at least twenty times."* JW letter to Donald Hall, September 25, 1973; *WP*, 394.

281 *He wanted the sense*: Interview with Franz Wright, May 23, 2001.

281 *"the magnificent Folies Bergère"*: JW journal, Paris, July 29, 1973.

281 *They often returned*: JW journal, July 31, 1973; and interview with Marshall Wright, October 17, 2006.

281 *When Marshall left Paris*: More than thirty years later, Marshall said only, "Texas was a bad scene." Ibid.

281 *"50-year employee"*: The *Times-Recorder* (Zanesville, Ohio), July 30, 1973.

281 *"stepped all unknowing"*: JW journal, Paris, June 17, 1977.

282 *He drafted another*: JW journal, August 18, 1973. See "The Language of the Present Moment."

282 *After arriving in Verona . . . own candle to Anne*: Interview with Anne Wright, Verona, July 20, 2004.

283 *"I've been writing"*: JW letter to John Logan, August 30, 1973, in *WP*, 392.

283 *Protests sprang up*: JW journal, Venice, September 13, 1973; and interview with Anne Wright, Venice, July 16, 2004. Concerning Neruda's murder, see Liam Stack, "New Mystery Surfaces," *New York Times*, November 7, 2015.

283 *"A dead girl"*: JW journal, draft poem, "Candle," October 2, 1973; see "Lighting a Candle for W. H. Auden."

284 *"It is so golden"*: JW letter to Robert Mezey, dated October 4, 1973 [likely written October 7, 1973].

284 *This first handwritten*: JW journal, October 22, 1973. See Hermann Hesse, "Farm," in *Wandering: Notes and Sketches*, trans. JW (New York: Farrar, Straus and Giroux, 1972), 46.

285 *The epigraph*: Virgil, Third *Georgic*, lines 66–67, see *The Georgics of Virgil*, trans. David Ferry (New York: Farrar, Straus and Giroux, 2005), 97. Wright's abbreviation of Virgil is found on the title page of Willa Cather's *My Ántonia* (Boston: Houghton Mifflin, 1954), where ellipses mark a deletion in the middle of the phrase. Since he had translated Virgil's poem himself (and knew much of Cather's novel by heart), Wright clearly preferred this version of Virgil's phrase.

285 *After Assisi, Florence*: Interview with Anne Wright, April 20, 2014; and JW letter to Franz Wright, from Rome, November 27, 1973, in *WP*, 399. The prose piece "A Letter to Franz Wright" is rewritten from the original letter.

285 *"two shepherds"*: Anne Wright open letter to friends, December 1974.

285 *"Underground, the hair"*: JW journal, Paris, January 6, 1974.

286 *They spent the night*: Anne Wright open letter to friends, December 1974; and JW letter to Jack Wright, from Paris, December 26, 1973.

23. Apologia for the Ohioan Tongue

287 *Open admissions*: Interview with Richard Barickman, May 20, 2005.

287 *"Dickens wrote"*: Ibid.

287 *"He took us seriously"*: Interview with Donna Masini, January 25, 2001.

288 *"He was a real performer"*: Interview with Kathy Purcell, August 14, 2014.

288 *"It doesn't say"*: JW letter to "Carol" [surname unknown], February 24, 1974.

288 *"decline into mawkishness"*: Edward Butscher, *The Georgia Review*, 1974, in *Clear Word*, 124.

288 *"That book was a mistake"*: JW, quoted in Alan Williamson, "An American Lyricist," *The New Republic*, 1983, in *HotL*, 411.

288 *"emotional exclamatoriness"*: Alan Williamson, *Shenandoah*, 1975, in *HotL*, 358.

288 *"straight, honest"*: Edward Engelberg, *The Southern Review*, 1974, in *HotL*, 356.

288 *"mannerism of sentimental"*: Williamson, "American Lyricist," in *HotL*, 412.

288 *"I think Jim"*: Interview with Jerome Mazzaro, February 6, 2003.

288 *"No more readings"*: JW journal, February 19, 1974.

289 *a dull joke*: "Wright's poetry indeed ain't much." William H. Pritchard, "Poetry Matters," *The Hudson Review* 26, no. 3 (Autumn 1973).

289 *Pritchard's arrogance*: See "Apologia for the Ohioan Tongue," JW journal, August 3, 1974.

289 *"Too cold for the snow"*: JW typescript, February 27, 1974. Wright later struck out these lines, as well as a disparaging reference to Pritchard by name.

290 *"'Hook' conveys"*: Stephen Yenser, "Open Secrets," *Parnassus: Poetry in Review*, 1978, in *HotL*, 325.

290 *Wright had not*: Jessie Lyons Wright died in Zanesville, Ohio, on March 2, 1974, at age seventy-six.

290 *Back in New York*: "Prayer," JW journal, March 8, 1974; and JW letter to Marshall Wright, March 8, 1974.

291 *That spring*: Interview with David Young, September 3, 2013; and JW letter to Franz Wright, November 27, 1973, in *WP*, 400.

291 *When Franz*: Young, September 3, 2013; interview with Franz Wright, May 23, 2001; and *Field* 10 (Spring 1974). Originally titled "Verona" and "Mantova," the poems would appear in sequence in *Pear Tree*.

291 *"You have brilliantly"*: Dr. William G. Caples, president of Kenyon College, awarding the Doctor of Humane Letters to JW, April 1974.

291 *The words startled*: Interview with Anne Wright, October 13, 2008.

291 *"it struck me"*: JW letter to Robert Bly, October 23, 1974, in *WP*, 410.

291 *After consulting*: Interview with Dr. Robert Segal, March 22, 2010; and JW letter to director of Doctors Hospital, May 11, 1974.

291 *"I quit cold turkey"*: JW letter to Stanley Kunitz, October 12, 1974, in *WP*, 409.

292 *"wretched bad writing"*: JW letter to Steven Berg at *APR*, May 27, 1974; *The American Poetry Review* 3, no. 3 (May/June 1974): 69; and JW letter of apology to Berg, December 5, 1974.

292 *"tired gray house"*: Dr. Thomas Hodge letter to JW, May 1974.

292 *"The Infidel"*: JW journal, June 9, 1974, in *CP*, 324.

292 *Richard Hugo and Bill Knott*: "On the Occasion of a Poem," *CP*, 303, 310.

293 *"I care about"*: JW letter to Robert Mezey, June 1974.

293 *"benevolence and grace . . . his last books"*: Mazzaro, February 6, 2003. *Two Citizens* was "a volume he willed into existence," Mazzaro felt, in the way that you force yourself to practice a difficult piano piece until it "becomes yours." That's why "the emotion of the book at times feels strained." Wright told Mazzaro that he realized the depth of his feeling for America at the international conference in Yugoslavia that he attended in August 1970.

293 *The love poems*: Kevin Stein notes that a copy of "Redwings" with corrections in Wright's hand includes lines addressing "Jenny" at the poem's conclusion. Stein, *James Wright: The Poetry of a Grown Man* (Athens: Ohio University Press, 1989), 146.

294 *"It was like my own . . . encapsulated energy"*: Interview with Joel Lipman, August 11, 2011; and Lipman e-mail to the author, January 24, 2011.

294 *"All this time"*: Anne Wright, undated private note attached to cover of Wright journal, summer 1974.

294–95 *"Wright was most attentive . . . between ideas"*: Lipman e-mail, January 24, 2011; and Lipman, August 11, 2011.

295 *"jaunty renditions"*: Jeanne Foster Hill, "The First Workshop: A Memoir of James Wright," *The American Poetry Review* 30, no. 4 (July/August 2001): 15; and interview with Hill, October 19, 2006. Hill mischaracterized Wright's graduate seminar as a "poetry workshop."

295 *"that drawing up"*: Lipman, August 11, 2011.

295 *"neither narrative . . . with contemplation"*: Hill, *The American Poetry Review*. Wright quoted examples from W. C. Williams, *Imaginations* (New York: New Directions, 1970).

295 *"listen more"*: Interview with Jeanne Foster Hill, October 19, 2006.

295 *"My work here"*: JW letter to Franz Wright, July 1, 1974.

295–96 *"I am having . . . the true path"*: JW letter to Robert Bly, July 4, 1974.

296 *"primarily for me"*: JW letter to Gerald Pincess, Hunter College English Department chair, July 20, 1974.

296 *"A Horatian Ode"*: JW journal, July 31, 1974. A typescript dated August 2 was published in the fall of 2001 in Robert Bly's journal *The Thousands*, no. 1 (Fall 2001), 74.

297 *"still as far away"*: JW journal, "My Father Died One Year Ago," August 4, 1974.

297 *"God damn all candles"*: JW journal, "My Mother," August 4, 1974.

297 *With any luck*: Calvin Bedient, *New York Times Book Review*, August 11, 1974, in *HotL*, 331.

297 *"All I want"*: JW journal, Milan, August 10, 1974: "Another Sophoclean Song."

297 *"Jenny my darkness"*: JW journal, Milan, August 11, 1974: "Strange Expression."

297 *Nothing slowed*: Wright transferred rough paragraphs or stanzas from a small three-by-five wire-bound notebook to another, larger journal he referred to as "Big Brownie," making minor edits as he wrote the fair copy.

298 *"She is dead"*: JW journal, Torri del Benaco, August 12, 1974.

298 *"I am alone. . . . his name would be Loss"*: JW journal, Torri del Benaco, August 13, 1974.

298 *"a book that I had"*: JW journal, Verona, August 23, 1974.

298 *"The flesh rages"*: Maxim Gorky, *Reminiscences of Tolstoi*, trans. Leonard Woolf and S. S. Koteliansky (Orono, ME: Puckerbrush, 1996), 58.

298 *During his first*: Describing the development of Wright's prose pieces over the course of that summer, Kevin Stein has written: "What results is a form that can incorporate the narration of actual experience, the expression of lyrical imagination, and the artist's own self-conscious awareness of the aesthetic process." Stein, *Grown Man*, 128.

298 *Wright sustained*: Interview with Louis Simpson, February 15, 2000, in "The Sound That Comes from Character," *The Georgia Review* 55, no. 3 (Fall 2001): 454.

298 *"The Lambs on the Boulder"*: JW journal, August 21, 1974.

299 *"The fruits of the Season"*: JW journal, August 22, 1974.

299 *"an herb of healing"*: JW inscription to Theodor Storm, *Pole Poppenspäler*, Padua, August 21, 1974.

299 *Coming across Storm's book*: JW journal, Verona, August 23, 1974: "this notebook is posted: the Uninvited Reader. I see no point in our wasting each other's time. / I value my privately written words as I trust you value your jugular vein. / If you invade my notebook, I hope you strangle on both."

299 *"force cheerfulness"*: JW journal, Torri del Benaco, August 13, 1974.

299 *"trying to sing himself"*: JW journal, Verona, August 23, 1974.

299 *"Written on a Big Cheap"*: JW postcard to Ann Sanfedele, August 31, 1974; and JW letter to Stuart Friebert, *Field* magazine, November 9, 1974.

299 *"One Last Look"*: JW journal, Verona, August 31, 1974.

300 *The overcrowded*: Interview with Anne Wright, January 18, 2001. "He really was very tense leaving Verona that time." Anne Wright, Verona, July 20, 2004.

300 *"The Silent Angel"*: JW journal, September 1, 1974.

300 *"In about five more hours"*: JW journal, September 2, 1974 (116, last page).

24. The Road Back

301 *"The Young Dickens"*: JW's teaching copy, inscribed at Hunter, 1974, of Graham Greene, *Collected Essays* (London: Penguin Books, 1970), see pp. 82 and 85.

301 *Within weeks*: APR published eight prose pieces (no. 3 [September/October 1974]: 3); see Stephen Berg, David Bonanno, and Arthur Vogelsang, eds., *The Body Electric: America's Best Poetry from 'The American Poetry Review'* (New York: W. W. Norton, 2000), 757–65.

301 *"My own classes have begun"*: JW letter to Franz Wright, September 12, 1974.

302 *"He seemed very balanced"*: Interview with Donna Masini, January 25, 2001.

302 *He confessed*: Interview with Anne Wright, October 13, 2008.

302 *Hypertension and exhaustion*: Interviews with Dr. Robert Segal, March 22, 2010, and Anne Wright, March 20, 2000.

302 *"I'm letting myself"*: JW letter to Franz Wright, September 29, 1974.

302 *The act of suicide*: Strangely, both sides of Wright's extensive correspondence with Sexton disappeared at the time of her death. In 1990, Diane Middlebrook wrote: "[The letters] were removed from Sexton's papers by some unknown hand before the files passed into Linda Sexton's keeping." Middlebrook, *Anne Sexton* (manuscript draft pages, with footnotes; shared by Middlebrook with author).

302 *Wright's struggle*: JW letter to Frederick Morgan, October 12, 1974.

302 *"Saying Dante Aloud"*: JW journal, October 19, 1974.

303 *"I feel more whole"*: JW letter to Robert Bly, October 23, 1974, in *WP*, 410. See also appendix to *WP*, 594.

303 *"utterly fearless"*: JW letter to Franz Wright, November 15, 1974.

303 *"as if he had turned"*: Robert Bly letter to Tomas Tranströmer, November 24, 1974, in *Airmail: The Letters of Robert Bly and Tomas Tranströmer* (Minneapolis: Graywolf, 2013), 271.

303 *He lobbied for*: JW letters to Louis Simpson and Helen Vendler, December 5 and 13, 1974. Gary Snyder, *Turtle Island* (New York: New Directions, 1974). *CP*, 105.

303 *"He never stopped"*: Interview with Franz Wright, May 23, 2001.

304 *"I felt that a lot"*: Interview with Philip Levine, December 15, 2004. In the company of others, Wright's open demeanor disappeared behind recitations of W. C. Fields or *Paradise Lost*. "It was a shield, in a way," one that "no intimacy could penetrate."

304 *"My own attacks"*: JW letter to Carolee Coombs-Stacy, January 10, 1975.

304 *"some of her soul"*: JW letter to Carolee Coombs-Stacy, February 25, 1975. Coombs-Stacy also revealed that she had named her daughter "Jenny," prompting Wright to tell her of his correspondence with "Jenny." He describes, in close detail, his intended pilgrimage to her imagined grave.

304 *"To Bee, Who Is Dead"*: JW journal, January 10, 1975.

305 *"a folio of favorite poets"*: JW journal, January 6, 1975.

305 *Ignatow had stressed*: APR finally published the portfolio in its May/June 1980 issue (vol. 9, no. 3) following Wright's death. Anselm Parlatore, Ann Sanfedele, Walter Hess, and Judith Johnson Sherwin also contributed work.

305 *"sense of camaraderie"*: Masini, January 25, 2001.

305 *In April 1975*: Interviews with Anne Wright, September 18, 2001, and Michael Graves, April 23, 2010.

305 *At the end of April*: Interview with Anne Wright, November 24, 2009; and Henry Hart, *James Dickey: The World as a Lie* (New York: Picador USA, 2000), 584.

306 *"a kind of ambient jealousy"*: Levine, December 15, 2004.

306 *But it was Wright's decision*: Anne Wright notes, 1975: "James reminds me he is responsible for AA decision."

306 *Back in January*: JW letter to Michael S. Harper, January 14, 1975, in *WP*, 417.

306 *"that there was going"*: Interview with Michael S. Harper, September 19, 2001.

306 *"I used to say"*: JW reading, Brown University, Providence, RI, May 9, 1975, recorded by Michael S. Harper.

307 *"my poor Jenny"*: JW journal, June 6, 1975.

307 *"The Road Back"*: JW journal, dated June 6–July 2, 1975. The title refers to *The Road Back* by Erich Maria Remarque, a sequel to *All Quiet on the Western Front*.

307 *"a house-guest. . . . good people"*: JW journal, June 12, 1975.

307 *"to condemn this book"*: JW journal, June 1975. See also JW letter to Richard Hugo, September 7, 1975, in *WP*, 426: "Although I didn't see the piece, I hear that somebody in the *Sewanee Review* wrote a review of my last book called 'The Collapse of James Wright.' I feel like Sugar Ray Robinson after his first fight with Randy Turpin."

307–308 *"what lies behind . . . before me, long ago"*: JW interview, April 1972; and "Ten Poems" (all uncollected), with the "Art of Poetry" interview, *The Paris Review* 62 (Summer 1975): 34–74.

308 *"He seemed so distant"*: Interview with Anne Wright, October 27, 2006.

308 *"melted the ice in me"*: JW journal, July 1, 1975.

308 *Throughout the conference*: Interview with Edward Morin, June 12, 2012. "[Wright] read from that [notebook] more than he did his own poems."

308 *"the vast swings"*: Interview with James Coleman, September 8, 2011.

308 *Kinnell then said*: Interview with Jeanne Foster Hill, October 19, 2006.

309 *"sort of shepherding him around"*: Interview with James Coleman, September 9, 2011.

309 *"He was very much"*: Hill, October 19, 2006.

309 *On the phone*: Ibid. Hill received "about twenty" letters from Wright between 1974 and 1978. "He called me a lot on the telephone, and I think he often called me when he was drunk."

309 *Wright's fragile state*: Interviews with Ira Sadoff, July 5, 2014, and Edward Morin, June 12, 2012. As Morin recalled, Wright "recognized how fragile—and frightened—he was, but he seemed to accept it. Or maybe he was just used to it."

309 *"Wright's poetry"*: Leslie Marmon Silko, preface to revised edition of *Ceremony* (New York: Viking, 1977; rev. ed. Penguin, 2006), xvi.

309 *"kind of battered"*: Anne Wright, September 18, 2001. "He always pulled himself together when Betty was around." Interview with Anne Wright, July 3, 2014.

310 *"in his post-summer"*: Elizabeth Kray, draft prose piece, undated [circa September 1975], in Elizabeth D. Kray Papers, Poets House Archives, Poets House, New York, NY.

310 *"painfully low"*: JW letter to Gary Gildner, September 21, 1975.

310 *"I think I have shed"*: JW inscription, October 7, 1975, Edward Thomas's *Collected Prose*. Wright quotes Chidiock Tichborne's "On the Eve of His Execution."

310 *"one of the secret spirits"*: JW interview, October 1971, in *CP*, 141.

310–11 *"at the Weeks Cemetery . . . who they are"*: JW typescript, October 12, 1975. That fall, when the book collector Burt Britton asked Wright to sketch a self-portrait, he drew a wavering pair of lines for the Ohio River with a third line to show the hills above it. He then added three simple crosses and the words "Weeks, Colerain, Ohio." Britton, *Self-Portrait: Book People Picture Themselves* (New York: Random House, 1976), 87. See Britton letter to JW, November 11, 1975.

311 *The line beneath*: Thomas's poem "The Ash Grove" concludes: "And I had what most I desired, without search or desert or cost." Edward Thomas, *The Annotated Collected Poems*, ed. Edna Longley (Newcastle, UK: Bloodaxe Books, 2003), 108.

311 *On the same day*: Merrill Leffler letter to JW, October 12, 1975.

311 *"just about every poem"*: Peter Serchuk, "On the Poet James Wright," *Modern Poetry Studies* (Vol. 10, Nos. 2, 3), 1981.

311 *"drug abuse"*: Anne Wright letter to Henry and Elizabeth Esterly, February 20, 1982. "[A]fter long silences from California, Lib finally told us Marshall was hospitalized for drug abuse. She has never told us anything more than that."

311 *Doctors now believed*: Liberty Kovacs letter to Social Services, February 1982, LK memoir, 322.

312 *But Wright and Anne*: After Marshall's two-week hospital stay, he spent five months in a residential treatment center and a further six months in a group home. According to Liberty, Marshall's condition was later determined to be a schizoaffective disorder, a term she used to describe her own family background as well as that of Wright and their two sons. LK memoir, 20, 322; and interview with Liberty Kovacs, March 7, 2010. In 1982, a second doctor identified effects related to brain injury, possibly resulting from the car accident Marshall had survived in Texas at the age of fourteen. Kovacs to Social Services, February 1982.

312 *"at just the right time"*: JW letter to Merrill Leffler, November 2, 1975, in *WP*, 431.

312 *"prose sketches"*: JW letter to Louis Simpson, November 30, 1975. "The language of prose is the most intense and musical language."

312 *"Every one of those"*: Interview with Merrill Leffler, October 16, 2002.

312 *"As the afternoon"*: Jane Cooper, public talk, "A Tribute to James Wright," Teachers and Writers Collaborative, New York, NY, December 13, 2000. Cooper's joint reading with Wright took place November 9, 1975, at the Long Island Historical Society in Brooklyn. Interview with Cooper, January 18, 2001.

312 *With only a few*: The three poets read at the 92nd Street Y Poetry Center on November 17, 1975. Unterberg Poetry Center recording.

313 *"the classical idea"*: JW journal, December 2, 1975.

25. *Redwings and Solitaries*

314 *"The classification of poems"*: Hayden Carruth, "The Question of Poetic Form," in *Selected Essays and Reviews* (Port Townsend, WA: Copper Canyon, 1996), 175.

314 *"I have never known"*: JW letter to Bernard Meredith, January 16, 1976.

314 *"Once I discovered"*: JW letter to Merrill Leffler, January 19, 1976. Carruth's *Hudson Review* essay had tried to defuse the argument between "fixed" forms and more open, "organic" ones. He suggested "outer" and "inner" as both more exact and less divisive terms.

315 *"the light of the river Adige."*: "The Secret of Light," 302.

315 *The conception*: Interview with Saundra Maley, October 16, 2002.

315 *"I don't see how"*: Robert Hass, "James Wright" (1977), in *Clear Word*, 220; *HotL*, 304.

315 *Wright was also*: JW letter to Sheriff, January 12, 1976, *WP*, 438.

315 *"the nine (!)"*: JW letter to Sheriff, February 12, 1976, in *WP*, 443.

315 *"He was a man"*: JW marginalia, teaching copy, *Monarch Notes: Don Quixote*.

316 *"all the way to"*: JW letter to Janice Thurn, May 4, 1976, in *WP*, 447.

316 *"twenty-nine contemporaries"*: William Heyen, ed., *American Poets in 1976* (New York: Bobbs-Merrill, 1976), 424–57.

316 *"Christ's Descent into Hell"*: Rainer Maria Rilke, *The Unknown Rilke: Expanded Edition*, trans. Franz Wright (Oberlin, OH: Oberlin College Press, 1990), 130; and JW letter to Franz Wright, May 2, 1976, in *WP*, 445. For Wright's 1960 translation of this Rilke poem, see appendix to *WP*, 588.

316 *"The sheer beauty"*: John Logan letter to JW, May 26, 1976.

316 *"I know of no other"*: John Logan, "The Prose of James Wright," *Ironwood* No. 10 (1977), 154.

316 *"uncluttered vision"*: JW letter to John Logan, June 1, 1976.

317 *"Goodbye to Ohio"*: JW typescript poem draft, circa June 1976.

317 *While Wright remained*: Interviews with Tom Flynn and Ed Ochester, both April 12, 2007. Flynn observed that by refusing to return to Martins Ferry, Wright could manipulate the geography inside his poems.

317 *"He had a Martins Ferry"*: Anne Wright, interviewed by Noah Adams, National Public Radio (1990). From "A Poet and His Hometown," first broadcast over National Public Radio in November 1990.

317 *"All the news"*: JW letter to Ann Sanfedele, August 4, 1976.

318 *"Every morning there"*: Interview with Anne Wright, November 1, 2002.

318 *"I'll be fine!"*: Interviews with Marshall Wright, October 17, 2006, and Liberty Kovacs and Marshall Wright, March 8, 2010.

318 *"I deliberately"*: Ibid.

318 *"If I ever find out"*: Anne Wright, quoting JW, November 1, 2002.

319 *"Our five days"*: JW letter to W. S. Merwin, September 25, 1976.

319 *"seeing the sun"*: JW journal, August 22, 1976. See also JW letter to Janice Thurn, September 25, 1976, in *WP*, 459.

319 *"a kind of spring"*: JW letter to Jack Wright, September 25, 1976, in *WP*, 457.

319 *On September 21*: JW letter to Donald Hall, September 21, 1976. Hall, *Kicking the Leaves* (New York: Harper & Row, 1978). When the book appeared in the fall of 1978, Wright told Hall, "It is your best book, and one of the finest books any and all of us have achieved. It is seamless, i.e., fulfilled, completed." JW letter to Hall, September 25, 1978. See also JW letter to Robert Bly, December 5, 1975, in *WP*, 435.

319 *"I don't feel"*: Robert Bly letter to JW, July 24, 1976.

320 *FOR REVISION OF*: JW typescript, with revisions, September 30, 1976. With minor changes, "Beautiful Ohio" is identical to the version Wright first drafted in prose.

321 *"Christ have mercy"*: Interviews with Sander Zulauf, July 5, 2000, and August 3, 2014; and interview with Anne Wright, October 30, 2016.

321 *Wright gave a measured*: JW reading, September 30, 1976, County College of Morris, *The First American Poetry Disc, Volume III: James Wright*, videotape copyright © 1987 County College of Morris, Randolph, NJ, produced by Sander Zulauf (available as "First American Poetry Series, Vol. III, James Wright" on youtube.com).

321 *"Everything Jim had . . . he couldn't help it"*: Hayden Carruth, public talk, Fourth Annual James Wright Poetry Festival, Martins Ferry, OH, May 4, 1984.

321 *"Jim was a good talker"*: Interview with Hayden Carruth, December 19, 2000. "He was very easy and fluent and witty and funny."

321 *Two weeks later*: JW letter to Carruth, October 25, 1976, in *WP*, 460. From the time they first met until Wright's death (a span of three and a half years), Carruth wrote two dozen letters to Wright, and received almost as many from Wright.

322 *"similar sense of"*: Carruth letter to JW, November 1, 1976. "I find in a poem like 'The Old Man Said Tomorrow' so much that touches my own personal verbal instincts, sound, rhythm, syntax, the whole thing (and which cannot be vocalized by the best reader in the world)."

322 *"I care about Orwell"*: JW letter to Edward Pell, October 25, 1976.

322 *"had so thoroughly immersed"*: Interview with Franz Wright, May 23, 2001.

322 *In November*: For an epigraph, Wright thought of using an excerpt from a passage in Orwell's *Coming Up for Air* that he quotes in his 1973 essay on Richard Hugo's work, "Secrets of the Inner Landscape" (*CP*, 298).

322 *"Sharp winter relaxes"*: Wright considered using the Horace couplet (*Odes*, I, 4) in Latin, as translated by J. V. Cunningham. The Ben Jonson couplet reads: "It is not growing, like a tree / In bulk, doth make man better bee." See Kevin Stein, *Poetry of a Grown Man* (Athens: Ohio University Press, 1989), 167, 200n9.

322 *"prepared to delete"*: JW journal, December 8, 1976. The final book includes thirty-seven poems, with paired prose pieces in "Two Moments in Rome" and "Two Moments in Venice."

322 *He shared copies*: JW, eight prose pieces in Michael Benedikt, ed., *The Prose Poem: An International Anthology* (New York: Laurel Edition/Dell, 1976), 484–96. Eleven American poets are represented, including Kenneth Patchen, David Ignatow, Robert Bly, and W. S. Merwin.

322–23 *"Since he's stopped drinking"*: Interview with Fran Quinn, May 17, 2003.

323 *"It was as if"*: Interview with Carolyn Kizer, April 15, 2000. Grace Schulman "didn't dare approach him" after readings, due to his "brusque, autocratic" public manner. Interview with Schulman, November 20, 2000.

323 *"finally reached the point"*: JW letter to Robert Bly, January 16, 1977.

323 *"is, at last, the only"*: JW letter to Hayden Carruth, November 14, 1976.

26. To cultivate the art of listening

324 *he wrote to*: JW letter to Marshall Wright and Liberty Kovacs, March 11, 1977.

325 *"to realize that most"*: JW, public talk, Academy of American Poets, New York, NY, March 30, 1977. Published in an edited version as "One Voice and Many" in *The New York Times Book Review*, March 18, 1984.

325 *"I found that the Italian"*: Robert Bly letter to JW, April 1, 1977, enclosing manuscript.

325 *"Chinese Poetry"*: "Chinese Poetry and the American Imagination," Academy of American Poets, April 21–23, 1977, cosponsored by the Asia Society and the Henry Luce Foundation.

325 *"endless abundance . . . violent stimulants"*: See "Some Notes on Chinese Poetry," in *CP*, 123. Wright quotes Wordsworth, preface to *Lyrical Ballads* (2nd ed., 1800).

326 *"the finest discussion"*: JW letter to Elizabeth Kray, April 26, 1977, in *WP*, 470.

326 *"American Spring Song"*: *The Selected Poems of Sherwood Anderson*, ed. Stuart Downs (Kent, OH: Kent State University Press, 2007), 1.

326 *"at the end of a war"*: JW reading, October 24, 1977, 92nd Street Y, New York, Unterberg Poetry Center recording.

326 *"greatest source"*: Interview with Stanley Plumly, October 15, 2002.

326 *"Wright recognizes"*: William Matthews, "The Continuity of James Wright's Poems" (1977), in *Clear Word*, 99.

326 *"the old dark knowledge"*: Wayne Dodd, "That Same Bodily Curve of the Spirit," *The Ohio Review* 43, no. 2 (Spring/Summer 1977): 59.

327 *"I am still praying"*: JW journal, Paris, June 16, 1977.

327 *"Remembering Owen"*: JW journal, Avallon, June 23, 1977; and typescript, Paris, August 15, 1977.

327 *"I must listen"*: JW journal, Dijon, June 28, 1977.

328 *"There is something"*: JW journal, Milan, June 29, 1977.

328 *"This morning"*: JW journal, Sirmione, July 1, 1977.

328 *"After a long still visit"*: "Wakening in Twilight," JW journal, Verona, July 9, 1977.

328 *"to begin dealing with"*: JW journal, Arezzo, July 16, 1977.

328 *Wright posted two letters*: JW letters to Michael di Capua and Michael Cuddihy, July 17, 1977.

329 *"One is never so alone"*: Louis Simpson, *Ships Going into the Blue* (Ann Arbor: University of Michigan Press, 1994), 114.

329 *"strange golden light"*: JW journal, Arezzo, July 24, 1977.

329 *"You know, he was"*: Interview with Anne Wright, Verona, July 20, 2004.

329 *"On American Poetry"*: JW journal, March 5, 1977.

330 *"this immense, welcoming"*: JW journal, Paris, August 6, 1977. See photograph of view from the study window in the Higginses' apartment.

330 *"a dream of comfort"*: JW journal, Paris, August 1, 1977.

330 *"the one they called for"*: JW journal, Paris, August 21, 1977.

330 *"an imitation"*: See "To a Visitor from My Home Town (an imitation of Walter von der Vogelweide)," *Assay* 14, no. 2 (Spring 1957), University of Washington. Shunk appears there, "The diver and the grappling hook" who "Raised to the skiff and shore" the body of a drowned friend.

330 *"It has been hounding"*: JW journal, Paris, August 23, 1977.

330 *"Few lines are written"*: JW journal, Paris, August 24, 1977.

331 *"indescribably to keep"*: JW journal, September 3 and 4, 1977.

331 *"his predecessor Sherwood Anderson"*: JW reading with Richard Eberhart, and Frank MacShane introducing Wright, Unterberg Poetry Center recording, 92nd Street Y, New York.

331 *"I spent eight years"*: Ibid.

331 *"really all right"*: JW letter to Hayden Carruth, October 29, 1977, in *WP*, 480.

331 *A marathon reading*: Betsy Fogelman Tighe memoir (unpublished draft). Fogelman sent Wright fifty cards and letters, many with poem drafts, over the next two years, and Wright responded with fifty-eight of his own.

332 *"You are to me"*: Betsy Fogelman letter to JW, November 3, 1977.

332 *"weeks of soaking"*: JW letter to Hayden Carruth, October 29, 1977, in *WP*, 480.

332 *"I specially value"*: JW letter to Franz Wright, October 30, 1977. Franz Wright's poem "The Wish" is from his first collection, *The One Whose Eyes Open When You Close Your Eyes* (1982), reprinted in *Earlier Poems* (New York: Alfred A. Knopf, 2007), 33.

332 *"subterranean" connection*: JW typescript, February 22, 1978, reverse side of draft, "Italy," revised July 29, 1978. See drafts, April 22, 1978, "Getting Out of Town Before It's Too Late" ("The Journey") and "On Shunk: The River at Cincinnati" on the same page.

333 *"the most serious"*: JW letter to Michael Cuddihy, November 14, 1977, in *WP*, 481.

333 *"It gave me odd feelings"*: JW letter to Michael Cuddihy, August 5, 1977.

333 *"I have been worrying"*: Robert Hass, "James Wright," in *Ironwood* 10 (1977), 74. *Clear Word*, 196. *Twentieth Century Pleasures* (New York: Ecco, 1984), 26. *HotL*, 278.

333 *"You can't not print this"*: Interview with Robert Hass, June 18, 2001. Hass believes that this tendency in Wright's poems is "probably connected to his alcoholism." Hass acknowledged that Lewis Hyde's groundbreaking study "Alcohol and Poetry: John Berryman and the Booze Talking," had influenced his thinking about Wright's work in his essay. Hyde's essay originally appeared in *The American Poetry Review* 4 (4) (July/August), 1975; reprinted in *Pushcart Prize Anthology* (New York: Penguin Books, 1987). Interview with Lewis Hyde, April 17, 2009.

333 *"the soundest and truest"*: JW letter to Robert Hass, March 18, 1978, in *WP*, 495.

333 *"I want to return"*: JW journal, November 18, 1977.

333 *Sounding beneath his words*: Juan Ramón Jiménez, translated by Robert Bly, in *Forty Poems of Juan Ramón Jiménez* (Madison, MN: Sixties Press, 1967), 81. St. Martin chose this version for his anthology *Roots and Wings*. See also Robert Bly, ed., *Lorca and Jiménez: Selected Poems* (Boston: Beacon Press, 1973), 77. Wright also knew the version by Carlos de Francisco Zea in *The Fifties* No. 2 (Summer 1959): 29. He copied the poem into his journal in Spanish and English on July 18, 1959.

27. A river flowing underground

335 *"I had my coffee"*: JW letter to Donald Hall, January 2, 1978, in *WP*, 490.

335 *"in this poet's cold"*: JW journal, January 8, 1978; and JW letter to Hayden Carruth, September 21, 1978. See Carruth, *Collected Shorter Poems 1946–1991* (Port Townsend, WA: Copper Canyon Press, 1992), 182.

335 *"We all wanted"*: Interview with Gerald Stern, November 7, 2002. See Galway Kinnell, "Jubilate," *The American Poetry Review* 40, no. 1 (January–February 2011): 5; and interview with Thomas Lux, June 21, 2014. Muriel Rukeyser read the poem's final section, but fainted at the podium, pulling down microphone cords and printed pages all around her. Refusing medical attention, Rukeyser finished her reading seated in a chair.

336 *"deeply disturbed"*: Interviews with Gibbons Ruark, October 29, 1999, and September 24, 2014; and interview with Anne Wright, September 25, 2014.

336 *"an unexpectedly weak book"*: Hugh Kenner, *New York Times Book Review*, February 12, 1978, in *HotL*, 363.

336 *In the* Saturday Review: Robert Pinsky, *Saturday Review*, January 21, 1978, in *HotL*, 365.

336 *"has put away any"*: Richard Howard, *New York Arts Journal* (February–March 1978), in *HotL*, 384.

336 *"perhaps better poems"*: Hayden Carruth, "The Passionate Few," *Harper's Magazine*, June 1978.

336 *"confusion of grief and loss"*: JW letter to Liberty Kovacs, March 5, 1978.

337 *"true serene music"*: Robert Bly letter to JW, February 27, 1978.

337 *"minor poet . . . I suppose"*: JW interviewed by Douglas John Henderson, Hunter College *Envoy* magazine, February 24, 1978, 1.

337 *"the dog days"*: JW letter to Diane Wakoski, March 20, 1978, in *WP*, 496.

338 *"Write out that spider"*: JW journal, March 21, 1978.

338 *"Getting Out of Town"*: JW journal, April 22, 1978.

338 *"Goodnight to John Shunk"*: JW typescript, April 26, 1978. "Wishes for My Son" was removed from the manuscript after Wright's death.

338 *"middle-aged roaring boy"*: Interview with James Reiss, December 5, 2011.

338 *"very oddly decorous"*: Interview with Stanley Plumly, October 15, 2002.

338 *"We don't approve"*: Interview with Anne Wright, March 23, 2000.

338 *"general chaos"*: Interview with Robert Bly, August 12, 2005.

339 *"getting ramshackle more"*: JW letter to Janice Thurn, June 7, 1978, in *WP*, 501.

339 *"To the Cicada"*: JW journal, July 8, 1978.

339 *"strange gentleness"*: JW typescript, March 28, 1978. *See* "In Idle Meditation," trans. Soame Jenyns, in *Selections from the Three Hundred Poems of the T'ang Dynasty* (London: John Murray, 1940), 44.

339 *In the middle of July*: JW letter to Liberty Kovacs, November 11, 1979. "I have been able, through the help of the AA program, to remain sober for a week less than sixteen months now."

339 *"absolutely marvelous"*: Interview with Anne Wright, September 18, 2001.

339 *"We're going soon"*: JW letter to Betsy Fogelman, August 2, 1978, in *WP*, 504.

339 *"simple, old-fashioned joy"*: JW letter to Carol Bly, August 5, 1978, in *WP*, 506.

340 *Betty Kray had press-ganged*: JW letter to Elizabeth Kray, August 7, 1978. The dual-language reading took place at the Public Library in New London, CT, August 23, 1978.

340 *"Perhaps the brilliant . . . flowing underground"*: JW, reverse side of typescript, February 22, 1978; revised July 29, 1978.

340 *The poem's final version*: D. H. Lawrence is a key presence behind this poem, from its earliest conception through its completion. Wright echoes Lawrence's line "Not I, not I, but the wind that blows through me!" from "The Song of a Man Who Has Come Through"—a poem Wright knew by heart. Another Lawrence poem, "Let the Dead Bury Their Dead—," sounds beneath the poem's concluding lines. Lawrence, *The Complete Poems*, ed. Pinto and Roberts (New York: Viking Press, 1964), 250, 440.

341 *"I kept getting"*: JW letter to Carol Bly, August 23, 1978.

341 *"Childhood Sketch"*: CP, 332. See William S. Saunders, *James Wright: An Introduction* (Columbus: Ohio Authors Series, 1979).

341 *"I am very happy"*: JW letter to Leslie Marmon Silko, August 28, 1978, in *Delicacy*, 3. See Truesdale, "On Which Side of the Green Wall," *Abraxas* 34 (Fall 1986), review of *Delicacy* (74): "The shifts in direction in [Wright's] work—which had clearly been going on long before these letters began—suggest that he was ready for this kind of friendship and the genuine dialogue that takes place in [his correspondence with Silko]."

341 *"He spoke in beautiful"*: Ruark, October 29, 1999.

342 *"Here I am"*: JW, quoted in interview with Anne Wright, July 13, 2004.

342 *"an attentive class"*: JW letter to Franz Wright, October 2, 1978.

342 *"Such a routine"*: JW letter to Hayden Carruth, September 21, 1978.

342 *"scattered"*: JW journal, September 28, 1978.

342 *"They stood not more . . . hand to touch"*: JW journal, September 16, 1978.

343 *"Written on a Big"*: JW reading, October 13, 1978, Loyola University, New Orleans. Interview with Bruce Henricksen, January 15, 2010. See Henricksen, obituary of JW, *New Orleans Review* (1980): "He thought it was just fine that the people of Verona sell pictures of Juliet's balcony to the unsuspecting. It helps keep something beautiful alive."

343 *"Unlike most speakers"*: Paul Dusseault, *Maroon*, Loyola University student newspaper, October 13, 1978, 2.

343 *"some madness . . . disciplined hope"*: JW interview, October 15, 1978, in *CP*, 172. The last phrase JW quotes is from the writer and critic Irving Howe.

343 *"Many things in"*: JW letter to Fogelman, October 9, 1978.

344 *"sheer tenacity"*: Leslie Marmon Silko letter to JW, September 9, 1978, in *Delicacy*, 4.

344 *"the rooster out of"*: Leslie Marmon Silko letter to JW, October 3, 1978, in *Delicacy*, 6.

344 *With her October 3 letter*: Leslie Marmon Silko, *Storyteller* (New York: Arcade, Little Brown, 1981), includes not only these poems and the title story she shared with Wright, but also an excerpt from her letter to Wright describing the rooster (p. 226).

344 *"I am closer to"*: JW letter to Leslie Marmon Silko, October 12, 1978, in *Delicacy*, 20, and *WP*, 508.

344 *In subtle ways*: See, for example, "Old Bud," "The Sumac in Ohio," and "Chilblain." See JW letter to Leslie Marmon Silko, November 16, 1978, in *Delicacy*, 30. Wright acknowledges how their "discussions of the relation between people and landscapes is very much at the heart of" his own recent poems.

344 *"I am extremely glad"*: JW letter to Leslie Marmon Silko, October 12, 1978, in *Delicacy*, 20, and *WP*, 508.

344 *"Attentiveness is also"*: JW essay "A Master of Silence: The Poetry of David Schubert," October 15, 1978, in *CP*, 97. Wright's comments on biography were deleted from the published text.

345 *These reflections show*: Max Picard, *The World of Silence*, trans. Stanley Godman (South Bend, IN: Gateway Editions, 1952). See JW journal, November 24 and 25, 1978.

345 *"a long and terrifying"*: JW letter to Leslie Marmon Silko, July 18, 1979, in *Delicacy*, 60 (corrected); and JW letter to Liberty Kovacs, October 21, 1978. The letter to Liberty from Wright that Marshall "intercepted" was dated October 15, 1978.

345 *"repetitive, confused"*: JW letter to Franz Wright, November 8, 1978.

345 *"our happy home"*: Marshall Wright letter to JW, undated, received November 2, 1978.

345 *Wright's letter to Franz*: JW letter to Franz Wright, November 8, 1978. "I'm sure you would have told Annie and me about [his marriage] eventually."

346 *"fairly good-humored"*: JW letter to Jack Wright, November 20, 1978.

346 *"Poet's Life at Odds with Verse"*: Doris B. Wiley, Philadelphia *Evening Bulletin*, Entertainment section, November 26, 1978, 14.

346 *"rare sincerity"*: Mark Strand, introduction to JW reading, Guggenheim Museum, November 28, 1978, *AAP* recording.

28. The silence of all the light

347 *"I have spent"*: Johann Wolfgang von Goethe, journal entry, October 19, 1786; in *Italian Journey*, trans. W. H. Auden and Elizabeth Mayer (New York: North Point Press, 1982), 96. Goethe was thirty-seven as he began his travels in Italy.

347 *"Simone [Weil] says"*: Herbert Read, "The Cult of Sincerity," *The Hudson Review* 21, no. 1 (Spring 1968). JW's copy includes marginalia.

347 *"These are the loveliest"*: JW journal, Paris, December 23, 1978, in *A Secret Field: Selections from the Final Journals of James Wright*, ed. Anne Wright (Durango, CO: Logbridge-Rhodes, 1985), 7.

348 *"Stop cursing"*: JW journal, Paris, December 30, 1978.

348 *Wright typed*: JW letter to Robert Bly, December 31, 1978, in *WP*, 513.

348 *Just as they stepped*: Interviews with Gibbons Ruark, October 29, 1999, May 30, 2007, and June 25, 2011; and Anne Wright journal, December 31, 1978. "He paid such beautiful attention to everything," Ruark marveled.

349 *"the legendary winter"*: JW letter to Leslie Marmon Silko, January 9, 1979, in *Delicacy*, 32.

349 *"Right at the dead"*: JW journal, Nice, January 11, 1979, in *Secret Field*, 8.

349 *"in an old, rambling"*: Galway Kinnell, public talk, "A Tribute to James Wright," Teachers and Writers Collaborative, New York, NY, December 13, 2000.

349 *"The chapel is astonishing"*: JW journal, Vence, January 14, 1979, in *Secret Field*, 8.

349 *"The rest of Europe"*: JW journal, Vence, January 15, 1979.

349 *"magical transformations"*: Interview with Galway Kinnell, April 27, 2005.

349 *"How can I feel"*: Wright had originally sketched a long prose piece from his journal entry that morning in Vence. He later redrafted the poem in verse. See JW journal, February 18, 1979.

350 *"without any irritable"*: John Keats, to George and Thomas Keats, December 21, 1817; *Selected Letters*, ed. L. Trilling (New York: Farrar, Straus and Young, 1951), 92. "I mean *Negative Capability*, that is, when a man is capable of being in uncertainties, mysteries, doubts, without any irritable reaching after fact and reason."

350 *"He was more present"*: Galway Kinnell, public talk, Kenyon College, Gambier, OH, March 26, 1983.

350 *"listen to what happens"*: JW journal, Nîmes, January 21, 1979. On March 18, in Verona, Wright typed James Joyce's poem "Tilly" as a prose paragraph, "to see what it *looks* like. I know what it sounds like."

350 *"This is one of those"*: JW letter to Betsy Fogelman, January 22, 1979.

350 In *"Leaving the Temple"*: Wright included an ivy leaf from Nîmes when he sent a copy of the poem to Betsy Fogelman months later. Betsy Fogelman Tighe memoir (unpublished draft).

350 *From Toulouse and Albi*: See Anne Wright, "Some French Tiles of Stone and Brick," in *The Summers of James and Annie Wright: Sketches and Mosaics* (New York: Sheep Meadow Press, 1981), 19.

351 *"a city I love"*: JW letter to Betsy Fogelman, February 3, 1979.

351 *Arriving in Amsterdam*: JW journal, Amsterdam, February 20, 1979, in *Secret Field*, 9.

351 *"the incredible purity of light"*: JW postcard to Betsy Fogelman, February 1979.

351 *"crowds of fathers"*: JW letter to Anne's mother, Louise Robinson, February 21, 1979.

351 *"I wonder if any"*: JW letter to Roger Hecht, March 7, 1979, in *WP*, 517.

351 *"The place took me"*: JW letter to Donald Hall, March 7, 1979, in *WP*, 518.

351 *"unutterably beautiful"*: JW to Anne Wright, journal, February 1979.

351 *"only a dim tower"*: JW letter to Leslie Marmon Silko, March 14, 1979, in *Delicacy*, 42, and *WP*, 519.

351 *craft of lacemaking*. JW letter to Leslie Marmon Silko, April 27, 1979, in *Delicacy*, 46.

352 *"the sun of early spring"*: JW journal, Paris, March 6, 1979, in *Secret Field*, 9.

352 *"As poets you and I"*: Hayden Carruth letter to JW, February 21, 1979.

352 *"Blessed peace!"* JW journal, en route to Verona from Paris, March 8, 1979.

353 *"a black snowdrift"*: "Above San Fermo," JW journal, Verona, March 22, 1979.

353 *"I asked my father"*: JW journal, Verona, March 22, 1979, in *Secret Field*, 10.

353 *"I felt at home"*: JW journal, Verona, March 24, 1979, in *Secret Field*, 11.

354 *"I have foundered"*: JW journal, Florence, March 31, 1979.

354 *"literally insane"*: JW journal, Florence, March 26, 1979.

354 *"comfortably and easily"*: JW journal, Rome, April 5, 1979.

354 *"weirdly silent places"*: JW letter to Hayden Carruth, April 3, 1979, in *WP*, 521.

354 *In five days*: "Contemplating the Front Steps of the Cathedral in Florence as the Century Dies," "Daphne," "The Vestal in the Forum," "In View of the Protestant Cemetery in Rome," and "Reading a 1979 Inscription on Belli's Monument."

354 *"The slow wind"*: JW journal, April 10, 1979. See Edward Hirsch, *HotL*, 387.

355 *"Every time you turn"*: JW journal, Naples, April 21, 1979.

355 *"We are now settled"*: JW journal, Taranto, April 23, 1979, in *Secret Field*, 11.

355 *"We walked for miles"*: JW letter to Franz Wright, May 4, 1979, in *WP*, 528. Wright knew Franz would hear the allusion to René Char.

356 *The film is based*: See JW letters to Michael Cuddihy, April 26, 1979, and Elizabeth Esterly, April 27, 1979. Exiled from Turin for anti-fascist activities in the mid-1930s, Levi in his memoir details his life among the destitute poor in a remote village in the southern Apennine Mountains.

356 *"Not all the naturalistic"*: JW letter to Gibbons Ruark, April 30, 1979.

356 *"where the very houses"*: JW journal, Lecce, May 2, 1979, in *Secret Field*, 12.

356 *"There is a festive air"*: Anne Wright journal, May 1979.

356 *"the futility of our anger"*: JW journal, Bari, May 15, 1979.

357 *"It is old, old"*: JW letter to Betsy Fogelman, May 23, 1979, in *WP*, 530.

357 *"as the twilight comes"*: JW journal, Fano, May 23, 1979.

357 *"The Sumac in Ohio"*: JW journal, Sirmione, May 27, 1979.

29. To gaze as deeply as I can

359 *"perhaps the happiest"*: Interview with Anne Wright, November 20, 1999.

359 *"I talk with my students"*: Leslie Marmon Silko letter to JW, May 10, 1979, in *Delicacy*, 48.

359 *"Much of that"*: JW letter to Leslie Marmon Silko, May 28, 1979, in *Delicacy*, 52. See also JW letter to Silko, July 29, 1979, in *Delicacy*, 63, and *WP*, 540. "I do declare, Leslie, something happens to you when you write with your characteristic warmth: you can sing like a bird."

359 *"almost an island"*: JW letter to Dr. Thomas Hodge, June 8, 1979, in *WP*, 536.

359 *His descriptions*: JW letter to Jack Wright, June 1, 1979, in *WP*, 531.

359 *"after a good deal"*: JW letter to Frederick Morgan, editor of *The Hudson Review*, June 1, 1979.

360 *"I wonder where words"*: JW journal, Sirmione, June 4, 1979, in *Secret Field*, 12.

360 *"I want and need"*: JW letter to Louis Simpson, May 21, 1979.

360 *"scarcely able to believe"*: JW letter to Janice Thurn, June 8, 1979, in *WP*, 535.

360 *"gift for solitude"*: JW letter to Robert Bly, June 8, 1979, in *WP*, 533.

360 *"The years are awfully"*: JW to Dr. Thomas Hodge, June 8, 1979.

360 *"inner relations"*: JW interview, September 30, 1979, in *CP*, 229. See Kathy Callaway, review of *This Journey* (1983), in *HotL*, 398.

360 *"May Morning"*: As Saskia Hamilton has written, "These hidden and open harmonies are suggestive of the modesty and power of his late style." Hamilton, "Listening to the Mourners," *The Kenyon Review* 29, no. 2 (Spring 2007): 191.

361 *"All I am doing"*: "An Italian Wasp," JW journal, Sirmione, June 13, 1979.

361 *At midday they*: JW letter to Betsy Fogelman, June 15, 1979.

361 *"Now they will"*: JW letter to Leslie Marmon Silko, June 15, 1979, in *Delicacy*, 55, and *WP*, 538.

361–62 *"I no longer think . . . I am content"*: JW journal, Sirmione, June 23, 1979, in *Secret Field*, 13 (corrected).

362 *"hot, humid, and crowded"*: Anne Wright, journal, June 27, 1979.

362 *"It is brutally hot"*: JW journal, Venice, June 28, 1979.

362 *"By God, when I die"*: JW to Anne Wright, recorded in her journal, July 2, 1979.

362 *"It is the day"*: JW journal, Siena, July 2, 1979. David Lyons, Uncle Sherman's son by a first marriage, had been a close companion of Wright's in childhood.

363 *"triumph for the dry weeds"*: JW journal, Siena, July 3, 1979, in *Secret Field*, 13 (corrected).

363 *"he seemed to dominate . . . always marginal"*: Frank MacShane, "James Wright: The Search for the Light," in *James Wright: A Profile*, ed. Frank Graziano and Peter Stitt (Durango, CO: Logbridge-Rhodes, 1988), 130.

363 *"golden as ever"*: JW journal, Arezzo, July 10, 1979.

363 *"an inescapable instance"*: JW journal, Florence, July 11, 1979.

363 *"I will be glad"*: JW journal, Arezzo, July 13, 1979.

364 *"in a way that he'd"*: Interview with Anne Wright, Verona, July 20, 2004.

364 *"This town is so noisy"*: JW journal, Venice, July 15, 1979.

364 *"Venice is strange"*: JW journal, Venice, July 16, 1979.

364 *"I am bone sick"*: JW letter to Michael di Capua, July 16, 1979.

364 *"and you, dear friend"*: Leslie Marmon Silko letter to JW, June 27, 1979, in *Delicacy*, 58.

364 *"in which, with great verbal"*: JW letter to Leslie Marmon Silko, July 18, 1979, in *Delicacy*, 60 (restored from original letter).

364 *"I am deeply moved"*: Leslie Marmon Silko letter to JW, July 28, 1979, in *Delicacy*, 64.

364 *"exhaustion of spirit"*: JW journal, Venice, July 21, 1979.

365 *"for I love the daybreak"*: JW letter to Janice Thurn, August 11, 1979.

365 *"The Sunlight Falling"*: JW journal, Moret-sur-Loing, July 26–27, 1979.

365 *They had talked*: Interview with Anne Wright, Moret-sur-Loing, July 9, 2011.

366 Trois Gymnopédies: Anne Wright journal, August 1979; and Anne Wright, memoir, "Gymnopedie No. 1," from "Fragments from a Journey," *The Kenyon Review*, new series vol. 7, no. 3 (1985), 36. The recording in the collection of Dr. Higgins was a performance by Aldo Ciccolini.

366 *"I can't—or won't"*: JW letter to Leslie Marmon Silko, August 8, 1979, in *Delicacy*, 68. Wright quotes a phrase from Virgil "that has stayed in my mind since I was a boy, likely a troubled boy, long ago, in Ohio—*sunt lacrimae rerum*—'These are the tears of things.'"

366 *"It has been"*: JW journal, Paris, August 15, 1979.

366 *"During these Paris days"*: Anne Wright journal, Paris, mid-August 1979.

366 *"To the Adriatic"*: JW journal, Paris, August 17, 1979.

367 *"This morning in Paris"*: JW letter to Franz Wright, August 18, 1979.

367 *"I am weary"*: JW journal, Paris, August 24, 1979.

367 *"Beside the Tour Magne"*: JW journal, Paris, August 28, 1979. The prose form gives "the kind of rough human context for [the image], and that's what makes a poem moving. A little roughness and literalness gives a poem poignancy and humanity, so he was able to do *both*." Interview with Franz Wright, May 23, 2001.

367 *"But first I have to return"*: JW journal, Paris, September 3, 1979. "But first I have to return to America, [a journey through ugliness and despair.] and resume my journey through [ugliness and despair.] the only life I have."

368 *"It is the last day"*: JW journal, Paris, September 4, 1979.

30. My true Ohio

369 *"a pile of busy mail"*: JW journal, September 5, 1979. "Chores, chores: the bone and sinew of the world."

369 *"It is good to write"*: Robert Bly letter to JW and Anne Wright, August 16, 1979.

369 *"gratitude for the"*: JW letter to Leslie Marmon Silko, August 23, 1979, in *Delicacy*, 74.

369 *"You are fearless"*: Leslie Marmon Silko letter to JW, September 12, 1979, in *Delicacy*, 77.

370 *"getting accustomed"*: JW letter to Michael Cuddihy, September 15, 1979, in *WP*, 543.

370 *"I must learn"*: JW journal, September 10, 1979.

370 *"They hid as long"*: JW journal, September 11, 1979.

370 *"I want to read"*: JW journal, September 18, 1979.

371 *"to stay sober"*: JW letter to Donald Hall, September 22, 1979.

371 *"Sometimes I think"*: JW journal, September 25, 1979.

371 *Smith was gathering*: Interview with Dave Smith, March 25, 2010; see Smith's interview with JW, September 30, 1979, *CP*, 191; and *Clear Word*, 3.

371 *It took Ruark's*: Gibbons Ruark, "With James Wright at the Grave of Edward Thomas," *The Cortland Review* (Spring 2003), cortlandreview.com.

371–72 *"peculiar kind of . . . what he is hearing"*: CP, 194–232.

372 *"I spoke more freely"*: JW journal, September 30, 1979.

372 *"something totally unpretentious"*: JW letter to Betsy Fogelman, October 4, 1979.

372 *"It was devastating"*: Interview with Anne Wright, July 20, 2004.

372 *"We are like an army"*: JW journal, Lake Minnewaska, October 6, 1979. See the first stanza of Horace's *Ode II*, 14:

> Ah! Posthumus, the years, the years
> Glide swiftly on, nor can our tears
> Or piety the wrinkl'd age forfend,
> Or for one hour retard th' inevitable end.

Christopher Smart, *Horace in English* (New York: Penguin Classics, 1996), 197.

373 *"He was very private"*: Interview with Anne Wright, July 20, 2004.

373 *"might make it possible"*: JW journal, October 2, 1979.

373 *"I reckon I'll read"*: JW journal, October 10, 1979.

373–74 *"an explorer and a poet . . . started by then"*: Robert Fitzgerald's introduction and JW reading, Harvard College Library, Cambridge, MA, October 11, 1979, Woodberry Poetry Room collection, Harvard University.

374 *"the pleasantest place"*: JW journal, October 11, 1979.

374 *"so monstrous"*: JW journal, September 10, 1979.

375 *"prescription for some stuff"*: JW journal, October 18, 1979.

375 *He had given*: Interview with Gibbons Ruark, May 30, 2007. Wright's journal shows multiple drafts in the last two weeks of October.

375 *"When I hear Shakespeare's"*: JW journal, November 4, 1979. *The Tempest*, act I, scene 2.

376 *"in good form"*: Interview with Gibbons Ruark, October 29, 1999.

376 *"It was a good"*: JW journal, November 1, 1979.

376 *"workaday New York"*: JW journal, December 4, 1979.

376 *"immediate, clear"*: JW letter to Mary Oliver, November 5, 1979, in *WP*, 546.

376 *"I felt, as he"*: Mary Oliver, letter to author, May 6, 2014.

376 *What progress Wright*: Interview with Anne Wright, November 18, 2014. Looking back, Anne found Wright's endurance remarkable "for a man who used to make such a terrible fuss over a head cold."

377 *"literally summoning up"*: JW journal, November 16, 1979.

377 *"basic condition"*: JW journal, November 17, 1979. "Epistle from the Amphitheatre" would be the final piece added to the manuscript.

377 *"struggling hard . . . feel driven"*: JW letter to Leslie Marmon Silko, November 18, 1979, in *Delicacy*, 87. "I miss you," Wright says in closing, "again, an odd thought, since we've never really met. But we will."

377 *A jubilant note*: Robert Bly letter to JW, November 15, 1979.

377 *In an interview*: Robert Bly interviewed by Michael Clifton, Indiana University, Bloomington, November 16, 1979, in Richard Jones and Kate Daniels, eds., *Of Solitude and Silence: Writings on Robert Bly* (Boston: Beacon Press, 1981), 84.

377 *"working frantically"*: JW letter to Robert Mezey, November 19, 1979, in *WP*, 547.

377 *"I feel so sick"*: JW journal, November 20, 1979.

377 *"Suggestions only"*: Hayden Carruth letter to JW, November 14, 1979. Wright also revised "Chilblain."

377 *"I see how necessary"*: JW journal, November 22, 1979.

377 *"It is an exceedingly"*: JW journal, November 25, 1979.

378 *"No matter which way"*: JW journal, November 28, 1979.

378 *"It is a grim time"*: JW journal, November 30, 1979.

378 *"oddly beautiful"*: JW journal, December 1, 1979.

378 *"I believe that"*: JW journal, December 2, 1979.

378 *"Really the only"*: JW journal, December 3, 1979.

378 *"M. E. Ketchum"*: JW journal, December 5, 1979.

379 *In plain, blunt*: JW journal, December 7, 1979.

379 *"horn beak . . . to kill"*: JW typescript, January 10, 1975, "To Bee, Who Is Dead." In an unpublished prose piece written in June 1975, Wright imagined his own death in the claws of a raptor. "Take one death with another, I dream of soaring myself with the soaring of the owl, knowing for a single instant what I have never known as a man: the terror, the magnificence, the welcoming power of the darkness, the brief and certain knowledge of what it feels like to rise above the earth and stay there as long as I live." "A Way to Go," JW journal, June 15, 1975.

379 *"TO THE SEA WIND . . . as moonlight"*: JW journal, December 7, 1979. Wright placed "To the Adriatic Wind, Becalmed" near the end of *This Journey*. It was first published in *The New Yorker* on December 7, 1981, exactly two years after this journal entry.

379 *"All the way into . . . the way / Down"*: "To the Adriatic Wind, Becalmed": JW journal, Paris, August 17, 1979.

380 *"I'm gonna beat this thing"*: Interview with Roland Flint, October 28, 1999. Sounding much like his old self, he then told Flint "two very funny limericks." Wright

also assured Robert Mezey, "I'm gonna beat this," when they met in New York later that month. Interview with Robert Mezey, October 14, 1999.

380 *Over the next four weeks*: JW journal, December 9, 1979; see also December 22, 1979; JW letter to Stephen Berg, December 26, 1979; and JW journal, January 1, 1980. Of the ten pieces Wright submitted to Berg, only two appeared in *APR*: "Camomilla" and "In a Field near Metaponto." *The American Poetry Review* 11 (January/February 1982).

380 *Though he first*: JW journal, December 12, 1979. Wright finally entrusted Hayden Carruth with the work.

380 *"a 50/50 chance"*: JW journal, December 10, 1979.

380 *"to my fascination . . . all this fuss"*: JW journal, December 11, 1979.

380 *"I was only sorry"*: JW journal, December 14, 1979.

380 *"It is like sending out"*: JW journal, December 16, 1979.

380 *"I want to share"*: JW letter to Leslie Marmon Silko, December 18, 1979, in *Delicacy*, 91.

381 *"Enter these nazis"*: JW journal, December 20, 1979.

381 *"the wise, despairing"*: JW journal, December 21, 1979. See also JW journal, July 15, 1979.

381 *"Well, in any event"*: JW journal, December 14, 1979.

381 *"[w]e live in the world"*: JW journal, May 17, 1977, reading Mark Strand's book *Darker*.

381 *"a glimpse of this"*: JW journal, Lititz, December 24, 1979.

382 *"entire day[s] of sunlight"*: JW journal, December 27, 1979.

382 *"We really have"*: JW, quoted in interview with Anne Wright, August 19, 2014.

382 *"There wasn't a sense"*: Interview with Gibbons Ruark, October 29, 1999. *See* Ruark, "Lost Letter to James Wright, with Thanks for a Map of Fano," in *Passing Through Customs: New and Selected Poems* (Baton Rouge: Louisiana State University Press, 1999), 67.

382 *As he and Wright talked . . . "to live quietly"*: Interview with Gibbons Ruark, April 12, 2007, and e-mail to author on May 12, 2007, quoting concurrent journals. Wright also read the poem he had given to Anne at Christmas, "Yes, But," and Yeats's "Adam's Curse." The books Wright kept close at hand included Orwell's *Collected Essays, Journalism and Letters*; Forster's *Two Cheers for Democracy*; Swift's *Gulliver's Travels*; *The Portable Dante*; Chaucer's *Canterbury Tales*; and Twain's *Huckleberry Finn*.

382 *"From that first day"*: Galway Kinnell letter to JW, December 16, 1979.

382 *"like a natural brother"*: JW letter to Galway Kinnell, December 31, 1979, in *WP*, 549.

383 *"I am becoming"*: JW journal, January 2, 1980. The entry concludes: "Well, all right, but I could surely use a rest from all this Eternal Truth for a while. There is nothing noble or spiritual about this truth. It is ugly, it is sad, the bones here ache without peace, and the truth stinks. Stinks. It stinks."

383 *More than five hundred poets*: Tom Buckley, "Honor Roll of American Poets Reads at White House," *New York Times*, January 4, 1980, A1.

383 *"even though he had"*: Interview with Grace Schulman, November 20, 2000.

383 *"but one look at him"*: Interview with Anne Wright, July 20, 2004.

383 *James Dickey*: Interview with Anne Wright, June 13, 2002; and Henry Hart, *James Dickey: The World as a Lie* (New York: Picador USA, 2000), 584. Dickey

sent a telegram to Wright in the hospital that Anne tore up before her husband saw it. It read, "I miss hearing your voice." Dickey telegram to JW, January 20, 1980.

383 *"There are just three of us"*: Richard Hugo, quoted in interview with Philip Levine, December 15, 2004. Three years later, Hugo would die of leukemia.

383 *"It struck me that"*: JW journal, January 3, 1980.

384 *"he had a kind of . . . see me now"*: Ruark, October 29, 1999.

384 *"I can understand more"*: JW journal, January 4, 1980.

384 *"it is the cause"*: JW journal, January 5, 1980.

384 *Leslie Silko, in her letter*: Leslie Marmon Silko letter to JW, January 3, 1980, in *Delicacy*, 92; and JW journal, January 8, 1980. "I think I lost any clear sense of what the doctors are doing."

384–85 *"a certain very dark"*: JW journal, December 31, 1979.

385 *"For the truth is"*: JW letter to Galway Kinnell, December 31, 1979, in *WP*, 549.

385 *"There must be a way"*: JW journal, January 9, 1980. The sentence concludes: "and all though trust of it mere illusion, no matter what it calls itself." Wright's handwriting is nearly illegible; the word "trust" is questionable.

31. These are my hopes

386 *"and in a real dark night"*: F. Scott Fitzgerald, *The Crack-Up* (New York: New Directions, 1956), 75.

386 *Of three books*: Interview with Anne Wright, July 20, 2004. A new novel by V. S. Naipaul, *A Bend in the River*—a Christmas gift from Anne—held a bookmark at page five. John Le Carré's *Smiley's People* also remained unfinished. Robert Bly knew that Wright held Orwell's example close to his heart, as a kind of moral center. Interview with Robert Bly, April 5, 2002.

386 *"ability to touch on grief"*: Robert Bly letter to JW, January 8, 1980. Already mourning Wright's illness, Bly's prose poem "Eleven O'Clock at Night" crafts a refrain from the phrase "for that there is no solution." It is the opening poem in Bly's *Reaching Out to the World: New & Selected Prose Poems* (Buffalo, NY: White Pine Press, 2009), 13. See also Bly, *Stealing Sugar from the Castle: Selected and New Poems, 1950–2013* (New York: W. W. Norton, 2013), 140.

387 *"It's far worse"*: JW, "Hospital Notes," January 15, 1980.

387 *In a letter to Hall*: Donald Hall letter to Robert Bly, January 18, 1980. Robert Bly papers, Andersen Library Archives.

387 *A succession of*: Robert Mezey, David Ignatow, Etheridge Knight, Louis Simpson, Lyle Tollefson, and Anthony Hecht, among many others, visited Wright in Mount Sinai.

387 *"I'd rather be in Philadelphia"*: Interviews with Philip Levine, December 15, 2004, and Mark Strand, April 30, 2010.

387 *"I could feel his eyes"*: E. L. Doctorow, "James Wright at Kenyon," in *Jack London, Hemingway, and the Constitution: Selected Essays, 1977–1992* (New York: Random House, 1993), 197.

387 *Overwhelmed by the sight*: Interview with E. L. Doctorow, March 19, 2002; and interviews with Anne Wright and Jean Valentine, March 20, 2000.

388 *"as truly horrible"*: JW, "Hospital Notes," January 26, 1980.

388 *"a stream of jokes"*: Carolyn Kizer, public talk, Saratoga, CA, March 22, 1997; interview, April 15, 2000; and Kizer, "Final Meeting," in *The Nearness of You* (Port Townsend, WA: Copper Canyon Press, 1986), 95.

388 *"alive and alert"*: Interview with Anne Wright, April 17, 2009.

388 *"I was afraid Robert"*: JW, "Hospital Notes," February 1, 1980.

388 *"a warmth, a kindness"*: Interview with Leslie Marmon Silko, January 31, 2011.

388 *"I had to leave"*: JW, "Hospital Notes," February 8, 1980.

389 *"tried to make New York"*: Betsy Fogelman Tighe memoir (unpublished draft).

389 *"big green Madonna manuscript"*: JW, "Hospital Notes," February 15, 1980.

389 *"one of the great"*: Interview with Galway Kinnell, January 30, 2002.

389 *"beautiful visit . . . much to me"*: JW, "Hospital Notes," February 15, 1980.

389 *Nearly destitute*: Interviews with Franz Wright, May 23, 2001, and Jean Valentine, March 20, 2000. Franz visited his father in Mount Sinai eleven times between February 19 and March 12, 1980, his last.

389 *"[Franz] seemed to get"*: JW, "Hospital Notes," February 1, 1980.

389 *"horribly prefigure"*: Franz Wright, May 23, 2001.

389 *"Dad, you're immortal"*: JW, "Hospital Notes," February 29, 1980; and interview with Ann Sanfedele, April 23, 2010. True to the comic banter they shared, Wright scribbled a note to Sanfedele: "I'm immortal—this weak. WEEK!" Responding to the knowing look Wright gave her, she countered, "No, he said you were *immoral*." As Sanfedele remembered, "Franz looked startled, but Jim gave as close to a laugh as you could get."

389 *Marshall then agreed with the doctor*: Interviews with Anne Wright, October 31, 2004, and Marshall Wright, October 17, 2006: "I knew from the questions he was asking me that I wasn't ready to see my dad. It could've upset him, and caused him pain or trauma, and I told that to the psychiatrist."

389 *Having neglected his medications*: Marshall Wright, October 17, 2006.

389 *Anne insisted*: Anne Wright, October 31, 2004. "I've never known if it was the right thing," Anne allowed. Interview with Anne Wright, June 30, 2005. Liberty Kovacs's claim that "his father refused to see [Marshall] when he was dying" (LK memoir, 326) ignores evidence to the contrary shared with her by the author in October 2006. After her book appeared in 2008, Kovacs conceded that Marshall had told her of his meeting with Wright's psychiatrist and that Anne had kept him from seeing his father (interview with Kovacs, March 8, 2010). Franz believed that his father had refused to see Marshall, despite Anne Wright's denials.

390 *"Be sure to keep"*: JW, "Hospital Notes," February 29, 1980.

390 *"As the days bleed"*: JW, "Hospital Notes," February 28, 1980.

390 *"2 or 3 strippings"*: JW, "Hospital Notes," February 29, 1980.

390 *"in a real dark night"*: JW, "Hospital Notes," March 2, 1980. Fitzgerald, *The Crack-Up*, 75.

390 *"Well, what do you think"*: Frank MacShane, to JW and Anne Wright, quoted in interview with Anne Wright, May 27, 2003.

390 *"Isn't it becoming"*: JW, "Hospital Notes," March 2, 1980.

390 *The moment came*: JW, "Hospital Notes," March 9, 1980. Wright told Irving Silver he had "solved the main problem of my new book" when he chose the title.

390 *When Moss heard*: JW, "Hospital Notes," March 17, 1980; interview with Anne Wright, March 30, 2008; and *The Summers of James and Annie Wright: Sketches and Mosaics* (New York: Sheep Meadow Press, 1981).

391 *"I must complete"*: JW, "Hospital Notes," March 7, 1980.

391 *"You're the only one"*: JW, "Hospital Notes," March 11, 1980.

391 *"They were kindred souls"*: Interview with Anne Wright, October 31, 2003. At Wright's memorial service, Braxton spoke of him as "my surrogate father."

391 *"a plain old-fashioned tranquilizer"*: JW, "Hospital Notes," March 14, 1980.

391 *"prepare them"*: JW, "Hospital Notes," March 16, 1980.

391 *"more or less done"*: JW, "Hospital Notes," March 16, 1980.

391 *"I'd like to go back to Italy"*: JW to nurse, quoted in interview with Anne Wright, May 6, 2007.

391 *"I would like to come"*: JW, "Hospital Notes," March 18, 1980.

392 *Though Young handed*: Interview with David Young, September 3, 2013.

392 *"dingier than ever"*: Interview with Anne Wright, December 16, 2014.

392 *"They didn't hurt me"*: JW, "Hospital Notes," March 21, 1980; and interview with Anne Wright, March 20, 2000.

392 *"Am I likely to die here?"*: JW, "Hospital Notes," March 21, 1980.

392 *"Well, this is it"*: JW, quoted in interview with Anne Wright, July 20, 2004.

392 *Strangely, the one book*: F. L. Lucas: *Tragedy: Serious Drama in Relation to Aristotle's 'Poetics'* (New York: Collier Books, 1957).

392 NERUDA FINEST: JW, "Hospital Notes," March 24, 1980. On March 19, Hardie St. Martin had been one of the last visitors to see Wright at Mount Sinai.

392 *"It was a relief"*: Donald Hall, introduction to *Above the River: The Complete Poems* (New York: Farrar, Straus and Giroux, 1990), xxxvi.

393 *"Don, talking to me"*: JW, inscription, March 22, 1980, in Hall, *String Too Short to Be Saved: Recollections of Summers on a New England Farm* (Boston: Nonpareil Books, 1979).

393 *"improvised a small ritual"*: Hall, introduction to *Above the River*, xxxvii; interview with Donald Hall, February 22, 1999; and interview with Karin East Marvin, January 22, 2011.

393 *"something stronger"*: JW, "Hospital Notes," March 22, 1980.

393 *"Nobody loved the town"*: Lillian Renzler, March 23, 1980, quoted by Van Horne, Wheeling *News Register*, March 30, 1980.

394 *In successive entries*: JW journal, April 30, 1962.

394 *"the special intervention"*: JW letter to Barbara Thompson, January 26, 1965. The poem's imagery foreshadows the "slender and fastidious" spider that "stepped into the center of air" in "The Journey."

394 *"I suppose the notebook"*: JW journal, March 23, 1965. Wright concludes this entry by quoting a passage from "Edward Thomas, whose writings I love beyond those of any other author in any language."

394 *"El viaje definitivo"*: Juan Ramón Jiménez, from *Poemas agrestes* (1910–1911); *Antolojía Poética*, edición de Vicente Gaos (Madrid: Ediciones Cátedra, 1975), no. 44, 96.

394 *"asking the blessing"*: JW letter to Prairie Dern, March 23, 1965. In a letter to Dern five days earlier, Wright confessed, "Plainly I sit at a crossroads." March 18, 1965.

394 *The words "journal"*: *Webster's Third New International Dictionary Unabridged* (Springfield, MA: Merriam-Webster, 1986). "I worked for two nights in the factory my father had worked in, and I quit," Wright said. "I thought it was too much for me to handle. I couldn't live that kind of life. It was just as hard for my father." *CP*, 199.

394 *"My book, my book"*: JW, to attending doctor, March 25, 1980, quoted in interviews with Anne Wright, May 6, 2007, and February 23, 2010. The doctor who phoned to tell her of Wright's death related the account of his rising from bed at sunrise.

Epilogue: One Last Look at the Adige: Verona in the Rain

395 *"an experimenter, an artist"*: Eric Page, *The New York Times*, Thursday, March 27, 1980.

395 *"It was an astonishing"*: Interview with Sander Zulauf, July 5, 2000.

395 *Few American poets*: Bruce Henricksen and Robert Johnson, eds., *From the Other World: Poems in Memory of James Wright* (Duluth, MN: Lost Hills Books, 2008), published forty-five poems dedicated to Wright, including work by Robert Bly, W. S. Merwin, Galway Kinnell, Sander Zulauf, Gibbons Ruark, Richard Hugo, Stanley Plumly, and C. K. Williams. There are dozens of other elegies to Wright, including poems by Jean Valentine, Derek Walcott, Hayden Carruth, David Ignatow, Denise Levertov, Franz Wright, Mary Oliver, Ai, Donna Masini, Larry Levis, Campbell McGrath, Carolyn Kizer, Louis Simpson, William Heyen, Diane Ackerman, Philip Appleman, Jane Cooper, Anthony Hecht, Marilyn Hacker, David Wagoner, Michael S. Harper, Gerald Stern, and many others.

396 *In its May/June issue*: *The American Poetry Review* 9, no. 3 (May/June 1980).

396 *"We left it as it was"*: Interview with Anne Wright, April 6, 2010. After Wright's death, a handful of poems were removed from the manuscript he had arranged. Wright had wanted the twin poems "Entering" and "Leaving the Temple in Nîmes" to be the first and last poems in the book. Bly, Carruth, and Mezey sent letters with comments on the manuscript, while Hall joined Anne and Kinnell in Vermont in July 1980. Interview with Galway Kinnell, January 30, 2002.

396 *After Anne submitted*: Interview with Anne Wright, March 30, 2008. Di Capua had also promised to publish Wright's *Collected Prose*, but dropped the book after Wright's death.

396 *Philip Levine then approached*: Interviews with Philip Levine, December 15, 2004, and Anne Wright, October 30, 2016.

396 *"That sense of astonishment"*: Edward Hirsch, *The New York Times Book Review*, April 18, 1982, in *HotL*, 387.

396 *"Wright achieved"*: Robert B. Shaw, *The Nation*, August 7, 1982, in *HotL*, 409.

397 *"The solution is not"*: Kathy Callaway, *Parnassus* (1983), in *HotL*, 391.

397 *"Wright is not a"*: John Haag, "Beyond the Green Wall," AWP's *The Writer's Chronicle* 25, no. 4 (February 1993): 16.

397 *"Clarity of feeling"*: Hayden Carruth, review of Wright's *Collected Prose*, in *Sitting In: Selected Writings on Jazz, Blues, and Related Topics* (Iowa City: University of Iowa Press, 1986), 118.

397 *"the expansive humanity"*: Interview with Marilyn Hacker, December 15, 2000.

397 *More than fifty*: Interview with Joel Lipman, August 11, 2011. The festival was first suggested by Lipman and continued with the support of the Martins Ferry Public Library and the Ohio Arts Council. Robert Fox, director of the OAC, was instrumental in supporting the idea. He worked with Mikey Rakay and the head librarian at the MFPL, John Storck, who was succeeded by Yvonne Myers, with help

from Tom Flynn. Anne Wright was a featured guest at every festival. The Twenty-Seventh Annual Festival took place in April 2007.

397 *"Behind all of them"*: Stanley Kunitz, interview, Tenth Annual James Wright Poetry Festival, Martins Ferry, OH, April 21, 1990.

398 *"You can't separate"*: Denise Levertov, public talk, Fourth Annual James Wright Poetry Festival, May 5, 1984.

398 *"It's penetrating . . . extraordinary mind"*: Interview with Gerald Stern, November 7, 2002.

398 *"Wright was born"*: Robert Bly, public talk, "Into Blossom," in conversation with Carolyn Kizer, Saratoga, CA, March 22, 1997. "Original rhythms appear in the smallest sentence of James Wright, and composers recognize it right away. So, that's some kind of musical genius."

398 *"We hunger for"*: W. Jackson Bate, *John Keats* (Cambridge, MA: Harvard University Press, 1963), 157.

398 *"I do think the book"*: Interview with Galway Kinnell, January 30, 2002.

399 *"this beautiful, unbelievable"*: Sonjia Urseth letter to JW, April 30, 1959.

399 *"What a dazzling gift"*: JW, marginalia on Sonjia Urseth letter, April 30, 1959. For Wright, the letter represented the ideal he had hoped for in his relationship with Urseth, recalling his role as a mentor to a prized student. Wright had recommended Urseth's short stories to the editor of *Botteghe Oscure*—just as Theodore Roethke had helped secure the publication of Wright's first poems in that journal four years earlier.

Acknowledgments

I missed the chance to meet the poet James Wright and have spent the years since his death trying to catch up with him. I first read his poems at Cornell University, when the inspiring poet and teacher Thomas Johnson sent me to the library to find *The Branch Will Not Break* after my first day in his classroom in September 1977. Months later I began a study of Wright's translations of Pablo Neruda and César Vallejo, fascinated by the effect their work had had on Wright's poetry. In June 1979 I met the poets Robert Bly and Fran Quinn, who encouraged me to talk with Wright when he returned from Europe. But my plan to interview Wright was postponed, and then canceled, by his illness.

In 1990, after producing various independent radio documentaries, I wanted to honor the publication of Wright's Complete Poems, *Above the River*, with an audio portrait. I recorded my first interviews with Bly and with Wright's widow, Anne, that spring, and spoke with many other poets, friends, and relatives of Wright's at the tenth annual James Wright Poetry Festival in Martins Ferry, Ohio. Since that time I have recorded more than two hundred interviews and gathered an archive of Wright's readings and public talks.

Anne Wright asked me to write the authorized biography in 2002, and my family and I traveled with her to Italy in July 2004; we later traveled together to Paris and Moret-sur-Loing in 2010. I also assisted Anne and Saundra Maley with editing Wright's Selected Letters, *A Wild Perfection*, published by Farrar, Straus and Giroux in 2005. During the years of research for this book, I spent many weeks at the Elmer L. Andersen Library at the University of Minnesota in Minneapolis, where Wright's papers are held. I am continually grateful to Cecily Marcus, Barbara Bezat, and the staff of the Literary Manuscripts/Upper Midwest Literary Archives.

I wish to thank Erik Storlie for hosting two separate gatherings of friends who knew Wright as part of the Dinkytown and Seven Corners community in Minneapolis in the late 1950s and early 1960s. I recorded two long afternoons of conversation in the summers of 2002 and 2003 that offer a group portrait of Wright at this difficult yet hugely productive period in his life. Among those who gathered in Erik's living room in Minneapolis were John Beauchamp, Bill Breer, Marv Davidov, Fred Hoffman, George Kliger, "Spider" John Koerner, James "Red" Nelson, Richard Quinn, Bruce Rubenstein, and Erik Storlie. Special thanks are due also to Harry Weber and his remarkable memory. Included here is a small fraction of their collective story, from a time when Minneapolis and St. Paul became a Midwest outpost for the nascent cultural revolution already underway in San Francisco and New York City.

I am especially indebted to the trust placed in me by Sonjia Urseth, who preserved her extraordinary correspondence with Wright from 1957 through 1959 and shared it with me before donating the collection to the Andersen Library Archives. I also wish to thank Carol Bly and Liberty Kovacs for generously sharing their memories of Wright as well as their private collections of photographs. Thanks also to Madeline Zulauf for her evocative photographs of Martins Ferry. Another excellent photographer, Terry Dagradi, contributed her time and skill to digitally archiving hundreds of images from many different sources over the years I worked on this biography, and I thank her with all my heart.

I have benefited from numerous grants and residencies over the past decade of work on this biography. I want to gratefully acknowledge the Corporation of Yaddo in Saratoga Springs, New York; the Anderson Center in Red Wing, Minnesota; and the Saltonstall Foundation for the Arts in Ithaca, New York, who granted me essential residency fellowships. I especially want to thank the MacDowell Colony in Peterborough, New Hampshire, and the artists whom I met there. Both at the beginning and during final editing, my time at MacDowell helped shape my thinking and made it possible to complete this work. The financial support of a New York Foundation for the Arts Fellowship in 2014 freed me to focus on the final chapters of the manuscript. Thanks to an Independent Arts Grant from the Puffin Foundation in Teaneck, New Jersey, in 1999, I purchased equipment to record in broadcast quality all the interviews for this biography. I also wish to thank the Leon Levy Center for Biography at the Graduate Center of the City University of New York for a biography clinic fellowship in 2013, and the community of writers in the Biographers International Organization.

I am indebted to Robert Bly and Fran Quinn for their encouragement and advice throughout the long genesis of this biography. Jean Valentine and Grace Schulman have also been important friends to me and my work. Gibbons Ruark and Robert Mezey have shown me great generosity and shared their deep understanding of Wright. I am saddened to know that many who contributed to this book will not read it, and wish to honor Roland Flint, Michael S. Harper, Galway Kinnell, Philip Levine, and C. K. Williams for their kindness and support.

I want to thank Robert Henriques for his unconditional enthusiasm and lifelong friendship, and Stanley Letovsky for practical suggestions and encouragement. The help of another good friend, Ronald Mendez-Clark, has also been invaluable to me; he has corrected my Spanish and shared his great knowledge of Latin American and Spanish literature. Susan Blue suggested many sources for genealogical research, and her advice and good sense spared me more than one interpersonal disaster. I also wish to thank Saundra Maley for her dedication to Wright's work and Laura Newbern for her friendship and love of poetry. Rose Ann Miller has been an enormous help to me as well. Robert Boyle and the staff of the Field Library in Peekskill, New York, have been generous with their time and assistance. I'm grateful to Tim Trewhella for his first-rate Internet sleuthing. Special thanks also to Lee Briccetti and the staff of Poets House in New York City.

This biography has benefited from the hands-on expertise of many fine readers and friends, including John Knight, my superb editor at Farrar, Straus and Giroux. Jonathan Galassi encouraged this book from the start, and his support has been crucial. Stuart Servetar has been a reader since I drafted the first paragraphs, and his uncompromising standards and good humor have sustained me. When I struggled with a draft too unwieldy to stand on its own, John Herman's keen editorial guidance helped me shape the narrative and clear the weeds. The marvelous Patti Gauch shared her comments on my final draft, and I am indebted to each of these thoughtful editors. My wife, Sarah Haviland, and our daughter, Emma, are not only skilled in navigating my private weather and peculiarities, but are expert readers as well. They have been my essential support and companions throughout, and their love means everything to me.

More than anyone, I want to thank Anne Wright for her tireless devotion to her husband's poetry and for entrusting me with this authorized biography. She has submitted to countless hours of interviews without complaint, and suggested many fruitful directions of inquiry. Her good humor and warmth have made this work a pleasure. Anne has generously shared the personal books and papers of Wright's still in her possession, as well as many dozens of photographs. The unrestricted access she has granted me to Wright's unpublished work has made this book possible.

Many other writers and readers have helped me think about Wright's life and his poems, and the endnotes to this biography name many to whom I am indebted. The following list includes all the people I have interviewed in person, over the phone, or via correspondence in the course of researching this biography, and I am grateful for their contributions: Richard Barickman, Aliki Barnstone, Willis Barnstone, Charles Baxter, John Beauchamp, James Bertolino, Carol Bly, Robert Bly, Ruth Bly, Marianne Boruch, Gigi Bradford, Lee Briccetti, William Breer, Frederick Brocklehurst, Michael Dennis Browne, Hayden Carruth, Sharon Chmielarz, James Coleman, Jane Cooper, Nicholas Crome, Marv Davidov, Laura Lee DeCinque, Jessica Pritt DeDomenicus, Madeline DeFrees, Chard deNiord, William DeVoti, Roland Dille, Stephen Dobyns, E. L. Doctorow, Rosamond du Pont, William Duffy, David Dunlap, Arthur Efron, Kathy Engel, Carolyn Epes, Clayton Eshleman, Peter Everwine, Howard Fink, Roland Flint, Thomas Flynn, Edwin Frank, Stuart Friebert, Richard Gibson, Jack Gilbert, Daniela Gioseffi, Richard Goldhurst, Susan Lamb Graham, Michael Graves, Alvin Greenberg, Marilyn Hacker, Donald Hall, Mary Ann Hanna, Charles G. Hanzlicek, Michael S. Harper, Jim Harrison, Robert Hass, Winona Hastwell, Brooks Haxton, Robert Hedin, Bruce Henricksen, William Heyen, Claude Higgins, Dr. Robert Higgins, Geoffrey Hill, Jeanne Foster Hill, Edward Hirsch, Richard Hodge, Dr. Thomas Hodge, Frederick Hoffman, William Holbrook, William Holmick, Howard Huelster, Lewis Hyde, Rod Jellema, Galway Kinnell, Carolyn Kizer, George Kliger, John Koerner, Liberty Kardules Kovacs, Lemoyne Krone, Maxine Kumin, Stanley Kunitz, Joseph Langland, Annie Lannum, Harley "Pete" Lannum, Li-Young Lee, Dr. Frank LeFever, Merrill Leffler, Philip Levine, Claire Lindenberger, Herbert Lindenberger, Joel Lipman, Thomas Lux, Elizabeth Macklin, Saundra Rose Maley, Dennis Maloney, Freya Manfred, Karin East Marvin, Donna Masini, Irving Massey, Jerome Mazzaro, Jane Giles McClung, Ronald Mendez-Clark, W. S. Merwin, Robert Mezey, Penny Wright Monroe, Thomas Monroe, Robert Morgan, Edward Morin, Jane Moss, Stanley Moss, Neil Myers, Yvonne Myers, Timothy Neal, James "Red" Nelson, Kathleen Norris, Ed Ochester, Mary Oliver, William Olsen, Michael Ondaatje, Nancy Paddock, Dr. Henry Parker, Jay Parini, Anselm Parlatore, Stanley Plumly, Phyllis Lyons Pritt, Dr. Eugene Pugatch, Kathy

Purcell, Paul Pyle, Fran Quinn, Richard Quinn, Sheila Ráshed, James Reiss, Jerome Rothenberg, Gibbons Ruark, Kay Ruark, Bruce Rubenstein, Mary Ruefle, Ira Sadoff, Ann Sanfedele, Nancy Sayles-Evarts, Peter Schmidt, John Schmitt, Franz Schneider, Grace Schulman, Shirley Scott, Morton Segal, Dr. Robert Segal, Hugh Seidman, Ronald Sharp, Leslie Marmon Silko, Louis Simpson, Jerow Smiley, Dave Smith, Thomas R. Smith, Gary Snyder, Kevin Stein, Gerald Stern, Peter Stitt, Tony Stoneburner, Erik Storlie, Mark Strand, John Suriano, Thom Tammaro, Annie Tanks, Thomas Tenney, Betsy Fogelman Tighe, Lyle Tollefson, Tomas Tranströmer, Michael True, C. W. "Bill" Truesdale, Joan Wurtele Truesdale, Rae Tufts, Sonjia Urseth, Jean Valentine, Gladys Van Horne, Therese Vezeridis, John Vrotsos, David Wagoner, Diane Wakoski, Anthony Walton, Harry Weber, Seymour Weissman, C. K. Williams, Anne Runk Wright, Elizabeth Wright, Franz Wright, Helen Wright, Jack Wright, Marshall Wright, David Young, and Sander Zulauf.

I transcribed the recollections and insights of the following people from recordings of public tributes to the poet, including appearances at the James Wright Poetry Festival and other interview sources. The majority of these recordings were made exclusively for this biography: Jon Anderson, Maggie Anderson, Mary Bly, Jonathan Chaves, Marilyn Chin, Billy Collins, Carol Conroy, David Dougherty, Les Douglas, Denise Duhamel, Cornelius Eady, Lynn Emanuel, Carolyn Forché, Jack Furniss, Ruth Gardner, Elton Glaser, Linda Gregg, Mark Gustafson, Patricia Hampl, Roger Hecht, Joe Heithaus, Andrew Hudgins, David Ignatow, Louis Jenkins, Garrison Keillor, John Knoepfle, Wayne Koestenbaum, Denise Levertov, Jan Heller Levi, John Logan, Campbell McGrath, Irene McKinney, Jim Moore, Thomas Owens, Joe Paddock, Linda Pastan, Charles Persky, Marge Wright Pyle, Carol Rubenstein, Richard Shelton, Edwin Spievack, Maura Stanton, Henry Taylor, Judith Vollmer, and Theodore "Ted" Wright.

Finally, there are a number of literary archives and individuals I want to acknowledge for sharing copies of audio recordings of Wright's readings and public talks. The transcriptions I've made from this material are at the heart of this biography. From Wright's private collection of recordings, courtesy of Anne Wright, I have transcribed his readings at Wesleyan University, Middletown, Connecticut, on October 10, 1968; Sir George Williams College in Montreal, Canada, on December 13, 1968; his sermon at the United Methodist Church in Old Chatham, New York, on April 27, 1969; his readings at the University of Colorado at Fort Collins on May 16 and 17, 1969; his reading at the Poetry Center of the University of Arizona at Tucson, February 21, 1973; his lecture on the work of David Schubert at the University of Delaware, Newark, on October 17, 1978; and his final reading at the Harvard College Library in Cambridge, Massachusetts, on October 11, 1979, now part of the Woodberry Poetry Room Audio Archive. Dave Smith kindly shared his original cassette recordings of Wright's reading at the University of Michigan, Ann Arbor, on April 11, 1969, and Wright's final interview, on September 30, 1979, in New York City. The Andersen Library Archives at the University of Minnesota in Minneapolis is the source for Wright's reading at a tribute to Robert Frost, dated February 22, 1963, as well as Roland Flint's interview with Wright and Robert Bly for the university radio station, recorded in late July 1967, and Robert Bly's reading in Minneapolis on January 27, 1968. The Academy of American Poets provided copies of Wright's readings in New York City on March 20, 1964, and October 28, 1978; his conversation "The Music of Poetry," dated March 2, 1967; his reading of poems by João Cabral de Melo Neto on October 21, 1969; and the lecture titled "One Voice and Many," dated March 30, 1977. The Library of Congress is the source for Wright's readings on May 25, 1958 (in Minneapolis), and December 5, 1966 (with Louis Simpson and James Dickey, in Washington, D.C.). The Unterberg Poetry Center of the 92nd Street Y in New York has an outstanding collection of recordings, and I thank them for sharing the following readings from the Poetry Center stage: Wright's appearance with Pablo Neruda, June 11, 1966; Wright's reading on November 21, 1966; as moderator for a reading by Michael Benedikt and Marge Piercy, November 4, 1968; with Pablo Neruda, April 12, 1972; and with Stanley Kunitz and Carolyn Kizer on February 14, 1977. The Poetry Center also recorded Louis Simpson, Robert Mezey, and Grace Schulman reading Wright's work on November 17, 1975. The Special Collections of the Library at the University of Washington in Seattle provided the Roethke Memorial Reading that Wright gave on May 25, 1972, and I thank them for the portions of that recording transcribed here. The Poetry Center and American Poetry Archives of San Francisco State University preserves another excellent archive of recordings, and provided copies of Wright's readings at the university dated April 26, 1965, and April 17, 1968. Sander Zulauf preserved a copy of Michael S. Harper's recording of Wright at Brown University on May 9, 1975, and I thank them both. Zulauf is also the producer of the video recording of Wright's reading on September 30, 1976, at the County College of Morris, Randolph, New Jersey (First American Poetry Series, Vol. III, which is available on YouTube). The Poetry Collection of the University Libraries, University at Buffalo, the State University of New York, has gathered an exceptional archive of recordings, and I thank them especially for providing copies of Wright's readings at the university on November 15, 1967; July 2, 1969; his discussion and interview with Allen DeLoach and Anselm Hollo dated August 12, 1969; his reading and interview at the State University of New York, Brockport, on September 23 and 24, 1970; his readings at the University at Buffalo on February 18 and 19, 1972; and the reading dated February 15, 1973, at Florida Technological University and Rollins College, with John Logan and Denise Levertov. All of the above-named institutions retain their respective copyrights to these recordings and their use here is by permission, for which I am grateful.

Index